APPLETON-CENTURY-CROFTS POLITICAL SCIENCE SERIES

Edited by R. Taylor Cole

INTERNATIONAL

POLITICS

POLITICAL SCIENCE SERIES

Edited by R. Taylor Cole

Vernon Van Dyke, *International Politics.*

Arthur W. Bromage, *Introduction to Municipal Government and Administration,* Second Edition. Fall, 1957.

Clyde F. Snider, *Local Government in Rural America.* Fall, 1957.

Elton Atwater, William Butz, Kent Forster, and Neal Riemer, *Problems of International Understanding and World Affairs,* in preparation.

International Politics

by

Vernon Van Dyke
State University of Iowa

New  York

APPLETON-CENTURY-CROFTS, INC.

Copyright © 1957 by

APPLETON-CENTURY-CROFTS, INC.

539-2

PREFACE

THE AIM OF THIS BOOK is to describe and explain the behavior of states in their relations with each other in as clear and coherent a manner as possible.

Two principal questions are asked. The first is, why do states behave as they do? This question concerns motivations and objectives, "why" being interpreted both in a "because of" and in an "in order to" sense. The second principal question is, by what methods and under what limiting conditions do states pursue their objectives? In other words, how and within what limits do they strive to get what they want? The limits referred to may be voluntarily accepted, imposed by other states, or imposed by circumstances beyond human control.

The book is based on the assumption that the problem of war is the major problem faced in international politics. Therefore, the treatment of the above questions is heavily influenced by a desire to gain and provide an understanding of the causes of war and the conditions of peace. To facilitate the achievement of this objective, international politics is discussed within the framework of an analogy with domestic politics. This reflects the view that the political process at the international level has much in common with the process at the national level, and that an understanding of the factors making for domestic peace or civil war will contribute to an understanding of comparable factors operating among countries.

The questions posed are dealt with on a general basis rather than in relation to specific countries. Either method might be employed. An examination and explanation of the actions and interactions of enough states over a long enough period of time—in other words, an examination of diplomatic history—should lead to the answers which are sought. In truth, this route to the answers is, in a sense, an imperative one, for it is only through knowledge of specific actions in specific circumstances that generalizations about behavior can be reached. But it is not necessary for everyone to retrace the same path. Once the study of history has progressed far enough to provide generalizations (or the basis for them), as it obviously has, it seems best to seize upon them and use them, always testing them to determine the extent to which they provide reliable guides

v

to an understanding of actual events, and always trying to perfect them so as to provide a basis for prediction. Thus, though the choice might reasonably have been otherwise, this book makes no effort to present diplomatic history, whether from the remote or from the immediate past; there is no discussion, for example, of the foreign policies of the major powers—so common in textbooks on international relations. The focus is on generalizations which the study of history has provided rather than on the myriad of factual details leading to them. Historical data are introduced here and there simply to illustrate the main points on which attention should center. And these main points are examined not only in the light of illustrative material from political history but also in the light of enriching data from other fields, especially from economics and psychology. It is hoped that clarity and understanding will thereby be enhanced.

In writing the book I have had valuable assistance from others. Special thanks go to Frederick S. Dunn, Director of the Center of International Studies at Princeton University, to Taylor Cole of Duke University, and to Arno Mayer of Brandeis University, all three having read the entire manuscript and offered welcome suggestions. Similarly, Lane Davis, James Murray, Arnold Rogow, and Paul Olson, all of the State University of Iowa, and Fred Sondermann of Colorado College read various chapters with the usual result, suggestions for improvement. Both Frank A. Beach of Yale University and Harold Guetzkow of the Carnegie Institute of Technology were good enough to offer comments on an early version of Chapter 8, "Psychological Factors in War and Peace." During the summers of 1955 and 1956 I had the privilege of directing seminars on the teaching of international politics under grants from the Ford Foundation, the members of the seminars being teachers of the subject themselves; it is perhaps needless to say that discussions with them proved to be of great benefit. Finally, thanks should go to the State University of Iowa, which generously granted me a research professorship for a semester and thus facilitated the completion of the work.

Any weaknesses and errors in the book, of course, remain my own.

V. V. D.

State University of Iowa

CONTENTS

Preface   v

PART I

POLITICS: DOMESTIC AND INTERNATIONAL

1. What Is Politics?   3

The Struggle for Power Within and Among Groups. The Struggle Over Conflicting "Interests" or "Values." Is Politics a Constant Struggle for Maximum Power? Is Power an End in Itself? The Power Struggle Involves Both Cooperation and Conflict. The Focus in the Study of Political Science and International Politics.

2. Domestic Politics, Peace, and Civil War   14

Government and Domestic Peace. Attitudes and Domestic Peace. Domestic Peace and the Desires of the Strong.

PART II

THE DYNAMICS OF INTERNATIONAL
POLITICS

3. Security and Sovereignty   29

The "Self" in "Self-Preservation." Security and Its Problems. Why Self-Preservation Is Desired. Security and Competing Interests. Preserving Sovereign Independence.

4. Nationalism and War   40

The Nation and the State. Loyalty to the Nation.

5. Ideological Motivations and Objectives   60

Liberalism. Fascism. Communism.

6. Economic Objectives and Economic Forces   88

Economic Considerations and Foreign Policies. Economic Theories of Imperialism. An Appraisal.

vii

7. **War and the Expectation of War** **111**

War and the Seeds of Future War. The Influence of the Expectation of War. Jingoism and Militarism. Schumpeter's Theory of Imperialism.

8. **Psychological Factors in War and Peace** **131**

Human Nature versus Learned Behavior. Drives, Motives, Attitudes, Interests, Values, and Ideologies. Some Psychoanalytic Explanations of Behavior. The Frustration-Aggression Theory. Lasswell's Political Type. Implications for International Politics.

9. **Common Objectives of States** **153**

Security and Sovereignty. Aggrandizement. Peace. Prosperity. The Protection and Promotion of Ideology. Justice. Power. The Classification of States by Motivation or Objective.

PART III

METHODS AND LIMITING CONDITIONS
IN INTERNATIONAL POLITICS

10. **Power** **175**

The Elements of Power. Short Cuts in the Calculation of Power. The Relativity of Power.

11. **The Distribution and Balancing of Power** **199**

The Purposes of Balancing Power. Assumptions Underlying the Principle of the Balance of Power. An Examination of the Fifth Assumption. Methods Employed in the Balancing of Power. The Search for a Preponderance of Power. An Appraisal of the Balance-of-Power Principle.

12. **Armaments and Disarmament** **226**

The Functions and Purposes of Armed Forces. Regulating and Limiting Armaments. Why States Propose Disarmament. Obstacles to Agreement on Disarmament. Disarmament and Political Settlement.

13. **The Pursuit of Objectives by Economic Means** **248**

Foreign Exchange. The International Exchange of Goods and Services. Foreign Investments. Economic Nationalism and Economic Internationalism.

14. **Diplomacy and Settling International Disputes** **268**

Recognition and the Establishment of Diplomatic Relationships. Some Ground Rules of Diplomatic Relationships. The Functions of Diplomats and Consuls. Amicable Methods of Handling International Problems. Non-Amicable Methods of Settlement. Diplomacy by Conference. The Choice of Methods.

15. **International Law, Morality, and Peaceful Change** **289**

What Is International Law? The International Legislative Process. The Scope and Content of International Law. Respect for Law and the Enforce-

ment of Law. The Functions of Law. The Role of Morality. The Problem
of Peaceful Change. The Outlawry of War.

16. The Utility of War 317

The Political Importance of War. The Incidence and Costs of War. Prospective Costs of Nuclear Warfare. Does War Remain a Useful Instrument?
Nuclear Weapons and the Level of Armaments.

17. Substitutes for War 337

The Dissemination of Education, Information, and Propaganda. Economic
Blandishments and Penalties.

18. International Organization for Peace and Security 356

The League of Nations: Structure and Powers. A Hypothetical "Maximalist" Interpretation of the Provisions for Collective Security. Actual Interpretations and Applications of Provisions for Collective Security. The
United Nations: Purposes, Structure, and Powers. Peaceful Change and
Permissive Action for Collective Security.

19. International Organization for Welfare 378

The General Assembly and the Economic and Social Council. The Specialized Agencies. The Value of International Welfare Activities.

20. The Treatment of Dependent Peoples 394

Traditional Types of Colonial and Quasi-colonial Relationships. Colonial
Imperialism and Native Welfare. Arrangements for Governing Colonies.
The League of Nations Mandate System. The United Nations and Colonial-
ism.

PART IV

PROSPECTS FOR PEACE

21. The Prospects of Peace: A Balance Sheet 413

The Problem of Government for the World. The Problem of Attitudes.
Security-Community. World Federalism. Crisis.

Appendix: International Documents

Charter of the United Nations 427

Statute of the International Court of Justice 450

Constitution of the United Nations Educational, Scientific and Cultural
Organisation 463

Universal Declaration of Human Rights 471

North Atlantic Treaty 476

Index 479

Part I

POLITICS: DOMESTIC
AND INTERNATIONAL

CHAPTER 1

What Is Politics?

ALL OF US are involved in international politics. There was a time when relations among states seemed to matter little to most Americans, but that time is past. When we pay federal taxes, whether as part of the price of a movie or under the payroll deduction plan, most of what we pay goes to meet the costs of armed forces and of aid to foreign states; we are paying for past and for possible future war. Selective service boards send us or our friends and relatives into service for Uncle Sam. Over all our lives hangs the possibility of personal involvement in war; we may have to fight or to produce the things that are needed to fight. Or, the job of surviving may be very real, if we live in a city subjected to nuclear attack. How we will live and whether we will live are questions that are as likely to be answered by statesmen and generals of our own and foreign countries as by any decision which we personally may make.

In some ways international politics seems very simple, and in some ways it is bewildering. It seems simple in that the language of newspapers and of foreign offices is generally language that we can understand; practitioners in the field are not in a little world of their own like the nuclear physicists, using words that can be understood only by the initiated. It seems simple, too, in that many of the most vital issues involved in relations among states are issues that can readily be grasped—where a boundary line should be placed on the map, whether the government of one state should be permitted to impose its conceptions and its will on the people of another state, whether an alliance should be made or war declared. Actually much of the language of international politics and most of the issues are more complex than they seem, but still the appearance of simplicity is there.

International politics seems bewildering too. Most of us have no particular animus toward a Russian Ivan, but still the possibility is before us that we may have to try to kill him. Most of us want a good education, a good job, personal freedom, and a life that is both comfortable and useful; yet we as a nation devote an astounding proportion of our resources, both human and material, to purposes which are more closely related to war than to the kind of life that we would prefer to lead. Over the past several decades, decisions made in Berlin, Tokyo, Moscow, and Peking have unleashed events which have increased the cost of living in Kansas and which have sent Hoosiers and Texans to Guadalcanal, Normandy, and Korea. Forces that seem beyond control appear to sweep people into battle in strange lands, even though these people would prefer never to leave their home towns except on vacation trips. Why should such things occur?

We must be neither deceived by the apparent simplicity of some aspects of international politics nor deterred by signs of bewildering complexity. Both may simply reflect incomplete and superficial understanding; a more sound and complete understanding is attainable.

THE STRUGGLE FOR POWER WITHIN AND AMONG GROUPS

Conflicting Needs and Wants

The starting point in politics, whether domestic or international, is the fact that people have needs and wants. From this, all else flows. Without the presence of needs and wants, politics would no more exist among men than among stones. They are the mainspring of politics.

There are, of course, many kinds of needs and wants. Not all of them relate to politics. But almost all are such as to bring people into contact with each other. Without contact with others one cannot get a meal or make a million dollars or hear good music or gain an understanding of the society one lives in. Contacts arising from efforts to satisfy needs and achieve wants frequently lead to the formation of groups. Groups are essential to politics, for politics is a group phenomenon. Robinson Crusoe could not play politics.

Whether the group is a family, a fraternity, a church, or a nation, the needs and wants of those involved are bound to differ. The members will have some needs and wants in common, or they would not constitute a group, but they will almost certainly be in disagreement concerning others. For instance, the members of a fraternity may agree in wanting a new house; there may be complete harmony on the point that the old house is unsatisfactory and that a new one is needed. Yet, when it comes to action for raising funds, deciding where to locate the new house, selecting the plans, and settling dozens of other issues, disagreements are bound to arise. Views concerning the best course of action and perhaps on the best way of organizing for action are bound to differ. One hundred per cent harmony in any group is very rare. This fact, too, is part of the foundation of politics. Disagreement is as essential to politics as are needs and wants and groups.

The disagreement must not be total. It must not be so complete and comprehensive as to exclude all possibility of cooperation or adjustment. It must not be so extreme as to break up the group, or terminate contact between groups, or produce literally a death struggle. For politics to exist, relationships within or among groups must fall somewhere between complete agreement and complete disagreement. There must be both common and contradictory desires.

Group Leadership and Group Policies

Politics does not flow automatically from all needs and wants occurring within or among groups and involving agreement-disagreement. There are personal, economic, esthetic, and other questions which are not political. Questions become political when they involve the determination or selection of group policy or group organization or group leadership. The worker who begs his boss for a raise is not in politics; he is engaged in a non-political, personal activity. But if he tries to secure the election of new trade union leadership—perhaps in the hope that they will call a strike so as to force the boss to increase wages—he is in politics. The stockbroker who argues with the Internal Revenue Service over the size of his income tax is not in politics, nor is he if he takes his case to court. But if he tries to persuade his Congressman to seek an amendment to the income tax law, he is in politics. Two Rotarians discussing the activities of their club for their mutual enlightenment are perhaps not being political, but if one of them urges the other to vote for Horatio Zilch as club president, or if he tries to persuade the other to support the making of a gift to the local Boy Scout troop, his activity becomes political.

Politics is oriented on action by a group. It is a relationship among members of a group, in their capacity as members of the group, oriented toward some action by the group. Or it is a relationship among different groups, oriented toward actions which concern that relationship. Politics arises from the very existence of groups and from the efforts of men to shape group policies and to create relationships under which their desires can be achieved to the maximum extent. It is "the art of influencing, manipulating, or controlling [groups] so as to advance the purposes of some against the opposition of others." [1]

Politics occurs in all groups. It occurs in university faculties, in service clubs, in trade unions, in boards of directors of corporations, in political parties, in the governmental bureaucracy, in legislatures, and among citizens or subjects grouped for purposes of government. It also occurs

[1] Quincy Wright, *The Study of International Relations* (New York, Appleton-Century-Crofts, 1955), p. 130.

among groups which are in contact with each other—among different
faculties within one university, among different branches or agencies of
government, and among governments themselves.

The Struggle for Power

If politics is oriented on group action and on the efforts of men to
achieve their desires through group action, this means that politics involves efforts on the part of some to influence or control the actions of
others. In fact, it always involves this. Efforts to influence or control
group policy, or the structure of group organization, or the selection of
group leadership—or efforts to influence or control relationships among
groups—constitute the essence of politics.

This is the basis for the common statement that politics is a struggle
for power. The truth of the statement is, of course, a matter of definition.
We can define power as the ability to influence or control the actions
of others—the ability to make one's will prevail. And we have said that
politics involves efforts on the part of some to influence or control the
actions of others. Thus, politics involves power; power becomes an
inescapable element in politics; all politics becomes power politics. In
fact, the phrase *power politics* becomes a redundant phrase, for the word
politics implies a power relationship. Assuming contradictory desires,
there will be a competitive effort to influence or control others so that
desires can be fulfilled. In other words, there will be a struggle for
power. Politics is a struggle over the determination of internal and
external policies of the group. It is a struggle over the plan of organization of the group—what offices and agencies and processes it will use,
and how it will use them, in determining and implementing its policies.
It is a struggle to determine who will lead. It is a struggle to determine
whose desires relating to group concerns will be fulfilled.

Politics, then, becomes a process taking place within and among groups
—a process in which power (influence and control over others) is gained,
maintained, and used. And the study of politics becomes the study of
this process.

The central question which the student of politics asks is, how is
power gained, maintained, and used? Or, if he wants to take a norma-
tive approach, he asks, how ought power be gained, maintained, and
used? These are the central questions regardless of the unit of politics
under consideration; they are applied to a study of politics in the local
post of the American Legion as well as to a study of politics in the
United Nations.

THE STRUGGLE OVER
CONFLICTING "INTERESTS" OR "VALUES"

Before proceeding further, it will probably be best to clear away some possible sources of doubt and confusion. Most discussions of politics, describing the basic source and purpose of political action, refer to the pursuit of "interests" or to the promotion of "values" rather than to the effort to satisfy needs and achieve wants. Politics is said to be a struggle in which individuals or classes or parties or nations strive to promote their interests through influencing or controlling group action. Or politics is said to be a struggle for the maximum realization of values through group action. These alternative approaches to the question are quite acceptable, and, since we will be using the concepts "interests" and "values" later, we may as well explore their meaning now.

Interests

The term *interests* may refer either to an objective or to a method of reaching an objective; it may refer to an end or to a means. This ambiguity often gives rise to confusion. Both the meaning of the term and the source of confusion can easily be illustrated. Suppose a person's objective is the acquisition of wealth; this is his end-interest. Given this end-interest, he can engage in rational and more or less scientific inquiry into appropriate methods—or hire others to do it for him. The inquiry would presumably reveal, on the one hand, that the construction of horse-drawn buggies would not bring wealth. On the other hand, it might reveal that the profits from the construction of houses would likely be high. Therefore, he would have an interest (a means-interest) in constructing houses, but not in making buggies.

To shift to a different illustration, suppose that the objective of the American people is to preserve the independence of the United States; this is an end-interest. Again, rational inquiry can occur to find appropriate methods. The inquiry might show that unilateral disarmament would put American independence in jeopardy, but that armaments and alliances would serve to protect it. Therefore, the American people have an interest (a means-interest) in maintaining armaments and alliances, but not in unilateral disarmament.

Note that in the above illustrations we started with assumptions. In the first wealth was assumed to be the person's end-interest, and in the second independence was assumed to be an end-interest. But are such assumptions necessarily valid? Can a person *know* that wealth is his end-interest, or can a people *know* that independence should be preserved? The answer is that the process of determining interests must begin with one or more assumptions; it must begin with one or more postulates or preferences. If a person is willing to start with the assumption that wealth is his end-interest, he is free to do so. He may, however, ask himself why he wants wealth, and then he is driven back in his thinking to some other assumption or postulate; perhaps he decides that he wants wealth in order to be able to promote human welfare or happiness, and then human welfare or happiness becomes his end-interest and wealth is transformed into a means-interest. Having accepted a new and more fundamental end-interest, he may then examine the question whether the acquisition of wealth is the best way to promote it—whether it is really a "true" means-interest, and he may or may not decide that it is. Similarly, those who assume that independence should be the end-interest of the American people may ask themselves why, and then they too will be driven back in their thinking to some other assumption or postulate; perhaps they too will find that they want independence as a means of promoting welfare or happiness, whether for the American people or for others as well; if this is so, independence is transformed into a means-interest, and inquiry may or may not show that it is a valid method of promoting the new end-interest.

We have engaged in this examination of the meaning of the concept "interests" so as to permit us to avoid some of the intellectual traps that it contains. Those who apply the concept without examining it carefully are inclined toward several errors. They are inclined to regard interests as tangible, material, or selfish, and to assign no place to altruism or social conscience; if they do acknowledge these qualities it is usually to treat them as deviant and dubious sources of political motivation. They are also inclined to think of interests as objectively determinable, as if they existed independently of any postulates or preferences. They speak of the "true interests" of a person or a people, which exist even if the individuals involved are not aware of them. In our terms, however, "interests" may be either selfish or altruistic. End-interests are always subjectively selected, and cannot be regarded as necessarily true or false; they are simply assumed or postulated. Only means-interests are objectively determinable, and they can be "true" only in the sense that they effectively promote the achievement of an end-interest which is assumed to be desirable. So interpreted, interests should coincide with needs and wants, and the two concepts can be used interchangeably in defining politics.

Values

Politics is also sometimes described as a struggle for the maximum realization of values through group action. The term *values*, like the term *interests*, is a source of confusion, for it is often applied loosely or given different meanings by different writers. At the simplest level, the term *value* is used as a synonym for needs and wants, for desires, or for interests. Whatever is needed or wanted, whatever is desired, or whatever is regarded as an interest is also a value. A value becomes a desired event, situation, relationship, or procedure.[2] It may denote an end (desirable for its own sake) or a means (desirable as an instrument). Those who use the term in this sense generally illustrate it with types of values, such as power, wealth, and well-being. This is the meaning implied in the above statement that politics is a struggle for the maximum realization of values, and the statement becomes quite compatible with the definition of politics already offered.

Alternatively, the word *value* sometimes serves to designate not what is desired but what is desirable. It is used to denote a conception of the desirable which influences the selection from available ends and means of action.[3] The word is thus given a moral connotation. The desirable will include only what is good or right. Wants, desires, or interests which are considered bad or wrong will not be values. If this definition is used, it becomes rather questionable to describe politics as a struggle for the maximum realization of values; the participants may think, of course, that what they desire is also desirable (i.e., good or right), but the detached observer can scarcely agree with them all.

In this book, unless otherwise indicated, we shall use the first of the above two meanings of the word *values;* it will denote what is desired.

IS POLITICS A CONSTANT STRUGGLE FOR MAXIMUM POWER?

The statement was made above that politics is a struggle for power. This calls for some discussion, for it might produce a misconception. It might suggest the concept of a "political man" analogous to the concept of an "economic man" which economists have used, and just as the behavior of the "economic man" was assumed to be guided exclusively by a search for maximum profits, so the behavior of the "political man" would presumably be guided exclusively by a constant search for maximum power. But if such an "economic man" ever existed, he has been rare; practically all men, even in the conduct of their business activities, are influenced by non-economic desires. Similarly, a "political man" who devoted himself exclusively and single-mindedly to the greatest possible increase in his power would be very rare.[4] The proposition that politics is a struggle for power does not mean that every individual and every group are constantly seeking maximum power.

[2] Harold D. Lasswell and Abraham Kaplan, *Power and Society* (New Haven, Yale University Press, 1950), pp. 16-17, 55-58.

[3] Clyde Kluckhohn and others, "Value and Value Orientations in the Theory of Action," in Talcott Parsons and Edward A. Shils, eds., *Toward a General Theory of Action* (Cambridge, Harvard University Press, 1951), p. 395.

[4] E. H. Carr, *The Twenty Years' Crisis 1919-1939* (London, Macmillan, New York, St. Martin's, 1949), p. 97.

In the first place, desires are not exclusively political. People have wants that are non-political in nature. They want material comforts, entertainment, esthetic and intellectual satisfactions, recognition, respect, and many other things that may or may not relate to politics. And in pursuing their other wants, they necessarily have to limit their pursuit of political power. The pursuit of maximum power is commonly incompatible with the fulfillment of non-political desires. Few are willing to forego all other desires so that a maximum of political power can be achieved.

In the second place, political desires themselves may be limited in character. Individuals are frequently indifferent to politics—and therefore to power—in some or all of the groups to which they belong. If not indifferent, they may well be satisfied with a modicum of influence or control; a person who becomes vice-president of a group does not necessarily want to be president, and a president does not necessarily want to be a dictator. Moreover, intergroup politics is not necessarily an all-out struggle for boundless power. Some groups, at least, have limited objectives and are satisfied with whatever power will permit them to achieve those objectives. For instance, if the lawyers can muster enough power to control state legislation on certain restricted matters, such as admission to the bar, they are likely to be satisfied; they are not likely to seek complete control over the state government for the bar association. A pressure group concerned with the tariff on imported textiles is not likely to seek enough power to permit it to dictate federal legislation concerning the allocation of wavelengths to radio broadcasting stations.

Therefore, though politics is a struggle for power, it is not to be pictured as a process involving constant and all-out struggle by all units involved for maximum power. The extent to which available energy and resources are devoted to the accumulation and use of power is likely to vary widely according to circumstances.

The point is significant. If every person or group involved in the political process strove constantly and exclusively for maximum power —if this were a law of politics—then there would be a basis for predicting future behavior. Each group could shape its policies in full knowledge of the dominant objective of every other group. There would be no place for sentiment or morality or friendship, or for non-political pursuits. Rather, there would be a constant and cold calculation of the power advantages to be gained from this move or that. Politics would be a ruthless process in which the power of one person or group would be restrained only by the adverse power of another person or group, or by adverse circumstance. Law and morality would be articles of convenience, to be observed or cast aside as expediency dictated.

There is no doubt that politics sometimes approaches this description, particularly where relationships involve nearly total disagreement on issues which both sides regard as vital. But it would be misleading to assume that acute struggle and tension are inevitable, or even normal, in politics.[5] Equally, it would be misleading to assume that, where acute political tension does exist, all efforts to alleviate it are necessarily futile.

IS POWER AN END IN ITSELF?

Another misconception might also arise from the statement that politics is a struggle for power. It is that power is the one and only objective —an end in itself. Of course, it may be. Individuals and groups sometimes take the view, as we shall later see, that the possession of power, that is, domination over others, is the ultimate goal of action. There are political movements which seem to be inspired by nothing else than an urge to power. This, however, is not always true. Recall the proposition that politics springs out of human needs and wants (desires). These desires are varied. Although they include the desire to dominate, they also include many others. They include the desire for material things, for the essentials and the comforts and the luxuries of life. They include the desire for order and for security. They include the desire for respect and esteem. They include the desire for civil rights and personal liberties. Power is always an objective, but it may be just a prerequisite to the achievement of other desires rather than the ultimate goal.

If power were always the end in itself, politics could be likened to a game the object of which is to select the current winner. It would presumably be a more bloody game than is chess or baseball, but still the outcome would be without moral significance. The victory of one participant in the game would be followed sooner or later by the victory of another, and life would be made up of endless rounds of meaningless struggle. Each victor would have demonstrated his power, and that would be that.

Although this kind of a situation is imaginable and although it is perhaps a theoretical possibility, it never exists in reality. Power may in practice be an end in itself for some participants in the struggle, but not for all of them. Most, if not all, want power so as to achieve more ultimate objectives, whether moral or material. The outcome of the power struggle at any one time represents not simply the victory of one side as an end in itself, but a decision as to whose desires can be achieved. It may have, in fact it is likely to have, moral significance to those involved. It determines how people will live. It determines what kind of society will exist. It determines what kind of a political, economic, and moral structure will prevail, what kind of civilization people will have. One need only look at the transformation which the Bolsheviks

[5] Arnold Wolfers, "The Pole of Power and the Pole of Indifference," *World Politics*, Vol. 4 (October, 1951), pp. 39-63; Carr, *op. cit.*, pp. 102 ff.

brought to Russian life or which the Nazis wrought in German life to see how fateful the political struggle may be to man's fate and progress. The struggle between the free world and the communist world is fraught with similar significance.

Thus, though politics is a struggle for power, it should not be regarded as this alone. The earlier statement is perhaps better: that it is a struggle to determine whose desires relating to group concerns will be fulfilled. It is not simply a game in which points are scored for the purpose of seeing who wins, but a process in which the most fundamental decisions are made concerning the kind of life that people will lead.

THE POWER STRUGGLE INVOLVES BOTH
COOPERATION AND CONFLICT

Attention should also be called to the fact that the power struggle is not necessarily a struggle of each against all. It is not to be assumed that every participant will be hostile to every other participant. This is rarely true, if ever. The power struggle involves cooperation as well as conflict. Persons and groups whose desires are identical or harmonious are likely to join forces in an effort to achieve what they want. Even where the desires of the participants are in conflict, there may be compromise and adjustment to permit joint efforts. Politics thus witnesses more or less intensive and effective cooperation among some individuals and groups in order that opposition to others can be more effective. Struggle between antagonists is matched by more or less harmony within each of the antagonistic groups. Politics involves friendly as well as hostile relationships.

THE FOCUS IN THE STUDY OF POLITICAL SCIENCE
AND INTERNATIONAL POLITICS

While politics occurs within all groups and among many of them, political activity is most prominent in connection with government. Though political science is concerned with politics wherever it occurs, it focuses primarily on the struggle among individuals and groups to influence or control government, and on the struggle among different governments. The student of political science wants to know how power is gained, maintained, and exercised everywhere, but especially how it is done within and among governments.

In international politics, we are primarily interested in the power struggle among the governments of sovereign states. In particular, we are interested in the problem of war. How does it happen that the international power struggle leads so frequently to war? Why do states wage war and how do they try to ward it off? This book is written on the assumption that peace is a value (desirable) but not necessarily the supreme value. A major purpose is to identify values relevant to peace and war, to explore the implications both of these values themselves and of methods of pursuing them, and to see whether and how adjustments might be made to reduce the role of violence in international affairs.

We shall start our inquiry in the more familiar domestic sphere. An understanding of international politics is likely to be improved by an understanding of domestic politics—where a power struggle also occurs and where civil war is sometimes fought.

SUGGESTED READINGS

CARR, E. H., *The Twenty Years' Crisis 1919-1939* (London, Macmillan, New York, St. Martin's, 1949).

DE GRAZIA, Alfred, *The Elements of Political Science* (New York, Knopf, 1952).

EASTON, David, *The Political System* (New York, Knopf, 1953).

LASSWELL, Harold, *Politics: Who Gets What, When, How* (New York, McGraw-Hill, 1936).

LASSWELL, Harold D., and KAPLAN, Abraham, *Power and Society* (New Haven, Yale University Press, 1950).

SNYDER, Richard C., and WILSON, H. Hubert, *Roots of Political Behavior* (New York, American Book, 1949).

WRIGHT, Quincy, *The Study of International Relations* (New York, Appleton-Century-Crofts, 1955).

CHAPTER 2

Domestic Politics, Peace, and Civil War

THE IMPRESSION IS COMMON that international politics is somehow very different from domestic politics. Particularly in democratic countries people usually think of domestic politics in terms of persuasion, peaceful legislation and administration, and periodic elections; they think of international politics in terms of war and the threat of war. There is a vague sense not only that international and domestic politics proceed on different levels involving different issues, but also that they are scarcely of the same genus.

There are differences between politics in the two areas, and very important ones. Among the differences—and probably the most important of them—is the fact that within countries government exists, whereas among countries it does not. Yet, though differences exist and are important, they should not be exaggerated. There are similarities, too, the overwhelming one being that a power struggle pervades both. The power struggle within countries sometimes erupts in civil war, just as the power struggle among countries sometimes involves international war.

The outstanding fact is that, for some countries, civil war is a much less frequent event than international war.[1] This fact suggests another which, while obvious, is strikingly important: that conditions and methods of action exist within those countries which somehow permit the power struggle to proceed by means that usually are peaceful. The question is, what are these conditions and methods? The answer to this question can certainly shed some light on the problem of reducing the prevalence of war in international politics.

---

[1] According to Quincy Wright, 70 of the 244 wars in which European states engaged from 1480 to 1941 were civil wars; the corresponding figures for non-European states are 12 out of 113. *A Study of War* (Chicago, The University of Chicago Press, 1942), Vol. I, p. 651.

GOVERNMENT AND DOMESTIC PEACE

Government is a vital factor in determining whether peace will prevail within countries or civil war occur.[2] Government includes many things. There is no need here to attempt a comprehensive description, but it is important to recall those aspects of government which contribute particularly to the preservation of domestic peace.

The Executive: Law Enforcement and Armed Peace

Government regularly includes an executive—whether it is a president, a prime minister, a dictator, or a king. One of the major tasks of the executive is to administer and enforce the law. Normally this task proceeds quite peacefully; once citizens and subjects know what the law is they usually abide by it. But the important thing for our purposes is that every government aims to equip its executive with the power to enforce law against the recalcitrant. What we call peace within countries does not involve the elimination of all violence; rather, peace involves an organization of violence. Peace is always armed. Governments disarm those subject to their jurisdiction; they regulate or forbid the possession of weapons by citizens and subjects, and they prohibit the creation of private or party armed forces. At the same time, they themselves maintain both police and military forces. In short, governments seek a monopoly of violence. They want the physical power in their own command to be so overwhelming as to give potential rebels no hope of success. And, in truth, as long as executive power is clearly overwhelming, it would be madness for hostile elements to rebel.

Suppose for a moment that some government should renounce all use of violence. How long would it remain a government? Persons or groups which wished to challenge its authority could no doubt succeed in doing so. And a determined group willing and able to resort to violence could no doubt completely overthrow and displace a government which committed itself to nothing but pacific methods. Or suppose that, while not renouncing violence, a government should fail to maintain overwhelming military power in relation to those subject to it; suppose that it should allow a hostile party or faction to develop an army or to subvert and win over to its own side the armed forces that are supposed to be loyal to the government. If those hostile to the government came to command sufficient military power to give them a good prospect of winning in civil war, they would at least be strongly tempted to initiate such a war.

This is illustrated by events in Spain in the 1930's. A democratic government existed which enacted various reforms. These reforms aroused

[2] See the discussion, "War and Vital Interests Inside the State," in J. L. Brierly, *The Outlook for International Law* (Oxford, Clarendon, 1944), pp. 46-60.

the antagonism of significant groups in the Spanish population, particularly the landlord group, much of the leadership of the Catholic Church, and a large proportion of the armed forces. These groups, intensely opposed to the government and believing that they commanded more military power than the government, rebelled. In the Civil War which followed they proved their military predominance, and their victory involved the overthrow of the democratic government and its replacement by a government headed by Franco, the rebel leader. Similarly in China the Nationalist regime of Chiang Kai-shek was unable to maintain overwhelming power vis-à-vis Communist forces. The latter rebelled, and after prolonged civil war drove the Nationalist regime from the mainland of China and established a Communist dictatorship in Peking.

Peace, then, depends to some extent on power relations within the country. The executive must have sufficient power at its command to enforce obedience. A peaceful country is a policeful country. It is usually not necessary for a government to develop its power to the uttermost, but it is necessary that it constantly maintain a preponderance that is overwhelming in relation to the power that can be mustered by any potential rebels. What we call peace, then, depends in part on the ratio of military power between the government and those who might be inclined to challenge the government in civil war.

Legislative Authority, Making Law a Reflection of the Desires of the Strong

In addition to a law-enforcing authority armed with superior power, government also includes a law-making authority—perhaps the executive itself if the country is dictatorial, or perhaps an elected legislature. Lawmaking has much to do with the questions of war and peace within any society. Probably the most serious and threatening disputes which arise are disputes over what the law should be. Should slavery be permitted or prohibited? Should trade unions be outlawed, or should collective bargaining with trade unions be required? Should the law provide for a socialist or for a capitalist system? Should minority groups, like the Negroes in America, have fully equal membership in society? In a time of depression and mass unemployment, should the law provide some form of aid, or should life proceed on "the devil take the hindmost" principle? During the past century, in one country or another, all these questions and many more like them have produced either threats of civil war or the actual outbreak of civil war.

The important thing in any society, if war is to be avoided, is that the law should be a reasonably accurate reflection of the desires of the strong.[3] The correlation between strength and law, as indicated above,

[3] For a more extended discussion of this proposition, see pp. 300-305 below, Chapter 15, and the sources there cited.

can be obtained in part by measures of the government to keep itself strong; as long as it has overwhelming police and military power at its command, it is under no compulsion to change the law. Yet, in a changing society a government which fails to change the law is likely to find it difficult to maintain a clear preponderance of power. Groups that are rising in the society will become more and more discontented with laws which confer advantages on groups that are declining. For instance, at one time trade unions were illegal in many states of the United States; at one time there was no attempt to regulate utilities or control monopolies; at one time there was no governmental effort to alleviate distress produced by economic depressions; at one time there was no federal income tax law. Now suppose that in none of these respects had the law been changed. Certainly discontent would have become widespread, and the position of the government would have become precarious. Workers would have become restive, and would have regarded government simply as an instrument through which employers maintained a system of repression and exploitation. Many consumers would have become enraged over the extortions of utilities and monopolies. The unemployed would have become bitter against a system which brought ruin to their lives. And the relatively poor would have resented a tax system which seemed disproportionately burdensome to them. Perhaps, despite all this, the government would have been able to maintain itself through repressive measures—through a rigid preservation of a monopoly of violence. However, mass discontent would have made this difficult. The discontented might well have found ways of organizing themselves for action against the government despite its measures of repression—just as various rebel groups in Russia managed to organize and act against the Tsar.

Rather than try to maintain the correlation between strength and law by exclusive concern for strength, most governments seek to maintain the adjustment at least in part through changing the law. Particularly in democratic countries, emphasis is placed on procedures through which influence and control over government can be transferred from groups that have lost strength to groups that have gained strength. There are periodic elections by which the desires of the voters are presumably determined. There are legislatures in which representation is given to parties or groups in rough proportion to their voting strength. Parties and groups which lose out in elections lose control of law-making and law-enforcing authority. Those with the greatest voting strength gain such control and, within constitutional limitations, can enact new law or amend old law to satisfy their desires. Dictatorial governments likewise have means of changing the law—even though it is simply the fiat of the dictator. In connection with all types of government, one of the main considerations in enacting and changing the law is that the law should be such, at a minimum, as to keep discontent below the point at which rebellion might break out.

The importance of adequate procedures for changing the law—or of permitting the strong to determine what the law should be—can scarcely be exaggerated; these procedures contribute mightily to the preservation of peace within the state. There is no way of knowing how often civil war would break out in the absence of such procedures; it would depend on many factors, including the speed with which change occurred in the distribution of strength among groups and classes within the society. Nevertheless, there can be no doubt that civil war would occur much more frequently than it does if government insisted rigorously on enforcing unchanging law. "No peace system can be expected to work for any length of time unless it contains adequate provision for bringing about changes in the status quo as required by changing conditions." [4] Elections and legislatures—or substitutes for them—are the fields of battle in which most of the disputes are resolved which might otherwise lead to the outbreak of violence or civil war.

In the international field, what we have just been discussing is commonly treated under the label "peaceful change." Richard Van Wagenen defines peaceful change as [5]

the resolving or adjustment of social problems, normally by institutionalized procedures, without resort to unauthorized physical force. It should be noted that the use of authorized physical force does not violate the concept of peaceful change.

He goes on to suggest that the term *policeful change* would be more appropriate than *peaceful change,* because the essential consideration is not whether the change is peaceful or warlike but rather whether it is authorized or unauthorized. Within countries governments authorize and may enforce change.

The Judiciary, Interpreting the Law and Maintaining an Expectation of Justice

Courts likewise are important instruments for the preservation of peace within countries. It is through them that the executive seeks to enforce criminal law, and through them (at least in most countries) that the citizen secures protection against arbitrary and illegal executive actions. Moreover, it is through them, in civil suits, that individuals can frequently secure the settlement of disputes between themselves. So far as domestic peace is concerned, the chief direct contribution of civil

[4] Frederick Sherwood Dunn, *Peaceful Change* (New York, Council on Foreign Relations, 1937), p. 2.

[5] Richard W. Van Wagenen, *Research in the International Organization Field* (Princeton, Center for Research on World Political Institutions, 1952), pp. 11, 14-15.

actions and the prosecution of those accused of crime is a reduction in scattered acts of individual violence. But it seems plausible to assume that civil war would be more likely if there were no judicial agencies to which appeal could be made for an interpretation and application of the law.

Courts, along with other governmental agencies, help to reduce the prospects of civil war especially by maintaining an expectation of justice. The existence of such an expectation of justice through political and governmental action is another of the important bases of peace within states. Whether within or among states, war is usually, though not always, a measure of last resort. As long as any substantial hope exists that strongly held desires can be fulfilled by peaceful political and governmental processes, civil war is not likely to occur. If people think that they can get what they regard as justice by resort to courts or to legislatures or to executive action, they are not likely to rebel. By maintaining institutions and procedures through which justice can be done, governments do a great deal to deter resort to violence.

Law Itself as a Reinforcement of Peace

There is another way, too, in which government contributes to domestic peace: it provides law. Hitherto, we have emphasized the importance to peace of means of enacting, amending, and interpreting law. But the very existence of law, whether it is statute or common law, likewise reinforces peace. In the first place, law helps to maintain domestic peace simply in providing reasonably clear statements of rights and duties; it is obvious that violence is more likely to occur where rights and duties are undefined or vague. Adjacent property owners, for instance, are more likely to get into a dispute over their respective obligations concerning a line fence if there is no law concerning the question than if there is a law regulating the question. Further, law reinforces peace through what may be called a socializing effect. Law helps to create and intensify the bonds of any society. Those living under one law are likely, more and more, to regard themselves as belonging to one society. Moreover, law will produce common bonds among them—particularly among those who believe that they derive benefits from the law. For instance, property owners will likely want to maintain the governmental and legal system under which their property rights are protected; parties to contracts will want to maintain the system under which they expect the contract to be interpreted and enforced; trade unions, if they regard their position in society as reasonably satisfactory, will oppose rebellion against the system, especially if the program of the rebels would render the position of trade unions less satisfactory. In short, law facilitates the development of a whole network of common interests, and the more intensive and extensive this network becomes the less likely is it that rebellion will occur.

ATTITUDES AND DOMESTIC PEACE

The preceding discussion brought out three principal points. The first was that peace within countries depends in part on the relative power positions of different groups and organizations; more specifically, that peace depends in part on governmental possession of military and police power that is overwhelming in relation to the physical power that can be mustered by any rebellious group. The second point was that peace also depends in part on the existence of peaceful procedures, whether judicial, legislative, or executive, through which people can get what they regard as justice; these procedures relate to making, amending, and interpreting the law. The third item called attention to the fact that the very existence of a system of law tends to reinforce peace.

All these points are important, but clearly they do not provide the whole story. A government might be able to maintain itself and preserve domestic peace simply on the basis of its command of violence and on the basis of executive, legislative, and judicial processes, but in fact governments do not like to rely on these factors alone, and they commonly do not do so. Peace within countries also depends upon the attitudes of people, not simply on government and the processes of government.

A Constitutional Consensus

In general, peace within countries is the more secure the more widely a common set of fundamental desires exists.[6] When the people of any country are at odds on the fundamental principles on the basis of which life will proceed, domestic peace is obviously endangered. In Russia under the tsars, for example, agreement on fundamental principles broke down. Some wanted to retain a tsar as an absolute ruler; others wanted democracy; others wanted to establish a dictatorship of the proletariat and ultimately a communist society. Reconciliation of these conflicting desires was impossible, and the question whose desires would prevail was finally answered on the battlefield. Similarly, before the French Revolution, before the American Civil War, before the Spanish Civil War —and, in fact, before every major civil conflict—sharp differences have developed on issues regarded as vital. Peace is precarious in any country when powerful elements in the population reject economic or political principles which the government seeks to uphold. But where there is general acceptance of the existing system, as there is in the United States and in most countries, domestic peace is reasonably secure.

What are the attitudes that are of fundamental importance? Perhaps

6 R. M. MacIver, *The Web of Government* (New York, Macmillan, 1947), pp. 3-6, 15-21, and *passim*.

the basic one concerns belief in law and order—belief in peace. In most countries people simply do not think in terms of possible civil war. Almost all of them conduct their affairs on the assumption that peace will be preserved—that the changes which occur will occur on the basis of peaceful processes. They tacitly subordinate all demands for change to a paramount desire that law and order should be maintained. They have a desire for peace that is supreme over any desire for change. And the very forgetfulness of the possibility of rebellion is the surest guarantee that rebellion will not occur. As we shall see later, in international politics the very expectation of war does much to bring war on. The absence of such an expectation within countries is probably the best assurance of domestic peace.

What is called a constitutional consensus underlies this belief in peace. In a democratic country the constitutional consensus will include such beliefs as the following: that paramount importance is to be attached, not to the government as such nor to the nation as such, but to the individual; therefore that respect for, and the promotion of, the dignity and worth and liberty and welfare of the individual should guide governmental activities; that the right to law-making and law-enforcing authority should be assigned in accordance with the outcome of free and fair elections; that the law should be obeyed; that there should be tolerance of minorities; and that minority parties should not be crushed or liquidated, but should be permitted to operate unhampered by discriminatory legal impediments to future electoral victory.[7]

Given general popular agreement on fundamental principles such as these, the possibility of civil war is rendered extremely remote. There may be—and really there are bound to be—intense disputes over the meaning of some of these principles and the best method of implementing them, but the principles themselves set limits on the ways of resolving such disputes. To resort to civil war as a method of settlement would be to abandon the principles themselves.

Society, the Public Interest, and Loyalty

Along with common attitudes on the supreme importance of peace and on such fundamental principles as those described above usually goes recognition of membership in a society in which individuals have obligations to each other. There is a belief that in some circumstances the individual—or perhaps a great many individuals—should accept risks and sacrifices in the interest of the rest.[8] The most extreme examples relate to international war. When a country is involved in foreign war, people

---

[7] Cf. "American Ideals and the American Conscience," in Gunnar Myrdal, *An American Dilemma* (New York, Harper, 1944), Vol. I, pp. 3-25.

[8] Cf. E. H. Carr, *The Twenty Years' Crisis 1919-1939* (London, Macmillan, New York, St. Martin's, 1949), pp. 166-169.

generally accept the view that it is right to ask some to risk their lives
in behalf of the good of the society as a whole; military preparations
against the possibility of future war commonly also require sacrifices
from some—for instance, in the form of military service—in order that
the interests of the rest may be served. In questions unrelated to war,
too, there is a recognition in many ways of the supremacy of common,
public interests over private interests. This is involved in the concomi-
tant of the principle of majority rule, that is, that the minority should
obey. It is involved in the idea that the law should be observed even by
those who consider it bad. The principle that the good of the many
transcends the good of the few is also reflected whenever the right of
eminent domain is exercised.

Accompanying this recognition of the transcendent importance of the
good of the whole society goes loyalty to certain symbols and principles
of that society. American society, like most others, is a national society.
Therefore we give great emphasis to certain national symbols. The most
important of them is the flag, but there are others, too. We maintain
national shrines, such as Mount Vernon, and various memorials, such as
the monuments to Washington, Jefferson, and Lincoln in Washington,
D.C. Visits to these shrines and memorials are supposed to kindle and
maintain loyalty to the society of which we are a part. Certain government buildings, particularly the White House and the Capitol, take on
symbolic significance in reminding us of common membership in one
society. National holidays, particularly the Fourth of July, and the sing-
ing of the national anthem serve the same purpose. The principles on
which our national life is based are set forth and symbolized in the
Constitution, which is therefore hallowed. Negatively, we encourage
loyalty to our society and the principles on which it is based by de-
nouncing and excoriating those who oppose our system—such as Hitler,
Stalin, and the Communists.

Response to national symbols and belief in the principles on which our
society is based commonly involve emotional overtones. Faith in the
flag and acceptance of constitutional doctrine take on a religious flavor.
Given attitudes of this sort, civil war becomes no more than a very remote
possibility.

Attitudes, then, reinforce government in maintaining peace within
countries. The relationship between the two is a reciprocal one. The
existence of common attitudes helps make government possible, and
governments themselves do a great deal to foster and preserve common
attitudes. Through the educational system, through public ceremonies,
through the exhortations of political leaders, and in many other ways,
governments try to develop, maintain, and intensify a sense of oneness
on the part of the people, a sense of loyalty to the society as a whole.

And, in varying degrees, governments try to suppress those whose activities undermine the sense of common loyalty. All governments make treason a crime. Many outlaw certain political movements regarded as seditious, such as the communist movement. All try to enforce some degree of respect to the national flag—for instance, by making desecration of the flag a punishable offense.

The existence of organized government and adherence by the people to a common set of fundamental attitudes, then, are the principal pillars on which peace within countries rests.

DOMESTIC PEACE AND THE DESIRES
OF THE STRONG

The proposition was made above that, if civil war is to be avoided, the law should be a reasonably accurate reflection of the desires of the strong. This idea calls for some elaboration and emphasis. People do not commonly think of the fact that within countries the strong rule, and so they put international politics—where the strong more obviously rule —in a class by itself. Actually, it is in the nature of all politics that the strong rule.

We have already described politics as a struggle for power; within countries, it is a struggle to gain and maintain control over governmental offices, with a view to exercising that control to promote the fulfillment of political desires. The group, perhaps a political party, or the amalgamation of groups that can muster predominant strength establishes its right to law-making and law-enforcing authority. Theoretically, the strong may be either a majority or a minority. The desires of a people may be so harmonious that the strong include virtually the entire population. Or, particularly in the light of modern technology and of the relatively new techniques of totalitarian control, the strong may constitute only a small proportion of the population.

Strength and the Right to
Rule in Democracies

The strength which gives the "right" to rule is measured in various ways. In democratic countries it is measured in the first instance through elections. Control over government is assigned on the basis of electoral appeal.

Suppose, however, that the distribution of ballots fails to reflect the distribution of military power. Suppose that a political party, such as the Communist Party, has managed to get itself into a position where it might overthrow the government in civil war even if it cannot win a majority of the votes. Or suppose that some sort of conspiracy against the democratically elected government exists, and that the conspirators have the support of most or all of the police and military forces. What kind of a position is the government then in?

In such a situation the government will exist only on the sufferance of those who, by whatever means, have secured a preponderance of military power. It may seek to save itself by making concessions to the opposition, and then the desires of the militarily strong will largely dominate. If it fails to make adequate concessions, it will face rebellion, and the strong will establish their right to rule in civil war.

It may be that the attitudes on which domestic peace rests will be influential enough to deter rebellion even on the part of those who have the power to rebel successfully. However, these attitudes themselves are not likely to survive indefinitely if the laws and the administration of those laws go flagrantly against the desires of the strong. Men are usually reluctant to undertake the risks of war, whether civil or international, but all history shows that they do sometimes accept those risks. Sooner or later, unless the government makes great concessions to the desires of the strong, the attitudes which deter rebellion will be abandoned and rebellion will occur.

Thus if the distribution of ballots does not correspond reasonably well with the distribution of military strength—if those who win elections do not possess a preponderance of military power—sooner or later civil war is likely to occur. Battlefields replace polling booths, and bullets replace ballots in determining who the strong are, and therefore who has the "right" to rule.

Strength and the Right to Rule in Dictatorships

The relationship between military power and control over government is all the more apparent in dictatorial countries. Dictators ordinarily establish their control over government simply because they can muster more physical power than others. They secure the "right" to rule through the threat or the use of force. Before the establishment of their "right" to rule, if they take another's property, the action is punishable as robbery; if they kill an opponent, the action is punishable as murder. After they secure control of the government they become the "legitimate" authorities, and the very same actions against the very same people are regarded as "legal" and are classified as taxation or confiscation or execution. Since they secured the "right" to rule through the threat or the use of force, this method of displacing them is suggested to others. Consequently, the dictator tries, within the limits of his own principles and objectives, to win the support of as many people as possible, and to repress, perhaps bloodily, those whose support he cannot gain. The latter, in turn, will seek to escape repression and, given propitious circumstances, may conspire and seek to overthrow the dictator. Given modern devices of totalitarian control, this is often an extremely difficult task, but if success is achieved, the "right" to rule is transferred. Control over government and therefore over law goes to those who are now the strong.

The principal points of this chapter can be summarized as follows. A power struggle goes on in politics within countries just as it does among countries. Within countries the power struggle is normally carried out by peaceful means; civil war is less frequent than international war. The power struggle within countries can be carried on by peaceful means for two main reasons:

1. Government exists. The government normally possesses a monopoly, or at least an overwhelming preponderance, of power, thus making rebellion futile and thus permitting the enforcement of law. Moreover, government involves institutions and procedures through which laws may be enacted, changed, interpreted, and administered.

2. Attitudes exist which reinforce peace. The presence of common desires and of common loyalties and the very assumption that the political process will be carried on peacefully all work together to relegate the possibility of civil war into the background.

Nevertheless, within countries the strong rule; the law normally reflects the desires of the strong. As the distribution of power within a country changes, as some groups rise in power while others fall, the law will be changed to reflect the new situation. It will be changed peacefully if adequate peaceful procedures are available. If adequate peaceful procedures are not available, then violence is sooner or later likely to occur. The strong will not indefinitely support a legal order which runs drastically counter to their desires.

SUGGESTED READINGS

CARR, E. H., *The Twenty Years' Crisis 1919-1939* (London, Macmillan, New York, St. Martin's, 1949).

DE GRAZIA, Alfred, *The Elements of Political Science* (New York, Knopf, 1952).

DE GRAZIA, Sebastian, *The Political Community* (Chicago, The University of Chicago Press, 1948).

HOOK, Sidney, "Violence," *Encyclopedia of the Social Sciences*, Vol. XV, pp. 264-267.

McKINLEY, Silas Bent, *Democracy and Military Power* (New York, Vanguard, 1941).

MERRIAM, Charles E., *Political Power* (New York, Whittlesey House, 1934).

RUSSELL, Bertrand, *Power, a New Social Analysis* (New York, Norton, 1938).

WATKINS, Frederick M., *The State as a Concept of Political Science* (New York, Harper, 1934).

WRIGHT, Quincy, *A Study of War* (Chicago, The University of Chicago Press, 1942).

Part II

THE DYNAMICS OF

INTERNATIONAL POLITICS

Introductory Note

IN THE SUCCEEDING CHAPTERS on the dynamics of international politics we shall be analyzing primarily the "why's" of state behavior. "Why" will be interpreted both in a "because of" sense and in an "in order to" sense; we shall treat causes and purposes, motivations and objectives. Later, in the chapters of Part III, the focus will be on the "how's" of state behavior—the methods employed to achieve the purposes.

In analyzing the "why's" we shall first discuss sovereignty and security, and the desire to preserve them. Then we shall deal with some ideas which those who act in the name of the state espouse and which presumably influence their decisions: the idea of the nation and the associated ideology of nationalism, and the ideas of liberals, fascists, and communists. Thereafter attention will be focused on the economic forces and objectives which in various circumstances contribute either to international cooperation or to international conflict. War itself, and the expectation of war, will be seen to play a significant role in causing war. The character of human nature will be analyzed with a view to assessing psychological factors making for peace and war. Finally, there will be a summary chapter listing and briefly discussing the various objectives that states commonly pursue.

CHAPTER 3

Security and Sovereignty

STATES GENERALLY seek self-preservation or security above all. They regard survival as their paramount interest. Normally they are willing to sacrifice every other interest, if need be, to promote this one effectively.

The words *self-preservation, security,* and *survival* appear to have plain, common-sense meanings, and to a large extent they do, but complexities and ambiguities are hidden in them which deserve to be explored. The meaning of concepts which play such an important role in international politics cannot simply be taken for granted. Further, if states put such stress on preserving themselves, it is proper to ask what leads them to do it and whether the objective is justifiable.

THE "SELF" IN "SELF-PRESERVATION"

When states seek self-preservation, precisely what is the "self" that is to be preserved? The answer is not always obvious.

Territory and People

Naturally, the self includes territory and the accompanying people. Self-preservation is regularly taken to require the preservation of "territorial integrity." The general rule is that states want to preserve their jurisdiction over whatever territory they possess.

However, different portions of a state's territory may not be regarded as equally valuable parts of the self, and states may in fact survive the loss even of territory that they regard as essential. Britain defended its colony, Burma, during World War II in the struggle for self-preservation, and then voluntarily granted it independence; Burma was apparently not an essential part of the self that was to be preserved. The United States did the same with regard to the Philippines. Poland survives as a state, but with boundary lines far different from those of 1939. Germany lost territory that it considered an essential part of its self after World War I but did not lose its character as a state. Frequently in history states have ceded or exchanged territory without any sign of a feeling that this was contrary to self-preservation. States holding trust territories under the United Nations are bound to promote their progressive development toward self-government or independence, which suggests that these territories are not essential parts of the self from the point of view of the administering powers.

Moreover, it is probably fair to say that the territorial self is sometimes defined to include land under the jurisdiction of another state. Thus, though France lost the provinces of Alsace-Lorraine to Germany in 1871, it maintained a moral claim to them and took them back after World War I. Similarly today neither the East Germans nor the West Germans are much influenced by existing boundary lines in defining Germany's real territorial self.

Thus, though states have self-preservation as a major objective, the territorial self that is to be preserved is subject to definition. It regularly includes territory thought of as the homeland, and it may include other territory as well. Perhaps the best statement is that, as a minimum, states want to avoid being compelled by external power to give up territory over which they actually have control and that, as a maximum, they want to be free to delimit their boundaries as they please.

Sovereignty and Equality

In addition to territory and people, the self that is to be preserved has another attribute usually described as sovereignty or independence. The meaning of these words is very elusive. This is indicated by the fact that the League of Nations accepted both Britain and its colony, India, as sovereign, and by the fact that the United Nations accepts as sovereign both the U.S.S.R. and two constituent republics within the U.S.S.R.

However, the term does have a legal meaning. From a legal point of view it denotes a status. A political entity which is free to make and enforce law as it sees fit, subject only to the requirements of international law, is said to possess sovereignty or independence. In other words, where law-making and law-enforcing authority is unlimited, except by international law, there sovereignty resides.[1] The fact that sovereigns are subject to international law implies that they are able to enter directly into relations with other states.

The legal conception of sovereignty can be clarified by considering political entities that are not sovereign. Among these are the political subdivisions into which states are divided. In this country, for example, the forty-eight states are not sovereign; the constitution not only limits

[1] Quincy Wright, *A Study of War* (Chicago, The University of Chicago Press, 1942), Vol. II, p. 896.

their law-making and law-enforcing authority, but it also confers on the federal government the right to make laws which will be enforced within the various states. Neither are counties and cities sovereign, for their authority is dependent on legislation enacted by state governments. Puerto Rico is not sovereign; rather, it is a dependent territory to which the United States has granted self-government. Similarly, the colonies or dependent territories within the British or other empires are not sovereign; they have been annexed by a "mother country" and have only such law-making and law-enforcing authority as the mother country permits them to have.

Not only do these various kinds of subordinate political entities have law-making and law-enforcing authority that is limited by some other political entity; another key fact is that they are not directly subject to international law. Their actions may violate international law, but responsibility for the violation rests with the sovereign. If a foreign government wishes to lodge a formal protest claiming, for example, that Iowa has violated a treaty obligation or a rule of general international law, it will address the protest not to Des Moines but to Washington, D.C. Similarly, protests concerning the actions of a British colony would go not to the colonial government but to London. In other words, non-sovereign, dependent political entities lack a capacity to enter freely into foreign relations; they lack the capacity to assume the rights and undertake the duties provided for in international law.

Thus it can be said that sovereignty involves two closely related elements: freedom to make and enforce domestic law, and a capacity to invoke rights and assume obligations under international law. It may be helpful to think of the sovereign as standing on a line across the middle of this page. The upper part of the page is the field of international law; the lower part is the field of domestic law. The sovereign is limited by regulations in the upper field of international law, but can do as he pleases in the lower field of domestic law. However, the line between the two fields is a shifting one. As international law develops, by treaty or otherwise, the line cuts across the page at a lower point. The sovereign is still there, subject to the one field of law and supreme over the other, but the line between the two fields has shifted. The field of domestic law has contracted, and the field of international law has expanded.

For example, international law now permits each state to deal with atomic energy as it sees fit. Each state is free to produce fissionable materials, from which atomic energy can be released. Each state is free to use atomic energy within its territory. Each state is free to manufacture nuclear weapons of any kind in any quantity. But states could change this situation through treaty agreement. The United States itself has proposed a plan under which a world Atomic Development Au-

thority would be created. Under the plan the ADA would have very
extensive control over all activities pertaining to fissionable materials
throughout the world. Suppose that such a plan were adopted. Suppose,
further, that activities pertaining to atomic energy should come to pene-
trate every aspect of the economic life of the United States or of other
parties to the treaty. This would mean that the ADA would have substantial authority over economic life in the countries involved. Sovereignty would thus lose much of its significance, though it would still
theoretically exist.

This kind of thing has actually happened, particularly in relations between rather backward countries and advanced countries. Great Britain,
for example, once concluded treaties with certain Malay states under
which these states became protectorates. Britain, as the protecting
power, gained various rights in connection with the governmental affairs
of its protectorates; among other things, it gained the right to conduct
their foreign relations. Nevertheless, Britain continued to recognize these
states as sovereign. They remained supreme over their domestic affairs,
but the domestic field had greatly contracted and the field of international law had greatly expanded. Thus their sovereignty lost much of
its significance.

Sovereign states are said to be equal.

Superficially, this statement looks absurd. States are obviously unequal
in many ways. They are unequal in terms of the size of their population
and territory. They are unequal in terms of resources, wealth, and power.
These inequalities are obvious. Not so obvious is the fact that states are
also unequal in terms of legal rights. Some states possess rights which
others do not have. This is illustrated by the above reference to British
relationships to certain Malay states; by treaty these states gave up certain rights to Britain. It is also illustrated, say, in the United Nations,
where some states have permanent seats on the Security Council and
others are elected for limited terms. It is often illustrated by the situation
of states defeated in war; the peace treaties imposed on them commonly
deny or limit rights which other states freely exercise, such as the right
to maintain armed forces of the size and kind that they want.

Actually, of course, the principle of the equality of states does not
mean that they are equal in every respect. Rather it means this: that
states are equally entitled to have their rights respected. In other words
whatever the rights of a state may be they are to be respected in the same
way in which the rights of other states are respected.[2]

The principal implication of this is that power, as such, gives no
special rights. One state has no right, simply because it is stronger, to
impose its will on another. Nor does a group of states have the right

[2] J. L. Brierly, *The Law of Nations* (Oxford, Clarendon, 1949), pp. 115-118.

to override the sovereign equality of any outside state; if the outside state is observing existing law, it is legally free to rest on its rights and to refuse to acquiesce in the demands or suggestions of others.

This point is tremendously important. To assure clarity it is desirable to make the same point in another way. Within democratic states, people are generally regarded as equal; our constitution assures to every person the equal protection of the laws. This is not, however, interpreted to prevent majority rule. Laws may be enacted and enforced on everyone, even though a substantial minority opposes the law. The principle of equality does not give the individual a right of veto on changes in the law.

In the international realm, the situation is different. The principle of sovereign equality is interpreted to mean that no changes in the law affecting the rights of a state may be made without its consent. International law itself is said to be based on the consent of the states which it binds. Treaties come into effect only when states agree to them, and they bind only those states that do agree. Unless some specific contrary arrangement has been agreed to, each state has a veto on the creation of new law affecting it. There is no international legislature which can enact law by majority vote.

Further, within states the principle of equality is not interpreted to forbid hailing an individual into court against his will. He can be sued, or he can be prosecuted for violation of criminal law. But here again the situation is different in the international realm. The principle of sovereign equality is interpreted to mean not only that a state may veto changes in the law affecting its rights, but also that a state cannot be hailed into court without its consent. There are, of course, judicial methods which states may use for the purpose of settling their disputes, but they are not obliged to accept such methods. They can neither be sued nor criminally prosecuted. If they take their case to court, it must be with the consent of all parties.

Finally, within states the principle of equality is held to be compatible with the existence of an executive organ of government which will enforce law. Among states this does not prevail. Although some halting steps have been taken toward the creation of international executive organs, particularly in the United Nations, such organs as now exist have very limited powers. Sovereign states have not wanted to place themselves under an international executive with effective power over them. Among the considerations deterring them has been the fear of losing the rights and privileges that sovereign equality provides.

A Political and Economic System

Square miles of land, numbers of people, and a legal status of sovereignty and equality fall far short of including all the aspects of the self which states seek to preserve. Within the various sovereign states, there are different traditions, different customs, and different ways of living. There are democratic governments, which vary more or less among themselves. There are oligarchies and dictatorships. Economic systems differ, the principles of communism, socialism, and capitalism being implemented in varying degrees in different countries. Scales of living and the distribution of wealth vary. The list of differences among the political and economic systems in different states is almost endless.

Within each country some or all people want to preserve the political and economic system under which they live. A dictator is likely to think that governing the state is a good thing for himself, and perhaps for others as well; he will not want the political system in which he has come to power to be destroyed. Where political power is held by an oligarchy or ruling class, the rulers involved are also likely to think that it is good and right to preserve the system under which they enjoy a privileged position. Similarly in democracies, where political power is widely dispersed, the politically influential are commonly jealous of the independence of their state and want to preserve its democratic system. Whatever the economic system, there will be some who are favored by it and who therefore want it preserved.

The self which is to be preserved thus normally includes a political and economic system—a social system; it includes a way of life, a culture. The aim of governments is not simply to preserve the state, but to preserve a particular kind of state. This sometimes raises a problem of priority, for measures which will perhaps contribute to the preservation of territorial integrity may be more or less incompatible with principles on which the social system is based. Should women be mobilized on the same basis as men when dire threat confronts the state? Should lies be told if it seems likely that they will render the state more secure? Should a country which prizes freedom adopt measures of regimentation to increase its survival capacity? Should surprise attack or "preventive" warfare be regarded, in principle, as proper? Or perhaps the question should be, in what circumstances, if any, should a state adopt methods of preserving territorial integrity and sovereignty which are incompatible with the principles by which it wants to live?

The fact that the self includes a particular type of social system also raises questions concerning relationships with foreign states. Should alliances be made with states which champion antithetical social systems? Should similar social systems be protected or promoted in other states? If a desirable kind of self is to be preserved, does this necessitate action, and, if so, what kind of action, to establish or maintain an appropriate world environment? We shall discuss these questions further in Chapter 5.

SECURITY AND ITS PROBLEMS

Although the terms *self-preservation, survival,* and *security* are sometimes used interchangeably, the term *security* often has a broader connotation. It relates not only to the ultimate desire that the state survive
but also to the desire that it should live without serious external threat
to interests or values which are regarded as important or vital.

The policies which states follow to promote their security rest on a
series of judgments and choices.[3] In the first place, the interests or values
to be rendered secure must be decided upon. We have listed what are
usually regarded as the basic ones in the above attempt to define the self
that is to be preserved; these items might be subdivided and other items
might be added. The list offered may appear to be an obvious one, yet
it is of some importance that each government decide explicitly for itself
precisely what it is that it wants to preserve and thereafter give conscious attention to the problems involved. Otherwise they may find themselves preserving something which is really not vital to them, or unprepared to preserve the vital.

In the second place, judgment must be exercised in identifying the
sources and appraising the extent of foreign threats to whatever it is that
is to be kept or rendered secure. This means that attention must be paid
to changing conditions which may affect relationships with other states,
and that estimates must be made of their intentions and capabilities. As
we shall see later, the tasks involved are very difficult.

In the third place, the degree of security aimed at must be decided
upon. Absolute security, involving the complete absence of any external
threat, is normally unobtainable. No security at all, involving complete
helplessness in the face of external threats, is normally unacceptable.
The security goal chosen must fall somewhere between these extremes.
Even under similar threats, different states seek different degrees of
security, which means that some devote a relatively high and others a
relatively low proportion of their resources to the security effort; it also
means that states differ in the emphasis which they put on alliances and
other international security arrangements.

In the fourth place, the methods of promoting security must be chosen
—a topic to be discussed in various chapters of Part III. Dangers may
be warded off or countered through negotiations with other states, which
implies that decisions must be made on the specific objectives to be
pursued and on the specific arguments and pressures to be employed.
Economic measures may be adopted to affect the power or welfare of
other states. Propaganda may be spread, and fifth columns may be devel-

[3] Arnold Wolfers, " 'National Security' as an Ambiguous Symbol," *Political Science
Quarterly,* Vol. 67 (December, 1952), pp. 481-502.

oped. Armed power may be increased or reduced at home, and military aid may be extended or denied to other states. Alliances and other agreements affecting security may be concluded. War itself may be waged in the name of security. The number and variety of available methods is very extensive, and they can be employed in various combinations. The choice of method is often both difficult and crucial.

WHY SELF-PRESERVATION IS DESIRED

Why do states seek to preserve themselves, and why do people make sacrifices for this purpose? Many considerations are involved, some rational and some non-rational. Within the same state, different persons and different classes may be moved by different considerations. Those who feel that the state serves their good may be expected to want to preserve it. Governmental leaders themselves will almost certainly be in this category. The ruling class, if any, is very likely to be. All the elites within the society, that is, all those who get the most of the best, usually want to preserve the political structure under which they enjoy a favored position. Perhaps almost the entire population of the state will believe on quite reasonable grounds that their interests will be served better if the state survives than if it should become a part of some larger political entity.

Further, rational expectations are usually supplemented by emotional forces—especially by nationalist and patriotic feelings, which we shall discuss in subsequent chapters. The emotional forces are commonly so strong that the desirability of preserving the state becomes a matter of faith. Even to raise the question whether the state should be preserved may produce the impression of apostasy or sacrilege. People in one country may be able to be dispassionate about whether a foreign people are really better off because they constitute an independent state, but the same people are unlikely to take a detached view of their own position. Americans, for example, may take it almost as a matter of course that the people of Western Europe would be better off if they would abandon the idea of national independence and join in a federation, but those who suggest that the American people themselves should take a comparable step risk being accused of virtual treason.

SECURITY AND COMPETING INTERESTS

There are qualifications to the general proposition that self-preservation, survival, or security constitute the paramount objective of states, and some of them should be enumerated. Political leaders and those who influence them sometimes place such stress on other objectives that they are willing to resort to aggressive war, thus risking the very existence of the state. The prospect of gain of some sort may appear to be great enough to justify the risk. Hitler and the Nazis illustrate this point. Individuals, groups, and whole social classes may place such stress on private or class interests that the question of the survival of the state becomes secondary if not insignificant. There are always some who are out to feather their own nests regardless of social need. Commonly there are dissident groups within the state who may welcome its extinction, even through foreign conquest. A privileged class which is in danger of losing out in a domestic political struggle may, in effect, abandon the idea of preserving the independence of the state if there is a good prospect that by so doing the social order under which they have prospered can be maintained. Conversely, a class which feels underprivileged may seek foreign aid and may compromise or abandon the principle of national independence if there is a good prospect that by so doing the desired domestic changes can be brought about. Thus, some conservatives in France in the late 1930's are said to have endorsed the slogan, "Better Hitler than Blum," that is, they are said to have taken the view that it would be better for France to be subjected to Germany under Hitler than for France to be ruled by socialists. Thus also communists needing Soviet help have often been willing to subordinate the question of the independence of the state to their paramount objective of achieving and maintaining the triumph of communism.

Governments and people regularly face a problem in allocating resources between their efforts in behalf of security and their efforts in behalf of welfare. Although people generally want security for their state, they also want to enjoy not only the necessities but also some of the comforts and luxuries of life. Prosperity, pleasure, and esthetic satisfactions are desired in some measure. To some extent the promotion of welfare is quite compatible with the promotion of security, for many measures contribute to both power and welfare simultaneously. Frequently, however, a choice must be made, and it is by no means a foregone conclusion that the choices will be for power or security rather than for welfare. Sometimes the politically influential are so insistent on what they regard as welfare that they neglect the security program.

Conscientious objectors do not make the survival of the state the paramount objective; in refusing to fight they reflect attachment to what they regard as a more important value. Moreover, the possibility of unlimited nuclear warfare is likely to lead many to ask whether anything—even the continued existence of the state—will justify the cost, and the question may expand the roll of conscientious objectors. Further, those endorsing international federation or world government are directly attacking the principle of state sovereignty; though they presumably wish to preserve the state against external aggression, they seek a voluntary abandonment of independence on certain agreed conditions.

They take heart from certain precedents illustrating the voluntary abandonment of sovereignty, such as the union of the original thirteen American states and the merger between the United States and the Republic of Texas.

Despite qualifications and exceptions, however, the general rule remains that the paramount objective of states in the field of international politics is self-preservation.

PRESERVING SOVEREIGN INDEPENDENCE

Human experience demonstrates that government and the state are necessary and inevitable; men cannot have a satisfactory life in anarchy. It does not demonstrate, however, that the world must be divided into precisely the states which exist, or, perhaps, that it must be divided at all. The world has not always been divided as it now is, and present divisions must be regarded as temporary. Political history is full of the stories of the rise and fall of states. Some states have been swallowed up by others, and sometimes the process has gone on, as it did in the days of Rome, until all the known world was included in one empire. At other times, empires have had to disgorge peoples who then established themselves in separate states with their own governments. States which have been divided have sometimes voluntarily united, and states which have been united have sometimes voluntarily divided. The shifting of boundary lines between states has occurred again and again. Mountains and seas are pretty well fixed on the map, but political boundaries recurrently change.

So far as the division of the world into states has a rational justification, it is to be found in the diversity of human aspirations, interests, and ways of thought and action. We Americans, with our own sovereign and independent state, can govern ourselves pretty much as we please. Were the United States to be united with Canada, both Americans and Canadians would have to make adjustments, many of which would be unwelcome on one or both sides. Were the union also to include other peoples, still greater reciprocal adjustments would be required. The division of the world into states permits the politically influential to govern each country as they see fit; it recognizes diversity and facilitates the creation and preservation of attitudes and practices which the different portions of mankind regard as desirable. If the world were united under one government, and if this world government were given significant functions and powers, its survival would be doubtful. Differences between communists and others, to say nothing of the multitude of other differences which divide the human race, would probably tear it asunder.

The state system has the advantage, then, of recognizing and reflecting human diversities, but it has powerful disadvantages as well. It results in substantial international anarchy. The principle of sovereign equality, as interpreted, has prevented the development among countries of anything really comparable to the governments which exist within countries. We have seen that, within countries, government constitutes one of the principal foundations of peace. Deprived of a central government, then, the world is much more likely to suffer war, with all the destruction and tragedy that it involves, than is an individual country. Likewise, an anarchic world can make only lame arrangements for the economic, social, and cultural services and functions which normally go with government.

In the international realm, therefore, one of the main problems is to develop world government, or to find substitutes which will be adequate in performing the functions that government normally performs, while at the same time permitting the survival of diversity. A world government which did not recognize and respect human diversity could not be established; if it were somehow established, it could not succeed. A world without one government, divided into states, reflects human diversities, but is plagued by war.

SUGGESTED READINGS

BRIERLY, J. L., *The Law of Nations* (Oxford, Clarendon, 1949).

GROSS, Feliks, *Foreign Policy Analysis* (New York, Philosophical Library, 1954).

HALLE, Louis J., *Civilization and Foreign Policy* (New York, Harper, 1955).

KEETON, George W., *National Sovereignty and International Order* (London, Peace Book Co., 1939).

WOLFERS, Arnold, " 'National Security' as an Ambiguous Symbol," *Political Science Quarterly*, Vol. 67 (December, 1952), pp. 481-502.

WRIGHT, Quincy, *A Study of War* (Chicago, The University of Chicago Press, 1942).

CHAPTER 4

Nationalism and War

THE ARGUMENT of the preceding chapter was based tacitly on the assumption that the units with which we deal in studying international politics are states. States were said to pursue the objective of self-preservation, survival, or security.

Though it is correct, in a way, to say that states are the units with which we deal, this is by no means the whole story. The sovereign state and its government are not living beings who can think or write or speak. We talk about the policies of states; we say that governments negotiate with each other; more generally, we speak of the behavior of states and governments. But such statements involve a considerable amount of fiction. No one could draw a picture of a state adopting a policy or of two governments negotiating.

The fact is that governments are made up of human beings and that the human beings who hold government offices act in the name of the state. It is not the government which thinks or acts; it is the men who compose the government. And they, in turn, are always influenced more or less by other men, the citizens or subjects, whose obedience and support they must have. In other words, if the policies of states are to be understood, one must understand the desires and thoughts and emotions which govern the actions of individual men. States behave as men decide that they should behave.

The proposition that the units with which we deal are states must be qualified in another way, too. Ever since the beginning of the western state system, the list of states into which the world is divided has undergone periodic change. New states have come into existence, and old states have disappeared. These changes have not all occurred as a result of the will or actions of states. Many of them have been brought about against the will of existing states by the revolutionary action of private groups. And, as with states, such groups behave as men decide that they should behave.

What influences the judgment and behavior of those who act in the name of the state or in the name of revolutionary movements is a long and complex subject. We shall be exploring it in a number of chapters. One of the factors is the idea of the nation and the ideology of nationalism. This factor is, in truth, probably the most important of all in influencing those who help determine what the policies of most states should be, and it has probably also been the most important of all in the revolutionary movements of modern times. The idea of the nation and the ideology of nationalism are therefore of great importance to an understanding of international politics.

The ideology of nationalism involves two rather simple basic propositions. The first is that all members of the nation—or at least all who are territorially concentrated—should be united in a political entity with distinctive status; almost always the status desired is that of sovereignty or independence. This proposition reflects the alleged right of national self-determination. The second is that all members of the nation should be loyal primarily to their nation or nation-state. We shall discuss these propositions in turn.

THE NATION AND THE STATE

Toward the close of World War I Woodrow Wilson declared: [1]

Peoples and provinces are not to be bartered about from sovereignty to sovereignty as if they were mere chattels and pawns in a game. . . . Peoples may now be dominated and governed only by their consent. Self-determination is not a mere phrase. It is an imperative principle of action, which statesmen will henceforth ignore at their peril.

The statement was an outgrowth of the democratic principle that people should form their own constitution and choose their own government. It is not unnatural that those who accept this principle should go on to say that groups of people, especially those located in border regions, should be permitted to decide to which state to attach themselves or whether to constitute a state of their own.

Wilson's Secretary of State, Robert Lansing, was hostile to such an extension of democratic principle. He held that the idea of self-determination was "loaded with dynamite," and said,

It will raise hopes which can never be realized. It will, I fear, cost thousands of lives. In the end it is bound to be discredited, to be called the dream of an idealist who failed to realize the danger until too late to check those who attempt to put the principle in force. What a calamity that the phrase was ever uttered! What misery it will cause!

[1] Wilson's and Lansing's views are quoted and discussed in Alfred Cobban, *National Self Determination* (Chicago, The University of Chicago Press, 1944), esp. pp. 19-22.

Wilson himself later appeared to regret having endorsed the principle of self-determination, saying that he had not known that nationalities existed which sought to have it applied to them. Nevertheless the principle continued to be endorsed by others. It was stated in clear-cut form in 1938 by a Slovak leader, Tuka. Slovakia at the time was included in the state of Czechoslovakia. The Germans under Hitler, appealing to nationalist principles, had already seized the western rim of Czechoslovakia, the Sudetenland, inhabited by German-speaking people. The remainder of Czechoslovakia was likewise threatened by Hitler, and in these circumstances nationalism came to the fore among the two million Slovaks inhabiting the eastern part of the state. Tuka declared: [2] "It is not only the sacred right but the duty of every nation to possess its own state. We must carry Slovak independence to its logical end." And carry it to the end they did. When Hitler seized the western provinces of Czechoslovakia in the spring of 1939, he recognized Slovakia as an independent state.

Why does nationalism develop? Obviously, it does not spring suddenly upon the scene. A whole people is not completely lacking in national consciousness at one moment and ardently nationalistic the next. What types or classes of people first adopt the attitude? Why? Why do others follow along? To answer such questions, we would have to plumb deeply into the wellsprings of human behavior. Presumably we would find that people become nationalists because they think that nationalism will serve some need or want; perhaps it is useful in promoting an economic interest, or in satisfying a craving for distinction and respect, or in providing a basis for social unity and order.[3] Rather than focusing on the reasons for the development of nationalism, however, we shall simply accept it as a phenomenon with important implications for international politics, and explore the implications.

If the principles of nationalism and self-determination were given general application, the theoretical end-point would be a world in which each nation constituted a state, provided that it wished to do so. Actually, however, general application of the principle is impossible, for it leads, necessarily or potentially, into a series of difficulties.

In the first place, it implies that the nation as a concept can be defined, and that a nation as an entity can be identified and set apart from other nations. Second, efforts to create a nation-state are likely to run counter to the territorial claims of other states; more specifically, empires and multinational states are threatened by the principle and are likely to resist its implementation. Third, it ignores considerations other than

---

[2] New York Times, December 11, 1938, p. 50, col. 5.
[3] See Hans Kohn, The Idea of Nationalism: A Study of Its Origins and Background (New York, Macmillan, 1944); Carlton J. H. Hayes, The Historical Evolution of Modern Nationalism (New York, Richard R. Smith, 1931).

nationality that are frequently important in the location of boundary lines—historic claims and economic and military desires. The fourth difficulty stems from the fact that nationalists are not always satisfied with the creation of a nation-state; rather, there is a tendency for nationalists to seek glory for the nation in the form of dominion over foreign territory and people. In other words, there is a tendency for nationalists to become imperialists, seeking to deny to others the right of independence which they claim for themselves. Struggle, perhaps involving war, is likely to ensue.

The Problem of Identifying Nations

The concept of the nation is vague.[4] The nation is not a physical substance the properties of which can be measured or analyzed in a scientific way. It exists in the external, physical world, to be sure, and therefore has objective attributes, but it also exists in part in the minds of men, and therefore it includes subjective elements. There is no one definition of the term which all would accept. The problem of identifying a nation is therefore often plagued with doubt and difficulty, as is the problem of determining on the map precisely where one nation ends and another one begins.

1. The vagueness of the identifying characteristics. All agree that the nation must include both people and territory. Precisely how many people and how much territory it would be impossible to say. The people must be in reasonably close contact with each other, and must regard themselves as constituting a distinct society, set apart from other societies, which are considered alien or foreign. Again it is impossible to say how intense this feeling of membership in a distinct society must be. Further, the attributes that distinguish one group of people from another vary a good deal. Most often it is language, although language is obviously far from reliable as a test of nationality; Englishmen and Americans speak the same language, but regard themselves as members of different nations, and the Swiss speak four different languages. Moreover, in some regions of the world languages shade off into each other so imperceptibly, through the dialects of border regions, that it is impossible to tell where the dividing line between them is. Race and color are sometimes cited as distinguishing nations from each other, but often people of different race or color are combined in one nation and people of the same race or color are divided into different nations. The same may be said with regard to religion as a distinguishing characteristic.

[4] Cf. Louis L. Snyder, *The Meaning of Nationalism* (New Brunswick, Rutgers University Press, 1954), pp. 14-55; Boyd C. Shafer, *Nationalism, Myth and Reality* (New York, Harcourt, Brace, 1955); E. H. Carr, *Nationalism and After* (New York, Macmillan, 1945); Royal Institute of International Affairs, *Nationalism* (London, Oxford, 1939); Carlton J. H. Hayes, *Essays on Nationalism* (New York, Macmillan, 1926).

Similarly, different traditions or customs or culture patterns sometimes set nations apart from each other, but they do not always do so. In short, the attributes that distinguish one nation from another are not always clearly discernible.

Another element essential to the existence of a nation is a desire on the part of its members for a distinctive political status. Though in rare cases they may be satisfied with a status providing some degree of self-government within a multinational framework, the usual demand is for complete independence or sovereignty. Either the people involved must have their own government, whatever its form, and constitute an independent state, or they must, as a general rule, aspire to self-government and independence. Again, however, it is impossible to say how widespread or how intense those desires must be before a nation can be said to exist.

For a nation to exist, there must be not only people, territory, a sense of membership in a distinct society, and a desire for common government within an independent state, but there must also be some degree of common feeling or will; there must be a sense of oneness, of unity, of common purpose; there must be a recognition of the existence of common bonds and common interests which set the national society apart from foreign societies. The people must believe that they have more in common with each other than with members of other societies. There must be a conception of a national self whose purposes are to be advanced and protected. If men thought of themselves primarily as farmers or factory workers or businessmen or clergymen, and identified themselves primarily with their counterparts all over the world, nations could not exist. To constitute a nation, they must think of themselves primarily as Americans, Frenchmen, Germans, and regard the bonds that tie them to the country as more important than any bonds that they may have with people in other countries.

In short, though some of the elements requisite to the existence of a nation are fixed and objectively determinable, others are impermanent and subjective. The existence of a nation depends in part on the attitudes of men. The nation is not divinely ordained, nor is it the product of some inescapable law of nature. Rather, people think nations into existence and could think them out of existence. The nation is a historically constituted society, created by the decisions of many men to create it.

2. *Resulting problems.* The nationalist proposition that all members of a nation should be included within an independent state thus meets with a serious difficulty at the outset. If there is no reliable definition of the term *nation,* how can nations be distinguished from each other? Further, in practice the difficulty is intensified. Even where the criteria of nationality are agreed to, it is often difficult or impossible to apply them.

In considerable sections of the world, people have no more national feeling than did the people of Europe in the Dark Ages. In border regions between clearly recognizable nations—for example, in the area where the Serbs, Greeks, and Bulgars border on each other—the distinguishing characteristics of nationality are sometimes so fused and intermixed that they no longer provide guidance for the drawing of political boundary lines. In still other areas, people of clearly distinct nationalities are so interspersed that it is impossible to locate a boundary in such a way as to put all members of each nationality on the same side of the line.

The significance of all this to international politics is rather simple and clear. If members of adjacent nations insist, as they commonly do, that state and national boundary lines shall coincide, and if there is no objective and reliable way of determining where one nation ends and the other begins, disputes are likely and the disputes may lead to war. Even assuming that each nation is willing to follow the principle of nationality in formulating its territorial claims, each is likely to make the most extensive claims for which it can find a shadow of justification, for it is not customary for nations to give each other the benefit of the doubt on such questions. Conflicting claims thus arise, and peaceful settlement of them has often proved to be impossible.

Problems of this kind have abounded in European history, particularly in the Balkans. For example, in 1911 nationalist aspirations led Greece, Serbia, Bulgaria, and later Montenegro to join in a Balkan League, the object of which was to seize territory from the Ottoman Empire. The parties agreed in advance to a division of the seized territory along lines of nationality, except for one area in Macedonia where their claims were in conflict; they could not agree what the limits of their respective nations were in relation to this contested zone. The prewar agreement was that the ultimate assignment of this zone should be left to the judgment of the Russian Tsar.

When the war against the Turks was over, however, Greece occupied Salonica, and Serbia occupied the contested Macedonian zone. Bulgaria was unwilling to allow either state to keep what it held, and it treacherously attacked them both. A Second Balkan War was therefore fought among the victors over the division of the spoils, a war in which Rumania also joined. The principle of nationality thus broke down as a basis for delimiting states; nationalist aspirations produced war not only against the imperial overlord, but also among the victor nations themselves. Power rather than principle ultimately determined where the various boundary lines should be.[5]

[5] A. J. Grant and Harold Temperley, *Europe in the Nineteenth and Twentieth Centuries* (New York, Longmans Green, 1952), pp. 375-380.

Nationalist Claims and Multinational States

The second difficulty with the principle that each nation should be free to constitute itself as a united and independent state is that it threatens empires and multinational states, and they are likely to resist its implementation.

The boundaries of states and of nations have never fully coincided, not when the idea of nationalism developed, and not yet today, even after a century and a half of changes in the political geography of the world.

That this is almost inevitable is implied in what has already been said. Where the dividing line between nations cannot be determined, or where people of clearly distinct nationalities are territorially interspersed with each other, there can be no identity of nation and state.

The same truth can be arrived at historically. As the nationalist idea that the nation and state should be coterminous spread over the world, it rarely found a situation where in fact they were coterminous. The idea first came to the fore in Europe at the time of the French Revolution. Few if any of the states of Europe were then nation-states. All of south-eastern Europe was included in two great empires, the Ottoman and the Hapsburg. The Poles were divided between Prussia, the Hapsburg Empire, and the Russian Empire. There were then no Germany and no Italy in a political sense; instead, the Germans and Italians were divided into many states. Neither was there a Belgium. Further, outside Europe the coming of nationalism has found few, if any, nation-states already in existence. At one time or another, European states have held most of the rest of the world as subject or colonial territory.

1. Irredentas and national minorities. Where the nation and state are not coterminous, *Irredentas* and national minorities are said to exist. The term *Irredenta* came into prominence while Italy was being united as a nation-state. The process of national unification was substantially completed by 1870, but many Italian-speaking people remained within the Austro-Hungarian Empire. From Rome's point of view the Italians who remained under alien rule constituted an Irredenta, that is, they were "unredeemed." One of the principal objects of Italian nationalists thereafter was to bring about the redemption of their compatriots by annexing them and the territory on which they lived to Italy. From Vienna's point of view, these Italians constituted a national minority. The term *national minority* designates a sizable but minority element in the population of the state; the minority is more or less concentrated in a given territory; its members may possess citizenship or nationality in a legal sense, but are not really regarded in a spiritual sense as comembers of the nation; rather, they are regarded either as constituting a nation which may want its independence or as belonging in a spiritual sense to some foreign nation-state, usually an adjacent one, which they may wish to join.

The fact that nation and state do not always coincide should be coupled with another one which is simple but all-important: that states commonly desire to retain territory which they possess. Though asserting nationalist claims for themselves, the European peoples have generally refused to concede the nationalist claims of others, whether within Europe or abroad, who were subject to their jurisdiction. Magnanimous grants of independence to subject people, or magnanimous cessions of territory designed to make possible the unification of another nation, have been very rare. Britain's grant of dominion status or independence since World War II to some of its former colonies in South Asia has been exceptional. Generally, states have acquiesced in nationalist demands which involved a loss of territory only when they had no choice —or, more specifically, only when they were compelled to do so by force. Time and again colonial peoples, like the Americans in 1776, have rebelled against imperial rule and demanded national independence. Time and again national minorities have been disloyal to the state in which they were located, and have engaged in revolutionary-nationalist uprisings to obtain their freedom. The foreign policies of a number of states have at various times been shaped so as to promote the redemption of Irredentas, and this has often led to war. When subject peoples are determined to free themselves from alien control, when nation-states are determined to redeem Irredentas, and when threatened governments are determined to preserve their rights, conflict is almost inevitable and the conflict may express itself in war.

2. *A corollary concerning divided nations.* A corollary proposition ought also to be made. There have been times when a nation, though not subject to alien rule, has been divided into different states. The governments of these different states commonly wish to preserve themselves. A contradiction develops, then, between nationalists seeking unification and governments seeking survival. In this situation the governments threatened by nationalism have sometimes joined hands to suppress it, as the German states did under the leadership of Metternich in the first half of the nineteenth century. More often one of the governments—the one regarding itself as in an especially favorable position —has become the champion of nationalism and has sought unification of the nation by subordinating or liquidating the other governments that stood in its way. Prussia under Bismarck played such a role, and so did Cavour, the Premier of Sardinia-Piedmont, in connection with the unification of Italy. Wars were involved in each case. Today Germany, Korea, and Vietnam are all divided.

3. *Making the state a nation.* Sometimes nationalists reverse the

proposition that the nation should be a state, and say that the state should be a nation. They seek to realize this desire in various ways. Many states restrict or prohibit the immigration of aliens; one of the reasons for doing so is a fear that large numbers of immigrants might adulterate the character of the nation. Thus, the United States has a quota system for regulating immigration, which for long was so devised as to restrict especially the immigration of those considered most likely to retain their alien ways after coming into the country. For several decades Orientals were prevented from immigrating at all. Similarly, Australia has what is called a "white Australia" policy, which seeks to preserve certain characteristics of the nation by barring Orientals. Once an immigrant comes into the country, those seeking national homogeneity want to bring about his assimilation: they do various things to induce him to drop distinctively alien culture patterns and to take on the language and customs of the nation that he has joined.

The regulation of immigration may prevent the creation of a new national minority, but does not solve the problem of a national minority which is already within the country. It must somehow be eliminated if the state is to be made into a homogeneous nation. Elimination may be attempted through assimilation, transfer, dispersal, or extermination. Assimilation has been the most common, although perhaps not the most successful, method. The effort here is to induce or force the minority to abandon its own language and customs and adopt those of the majority; the hope is that eventually the minority will cease to be distinguishable as such, and that the loyalties of the people involved will go to the nation-state which they have fully joined. Thus the Tsar tried to "Russify" some of the minorities under his jurisdiction, and Mussolini tried to "Italianize" the German-speaking inhabitants of South Tyrol—an Austrian province transferred to Italy after World War I.

The transfer of populations, designed to eliminate national minorities, may be voluntary or involuntary. Members of the national minority may simply be given the right to move out of the country—as with the Hungarian "optants" who found themselves in Rumania after a shift in the boundary line following World War I; these Hungarians were given the right to choose between Hungarian and Rumanian citizenship, but if they chose to retain Hungarian citizenship they had to abandon their homes and move across to the Hungarian side of the new boundary line. Involuntary transfers of population may result from persecutory measures which leave the people involved with little choice but to flee, or they may result from direct governmental action. Greece and Turkey made a direct attack on the problem after World War I, when they formally agreed to an exchange of populations; under the agreement, Greeks in Turkey were deported to Greece, and Turks in Greece were deported to Turkey; people who had lived all their lives in a given home suddenly found themselves uprooted and sent to another country in response to the demands of nationalism.

Dispersal as a means of eliminating a national minority has been practiced mainly, if not exclusively, in the Soviet Union. During World War II the Soviet government uprooted and dispersed over its own territory four different minority groups, apparently on suspicion of disloyalty, and a similar fate evidently befell a substantial portion of the people of the Baltic Republics. Extermination as a method of eliminating a people regarded as a national minority was attempted by the Nazis against the Jews.

Both the seriousness and the intractability of the problem of national minorities are reflected in European experience after World War I. The very fact that Greece and Turkey would exchange minorities suggests their fear that the persistence of the problem would impair good relations between them. Similar fears led the victors in World War I to require that several of the states in eastern and southeastern Europe agree to special treaties designed to protect remaining minorities against certain kinds of discriminatory treatment. No effective way of enforcing these treaties, however, was ever found, and in the 1930's Poland denounced its obligation. The German minorities in eastern Europe became an acute problem with the rise of Nazi power. Hitler placed great emphasis on the alleged mistreatment of them in Czechoslovakia and Poland, probably more as an excuse than as a reason for an aggressive program.

4. Plebiscites as instruments of self-determination. The effort to make the nation and the state coterminous has sometimes—especially after World War I—involved the use of plebiscites, that is, the people in question have been asked to choose their future status by voting. Thus, when Germany protested the plan to transfer the province of Upper Silesia to Poland after World War I, the Allies agreed to let the people of the province vote on whether they wanted to be included in Germany or Poland.

Although superficially attractive in terms of democratic principles, the idea of holding plebiscites to determine the national status of a given group of people runs into a number of practical difficulties.[6] The overwhelming one is that the government which now rules the territory in question is almost certain to oppose any steps which will threaten its control. The proposition made above is applicable here again: that governments ordinarily want to keep what they have. Imperial countries generally react in horror at the thought of giving colonial peoples their choice of independence. Countries involving a mixture of races or of nationalities do not ordinarily want to permit the secession of any portion

---

[6] See Cobban, *op. cit.*, pp. 25-27, and the references there cited.

of the population. Moreover, a government which is in a position to seize territory that it wants may well do so without risking an adverse vote in a plebiscite.

The result is that the usefulness of plebiscites is limited. They have been conducted mainly in territories of states defeated in war when the victors could not agree on outright seizure and when the claimant state was deterred, for whatever reasons, from defying its allies. Most of the territorial transfers in Europe after World War I and all those after World War II have occurred without the benefit of plebiscites. The plebiscites which were held after World War I related exclusively to portions of German territory claimed by Belgium, Denmark, and Poland, respectively.

There is another general difficulty in the use of plebiscites. They naturally can take into account only the wishes of the people who vote. This may mean that the economic and strategic interests and the historic claims of one or more states will be ignored. Such considerations are sometimes held to be so vital as to preclude the use of plebiscites. More will be said on this topic in a moment.

Even if these difficulties with plebiscites are somehow overcome, problems still remain. Within which territorial unit will the plebiscite be held? By adjusting its size appropriately, or by something analogous to gerrymandering, the outcome frequently can be largely predetermined. Who will be permitted to vote? The answer to this question might also determine the outcome, especially where transfers of population have occurred. Alsace-Lorraine, for instance, would undoubtedly have voted to remain with France in 1871, when Germany seized it. However, by 1919 enough Frenchmen had emigrated and enough Germans had immigrated to produce some doubt as to the result of a plebiscite, had one been held. Who will supervise or administer the plebiscite, and how will its freedom and fairness be assured? Strong national passions are likely to be involved, and partisans of one side or another are likely to attempt to control the outcome through intimidation or fraud. Supervision by outside powers, presumably neutral, is perhaps the answer, but the supervisory personnel will then be strangers whose regulations and controls may be circumvented by adept, local political leaders. What can be done if the people involved are unfamiliar with democratic electoral processes? If all these problems are solved and a plebiscite held, should the entire area involved be awarded as a unit in accordance with the wishes of the majority, or should the area be divided so as to place each local voting district, so far as possible, within the state of its choice? Finally, on what occasions should plebiscites be permitted and who would decide when to permit them? Frequent shifts of territory from one state to another would obviously cause undesirable instability.

It is, of course, possible that the various technical problems connected with plebiscites can be solved with reasonable satisfaction. The fact remains, however, that it is difficult to do so, and this perhaps explains why there has been no attempt to use plebiscites in connection with the territorial problems which emerged in Europe after World War II.

Self-determination through plebiscites is therefore hardly a complete solution to the territorial problems which nationalism involves. Nationalist claims of colonial peoples and of minorities within advanced states are likely to continue to be sources of friction and perhaps war.

Non-nationalist Considerations and National Boundaries

A third major difficulty in the proposition that the nation and the state should coincide comes from its neglect of considerations other than nationality. Nationalists themselves would grant that historic claims and economic and military needs should all be taken into account in fixing boundary lines, yet the principles of nationalism provide no solution for the problems involved. Consider, for example, former German territory now lying to the east of the Oder-Neisse line. For the most part, German people have been driven from this territory and have been replaced by Poles and others. Suppose that this situation persists for many decades. Let it not be assumed that Germany will abandon its claims to this territory simply because it has come to be inhabited by people of another nationality. Given the opportunity to make its voice heard, Germany is likely to say that its historic claim is paramount over every other consideration. The recovery of territory lost in previous wars is a common objective of states, regardless of changes in the nationality of the inhabitants of the territory.

Economic and military desires likewise compete with considerations of nationality in the fixing of boundary lines. Most governments are concerned about both the wealth of their citizens and the economic basis of power; they may therefore wish to bring areas under their control because of the economic advantage to be derived, regardless of the nationality of the inhabitants. Moreover, when boundaries are being located, concern for the economic livelihood of the people in border regions may compete with purely nationalist considerations in influencing the decision made.

Military considerations are probably even more important. Assuming future war as a possibility, governments seek security. Among other things, this involves a desire for strategically defensible frontiers. Thus, after World War I, Italy not only wanted to include all Italians within its new borders, but also sought a frontier on the Brenner Pass in the Alps. That this involved the annexation of territory inhabited by German-speaking people made little difference in Rome, so long as Italy was made militarily more secure and powerful. Similarly, after World War I, Czechoslovakia received the Sudetenland even though its inhabitants were Germanic, largely because the territory included the mountainous rim on which the defense of the state had to rest. Losing this region to Hitler in 1938, Czechoslovakia was awarded it again after World War II. Military considerations have likewise influenced the fate of much additional territory during and since World War II. The Soviet Union has gained and regained territories both in the Far East and in Europe, largely to enhance its security. Poland has theoretically been compensated for its territorial losses to the Soviet Union by the acquisition of former German territory. The United States has taken numerous Pacific islands which were previously under the control of Japan, most of them being held in the form of a trust territory. In all these territorial transfers, nationality considerations had scant significance.

Contradictions between nationalist claims, on the one hand, and historic, economic, and military considerations, on the other, are virtually inevitable. The problems may be temporarily resolved, usually by letting the powerful have their way, but new solutions are likely to be sought later when power relationships have changed. The demand for new solutions is almost certain to involve friction and perhaps war.

Nationalism and Imperialism

Experience has revealed a fourth major difficulty in the nationalist proposition that each nation should constitute a united and independent state. It is that nationalists are often not satisfied to be nationalists in the strict sense. Rather, they tend to become imperialists, that is, they seek control over territory beyond the confines of the nation. They become advocates of extranational expansionism. As a French writer puts it, "Patriotism, conventionally defined as love of country, turns out rather obviously to stand for love of more country." [7]

Although perhaps not inevitable, the desire for extranational expansion is a common characteristic of nationalism and a natural one. It stems from a number of sources, most of which will be discussed elsewhere; imperialism is a broad subject.

Nationalists sometimes seek extranational expansionism out of concern for the security of the nation, thinking that the acquisition of a given piece of foreign territory will be strategically advantageous. Sometimes they seek extranational expansionism for economic reasons: they want to control foreign territories in which important raw materials are located, or in which investments can be profitably made, or to which surplus products can be sold, or to which surplus population can migrate.

[7] René Johannet, quoted by Quincy Wright, A Study of War (Chicago, The University of Chicago Press, 1942), Vol. II, p. 1038, footnote 81.

Sometimes, if the nation is in some way disunited or beset by domestic dissension, they seek foreign adventure as a means of promoting national unity.

However sound or unsound these reasons for extranational expansionism may be in specific instances, they are relatively rational. Irrational and emotional forces are also often powerful. The nationalist glorifies the nation. He identifies himself with its fortunes, and wants for it a place in the sun so that he can bask in its reflected rays. Defeat for the nation is ignominy for such an individual, and victory for the nation gives him prestige. National honor and pride become intertwined with personal honor and pride. It may or may not be true that individuals who thus identify themselves with the nation could secure full satisfaction out of its cultural, scientific, or other such achievements. The fact is that they often do not. Rather, they commonly interpret glory in terms of conquest and dominion, in terms of size and power.

In glorifying the nation the nationalist is also likely to glorify the principles on which the life of the nation is based. These principles he is likely to regard as moral and good; since they are good for him and his nation, he may assume that they would be good for all the world. Contrary principles espoused abroad may come to be regarded not merely as less desirable but as positively bad and evil. A missionary and crusading spirit may well enter in, the nationalist becoming convinced that it is his duty to give light and guidance to the backward and benighted. The French revolutionists of 1789, determined at the outset to gain liberty, equality, and fraternity for themselves, soon found themselves caught up in a crusade to spread the blessings of these principles over all of Europe, if not over the world. Englishmen responded to Rudyard Kipling's plea on the White Man's Burden:

> Take up the White Man's Burden—
> Send forth the best ye breed—
> Go bind your sons to exile
> To serve your captives' need.

A similar spirit has existed in the United States at various times; an extreme form of it is illustrated in the following declaration by former Senator Albert J. Beveridge: [8]

God has made us [the English-speaking and Teutonic peoples] the master organizers of the world to establish system where chaos reigns. He has given us the spirit of progress to overwhelm the forces of reaction throughout the earth. He has made us adepts in government that we may administer government among savage and senile peoples. Were it not for such a force as this the world would relapse into barbarism and night. And of all our race He has marked the American people as His chosen nation finally to lead in the regeneration of the world.

[8] *Congressional Record*, Vol. 33, Part 1 (January 9, 1900), p. 711.

President McKinley justified the taking of the Philippines partly on the basis of such considerations as these. Generally speaking, imperialism commonly involves national pride: a belief that the principles and practices associated with one's own nation are superior to contrary principles and practices, and that they should therefore be made to prevail universally.

The nationalist proposition that each nation should constitute a united and independent state is thus fraught with difficulties. The problem of defining the concept of the nation and the problem of actually identifying nations are plaguing. If these problems are solved, there remains almost inevitable conflict between the "rights" asserted by nationalists and the rights possessed by those established states which include national minorities or which rule over colonial territory. Likewise, disagreement, friction, and possible war are inherent in the fact that historic claims and economic and military-strategic desires sometimes run counter to claims based on nationality. Finally, nationalism fails to provide a basis for a stable international order because of its tendency to develop into imperialism.

The fact is that the questions whether a particular state should exist and, if so, what its boundary lines should be have more commonly been decided on the basis of war and threats of war than on the basis of common consent that the principle of nationality and consequent nationalist claims ought to be respected. This is to say that the political geography of the world has been fixed, however temporarily, more by power than by principle. If power is a more important factor than principle, it is not surprising that the principle has never been fully implemented; it would not be surprising if it never were. The principle that each nation should constitute a united and independent state invites unending conflict.

LOYALTY TO THE NATION

The second main proposition to which all nationalists agree is that the individual should be loyal primarily to his nation, above all where relationships with foreign nations are involved.[9] The question is, what does loyalty require? A universal requirement has already been discussed: that the patriot shall endorse and uphold the idea that the nation should be united in a distinct political entity, usually an independent state. Beyond this point, the meaning of loyalty varies, de-

[9] For a discussion of the meaning, sources, and expression of loyalty, and of interrelations among loyalties, see Harold Guetzkow, *Multiple Loyalties: Theoretical Approach to a Problem in International Organization* (Princeton, Center for Research on World Political Institutions, 1955).

pending on who defines the term. Governments may define loyalty in one way, privately organized groups and organizations in another, and the individual nationalist may adopt a personal definition of his own.

Governmental Definitions of Loyalty

Governments in defining national loyalty always require general obedience to law, and support for the constitution. In dictatorial countries this is likely to mean that any word or act will be regarded as disloyal if it in any way impedes achievement of the purposes of the government and, above all, if it might contribute to the downfall of the government. In other words, loyalty to the nation is defined to mean loyalty to the particular government which rules the nation. In democratic countries, the usual governmental definition of loyalty is not so sweeping. In the United States, for example, no question of national loyalty is involved if one seeks to bring about the defeat of the party in power at the next election. But it is disloyal to advocate the overthrow of the government by force and violence. The offense against the requirements of national loyalty is particularly heinous if those advocating such overthrow are associated in any way with a foreign power. The ultimate form of disloyalty, from the point of view of governments, is treason.

Not only do governments define loyalty to prohibit certain things like subversion and treason, but they also define it to require certain things in a positive way. This is true above all in connection with military affairs. Where foreign danger to the nation exists, service on behalf of the nation becomes a paramount obligation of the patriot. He is expected not only to support the idea of national defense, but to give service for national defense if he is called upon to do so. Governments expect loyalty to the nation to supersede literally all other loyalties. They require those who owe them allegiance to leave home and family, school and career, in order that the national cause may be served. They extol sentiment such as that attributed to Nathan Hale, who is said to have regretted that he had but one life to give for his country.

Most democratic governments respect the views of those citizens whose religious or ethical beliefs prohibit or restrict the rendering of military service. That is, they permit the individual to put loyalty to his interpretation of the injunctions of God or conscience ahead of loyalty to the nation or state. They therefore grant the right of conscientious objection to military service, and may arrange alternative types of service for conscientious objectors to perform. Generally, however, governments simply imprison or otherwise punish those who place loyalty to anything else ahead of loyalty to the nation.

Private Definitions of Loyalty

Private organizations and individuals, in defining national loyalty, may or may not agree with the definition advanced by the government.[10] Some go beyond the government in fixing the demands of loyalty, and at the other extreme some disagree totally with the government on the subject. Militantly patriotic organizations and individuals often go beyond governmental requirements. In the United States, for example, the government does not interpret loyalty to require support for a capitalist or free enterprise system, but some "100 per cent Americans" do. They regard the particular economic system that the country has had as so precious and essential an aspect of the nation that they denounce advocacy of socialism as disloyal. A few have gone so far as to claim not only that the advocacy of socialism is disloyal, but also that it is subversive to include books about socialism or communism in libraries or to teach about them in schools. In the days of the League of Nations there was much opposition to American membership, some of it based on a fear that membership might somehow lead to a loss of national sovereignty and independence; there is some opposition to the United Nations today on the same ground. Loyalty to an international organization is not to supersede loyalty to the nation.

At the other extreme, some private individuals and organizations completely reject their government's definition of the requirements of loyalty. Consider, for example, the position of a German nationalist in the part of Germany under communist dictatorship. He has considerable reason for regarding the communist dictatorship as an instrument of the Kremlin —an instrument through which Russians control East Germany. From his point of view, therefore, East Germany is under hated alien rule. Further, he is likely to blame both the Russians and their German accomplices for the fact that Germany remains divided. In this situation, what does nationalism require of him? Thinking that the German Communists who constitute the government have betrayed the country, he may conclude that, as a good patriot, he must seek their overthrow. Perhaps he will decide that he can do this best by fleeing to West Germany. There he may join with others in efforts designed to liberate his part of Germany from foreign rulers and native traitors. He may make radio broadcasts, encouraging dissidence and perhaps rebellion in East Germany. He may engage in various plots or conspiracies against "his" government. He may even try to bring about war in the hope that East Germany can thus be liberated and all Germany united once more. Or the German nationalist may elect to stay within East Germany, there to carry on activities

10 Henry Steele Commager, *Freedom, Loyalty, Dissent* (New York, Oxford, 1954), esp. pp. 135-155.

which will be officially regarded as subversive and there to engage in sabotage against his own government if war should come. Whichever course of action he takes, the communist dictatorship will regard him as a traitor, but from his own point of view he will be serving the national cause which the Communists have betrayed.

Thus loyalty to the nation may be interpreted differently. The general requirement is that the interests of the nation should be served, but what is in the interest of the nation is a question on which patriots may differ.

The Inculcation of Loyalty

It goes without saying that those who concern themselves with the meaning of loyalty are likely to engage in activities designed to secure general acceptance of their ideas. Governments do so, and often do it very vigorously. They commonly use public schools for the purpose, insisting that teachers and textbooks shall inculcate loyalty at least to the constitutional system of the country if not to the government itself. The teachers themselves are to be loyal nationalists, not disloyal or subversive. Textbooks are to present and discuss the utterances of the founding fathers and the traditions of the country in a favorable light. Perhaps there will be a requirement that, on occasion, the national anthem be sung, the flag saluted, or pledges of allegiance given. Outside the schools, governments or the dominant political party may organize youth movements to capture the minds of the young. They may regulate or control means of mass communication—the press, radio, television, movies—to see to it that subversion is avoided and loyalty inculcated. They always establish national shrines and declare national holidays to commemorate persons or principles or past events which have been significant in the life of the nation, hoping that such memorials and the ceremonies connected with them will create or reinforce national loyalties.

The efforts of private organizations and individuals to inculcate loyalty will reflect their conception of the meaning of the term. If they agree with the government's definition, they will simply reinforce and extend the government's program. In most countries, whether because the people control the government or because the government shapes popular attitudes, substantial agreement with the government's definition exists. Thus private organizations often voluntarily assist in inculcating and maintaining a spirit of loyalty to the nation, according to the official definition. So, commonly, do the press, the radio, and other means of mass communication even if they are under private control. Those who adopt a more extreme definition of loyalty than the government are likely to try to secure general conformity with their views. Thus the American Legion or the D.A.R. may try to prevent "radicals" from speaking at public meetings or to prevent the use of "socialistic" books in the schools.

In the case of persons suspected of supporting or sympathizing with communism, pressures may be brought to bear to exclude them from radio broadcasting, even if the program involved is purely for entertainment purposes. Similarly, people who reject the government's definition of loyalty and who think that loyalty to the nation requires the overthrow of the government may do what they can to secure the acceptance and support of others for their views.

Conclusions Concerning Loyalty

Two principal conclusions are to be drawn from this discussion of national loyalty. The first is that under the nation-state system governments seek and usually obtain the fervent loyalty of the people under their jurisdiction. A "nation of patriots" is the ideal of the nationalist. For Americans, "politics" should stop at the water's edge. In Britain, during World War II, a "national" government was formed: a coalition government involving the submergence of partisan rivalries. In other countries too, in times of crisis, national unity in the face of foreign danger has been the watchword. National loyalty and patriotism thus provide a basis for unity and power.

The second conclusion is intimately related. It is that, if primary loyalty goes to the nation, loyalty to anything other than the nation must be secondary or non-existent. This has very serious implications for the problem of international peace. We said in Chapter 2 that attitudes reinforce government in maintaining peace within countries. Where the nation constitutes a state, loyalty to the nation-state is one of the most significant and potent of these attitudes. Nationalism thus commonly makes an immense contribution to the preservation of domestic peace. However, national loyalty is usually interpreted in a way that precludes international loyalties, and so it tends to prevent the development of attitudes which might reinforce international peace. The idea of sovereignty and the idea of nationalism work together to keep the world as a whole deprived of the bases of peace which people within countries enjoy. They are major obstacles to the development of an international political structure which might be effective in reducing the role of war.

¶ Nationalism is the strongest ideology extant. It is the most potent of the dynamic forces which guide the behavior of statesmen. Desires connected with nationalism—to establish the nation as an independent state, to complete the unification of the nation, to create national homogeneity, to preserve the territorial integrity or independence of the nation, or to glorify the nation through foreign aggrandizement—have influenced international relations in the last century and a half to an extent which would be difficult to exaggerate. By every sign they will continue to do so.

Although all nationalists subscribe to the two main propositions which we have been discussing in this chapter, they differ among themselves on related issues. Some of the differences stem from the ideology to which they subscribe and will become apparent in the following chapter.

SUGGESTED READINGS

BROWN, Delmer M., *Nationalism in Japan* (Berkeley, University of California Press, 1955).

CARR, E. H., *Conditions of Peace* (New York, Macmillan, 1944).

CARR, E. H., *Nationalism and After* (New York, Macmillan, 1945).

CHADWICK, H. Munro, *The Nationalities of Europe and the Growth of National Ideologies* (New York, Macmillan, 1946).

CLAUDE, Inis L., *National Minorities* (Cambridge, Harvard University Press, 1955).

COBBAN, Alfred, *National Self-Determination* (Chicago, The University of Chicago Press, 1944).

COMMAGER, Henry S., *Freedom, Loyalty, Dissent* (New York, Oxford, 1954).

DEUTSCH, Karl W., *Nationalism and Social Communication* (New York, Wiley, 1953).

GRODZINS, Morton, *The Loyal and the Disloyal* (Chicago, The University of Chicago Press, 1956).

GUETZKOW, Harold, *Multiple Loyalties: Theoretical Approach to a Problem in International Organization* (Princeton, Center for Research on World Political Institutions, 1955).

HAYES, Carlton J. H., *Essays on Nationalism* (New York, Macmillan, 1926).

HAYES, Carlton J. H., *The Historical Evolution of Modern Nationalism* (New York, Richard R. Smith, 1931).

KOHN, Hans, *The Idea of Nationalism: A Study of Its Origins and Background* (New York, Macmillan, 1944).

KOHN, Hans, *Nationalism: Its Meaning and History* (New York, Van Nostrand, 1955).

Nationalism, Royal Institute of International Affairs (London, Oxford, 1939).

SHAFER, Boyd C., *Nationalism, Myth and Reality* (New York, Harcourt, Brace, 1955).

SNYDER, Louis L., *The Meaning of Nationalism* (New Brunswick, Rutgers University Press, 1954).

ZNANIECKI, Florian, *Modern Nationalities: A Sociological Study* (Urbana, University of Illinois Press, 1952).

CHAPTER 5

Ideological Motivations and Objectives

IN DISCUSSING NATIONALISM we have already been discussing ideology, for nationalism is an ideology. We have seen how nationalist ideas affect political life within states and, even more, how they lead to friction and conflict among states. Other ideologies operate similarly. We shall discuss liberalism, fascism, and communism.

Certain assumptions underlying the discussion should be made explicit: that ideas influence action; that the desire to promote or defend certain principles is a factor in the power struggle; that the ideology of a state—liberal, fascist, communist, or whatever—helps to determine both the methods it will adopt and the objectives it will pursue in foreign affairs.

The point will perhaps be clearer if the situation within countries is recalled. We have seen that politics within countries involves struggle over the principles on the basis of which political, economic, and social life should proceed. Some may want democracy, others dictatorship. Some may want free enterprise, others socialism. As long as significant portions of the population disagree on such fundamental questions, there is danger of civil war. Those favored by the existing system will want to preserve it, but those who think that another system would make life better for themselves will want change. If most or all the people ever agree on one common set of fundamental principles, domestic peace is made relatively secure.

The situation is similar among countries. Whatever the prevailing ideology within the state, the government is likely to regard it as good and to want to preserve it. A government based on liberal-democratic principles will want to preserve those principles; a fascist dictator will want to preserve fascism, and so on. Where the social system in a number of states is based on the same set of ideological principles, the governments involved have a common interest in preserving the conditions that permit the survival of the ideology; thus a basis of cooperation is provided. Conversely, where ideologies are antithetical—and particularly where one or more of them calls for the aggressive extension of certain principles over the world—a basis is laid for hostility and conflict.

Although ideas influence action, they are not necessarily the ultimate or the sole mainspring of action. They themselves may be reflections of something more basic, as when the rich man objects in principle to the graduated income tax, or they may be rationalizations of desires which it would be improper to express publicly, as when a politician who is greedy for personal power professes concern only for the public interest. Whether or not a particular idea is developed or endorsed does not depend only on the native ability of men to think or on the intrinsic merit of the idea; to be endorsed, ideas must somehow correspond to personal and social wants and needs. There is an interplay between economic, social, and psychological conditions, on the one hand, and the ideas that men develop and endorse, on the other. An emperor is not likely to endorse the ideas of nationalism, and a millionaire is not likely to endorse communism. Ideas alone thus do not provide a full explanation of political behavior.

Even so, they are significant. Though they may be reflections of something more basic or rationalizations of secret desire, knowledge of them frequently makes the behavior of states more understandable and more nearly predictable. Moreover, ideologies which originally are reflections or rationalizations may take on an independent force of their own and continue to influence action long after the reasons for endorsing them have disappeared. Nationalism itself, for example, was originally championed largely by the rising merchant class as a tool in its struggle against certain vestiges of feudalism, but it continues as a powerful force, evoking support from all classes and influencing their conduct.

Aside from nationalism, two of the most potent ideologies in the world are those of liberalism and communism. Fascism, weakened by the defeat of its champions in World War II, plays a lesser role, but it is scarcely safe to assume that it will not revive; in any event it is desirable to give some attention to it if only to see to what extremes certain ideas may lead. One of the questions confronted in liberalism and fascism, and in nationalism as well, concerns the relationship of the individual to the state. If the individual is to give primary loyalty to the nation-state, which comes first, the individual or the nation-state? Is supreme importance to be attached to the nation or to the individual human being? Is one the master and the other the servant? If so, which is which? If not, what is the relationship between the two?

LIBERALISM

Basic Principles

The basic assumption of the liberal is that the individual human being is of supreme value. The goal of the liberal is to enable every human being to develop his own capacities and talents to the utmost, to achieve the maximum satisfaction of his needs and desires, to permit each individual to realize his conception of perfection. There is no order of priority among individuals for these purposes. There is no belief that nature has made some human beings better than others and that therefore some are naturally entitled to special privilege. Rather the equality of men is assumed, and the liberal, if he had his way, would give all men of all races equal opportunity to perfect themselves. Moreover, liberals deny the existence of any objective or scientific way of determining what men should be like; they have no mold into which to cast the human personality so as to make it ideal. They do not claim to know what is good for men. Rather they would let each man determine for himself what he thinks is good for him, and they would let him seek his own good. Liberty is thus essential. The individual must be free to decide what he wants, and free to seek what he wants. Limits have to be imposed so that one individual, in pursuing his own desires, does not interfere unduly or unfairly with other individuals; it may be, too, that instead of simply minimizing restraints on individuals so that they can seek their own good, society will take positive action to promote the achievement of what the majority regard as good. But still the end-point is the good of the individual.

Holding views such as these, liberals are bound to go on to say that social customs and practices and institutions, and the ideologies accompanying them, are good or bad depending on their relationship to the individual's pursuit of self-perfection. Things which oppress or suppress or subordinate the individual are bad, and things which facilitate the promotion of individual welfare are good. They must be judged, on as rational a basis as possible, according to their effectiveness in serving men. It is on this basis that the liberal judges forms of government, for instance. Those which are repressive or oppressive are bad, and those which maximize the freedom and opportunity of individuals to pursue their own welfare are good. With liberalism therefore goes a belief that government should be democratic.

Where do the nation-state and nationalism fit into the liberal's framework? [1] The liberal, speaking as a liberal, must treat them from a utilitarian point of view. If the nation-state and the ideas of nationalism are good for the individual, they are good. If they are bad for the individual,

---

[1] See the discussion of liberal nationalism in Carlton J. H. Hayes, *The Historical Evolution of Modern Nationalism* (New York, Richard R. Smith, 1931), pp. 120-163.

they are bad. They do not justify their own existence except in serving the individual. Thus the liberal has a clear answer to the question, "Which comes first?" He says that the individual does, and that the nation-state is therefore secondary and subordinate.

Nevertheless, the answer is really not as clear nor as definitive as it seems. The liberal nationalist, regarding the nation-state as a useful instrument for the protection and promotion of the welfare of the individual, naturally wants to preserve it. He probably will also want to preserve, in the main, the social and political system associated with the nation-state. What then happens to the individual whose words or actions either make it more difficult for the nation-state to survive or tend positively to undermine it? Further, though regarding the nation-state and its accompanying institutions and practices as means of serving the individual, the liberal rather naturally tends to turn the means into an end in itself. When he glorifies the nation-state, even as a means, does he not thereby attach value to it, and may he not thereby attach so much value to it that its preservation becomes the supreme end? If he does this, the question may be asked again: what happens to the individual? May he not be relegated to a place of secondary importance? May he not become the servant rather than the master?

Liberalism requires that the individual be afforded certain rights: the right to freedom of speech, press, and religion, the right to own property, the right to due process of law, the right to organize into trade unions and to strike, and so on. What happens to such rights when the nation-state is in danger? Are they to be modified or abolished?

The right of trade unions to call strikes is a good case in point. Suppose that in time of extreme national emergency—perhaps in time of war—the railway unions call a strike. Now, the whole economy of any advanced country is dependent on railroads. If the trains do not run, the country will be paralyzed. An extended strike in wartime might lead to complete national disaster. Will the right to strike be upheld even then? The question puts the liberal nationalist in a dilemma. If he denies the right to strike, he goes against a fundamental tenet of his creed, but if he upholds the right to strike it is conceivable that his country will be conquered. Conquest by a communist state, to assume the worst, would mean not only the virtual or complete elimination of the independence of the nation-state, but also the abolition of most of the rights which the liberal holds dear.

The liberal may confront the same kind of dilemma in connection with many other issues. In the broadest possible terms, he may be driven to choose, at least temporarily, between the preservation of democracy and the preservation of the nation-state. In every national emergency the tendency in democracy is to concentrate power in the hands of the executive. The greater the emergency, the greater is this tendency. In

time of war, if the nation-state is in mortal peril, democratic procedures
may be too slow and unreliable to afford a maximum chance of countering the threat. Will the liberal then stick to democratic procedures and
individual rights, or will he sacrifice all so as to give the nation-state
the best chance of survival?

In actual practice, the tendency of liberals when faced with such
dilemmas has been to attach increased value to the nation-state. When
the social and political life of the country is going smoothly and when
no serious external threats exist, democracy can be enjoyed to the full,
and substantially free rein can be given to individuals in the pursuit of
their welfare. But in times of stress, the idea of loyalty to the nation-
state and the idea of subordinating individual welfare to the common
national good take on added significance. The possibility is that the
emphasis on the nation-state might go so far as to make it, rather than
the individual, the object of supreme value. Then emotional attachment
to the nation may replace belief in the worth and dignity of man; glorification of the nation may replace glorification of the individual. And,
whatever the glorification of the nation might mean, it has often in practice meant the enhancement of the power of the nation and the subjection of the individual. "Nationalism has more often than not been the
enemy of democratic institutions." [2]

Implications for International Politics

The implications of liberal nationalism are important to international
politics in several ways, not all of them being consistent with each other.
Generally, it is probably true to say that liberalism itself makes for peace
and cooperation among nations. The idea of equal respect for individuals as human beings and the idea of tolerance theoretically preclude
any assertion of racial or national superiority which assumes a right to
rule over foreign peoples. The idea that the paramount object is to
promote the freedom and welfare of men generally militates against a
deliberate resort to aggressive war. In fact there is some evidence that
stress on individual welfare, on individual rights, and on the value of
human life has sometimes gone so far as to lead to a neglect of power
considerations. Faced with a choice between guns and butter, the liberal
is inclined to choose butter, perhaps to the peril of his nation. Faced
with a choice between appeasement and resistance to a foreign threat
at the risk of war, the liberal may be inclined toward appeasement, for
war threatens most of the values he holds dear. In recent decades particularly, the liberal democracies have been very reluctant to engage
in military preparations and to participate in war.

Nevertheless, liberal nationalism is, after all, a form of nationalism. It

[2] Alfred Cobban, *National Self-Determination* (Chicago, The University of Chicago
Press, 1944, copyright 1944 by the University of Chicago), p. 65.

shares with other forms of nationalism an emphasis on the unity of the nation in an independent state. Where the nation is divided or under foreign rule, even liberal nationalists may put more emphasis on the nation than on their liberalism, and may therefore favor militant and aggressive policies to achieve satisfaction of nationalist aspirations. They may be obsessed with the problem of "redeeming" an Irredenta or reducing somehow any dangers which may be occasioned by the presence of a national minority. Moreover, liberalism is in some ways a source of conflict, for it invites the competitive pursuit of private interests. This has several potential implications. It may lead to strife and disunity within the nation so extreme as to threaten a national breakdown; it is an old trick of governments in such a situation to find a foreign enemy and then to issue patriotic appeals to unity in the face of the common enemy. Or it may lead to the disappointment and frustration of many —of those unsuccessful in the competitive pursuit of private interest; this may produce different reactions, among them a resort to an extreme identification with the nation and a demand that the nation obtain a place in the sun from which glory can be reflected on its members. In other words, liberalism may lead to such divisions and frustrations in society that it will be neglected on behalf of nationalism, and perhaps a bellicose nationalism at that. Moreover, there have been many individuals and groups who, in the pursuit of their interests, have completely forgotten that they were liberals (if, indeed, they were) and have sought their own advantage regardless of the effect on others. Much misery has resulted both within the countries ostensibly endorsing liberalism and within colonial areas over which they have established their frequently illiberal rule.

Even liberal nationalism may have in it an element of missionary fervor. Convinced that the principles for which he stands are good for him and for his own society, the liberal is also inclined to think that they would be good for all the world. If his principles are good, it is not a very big jump to the conclusion that contrary principles are bad. Foreign governments that champion contrary principles may be regarded as reactionary and oppressive, as obstacles to the forward march of mankind toward a perfect society, and peoples subject to such governments may be regarded as deserving liberation. Formally, at least, it is not that the liberal wants to impose his conception of private good on individuals abroad, but that he wants them to have a social system which provides freedom. The thought has sometimes even been advanced that people should be forced to be free.

Finally, liberal nationalists are also men. As such, they love and hate; they are altruistic and selfish; they are merciful and ruthless; they are compassionate and lustful; they seek harmonious cooperation with their fellow men, yet seek to dominate.

In short, though liberalism with its stress on the worth and welfare of the individual may modify the extremes of nationalism and may in some respects make for international cooperation and harmony rather than for war, it by no means provides an assurance of peace.

Declared Objectives of Liberal Statesmen

Improved understanding of the relationship between liberalism and foreign policy may come from a brief sketch of the way in which liberal-democratic leaders spell out their conception of the proper objectives (goal-values) of their states. For this purpose we could focus almost equally well on the pronouncements of a number of different statesmen active at various times. It will suffice, however, to cite statements by recent American and British leaders for illustration. From among them, the choice falls primarily on Dean Acheson and Sir Winston Churchill, mainly because they gave unusually pointed and complete expression of their views. The symbols which they emphasized were peace, security, freedom, and well-being.

1. Peace. Peace is obviously desired. The ideology of liberal democracy contains no glorification of war, which distinguishes it from fascism, and even little explicit recognition of war as a useful instrument of policy. At the same time, liberal-democratic statesmen obviously do not make the avoidance of war their supreme objective. They desire peace but do not put it at the top of the hierarchy of values. This is confirmed by the very fact that they prepare for war and sometimes lead their states in war. It is also revealed in the definitions of peace that they employ. Sometimes they equate peace with law and order, which presupposes enforcement action—perhaps on a scale so extensive as to amount to war; for example, among the objectives for which the Korean war was fought was the enforcement of law and order. More often, liberal-democratic statesmen equate peace with the absence of war, but when they do they make it clear that they do not desire peace at any price. Otherwise, they presumably could have peace simply by giving in to whatever demands were made against them—which might mean the peace of slavery or of the grave. No statesman is so utterly devoted to peace that he would pay such a price for it. Liberal-democratic statesmen want to avoid war, but they regard some values as so precious that they are willing to wage war to preserve them if it becomes necessary to do so.

2. Security. What are these other values? Security is one of them. All statesmen seek security. But security for what? American statesmen commonly say security for the nation, and then they may spell out the concept further. Dean Acheson as Secretary of State did so. His view was that "the primary objective of any government is necessarily the security of its territory and people," and he went further.[3] He identified national security also with "the broadest kind of security for our free and democratic way of life." He spoke not only of preserving the country, but also of preserving it "as the kind of country which we know and love." With an even more sweeping view, and with an eye on Soviet and communist power, he declared, "We are faced with a threat not only to our country but to the civilization in which we live and to the whole physical environment in which that civilization can exist." Thus, security implied to him not merely such things as preserving territory or safeguarding the nation against a forced alienation of independence, but also preserving those conditions and practices and attitudes at home and abroad which are essential to the existence of the kind of society that the American people want to have. Security involves ideology as well as territory.

3. *Freedom.* The ideological element in the liberal-democratic conception is brought out even more clearly by the emphasis commonly given to freedom, and, more generally, to individual human values. Again statements by Dean Acheson as Secretary of State provide good illustrations. He explicitly stated some liberal postulates: "The free society values the individual as an end in himself." "The fundamental moral value on which our society rests is the brotherhood of man." Building on these postulates, he insisted on freedom for the individual. "Our first line of action," he declared, "... is to demonstrate that our own faith in freedom is a burning and a fighting faith. We are children of freedom. We cannot be safe except in an environment of freedom. We believe in freedom as fundamentally as we believe anything in this world." He described freedom as

... the very breath of life itself [and] ... the gateway of opportunity. Free men have the opportunity to better their lives, to abolish poverty, and to live in human dignity. Freedom is the climate in which men can work to fulfill all the affirmative aspirations and values of their lives. When people ask us, "What is it you are for, you men of the free world?" Then we say, "We're for freedom, because freedom is the key to everything else we want."

In this light it is rather natural that Acheson should have sought to justify many individual policies in terms of their contribution to freedom. He justified the Point Four program as an aid through which people could "improve their material welfare and at the same time live as free men, retain their personal dignity and independence, and develop to the

[3] Statements by Acheson are quoted mainly from *Strengthening the Forces of Freedom, Selected Speeches and Statements of Secretary of State Acheson,* Department of State Publication 3852, General Foreign Policy Series 28 (1950), and *Strengthening the Forces of Freedom,* Supplement, Publication 3852a. Cf. also *State Department Bulletin.*

full extent of their individual capacities." Similarly, Acheson described the North Atlantic Treaty as "far more than a defensive arrangement." He found its "ethical essence" in the common resolve of its parties to preserve and strengthen "tolerance, restraint, and freedom—the really vital things with which we are concerned." The treaty was "an affirmation of the moral and spiritual values" which its parties had in common. What the treaty seeks to preserve, said Acheson, "is the opportunity for a living heritage of freedom to continue to grow." His attitude reflected terms of the treaty. In its preamble, the parties express their determination "to safe-guard the freedom, common heritage and civilization of their peoples, founded on the principles of democracy, individual liberty and the rule of law." Article 2 declares that "the parties will contribute toward the further development of peaceful and friendly international relations by strengthening their free institutions, by bringing about a better understanding of the principles upon which these institutions are founded, and by promoting conditions of stability and well-being." John Foster Dulles as Secretary of State has made similar statements, illustrated by the following: [4]

The broad goal of our foreign policy is to enable the people of the United States to enjoy in peace the blessings of liberty. Under present world conditions we cannot achieve that goal by thinking just of ourselves. We must help other peoples to be free.

British statesmen also emphasize the idea of freedom. Winston Churchill in particular has played repeatedly on the word. He pictured Britain after the fall of France as bearing "the proud but awful responsibility of keeping the Flag of Freedom flying in the Old World till the forces of the New World could arrive." The restoration and rebuilding of Europe after the war was, to him, "animated and guided by the kindred themes of Liberty and Democracy." In his Iron Curtain speech he called upon both Britain and the United States to follow foreign policies designed to promote "the safety and welfare, the freedom and progress, of all the homes and families of all the men and women in all the lands." More positively, he wanted to seek "the permanent prevention of war and the establishment of conditions of freedom and democracy as rapidly as possible in all countries." Later he declared, "It is not against any race or nation that we range ourselves. It is against tyranny, in all its forms." Again and again he referred to "the causes of freedom and democracy which we seek to serve." [5]

There has also been a spelling out of the meaning of freedom. Acheson

[4] *State Department Bulletin*, Vol. 32 (February 28, 1955), p. 327.
[5] Randolph S. Churchill, ed., *The Sinews of Peace, Post-War Speeches by Winston S. Churchill* (Boston, Houghton Mifflin, 1949), pp. 42, 94, 103; Winston S. Churchill, *Europe Unite, Speeches 1947 and 1948* (London, Cassell, 1950), p. 318.

held, in the first place, that it requires political democracy. It calls for "a world in which each citizen participates freely in determining period-ically the identity of the members of his government." He asserted it to be "our faith—our deepest conviction—that representative and respon-sible government is more deeply in accord with man's nature than any other system of government." In the second place, Acheson held that freedom has economic aspects, requiring a certain minimum standard of living; the purpose of the Point Four program, he held, was to aid people in winning their struggle for daily bread, "not merely to gain the material things themselves," but "to gain them so that the victory over nature sets minds and spirits free." The third aspect of freedom that he emphasized was religious freedom.

In words, at least, liberal-democratic statesmen often seem as much interested in freedom abroad as in freedom at home. Thus Acheson de-clared, "We believe that all people in the world are entitled to as much freedom, to develop in their own way, as we want ourselves." He be-lieved the principles of democracy, individual liberty, and the rule of law to be principles of "universal validity." Former President Harry S. Truman held similar attitudes. Presenting the case for the Mutual Secu-rity Program in 1952, Truman expressed the view that "no nation . . . can undertake policies which are not squarely and solidly based on national self-interest." But he thought that it would be "a misrepresentation of the American people to suppose that self-interest—even wise and en-lightened self-interest—is the only cause of our concern with the outside world." He went on to say that "we have been dedicated through our history to the belief that responsible men deserve a democratic govern-ment and a free society." He warned against deserting the cause of democracy. He asked that, by rising to our historic traditions, we "add powerful momentum to the democratic counter-offensive which inspires in the people of the world a sense of their own destiny as free men—and which will in the end burst the bonds of tyranny everywhere on earth." [6]

In action, altruistic concern for freedom abroad has been less pro-nounced. In fact, Western democracies have displayed a willingness to tolerate and even to abet the suppression of freedom at times. Portugal was included as a party to the North Atlantic Treaty even though its government is undemocratic. Objections from France and Britain, based on ideological considerations, prevented the inclusion of Franco's Spain, but the United States made a bilateral defense arrangement with Spain nevertheless. The United States, Britain, and France joined in a program of aid to Tito's Communist dictatorship in Yugoslavia. When debate arose in the United States some years ago over the question whether aid should be denied to Greece and Turkey because of the attenuated char-

[6] *State Department Bulletin*, Vol. 26 (March 17, 1952), pp. 403, 410, 411.

acter of their democracy, Acheson declared that we were not in a position to "go from one country to another with a piece of litmus paper and
see whether everything is true blue." "The only question we should ask,"
he said, "is whether they are determined to protect their independence
against Communist aggression, and, if they are, we should recognize our
basic unity with them on this point."

In practice, then, liberal-democratic statesmen are more concerned
with "our" freedom than with "their" freedom, and they are sometimes
willing to promote "our" freedom by exchanging help with dictators.

4. *Well-being.* In addition to stressing a desire for peace, security, and
freedom, liberal-democratic statesmen commonly also espouse the promotion of welfare or well-being as an object of foreign policy. Thus
former President Truman thought it

... vital that the democratic nations show their concern for the well-being of
men everywhere and their desire for a better life for mankind. . . . In this way,
and in this way only, can we make human liberty secure against the forces
which threaten it throughout the world today.

Acheson expressed the view that "there can be no lasting peace, no real
security, while hunger, disease, and despair hold millions in their grip.
Every people must have a stake in peace worth defending." President
Dwight D. Eisenhower summed up American objectives in saying that [7]

We must continue to work with other countries to insure that each free
nation remains free, secure from external aggression and subversion, able to
develop a society marked by human welfare, individual liberty, and a rising
standard of living. . . .
    Peace with justice remains the sole objective. . . .

5. *The operational significance of declared objectives.* It is natural
that Western statesmen should stress such symbols as these, for they are
symbols which pervade the Western liberal and Christian tradition. But
what operational significance do they have? Does the desire for peace,
security, freedom, and well-being actually influence decisions concerning foreign affairs, and if so to what extent?

In considering this question a caveat should be entered at the outset.
It is not to be expected that the presence of such desires would completely account for all decisions made. An aspiration is not a policy, nor
is a desire to reach a particular goal always accompanied by knowledge
of how to do it. Several different roads may be thought to lead to Rome,
and a determination to get there will not, alone, dictate the choice among
them. The destination or goal is only one of many factors which are
likely to influence particular decisions.

[7] *State Department Bulletin,* Vol. 34 (April 2, 1956), p. 545.

Further, it should be remembered that no statesman—and least of all a democratic statesman—is free to act entirely as he pleases. He is subject to pressures of many sorts, both domestic and foreign. Some of these pressures, and perhaps powerful ones, may be exerted by those more interested in other values than in those which governmental leaders officially proclaim. Foreign governments willing to join in security measures may or may not be interested in freedom. Domestic pressure groups may be more interested in profits and privilege. Private interests are forever trying to sell themselves as public interests, and sometimes they succeed.

These considerations indicate that the operational role of liberal-democratic principles in guiding foreign policy is necessarily limited. Whether any role remains for them at all is a question which must be divided into two parts. Using the United States for purposes of illustration, does it in fact seek such values as peace, security, freedom, and well-being for itself? Does it also seek to promote such values for others?

That the United States seeks such values for itself, and that the desire to achieve or maintain them influences decisions, can scarcely be doubted. Security for the nation in its various attributes is obviously desired. Existing freedom is obviously cherished and to be defended. No one would doubt that the United States seeks well-being for itself. Periodic resort to war calls into question the operational significance of the desire for peace, but does not necessarily deny it, for peace is never put at the top of the hierarchy of values.

The question might be broken down still further. The above comments are made on the assumption that the United States is a unit, and in a sense it is. At the same time, it consists of individuals and groups whose desires and interests are sometimes contradictory. A foreign policy cannot serve them all equally well. A tariff may mean higher profits for one man and higher prices for another. A program of economic aid to a foreign country may increase one man's business and another man's taxes. A decision to increase the size of the armed forces may serve to protect freedom in general but means increased regimentation for those who are drafted. If we were to plumb the question of the objectives of foreign policy to the bottom, we would have to ask precisely whose desires within the country are reflected by each decision made and whose interests are served. It must suffice, however, simply to say that the values referred to above are values which liberal-democratic governments do and must seek to promote for some or all of their citizens.

Another incidental but significant point should also be made. The objectives which liberal-democratic statesmen seek to achieve relate in part to material self-interest. But moral values are also involved. The desire to preserve a particular way of life, the desire to preserve freedom, and even the desire to promote well-being have moral overtones. The fact is that people can be, and often are, as much aroused over the problem of preserving or promoting certain moral values like political or religious freedom as they are over the problem of promoting or defending their material welfare. The promotion of what might be called moral self-interest may be as much an object of diplomacy as the promotion of material self-interest. Politics is a struggle for power, but power may be desired in the defense or promotion of what is considered to be morally good. As indicated above, the pronouncements of liberal-democratic statesmen are filled with references to issues in international politics which are essentially moral issues.

Let it be granted, then, that liberal-democratic statesmen pursue what they consider to be the material and moral self-interest of the countries they represent. Do they also seek to promote the good of others on an altruistic basis? This question is much more difficult. Democratic statesmen commonly state their goals in cosmic terms, as if they are as much concerned for all mankind as for their own nation; if their words are to be believed, pure altruism often influences their policies. Perhaps there have been cases where a pure spirit of charity has inspired action, or where unselfish missionary zeal has been influential. Crusading for "the right" has perhaps occurred. Sympathy for the victims of "the Huns" no doubt led many Americans to take stands from 1914 to 1917 which contributed to the entrance of the United States into World War I. Moral indignation aroused by the Nazi assault on principles sacred to the Anglo-American tradition may likewise have played a role in leading both Britain and the United States into World War II. Such interpretations are difficult to establish or refute. Except perhaps for such episodes—and they are obviously of great significance—evidence of clear and substantial self-sacrifice on the part of any nation is difficult to find. In connection with recent American foreign policies, for example, it is easier to think of cases where the United States has aligned itself with exploitative and oppressive regimes for selfish purposes than to think of clear and significant examples of moralistic unselfishness. The question is whether, in connection with the foreign policies of states, benefit for others does not occur more as a byproduct of the pursuit of self-interest than as a result of deliberate altruism. Even if this is so, however, the benefit given is not without significance. Moreover, there is an automatic gain for peace and welfare when states define their own interests in such a way that the pursuit of them serves rather than contradicts the interests of others.

FASCISM

Fascist thought starts with an assumption diametrically opposed to that underlying liberal thought. Where the liberals postulate the supreme value of the individual, fascists postulate the supreme value of the nation-state or, as in Nazi Germany, the *Volk*. Where the liberals appraise the nation in terms of its utility in promoting the welfare of individual human beings, the fascists appraise the individual in terms of his utility to the nation. To the fascist, it is the nation which comes first, the individual being secondary and subordinate, deriving such rights as he has from service to the nation or to the racial society. The Italian fascists went on from this point to endow the nation-state with a life of its own, distinct from the lives of the human beings who composed it. They regarded the nation not simply as an aggregation of individuals but as a corporate body, a living organism, a Being. The Charter of Labor formulated in Mussolini's time most clearly expressed this conception. It asserted that [8]

the Italian nation is an organism having ends, life, and means of action superior to those of the separate individuals or groups of individuals which compose it. It is a moral, political, and economic unity that is integrally realized in the fascist state.

This kind of an outlook involves obvious fiction. It flies in the face of reason. It is based on a mysticism, deriving belief from emotion or feeling. So also was the attitude of the German Nazis, who placed supreme value on race.

Far from denying the mystical basis of their beliefs, the fascists and Nazis affirmed it and gloried in it. They were contemptuous of reason, extoling instinct, intuition, or drive of will. They deliberately and avowedly created a myth, believing that people would more likely do great things when inspired by a myth than when guided by reason. Thus the Nazis decried the fact that the nation which they took over had become a nation without a myth, and they regarded it as their mission to create "by means of a new myth a new standard of value by which all things are to be judged." Their view was that: [9]

During great historical movements the forces of nature operating in the human soul overleap the confining wall of logic. . . . The life of a race or a nation is not a logically developing system, nor yet a process which takes place in strict accord with natural laws. It is rather the unfolding of a mystical synthesis, an activity of the soul, which cannot be explained by logical formulae.

[8] Herbert W. Schneider, *Making the Fascist State* (New York, Oxford, 1928), p. 333.
[9] Quoted by William M. McGovern, *From Luther to Hitler* (Boston, Houghton Mifflin, 1941), p. 627.

On this non-rational basis the fascists and Nazis proceeded to glorify the nation-state or the ethnic *Volk* organized in the nation-state. It became the supreme value, its greatness the supreme end. Thus Mussolini declared: [10]

> We have created our myth. . . . Our myth is the nation, our myth is the greatness of the nation. . . . The foundation of Fascism is the conception of the State, its character, its duty, and its aim. Fascism conceives of the State as an absolute, in comparison with which all individuals or groups are relative, only to be conceived of in their relation to the state. . . . Everything for the state; nothing against the state; nothing outside the state.

In their ecstatic frenzy for the power of the nation or race, the fascists and Nazis of course lost sight of the individual. He was simply a tool, perhaps useful or perhaps harmful to the pursuit of extrahuman ends. He had no value simply as a human being. No more possessing a soul than does a pig or a horse, he could be slaughtered or worked according to the convenience of his masters. He really lost his individuality, being either absorbed into the body of the nation-state or treated as an animal fit only for slavery or death. "There are no longer any private people. All and every one are Adolf Hitler's soldiers." "All honor, after all, is political honor; with the honor of one's country, one's own is lost as well." [11]

The implications of fascist or Nazi nationalism for international relations are both more clear-cut and more extreme than those of liberalism. Positing the nation and the greatness of the nation as the supreme value, Mussolini went on to assert: [12]

> The Fascist State is an embodied will to power. . . . For Fascism, the growth of empire, that is to say the expansion of the nation, is an essential manifestation of vitality, and its opposite is a sign of decadence.

Hitler arrived at the same general conclusion on the basis of his racial myth. He believed in the "worth of Blood," and held that differences in Blood created differences in the value of races and men. The "basic idea of nature" was to him "aristocratic," those endowed with the best blood being the aristocracy entitled to rule over the others and those possessing the worst blood being subhuman and entitled only to die. "A State which, in the epoch of race poisoning, dedicates itself to the cherishing of its best racial elements, must some day be master of the world." Hitler felt an "obligation in accordance with the Eternal Will

---

[10] Herman Finer, *Mussolini's Italy* (New York, Holt, 1935), p. 218; Benito Mussolini, "The Political and Social Doctrine of Fascism," *International Conciliation*, No. 306 (January, 1935), p. 13.

[11] Statements by S. Behn and Robert Ley, quoted by Aurel Kolnai, *The War Against the West* (New York, Viking, 1938), p. 169.

[12] Mussolini, *op. cit.*, p. 16.

that dominates this universe to promote the victory of the better and stronger, and to demand the submission of the worse and the weaker." [13] The acceptance of such attitudes by a government controlling considerable power makes war virtually inevitable.

COMMUNISM

The element of missionary zeal is much more prominent in communism than in liberalism or even in fascism. The explicitly declared purpose of communists is world revolution.

The "Science" of Marxism

Underlying the demand for world revolution is a rejection of the tolerance and freedom which liberals proclaim. Rejection of such values is based on faith in the "science" of Marxism. Lenin, a leading apostle of Marx and still revered by communists as the founder of Russian Bolshevism, long ago declared,[14]

... The theory of Marx is the objective truth. ... Following in the direction of the Marxian theory, we shall draw nearer and nearer to the objective truth (without exhausting it); following another path, we shall arrive at confusion and falsehood.

Subscribing to the same view, Stalin depicted communism as a science which reveals the laws of historical development, a science which permits the discovery of "authentic data" about society, data "having the validity of objective truths." According to the journal issued by the Cominform—an international organization of communist parties existing from 1947 to 1956—"Marxism-Leninism is all-powerful because it is correct."

In other words, communists regard themselves as having a relationship to society similar to that of a medical doctor.[15] They believe that they have a science which permits them to diagnose social ills and prescribe remedies just as a doctor does with human patients. Moreover, they believe that they alone are in a position to do this; non-Marxist approaches lead only to "confusion and falsehood." Just as quacks are prevented from practicing medicine because of the damage to patients which they might do, so, according to the communists, those not guided by Marxism-Leninism should be barred from political activity and de-

[13] Adolf Hitler, *Mein Kampf* (New York, Reynal & Hitchcock, 1939), pp. 103, 580, 994.

[14] V. I. Lenin, *Collected Works* (New York, International, 1927-1932), Vol. XIII, p. 114.

[15] Several passages in this discussion of communism are repeated from the author's chapter, "The Foreign Relations of the Soviet Union," in Charles P. Schleicher, *Introduction to International Relations* (New York, Prentice-Hall, 1954).

prived of political influence. Armed with "truth" provided by "science," communists believe that they know what is good for mankind, who and what obstruct the achievement of the good, and how to overcome all obstacles to world-wide triumph.

Alleged Contradictions in Capitalism

According to the science of Marxism-Leninism, capitalism, though once a progressive system, has lost its usefulness and become a barrier to human progress. It is said to be beset by a series of contradictions which doom it to destruction, if only the communists give the forces of history a little help. The basic alleged contradiction is between the private ownership of the means of production and the social nature of the productive process. The claim is that, if production requires cooperative group effort, then it is contradictory to have the means of production under individual ownership. From this basic contradiction, others are said to flow: between classes, between imperialist states and colonies, among imperialist states themselves, and between the capitalist world and the communist world, once the latter emerges.[16]

All history, to communists, is the history of class struggle. In a capitalist system, the owning class (the bourgeoisie) is said to be dominant, both economically and politically. Owning the means of production, it employs others and makes them "wage slaves." Employers are held to be exploiters, failing to pay the workers their just due. Further, the owners of the means of production get control of the state; the machinery of government thus allegedly becomes an instrument in the hands of the bourgeoisie, used to maintain and enhance its privileges. Through the state the owners impose their oppressive rule. The bourgeoisie thus consists of exploiters and oppressors, and the workers constitute the exploited and oppressed.

Particularly among the industrial workers, the proletariat, class consciousness arises. The proletariat becomes aware of the fact that it is being exploited and oppressed and of the fact that a different kind of economic and political system is possible—a system in which exploitation and oppression would not occur. A struggle then ensues between the bourgeoisie and the proletariat; control over the government is the immediate issue. Claiming to know the "true interests" of the proletariat on the basis of the "science" of Marxism, the communists become the self-styled "vanguard" of the proletariat in this struggle. Their immediate object is revolution, that is, the seizure of state power.

Other contradictions impinge upon this struggle and facilitate the vic

[16] For a brief summary of communist theory see Historicus, "Stalin on Revolution," *Foreign Affairs*, Vol. 27 (January, 1949), pp. 175-214; cf. R. N. Carew Hunt, *The Theory and Practice of Communism* (London, Geoffrey Bles, 1950).

tory of the proletariat. Capitalism is said to lead necessarily into imperialism, and thus to the reduction of foreign peoples to colonial or semicolonial status. Colonial peoples are then exploited and oppressed, just as is the proletariat in the imperialist country itself. They, too, engage in a struggle against their exploiters and oppressors, striving to throw off the yoke of imperialism and secure national independence. They are thus allies in the class struggle, every victory they win contributing to the eventual triumph of the revolution within the imperialist country itself.

Further, according to communist theory, imperialist states inevitably become involved in struggle with each other. Driven to imperialism, they compete with each other in the search for colonies; they struggle over the division of the world, and, once the world is divided up, they struggle over a redivision. Wars occur in the process, weakening one or more of the imperialist states involved and facilitating a revolutionary seizure of power.

Finally, once revolution has occurred in one or more of the capitalist countries, a new contradiction arises, a contradiction between the two worlds of socialism and capitalism. According to the Marxist-Leninist point of view, capitalism will be weakened by the very fact that part of the world has been removed from its sphere of exploitation. Further, the communists are convinced that their system will work better than any other, and that the very example of their success will contribute to revolution elsewhere. Moreover, as will be seen in a moment, communist theory makes it a prime duty of the socialist state to promote revolution abroad.

Communists believe both that the various contradictions make their ultimate victory inevitable and that they must organize and work to achieve victory. They must act as the agents of history in giving effect to its ineluctable laws. Their party must consist of selected and strictly disciplined revolutionaries, thoroughly dedicated to their cause. They must be willing to use literally any means that will promote their triumph, for the end will justify the means. Existing laws may be disregarded, for they are laws enacted for the benefit of the bourgeoisie. Prevailing morality may be ignored, for morality, too, is simply a class instrument. For communists, anything will be moral "which serves to destroy the old exploiting society and to unite all the toilers around the proletariat." The party must work openly where the laws permit, but in any event it must also have an underground apparatus which can persist in revolutionary activity despite repression on the part of the bourgeois state. Crime and sin are dismissed as concepts of the class enemy; nothing will be really criminal or sinful which serves the cause. Deception, robbery, murder, and treason are all justifiable.

Democracy Means Dictatorship

Communists endorse democracy, but give the word their own special meaning. In fact, they deny that there is any such thing as democracy pure and simple. The state is a class instrument, and the principles on the basis of which the state is governed are class principles. Where democracy exists under capitalism, it is therefore bourgeois democracy, just as a capitalist state is bourgeois. And bourgeois democracy, Lenin long ago declared,[17]

... is always bound by the narrow framework of capitalist exploitation, and consequently always remains in reality a democracy for the minority, only for the possessing classes, only for the rich. Freedom in a capitalist society always remains just about the same as it was in the ancient Greek republics: freedom for the slave owners.

There might be freedom within the bourgeoisie; the ruling bourgeois party in a democracy might permit other bourgeois parties to operate, but a real challenge to bourgeois rule would be met by martial law and the threat or the use of violence. In short, Lenin held, "The most democratic bourgeois republic was never, nor could it be, anything else than [a] dictatorship of the bourgeoisie." [18]

Communists demand the transfer of power to the proletariat, proposing to replace the dictatorship of the bourgeoisie with a dictatorship of the proletariat. The function assigned to the dictatorship of the proletariat is to "expropriate the expropriators," that is, to socialize the means of production; this involves the liquidation of the bourgeoisie as a class. The ultimate goal is the creation of a classless (one-class) society in which exploitation and oppression will be eliminated. Such a society would operate on the basis of the principle, "From each according to his ability, to each according to his need." Class divisions having disappeared, there would be no more need for the state; it would wither away.

Communists engage in some subtle sleight of hand in connection with demand for a transfer of power to the proletariat and for the liquidation of the bourgeoisie. When power goes to the proletariat, precisely who gets it? Who are included in the bourgeoisie? The answer to the first question is that power goes actually to the communists. It goes to the communists not because they have been elected to represent the proletariat but because the "science" of Marxism-Leninism designates them as the "vanguard" of the proletariat. They constitute themselves as a self-appointed elite. It is a dictatorship of communists which they establish, acting in the name of the proletariat. The answer to the second question (Who are included in the bourgeoisie?) is equally arrogant.

[17] V. I. Lenin, op. cit., Vol. XXI, Bk. 2, p. 217.
[18] Selected Works (New York, International, 1935-1938), Vol. X, p. 35.

The revolutionary struggle is ostensibly between the proletariat and the bourgeoisie. The communists assert that they speak for the proletariat. Those who are against the communists must therefore be for the bourgeoisie. They are bourgeois, and are therefore to be liquidated.

Nevertheless, the dictatorship of the proletariat is ostensibly democratic, is "a million times more democratic than the most democratic bourgeois republic." It is democratic not because it has the electoral support of any particular portion of the people nor because it wins out in electoral competition with other parties. Rather it is democratic because it serves the "true interests" of the masses of the people, these true interests being determined not by the people themselves but by those schooled in the "science" of Marxism-Leninism.

> The democratic or anti-democratic nature of public life of a state, of a government's policy, is determined not by the number of parties but by the substance of the policy of this state, of these parties—by whether this or that policy is carried out in the interests of the people, in the interests of its overwhelming majority, or in the interests of its minority.[19]

Extending the Revolution

The communists expect to triumph now in one country and now in another, the revolutionary tide ebbing and flowing in correlation with periods of stability and crisis in the capitalist system. There is no timetable in accordance with which this historical process is expected to unfold, but there is no doubt in the minds of the faithful that world triumph finally will be theirs. There is ultimately to be "the closest union and complete merging of the workmen and peasants of all nations into a single world-wide Soviet Republic."

How will triumph in the various countries be achieved? And what of relationships between those countries in which the revolution has already triumphed and those in which non-communist regimes still prevail? The emphasis in Marxist-Leninist theory is on the expectation that the communist party of each country will play the major role in seizing power for itself; for long the assumption was that the seizure would occur through revolution. But still an international duty—a world mission—is assigned to the country in which the revolution first triumphs. Lenin long ago declared: [20]

> The victorious proletariat of that country, having expropriated the capitalists and organized socialist production at home, would rise against the rest of the capitalist world, attracting the oppressed classes of other countries, raising among them revolts against the capitalists, launching, in case of necessity, armed forces against the exploiting classes and their states.

[19] Georgi Aleksandrov, *The Pattern of Soviet Democracy* (Washington, Public Affairs Press, 1948), p. 23.
[20] *Collected Works*, Vol. XVIII, p. 272; Vol. XX, Bk. 1, p. 145; cf. also J. V. Stalin, *Leninism* (London, Communist Party of Great Britain, 1928), Vol. I, p. 56.

Once the Bolsheviks had seized power in Russia in 1917, Lenin declared it "inconceivable that the Soviet Republic should continue to exist interminably side by side with imperialist states. Ultimately one or the other must conquer. Pending this development a number of terrible clashes between the Soviet Republic and the bourgeois states must inevitably occur." He championed "proletarian internationalism," which he defined as "hard work at developing the revolutionary movement and the revolutionary struggle in one's own land, and the support (by propaganda, sympathy, material aid) of such, and only such struggles and policies in every country without exception."

In line with this conception of proletarian internationalism, Lenin encouraged the formation of communist parties abroad and led in the establishment of an international organization of those parties, called the Third International, in 1919. Acceptance of the "science" of Marxism-Leninism was, of course, prerequisite to membership in the organization. Soviet leaders naturally set themselves up as the supreme interpreters of the science, as revealers of the "truth." Able, as they were, to lend prestige and to give financial, diplomatic, and military support to non-Soviet parties, they established their control over the international movement. Loyalty to the Soviet Union and its leadership became the touchstone for foreign communists. Foreign parties became fifth columns abroad, controlled from Moscow. Although the Third International was formally in existence only until 1943, its dissolution did not substantially change the situation.

The extreme to which Lenin was willing to go in promoting the triumph of the communist ideology is indicated by the fact that he endorsed not only civil but also international war as appropriate methods in the struggle. He was not concerned with the question whether international wars were aggressive or defensive; the question was whether they were "just" or "unjust." "Just" wars included, among others, those "waged . . . to liberate the people from capitalist slavery, or, lastly, to liberate colonies and dependent countries from the yoke of imperialism." He took the view that, "if war is waged by the proletariat after it has conquered the bourgeoisie in its own country and is waged with the object of strengthening and extending socialism, such a war is legitimate and 'holy.' " Along the same lines, a Congress of the Third International later enacted a resolution denying the existence of any contradiction "between the Soviet Government's preparations for defense and for revolutionary war and a consistent peace policy." "Revolutionary war of the proletarian dictatorship," it declared, "is but a continuation of revolutionary peace policy 'by other means.' " [21]

[21] *History of the Communist Party of the Soviet Union* (*Bolsheviks*), *Short Course* (New York, International, 1939), pp. 167-168; V. I. Lenin, *Selected Works,* Vol. VII, p. 357; Communist International, *The Struggle Against Imperialist War and the Tasks*

Events since World War II illustrate both the role of domestic revolutionary forces and the role of the Soviet Union in promoting the geographical extension of communism. In China triumph was achieved largely through domestic revolutionary efforts, though the Soviet Union gave some assistance and though Soviet power may have deterred more drastic counterrevolutionary action on the part of Western states. In North Korea Soviet assistance was overt, and the North Korean attempt to spread revolution throughout the peninsula by aggressive war was presumably endorsed (certainly it was supported) by Moscow. In Eastern Europe the Communists came to power largely if not exclusively because of the presence or proximity of the Red Army. It is probably the precedents in Eastern Europe, plus the growing power of the Soviet Union, which provide the basis for the present official view that in some countries victory may be achieved without violent revolution. The general point is that violent revolution is necessary only where the bourgeoisie resist; if the resistance of the bourgeoisie is paralyzed, actual revolutionary war becomes unnecessary. Khrushchev has even suggested that at times the communists may win out in a "normal" electoral and parliamentary struggle.[22] Read in the light of Marxism-Leninism, his statements suggest the possibility that the Soviet Union itself might act to paralyze opposition to communists in other countries, as it did in Eastern Europe after World War II, or that it might stand poised with nuclear weapons to prevent the United States from going to the assistance of a besieged government.

Coexistence and Peace

Though expecting and demanding world revolution, communists also stress coexistence and peace. The meaning assigned to these words is uncertain. Like the word *democracy*, they are subject to definition and may be given a peculiarly communist meaning. We have already noted how, in the communist lexicon, peace may call for revolutionary war —war to eliminate capitalism as the alleged cause of war. Endorsement of the principle of coexistence might mean a promise of enduring tolerance of differences (which is scarcely to be expected of communists); it might mean a promise that communist dictatorships will confine their struggle against capitalism on the international level to peaceful competition (and this is the meaning which Khrushchev publicly espouses); or it might mean simply a recognition of the necessity of living together on a temporary basis until one side can kill the other off.

---

of the Communists, Resolutions of the Sixth World Congress, July-August, 1928 (New York, Workers Library, 1934), p. 33.

[22] "Report of the Central Committee of the Communist Party of the Soviet Union to the Twentieth Party Congress," *For A Lasting Peace, For A People's Democracy,* February 17, 1956, p. 3.

Attitudes Toward Nationalism

With the objective of world revolution, and with the slogan "Workers of the world, unite!" communism is internationalist in outlook. What attitude does it take toward nationalism? Its opposition to "imperialism" led it from the first to favor nationalist movements in colonies because of the prospect that such movements would weaken capitalist states, but the early attitude toward nationalism in the advanced countries was one of contempt. Nationalism was regarded as an ideology developed by the merchant class in its struggle against feudalism, and retained as a device for persuading the workers under capitalism to support the bourgeois governments which held them in subjection. Nationalism, like religion, was opium for the people. In more recent years, however, this line has changed, and communists often play the role of national chauvinists.

The point can be illustrated by reference to the propaganda of the French Communist Party, which styles itself the great defender of the national independence and sovereignty of France.[23]

The initial thesis which the French Communists offer in support of their nationalist line is that the French bourgeoisie and the governing groups generally have betrayed and are betraying the nation. The bourgeoisie, according to the Communists, was patriotic as long as it was a young and rising class, as long as it was interested in the establishment and preservation of a national market, but that time, allegedly, has long since passed. In recent years, according to the Communist line, fear of the people has come to dominate the ruling classes in Europe—fear of the rising working class and fear of colonial movements for national liberation. The ruling classes are said to fear that their own independent national governments are no longer effective instruments for maintaining their position and privileges, and since national governments have lost their utility, the ruling classes are impelled to depart from the national framework and seek safety in international arrangements, abandoning sovereignty and independence in the process. Thus through such instruments as the North Atlantic Treaty and the Council of Europe, they create a new Holy Alliance designed to preserve reactionary institutions and practices. For class advantage they sell the nation out to American imperialism.

With the nation thus allegedly threatened by the treason of the privileged class and by grasping American imperialism, it is the working class which, according to the Communists, comes to the rescue. Of course, the

---

[23] Subsequent paragraphs on the attitude of the French Communists toward nationalism are taken from the author's study, "The Communists and the Foreign Relations of France," in Edward Mead Earle, ed., *Modern France* (Princeton, Princeton University Press, 1951), pp. 240-247. The French sources used are there cited.

Communists admit that the working class, like the bourgeoisie, has a class interest to serve, but they claim that the interests of the working class coincide with, whereas the interests of the bourgeoisie contradict, those of the nation. Therefore, to promote the interests of the bourgeoisie is to betray the nation, but to promote the interests of the working class is to serve the nation. The working class has become the "national class par excellence"; it is the "only authentic national class." "The working class itself incarnates the national interests of the fatherland which the false elites and the ruling classes have betrayed."

Supporting this view, the Communists refer to the fact that the working class is numerous, but they do not rest their argument on this point. This is not a case where a majority determines the national interest. The "economic and political role" of the working class is "even more important" than its numbers in making it the national class. The working class is the national class, in addition, "because . . . it is the rising class, the class which will put an end to the exploitation of one nation by another and which, in giving *la patrie* a human and fraternal content, will permit it to flower freely." In other words, the "science" of Marxism-Leninism operates again. Just as the Communists claim to know the "true interests" of the various classes, so do they claim to know the "true interests" of the nation. Only those who agree with the Marxist-Leninist view can be patriots.

From the French communist point of view, preservation of national independence and sovereignty has operational significance only in relations with the capitalist world. It is only from the capitalist side that threats to the nation come. "There exists no conflict of interests between the workers of the different nations." Proletarian internationalism requires solidarity with the Soviet Union, but such solidarity is perfectly compatible with national patriotism, because Soviet interests "never conflict with the interests of the people of France." Not only do the French Communists deny a conflict of interests between France and the Soviet Union, but they declare that France can preserve its national independence only by aligning itself with the Soviet Union. "There is no national independence without international solidarity in the anti-imperialist camp in general and among the communist parties in particular."

Some other communist parties have developed a jealous regard for national independence, which is asserted against the Soviet Union. Thus nationalism played a major role in the break between the Soviet Union and Tito's Yugoslavia in 1948, and in 1956 it came to the fore in other countries of Eastern and Southeastern Europe, especially in Hungary and Poland.

Status of the Individual

Discussing the theories of liberalism and fascism we took up the question, which comes first, the nation-state or the individual. In connection with communism, the question is which comes first, the individual or the revolutionary cause. Communists themselves give the question little attention. Though their ultimate objective is a society in which individual welfare will be served, they are so preoccupied with what they consider to be the urgent revolutionary task that the individual gets short shrift. The attitude is akin to that of the fascists. If the individual has value, he derives it from service to the cause. He is to be used, manipulated, or doomed to die in accordance with the alleged requirements of the world historic mission which communists claim to serve. In the effort to remake the world, there is no place for tolerance or compassion. Fanatically convinced that they know the true interests of social classes, of peoples, and of all mankind, communists have proved their capacity to destroy the lives of millions and millions of people (figuratively and literally) while unctuously proclaiming that they fight on the side of the Lord. It is scarcely an answer to say that communist crimes against humanity are to be attributed to Stalin, whom the communists have now demoted, for the system produced him and lent itself to his ruthless and bloody program; moreover, similar practices accompany communism in countries other than the Soviet Union. The question is whether the good society which communists envision can be achieved by such methods.

The Ideology: An Operational Guide?

So far we have been assuming that ideology really guides the actions of communist statesmen in the foreign field. Though the assumption is probably sound, it is nevertheless subject to question; as yet it can scarcely be either proved or disproved in a definitive sense. Most of the actions of the U.S.S.R., at least, could be explained in terms of motivations and objectives common to all states, for example, the desire for security, for power, for empire, and for economic advantage.

Changes which have occurred in the words and policies of the Soviet leadership since the death of Stalin add to the difficulty of determining "real" Soviet objectives. There have been efforts to relax international tensions and reduce the danger of war. Moscow's control over the communist governments of Eastern and Southeastern Europe, and over foreign communist parties generally, has apparently been somewhat loosened. The potentially catastrophic nature of unlimited nuclear warfare has been acknowledged. There has been renewed emphasis on peaceful competition and coexistence. Whereas Stalin himself was generally regarded as a coldly calculating individual rather than a person, like Hitler, who emphasized intuition, his successors give the impression of being flexible and even more reasonable. What will come of all this remains to be seen.

Although there may be doubts about the real motivations and objectives of communist states, it is worth emphasizing that the rulers of those states say that Marxism-Leninism is their guide, and, even if the ideology is simply a tool which they use to serve their own private purposes, it is a tool which has stood them in good stead and which they seem unlikely to cast aside.[24]

Implications for International Politics

Assuming that ideology actually guides the behavior of communist states, what are the implications for international politics? In the first place, communism has provided the Soviet government (and now also provides the Peking regime) with a basis for the development of fifth columns—some of them very powerful—in other countries. Aggression by subversion has taken a much more prominent place in world affairs than ever before. In the second place, communism has provided a basis for cooperation among those states endorsing it, and may continue to do so. However, so far as the cooperation has had an ideological base it has rested on acceptance of the "truth" as revealed by science to the Kremlin; rejection of the Kremlin's conception of "truth" might well lead to something in the nature of religious wars. Internecine struggles within various communist parties, especially the Soviet party, provide little basis for expecting peace even if all the world should go communist. In the third place, and most important of all, statesmen whose thoughts are shaped by Marxist-Leninist theory must, somehow and some time, seek the overthrow of non-communist governments. They must assume the existence of basic and irreconcilable mutual antagonism in relations with such governments; neither side can expect fundamental reconciliation and trusting cooperation with the other.

Differences between the policies of liberal-democratic and communist states are usually not as complete as the above sketch suggests. The basic objective of every state is normally to preserve and protect itself against external attack, or, more generally, to avoid having an outside will imposed upon it. In other words, all states, including communist states, seek to preserve their independence and their security. Moreover, though communism endorses aggressive civil and international war as a useful instrument of policy, it would be unsound to infer from this that communist governments are forever plotting war. The Soviet leaders long ago accepted the principle that they would not undertake serious risks and costs simply to promote revolution abroad. In any event, govern-

[24] For an intensive analysis of the behavioral code of the Russian Bolsheviks, see Nathan Leites, A Study of Bolshevism (Glencoe, Free Press, 1953).

ments do not ordinarily go to war unless they see a good prospect of winning. Aware of the potential destructiveness of nuclear warfare, and denied substantial hope of victory, even a communist government may be devoted to peace. Further, even though world revolution is the communist objective, neither the Soviet nor any other communist government can pursue this objective forever in utter disregard of the people under its control; some minimum standard of well-being must be maintained, and there will be pressures for something above a minimum standard. Concentration on world revolution and an all-out effort to promote it may be possible for a time, but zeal and sacrifice for the achievement of a single objective cannot be maintained indefinitely. Human desires are too varied, and human beings are too concerned with their own personal interests, to permit this.

Though differences between the policies of liberal-democratic and communist states are perhaps not as great as the ideologies suggest, they are nevertheless sharp. The basic difference probably derives from the fact that liberal-democrats do not claim to know the "truth" whereas the communists do. Not claiming to possess "truth," not asserting absolute knowledge of the interests of individual men or of society, the liberal emphasizes procedures by which decisions should be made and certain limitations within which decisions should be made. He stresses majority rule, minority rights, and constitutional safeguards of liberty. He seeks to keep the future open, to maintain conditions under which individuals can choose the paths which seem likely to lead to satisfaction. Emphasizing liberty he must also emphasize tolerance of differing ideas and practices to which liberty leads. His world is one of diversity, involving respect for the choices of others so long as they do not unduly impair his own freedom to choose. He must insist upon restraint, for liberty is like a kite which is kept flying by the string which holds it down.

The communist is intolerant. Claiming to know what should be done, why should he tolerate error? Why should he permit liberty, when liberty may lead to wrong choices? Why keep the future open, when he knows without doubt what it should be? His duty is, rather, to remake individual men and whole societies—to remake the world—in accordance with the prescriptions of science. In the titanic struggle to remake mankind, he does not even grant the right of silence; those who are not liquidated must be compelled to shout, if not to work, for the cause. He permits diversity only where the obstacles to its elimination are too great to be overcome. Commanding "truth," he has no respect for what he regards as error. Such restraint as he displays reflects only his prudence rather than respect for the right of others to be wrong.

Both liberal-democracy and communism may thus make for either cooperation or conflict among states. Each ideology facilitates cooperation among those adhering to it. At the same time, each ideology is a challenge—each is subversive—to the other. This very fact makes for friction and conflict, and the prospect of conflict is greatly enhanced by the belief of communists that it is their historic mission to overthrow non-communist systems and bring world-wide triumph to their cause.

SUGGESTED READINGS

CARR, E. H., *Conditions of Peace* (New York, Macmillan, 1944).

COLE, Taylor, ed., *European Political Systems* (New York, Knopf, 1953).

COOK, Thomas I., and MOOS, Malcolm, *Power Through Purpose* (Baltimore, Johns Hopkins Press, 1954).

EBENSTEIN, William, *Today's Isms: Communism, Fascism, Capitalism, Socialism* (New York, Prentice-Hall, 1954).

FRIEDRICH, Carl J., *Totalitarianism* (Cambridge, Harvard University Press, 1954).

GROSS, Feliks, ed., *European Ideologies* (New York, Philosophical Library, 1948).

HUNT, R. N. Carew, *The Theory and Practice of Communism* (London, Geoffrey Bles, 1950).

MARSHALL, Charles B., *The Limits of Foreign Policy* (New York, Holt, 1954).

MORGENTHAU, Hans J., *In Defense of the National Interest* (New York, Knopf, 1951).

MORGENTHAU, Hans J., "Another 'Great Debate': The National Interest of the United States," *American Political Science Review*, Vol. 46 (December, 1952), pp. 961-988.

MUSSOLINI, Benito, "The Political and Social Doctrine of Fascism," *International Conciliation*, No. 306, January, 1935.

NORTHROP, F. S. C., *The Meeting of East and West, an Inquiry Concerning World Understanding* (New York, Macmillan, 1946).

NORTHROP, F. S. C., *The Taming of the Nations, a Study of the Cultural Base of International Policy* (New York, Macmillan, 1952).

OSGOOD, Robert E., *Ideals and Self-Interest in America's Foreign Relations* (Chicago, The University of Chicago Press, 1953).

TANNENBAUM, Frank, *The American Tradition in Foreign Policy* (Norman, University of Oklahoma Press, 1955).

CHAPTER 6

Economic Objectives
and Economic Forces

ANY INQUIRY into the question why states behave as they do—and that is the inquiry in which we are engaged—must take economic factors into account. They obviously play a significant role in international politics, just as they do in domestic politics.

There is danger of confusion in considering the subject, so we must be clear on what we are and what we are not discussing. The object in this chapter is to explain and assess the influence of economic considerations and economic forces on foreign policies. We want to know to what extent and in what ways economic factors make for cooperation or conflict among states. We want to know how and in what ways international relations are affected by the desire to retain or secure control over scarce resources. We want to know what follows in the international field from the fact that men desire wealth and from the fact that they operate under a particular kind of economic system—under capitalism, in particular.

Of course, economics plays not only an influential but also an instrumental role. It is not only a determinant of foreign policy but also a tool of foreign policy. A state may pursue objectives selected for economic reasons, or it may adopt economic methods in pursuing objectives selected for whatever reasons. We are here interested in the influential role of economics, not in its instrumental role. For example, we are not interested in the economic methods by which governments may seek to win friends or influence people; we are not interested in the economic methods by which the power of a state may be increased or reduced. Discussion of economic methods for the promotion of political purposes will be reserved for a later chapter.

The influence of economic considerations and forces on the behavior of states is in some respects a highly controversial subject. Economic determinists, and particularly the Marxists, interpret and explain virtually all political actions, domestic and international, in economic terms. Others reject such sweeping views, yet grant that economic factors play a powerful role. We shall first deal with the less controversial aspects of the subject, and then discuss economic theories of imperialism and war.

ECONOMIC CONSIDERATIONS AND FOREIGN POLICIES

That men desire the necessities and comforts and luxuries of life goes without saying. If they could secure all that they wanted within their own countries, the pursuit of economic objectives would presumably have less impact on international politics. The fact is, however, that many of the things that people want can be secured only, or more advantageously, in foreign countries. Resources are not distributed among countries in proportion to the demand for them. Raw materials in short supply in one country may exist in abundance in another; Britain, for example, produces no oil, but various states in the Middle East produce far more than they require. Climate and soil may permit one country to produce agricultural commodities which can only be produced with difficulty, if at all, in another; coffee, for example, can be grown in Brazil, but not in the United States. There are differences among nations in the productive skills and productive facilities available; the Swiss, for example, possess in an unusual degree the skills and facilities necessary for watchmaking, yet do not manufacture automobiles. More generally, differences exist among countries in the possession of capital available for investment and in the rate of profit that can be secured on investments.

International commercial and financial relationships develop naturally and almost inevitably out of factors such as these. Needing oil, the British go abroad to buy it. Wanting coffee, Americans import it from Brazil and elsewhere. Desiring watches, the people of many countries secure them from Switzerland. Requiring capital for the development of their resources, governments and private entrepreneurs often seek to attract foreign investors or to borrow abroad.

These statements are all rather simple and obvious, yet they are fraught with great significance to international politics. Governments themselves desire revenue, and they commonly look upon international commercial activities, particularly on the importation of goods from abroad, as a source of revenue. At the same time, governments commonly seek to protect the domestic economy against the possible adverse effects of foreign trade. More important to an explanation of the impact of economic pursuits on international relations is the fact that individuals who go abroad do not always leave their own governments entirely behind them. It is said that a Chinese emperor in the eighteenth century was unmoved by the fact that a number of Chinese traders had been killed in Java; he said that he was not interested in the fate of those who were so greedy for gain that they left the Heavenly Kingdom and went abroad among barbarians to seek it. This kind of attitude is alien to the western world. Tourists and traders who go abroad—and often even emigrants —take the flag with them, in effect, and the flag also follows the dollar. Governments are concerned with the wealth and well-being of their citizens abroad, and with the security of their lives and property. They therefore commonly seek to promote the economic activities of their citizens abroad, to see to it that justice is done to them in foreign countries, and generally to facilitate profitable and desirable international trade. Citizens abroad, in turn, look to their home governments for protection, and sometimes seek even more than protection, as will be shown below.

These attitudes are basic to an explanation of the influence of the pursuit of economic objectives on the behavior of states. Sometimes they produce cooperation among states in service to the mutual advantage of their citizens. Often, however, the activities of citizens abroad lead to international friction and conflict.

The Economic Factor in Colonial Imperialism

The establishment of European colonies abroad—involving the conquest of most of the rest of the world since the fifteenth century— resulted from the pursuit of a number of different objectives. The first explorers crossed the seas partly out of pure curiosity. They and their successors, having contacted alien lands and peoples, pressed on partly out of a desire to extend the Christian religion, or to secure religious liberty for themselves, or, more recently, to take up the alleged White Man's Burden. Many colonies were seized either because the possession of colonies was thought to lend glory to king or nation or because of their strategic value in rendering existing possessions more secure. There is no simple explanation of overseas imperialism. Yet among the factors which have operated, economic considerations have certainly been powerful.

1. The search for profits and the seizure of colonies. Economic objectives were particularly important in the early expansion of Europe across the seas. Voyages down the African coast sponsored by Prince Henry the Navigator were encouraged when the first ships returned with gold dust and Negro slaves. Later expeditions were lured on by thought of the riches to be obtained from importing the spices and other rare products of India and the East. Once the Portuguese reached India, they found that they could not capitalize on their discovery merely through peaceful trade. They had to destroy the fleets of the Arab merchants and to establish naval bases on the shores of India and other eastern lands. These things they did, enriching themselves and establishing colonies, some of which Portugal retains, though in some jeopardy, to this day.

Later the Dutch entered the trade, the States-General creating the Dutch East India Co. in 1602 and authorizing it to make war or peace, seize foreign ships, establish colonies, construct forts, and coin money. The British likewise entered with their East India Co. Soon the two were fighting each other as well as the Portuguese while reducing the peoples of the East to colonial subjection. Gradually the Dutch, in an effort to make their trade secure, established political control over the East Indies, which they retained until after World War II. The British, and later the French, developed their trade and power primarily in India, the British eventually winning out and reducing all India to colonial control. It should be noted that neither the Dutch nor the British began their activities in the East for the purpose of establishing empire. Rather, the main purpose was profit, but once European lives and property were at stake in the East, activities could not remain purely commercial. To protect themselves and their interests, the Europeans felt compelled to take part in the political and military affairs of the governments and peoples of the region, and this in turn led gradually to the establishment of colonial controls.

Similar developments occurred in relationship to the western hemisphere. Desire to find a way to the Indies and to the profits to be secured through trade with them played a major role in the voyages of Columbus and others who sailed west across the Atlantic. It took much exploring before what someone has called the "depressing fact" became clear that the route to the West led only to a sparsely populated new world. Meantime the explorers laid claim to newly discovered lands on behalf of the crown which sponsored their voyages. Adventurers and settlers took up residence temporarily or permanently across the seas, extending the realm of European control. Spanish *conquistadores* established the "silver empire," looting the wealth of the Aztecs and Incas and winning a vast empire for Spain. Colonizers set out from Britain for North America, usually sponsored by a joint stock company. There were a number of arguments for sponsoring such colonization, the most important being economic. "The colonies were to enrich the investors, and the realm in general, by producing commodities which were in demand in Europe; to enrich the Crown by means of customs duties; and to enrich the merchants and manufacturers of England by serving as markets for English products."[1] Britain and Spain, especially, enacted navigation and other acts designed to preserve for their own people the profits of trade with

[1] J. H. Parry, *Europe and a Wider World* (London, Hutchinson's University Library, 1949), p. 108.

the colonies and to enhance the revenues which the governments themselves would derive from that trade. The French and Dutch were likewise lured on largely by the prospects of profit to participate in the exploration and colonization of the new world.

In the western hemisphere, as in the East Indies, the pursuit of wealth led to conflict both with native peoples and among the European countries involved. Privateering, bordering on piracy, was common for long periods in the relationships between the ships of different European countries in the Atlantic. Numerous colonial wars were fought among the imperial powers.

During the nineteenth century the European powers reduced one part of Africa after another to colonial control. The motivating considerations in most of the acts of expansion were mixed. The desire for profits certainly entered. When King Leopold II of Belgium took steps leading to the establishment of the Congo Free State, of which he became King, he professed the most altruistic motives: [2] "To open to civilization the only part of our globe where it has not yet penetrated, to pierce the darkness which envelopes whole populations, is a crusade, if I may say so, a crusade worthy of this century of progress." In fact, however, his rule over the natives of the Congo turned out to be ruthless and inhumane, though very profitable. He and others associated with him made millions of dollars. Whatever Leopold's original motives, his actions eventually led to the acquisition of the Congo Free State by Belgium as a colony. Elsewhere in Africa, too, the desire for profit, the desire to protect the lives and property of citizens who themselves were pursuing profit, the desire for prestige and power, ostensible response to the idea of the White Man's Burden, and other considerations combined to produce imperialism. By the end of the century very little of the continent remained free.

2. *The role of population pressure.* The pressure of population on resources has figured, especially in more recent times, as both a reason and an excuse for imperialism. Note that it is not population density which is necessarily involved; the pressure of population on resources may be great even in sparsely settled territories. Note too that there is no direct correlation even between pressure of population on resources and imperialism; many countries where such pressure is great have been non-imperialistic. Something must be added to population pressure before imperialism is produced, and even then it may or may not materialize. Perhaps the most general formulation is this: when the politically influential believe that scales of living are unduly low, that resources in the homeland provide an inadequate basis for improvement, and that improvement could be accomplished through a program of territorial

[2] Parker Thomas Moon, *Imperialism and World Politics* (New York, Macmillan, 1927), pp. 75-97.

aggrandizement, the stage is set for an expansionist program.[3] Japan's imperialism is frequently explained in these terms, the allegation being that she needed colonial territories both as an outlet for surplus population and as a source of raw materials. In the period between the wars Mussolini cited population pressure in Italy as a factor necessitating territorial expansion—and at the same time tried to encourage population growth so as to obtain the manpower which a program of aggrandizement seemed to require. In fact, migration from an imperialist country to its colonies has rarely if ever served significantly to reduce population pressure, but belief that it would may at times have stimulated colonial ventures.[4]

3. *Economic factors in American imperialism.* The history of American foreign relations offers numerous examples of the influence of economic considerations in producing imperialism, whether it took the form of the acquisition of territory or of military intervention in the affairs of other states. While Texas was still a part of Mexico, people from the United States emigrated to the territory primarily for economic reasons. They naturally took their own language and customs and expectations with them. In a sense they constituted an alien fifth column infiltrating the territory of a friendly state. Mexican rule proved uncongenial and eventually unacceptable to them. They rebelled, established their independence, and later secured admission into the United States. War between the United States and Mexico developed over the issue.

Hawaii became a possession of the United States by a somewhat similar process. Missionaries began the penetration of the islands, and were soon followed by traders and pineapple growers. Again a clash of cultures developed, and the Americans on the island—with unauthorized help from local United States representatives—eventually rebelled against the native government and seized control. Cleveland, inaugurated as President soon after the Hawaiian revolution, had pangs of conscience over the role of the United States in the events and tried to find a way to restore a legitimate Hawaiian regime, but he could not do so without placing the lives of the American rebels in jeopardy. The revolutionary government therefore survived, and in the surge of American imperialism at the time of the Spanish-American War it secured the annexation of Hawaii to the United States.

American advocates of the annexation of the Philippines after the Spanish-American War used economic arguments, among others, to support their program. They were enamored of the possibilities of trade in the Far East, and thought that control of the Philippine Islands would facilitate the penetration of markets in the region. Senator Albert J.

[3] Warren S. Thompson, *Population Problems* (New York, McGraw-Hill, 1953), pp. 359-360.
[4] Grover Clark, *A Place in the Sun* (New York, Macmillan, 1936), pp. 85-129.

Beveridge, a leading exponent of annexation, made perhaps the most flamboyant plea, appealing at once to economic considerations, to the idea of the White Man's Burden, and to national chauvinism: [5]

American factories are making more than the American people can use; American soil is producing more than they can consume. Fate has written our policy for us; the trade of the world must and shall be ours. And we will get it as our mother [England] showed us how. We will establish trading posts throughout the world as distributing points for American products. We will cover the ocean with our merchant marine. We will build a navy to the measure of our greatness. Great colonies, governing themselves, flying our flag and trading with us, will grow about our posts of trade. Our institutions will follow our flag on the wings of our commerce. And American law, American order, American civilization, and the American flag will plant themselves on shores hitherto bloody and benighted, but by those agencies of God henceforth to be made beautiful and bright.

In these cases—Texas, Hawaii, and the Philippines—it is obvious that the economic argument alone does not explain the imperialistic expansion which occurred. In each one, considerations of national pride and a longing for something vaguely regarded as greatness clearly played a significant role.

The United States on numerous occasions has been involved in friction and conflict with several of the Caribbean republics. Again non-economic considerations have often entered. The desire to forestall European intervention, to safeguard the route through Panama, and perhaps the psychological satisfaction derived from dominance have all played a role. But economic considerations have usually been important in the difficulties which have arisen. One of the most flagrant examples is that relating to Nicaragua in the period from 1909 to 1912. American business concerns operating there, dissatisfied with the government of President Zelaya, apparently encouraged and financed revolution against it. The United States government officially intervened to support the revolutionaries in the struggle that ensued. The justification for the intervention, which prevented Zelaya's forces from re-establishing control over the port city of Bluefields, was that American life and property there would be endangered if the rebel forces were defeated. In other words, by military action the United States assured the rebels a safe haven in Bluefields. Later, when the legitimate government sought to blockade the port so as to prevent "the revolution from continuing to receive, as before, arms, supplies, and funds from New Orleans," the United States frustrated the action by threatening war. Unable to cope with American support for the rebels, both President Zelaya and his legitimate successor abandoned the struggle and fled the country. The rebels thus won out.

[5] Claude G. Bowers, *Beveridge and the Progressive Era* (New York, Literary Guild, 1932), p. 69.

Negotiations with the rebel government led to agreement between the United States and Nicaragua satisfactory to American commercial interests operating in the country. Soon the former secretary of one of the American concerns became Nicaragua's president.[6]

This is a clear instance in which the actions of a state were influenced by the economic interests of its nationals abroad. Similarly, American relations with Mexico were strained for over a decade after the 1917 Mexican constitution asserted national ownership over subsoil deposits, including ownership of oil under land owned or leased by American companies. Mixed considerations—among them economic ones—led to American intervention in Cuba, the Dominican Republic, Haiti, and Panama.

4. *The relative influence of economic and political factors.* The developments and episodes described above scarcely permit any generalization other than that sometimes and to some extent economic factors have contributed to international friction, colonial imperialism, and war. Systematic studies have been made, however, from which more pointed conclusions have been drawn. Jacob Viner, for example, has investigated relationships between international finance and balance-of-power diplomacy, mainly in Europe, from 1880 to 1914. In all the transactions studied he found that the bankers, far from taking the initiative in actions which dragged governments into difficulties, were "passive and in some cases unwilling instruments of the diplomats."

... The bankers in general seem to have been pacifically inclined, and to have been much more favorably disposed than were their governments to international cooperation and reconciliation. . . . Bankers rarely favor an aggressive policy toward powerful adversaries, or even toward weak countries if the latter have powerful friends. Whatever their attitude toward weak and friendless countries, in the diplomacy of the Great Powers they are a pacific influence. ... For the claim sometimes made that the bankers exercised a controlling influence over pre-war diplomacy, the available source material offers not the slightest degree of support.[7]

Similarly, Eugene Staley, in his *War and the Private Investor,* made an analysis of all cases roughly in the half-century after 1880 in which pressures from private traders and investors are alleged to have been the source of serious international disputes. Only rarely did he find that

[6] Charles A. Beard, *The Idea of National Interest* (New York, Macmillan, 1934), pp. 170-182. Cf. Samuel Flagg Bemis, *The Latin American Policy of the United States* (New York, Harcourt, Brace, 1943), pp. 161-163. In a sense the American practice of extending diplomatic protection to its citizens in Caribbean countries, sometimes involving military intervention, served as a substitute for reducing them to the status of colonies. See pp. 303-304, below.

[7] Jacob Viner, "International Finance and Balance of Power Diplomacy, 1880-1914," *Southwestern Political and Social Science Quarterly,* Vol. 9 (March, 1929), pp. 450-451.

the economic factor operated alone, and often he discovered it to be less influential than political factors. Where serious disputes arose such factors as concern for national power and prestige almost always supplemented economic factors in producing difficulties. This was particularly true in relationships among the great powers. Where the potential antagonist was a great power, and where no significant military or political interest was involved, governments extended only hesitant support, if any at all, to citizens trading and investing abroad. They did not want to fight a major war, or seriously to risk it, solely for the benefit of a few. Several statements by Staley are in point: [8]

Private investments seeking purely business advantage (i.e., unmotivated by political expansionism, balance of power strategy, military considerations, or other reasons of state) have rarely of themselves brought great powers into serious political clashes.

Where there has been really serious friction between major powers over investment matters, examination will disclose in most instances that the political opposition existed before the investment issue arose, and either expressed itself through them or crystallized around them.

Investments used in the service of naval and political strategy, colonial expansion, quests for national glory, and the like, have been more productive of international friction in the past than investments actuated solely by private profit motives.

The Moroccan crisis of 1911 is one of the few incidents in which a private enterpriser has dragged an unwilling government into serious diplomatic difficulties. There is every evidence that the German government wanted the German concern involved in this case to reach an amicable understanding with its French counterpart. The French government took a similar view. Nevertheless, the German firm persisted with incomprehensible stubbornness in rejecting even the most generous offers; at the same time it engaged in a propaganda campaign, arousing German nationalist and patriotic emotion over the issue. A serious crisis ensued in the relations between Germany and France; it was resolved peacefully, yet it certainly contributed to an embitterment of relationships. The very rarity of such a case, however, is at least as significant as the fact of its occurrence.

The influential role of the economic factor in recent times has been somewhat greater in relationships between great powers and small, "backward" countries. As Staley puts it,[9] "Private investments have been important as instigators (as distinguished from tools) of diplomatic action mainly in connection with the relations of relatively weak capital-importing countries with relatively strong capital-exporting countries."

[8] Eugene Staley, *War and the Private Investor* (Garden City, Doubleday, Doran, 1935), pp. xvi, 359, 360.
[9] *Ibid.*, p. 366.

Most of the episodes described on the preceding pages illustrate the point.

5. *Exploitation, mutual advantage, and struggles for independence.* The above examples alluded only to cases of more or less active or aggressive measures on the part of imperialist countries. Two comments might be added. In the first place, it should not be assumed that all economic relationships between great powers and "backward" areas—even when the latter become colonies—are necessarily to the disadvantage of the weaker party. Many such relationships have provided mutual benefit. In economic relationships profit for one side does not necessarily mean loss for the other. Even in the colonial field, where considerable exploitation of native peoples has obviously occurred, the record is not all black, for often the material progress—and sometimes the political progress—of colonial peoples has been promoted.

The second comment contradicts the first, in a sense, yet it is still true. It is that the establishment of colonial or quasi-colonial relationships has often led to long-range difficulties. Colonial peoples have commonly become resentful both of white settlers who have entered their territory and of the alien governments to which they are subjected. In recent decades anti-imperialist nationalism has become an extremely potent force in much of the colonial world; almost pathological hatred of the imperial overlord has sometimes developed. The reduction of "backward" people to colonial control has therefore often been followed, sooner or later, with bitter, if not with violent, struggles for independence. Imperialism in times past remade the political geography of the world, and in more recent times anti-imperialist nationalism has been remaking it again. The conflict of colonial imperialism and anti-imperialist nationalism still goes on.

International Effects of Domestic Economic Measures

International relations are affected by the pursuit of economic objectives at home as well as by the pursuit of economic objectives abroad. Governments are concerned not only with the prosperity and well-being of nationals doing business in foreign countries but also with the prosperity and well-being of citizens within the country. They want to prevent foreign trade from having an adverse effect on the domestic economy; they sometimes regulate the character and extent of participation by foreigners in domestic economic life; and they normally seek to maintain or improve the level of domestic well-being. Measures taken for any of these reasons may produce repercussions abroad.

1. *Protection of domestic producers.* During the seventeenth and eighteenth centuries the countries of western Europe regulated foreign trade relationships on the basis of the principles of mercantilism. Both power and plenty were the objectives, and a long-run harmony between

the two was assumed.[10] Money was thought to command them both, so foreign trade relationships were regulated with a view to amassing money. A so-called favorable balance of trade was sought, mainly by encouraging exports and restricting imports. Though the theory alleged to justify mercantilist methods has been proved unsound, some of them are still employed.

Tariffs are the traditional device for protecting the domestic economy —or simply of conferring advantage on special interest groups at the expense of others. More recently, states have resorted to fixing quotas on imports, that is, to specifying that no more than a certain quantity of an item can be imported in a given period of time. They have also resorted to exchange controls, to regulating the purchase of foreign currencies needed to pay for imports. Furthermore, sanitary regulations are sometimes imposed; whether the desire to protect domestic plant and animal life from disease is the real or only the ostensible reason, the effect is to curtail imports.

Although perhaps protecting the domestic economy, tariffs, quotas, exchange controls, and sanitary regulations are likely to do damage to other countries. A reduction in one country's imports means a reduction in another country's exports. An increase in the United States' tariff on watches amounts to an attack on the prosperity of Switzerland. A French quota on the importation of automobiles reduces profits in Detroit. British exchange controls which restrict the importation of cotton from the United States help cause unemployment in the South. An American ban on the importation of Argentine beef because of the presence of hoof-and-mouth disease in Patagonia contributes to depression in Argentina. Not only do these measures sometimes reduce trade, but, of course, they curtail increases in trade which might otherwise occur.

The adoption of protective devices often leads to international protest. Governments do not like to have their economies damaged or undermined from abroad. They do not like it when others seek to "export unemployment." Some thirty different countries protested to the United States when the Smoot-Hawley tariff was enacted in 1930. A country shut out from foreign markets—and therefore substantially prevented from buying the things it needs abroad—may take drastic measures to remedy the situation. It may retaliate in kind, or it may take even more extreme measures. As Jacob Viner puts it,[11] "Trade barriers ... are undoubtedly the major economic contribution, directly or indirectly, to international conflict, tension, and war." There is no doubt that the pro-

[10] Jacob Viner, "Power Versus Plenty as Objectives of Foreign Policy in the Seventeenth and Eighteenth Centuries," *World Politics,* Vol. 1 (October, 1948), esp. p. 10.

[11] Jacob Viner, "The Economic Problem," in George B. de Huszar, ed., *New Perspectives on Peace* (Chicago, The University of Chicago Press, 1944, copyright 1944 by the University of Chicago), p. 102.

tective measures taken by other countries played a role in producing the economic difficulties which contributed, however significantly, to both German and Japanese aggressiveness in the 1930's.

These problems sometimes lead also to international cooperation. After all, there is clear mutual advantage to be secured through international trade. Since 1934 the United States has taken the lead in efforts to secure a general relaxation of trade barriers. The Reciprocal Trade Agreement program has produced a large number of bilateral agreements in which the parties agree to reduce certain specified tariff rates, or to levy no tariff at all on certain specified items. Moreover, these agreements include a most-favored-nation clause, binding the parties to extend to each other any tariff concessions granted to other states. Tariff reductions called for in bilateral agreements are therefore generalized. Since World War II there has been considerable cooperation, especially among the states of the West, designed not only to bring about a reduction in tariffs but also to eliminate or reduce other barriers to trade.

2. *Regulation of foreign participation in economic life.* Governmental regulations of the character and extent of participation by foreigners in domestic economic life are far less significant than trade barriers to international politics. Moreover, such regulations are usually designed to promote objectives which are more political than economic, as when governments are moved by national pride or by concern for security to prevent aliens from securing control over vital sectors of economic life. Nationalist and racialist factors often enter. Former American policies concerning the immigration of Orientals, and concerning the treatment of those who had already entered the country, provide a case in point. Welcomed when cheap labor was needed, the Chinese were excluded from the country when fear developed, especially in the trade unions, that their willingness to accept low wages would depress the scale of living of American workers. The Japanese were likewise subjected to discrimination for various reasons, including economic ones. Diplomatic difficulties ensued, leading to a gentlemen's agreement between the United States and Japan under which the latter agreed to deny passports to its nationals wishing to emigrate to the United States. Later, California and other states enacted legislation prohibiting aliens ineligible for citizenship (principally the Chinese and Japanese) from owning or leasing land for agricultural purposes. Still later the federal government heaped indignity on both China and Japan through the immigration law of 1924; while permitting immigration from other countries on a quota basis, the law entirely prohibited immigration from these and other Oriental countries. There was resentment over this especially in Japan, and the resentment was undoubtedly a factor in the exacerbation of relations with Japan which later occurred.

Regulations concerning the participation of foreigners in domestic economic life have also contributed to other episodes involving international friction. Economic considerations were among those which induced the Boer Republic to enact legislation discriminating against aliens, and this legislation in turn helped to bring on the Boer War. Economic considerations have commonly also figured among those leading to the socialization or nationalization of resources or industries—for example, by the Bolsheviks after the October Revolution, by the Mexicans in connection with subsoil deposits and the oil industry, and by Iran of the Anglo-Iranian Oil Co. The implications for international politics are obvious.

3. *Deficit financing and war preparations.* Governmental efforts to maintain or improve the general level of domestic prosperity are probably most serious for international relations when they involve an armaments program. It should not be forgotten that such a program may be designed for pump-priming as well as for power. When governments try to spend themselves out of depressions, or spend to avoid depressions, they sometimes find it easier to spend on armaments than on anything else. People may be divided about the wisdom of adopting a work-relief program or providing a dole; they are less likely to be divided over proposals to increase the power of the armed establishments, particularly if a foreign enemy exists or can be created. As a writer in *Punch* put it many years ago,

> The heart of a nation, as never before,
> Is united when making munitions of war.

The United States Congress in 1934 explicitly declared that one of its purposes in appropriating money for the construction of naval vessels was to provide work. Usually, however, such explicit admissions are not made. It becomes difficult to tell, therefore, where concern for power stops and where the desire to provide employment begins in influencing governments to enact arms programs. Hitler's rearmament of Germany in the 1930's certainly was a major factor in eliminating unemployment in the country, whether or not this was a conscious purpose. Certainly, too, the armaments program in the United States has come to be so important an element in the national economy that changes must be considered not only in terms of military needs but also in terms of the prospective effects on the level of prosperity.

It should be pointed out, however, that pump-priming is called for only in deflationary periods. Further, advances made in the field of economics in recent years have revealed means of curbing deflation which are superior to large-scale armaments expenditures. It is therefore not to be assumed, whether in periods of deflation or inflation, that armaments programs are undertaken (solely, largely, or at all) for economic reasons. Dangers to national security may be very real.

To sum up, we have seen that the pursuit of economic objectives both abroad and at home may influence foreign policies and contribute to international friction and war. Citizens who travel or trade or invest abroad sometimes drag their governments after them into colonial ventures or into difficulties with foreign states; this occurs more often in relations between strong and weak powers than in relations between strong powers themselves. Governments seeking to promote domestic prosperity sometimes take measures which create international friction and increase the probability of war; they enact trade controls which undermine prosperity abroad, they discriminate against aliens in domestic economic life, and they may use armaments programs to relieve or avert unemployment. Conversely, too, states sometimes cooperate with each other in the pursuit of common economic interests.

4. *State-controlled economies and the problem of war.* This discussion of the relationship between economic forces and the behavior of states has so far related mainly to free-enterprise economies. Is there reason to believe that the establishment of state-controlled economies would materially reduce the role of economic factors in contributing to international friction and war? Probably not, if the world continued to be divided into sovereign states. Conflicts of economic interest among the various states would still exist, and the very fact of state control over the economy would automatically make such conflicts intergovernmental. In private enterprise many of the quarrels which arise because of international commercial activities remain private quarrels, settled by negotiation among the persons involved or by established judicial procedures. State control would transform such quarrels into public quarrels, necessarily exacerbating international relations. It is argued, in fact, that peace is more likely to be promoted through a reduction rather than through an extension of governmental participation in economic life. Thus, Jacob Viner declares that [12] "for a world of autonomous nation-states ... economic factors can be prevented from breeding war if, and only if, private enterprise is freed from extensive state control other than state control intended to keep enterprise private and competitive."

Consider, for example, the position of a government which plans and controls the national economy when, as is almost inevitably the case, the success of the plan depends on the sale of certain goods abroad and the receipt of essential materials in exchange. To be more specific, suppose that the success of an economic plan in a powerful state depends upon the importation of oil from an adjacent weak state. Suppose further that for some reason supplies of oil from the weak state are threatened or cut off. An international political issue immediately arises. Various solutions may, of course, be available. The point is that there is no

[12] Jacob Viner, "International Relations Between State-Controlled National Economies," *American Economic Review,* Vol. 34, Part 2 (March, 1944), p. 328.

reason to think that state planning and state control will make international difficulties less likely; the reverse is probably true. The powerful state in this situation will at least be strongly tempted to intervene in the weak state, and perhaps to annex it.

Nor is it necessarily true that the achievement of the communist dream of a classless society would reduce the occasions for international friction and conflict. Again, and completely aside from other features of the communist program which make for war, the reverse of this expectation is more likely to be true. As Jacob Viner puts it,[13]

... There are substantial grounds for expecting classless societies, if organized on a national basis, to be readier to engage in war than bourgeois capitalist societies. ... As compared to class-divided states, a classless state will be more unified with respect to national policy because of the absence of internal conflicts of class interest and the absence of opposition parties organized on class lines and tending even to take antinational positions. It is hard to think of any economic ground for going to war which may not be as much present in a world of classless nation-states as in a world of capitalist states, and there is no basis for supposing that classless societies would not share with capitalist societies most of the political or sentimental or moral reasons for going to war, while producing some novel ones of their own.

In short, in view of the probability that some degree of state intervention in economic life is likely to continue indefinitely, economic factors influencing the behavior of states are likely to continue to operate. The adoption of socialist proposals might well accentuate rather than reduce the economic sources of international friction and war.

ECONOMIC THEORIES OF IMPERIALISM

It is one thing to say that economic factors sometimes contribute to the development of friction or the outbreak of war among states, and quite another thing to explain friction and war mainly or exclusively in economic terms. This is what some do. There are theories of imperialism and war which presume to explain these phenomena as resulting entirely—or nearly so—from economic relationships and economic forces.

Theories of this type divide into two main classes, one treating imperialism as a policy and the other treating it as a stage of history. When imperialism is treated as a policy, the implication is that it results from choices which men make; under this kind of theory, imperialism could be avoided if men would only make different choices. When imperialism is treated as a stage of history, the implication is that it is a natural and necessary aspect of the development of capitalism; given a capitalist system, imperialism thus becomes unavoidable.

[13] "The Economic Problem," *loc. cit.*, p. 96.

Imperialism as a Policy

Perhaps the most influential economic theory treating imperialism as a policy rests on the idea of overproduction-underconsumption, that is, on the idea that a capitalist country tends to produce more than it can consume. There results, it is argued, a surplus of goods and a surplus of capital, and the presence of the surpluses in turn leads to a search for foreign markets in which the surplus goods can be sold and the surplus capital invested. Out of the search, imperialism and war are said to arise.

According to the proponents of the overproduction-underconsumption thesis, of whom J. A. Hobson, an English economist, has been the most influential, capitalism commonly involves "a distribution of general income which puts too small a share in the hands of the working classes, too large a share in the hands of the employing and owning classes." [14] The employing and owning classes, possessing "too large" a share of the total income, will either invest or save much of their share. If they save it, there will be products on the market for which there is inadequate effective demand. If they invest it within the country in factories and other means of production, they will simply accentuate the difficulty, creating still more surpluses for which effective demand will be inadequate. If the working classes—the mass of the consumers—had a greater share of the national income, they might buy up the products which otherwise are surplus, but the distribution of income is said to prevent them from doing so. Thus, in Hobson's words,[15]

Everywhere appear excessive powers of production, excessive capital in search of investment. It is admitted by all business men that the growth of the powers of production in their country exceeds the growth in consumption, that more goods can be produced than can be sold at a profit, and that more capital exists than can find remunerative investment.

What is the way out? According to Hobson, the way out which is commonly chosen is imperialism. "It is this economic condition of affairs," he said, "that forms the taproot of imperialism." Those with surplus products and surplus capital seek to sell or invest abroad. "Imperialism is the endeavor of the great controllers of industry to broaden the channel for the flow of their surplus wealth by seeking foreign markets and foreign investments to take off the goods and capital they cannot sell or use at home." [16]

Hobson did not argue that the economic factor operated alone in producing imperialism. He pictured finance as the "governor" rather than

[14] J. A. Hobson, *Imperialism* (London, George Allen & Unwin, 1938), p. vii.
[15] *Ibid.*, p. 81.
[16] *Ibid.*, p. 85.

the "fuel" of the imperial engine. It did less to generate imperialist strivings than to direct and concentrate them. "Finance manipulates the patriotic forces which politicians, soldiers, philanthropists, and traders generate; the enthusiasm for expansion which issues from these sources, though strong and genuine, is irregular and blind; the financial interest has those qualities of concentration and clear-sighted calculation which are needed to set Imperialism to work." [17]

Neither did Hobson argue that imperialism is necessarily of economic benefit to the imperialist country as a whole. Rather, he took the view that imperialism is "bad business for the nation"; its risks and costs are greater than the rewards which come to the country as a whole. Yet, though imperialism is "irrational from the standpoint of the whole nation, it is rational enough from the standpoint of certain classes in the nation." Some stand to gain, and they manipulate public policy so as to secure gain for themselves even though others suffer. According to Hobson,[18] "The famous words of Sir Thomas More are as true now as when he wrote them: 'Everywhere do I perceive a certain conspiracy of rich men seeking their own advantage under the name and pretext of the commonwealth.'"

Finally, as already suggested, Hobson did not argue that imperialism is inevitable under capitalism. Rather, it results from "a false economy of distribution," a wrong distribution of income. "Imperialism is the fruit of this false economy; 'social reform' is its remedy. The primary purpose of 'social reform' ... is to raise the wholesome standard of private and public consumption for a nation, so as to enable the nation to live up to its highest standard of production." [19] Hobson declared that a completely socialist state which kept good books would soon discard imperialism, and that an intelligent laissez-faire democracy which gave duly proportionate weight in its policy to all economic interests alike would do the same.

John Maynard Keynes's *The General Theory of Employment, Interest and Money* contains an explanation of imperialism and war similar in some respects to that of Hobson. Keynes pointed out [20] that in a laissez-faire capitalist system "full, or even approximately full, employment is of rare and short-lived occurrence." Though governments desire to alleviate or eliminate unemployment, traditional laissez-faire theories provide them with no orthodox means of doing so. If they are to reduce unemployment they are therefore impelled to struggle for an export surplus

[17] *Ibid.*, p. 59.
[18] *Ibid.*, p. 46.
[19] *Ibid.*, p. 88.
[20] John Maynard Keynes, *The General Theory of Employment, Interest and Money* (New York, Harcourt, Brace, 1936), esp. pp. 250, 349, 381-383. For a discussion of various economic explanations of imperialism, see E. M. Winslow, *The Pattern of Imperialism* (New York, Columbia University Press, 1948).

and for an import of the monetary metal at the expense of their neighbors. International trade thus became to him "a desperate expedient to maintain employment at home by forcing sales on foreign markets and restricting purchases, which, if successful, will merely shift the problem of unemployment to the neighbor which is worsted in the struggle."

Never in history [he said] was there a method devised of such efficacy for setting each country's advantage at variance with its neighbors' as the international gold (or, formerly, silver) standard. For it made domestic prosperity directly dependent on a competitive pursuit of markets and a competitive appetite for the precious metals. [The struggle] has tended to become increasingly internecine.

Keynes recognized that war had "several causes," but over and above the others he placed the economic causes, "namely, the pressure of population and the competitive struggle for markets." He argued, however, as did Hobson, that the economic causes of war could be counteracted within the framework of the capitalist system.

Imperialism as a Stage of History

Of the Marxists, and of those who regard imperialism as an inevitable stage in the development of capitalism, Lenin, the Russian Bolshevik leader, has been most influential. His explanation of imperialism and war depended neither on the idea of underconsumption nor on the idea that capitalist states are driven to seek foreign markets as a means of reducing unemployment. Rather, he based his theory on the "general and fundamental law" that under capitalism both the means of production and the money available for investment are concentrated in fewer and fewer hands. In other words, capitalist economies come to be dominated by monopolies or trusts, supplemented internationally by cartels. At some point in this process capitalism is transformed into imperialism. According to Lenin's "briefest possible definition," imperialism is "the monopoly stage of capitalism."

Capitalism in its monopolist or imperialist stage, according to Lenin, is necessarily expansionist. It is expansionist in part because the monopolists come to control "surplus" capital. They will not use the surplus for the purpose of raising the standard of living of the masses, for this would mean a decline in profits. They cannot keep on investing within a strictly national economy, because as capitalism matures the rate of profit on investments within the country tends to decline. So they invest abroad, in less advanced countries, where the rate of profit promises to be higher. Having invested, they want their investment to be secure. "The necessity of exporting capital gives an impetus to the conquest of colonies, for in the colonial market it is easier to eliminate competition, to make sure of orders, to strengthen the necessary 'connection,' etc., by monopolist methods (and sometimes it is the only way)."

Monopoly capitalism is also expansionist, Lenin held, because of the need for foreign raw materials and because of the competition among capitalists of various countries for control over them. "Colonial possession alone gives complete guarantee of success to the monopolies against all the risks of the struggle with competitors. . . . The more capitalism is developed, the more the need for raw materials is felt, the more bitter competition becomes, and the more feverishly the hunt for raw materials proceeds throughout the whole world, the more desperate becomes the struggle for the acquisition of colonies."

As the reference to the acquisition of colonies suggests, Lenin was not speaking solely of economic expansion. Under his analysis, monopoly capitalists dominated not only the economic but also the political life of imperialist countries. In general, he regarded all governments simply as instruments of a ruling class. Whether governments were monarchical or republican, dictatorial or democratic—in fact, regardless of their form —they would be class instruments in societies divided into classes. Under monopoly capitalism, they would be tools of the monopolists. Thus, if the monopolists wanted to render their foreign investments secure, and if they wanted to gain control over the sources of needed raw materials, they would simply use government to serve this end. Whether the nation as a whole gained or lost through imperialist expansion was an irrelevant question; it was only the interests of the monopolists which counted. Thus through their economic power and through their use of the state the monopoly capitalists engaged in struggles for territorial expansion. The fundamental forces at work were economic, but Lenin admitted the existence of a "non-economic superstructure" which stimulated the striving for colonial conquest. What he meant was that the monopoly capitalists developed ideologies and principles which justified and reinforced their pursuit of economic interests.

In Lenin's description, the process of imperialism went on until the whole world had been divided up among the imperialist powers, but even then it did not stop. Enduring stability was out of the question. Lenin held that capitalism develops unevenly in different countries. Power relationships among countries therefore change, and as they change there are demands for a redivision of the world. Imperialist countries which in the days of their strength seized foreign territories are thus compelled to disgorge their gains when other imperialist countries become more powerful.

Lenin simply assumed that wars arise naturally out of the imperialist struggle. He thought it "naive" to talk about peace under imperialism. There would be wars among the imperialist states themselves over the division and redivision of the world, and wars between imperialist states and the colonial areas. Nowhere did he explicitly claim that all wars arise out of economic causes even under capitalism; in fact, when explaining the origin of particular wars he cited reasons which seem to have little to do with capitalism or with economics. Nevertheless, the inference of his argument was that wars would be inevitable as long as capitalism endured.[21]

AN APPRAISAL

There is no denying the fact that economic forces and economic considerations sometimes contribute to international friction and war, just as do many other forces and considerations. The principal question is whether any of the theories presuming to explain war largely or exclusively in economic terms is sound.

It is rather striking that none of those who stress economic theories of imperialism and war have developed or defended those theories on the basis of a serious analysis of the formulation of foreign policies or the actual developments leading to the outbreak of war. None of them traces the precise route from the existence of an economic desire to the firing of the first shot. Rather, they engage in economic analysis, and are satisfied when they have found an economic desire or circumstance which makes resort to war more or less plausible. They are then inclined to assume that, when war occurs, it occurs because of the reasons they have found plausible.

In contrast, those who approach the question of the causes of imperialism and war through a study of the formulation and execution of foreign policies in concrete situations rarely emerge with an answer that is exclusively economic. Almost always non-economic factors are found to be heavily involved, and very often they appear to play a decisive role.

Certainly studies such as those made by Viner and Staley, referred to earlier in this chapter, have refuted any theory which ascribes imperialism and war, as a general rule, to the influence of particular and identifiable capitalists on government. As Staley demonstrates, it is the exception rather than the rule when serious friction and war can be explained on this basis. Governments rarely undertake serious risks promoting or protecting the interests of individual persons, groups, or corporations, except when those interests coincide with larger interests of the state. To the extent that Hobson's theory, or any other theory, rests on the idea that war generally results from a conspiracy of rich men seeking personal profit, it is plainly unsound.

Moreover, differences in the behavior of the various capitalist states render any theory questionable that ascribes war to capitalism as such. Switzerland and Sweden, which Lenin would have regarded as cap-

[21] E. Varga and L. Mendelsohn, eds., *New Data for V. I. Lenin's "Imperialism, The Highest Stage of Capitalism"* (New York, International, 1940), esp. pp. 138-140, 182, 186, 192; cf. Lionel Robbins, *The Economic Causes of War* (London, Jonathan Cape, 1939).

italist, have avoided participation in war for almost a century and a half, and have not pursued imperialistic policies. In the twentieth century, Denmark, the Netherlands, and a number of other states commonly regarded as capitalist have not been imperialistic in the sense of acquiring colonies, and have become involved in war only because they were attacked. If underconsumption or unemployment or monopoly capitalism were a compelling cause of imperialism and war, how can so many states have avoided its force? It is no answer to say that the states named are too small to fight, for they could have allied themselves with more powerful neighbors.

Further, it is plain that wars occur under capitalism which are hardly explicable in terms of any of the economic theories that have been advanced. Certainly none of them explains in any direct way the Spanish-American War, the Russo-Japanese War of 1904-1905, the Turco-Italian War of 1911, or the Balkan Wars. Lenin to the contrary notwithstanding, they hardly explain the Austrian attack on Serbia in 1914 and the subsequent transformation of this war into World War I. Nor, to take a more recent illustration, do they explain the North Korean aggression of 1950. The very fact that wars have occurred throughout history, waged by both capitalist and non-capitalist powers, demonstrates that causes of war operate which are independent of capitalism.

Lenin's theory is particularly vulnerable. It is simply not true in any meaningful sense that monopolists control government as a regular matter in advanced capitalist countries. For the United States, one need only recall Roosevelt's New Deal and Truman's election in 1948—major events which are hardly attributable to Wall Street. For Britain it is sufficient to recall the election of a Labor government with a socialist program after World War II. If it is contended that the New Deal in the United States and the Labor program in Britain are simply alternative expressions of the political power of monopolists, the obvious answer is that the monopolists are sharply divided against themselves, favoring quite different types of economic policies with different implications for international politics. The record shows that capitalist democracies tend to become welfare states, a possibility which Lenin's analysis denies. Moreover, since World War II the actions of the Soviet Union on the one hand and of the Western powers on the other scarcely lend credence to the view that imperialism is peculiarly associated with capitalism.

The views of Hobson and Keynes were not so extreme. Although Hobson no doubt exaggerated and distorted the role of economic factors in producing imperialism and war, both he and Keynes granted that non-economic factors were also in part responsible. Moreover, both granted the possibility of reforms within the framework of capitalism that would reduce or eliminate economic forces which, among others, make for war, and the development of the idea of the welfare state has in fact been accompanied by such reforms.

It might be noted that Quincy Wright, though of course granting that economic factors sometimes help produce imperialism and war, does not associate these phenomena especially with capitalism. In fact, the reverse is true. He says: [22]

Capitalistic societies have been the most peaceful forms of societies yet developed. . . . Wars have occurred during the periods of capitalistic dominance, but they have been least frequent in the areas most completely organized under that system. . . . In the modern period, in which alone capitalism has been fully developed, war has more frequently been initiated by states dominated by agrarianism or by socialism than by those dominated by capitalism.

It is perhaps understandable that those who have stressed economic causes of war should have neglected to point out that economic pressures actually work both ways. While bringing economic advantage to some, war brings loss and destruction to others. Major wars necessarily disrupt trade patterns, both within and among states. War means the severance of trade with the enemy and the actual or potential loss of investments in enemy territory. The fact is that the economic interests of traders and investors have often led them to exert their influence on behalf of peace. Moreover, even those who stand to gain economically from war may recoil from it for non-economic reasons.

It is said that when Japan's capitulation was announced in 1945 a lady in a Detroit bakery expressed the wish that the war might have continued for a few more months until the mortgage on her house had been paid off. A pie was thrown in her face. Both her wish and the reaction to it are significant in connection with the economic factor as a cause of war.

SUGGESTED READINGS

BEARD, Charles A., *The Idea of National Interest* (New York, Macmillan, 1934).

CLARK, Grover, *A Place in the Sun* (New York, Macmillan, 1936).

HOBSON, J. A., *Imperialism* (London, George Allen & Unwin, 1938).

KNORR, Klaus, "Theories of Imperialism," *World Politics,* Vol. 4 (April, 1952), pp. 402-431.

LANGER, William L., *The Diplomacy of Imperialism, 1890-1902* (New York, Knopf, 1935).

MOON, Parker Thomas, *Imperialism and World Politics* (New York, Macmillan, 1926).

PARRY, J. H., *Europe and a Wider World* (London, Hutchinson's University Library, 1949).

ROBBINS, Lionel, *The Economic Causes of War* (London, Jonathan Cape, 1939).

[22] Wright, *A Study of War* (Chicago, The University of Chicago Press, 1942, copyright 1942 by the University of Chicago), Vol. II, pp. 1162-1164.

STALEY, Eugene, *War and the Private Investor* (Garden City, Doubleday, Doran, 1935).

VARGA, E., and MENDELSOHN, L., eds., *New Data for V. I. Lenin's "Imperialism, The Highest Stage of Capitalism"* (New York, International, 1940).

VINER, Jacob, "The Economic Problem," in DE HUSZAR, George B., ed., *New Perspectives on Peace* (Chicago, The University of Chicago Press, 1944).

WINSLOW, E. M., *The Pattern of Imperialism* (New York, Columbia University Press, 1948).

CHAPTER 7

War and the
Expectation of War

MANY YEARS AGO an English writer, R. G. Hawtrey, made the rather enigmatic statement that "the principal cause of war is war itself." He explained himself to some extent as follows: [1]

When I say that the principal cause of war is war itself, I mean that the aim for which war is judged worth while is most often something which itself affects military power. Just as in military operations each side aims at getting anything which will give it a military advantage, so in diplomacy each side aims at getting anything which will enhance its power. Diplomacy is potential war. It is permeated by the struggle for power, and when potential breaks into actual war, that is usually because irreconcilable claims have been made to some element of power, and neither can claim such preponderance as to compel the other to give way by a mere threat.

This explanation is helpful, but it by no means exhausts the subject. Hawtrey's own explanation bears some clarification, and additional implications of his central proposition can be found.

Our purposes will be served best if we broaden Hawtrey's proposition a little and then explore its meaning. We can say that war and the expectation of war exert a major influence on the behavior of states. Both past war and the expectation of future war are involved, and they not only help cause war but they also help to shape foreign policies and international relationships both in peacetime and in wartime. If it were not for the fact that wars occur and are expected to occur, states would behave very differently than they do.

[1] R. G. Hawtrey, *Economic Aspects of Sovereignty* (New York, Longmans Green, 1930), p. 107.

WAR AND THE
SEEDS OF FUTURE WAR

War affects the behavior of states and sows the seeds of future war in various ways.

Struggles over Peace Terms

War is likely to produce tensions among the victors—and it may produce new war—because of disagreements over the terms of a peace settlement. This is, of course, not to be expected if the war has involved only two states and if one of them has emerged as a clear victor; however, if there are two or more states on the winning side, the problem of arriving at a peace settlement may involve serious difficulties among them. Each will want to satisfy the aspirations which led it to go to war or which it developed during the course of the war. Expecting (or planning) future war, each will want to assure for itself a strong power position. The resulting desires and demands of one victor may be incompatible with those of another. A struggle will then ensue, involving international tension and possibly leading to war.

One of the best illustrations dates from the Balkan wars of 1912-1913. Once the first war was over (against the Ottoman Empire), the victors fell out among themselves over the division of the spoils, and a new war ensued, this one among the victors. Similar strains in the fabric of allied relationships have been evident after each of the general wars in the last century and a half. During the Congress of Vienna after the Napoleonic wars, three of the principal powers actually made an alliance against the remaining two, and there was real danger that the struggle over the terms of peace would lead to new war. During the Paris Peace Conference after World War I, tension developed especially over the demands of Italy. After World War II, there was no attempt to arrive at a general settlement in one conference, but great tension soon developed over various aspects of the piecemeal settlement. "Cold war" set in between East and West, and hot war occurred in Korea.

Dissatisfactions of Parties to the Peace Settlement

Once a peace settlement is made, its terms are likely to be unsatisfactory to some states, and the dissatisfied may then pursue policies designed to upset the settlement. Some of the victorious states themselves may be dissatisfied, even though they formally agreed to the peace terms. After World War I, for example, many Italians took the view that Italy had "won the war, but lost the peace." Under Mussolini, Italy became a revisionist power, and ultimately joined Germany in attacks on the peace treaties. Defeated states are, of course, most likely to resent a peace settlement and to seek change in it. France never reconciled itself to the loss of Alsace-Lorraine after the Franco-Prussian War in 1871. The Versailles settlement, in turn, embittered Germany and contributed to the rise of Nazism with its aggressive foreign policy. If the division of Germany which occurred after World War II can be called a settlement, certainly it is one which Germans and others will seek to upset.

Dissatisfactions of Former Neutrals

Neutrals in war may be dissatisfied with its outcome, and may seek change. They may see danger for themselves in the new power relationships established as a result of war. A country which felt reasonably secure as long as a potential enemy was held in check by a third power may suddenly become insecure if the third power itself is defeated. Thus, for example, France felt reasonably secure against Prussia as long as Austria seemed able to hold Bismarck in check, but after the Seven Weeks' War many Frenchmen demanded "Revenge for Sadowa," that is, they sought somehow to regain security for France after the battle in which Austria was decisively defeated; their attitude contributed to the coming of the Franco-Prussian War. The same kind of considerations sometimes lead neutrals to enter a war which is already in progress, as will be noted below.

The Diversion or Reduction of Power, and Demands for Change in Situations Maintained by Power

Another point is closely related. It is that whenever a given situation is maintained more by power than by consent, there are likely to be demands for change whenever the power is diverted or significantly reduced. War and the threat of war may divert or reduce power, and may therefore be an occasion or a cause of troubles outside the original area of friction. Examples of the operation of this principle are numerous. After the Crimean War the victors (Britain, France, and Sardinia) prohibited Russia from fortifying the shores of the Black Sea or maintaining naval vessels on its waters, but when the Franco-Prussian War occurred Russia defied the prohibition, and the Crimean victors were too preoccupied in western Europe to enforce it. Likewise during the Franco-Prussian War French power could no longer preserve the Pope's control over the area of Rome; Italian nationalists were thus free to take —and did take—one more step toward the unification of Italy. A Japanese leader offered a very cynical version of the principle under discussion many decades ago; anticipating troubles in Europe (which eventually took the form of World War I), he looked forward to them. He saw that the diversion of European power from the Far East would leave Japan relatively free to work its will, and he declared,[2] "When there is a fire in a jeweler's shop, the neighbors are not to be blamed for helping themselves." Japan subsequently utilized World War I as the occasion for taking over German rights in the Pacific and Far East, and for making its Twenty-one Demands on China. Similarly, while the powers of Western Europe were locked in struggle during the early stages of World War II, the Soviet Union took advantage of the situation to fight a war against Finland and to annex Estonia, Latvia, Lithuania, and parts of Poland and Rumania.

The same kind of thing sometimes occurs in relations between an imperial country and its colonies. For example, when Spanish power declined drastically during the Napoleonic wars, most of Spain's colonies in the western hemisphere revolted and established their independence. When the power of France, the Netherlands, and Britain declined during World War II, all three faced severe colonial difficulties. It is probably more than a coincidence that the British granted independence (or dominion status with the right of secession from the Commonwealth) to Burma, Ceylon, India, and Pakistan after the relative decline of British power in World War II. More certainly, it was the relative decline in Dutch and French power which made feasible the rebellions that confronted the two countries after World War II in Indonesia and Indochina, respectively.

War, Domestic Change, and Future Troubles

War on any considerable scale necessarily has a significant impact on the social, economic, and political situation within the belligerent countries, especially in those which are defeated. This, in turn, is likely to affect their subsequent behavior. It was World War I which permitted the Bolsheviks to seize power in Russia, and World War II which provided the occasion for an extension of communist control in Eastern and Southeastern Europe, China, and North Korea. These developments have obviously had a tremendous impact on international politics, leading both to cold and to hot war. Similarly, World War I and its aftermath produced changes in Germany which facilitated the rise of Hitlerism and thus contributed to the coming of World War II.

Success in War Recommends War

War affects the behavior of states by the very example and lessons which it involves. Gains made by one state through war recommend the use of war to other states as an instrument of policy. In a sense, war is sometimes contagious. Consider, for example, the record of the 1930's. Japan's success in Manchuria and China certainly encouraged Musso-

---

[2] H. F. MacNair, *The Real Conflict between China and Japan* (Chicago, The University of Chicago Press, 1938, copyright 1938 by the University of Chicago), p. 111.

lini to think that he could engage in aggression against Ethiopia without encountering substantial opposition from other powers. Success in Ethiopia, in turn, encouraged both Italian and German intervention in the so-called Civil War in Spain. Cumulative successes encouraged Hitler's aggressiveness, leading to World War II. Although no one can know what might have been, it seems to be a fair guess that the early frustration of Japan's program by a combination of powers determined to suppress any aggression might have deterred Mussolini and Hitler from taking the course they subsequently did take. The assumption that successful war encourages more war is certainly one of the factors that induced President Truman to order American intervention in Korea in 1950; he hoped that the defeat of one communist act of aggression would discourage similar subsequent acts.

War and the Assumption of Violence

Finally, the occurrence of war strengthens the expectation that it will recur. It confirms a basic assumption on which statesmen must operate —the assumption of violence. And, as we shall see, this expectation and this assumption have a profound effect on foreign policies and do much to bring war on.

It might be noted that there is little that is automatic or inevitable about the effect of war on the behavior of states. Almost all the above propositions suggest what may happen rather than what definitely will happen. No law of politics is involved. Though quarrels among victorious allies over the peace settlement usually occur, they are not always serious; for example, the victors in the Crimean War had no great difficulty in agreeing on the terms to be imposed. Defeated states do not always seek to upset a peace settlement imposed upon them; Bismarck's terms to Austria-Hungary after the Seven Weeks' War, for example, were so generous that it was soon possible for him to make an ally of his former enemy. Similarly, after World War II, though former allies have become actual or potential enemies, former enemies have in a number of cases become allies. Colonies do not always rebel when the mother country is in difficulty, else many of the colonial difficulties that occurred after World War II would have occurred after World War I, if not before. This discussion of war and the seeds of war has dealt with tendencies and possibilities, not with certainties. Even if war did always sow the seeds of future war, the future war might never come. After all, seeds do not always sprout.

Another warning note might be entered. The statement that war is likely to influence future behavior obviously does not mean it will be the only influencing factor. The statement that war is a cause of certain developments does not necessarily mean that it is the only cause. The statement that war is an occasion for certain developments—such as re-bellion on the part of a colony—clearly implies that other factors are also operating. The dynamics of international politics are complex.

THE INFLUENCE OF THE
EXPECTATION OF WAR

A Domestic Analogy

In Chapter 2 we saw that one of the attitudes which contributes mightily to the preservation of peace within countries is the very assump-tion that peace will prevail. Within stable countries, people normally assume that disputes which arise will be settled without resort to vio-lence. Individuals do not ordinarily carry lethal weapons, and political leaders do not ordinarily calculate their moves in terms of possible civil war.

Suppose that the situation were different. Suppose that every time a hand was raised, one would have to fear that it might contain a dagger. Suppose that anyone reaching into a pocket was suspected of reaching for a gun. Suppose that the usual consequence of a personal antagonism or a grudge was an effort to injure or to kill. Would not the very atmos-phere of aggression and suspicion and fear accentuate violence? A person would have to arm himself and train himself to use arms. With death as the possible consequence of inaction, he would have to act quickly and decisively on the slightest sign of a need for self-defense. He would have to act and then inquire whether the need for action was real.

Similarly, if political leaders regularly assumed the possibility of civil war, they would have to jockey for advantage, or at least for safety, in terms of military power. Command over votes would not be enough. A political leader who saw an opportunity to strike in such a way as to establish his power definitely or to eliminate a threat to his position would at least be strongly tempted to do so. One who saw the distribu-tion of power shifting against him would be tempted to strike while victory seemed possible of achievement. Concern for power and security, concern for survival, would tend to overshadow what are normally re-garded as the substantive issues of politics. It can hardly be doubted that in such a situation civil war would be more common than it in fact is.

The same kind of considerations apply in the international field. Be-tween some countries—the United States and Canada, for example—there is no expectation of war and therefore no power struggle in a military sense. But between other countries—the United States and the Soviet Union, for example—the expectation of war is ever-present; even if neither side really wants war, which may or may not be true in this instance, each must regard it as a distinct possibility.

Types of Preparedness Measures

Assuming that defensive war may be necessary, states must prepare for it. They must seek to maintain or build up their power, exerting themselves more or less in proportion to their estimate of the extent and imminence of the danger.

Discussion of the elements of power, and therefore of the various areas of activity in connection with an effort to maintain or increase power, will be postponed until later. But the most prominent of these areas of activity must be mentioned here. Expecting war, states must make military, economic, psychological, and diplomatic preparations.

The character of the military preparations normally made is fairly obvious. States which feel threatened seek to build up their armed establishments. They train men, plan strategy, develop new weapons, manufacture the thousands of items needed in war, and seek to build up the morale of the armed forces, perhaps by inculcating hate of the prospective enemy.

Economic preparations are usually labeled as manifestations of *economic nationalism*—a term which denotes "the point of view that it ought to be the object of statesmanship in economic matters to increase the power rather than the economic well-being of a given society." Various kinds of economic regulations and activities may increase power. Tariffs, quotas, exchange controls, and the licensing of foreign trade are devices to this end. State subsidies, special concessions on taxes, or other measures may be employed to develop and support economic activities which are of special significance to the power of the state, like the operation of a merchant marine or airlines, or the production of synthetic oil or rubber. The state itself may engage extensively in vital economic activities, as the United States has done in the field of atomic energy and in connection with the stockpiling of strategic materials. It may control foreign trade and foreign investments in such a way as to strengthen potential allies and weaken potential enemies. It may engage in pronatalist policies, seeking to increase the human war potential, as Hitler and Mussolini did. And economic nationalism may merge into imperialism if the government seeks to secure political control over foreign sources of supply of essential materials.

Psychological preparations are expressed in propaganda, generally designed to convince the people of the state that the cause for which it stands is just and that this righteous cause is threatened by an outside power, which is evil. Love for the country and devotion to its cause are obviously desirable if the mobilization of power is to be adequate; suspicion, distrust, and hatred of the potential enemy are also to be desired.

Diplomatic preparations usually involve efforts to isolate the potential enemy, if possible, or to cut it off from outside support to the greatest extent possible. At the same time, they involve efforts to win friends and allies. Moreover, diplomacy must be so conducted as to put the country in the best possible light when and if war comes.

Effects of Preparedness Measures

States following defensive policies and engaging in these preparations normally justify them in the name of peace. The hope is that the power of the state can be made so great, as compared to the power of the potential enemy, that it will not dare attack. Preparations for war sometimes have this effect; perhaps they usually do—it is difficult to say when a war has been averted which otherwise would have occurred. But certainly also such preparations have an opposite effect. A state engaged in them is unlikely to be able to convince its potential antagonist that its purposes are purely defensive; even if it does succeed in doing so, the other state is bound to wonder how long those purposes will remain defensive. The antagonist is therefore likely to build up its own power, if only as a precautionary measure. In so doing, it accentuates already existing fears, and so encourages still more vigorous preparations in the other state. A vicious circle is thus created, a so-called armaments race. Thought of the possibility of war begins to dominate domestic and foreign policy in the states involved. Every move is appraised in terms of its effect on power relationships. There is an inclination to read a hostile intent into the various moves of the potential antagonist. Both international tensions and personal anxieties are likely to become acute, and they may become intolerable.

War tends to break out in such circumstances. Perhaps one side will make a move which the other regards as aggressive. Perhaps one side, assuming that war has become virtually inevitable and fearing that it will lose out in a prolonged armaments race, will decide to precipitate hostilities, that is, to wage a preventive war. Psychological factors strengthen the temptation to do this, for the anxieties of peace sometimes seem greater than the horrors of war. Many observers of the British scene in the fall of 1939 noted that the declaration of war seemed to bring relief.

States which recognize the possibility of war but desire to avoid it are thus in something of a dilemma. On the one hand, if they neglect their power and allow themselves to get into an inferior power position, they invite inadmissible demands if not attack. On the other hand, if they pay great attention to power relationships and seek to develop a safe power position, they may create or accentuate tensions and thus help to bring on the war which they seek to avoid. A middle course is obviously desirable, but precisely what constitutes a middle course in a necessarily vague situation is a question on which even those trained to judge such matters may differ.

Fears of Third States and the Extension of War

Not only does the expectation of war lead to preparation for war, which may help to bring it on. Fears for the future also often lead to the extension of existing wars. Once war has broken out between any two states, its outcome will be of concern to other states. This might not be so if it were known that the war would be the last one ever to be fought, but if future wars are to be expected the possible results of an existing war must be appraised in this light.

1. *A hypothetical illustration.* Suppose that there were only three states, A, B, and C. They do not command precisely the same amount of power, but the differences are not great. Now suppose that state A attacks state B. If state C could be sure of living in peace regardless of the outcome of the struggle between A and B, it might well remain neutral, but it cannot be sure of this. All history teaches it that it must assume the possibility of future war. The outcome of the present war is therefore of vital importance. If A should conquer and annex B, C might not be able to survive future war. A would have gained such power as to render C helpless. By all means, state C must try to prevent such a development. C may have no particular interest in the issues over which A and B are fighting, but this makes no great difference. The overwhelmingly important requirement is that C maintain a relative power position that will permit it to survive.

There are various ways in which C can attempt to do this. If the belligerents are fairly evenly matched and seem headed for a stalemate, C can bide its time. If state A seems to be headed for victory, C can give aid to State B. Perhaps the aid can be in the form of supplies or perhaps C can formally join in the war on the side of B on mutually agreeable terms regarding the ultimate peace settlement. Or C could join with A in despoiling B if mutually agreeable terms were arrived at.

In other words, recognizing the possibility of future war, C must attempt to prevent an outcome of the existing war that would have a serious adverse effect on its own relative power position. The attempt may well involve C itself in the war. In this example the expectation of future war has led to an extension of the existing war.

This helps to explain what Mr. Hawtrey meant when he said that "the aim for which war is judged worth while is most often something which itself affects military power." If, in the hypothetical case described above, state C should enter the war, it would not be fighting, immediately at least, for freedom or justice or wealth or any similar value, for nothing which it holds dear has been attacked; rather it would be fighting to maintain a relative power position that would permit it to maintain its values if they were threatened in the future.

2. *Illustrations from the two world wars.* History is full of illustrations of the operation of these considerations. Of course, third states may enter a war to promote immediate interest or advantage, but a large proportion of them do so to protect themselves against putative future dangers—dangers which might or might not in fact develop. If an enigmatic statement is permitted, it might be said that states are often fighting a future war rather than a present one, that is, they fight now rather than later because of a fear that if they wait their chances of victory will have been reduced.

Consider World War I, for example. It began with an attack by Austria-Hungary on Serbia. How did this war between two states in the heart of Europe turn into a world war? Among the numerous operative factors, the concern of other states for their future relative power position was certainly important. Russia and France had agreed that it was vital to them to preserve a "balance" of power. We shall discuss this concept more fully later; here it suffices to say that they had agreed that they must maintain a distribution of power that would leave them reasonably safe. They had further agreed that changes in the Balkans might make the distribution of power unsafe. When Austria-Hungary attacked Serbia, therefore, Russia and France immediately became concerned. Russia, especially, feared that Austria-Hungary would win, that Austria-Hungary would be strengthened by victory, and that an increase in Austro-Hungarian power would be dangerous for the future. Other influences also operated, of course. Together they led to Russian mobilization, the obvious Russian intention being to intervene in the war.

This alarmed Germany, for Russia and Serbia combined might defeat its ally, Austria-Hungary. Then Germany might be left in a relatively less favorable power position. Germany was not attacked; there was no immediate menace to her, but she feared for the future. This fear, among other considerations, led her to deliver ultimatums both to Russia and to Russia's ally, France. So, almost immediately, the war between Austria-Hungary and Serbia was extended over most of the continent of Europe.

When Germany attacked Belgium in an effort to get at and crush France, Britain became involved. There was no attack on Britain. Had she chosen to do so, she in all probability could have remained neutral in the war, but the war might then have ended with Germany and Austria-Hungary dominant on the continent, with bases just across the Channel from which mortal attacks might in the future be launched on Britain. It had always been British policy to prevent any such development, and the policy was continued in 1914. Britain entered the war largely to ward off the danger which might develop in the future out of a victory on the part of the Central Powers.

Similar considerations were among those which finally induced the

United States to abandon neutrality and declare war. Secretary of State, Robert Lansing, gave clear expression to them in 1916: [3]

It is my opinion that the military oligarchy which rules Germany is a bitter enemy of democracy in every form; that, if that oligarchy triumphs over the liberal governments of Great Britain and France, it will then turn upon us as its next obstacle to imperial rule over the world; and that it is safer and surer and wiser for us to be one of many enemies than to be in the future alone against a victorious Germany.

Nothing could be more explicit in showing that the expectation of future war contributed to an extension of the existing one.

Virtually the same sequence occurred in connection with World War II. In the fall of 1939 Germany attacked Poland. She did not attack France and Britain, yet they declared war. Why? Among other things, they believed that an increase in Germany's power would ultimately endanger them. Each felt, as Lansing had before, that it was "safer and surer and wiser . . . to be one of many enemies than to be in the future alone against a victorious Germany." In guiding American policy Franklin D. Roosevelt was influenced by the same thoughts. In his State of the Union message in 1940 he declared that [4] "it becomes clearer and clearer that the future world will be a shabby and dangerous place to live in—even for Americans to live in—if it is ruled by force in the hands of a few." A defense policy based on withdrawal within our own boundaries would, he declared, merely "invite future attack." He thought it a delusion that the United States could safely be permitted "to become a lone island, a lone island in a world dominated by the philosophy of force."

Such an island represents . . . a helpless nightmare, the helpless nightmare of people without freedom; yes, the nightmare of a people lodged in prison, handcuffed, hungry, and fed through the bars from day to day by the contemptuous and unpitying masters of other continents.

In another address Roosevelt declared:

If Great Britain goes down, the Axis powers will control the continents of Europe, Asia, Africa, Australasia, and the high seas—and they will be in a position to bring enormous military and naval resources against this hemisphere. It is no exaggeration to say that all of us in the Americas would be living at the point of a gun—a gun loaded with explosive bullets, economic as well as military.

Thus the United States took the road to war in part because it feared the results of a future war fought in less favorable circumstances. It fought, in part, against hypothetical future danger.

[3] Robert Lansing, *War Memoirs* (Indianapolis, Bobbs-Merrill, 1935), p. 103. The influence of the expectation of war is also discussed in E. H. Carr, *The Twenty Years' Crisis* (London, Macmillan, New York, St. Martin's, 1949), pp. 109-113.
[4] Franklin D. Roosevelt, *Roosevelt's Foreign Policy, 1933-1941* (New York, Wilfred Funk, 1942), pp. 214, 242, 251, 312.

The same kinds of considerations have operated since World War II. American Secretaries of State have referred again and again to the danger that the future would bring if communists loyal to Moscow were to come to power throughout Europe or throughout Asia. One of the objectives of the containment policy has been to prevent such a shift in the distribution of power from occurring. The possibility of future war is one of the main determinants of present policy.

Wars seem to spread especially when they involve at least one great power on each side for a significant period of time. Quincy Wright reports that during the past three centuries [5] "there have been fourteen periods in which war existed with a great power on each side for over two years." In eleven of the fourteen, every other great power became involved. Among the factors operating, concern over the distribution of power which would follow the war was undoubtedly significant.

Future Security and Present War Aims

Once states become involved in war, there is a tendency for them to develop objectives which have little or nothing to do with their initial decision to fight. In particular, victors commonly seize territory from the defeated even though they did not go to war for that purpose. The British Empire was built up to quite an extent in this way, governments in London seizing on the opportunities that victory provided to take territory which was either commercially or strategically valuable. The United States has done the same thing. Certainly few Americans entered the Spanish-American War with a view to annexing the Philippines, yet this is what occurred at the end of the war. Certainly too, the desire to take Japanese territory had nothing to do with American participation in World War II, yet at the war's end the United States secured the former Japanese mandated islands under a trusteeship arrangement and simply remained in occupation of the Ryukyu Islands, including Okinawa.

The expectation of future war is among the factors contributing to such aggrandizement. Assuming that more war will occur, those who make decisions on high policy are necessarily under pressure to shape each peace settlement in such a way as to promote future security or future victory. Seizures of foreign territory—defensive imperialism—may serve this purpose.

JINGOISM AND MILITARISM

A number of attitudes and motivating forces sometimes become closely associated with the thought and expectation of war. Whatever the causes of their development, they may well play an influential role.

[5] Quincy Wright, *A Study of War* (Chicago, The University of Chicago Press, 1942, copyright by the University of Chicago), Vol. I, p. 240.

Jingoism

Jingoism is perhaps the most transient and superficial of these attitudes and forces. The term entered the English language in the course of an Anglo-Russian crisis in 1878. Russia had defeated the Ottoman Empire, and threatened a penetration of its power to the Mediterranean. This Britain was determined to prevent. In the course of the agitation over the issue a jingle appeared in England, declaring:

> We don't want to fight, but by jingo if we do
> We've got the ships, we've got the men, we've got the money, too.

Ever since, the term *jingoism* has served to denote a cocky and bellicose national spirit, one which almost invites and welcomes war. Whipped up by what is taken to be a challenge from abroad, it involves brash willingness and even eagerness to take up the challenge. A government controlled by jingoists has a chip on its shoulder and is spoiling for a fight. Such an outlook obviously makes war more likely.

Militarism: The Use of Armed Forces for Other than Military Purposes

Militarism is a rather vague concept. It refers to an attitude or spirit which is more stable and durable than jingoism. In its least significant form it denotes various attitudes and practices associated with armies and wars, yet transcending true military purposes.[6] It regards armed establishments as having purposes to which security and war are incidental and peripheral. There was a time in Europe, for example, when some of the royalty regarded armies (or units thereof) more or less as playthings. They derived gratification out of command itself and out of the ceremony and display associated with peacetime military activity. The attitude is typified by the Russian grand duke who said that he hated war "because it spoils armies." [7]

In Europe and elsewhere, armies have also served as means of providing status, honor, and income to the nobility or to others. Until fairly recent times in some of the European countries, commissions as officers in the armed forces were reserved for the nobility, the needs of the service and the competence of the individual having little to do with the appointments made. Commissions were often sinecures, granted more as favors or rewards or as bribes designed to assure the support of the recipient for king or government than because of military need. Sometimes far more officers were appointed than were needed. Conversely, sometimes the principle that officers must be noblemen restricted a military expansion regarded as desirable. In the decade before World War I,

---

[6] Alfred Vagts, *A History of Militarism* (New York, Norton, 1937), p. 11.
[7] *Ibid.*, p. 13.

for example, Germany curtailed the expansion of its army "because not enough officers 'of class' could be found, and the military were unwilling to descend to 'little-suited elements' and thus expose the officer body to 'democratization.'" [8]

Militarism, both in its mild and in its more serious forms, may include the idea that military activity is a good means of promoting values and instilling virtues regarded as desirable. Military training has often been described as a device for inculcating loyalty, discipline, and a sense of civic responsibility, and as a means of promoting health, physical hardihood, and education. Soldiers are often looked upon as being somehow more heroic than civilians, additional prestige going to the man because of the uniform he wears. Military service, in peace as well as in war, is regarded as ennobling.

These manifestations of militarism may or may not have much to do with international politics. So long as armies remain playthings, or means of providing status, honor, and income, or devices for promoting domestic values or instilling virtues, they are of relatively small moment on the world scene. Accompanying these purposes of armies, however, there may be tendencies which promote resort to war. After all, few would argue that these functions fully justify the existence of armies. Those who wish armies to serve these purposes must therefore find some ulterior justification. They may thus be inclined to create or magnify foreign dangers and perhaps to bring about actual war. Moreover, a military caste—whether or not consisting of noblemen—may be inclined to regard war as a kind of glorified sport.

Militarism: Emphasis on War as a Method or a Goal

More significantly for our purposes militarism may involve one or more of several attitudes which make war more likely. The militarist may regard war and the preparation for war "as the chief instruments of foreign policy and the highest form of public service." [9] He may extol and glorify military exploits. He may welcome foreign danger and foreign war as means of promoting domestic unity, and he may regard war as good in and of itself.

1. War as normal. It is perhaps natural that repeated war and threats of war should militarize thought and life, that they should make war appear almost as a normal instrument of foreign policy and as a normal pursuit. The whole life of a people—the social, political, and economic structure—may be so conditioned by war that war becomes a habit or a necessity. Schumpeter's theory of imperialism, to be discussed below,

[8] *Ibid.,* p. 221.
[9] C. Delisle Burns, "Militarism," *Encyclopedia of the Social Sciences,* Vol. X, pp. 446-451.

is based on this proposition. It is also perhaps natural that in an atmosphere of war added weight is commonly given in the councils of state to the generals and admirals. No one knows with any certainty what the significance of this may be; perhaps no generalization could be sound, for generals and admirals are not all of one stripe. But there is common speculation that, accustomed to thinking in military terms, they will be more inclined than others to see and to seek military solutions to pending and prospective problems.

2. *War as a source of glory.* Pride in past military exploits is a common phenomenon. Among the heroes in the history of every country, victorious military leaders are accorded a high place. Whether they fought aggressively or defensively makes little difference. Whether they contributed in any significant way to the cultural or material betterment of their country or of mankind is a question which is commonly neglected or ignored. The destruction and death that they wrought are forgotten. Whether their cause was good or bad, their memory is honored at least in the country in whose name they fought. Those who conquer are considered great. Defeat disgraces the leader involved and casts down the pride of the country from which he comes. The usual remedy is victory, perhaps in another war.

Surely such attitudes affect current behavior. If war has been a historic path to glory, it is recommended to those of the present and future who seek glory, and they are numerous. Perhaps no one would deliberately begin a war for the sake of the glory it might bring, but certainly the view that war, and more especially victory, are glorious must condition the thoughts of military and civil leaders—and even of the rank-and-file citizens—who make the fateful decisions concerning peace and war. People are drawn to do those things which bring praise.

It might be recalled that Frederick the Great, dispatching his officers to war in 1740, sped them on to what he called the "rendezvous of fame, whither I shall follow you without delay." Some months later he explained that [10]

My youth, the fire of passions, the desire for glory, yes, to be frank, even curiosity, finally a secret instinct has torn me away from the delights of tranquillity. The satisfaction of seeing my name in the papers and later in history has seduced me.

3. *War as a unifying activity.* War long ago demonstrated its usefulness as a means of producing or reinforcing social cohesion and political unity within belligerent countries. It is a recognized means through which a government threatened by domestic discontent and disaffection can seek to strengthen its position. If the government can direct antagonisms abroad and occupy people with foreign war, they are less likely

[10] G. P. Gooch, *Frederick the Great* (New York, Knopf, 1947), pp. 12, 15.

to engage in domestic, internecine strife. This function of war has frequently been noted. An observer in 1604 is said to have described "forreigne warre" as "a sovereigne medecine for domesticall inconveniences." [11] Shakespeare ascribed similar thoughts to King Henry IV, who in the play advised his successor as follows:

> I . . . had a purpose now
> To lead out many to the Holy Land
> Lest rest and lying still might make them look
> Too near unto my state. Therefore, my Harry,
> Be it thy course to busy giddy minds
> With foreign quarrels; that action hence born out
> May waste the memory of former days.

There are, of course, more recent illustrations. Secretary of State Seward early in Lincoln's first administration submitted "Some Thoughts for the President's Consideration," urging a militant foreign policy and probable war. His belief apparently was that foreign war would be a cure for internal dissension. Some interpreters believe that Bismarck shifted to a policy of overseas imperialism in the hope that it would serve as a "lightning rod for the Social-Democratic danger" and generally as a means of promoting domestic unity.[12]

A Japanese diplomat is said to have explained Japan's resort to war against China in 1894 as a means of improving the situation at home "by arousing the patriotic sentiment of our people and more strongly attaching them to the Government." [13] Before the Russo-Japanese War of 1904-1905, the Russian Minister of the Interior expressed the view that [14] "we need a small victorious war to stem the tide of revolution." Hitler before his accession to power publicly declared,[15]

If I wish to bind our people together in unity, I must first create a new front which has a common enemy before it, so that every one knows that we must be one, since this enemy is the enemy of us all.

4. *War as good in itself.* Militarism in its most extreme form glorifies war as good in itself. In recent times, the attitude is illustrated best in fascist and Nazi writings. Mussolini, for example, expressed himself as follows: [16]

[11] Quoted by Jacob Viner, "International Relations between State-Controlled National Economies," *American Economic Review*, Vol. 34, Part 2 (March, 1944), p. 326.

[12] Vagts, *op. cit.*, p. 418.

[13] *Ibid.*, p. 421.

[14] D. J. Dallin, *The Rise of Russia in Asia* (New Haven, Yale University Press, 1949), p. 79.

[15] Frederick L. Schuman, "The Third Reich's Road to War," *Annals of the American Academy of Political and Social Science*, Vol. 175 (September, 1934), p. 34.

[16] Benito Mussolini, "The Political and Social Doctrine of Fascism," *International Conciliation*, No. 306 (January, 1935), pp. 7-8.

Fascism, the more it considers and observes the future and the development of humanity quite apart from political considerations of the moment, believes neither in the possibility nor the utility of perpetual peace. It thus repudiates the doctrine of Pacifism—born of a renunciation of the struggle—as an act of cowardice in the face of sacrifice. War alone brings up to its highest tension all human energy and puts the stamp of nobility upon the peoples who have the courage to meet it.

E. Banse, a Nazi writer, took a similar position: [17]

War means the highest intensification not of the material means only, but of all spiritual energies of the age as well. . . . War provides the ground on which the human soul may manifest itself at its fullest height, in richer forms and surging from more profound wells than it might in any scientific or artistic exploit as such. Nowhere else can the will, the achievements of a race or a state rise into being thus integrally as in war. War is a purifying bath of steel, breeding new impulses, and an infallible test of fitness.

Similarly, Robert Ley, head of the German Labor Front under Hitler, described war as "an expression of the highest and best in manhood." [18]

It is difficult to say how widespread each of these attitudes toward war may be. Their prevalence varies in different times and in different countries. The point need not be labored, however, that where such attitudes exist—and particularly when they are entertained by individuals with considerable influence over foreign policy—the implications for international politics are profound.

SCHUMPETER'S THEORY OF IMPERIALISM

His Definition: "Objectless" Expansionism

The above discussion of militarism leads naturally into a discussion of Schumpeter's theory of imperialism. Note should be made first of all of the definition of imperialism which Schumpeter adopted, for it is a restrictive one. He excluded from consideration many acts and policies which others describe as imperialist. He refused to call a policy imperialist when it appeared reasonable, that is, when it was designed to promote a "concrete interest." Thus his theory does not cover policies which a landlocked state might pursue to obtain access to the sea, or policies which a state in need of land or raw materials might pursue to get them. He acknowledged that there are reasons for every aggressive policy, but insisted on calling such policies imperialist only when the true cause of them lies beyond the reasons given and is not included among the war aims.

Whenever the word imperialism is used [said Schumpeter], there is always the implication . . . of an aggressiveness, the true reasons for which do not lie

[17] Quoted by Aurel Kolnai, *The War Against the West* (New York, Viking, 1938), p. 411.
[18] *New York Times,* March 28, 1940, p. 3, col. 3.

in the aims which are temporarily being pursued; of an aggressiveness that is only kindled anew by each success; of an aggressiveness for its own sake, as reflected in such terms as "hegemony," "world dominion," and so forth. And history, in truth, shows us nations and classes—most nations furnish an example at some time or other—that seek expansion for the sake of expanding, war for the sake of fighting, victory for the sake of winning, dominion for the sake of ruling.[19]

Regarding expansion for its own sake as really objectless, Schumpeter defined imperialism as "the objectless disposition on the part of a state to unlimited forcible expansion."[20] He declared that "numberless wars —perhaps the majority of all wars—have been waged without adequate 'reason'—not so much from the moral viewpoint as from that of reasoned and reasonable interest."[21]

Underlying Reasons for "Objectless" Expansion

There must be reasons, of course, even for objectless expansion, whether or not those involved are conscious of them; Schumpeter's object was to reveal the reasons. To do this, he examined a series of examples of imperialism in ancient and modern times. He found that states which became imperialist faced needs and desires at some time which led them to create a war machine and to wage war. Initially the war machine and the wars fought were designed to promote "concrete interests," and therefore state policies were, by Schumpeter's definition, non-imperialistic. But the very existence of the war machine and the very prosecution of war resulted in conditioning both attitudes and the social structure of the state. Economic, political, and social life became more or less adjusted and adapted to the needs of war. Then, when "concrete interests" had been served and reasons for war had disappeared, there was a threat of maladjustment. A social order geared to war would be out of place if international relations became harmonious. Of course, the social structure might be changed and adapted to conditions of peace, but such readjustment threatened rulers and vested interests generally; rather than run the risks of peace, they sometimes preferred to wage war even though no "concrete interest" would be served thereby. "Created by wars that required it, the machine now created the wars it required."[22]

Schumpeter summarized his findings in three points. First, he held[23] "that 'objectless' tendencies toward forcible expansion, without definite, utilitarian limits—that is, non-rational and irrational, purely instinctual

[19] Joseph A. Schumpeter, *Imperialism and Social Classes* (New York, Augustus M. Kelley, 1951, copyright 1951 by Elizabeth Boody Schumpeter; quotations by permission of the trustees of the estate of Elizabeth B. Schumpeter), p. 6. Cf. Klaus Knorr, "Theories of Imperialism," *World Politics*, Vol. 4 (April, 1952), pp. 402-431.

[20] Schumpeter, *op. cit.*, p. 7.

[21] *Ibid.*, p. 83.

[22] *Ibid.*, p. 33.

[23] *Ibid.*, pp. 83-84.

inclinations toward war and conquest—play a very large role in the history of mankind." Second, he found the explanation of this drive toward war "in the vital needs of situations that molded peoples and classes into warriors—if they wanted to avoid extinction—and in the fact that psychological dispositions and social structures acquired in the dim past in such situations, once firmly established, tend to maintain themselves and to continue in effect long after they have lost their meaning and their life-preserving functions." Third, he found that the survival of warlike dispositions and structures is due both to the "domestic interests of ruling classes [and to] the influence of all those who stand to gain individually from a war policy, whether economically or socially."

Schumpeter drew his prime illustrations of this sequence from antiquity, but argued that it operates also in modern times. He explained the wars of Louis XIV in these terms. He assumed that, by the end of France's war with Spain in 1659, the "concrete interests" of France had been served; there was no serious external threat, and disarmament might have occurred. "But the foundations of royal power rested on [the] military character of the state and on the social factors and psychological tendencies it expressed." In particular, Louis XIV felt compelled to cater to the aristocracy for its support.

Unless the nobles were to be allowed to revolt, they had to be kept busy. Now all the noble families whose members were amusing themselves at Versailles could look back on a warlike past, martial ideas and phrases, bellicose instincts. To ninety-nine out of a hundred of them, "action" meant military action. If civil war was to be avoided, then external wars were required. . . .

Thus the belligerence and war policy of the autocratic state are explained from the necessities of its social structure, from the inherited dispositions of its ruling class, rather than from the immediate advantages to be derived by conquest.[24]

The Anti-Imperialistic Nature of Capitalism

Though tracing the forces making for imperialism down to modern times, Schumpeter contended that they are declining in strength. To him, imperialism was "atavistic in character."

It . . . stems from the living conditions, not of the present, but of the past— or, put in terms of the economic interpretation of history, from past rather than present relations of production. It is an atavism in the social structure, in individual, psychological habits of emotional reaction. Since the vital needs that created it have passed away for good, it too must gradually disappear, even though every warlike involvement, no matter how non-imperialist in character, tends to revive it.[25]

In contrast to Lenin and others, Schumpeter argued that capitalism is anti-imperialistic. Under it people are "democratized, individualized, and

24 *Ibid.*, pp. 76-77.
25 *Ibid.*, pp. 84-85.

rationalized," and "everything that is purely instinctual, everything inso-
far as it is purely instinctual, is driven into the background by this
development." [26] Thus, throughout the world of capitalism, there has
arisen opposition to war. Peace movements have appeared. When war is
fought it must be fought in the name of defense against attack; imperialism must be repudiated, or ascribed exclusively to the enemy.
Schumpeter acknowledged that developments may occur under capitalism producing economic causes of war; specifically, he cited tariffs and
other trade barriers as elements permitting the development of monopolies, which in turn required export markets for their most profitable
operation, and he granted that the competitive struggle for export markets might lead to friction and war. But he described trade barriers
themselves as essentially atavistic, resulting from attitudes surviving from
the precapitalist period more than from attitudes developed under capitalism, and he thought that gradually such attitudes would disappear.
He held it to be [27] "a basic fallacy to describe imperialism as a necessary
phase of capitalism, or even to speak of the development of capitalism
into imperialism." He held that under capitalism, "imperialisms will
wither and die."

Schumpeter's study of imperialism was first published in 1919. Events
since then, especially the rise of fascism, Nazism, and perhaps communism, give rise to the question whether he may not have been too
optimistic about the democratizing, individualizing, and rationalizing
effect of capitalism, and about its tendency to make imperialisms wither
and die. Perhaps, too, he exaggerated when he said that "numberless
wars—perhaps a majority of all wars" are to be explained by his theory.
Yet, even if the theory explains only a few wars—or even if the factors
on which he dwelt serve merely to reinforce others which made for war
—his contribution to an understanding of the behavior of states is significant.

SUGGESTED READINGS

ALLPORT, Gordon W., "The Role of Expectancy," in CANTRIL, Hadley, ed.,
  Tensions That Cause War (Urbana, University of Illinois Press, 1951).
BURNS, C. Delisle, "Militarism," Encyclopedia of the Social Sciences, Vol. X,
  pp. 446-451.
CARR, E. H., The Twenty Years' Crisis (London, Macmillan, New York, St.
  Martin's, 1949).
LASSWELL, Harold, World Politics and Personal Insecurity (New York, Whittle-
  sey House, 1935), esp. Chapters III and IV.
SCHUMPETER, Joseph A., Imperialism and Social Classes (New York, Augustus
  M. Kelley, 1951).
VAGTS, Alfred, A History of Militarism (New York, Norton, 1937).

[26] Ibid., p. 89.
[27] Ibid., pp. 118, 130.

CHAPTER 8

Psychological Factors in War and Peace

We have been discussing the behavior of states. This has involved a fiction for, strictly speaking, states do not behave. The state is an abstraction and—fascist theory to the contrary notwithstanding—is not a living thing. The state, therefore, does not think or feel or act. The thinking and feeling and acting which constitute what we call the behavior of states are done by individual human beings. They are done by those officially charged with authority to make decisions on behalf of the state, by advisers of the decision-makers, and by all those throughout the population who, by vote or otherwise, influence public policy. This being so, if we wish to understand what we call the behavior of states we must understand the factors, at least the major ones, which help to explain the political attitudes and actions of individual men.

This thought is, of course, not a new one. We have been proceeding on the basis of it all along. We said that some or all men in each state like the idea of sovereignty, and that one of the major objectives of those controlling public policy is to preserve sovereignty and security. We discussed nationalism and patriotism and the ideological conflict in terms of the thoughts of men. We took up the question of the extent to which men's behavior is governed by economic conditions, and therefore of the extent to which state policy is determined by economic factors. In the preceding chapter we discussed the effect of war and the expectation of war on state policy (i.e., on the thoughts of those who make decisions in the name of the state).

Thus, in seeking to explain the behavior of states, we have already been discussing the attitudes of individual men and some of the forces and conditions which help shape those attitudes. In this chapter, however, we shall be even more explicit in directing attention to the individual person. Psychologists, psychoanalysts, and psychiatrists have much to say on the question of human behavior. They do not all agree with each other. Some of them take the modest view that their science has not yet reached a stage permitting them to say anything that is valid and reliable on the questions which interest students of politics. Nevertheless, many of the findings of psychology are significant, if true, and it is worth while to give attention to them.

HUMAN NATURE VERSUS LEARNED BEHAVIOR

The Importance of the Learning Process

It is sometimes said that "you can't change human nature" and that "human nature makes war inevitable." Few psychologists, if any, would agree with either proposition. In fact, many psychologists would question whether there is any such thing as human nature in the sense of biologically determined behavior patterns which are common to all mankind. They point out that man, as compared to other animals, is least controlled by instinct; man is guided and controlled far more by what he learns than by what he biologically is. His personal attributes are determined less by the fact that he is human than by the fact that he has certain experiences in a given environment. The behavior of human beings, then, is shaped less by heredity than by what they learn. The culture into which they are born and in which they live does more to influence their behavior than do their genes and chromosomes. As Mark May puts it,[1] "Man's biological nature is neither good nor bad, aggressive nor submissive, warlike nor peaceful, but neutral in these respects." Man may develop in any of a number of different directions "depending on what he is compelled to learn by his environment and by his culture. It is a mistake to assume that he can learn war more easily than peace. His learning machinery is not prejudiced. . . . The bias is in his social environment."

A Theory of Learning

Modern psychology depicts man as being animated by drives which stimulate action. A few of these drives, the primary drives, are innate; most of them, the secondary drives, are acquired or derivative. Even in connection with the drives themselves, social conditioning plays a major role. Hunger is a primary drive, but social conditioning refines the crude desire for food into a desire for particular kinds of food. The secondary drives, such as fear, ambition, and pride, all develop as a result of a learning process.

Responding to drives, man acts. Some actions do not fulfill his needs or satisfy his wants; they do not reduce the force of his drive. He thus

[1] Mark A. May, *A Social Psychology of War and Peace* (New Haven, Yale University Press, 1943), p. 20.

learns that it is useless to repeat such actions. Others lead to satisfaction; they are drive-reducing. In similar future situations, such actions are to be repeated. Through trial and error, and through the example and instruction of others, men learn what kinds of behavior will (and will not) lead to the desired result in given kinds of situations. If aggression is rewarded with considerable regularity, the individual learns to be aggressive. If submissiveness is more often rewarded, the individual learns to be submissive. Or, more correctly, he gradually learns in which situations aggressiveness is most likely to pay and in which situations submissiveness is most likely to produce the desired reward. In other words, not only the drives which stimulate action but also the particular kinds of action which are appropriate and rewarding are largely determined by social forces.[2] If this is true, peace and war result much more from the acquired than from the innate characteristics of men. If men fight, it is largely because they have learned that fighting may produce rewards. In the cultures with which we deal in international politics men learn many of the same things, and there is therefore considerable similarity in drives and responses; still, strictly speaking, it is socially conditioned behavior rather than human nature with which we are concerned.

DRIVES, MOTIVES, ATTITUDES, INTERESTS, VALUES, AND IDEOLOGIES

The preceding discussion refers to *drives* without defining the term. Previous chapters refer to *motives, attitudes, interests,* and *values.* If the psychological factors in war and peace are to be understood and are to be related to previous and subsequent discussions, these concepts and the relationship among them must also be understood. For our purposes, the following definitions seem most useful.

Drives and Motives

The term *drive* denotes an internal condition of an organism—a condition of the body. Drives have to do with "bodily states of tension" and with the arousal of energy for action designed to relieve that tension. "Drives are bodily states felt as restlessness, which initiate tendencies to activity."[3]

Motives give direction to the use of energy. Men learn that the achievement of particular goals will relieve the states of tension accompanying drives; they learn that achievement of the goal will be drive-reducing. They thus develop motives, which orient action toward goals. Motivation

[2] *Ibid.,* pp. 25-26; Neal E. Miller and John Dollard, *Social Learning and Imitation* (New Haven, Yale University Press, 1941), pp. 1-36. Cf. Ernest R. Hilgard, *Theories of Learning,* 2nd ed. (New York, Appleton-Century-Crofts, 1956).

[3] Theodore M. Newcomb, *Social Psychology* (New York, Dryden, 1950), pp. 80, 112.

may be strong or weak, depending on the strength of drives; if the internal conditions determining the strength of drives can be manipulated, the strength of motivation will change accordingly. For example, given a hunger drive, men learn that food will be drive-reducing. In hunger the consumption of food then becomes a goal. Motive will selectively direct the use of energy toward the achievement of the desired goal. Once food is consumed, the strength of the hunger drive and thus the strength of the accompanying motivation are reduced.

There is an important qualification to this principle. Some motives seem to continue to operate in their own right, independently of the drives which they originally served to reduce. Or, to put it somewhat differently, motives (or the goals on which they are oriented) sometimes call new drives, acquired drives, into existence. For example, man learns that actions regarded in his culture as bad or wrong bring penalties, whereas actions regarded as good and right bring approval and praise. On this basis conceptions of right and wrong, good and bad, develop; in fact, there develops a whole "complex system of desires which provide the basis for conformity, morals, and conscience." [4]

Attitudes

Just as drives contribute to the development of motives, so do motives contribute to the development of attitudes. An attitude involves an object or a symbol (e.g., the national territory or the national flag) around which various motives cluster. An attitude is a "state of readiness for motive arousal." To put it more understandably, an attitude relates to a predisposition. "An individual's attitude toward something is his predisposition to perform, perceive, think, and feel in relation to it." Like a motive, an attitude refers to the direction of behavior. It differs from a motive in two ways. First, it may exist even if relevant drives have been removed, though it promises the arousal of motivation and drive under certain circumstances. Second, an attitude is more persistent and general than a motive. Motives are temporary (though sometimes recurrent) and relatively specific.[5] It is not unusual for certain attitudes to become predominant. Individuals become Dodger fans or misers or religious zealots or political fanatics. They may organize their lives—and seek to organize the lives of others—on the basis of a given attitude or cluster of attitudes.

Attitudes and clusters of attitudes delineate values, in either or both of the meanings described in Chapter 1. They reflect or express both what is desired and what is considered desirable. Attitudes toward such things as power and wealth, nation and state, law and order, may make values out of all of them, in one or both senses.

[4] *Ibid.*, p. 125.
[5] *Ibid.*, pp. 118-121.

Interests and Values

Similarly, attitudes and clusters of attitudes delineate interests— whether what we have called end-interests or means-interests.

A point made in Chapter 1 with regard to values and interests will perhaps now be clearer. It is that for the most part they are subjectively and culturally determined, not ordained by nature. They are adopted largely as a result of the learning process. So far as they designate ultimate ends, they are simply posited as desired or desirable, and there is no objective or scientific way of proving that they should be posited. So far as they designate means of promoting the achievement of given ends, scientific investigation may be an instrument of the learning process to determine how effective they will probably be.

To apply the point explicitly to international politics, recall that states are sometimes said to pursue their interests. Assuming that the state is an entity which can have interests (an assumption which itself is rather questionable), how can they be determined? The answer is that end-interests must be posited, and no one can *know* whether or not they are *true*. Means-interests, actually or potentially, are subject to validation by objective or scientific methods.

Ideology

Speaking figuratively and somewhat inaccurately, we have now constructed most of a pyramid. Successive layers of the pyramid, from the bottom up, are composed of drives, motives, and attitudes. The attitude layer is an important one, including as it does conceptions of values and interests. At the top of the pyramid, whether constituting a separate layer or simply the peak of the attitude layer, comes an ideology. An ideology is a coherent value system, the term *value* here denoting a conception of the desirable which influences the selection from available ends and means of action.

SOME PSYCHOANALYTIC EXPLANATIONS OF BEHAVIOR

People do not necessarily want the same things. Even within one culture there are variations in human experiences and in the learning process which produce variations in acquired drives, in motives, in attitudes, in values, and in ideologies. Between cultures the differences are much greater. In some cultures there is substantial moderation and harmony in human relationships; in others there is habitual suspicion, ill-feeling, and hate. In some there is great stress on the acquisition of wealth; in others this is unknown or, even more, there may be stress on the giving away or destruction of wealth. In some, homicide, suicide, and war are common events, and in others they are very rare. Such differences emphasize the point made earlier: that human behavior reflects a socially conditioned learning process far more than it reflects anything which could be called human nature.[6]

Nevertheless, there are some innate drives which are common to all mankind, and among the major cultures of the world today there is considerable similarity in the acquired drives. There is likewise considerable similarity in the values which people come to endorse. For our purposes it is unnecessary to attempt a comprehensive listing of drives or values, or even to try to classify them in broad categories.[7] However, we can learn something by examining the findings of some students of human behavior. The boldest among them are probably the psychoanalysts.

Freud: Eros and Thanatos

Sigmund Freud led in the development of psychoanalysis. We must limit our reference here to just one aspect of his findings. He was tremendously impressed with the prevalence among his patients of intense drives of love and hate, of which the individuals themselves were often unconscious—so impressed that he came to regard these drives as instinctive or innate. He postulated the existence of what he called Eros, the impulse of love and of life, and the simultaneous existence of Thanatos, the impulse toward death or destruction. He became convinced that man has an innate drive toward evil, aggressiveness, destructiveness, and cruelty.

... Men are not gentle, friendly creatures wishing for love, who simply defend themselves if they are attacked. ... A powerful measure of desire for aggression has to be reckoned as part of their instinctual endowment. The result is that their neighbor is to them not only a possible helper or sexual object, but also a temptation to them to gratify their aggressiveness on him, to exploit his capacity for work without recompense, to use him sexually without his consent, to seize his possessions, to humiliate him, to cause him pain, to torture and kill him. *Homo homini lupus;* who has the courage to dispute it in the face of all the evidence in his own life and in history? This aggressive cruelty ... manifests itself spontaneously and reveals men as savage beasts to whom the thought of sparing their own kind is alien. Anyone who calls to mind the atrocities of the early migrations, of the invasion of the Huns or by the so-called Mongols under Jenghiz Khan and Tamurlane, of the sack of Jerusalem by the pious Crusaders, even indeed the horrors of the last world-war, will have to bow his head humbly before the truth of this view of man. ... Civilised society is perpetually menaced with disintegration through this primary hostility of men towards one another.[8]

---

[6] For excellent illustrations of cultural differences, see Ruth Benedict, *Patterns of Culture* (Boston, Houghton Mifflin, 1934).

[7] For a sample effort to do this, see Edward Chace Tolman, *Drives Toward War* (New York, Appleton-Century, 1942), pp. 9, 10, 28; cf. also Otto Klineberg, *Social Psychology* (New York, Holt, 1940), pp. 66-163.

[8] Sigmund Freud, *Civilisation and Its Discontents* (London, Hogarth, 1949), pp. 85-86.

As suggested earlier, Freud was probably wrong in holding that the cruel and destructive behavior of men is attributable to instinct. It results, rather, from a socially conditioned learning process. Those who find such behavior distressing may derive hope from this and look for long-run change, but in the short run the origin of cruelty and aggressiveness makes little difference.

Alfred Adler: Inferiority and Superiority

Alfred Adler was another early psychoanalyst. He sometimes styled himself [9] the "father of the inferiority complex," and declared it to be his "most general supposition that the psyche has as its objective the goal of superiority." He posited the proposition that the individual is predominantly "guided and spurred on by his longing for superiority." From this basic postulate, Adler and his disciples proceeded to explain the loves and hates and fears of men. His prescription for the good of men was "the conscious evolution of a feeling for the common weal and the conscious destruction of the will-to-power."

Karen Horney: The Search for Glory

Karen Horney, another prominent psychoanalyst, identified herself more with Sigmund Freud than with Adler, but the premise with which she started is similar to that of Adler. Her premise was that in our culture the individual develops "an urgent need to lift himself above others." Disappointed with his "real self," he creates "an idealized image of himself," which he endows "with unlimited powers and with exalted faculties; he becomes a hero, a genius, a supreme lover, a saint, a god." He becomes a Walter Mitty. The qualities of the idealized image may remain in the background, permitting "healthy striving" without significant neuroticism. But neuroticism develops when the qualities of the idealized image are permitted to come to the fore, leading perhaps to a Dr. Jekyll and Mr. Hyde type of personality. Neuroticism triumphs when the real self is forgotten and when the individual regards his ideal self as real.

Since the idealized image regularly provides for self-glorification, the search for glory becomes the comprehensive and dominant drive. According to Horney, this involves a drive toward perfection, toward external success, and toward vindictive triumph. The drive for perfection involves an assumption of omnipotence, an assumption that anything is possible for the idealized self. The drive toward external success, involving neurotic ambition, requires that one excel—whether in intellectual or artistic activities, in social relationships, in saintliness, in leadership, or whatever. The chief aim of the drive toward vindictive triumph "is to put

[9] Alfred Adler, *The Practice and Theory of Individual Psychology* (New York, Harcourt, Brace, 1929), esp. pp. 7-15.

others to shame or defeat them through one's very success; or to attain the power, by rising to prominence, to inflict suffering upon them— mostly of a humiliating kind." Or the drive toward vindictive triumph may manifest itself in efforts to frustrate, outwit, or defeat others in personal relations. It is a vindictive drive, according to Horney,[10] "because the motivating force stems from impulses to take revenge for humiliations suffered in childhood—impulses which are reinforced during the later neurotic development."

Among recent historical figures Hitler is a good illustration of a person who went through humiliating experiences and gave his whole life to a fanatic desire to triumph over an ever-increasing mass of people. In his case vicious circles, constantly increasing the need, are clearly discernible. One of these develops from the fact that he could think only in categories of triumph and defeat. Hence the fear of defeat made further triumphs always necessary. Moreover, the feeling of grandeur, increasing with every triumph, rendered it increasingly intolerable that anybody, or even any nation, should not recognize his grandeur.

What proportion of people may suffer from such neuroticism Horney does not say, though the implication is that tendencies of this sort are endemic in modern society.

Erich Fromm: Escape from Insignificance

In one of the most interesting efforts to apply the intuitions and insights of psychoanalysis to the political process, Erich Fromm selects for emphasis the necessity which men feel to "belong," to "avoid isolation and moral aloneness," to avoid powerlessness and insignificance.[11] He argues that the development of Protestantism and capitalism, though enhancing freedom from regimentation, has produced the very things that men want to avoid. Alone, insignificant, and powerless in modern society, men cannot go on bearing the burden of freedom as long as it is interpreted in a negative way, as freedom from restraint or interference. "They cannot go on bearing the burden of 'freedom from'; they must try to escape from freedom altogether unless they can progress from negative to positive freedom." [12] There are three mechanisms of escape: authoritarianism, destructiveness, and automaton conformity.

Authoritarianism is said to develop from

... the tendency to give up the independence of one's own individual self and to fuse one's self with somebody or something outside of oneself in order to acquire the strength which the individual self is lacking. ... The more distinct forms of this mechanism are to be found in the striving for submission and

[10] Karen Horney, *Neurosis and Human Growth* (New York, Norton, 1950), esp. pp. 21-27.
[11] Erich Fromm, *Escape from Freedom* (New York, Rinehart, 1941), pp. 22-23.
[12] *Ibid.*, p. 134.

domination, or, as we would rather put it, in the masochistic and sadistic strivings as they exist in varying degrees in normal and neurotic persons respectively.

Masochism, as Fromm defines it, aims "at dissolving oneself in an overwhelmingly strong power and participating in its strength and glory"; sadism aims "at unrestricted power over another person more or less mixed with destructiveness." Fromm speaks of a sado-masochistic person as having an "authoritarian character." He is both ready to submit to power, that is, to domination by the strong, and at the same time ready to impose power, to attack, to dominate, and to humiliate the weak.[13]

Destructiveness Fromm attributes not only to isolation and powerlessness but also to "anxiety and the thwarting of life."

Life has an inner dynamism of its own; it tends to grow, to be expressed, to be lived. It seems that if this tendency is thwarted the energy directed toward life undergoes a process of decomposition and changes into energies directed toward destruction. . . . The more the drive toward life is thwarted, the stronger is the drive toward destruction.[14]

The third mechanism of escape, automaton conformity, is almost self-explanatory. By this means, the individual loses his sense of isolation by ceasing to be himself and by becoming "exactly as all others are and as they expect him to be." The distinction between the self and society thus disappears.[15]

The personality characteristics described by Freud, Adler, Horney, and Fromm may, of course, be expressed in non-political pursuits. Not everyone who feels an urge to lift himself above others or to belong need satisfy his desires through political action. Moreover, those who enter the political arena may secure their satisfactions exclusively within the realm of domestic politics. However, the realm of international politics obviously includes opportunities to express Eros and Thanatos, and to seek superiority and glory. It is noteworthy that both Freud and Horney illustrated their analyses by citing political leaders (Genghis Khan and Hitler) who profoundly affected the course of world affairs. Fromm's whole book was an effort to explain the development of fascism, which obviously had international implications. Since the decisions affecting international politics are made by human beings and not by an abstract entity called the state, the personality characteristics of the human beings involved are bound to have effect.

[13] *Ibid.*, pp. 141-142, 164-168, 221.
[14] *Ibid.*, pp. 183-184.
[15] *Ibid.*, pp. 185-186.

THE FRUSTRATION-AGGRESSION THEORY

The Importance of Other People and the Group

Action in response to drives usually involves contact with other people, and usually a drive can be satisfied or reduced only if some other people provide assistance. Neither an infant nor, in a complex industrial civilization, an adult can meet even his most elementary needs by his own unaided efforts. If interpersonal relations could somehow be cut off, if all human beings could be isolated from each other, a substantial portion of them would starve, to say nothing of the lesser deprivations which they would suffer. Survival and other satisfactions are not only personal but also interpersonal or group matters. Cooperation and mutual aid are recognized essentials of a satisfactory life.

Securing satisfactions through group relationships, the individual learns to identify himself with the group. He comes to regard himself as a member of the group and to believe that his wants and needs can be satisfied only, or best, through association with the group. A sense of solidarity with the group thus develops. The individual learns to be loyal to the group. He develops a sense of duty or obligation. Through penalties and rewards he learns that he must help sustain the group both against internal disruption and against external attack, lest the satisfactions associated with membership in the group be lost. He learns that peace should be maintained within the group, that reliance should be placed on peaceful processes for the resolution of any conflicts which arise. The general trend in history has been toward the enlargement of the peace group—from family through clan or tribe to the modern nation-states and empires. The problem of extending the peace group to include mankind is, in part, the problem of teaching men to believe that this would give fuller and surer satisfaction to their wants and needs.[16]

The Inevitability of Frustration

The social conditioning of the individual and the development of group loyalties do not occur without great strains and tensions. Whereas many values can be obtained through cooperation and mutual aid, the search for others involves competition. Not everyone can have enough. One man's gain may be another man's loss. Similarly, if the desire for superiority or the search for glory is the dominant drive, all men cannot be satisfied in equal measure. The result is frustration, that is, in varying degrees men find themselves unable to secure what they want.

[16] Cf. Harold Guetzkow, *Multiple Loyalties: Theoretical Approach to a Problem in International Organization* (Princeton, Center for Research on World Political Institutions, 1955).

Aggression and Its Targets

Theories explaining the effect of frustration on human behavior are still in a tentative stage.[17] It is generally agreed, however, that frustration often leads to aggression. The aggression may be overt or covert—covert aggression taking the form, perhaps, of a plan for revenge which is never executed. The aggression may be undirected, as when one swears, or it may be directed. When it is directed, various targets may be chosen. The individual himself may be the target, that is, the aggression is directed inward. Or the external source of the frustration—perhaps another person—may be the target. Or an entirely innocent person or object may become the target; then a displacement of the aggression is said to occur.

1. Self-blame and projection. When the self is made the target, there is likely to be a feeling of guilt or sin or inadequacy of some variety. In extreme cases this leads to suicide. There is, however, a mechanism by which self-blame and hatred of the self can be alleviated or avoided. The individual can simply imagine that it is someone else who is blaming and hating him; he "projects" onto others his own tendencies to punish himself. They are plotting against him, persecuting him. It is they, therefore, not he, who deserve punishment. Those who see evil in themselves, whether they are frustrated or not, may likewise project the evil onto others: not my intentions, but theirs, are bad; it is their aspirations which are wicked and destructive.

The advantage of this mechanism is . . . obvious. It reduces anxiety to force the enemy outside the gate of one's soul. It is better to hate other people for meanness and to bear the fear of their ill-will than to hate oneself. . . . To see wickedness in others, though terrifying, is better than to be divided against oneself. It avoids the terrible burden of guilt.[18]

2. The displacement of aggressions. When aggression is directed against the source of frustration it is directed against whatever it is (animate or inanimate) that stands in the way of the achievement of desires. Thus a child denied candy by the mother may strike at her. Displacement is a more involved process. Suppose, for example, that a student is frustrated by his professor. Suppose, further, that in the circumstances it is not politic for the student to direct an aggressive response at the professor. The student may then turn unconsciously to a safer target. Instead of releasing his aggression against the professor, he

[17] John Dollard and others, *Frustration and Aggression* (New Haven, Yale University Press, 1939); N. R. Maier, *Frustration, the Study of Behavior Without a Goal* (New York, McGraw-Hill, 1949); Hilde Himmelweit, "Frustration and Aggression, a Review of Recent Experimental Work," in T. H. Pear, ed., *Psychological Factors of Peace and War* (London, Hutchinson, 1950), pp. 159-191.

[18] E. F. M. Durbin and John Bowlby, *Personal Aggressiveness and War* (New York, Columbia University Press, 1939), p. 23.

may take it out in some way on a classmate. In turn, a professor frustrated by his students may displace his aggressions on his wife. It is not unusual for aggressive impulses generated by a series of frustrations to be bottled up or repressed until they are finally released all together on a single hapless target. Then aggressive responses are far out of proportion to the nature of the offense.[19]

3. *Displacement, Thanatos, and sadism.* It is perhaps in these terms that Freud's conception of Thanatos should be explained. Perhaps, too, the frustration-aggression theory explains such episodes as the lynching of a colored woman in the United States in 1918. She was lynched "because she had remarked that 'if she knew the names of the persons who lynched her husband the Saturday before, she would have them prosecuted,' and for no other reason."

This woman was in the eighth month of pregnancy. She was hung head downward from a tree by her ankles. "Gasoline from the automobiles was thrown on her clothing, and while she writhed in agony the mob howled in glee; a match was applied and the clothing burned from her person. . . . While she was yet alive, a knife, evidently one such as is used in splitting hogs, was taken and the woman's abdomen was cut open, the unborn babe falling from her womb to the ground. The infant's head was crushed by a member of the mob with his heel."[20]

Similar sadism was clearly at work in producing the extermination of Jews in the Nazi gas chambers. Others in addition to Fromm are convinced that many Germans were attracted to the Nazi movement because of destructive impulses.

Many are convinced (and base this conviction on long personal experience) that the most effective instrument in the Nazi propagandist's hands has been the spectacle of cruelty. When masses of men have been repressed for a long time by adverse social, political and economic conditions, they seem to accept the open expression—above all the open demonstration—of hatred with deep satisfaction. . . . When the Nazis drove dissenters—or imaginary dissenters— from their meetings with cudgels, their audiences grew larger. Few people in Germany were at bottom anti-Semitic, but the joy large numbers felt in promises of blood-curdling treatment to be meted out to the helpless minority made them responsive to the suggestion. Smashing windows and street fighting were relied upon to win the crowd. . . . "We shall reach our goal," declared Goebbels, "when we have the courage to laugh as we destroy, as we smash, whatever was sacred to us as tradition, as education, as friendship, and as human affection."[21]

4. *Some qualifications and caveats.* It should not be assumed that aggressive behavior results exclusively from frustration and that it will

[19] Dollard and others, *op. cit.*, pp. 39-54.
[20] Pryns Hopkins, *The Psychology of Social Movements* (London, George Allen & Unwin, 1938), pp. 109-110.
[21] Adolf Hitler, *Mein Kampf* (New York, Reynal & Hitchcock, 1939), footnote, pp. 231-233. For a more comprehensive explanation of the motivations leading Germans to support the Nazis, see Fromm, *op. cit.;* also May, *op. cit.*, pp. 179-187.

necessarily end when frustration is no longer encountered. Neither should it be assumed that the problem of aggressiveness might be solved by somehow providing targets on which aggressions can be displaced harmlessly. Rather, aggression often becomes the normal and habitual means by which an individual attempts to secure what he wants. In many situations, aggressive attitudes tend to be general, extending over large areas of conduct regardless of opportunities for harmless displacement.[22] Moreover, the very nature of some of the goals which men pursue makes aggressive behavior of some sort rational and logical. If men placed greater value on brotherly love and were possessed of a passion for personal anonymity, political life within and among countries would be far different from what it is.

The Significance of Projection and Displacement in Political Life

Projection and displacement obviously play a significant role not only in private interpersonal relations but also in public affairs. The story is told of a psychiatrist whose prescription for a neurotic patient was that he should engage in soapbox oratory against almost anything he pleased. He might denounce Wall Street or the Communists, capitalism or creeping socialism, Republicans or Democrats. The point was to release repressed feelings of hatred and repressed impulses to aggression. Of course, the story ends with the report that the patient showed marked improvement after following his psychiatrist's advice. No one has yet devised a way of measuring the prevalence of this kind of motivation for political behavior, but surely it is common. What proportion of the political fanatics have an intelligent grasp of the issues on which they take their stand? What proportion of them, conversely, simply need some outlet for their aggressions, no matter what the target may be? One can scarcely read Nazi diatribes against the so-called Jewish pluto-democracies, or Soviet communist diatribes against the so-called imperialist warmongers without thinking that they reflect deliberate efforts to bring about a displacement of aggressions onto foreign targets. Scapegoats are sometimes useful, even if creating them causes international complications. Projection is also apparent in the international field, above all in the list of evil practices and intentions that communists attribute to the capitalist world.

Animism

Projection and displacement overlap with, if they do not account for, another non-rational phenomenon, revealed especially by anthropological research.

[22] H. J. Eysenck, "War and Aggressiveness: A Survey of Social Attitude Studies," in Pear, *op. cit.*, pp. 52-53.

It consists in the universal tendency to attribute all events in the world to the deliberate activity of human or para-human will. All happenings, whether natural and inevitable, or human and voluntary, are attributed to the will of some being either human or anthropomorphically divine. If a thunderstorm occurs, or a hurricane visits a village, or a man is killed by a tiger, the evil is attributed either to the magic of a neighboring tribe or the ill-will of demons and gods. In the same way, good fortune, however natural, is attributed to the deliberate intention of some other human being. This universal tendency in the human mind is termed animism.[23]

Illustrations of animism abound in primitive societies. Relevant activities often take the form of ceremonies to drive away spirits or appease gods who are held to bring evil to men. But they are also often directed against other human beings who are regarded as masters of magic or witchcraft.

The Motu of southeast New Guinea have a superstitious fear of the neighboring Koitapu, to the magical power of whom they attribute any calamity befalling them. In 1876 they lost much of their sago in a storm at sea, their frail canoes being unable to withstand the rough water and carry the cargo. They charged the Koitapu with bewitching their canoes and killed many of them in revenge. Again, in 1878, after a prolonged drought, for which they held a Koitapu village responsible, they attacked the village and killed all they could.[24]

A little reflection suggests that animism is hardly confined to primitive societies. The Nazis who killed Jews were no more rational than the Motu who killed the Koitapu. The same is probably true of the Russian Communists who starved the kulaks in connection with the collectivization of agriculture and who brought about the great purge of the late 1930's. It is a commonplace in American politics that voters in a drought-stricken area are likely to turn against the party in power at the next election. There may be some elements of animism in the denunciations which communists and non-communists currently exchange. Durbin and Bowlby declare,[25] "We think it difficult to exaggerate the frequency and importance of this cause of fighting in human societies of all degrees of civilization."

Man's Inhumanity

After briefly surveying events in the period between the two World Wars, Durbin and Bowlby conclude,[26] "No group of animals could be more aggressive or more ruthless in their aggression than the adult members of the human race." They do, however, find two differences between the aggression of more primitive beings and that of adult men.

[23] Durbin and Bowlby, op. cit., p. 13.
[24] Maurice R. Davie, The Evolution of War (New Haven, Yale University Press, 1929), p. 115.
[25] Durbin and Bowlby, op. cit., p. 14.
[26] Ibid., pp. 12-13.

In the first place the aggression of adults is normally a group activity. Murder and assault are restricted to a small criminal minority. Adults kill and torture each other only when organized into political parties, or economic classes, or religious denominations, or nation states. A moral distinction is always made between the individual killing for himself and the same individual killing for some real or supposed group interest.

In the second place, the adult powers of imagination and reason are brought to the service of the aggressive intention. Apes and children when they fight, simply fight. Men and women first construct towering systems of theology and religion, complex analyses of racial character and class structure, or moralities of group life and virility before they kill one another. Thus they fight for Protestantism or Mohammedanism, for the emancipation of the world proletariat or for the salvation of the Nordic culture, for nation or for kind. Men will die like flies for theories and exterminate each other with every instrument of destruction for abstractions.

Adult fighting, in other words, is a product of society, culture, and adherence to principle.

In mitigation of these severe conclusions on man's inhumanity to man, it might be pointed out that even within the same country aggressiveness and cruelty are not evenly distributed. Some individuals and some classes appear to develop these qualities to a far greater extent than others. Some are guided primarily by Eros, others by Thanatos. It was a small minority in Germany, for example, which led the way in the Nazi program of anti-Semitism and external aggression. To be sure, this small minority evoked the support of a large proportion of the population, but even at the height of Hitler's success many Germans found his actions abhorrent. Similarly, although many Americans seem to enjoy suffering and destruction—goading TV wrestlers and prize fighters to commit mayhem on each other, and attending the 500-mile automobile races in Indianapolis to see cars smashed and drivers killed—outbreaks of serious domestic violence are rare; the proportion of the population participating in such activities as the lynching described above is very small. Difficulties in securing volunteers for the armed services suggest that blood lust is relatively rare as a dominant drive.

LASSWELL'S POLITICAL TYPE

Harold D. Lasswell has probably made the most sustained and successful effort to relate the study of human psychology explicitly to political problems. Two related aspects of his work are especially pertinent for our present purposes.

Values Pursued

In the first place, he lists and defines values (desires, interests) which he regards as especially significant to the study of political behavior. They fall into two groups: the welfare values and the deference values.

Among the welfare values we are especially concerned with well-being, wealth, skill, and enlightenment. By *well-being* is meant the health and safety of the organism. *Wealth* is income: services of goods and persons accruing to the individual in any way whatever. *Skill* is proficiency in any practice whatever, whether in arts or crafts, trade or profession. By *enlightenment* we mean knowledge, insight, and information concerning personal and cultural relations.

Most important among the deference values, for political science, is *power*. Other important deference values are respect, rectitude, and affection. *Respect* is the value of status, of honor, recognition, prestige, the "glory" or "reputation" which Hobbes classes with gain and safety as one of the three fundamental human motivations. *Rectitude* comprises the moral values—virtue, goodness, righteousness, and so on. *Affection*, finally, includes the values of love and friendship.[27]

Lasswell defines power as participation in the making of decisions—a decision being a policy involving severe sanctions or deprivations.[28] Similarly, he uses the term to designate "relations in which severe deprivations are expected to follow the breach of a pattern of conduct." [29]

Each value which he lists may be desired either for its own sake or because it is useful in the pursuit of other values. Lasswell makes no general assumption concerning the order of priority that individuals and groups assign to these values, or about the relative intensity with which they are pursued. In fact, he warns against sweeping generalizations.[30]

It is impossible to assign a universally dominant role to some one value or other. No single principle of motivation can be elaborated into a tenable "philosophy of history"—as though always and everywhere human conduct can be interpreted as a striving only for economic gain, or for political power, or for prestige and glory, or for love and affection. In a specific situation, any or all of these—and others as well—might be involved in different degrees. What values are operative to what extent can be determined only by specific empirical inquiry.

This observation obviously calls into question some of the theories described earlier in this chapter, especially those of Karen Horney. Similarly, it adds to the doubts already expressed in the chapter "Economic Objectives and Economic Forces" concerning theories which purport to explain imperialism and war largely or exclusively in economic terms. With men pursuing a number of different values (and Lasswell's list does not presume to be exhaustive) an understanding of politics becomes more difficult to achieve. At the same time, it is helpful to be alert to the range of values that help shape behavior.

---

[27] Harold D. Lasswell and Abraham Kaplan, *Power and Society* (New Haven, Yale University Press, 1950), pp. 55-56.

[28] *Ibid.*, pp. 74-75.

[29] Harold D. Lasswell, *Power and Personality* (New York, Norton, 1948), p. 12.

[30] Lasswell and Kaplan, *op. cit.*, p. 57.

Deference Values, Especially Power, and the Political Type

Though heeding his own warning that no one value plays a universally dominant role, Lasswell is inclined to put special emphasis on the deference values. More particularly, he treats the desire for power as a ubiquitous political phenomenon, and he assumes that it is dominant in guiding the behavior of some individuals. To facilitate an understanding of such individuals, he constructs a model—a fictitious person—of what he calls the political type. The political type is the power seeker. "The notion of a political type is that of a developmental type who passes through a distinctive career line in which the power opportunities of each situation are selected in preference to other opportunities." The basic characteristic of the political type is "the accentuation of power in relation to other values within the personality when compared with other persons." More broadly, the political type feels an intense and ungratified craving for deference. He seeks to gratify these cravings through political activity, and rationalizes his activity in terms of the public interest.[31]

There is no implication that all those who are active in politics, or even all those who hold leading political positions, are political types in Lasswell's sense. Throughout history, examples abound of individuals who have sought to give up power rather than expand it. At the same time, there are also many instances of individuals who have been driven on by a craving for power which seemed insatiable. In some the lust for power has been so intense as to create a merciless disregard and even contempt for the interests and welfare of other men. "According to our speculative model, the perfect power type is wholly absorbed with advancing the value position of the 'sacred me' (not 'us'). Hence he sacrifices anyone and everyone at convenience for his power, and does not conceive of power as a means of advancing the value position of family, neighborhood, nation or any other group."[32] Endless accumulation of power becomes an all-consuming passion. The question is why? Why do some persons tend toward the extreme of Lasswell's political type?

The Sources of the Craving for Power

Lasswell's hypothesis is that "low estimates of the self" are at the bottom of the craving for power. The individual somehow feels deprived; he does not command the values which, for some reason, he thinks he should command. Perhaps he suffers from a physical handicap, a lack of well-being. Perhaps his income is low. Or perhaps, while thinking that he deserves deference, he feels that he does not actually obtain it—that

[31] Lasswell, *op. cit.*, pp. 21, 22, 38.
[32] *Ibid.*, p. 56.

others hold him in unduly low esteem. Alternatively, if the individual does not feel currently deprived, he may fear the loss of values in the future.

In some circumstances the individual accepts the actual or threatened deprivation without struggle; he becomes reconciled to low estimates of the self. In other circumstances he seeks to compensate for deprivation or to safeguard himself against future deprivation which he fears. The struggle for compensation or for a guarantee for the future takes the form of a struggle for power. Power is expected to overcome low estimates of the self. Lasswell's summary statement is as follows: [33]

> The accentuation of power is to be understood as a compensatory reaction against low estimates of the self (especially when coexisting with high self-estimates); and the reaction occurs when opportunities exist both for the displacement of ungratified cravings from the primary circle to public targets and for the rationalization of these displacements in the public interest.

Appropriate skills, of course, must also be possessed.

The same factors that lead individuals to crave power are also said to operate on groups. Individuals identify themselves with the group, and want it to command welfare and deference values in which they can share. The respect which individuals feel that they command, for example, varies with the respect commanded by a group with which they are identified. The nation or state is commonly the most important among such groups. When estimates of its value position are low, or when there is fear for its future value position, the stage is set for a compensatory struggle for power. The point is illustrated by the statement of a Nazi leader at a congress of the League for Germans Abroad in the 1930's: [34] "We have a common fate. Your star became dim with Germany's decline. When Germany came to be held in contempt, your prestige disappeared." It is also illustrated currently by demands on the part of colonial peoples for independence.

> The desire for respect is now understood to be one of the most important influences on men's conduct. Social tensions arise from resentment at not being respected as much as from any other source. Movements to give freedom to dependent peoples derive their strength primarily from the desire on the part of these peoples to participate in the sharing of respect.[35]

Healthy and Sick Personalities

Lasswell's political type represents an extreme which few, if any, individuals or groups actually reach. In his conception people range in their desire for power from some undetermined minimum to an absolute

[33] *Ibid.*, p. 53.
[34] Rudolf Hess, *Reden* (München, Zentralverlag der N.S.D.A.P., 1940), p. 264.
[35] Frederick Sherwood Dunn, *War and the Minds of Men* (New York, Harper, 1950), p. 41.

maximum. What proportion of individuals within any society and throughout the world are grouped at different points along the power scale is unknown. Further, the question how they should ideally be distributed along the scale can be answered only on the basis of some assumptions concerning the nature of the good society. In most conceptions of the good society, there would be a cutting point somewhere along the scale; individuals on one side of the cutting point would be regarded as having socially desirable or healthy personalities, and those on the other side (i.e., those who come closest to being political types) would be regarded as having sick personalities. Measures might then be taken to promote the development of healthy personalities and to exclude sick personalities from positions of political influence and control. The effect on the course of history might well be great. Plainly, by standards most likely to be acceptable to believers in liberalism and democracy, many of those who have done much to shape history in the past have been sick.

Lasswell's explanation of the sources of the lust for power obviously has something in common with psychoanalytical explanations of behavior and with the frustration-aggression theory. He does not generalize as much as Karen Horney, for example, but his political type could well be a person who, in her terms, is dominated by a drive for self-glorification. Similarly, low estimates of the self presumably mean frustration for the individual, and the compensatory striving for power presumably involves aggression.

IMPLICATIONS FOR INTERNATIONAL POLITICS

Some implications of the study of human psychology for international politics are reasonably clear, and others are shrouded in uncertainty and doubt.

Long-Run Possibilities

In the long run, perhaps the most important point is that human behavior is largely a reflection of the learning process. This process largely governs the selection of values, the order of priority among them, and the intensity with which they are pursued. It, rather than instinct, is the source of what Freud called Eros and Thanatos, of what Adler called the goal of superiority, of what Horney called the individual's feeling of an urgent need to lift himself above others, and of what Fromm called the desire of men to avoid powerlessness and insignificance. The learning process, moreover, largely governs the selection of methods for satisfying needs and wants, and the nature of reactions to frustration. It is on the basis of the learning process that estimates of the self are made and that reactions to low estimates of the self are selected. If the learning process governs so much of human behavior, it obviously follows that behavior can be shaped and changed. Very little of what men do is really inevitable.

Identification with the nation and loyalty to it are among the things learned. There is nothing in the nature of man which precludes identification with larger entities, up to and including the world as a whole. Loyalties could theoretically be developed to an entity encompassing all mankind.

These thoughts suggest the possibility of developing a peaceful and stable world order comprised of harmonious and good societies. The very expression of the thought, however, is enough to suggest how far men are from achieving such a goal.

Short-Run Dangers from "Mad Caesars"

For the short run, little can be said with real assurance. Presumably a fairly high proportion of those who rise to the top politically throughout the world are driven on by some such desires as those emphasized by Freud, Adler, Horney, and Fromm. It seems plausible to assume that many are driven on by frustration, reacting to it in aggressive ways. Displacement of aggressive impulses, projection, and what Durbin and Bowlby call animism appear to be common in political life. Obviously there are many in public life in various countries with tendencies toward the extreme illustrated by Lasswell's political type.

There have been many "mad Caesars" in history—sick personalities in positions of great political power. Some have ruled in states so small and weak that the damage they have done was almost automatically restricted; others have had great military power behind them, and have been able to do damage on a far-reaching scale. Genghis Khan might be cited, along with his statement that [36]

... a man's highest job in life is to break his enemies, to drive them before him, to take from them all the things that have been theirs, to hear the weeping of those who cherished them, to take their horses between his knees, and to press in his arms the most desirable of their women.

Hitler was no doubt a sick person in the sense that the word is being used here. Probably Stalin was, as well. Reporting to the Twentieth Congress of the Communist Party of the Soviet Union, Khrushchev is said to have described Stalin as [37] "a very distrustful man, sickly suspicious.... Everywhere and in everything he saw 'enemies,' 'two-facers,' and 'spies.'... His persecution mania reached unbelievable dimensions." Khrushchev also referred to Stalin's "mania for greatness," and asserted that he "completely lost consciousness of reality."

[36] Quoted by Lasswell, op. cit., p. 43.
[37] New York Times, June 5, 1956, p. 15. cols. 1, 7, 8.

Where sick personalities have autocratic control over great military power, the danger to the world is obviously very real. With the development of nuclear weapons and the prospect that most states will come to possess them, the proportion of statesmen who are in a position to do great damage will certainly increase.

Of course, statesmen do not act alone. They always have advisers, even the "mad Caesars." Frequently they share power with many others—with an oligarchy or an elite. In democracies the whole electorate, and especially the elected representatives of the people, share in decision-making. The more power is shared the less likely is it that the special personality characteristics of some one leader will be decisive. His actions will be influenced and perhaps controlled by those who participate in shaping public policy. In most governments, most of the time, very strenuous efforts are made to see to it that issues, above all issues involving questions of war and peace, are thoroughly and rationally considered by a large number of able people. The chance that unconscious or subconscious or irrational motives will control decisions on fateful issues is small, yet it happens.

Even democracy does not necessarily assure wisdom and rationality. Just as all members of the Motu tribe may have believed that the Koitapu bewitched their canoes, so may all or most members even of advanced societies share in the drives, motives, and attitudes of their leaders. The advisers of a "mad Caesar" may to some extent share his personality characteristics. Identifying with the nation or state, they may seek glory and power through it. The group as a whole may approach the characteristics of the political type. Low estimates of the individual or group self may lead to a compensatory struggle for power. Humble citizens may be frustrated, and be ready to displace their aggressions onto a foreign enemy. The problem of shaping the development of the human personality in such a way as to obtain socially desirable responses to stimuli in interpersonal and intergroup relations is not an easy one to solve.

Dangers in Psychological Approaches

Psychological approaches to politics, domestic or international, can easily give wrong impressions. One of them is that there are no real political issues. Especially when considerable attention is paid to the irrational aspects of behavior, the tendency is to conclude that if statesmen and others would only consult psychiatrists and accept psychotherapy the troubles of the world would be over. On the other hand, the conclusion may be that a focus on the learning process, with a view to creating healthy personalities, would permit the solution of all problems. In truth, these conclusions have a measure of truth in them, but the problem of creating a desirable world order is far too complex to be solved in these ways alone. Not all behavior is irrational. Neuroticism does not dominate the world scene. People with quite healthy personalities sometimes clash. The simple fact is that thoroughly rational people may want different things, or, when they want the same thing, there may not be enough of it to go around. Moreover, even if there is potentially enough to go around, it may be impossible to secure agreement on the best way of making it available. Problems arising out of such situations are quite real. Their solution may be complicated by the presence of irrational or neurotic behavior, but even the most perfectly adjusted and rational people would scarcely find answers that are easy and pat. If answers are to be found, the resources of many fields in addition to the field of psychology will have to be taxed.

SUGGESTED READINGS

BENEDICT, Ruth, *Patterns of Culture* (Boston, Houghton Mifflin, 1934).

CANTRIL, Hadley, ed., *Tensions That Cause War* (Urbana, University of Illinois Press, 1951).

DAVIE, Maurice R., *The Evolution of War* (New Haven, Yale University Press, 1929).

DURBIN, E. F. M., and BOWLBY, John, *Personal Aggressiveness and War* (New York, Columbia University Press, 1939).

FREUD, Sigmund, *Civilization and Its Discontents* (London, Hogarth, 1949).

FROMM, Erich, *Escape from Freedom* (New York, Rinehart, 1941).

GLOVER, Edward, *War, Sadism, and Pacifism* (London, George Allen & Unwin, 1947).

HORNEY, Karen, *Neurosis and Human Growth* (New York, Norton, 1950).

KLINEBERG, Otto, *Tensions Affecting International Understanding, a Survey of Research* (New York, Social Science Research Council, 1950).

LASSWELL, Harold D., *Power and Personality* (New York, Norton, 1948).

LASSWELL, Harold D., and KAPLAN, Abraham, *Power and Society* (New Haven, Yale University Press, 1950).

MAY, Mark A., *A Social Psychology of War and Peace* (New Haven, Yale University Press, 1943).

MURPHY, Gardner, ed., *Human Nature and Enduring Peace* (New York, Reynal & Hitchcock, 1945).

PEAR, T. H., ed., *Psychological Factors of Peace and War* (New York, Philosophical Library, 1950).

TOLMAN, Edward Chace, *Drives Toward War* (New York, Appleton-Century, 1942).

WEST, Ranyard, *Conscience and Society* (London, Methuen, 1951).

CHAPTER 9

Common Objectives of States

In the preceding chapters we have been analyzing the dynamics of international politics; we have been trying to find out what forces and conditions make states behave as they do. We discussed the desire of states to preserve their security and sovereignty. We discussed nationalism and some of the ideas connected with it, such as self-determination and patriotism. We discussed the ideological conflict, in particular the influence of liberal and communist ideas on the formulation and execution of foreign policies. Then came discussions of the role of economic factors, the role of war itself and of the expectation of war, and finally the role of psychological factors.

Three observations should be made about this list of topics. In the first place, it is not a complete list. Who knows how many factors affect the behavior of states? Some would insist that climate is the ultimate determinant. Some would want stress placed on geography, or on the implications of scientific and technological developments. Some would say that religion and morality should be included. The list of relevant topics might conceivably include even astrology. Yet, though the topics discussed do not include all which are or might be relevant, they no doubt include the most important of them.

In the second place, there has been no effort to rank the various topics in an order that reflects their influence on the behavior of states. It would be extremely difficult to determine their order of importance in relation to the policies of only one state in one particular situation. To attempt a generalization which would be applicable to all states and all policies would be out of the question.

In the third place, there has been no effort to discriminate rigorously between influencing factors which may be fundamental and factors which may be derivative or superficial. Are ideologies fundamental, or do they simply reflect class or other interests based on economics? Is nationalism fundamental, or is it simply a reflection of economic or psychological needs? Are war and the expectation of war fundamental, or do they simply reflect the fact that the world is divided into sovereign states? There is no agreement on such questions. To specify an ultimate factor or to list a group of ultimate factors which control the behavior of states would be quite arbitrary. In any case influencing factors which originally were derivative have often achieved independence and have come to exert influence in their own right. In the present state of knowledge all that can be said with assurance is that all the elements discussed do influence the behavior of states, and collectively they appear to be the most important influencing factors.

The purpose in this chapter is to present a summary statement and discussion of the objectives that states commonly pursue. In part, this will involve a synthesis of what has been said in the preceding chapters on the dynamics of international politics. In part, pursuing different categories of thought, it will involve a somewhat different angle of approach to the general question of what makes states behave as they do.

SECURITY AND SOVEREIGNTY

The paramount objective of every state, as a general rule, is self-preservation or survival. More broadly, the objective is security. When necessary, governments normally sacrifice every other objective, and require that citizens and subjects do likewise, to preserve the state. Peace is often sacrificed for this purpose; states wage war, if survival requires it. Efforts to enhance prosperity are also curtailed or abandoned, if survival is at stake. The greater the threat of destruction, the stronger will be the tendency to abandon political and economic principles and practices, such as free speech, free enterprise, and free elections, which seem to stand in the way of survival. Those moral and religious principles which interfere seriously with measures for self-preservation are likely to be reinterpreted. At the same time, citizens of the state who can contribute to its preservation are expected and required to do so, even though it cost them their lives.

Although these generalizations are sound, they are subject to interpretation and qualification. What are the attributes of the self that is to be preserved? Precisely what is to be rendered secure, and how much security is desired? In the eyes of individuals and governments, what desires sometimes qualify or supersede the desire for security?

We have seen that the self which is to be preserved regularly includes territory and people, though it is often difficult to say precisely what territory and people. Generally, the territorial self is defined in terms of the status quo, but it may also be defined in terms of a past situation or a future expectation. The basic proposition is that governments wish to retain what they have, or, more accurately, to avoid being compelled by other states to give up what they have. It is an involuntary loss which is to be guarded against especially.

The self also regularly includes sovereignty and equality. Sovereignty, it will be recalled, denotes the status of an entity supreme over domestic law but subject to international law. Each state wants to be able to fix and enforce law within its own domain as it pleases; it wants to retain an area of law over which it is supreme. There is therefore a strong tendency to restrict the development of international law and of international executive, legislative, and judicial agencies. Equality means that the rights of one state are entitled to as much respect as the rights of any other state; there is a determination to maintain the principle, in which even the most powerful acquiesce, that power as such gives no special rights. Title to sovereignty and equality is commonly regarded as so precious that it is to be preserved at any cost. However, just as territory is sometimes ceded voluntarily without any sense of damage to the territorial self, so are treaties sometimes voluntarily accepted which restrict the sphere of sovereignty and establish unequal rights.

The self is also usually considered as including a particular political and economic system. States want to avoid being compelled by external pressures to modify the social system under which they live. Communist states want the world to be safe for communism, and democratic states want the world to be safe for democracy. The elites in every society (i.e., those who get the most of the best) are almost certain to think that the system under which they have secured privileges should be preserved, and others may share the belief; the social system or way of life becomes an essential part of the self whose survival is sought. Perhaps, in addition, attempts may be made to extend the social system to other states.

Security is a somewhat broader concept than self-preservation or survival. It relates not only to the ultimate desire that the state survive but also to the desire that it should live without serious external threat to values or interests which are regarded as important or vital. The concept is a vague one. The values or interests to be kept secure must be selected and defined; the nature and extent of foreign threats must be appraised; the degree of security sought must be determined; and the methods of promoting security must be selected. Each step involves judgment and choice. States may make judgments and choices which render the concept incapable of general application; a number of states, all genuinely seeking security, may do it in such a way that security for one means insecurity for another. International friction and war may develop out of incompatible conceptions of the requirements of security.

Whether all existing states should be preserved or kept secure is a question about which detached observers might well have doubts. It is difficult to believe that a rational, omniscient, and omnipotent being would divide the world precisely as it is divided; such a being would presumably amalgamate or federate many states, possibly all of them. But the situation is somewhat analogous to that faced by the director of a children's camp who, when confronted with problems of children whom he did not like, said that he always had to keep reminding himself that somebody loved every precious one of them, even though he could not see why; he could not disregard them without unpleasant consequences. Similar forces operate in relation to love for, or loyalty to, the state. It may be based on rational or irrational considerations, or both, but still it exists.

However, as we have seen in Chapter 3, there are qualifications to the proposition that governments and people attach paramount value to the preservation of the state. Sometimes there is a willingness to risk the very existence of the state in an effort to achieve other values. On rare occasions some states have voluntarily accepted annexation by, or amalgamation with, other states. Sometimes there are disaffected elements in the population (e.g., national minorities, colonial peoples, communists in a non-communist state, and non-communists in a communist state) who attach little or no value to the preservation of the state. Conscientious objectors refuse to defend the state by military means. Advocates of one or another form of international federation or world government, though presumably willing to defend the state against external threats, nevertheless want it to go out of existence as a sovereign entity on agreed conditions.

But despite qualifications and exceptions, the general rule is that states seek self-preservation and security above all.

AGGRANDIZEMENT

In modern times it is rare for statesmen to say that they seek territorial aggrandizement, yet it is obvious that they engage in it. A number of reasons have been given in the preceding chapters. Nationalism itself calls for expansion on the part of those states which do not already encompass what is deemed to be national territory. Messianic movements, whether religious or secular, likewise sometimes call for expansion. Islam was extended by military means, in part for the greater glory of Allah. Various Christian statesmen, more in earlier than in recent times, have been moved to engage in expansion ostensibly to save foreign souls. A *mission civilisatrice* or the idea of taking up the White Man's Burden has sometimes been cited as an excuse or reason for aggrandizement, as in King Leopold's venture into the region of the Congo and as in Mussolini's attack on Ethiopia. Economic penetration has frequently led to the establishment of political control, particularly for weak and backward countries. The habit of war and domestic economic and political conditions that help bring war on have produced wars which in turn have led to aggrandizement. Schumpeter's theory of imperialism rests on this fact.

War and the expectation of war have combined with the desire for survival or security in bringing about many acts of aggrandizement. Machiavelli long ago observed that [1] "fear to lose stirs the same passions in men as the desire to gain, as men do not believe themselves sure of what they already possess except by acquiring more." Thomas Hobbes endorsed this observation in paraphrasing it.[2] Even the most superficial survey of diplomatic history establishes its truth. It is rare for war to break out simply because a state desires control over a strategic point which may be of value in future war, but once war has broken out, for whatever reasons, belligerents commonly seek to take advantage of the opportunities which it provides for seizing strategically desirable territory from the enemy. Neutrals may enter a war partly for this reason, as Japan did in relation to World War I.

On top of all this, aggrandizement sometimes occurs because of cultural and psychological forces which produce in many men a craving for power and glory. Such men are no doubt disproportionately represented among the statesmen of the world, for some measure of this craving is practically prerequisite to achieving or retaining positions of political responsibility. The craving is illustrated in a conversation which, according to Plutarch, took place between Cineas and Pyrrhus, when Pyrrhus was preparing to invade Italy.[3]

"The Romans, sir [said Cineas], are reported to be great warriors and conquerors of many warlike nations; if God permit us to overcome them, how should we use our victory?"

"You ask," said Pyrrhus, "a thing evident of itself. The Romans once conquered, there is neither Greek nor barbarian city that will resist us, but we shall presently be masters of all Italy, the extent and resources and strength of which any one should rather profess to be ignorant of than yourself."

Cineas after a little pause, "And having subdued Italy, what shall we do next?"

Pyrrhus not yet discovering his intention, "Sicily," he replied, "next holds out her arms to receive us, a wealthy and populous island, and easy to be gained. . . ."

"You speak," said Cineas, "what is perfectly probable, but will the possession of Sicily put an end to the war?"

"God grant us," answered Pyrrhus, "victory and success in that, and we will use these as forerunners of greater things; who could forbear from Libya and Carthage then within reach . . .? These conquests once perfected, will any

---

[1] Niccolo Machiavelli, *The Prince* and *The Discourses* (New York, Modern Library, 1940), p. 124. This general thesis is developed particularly by John H. Herz, *Political Realism and Political Idealism* (Chicago, The University of Chicago Press, 1951).

[2] Thomas Hobbes, *Leviathan* (Oxford, Blackwell, 1946), p. 64.

[3] Plutarch's *Complete Works, Parallel Lives*, Vol. II (New York, Crowell, 1909), pp. 54-55.

assert that of the enemies who now pretend to despise us, any one will dare to make further resistance?"

"None," replied Cineas, "for then it is manifest we may with such mighty forces regain Macedon, and make an absolute conquest of Greece; and when all these are in our power what shall we do then?"

Said Pyrrhus, smiling, "We will live at our ease, my dear friend, and drink all day, and divert ourselves with pleasant conversation."

When Cineas had led Pyrrhus with his argument to this point: "And what hinders us now, sir, if we have a mind to be merry, and entertain one another, since we have at hand without trouble all those necessary things, to which through much blood and great labor, and infinite hazards and mischief done to ourselves and to others, we design at last to arrive?"

Such reasonings rather troubled Pyrrhus with the thought of the happiness he was quitting, than any way altered his purpose, being unable to abandon the hopes of what he so much desired.

Whether this account is fanciful or factual, the desire for aggrandizement as a satisfaction in itself has certainly played a significant role in history. Before becoming King of Prussia, Frederick the Great envisaged himself as always advancing "from country to country, from conquest to conquest, selecting, like Alexander, new worlds to conquer." Later he declared, "The policy of great monarchies has never varied. Their fundamental principle has been ceaseless aggrandizement." "The passions of princes," he said, "know no other restraint than the limit of their power." [4] Napoleon seemed to be similarly motivated. Speaking to French sailors in 1797 he declared,[5] "Comrades, when we have secured peace for the continent, we shall join you in conquering the freedom of the seas. . . . Without you, we can carry the glory of the French name only to a small portion of the continent; with you we shall sail the seas and the most remote regions shall behold our national glory." On another occasion he said, "We must go to the Orient. All great glories are won there. . . . Europe is a mole-hill. There have never been great revolutions and great empires except in the Orient, where six hundred million men live." Hitler explained himself largely in terms of racial principle, but it is implicit in what he said that he sought glory and power through aggrandizement: "The pacifist-humane idea is perhaps quite good whenever the man of the highest standard has previously conquered and subjected the world to a degree that makes him the only master of this globe." "The Nordic race has a right to rule the world. We must make this right a guiding star of our foreign policy." [6]

[4] G. P. Gooch, *Frederick the Great* (New York, Knopf, 1947), pp. 283-284; Hans Kohn, *The Idea of Nationalism* (New York, Macmillan, 1944), p. 362.

[5] George Gordon Andrews, *Napoleon in Review* (New York, Knopf, 1939), pp. 176-177.

[6] Adolf Hitler, *Mein Kampf* (New York, Reynal & Hitchcock, 1939), pp. 394-395. The second statement, attributed to Hitler, is quoted from Frederick L. Schuman, *The Nazi Dictatorship* (New York, Knopf, 1935), p. 128.

The various forces making for expansion are so strong and have been so often manifested in history that some describe expansion as a virtual law of politics. Martin Wight, for example, declares: [7]

It is the general nature of all Powers to expand. The energies of their inhabitants expand economically, culturally, and politically, and unless there is a strong counter-reason, all these tendencies will be summed up in territorial expansion. . . .

Wight goes on to say that "every Power tends to expand until it reaches an equilibrium that is the product of two factors: external pressure and internal organization." In other words, they continue to expand as long as internal organization and resources permit the mustering of the necessary strength, or until they are stopped by some countervailing force. The countervailing force might be a natural barrier, such as an ocean or a mountain chain, or the armed might of other states. Similar conclusions will be cited below when power as an objective of states is discussed.

It is a historic fact that some states have set out on programs of aggrandizement without evident limits. World conquest seems to have been the goal, but to transform such intermittent and scattered efforts into a law of politics is too extreme, and even to describe it as a general tendency is questionable. Probably most statesmen most of the time give no thought to the possibility of taking other people's territory. Other values and goals are often more important. Yet the desire for aggrandizement, though not universal and constant, has appeared frequently enough that it must be listed among the significant goals that states sometimes seek.

PEACE

Statesmen frequently say that they seek peace. Affirmations of a desire for peace have become almost a universal feature of diplomacy. In many treaties, including the Charter of the United Nations, states have pledged themselves to peace. War itself is sometimes said to be fought on behalf of peace, as when President Truman declared that "our men [in Korea] are fighting for the proposition that peace shall be the law of this earth." [8] In most countries, and particularly in democratic countries, popular sentiment virtually compels the endorsement of peace. Even Hitler, while making statements which the discerning could only interpret as endorsements of war, also felt it necessary to make rather frequent protestations of a desire for peace.

As usually defined, peace means the absence of war. Yet, when statesmen and others say that they seek peace, so defined, there is always an

[7] Martin Wight, *Power Politics*, "Looking Forward" Pamphlets, No. 8 (London, Royal Institute of International Affairs, 1946), pp. 39-40.
[8] *State Department Bulletin*, Vol. 23 (September 11, 1950), p. 407.

explicit or implicit proviso. No statesman wants peace at any price. There are always some things which they want more than they want peace. It may be survival or security; it may be unification of the nation or other aggrandizement; it may be the protection and promotion of commercial interests or ideological principles; it may be freedom or justice. The very fact that wars occur demonstrates that peace is not the paramount value. This is not to say that professions of a desire for peace are necessarily hypocritical, although sometimes they undoubtedly are. It is rather to say that, although statesmen and others commonly want peace, they regularly want other things more. They want peace, provided that it is compatible with the preservation and promotion of other values which are more precious.

This point is obvious and simple, yet it is one which is often ignored, and the results of ignoring it are sometimes unfortunate. The objective of peace calls for international negotiation, and successful negotiation commonly requires compromise. The danger is that, if peace is made an absolute value and war is ruled out as a possibility, compromise may lead to futile concessions and appeasement. It is perhaps no accident that the British Prime Minister who declared in 1938 that peace was the greatest interest of the British Empire should have been the principal author of the policy of appeasing Hitler. Moreover, it is easy, however unsound, to jump from the premise that peace is the objective to the conclusion that armaments and a military establishment are unnecessary. The American peace movement between the wars, for example, was largely a movement for disarmament. The danger in this is that the state will find itself in a position of weakness when it realizes that it regards some values as more precious than peace and when it feels bound to fight for them.

Peace is not always defined negatively, as the absence of war. Sometimes it is given a positive meaning; it is equated to law and order or to order and justice. In this sense, peace presupposes law and recognized means of changing, interpreting, and enforcing law. In other words, it presupposes governmental or quasi-governmental organization. This in turn may involve police action to enforce law, and the police action may be on a scale so extensive that the acts involved become indistinguishable from acts of war. Thus, by one interpretation peace is the antithesis of war. By the second, it may require enforcement action, perhaps including virtual war. It is the latter meaning of the word *peace* which President Truman evidently had in mind when he said that American forces in Korea were fighting for peace.

The creation of such institutions as the League of Nations, the United Nations, and the International Court of Justice testifies to the fact that states sometimes seek peace defined as a situation of law and order, just as they sometimes seek it defined as the absence of war, but provisos and qualifications arise again. States are commonly willing to insist that their own legal rights must be respected and to take action to enforce their own rights. When they are convinced that attacks on the legal rights of other states involve serious potential menace to their own rights and interests, they may join in action, including military action, against the aggressor; the defense of national interest may then parade under the cover of support for law and order or support for an international organization. When they are not convinced that attacks on other states involve menace to themselves, they may give verbal support to the principle that law and order are to be preserved, but participation in enforcement action is another matter. It will occur, if at all, only on the condition that risks and costs in terms of objectives other than peace are not too severe. This general question will be discussed more fully in a later chapter.

In sum, peace is among the objectives that states pursue, but their pursuit of it is not unqualified. When peace is defined as the absence of war, states sometimes abandon it and go to war for the preservation or promotion of goals deemed more important. When it is defined as a situation of law and order, to be supported by war (police action) if necessary, states usually abandon it when the prospective short-run risks and costs in terms of other values appear to be greater than the prospective gains.

PROSPERITY

Protection and promotion of the economic well-being of some or all of the population constitute a regular objective of states, pursued by means of both domestic and foreign policies. This proposition holds, regardless of the economic system involved.

Pursuit of prosperity through foreign policy contributes to both cooperation and conflict in international affairs. In many ways the economic interests of states are mutual. The exchange of goods and services, and the borrowing and lending of money, commonly serve the mutual advantage of individuals, whether they occur within countries or among countries. In economic relationships one man's gain is not necessarily another man's loss. All involved have a common interest in developing and maintaining conditions in which mutual advantage is served, and international cooperation in peace is normally one of those conditions.

At the same time, economic activities are competitive. Those with things to sell compete for markets. Those who want to buy scarce products compete for available supplies. Sellers and buyers compete with each other in the sense of bargaining over prices and other terms of transactions. In international affairs several types of problems are likely to accentuate the frictions that commonly accompany competition. There are the problems attendant on the fact that different currencies are involved. There are the problems created for one country when another establishes trade regulations and barriers for its own advantage. There are the problems which arise when economic relationships develop between peoples with differing power positions, differing cultures, and differing conceptions of the rules and principles by which relationships should be governed.

The very fact of competition means tension among individuals involved. Because of the pressure of special interests or because the over-all outcome of the competitive struggle is likely to affect whole populations, the tension which arises from international commercial activities spreads in some degree to foreign offices. They commonly seek a peaceful adjustment of difficulties. After all, war is rarely profitable to a country as a whole, and is unlikely to be profitable even to a ruling class as a whole. Non-economic factors usually become involved in policies and negotiations on economic questions, perhaps reinforcing factors making for peaceful adjustment and perhaps reinforcing factors making for conflict. War sometimes ensues.

It is one thing to acknowledge that economic considerations exert a substantial influence on foreign policies and quite another to contend that economic conditions and forces control foreign policies. Marxists generally make this claim, though they differ among themselves in explaining and supporting the conclusion they reach. The extreme view that all wars under capitalism are economic in origin is not supported by historical evidence; nor, in the light of the numerous factors influencing the behavior of states, is such a claim even superficially plausible.

THE PROTECTION AND PROMOTION OF IDEOLOGY

Along with sovereignty goes the right of each state to establish and maintain the social, economic, and political system of its choice, which implies adherence to the ideology of its choice. One of the regular objectives of states is to preserve this right and to preserve the favored ideology. When states adhere to substantially the same ideology, this causes no difficulty; in fact, it constitutes a force making for cooperation. However, sharp ideological differences are a source of discord and possible war.

The reasons for this are fairly obvious. No social system and no ideology are totally good or totally bad. In varying proportions, there are good and bad features in each. Moreover, no social system operates through the years with uniform success and effectiveness; economic, political, and other difficulties periodically arise. The natural consequence of the bad features of a system and of its periodic special difficulties is that it will not evoke loyalty uniformly among different groups and classes. Varying proportions of the population of every state are always more or less disaffected. Given some knowledge of an alien ideology, some or all of the disaffected will be attracted by it. The very existence and example of an alien social system and an alien ideology are therefore to some extent subversive. The subversive influence may be so slight as to be politically insignificant (Oriental ideologies, for example, have never produced much impact in the West), or it may be so great as to produce intense demands for change. The ideology of the French Revolution proved to be quite subversive to the monarchical system in Europe, and today liberalism and communism are subversive of each other.

The threat of an alien ideology is all the greater when its adherents are imbued with missionary fervor and, even more, when they receive support and encouragement from their government in efforts to extend the ideology abroad. Aggression by subversion is no more welcome than aggression by military means. The more threatening it becomes, the greater becomes the prospect of war.

It might be noted that domestic and international factors combine in creating a threat of war rising from subversive influences. A country with faith in its own ideology and hope for the future need have little fear of the subversive influence of an alien ideology, and international relations need not be troubled by a theoretical ideological conflict. However, a country without faith and hope, or a country with allies who are without faith and hope, has much to fear. International tensions arising out of an ideological conflict are as much a measure of domestic doubts and insecurities as of efforts from abroad to create revolution.

JUSTICE

All states profess to seek justice for themselves and to desire it for others. To the extent that international law is deemed to incorporate justice, support for justice becomes support for law and order. Where international law is deemed to be unjust, support for justice involves demands for change, and demands for change may lead to conflict and war.

Even within countries where there is at least vague agreement on standards of justice, it is often difficult to determine precisely what would be just in concrete circumstances. There are judicial struggles over what the law is and legislative struggles over what the law should be. These are struggles to determine the official definition of justice. Where there is little or no agreement on standards of justice, the struggles are naturally all the more intense and are all the more likely to be resolved on the basis of power. The official definition of justice then becomes a reflection of the desires of the strong.

The struggle over justice among countries is similar to the struggle over justice within countries. Where international law is deemed to incorporate justice, the struggle over the application of law can be a judicial matter. Where there is general agreement on standards of justice but belief that existing law scarcely reflects those standards, there is basis for negotiation and agreement. But where conceptions of justice are markedly different, resolution of such disputes as arise will occur on the basis of a power struggle which may take the form of war.

Among some countries, particularly among those with similar ideologies, standards of justice are likely to be similar, and there is a fair prospect that the struggle for justice will be conducted by peaceful means. Among other countries, particularly among those with radically differing ideologies, standards of justice are so divergent that the settlement of disputes becomes almost automatically a question of power, whether brought to bear in conjunction with diplomatic negotiations or on the battlefield.

Dedication to justice and the fact of differing conceptions of justice are well illustrated in statements made on successive days in June, 1945, by Premier Suzuki of Japan and by General Eisenhower. The war with Germany had already ended, but the war with Japan was still in progress. Premier Suzuki's statement was as follows: [9]

From the very beginning the Greater East Asia war has been a holy war. . . . "Our fundamental policy is based on justice and righteousness. . . ." This means that Japan is fighting a war to uphold the principle of human justice and we must fight to the last.

Eisenhower spoke the next day, presumably without knowing of Suzuki's statement. "This was a holy war. More than any other war in history, this war has been an array of the forces of evil against those of righteousness." [10]

There is no reason to impugn the sincerity of either spokesman. It is probable that both conscientiously believed what they said. When conceptions of justice held in different states are so contradictory, it is understandable that the pursuit of justice leads to international difficulties.

POWER

What Is Power?

In Chapter 1 we defined power as the ability to make one's will prevail, the ability to achieve desires. By this definition it is axiomatic that the possession of power is one of the objectives of states. The existence of a desire connotes the existence of a desire to achieve it, that is, it con-

[9] *New York Times*, June 10, 1945, p. 3, col. 2.
[10] *Ibid.*, June 11, 1945, p. 5, col. 4.

notes a desire for power. States which have desires seek power just as people who are hungry seek food.

This definition of power is a very broad one. Under it, power can take many forms and be exerted in many ways. Thus it might take the form of knowledge used to induce a foreign statesman to adopt a desired policy. It might take the form of a radio broadcasting station used to make a foreign people believe what one wants them to believe. It might take the form of cotton used in trade to give effect to a desire to import coffee. Obviously, it might also take military form.

Now power does take all these forms and many others, but, though it may be true to say that the struggle to produce cotton and the struggle to develop military might are both forms of a struggle for power, it is also a little confusing. For present purposes, therefore, we shall restrict the discussion to certain forms and expressions of power. Specifically, we shall discuss the extent to which states seek to develop and maintain an ability to enforce respect for their rights and obedience to their desires. Enforcement of respect and obedience might occur through economic or military pressures, including war, or through territorial aggrandizement, discussed above.

The Desire for Power
as an End and as a Means

States clearly desire some power in this narrower sense. Whether they want security or aggrandizement or national unity or prosperity or justice or almost anything else, the ability to enforce respect, if not obedience, is the surest basis for achieving it. A state which is unable to enforce respect for its rights lives at the mercy of its neighbors. They may, of course, permit it to survive; rivalries among the neighbors may prevent any one of them from attacking even a powerless state, or their adherence to certain principles of law or morality may operate for the benefit of the weak. However, states do not like to have to rely on such uncertain prospects if they can avoid it. They prefer to command power, and if their own power is inadequate for their purposes they are likely to seek allies. Concern for relative power position is regularly among the considerations that influence decisions on both domestic and foreign policy; especially in times of international tension, this concern may be the dominant factor in decision-making. Concern for power, in fact, is the irreducible common denominator of the foreign and domestic politics of states. Both a state seeking security and a state seeking aggrandizement must command power.

Not only is power necessary as a means for the achievement of objectives; it may well be an end in itself. It may become an end simply because it is pursued so regularly as a means and because it proves itself so regularly to be useful that it tends to take on value in itself. It may become an end, too, as a result of psychological forces at work in those who participate in the decision-making process.

The importance which states attach to power is demonstrated by the phrase "power politics," which has come to be used especially in connection with international relationships. We have already noted that, in truth, all politics is automatically power politics. But the phrase also has a special meaning, designating "the politics of force—the conduct of international relations by force or threat of force without consideration of right and justice." [11] The importance of power is demonstrated even more by the very fact that states are called powers. The terms *state* and *power* are used synonymously. We speak of world powers and great powers and small powers. "A Great [or a world] Power is a Power with general interests, and with such strength that it can attempt to advance or protect those interests in every sphere. . . . Small Powers are Powers with the means of defending only limited interests, and of most of them it is true that they possess only limited interests." [12] Great powers normally achieve (and lose) their status in war. The importance of power in politics is also attested by the universal view that, whatever else international politics may be, it is also a struggle for power.

How Much Power?

The question is, how much power? Is it absolute ability to command obedience and respect which is desired, or are there limits beyond which states do not care to go? The questions are similar to those raised above in connection with the discussion of aggrandizement as an objective.

Just as many have seen no limits to the craving for aggrandizement, so have many seen no limits to the lust for power. Whether attributing the lust for power to psychological or economic or political or other forces, some observers in all periods of history have taken the view that it is insatiable. During the Peloponnesian Wars, according to Thucydides, an Athenian spokesman declared,[13] "Of the gods we believe, and of men we know, that by a necessary law of their nature they rule wherever they can." Thomas Hobbes described [14] "a perpetual and restless desire for power after power, that ceaseth only in death," as "a general inclination of all mankind." Bertrand Russell asserts,[15] "Men desire to expand, and their desires in this respect are limited only by what imagination suggests as possible. Every man would like to be God. . . . Of the infinite desires of man, the chief are the desires for power and

[11] Wight, *op. cit.*, p. 11.

[12] *Ibid.*, pp. 18, 27.

[13] Thucydides' *History of the Peloponnesian War*, tr. by Richard Crawley (New York, Dutton, 1910), Bk. V, Chap. 17, #105, p. 397.

[14] Hobbes, *op. cit.*, p. 64.

[15] Bertrand Russell, *Power, a New Social Analysis* (New York, Norton, 1938), p. 11.

glory." Bertrand de Jouvenel asks rhetorically,[16] "Can it be doubted ... that Power administers to conquer and conquers to administer? The instinct of growth is proper to Power; it is a part of its essence."

Such generalizations, however, are somewhat too glib and simple to be true. Hobbes himself spoke only of an inclination of men, and not of an absolute law of human behavior; even then he modified his statement:

> Kings whose power is greatest turn their endeavours to the assuring it at home by laws, or abroad by wars; and when that is done there succeedeth a new desire; in some, of fame from new conquest; in others, of ease and sensual pleasure; in others, of admiration, or being flattered for excellence in some art, or other ability of the mind.

In short, as Hobbes saw it, kings pursued various objectives, including ease, sensual pleasure, admiration, and flattery; these appear to have little to do with a power quest. Bertrand Russell, too, spoke of the "infinite desires" of men, granting that there are others beside power and glory.

In fact, other desires than the desire for power do exist, and pursuit of them precludes an effort to maximize power. To revert to the formulations of Lasswell, listing various welfare and deference values,[17] it is clear that the pursuit of some of these values is often incompatible with the pursuit of unlimited power. The study of psychology reveals that human behavior is influenced by a whole galaxy of innate and acquired drives many of which militate against the concentration of all resources on an effort to develop maximum power.

Even in societies placing great emphasis on power, such as Germany under the Nazis, various forces interfere with a really total mobilization and an all-out drive for power. Attitudes toward the role of women generally preclude full exploitation of their power-potential. Popular demand for many of the comforts and luxuries of life cannot be wholly ignored even by the most power-hungry dictator. Personal rivalries, the pursuit of private interests, and class conflict are likely to impede achievement of the theoretical maximum of power.

True, there have been in history both "mad Caesars," with psychopathic cravings for power, and "hysterical Caesars" with psychopathic fears which led to defensive imperialism. Enough rulers have sought apparently unlimited power and territorial aggrandizement to give reason to suspect that they may exist today and will appear in the future. Still, there have also been many rulers so avid for the pleasures of life, and many governments so concerned with such values as prosperity and peace, that they have neglected the power of the state.

Perhaps the best statement is that governmental attitudes range be-

[16] Bertrand de Jouvenel, *On Power* (New York, Viking, 1949), p. 137.
[17] Cf. Chapter 8, above, p. 146.

tween two theoretical extremes, the one calling for an all-out struggle for maximum power and the other reflecting a complete indifference to power.[18] In practice, neither extreme is ever reached. Accurate methods for measuring attitudes contributing to the power drive have not been developed, but it is a fair guess that during most of the twentieth century the attitude of at least one or another of the great powers has been closer to the first extreme than to the second. And a drive for maximum power by one major state is of tremendous importance in influencing the policies of all states. Prudent governments do and must take care lest their relative power position becomes such as to preclude the effective defense of cherished values.

THE CLASSIFICATION OF STATES
BY MOTIVATION OR OBJECTIVE

The motivations and objectives of each state are bound to differ more or less from the motivations and objectives of every other state. Nevertheless, common elements do often exist which permit the classification of states into groups.

Power States and Welfare States

Sometimes states are divided into those which pursue power (guns) and those which pursue welfare (butter). The validity of the classification depends upon the thought that lies behind it. It is invalid and misleading if it rests on the assumption that an absolute distinction can be made between states on this basis. All states pursue power in some degree, which means that all of them give up butter to some extent for guns. Those known as welfare states may simply be those which are rich in resources; being rich, they can have guns, and butter too. In this situation, the power states may simply be those which cannot afford both. The classification may be a valid one, however, if it is thought of in relative rather than absolute terms. After all, states which are roughly equal in resources sometimes give varying degrees of emphasis to welfare and power, respectively, and the variation may reflect significant differences in values or ideologies.[19]

"Haves" and "Have-nots"

Some years ago it was common to classify states into the "haves" and the "have-nots"; the "haves," of course, were those states relatively rich in material resources and affording relatively high standards of living; the rest were "have-nots." The assumption was that the "haves" would,

[18] Arnold Wolfers, "The Pole of Power and the Pole of Indifference," *World Politics*, Vol. 4 (October, 1951), pp. 39-63.
[19] E. H. Carr, *The Twenty Years' Crisis 1919-1939* (London, Macmillan, New York, St. Martin's, 1949), pp. 119-120.

as a general rule, follow pacific and defensive policies, whereas the "have-nots" would be inclined toward aggression. This basis of classification, however, has fallen into disuse, and for good reasons.[20] Material resources and standards of living do not, in and of themselves, provide a reliable basis for classification or prediction. The poorest states have not historically been the most aggressive, nor have the richest states been the most pacific. Until very recent years, for example, China was an anvil rather than a hammer in international politics despite her poverty. Ethiopia, though poorer than Italy, was a victim of aggression and not the aggressor. Neither the Central Powers of World War I nor the Axis Powers of World War II were really "have-nots" in terms of relative standards of living. A little consideration suggests that the extremely poor scarcely can be aggressive, at least without outside help, for they do not have the wherewithal with which to fight. Moreover, there is no necessary relationship between actual standards of living and feelings of deprivation. Those who know of nothing better are likely to be apathetic in their poverty, whereas those who live fairly well may be bitterly discontented and aggressive if they think that they deserve a better lot and have hope of achieving it. It is not so much the nature of one's existence as the nature of one's aspirations which influence behavior.[21]

Satiated and Unsatiated States

Bismarck once described Germany as a "satiated" state, the inference being that states are sometimes "unsatiated." These terms have been used ever since. The assumption is that satiated states, like the "haves," pursue defensive and pacific policies, whereas the unsatiated, like the "have-nots," are aggressively inclined. The chief difference between the two bases of classification is that the question of having or not having relates simply to the objective facts of a state's situation, whereas the question of satiation also includes the attitude of a government toward those facts. Since foreign policies derive from governmental attitudes, the classification of states as satiated or unsatiated provides a somewhat better guide to their probable behavior.

Status Quo and Revisionist Powers

States are also sometimes classified as "status quo" or "revisionist" powers. Status quo powers follow policies designed generally to maintain an existing situation. They may or may not "have" much in this situation, and they may or may not be satiated, but they assume that any change would likely be to their disadvantage. The situation they want to

[20] Cf. Frederick Sherwood Dunn, *Peaceful Change* (New York, Council on Foreign Relations, 1937), pp. 4-8.
[21] Eric Hoffer, *The True Believer* (New York, Harper, 1951), pp. 8-9.

maintain is usually one which has been established by treaty. Status quo powers thus are supporters of existing law, and they pursue defensive policies. Revisionist powers, on the other hand, seek change. They may already "have" a great deal but are still unsatiated. The change which they seek usually relates to a treaty. They thus seek to overthrow at least some aspects of existing law, and they are inclined toward militant and aggressive policies. The terms *status quo* and *revisionist*, it might be noted, assume the existence of some settled or fixed situation. Following the Paris peace settlement after World War I, France could properly be called a status quo power, for she wanted to maintain the settlement. Later, Germany and Italy could properly be called revisionist powers, for they wanted to upset the settlement. Since World War II, however, so many situations remain fluid and unsettled that only confusion can result from trying to classify states according to these categories.

Status Quo and Imperialist Powers

The term *status quo power* has a somewhat different meaning in another context. Sometimes it is used as the antonym of the term *imperialist power*. In this context, a status quo power is one which seeks to preserve or restore or moderately improve a given power relationship. The given power relationship may be the existing one or one which existed at a certain time in the recent past. States following a status quo policy are thus states which aim to keep the order of power in what is regarded as a customary pattern or to restore it to that pattern after temporary disruption. They are, in general, defensive and pacific. An imperialist power, on the contrary, is defined in this context as one which seeks to upset a given power relationship for its own advantage. It regards its given or customary power position as unsatisfactory and inferior, and it aims to move from inferiority to superiority.[22] It is likely to be militant and aggressive. According to these definitions, as to those of the preceding paragraph, France was a status quo power in the interwar period, and Germany and Italy were imperialist. For the period since World War II, the non-communist part of the world should probably be classified as following status quo policies, whereas the Soviet Union and other communist states should probably be described as imperialist.

These classifications for the period since World War II are stated as probable rather than certain because they reflect a judgment of Western and Soviet aims and intentions. It is assumed that the West is trying to retain or restore what it regards as a customary order of power, and that the communist bloc is attempting to create a new order of power in which it will have a superior rather than an inferior position. This assumption

[22] Cf. Hans Morgenthau, *Politics Among Nations* (New York, Knopf, 1954), pp. 36-37.

might be wrong. The possibility calls attention to one of the crucial questions in conducting diplomacy: how to determine whether another state seeking change or adjustment is really imperialist and therefore potentially dangerous, or whether it can be satisfied and induced to support the status quo, defined either as a legal situation or as an order of power, once concessions have been made. This is a problem which will come up again in Part III.

Arnold Wolfers suggests a variation to this basis for classifying states. He describes states as pursuing three types of goals,[23] "goals of national self-extension," "goals of national self-preservation," and "goals of national self-abnegation." Goals of national self-extension call for change in the status quo, however defined, and therefore require great emphasis on power. Goals of self-preservation usually call for preservation of the status quo, and require varying degrees of concern for power. Goals of self-abnegation, such as the pursuit of human justice or universal well-being or the preservation of a civilization which transcends national frontiers, may or may not require concern for power. There might be sacrificial efforts which disregard considerations of power, or there might be sacrificial efforts among allies, for example, which are designed to facilitate the mobilization of maximum power against a common enemy. Goals of national self-abnegation may or may not be covers for the pursuit of goals of one of the first two types.

SUGGESTED READINGS

CARR, E. H., *The Twenty Years' Crisis 1919-1939* (London, Macmillan, New York, St. Martin's, 1949).

DE JOUVENEL, Bertrand, *On Power* (New York, Viking, 1949).

EMENY, Brooks, *Mainsprings of World Politics*, Headline Series, No. 42 (New York, Foreign Policy Association, 1943).

GROSS, Feliks, *Foreign Policy Analysis* (New York, Philosophical Library, 1954).

MACHIAVELLI, Niccolo, *The Prince* and *The Discourses* (New York, Modern Library, 1950).

HERZ, John H., *Political Realism and Political Idealism* (Chicago, The University of Chicago Press, 1951).

HOBBES, Thomas, *Leviathan* (Oxford, Blackwell, 1946).

RUSSELL, Bertrand, *Power, a New Social Analysis* (New York, Norton, 1938).

THUCYDIDES, *History of the Peloponnesian War*, tr. by Richard Crawley (New York, Dutton, 1910).

WIGHT, Martin, *Power Politics*, "Looking Forward" Pamphlets, No. 8 (London, Royal Institute of International Affairs, 1946).

WOLFERS, Arnold, "The Pole of Power and the Pole of Indifference," *World Politics*, Vol. 4 (October, 1951), pp. 39-63.

WOLFERS, Arnold, and MARTIN, Laurence W., *The Anglo-American Tradition in Foreign Affairs* (New Haven, Yale University Press, 1956).

[23] Wolfers, *op. cit.*, pp. 50-57.

Part III

METHODS AND LIMITING CONDITIONS

IN INTERNATIONAL POLITICS

Introductory Note

In ANALYZING the dynamics of international politics in Part II, we have been dealing with the motivations and objectives of those who make decisions in the name of the state. We have been focusing on the question, why states behave as they do.

In Part III we shall deal with the methods by which states pursue their objectives and the limits under which they act. We shall focus on the question, what states do and how they do it.

The dividing line between Part II and Part III is neither absolute nor clear-cut. Questions concerning the why, what, and how of behavior are closely interrelated. Ends and means interact on each other, and means may become ends. Nevertheless, as will be seen, there are differences in subject matter between the two Parts, and even where the subject matter is similar, there will be differences in focus and emphasis.

CHAPTER 10

Power

POWER, AS WE HAVE ALREADY SEEN, is both an end and a means in international politics. It is the capstone among the objectives which states pursue and the cornerstone among the methods which they employ. It is necessary to security, aggrandizement, peace, prosperity, justice, and to the achievement of most of the other objectives which states have. It is also a limiting condition in international politics, for a state can do no more than its power permits it to do. Both natural obstacles and the adverse power of other states prevent any one state from achieving omnipotence and therefore prevent a state from completely working its will.

We have already defined power. We have said that in the broadest sense it is the ability of a state to make its will prevail and that in a narrower sense it is the ability to enforce respect and command obedience. We have not yet analyzed the component elements of power, however defined. That is the purpose of this chapter, on the basis of the broader definition. What must a state have to be strong? What factors must be taken into account in calculating the power of a state? We are interested in present power, in mobilizable power, and in long-range trends, for statesmanship must be guided not only by existing facts but also by future probabilities. The truth of this and the reasons for it will be made clearer later on.

Power is a complex phenomenon. Many elements contribute to it or detract from it. We shall describe these elements under the following headings: (1) the geographic base; (2) the demographic base; (3) productive capacity: resources and plant; (4) transportation and communications; (5) scientific and inventive potentialities; (6) the political system; (7) the economic system; (8) strategic position; (9) ideas; (10) intelligence; (11) armed establishments and military leadership; and (12) the wisdom of leadership. This breakdown of the elements of power is rather arbitrary and involves some overlapping; other categories might also be used.[1] In addition to discussing these elements of power, we shall also discuss possible short cuts in the calculation of power and the fact of the relativity of power.

THE ELEMENTS OF POWER

The Geographic Base

Among the factors which govern the strength and weakness of states, climate, natural resources, topography, size, and location in relation to the oceans and other states play important roles.

1. *Climate and natural resources.* The importance of climate is rather obvious. The Antarctic and the Sahara are clearly not suitable for the development of great power. All desert and tropical regions are handicapped from a power point of view. A temperate climate is most propitious. "In general, history is made . . . between 25° and 60° north latitude." [2]

Natural resources for agricultural and industrial production are likewise of great importance. Fertile, arable soil is basic to agricultural production. Metallic ores, like iron ore, are vital. With modern technology, inanimate sources of energy like coal and oil are essential to all kinds of productive activity. A country without a good supply of such resources within its own borders is vulnerable to outside pressures, and a country without access to them is doomed to weakness. Unless and until rather drastic technological changes occur, it is almost unthinkable that great power could develop in areas such as the Near and Middle East, which nature has not provided with anything like a balanced and adequate supply of natural resources. Such countries as Britain, Germany, the U.S.S.R., and the United States have been great powers for a number of reasons; among them a supply of raw materials adequate for the development of strength has been of great significance. Sometimes, too, their power has rested on their ability to withhold certain resources from other states in need of them.

2. *Topography and frontiers.* The power of a state is also in part a function of topography. More specifically, topography may influence the size and shape of a state and the defensive-offensive potentialities of its frontiers. The influence of topography on size and shape is demonstrated

---

[1] For various contributions to a discussion of the question, why some states are strong and others weak, see Harold and Margaret Sprout, *Foundations of National Power* (New York, Van Nostrand, 1951), pp. 104-148. This book also contains excellent reading material on the power position of the various countries and regions of the world. See also Stephen B. Jones, "The Power Inventory and National Strategy," *World Politics*, Vol. 6 (July, 1954), pp. 421-452.

[2] Nicholas J. Spykman, "Geography and Foreign Policy, I," *American Political Science Review*, Vol. 32 (February, 1938), p. 41; see also the second installment of this study in the April, 1938, issue of the same journal.

by the fact that the expansion of many states is stopped by geographical obstacles, particularly by mountains and seas, and that where expansion occurs it tends to occur where the least serious natural obstacles exist. The location of the Pacific shore fixed the "manifest destiny" of the United States, and also fixed the practical limits of the eastward expansion of Russia. The Alps, the Pyrenees, and adjacent waters did much to fix the size and shape of France. States do not ordinarily expand beyond natural barriers that offer serious obstacles to an effective internal system of communication and transportation; where such expansion does occur, decentralization, or even disintegration, is likely to follow. It is no accident that Switzerland has a relatively decentralized system of government, and that imperial countries have had difficulty retaining control of overseas colonies.

The possession of strategically desirable frontiers is an obvious asset to the power of a state. For defensive purposes, mountain chains and oceans are desirable as boundaries. When Czechoslovakia was established as a state, its western boundary was placed in the Sudeten Mountains rather than on the Bohemian plain, even though this meant the inclusion of a large Germanic minority in the Slavic state; military-strategic considerations based on topography were more important than the principle of nationality. Hitler, thinking in terms of aggrandizement, insisted on the transfer of the Sudetenland to Germany—a transfer which left the remainder of Czechoslovakia in a virtually indefensible military position. Similarly, after World War I, Italy secured a boundary on the Brenner Pass in the Alps, even though this meant the inclusion within Italy of the Austrian province of South Tyrol. Today, Spain and Portugal are regarded as the continental European countries least likely to be occupied by the Red Army in the event of World War III, primarily because the Pyrenees constitute such an imposing obstacle to an invader. India and Pakistan are in a better power position than they otherwise would be because the Himalayan Mountains stand in the way of potential Soviet or Chinese invaders.

3. *Size and location.* Pure size is important to power. Great size does not necessarily assure great power, as Brazil attests, but it usually creates the possibility of great power. Great size commonly implies the presence of large expanses of arable land, a considerable variety and quantity of raw materials, and thus the capacity to sustain a large population. Liechtenstein and Luxembourg can scarcely expect ever to be great powers, if for no other reason than that their small size denies them the necessary economic and demographic base. In terms of military strategy, great size is important because it allows room for retreat and maneuver. Large states, when at war, can buy time with space, that is, they can retreat before the enemy, escaping crushing blows, and still have space left in which to mobilize power and organize for counterattack. Both China and

the Soviet Union did this in World War II; if they had not had great reaches of land at their disposal, they would surely have succumbed or would have had to establish governments-in-exile, as many smaller countries did. Hitler conquered far more Russian than Polish territory, but Russia still had space left, and Hitler's logistical problems increased with his conquests. Generally, small countries which were subjected to heavy attack in World War II were quickly overrun.

Geographic location is obviously significant to the power of a state, but generalizations on the point are hazardous. A given location may make either for strength or weakness, depending on time and circumstance. We must therefore deal with concrete examples, though few can be found which are representative of a class. Belgium and Poland have historically been in dangerous positions, being relatively small states located between powerful neighbors. Switzerland's position, though somewhat similar, has proved to be less dangerous. Britain, France, and the United States, possessing considerable populations and productive power, have undoubtedly derived advantage from their location on the Atlantic Ocean; Cuba, though likewise located on the Atlantic, has scarcely derived similar advantage from a power point of view. Britain is an island state, and this fact in combination with others has until recently made her relatively safe from invasion, but the insular character of Ceylon and the East Indies did not save them from conquest. Britain lies in close proximity to the maritime routes to the principal ports of Europe, and, with great naval power, she can use this location in imposing a blockade on those ports. She also derives power from the possession of Gibraltar, Malta, Singapore, and other points strategically placed in relation to important shipping routes. At the same time, a weak state located in a highly strategic area is more likely to suffer from the fact than to gain. Egypt, strategically located, was for decades under varying degrees of foreign control, whereas Ethiopia has remained independent in part because its territory was of such little strategic significance. Colombia lost Panama, and Panama itself was obliged to turn the Canal Zone over to the United States. A strategic location, thus, is likely to be a power asset to the strong, but a liability to the weak.

The United States derives defensive strength from its remoteness from other centers of great power; nevertheless, distance turns out to be a source of weakness when the problem is to bring American power to bear abroad. China's location was disadvantageous during World War II, when she was remote from her friends and close to a powerful enemy, but the same location has apparently become an advantage; as a Communist state, she is close to a powerful friend and remote from major enemies. The republics of the Caribbean and of Central America are so located as to be militarily helpless in the face of American power, yet their fate has been substantially different from the fate of the countries of eastern and southeastern Europe, which stood helpless in the face of Soviet power at the close of World War II. Many more statements like these could be made concerning the significance of geographic location to the power of states. They substantiate the rather obvious point that location is significant to power, but they hardly lead to a single sound generalization.

4. *The relevance of technological conditions.* The importance of topography, size, and location must be appraised in terms of other factors, and especially in terms of the level of technology achieved. With the developments of the last century in the fields of communication and transportation, rivers have almost lost significance as defensive bastions, and neither mountains nor oceans have the significance they once had. As late as World War II the United States and the heart of the Soviet Union were regarded as immune from attack, but now civil defense is an urgent problem both in Chicago and in Tomsk. A few years ago, attack across the Arctic was out of the question, but now it is simply assumed that the Arctic will be a route for aerial attacks when and if World War III comes. The prospect that the Red Army might, like the *Wehrmacht,* have difficulty crossing the English Channel is of little comfort, considering the fact that bombers and guided missiles carrying atomic warheads can wipe out a substantial portion of Britain's population.

5. *Generalizations on the significance of location.* Despite difficulties, generalizations on the political significance of geographic location are sometimes made. Among the simplest of them is the assumption that in Europe, down to World War II, a state would be an enemy of its neighbor and a friend of its neighbor's neighbor; for example, France would be an enemy of Germany, but a friend of Germany's neighbor, Poland (or Russia). The example itself is true, but the generalization is hardly sound. Germany and Austria-Hungary were friends even though they were neighbors; so were Britain and France; and so were Austria-Hungary and Italy. France was not a friend of Austria-Hungary, even though the latter was its neighbor's neighbor.

It is sometimes said that since World War II this generalization can be reversed, indicating that a state will be the friend of its neighbor and the enemy of its neighbor's neighbor. Thus the states of Western Europe group themselves together in alignment with the United States, and the states of Eastern Europe group themselves together in alignment with the Soviet Union. Again the example is true, but the generalization must be qualified. Turkey is aligned with the West, even though it is adjacent to the Soviet Union. Similarly, Iran and Finland, though contiguous to the Soviet Union, have avoided absorption into the Soviet bloc, whatever their relationship to the West may be. Switzerland and Sweden remain neutral.

At the close of World War I, Sir Halford Mackinder attempted a much more sweeping generalization. He thought that [3] "the grouping of lands and seas, and of fertility and natural pathways, is such as to lend itself to the growth of empires, and in the end of a single world-empire." He pictured the continents of Europe, Asia, and Africa as a great "World-Island," having North America, South America, and Australia as its satellites. Within the world-island he found a "Heartland," including the vast area lying east and north of a line running from the Baltic Sea through the Lower Danube, the Black Sea, Asia Minor, Iran, Tibet, and Mongolia. In other words, the heartland included roughly the present Soviet Union, with additions to the West and South. It was "the region to which, under modern conditions, sea power can be refused access." [4] Within the heartland, according to Mackinder, the key area was eastern Europe, and he declared that when the statesmen of the victorious powers of World War I were shaping the terms of peace "some airy cherub should whisper to them from time to time this saying:" [5]

> Who rules East Europe commands the Heartland:
> Who rules the Heartland commands the World-Island:
> Who rules the World-Island commands the World.

Mackinder, however, could present no really convincing evidence to support such geographical determinism. Nicholas J. Spykman, examining Mackinder's dictum, labeled it false, and proposed one of his own: [6] "Who controls the Rimland [i.e., the peripheral countries of the Eurasian land mass] rules Eurasia; who rules Eurasia controls the destinies of the world." Both assertions, however, rest on many assumptions which may or may not be, or remain, sound, for the elements of power are not all determined by geography.

Mackinder's writings had considerable influence on Karl Haushofer, a leading German exponent of *Geopolitik* in Hitler's time. But geopolitics, as interpreted by Haushofer and his disciples, was less a study of how geography affects power and international politics than a study of how knowledge of geography might serve to promote the territorial aggrandizement of Germany.[7] It is thus scarcely relevant to an analysis of the component elements of power.

[3] Sir Halford J. Mackinder, *Democratic Ideals and Reality* (New York, Holt, 1942), p. 2.

[4] *Ibid.*, p. 110.

[5] *Ibid.*, p. 150.

[6] Nicholas J. Spykman, *The Geography of the Peace* (New York, Harcourt, Brace, 1944), p. 43; see also H. W. Weigert's critique of Mackinder in Sprout, *op. cit.*, pp. 174-179.

[7] See Derwent Whittlesey, *German Strategy of World Conquest* (New York, Farrar & Rinehart, 1942), esp. pp. 79-101.

The Demographic Base

1. Power and manpower. Obviously, although it would be wrong to say that states possess power in proportion to their population, they can scarcely be great powers unless they have large populations. India is not a great power, though its population is huge. Among the factors in the decline of France is the fact that Germany has outgrown her in terms of population. Britain, too, has declined relatively, though the support which she receives from overseas populations in the Commonwealth and Empire buoys her up. A major element in the power of the Soviet Union and in the power-potential of China is the great reservoir of manpower at their disposal. The United States is in a good position in terms of population, though it needs the support of allies if it is to come close to matching the manpower of the communist states.

Differences in sex-distribution in the population of various countries are so slight that they have little impact on power relationships, though there may be significant disparity in the productive employment of women. Similarly, among the advanced countries standards of health are so nearly uniform that power relationships are largely unaffected; among the major powers China perhaps faces the greatest health problem, with a high proportion of its population more or less weakened by disease. Differences in age-distribution are sometimes considerable. Both migration and differential birth and death rates leave some countries with a high proportion of the population in the lower-age groups and other countries with a high proportion in the upper-age groups. People in the upper-age groups constitute a much higher proportion of the population in the countries of Western Europe, for example, than in the countries of Eastern Europe.[8] The facts about age-distribution are better known than their consequences. One consequence of some importance is that there will be a higher proportion of men of military age in a young than in an old population. But which type of population will really be more productive and which will possess in greater measure the other skills and virtues contributing to power are questions about which too little is known. The usual assumption is that a younger population will be more productive and stronger.

Perhaps most important of all, the skills of a population must be considered in calculating a country's power. An illiterate population untutored in modern agricultural methods and unable to use modern machinery provides a poor base for power. One of the major problems of the Soviet Union has been to reduce these sources of weakness, and

[8] Frank W. Notestein and others, *The Future Population of Europe and the Soviet Union* (Geneva, League of Nations, 1944), esp. pp. 108-116; Warren S. Thompson, *Population Problems* (New York, McGraw-Hill, 1953), esp. Chapters VI and XVII.

the same problem in even more intense form confronts both China and India, to say nothing of many of the smaller countries of the world. In some degree, it confronts all countries. The complicated weapons of modern war can neither be manufactured nor be maintained, and armed forces cannot be effectively commanded, unless a considerable portion of the population is literate and in possession of various mechanical and other skills.

2. *Population projections.* For the purpose of projecting power calculations into the future, which all statesmen must do, population projections are useful. Such projections, based on hypothetical future birth and death rates suggested by past trends, indicate roughly the probable size and age-distribution of a population some twenty or more years hence. One of the overbrooding facts of the present East-West struggle is that such estimates reveal the prospect of an increasing manpower advantage for the communist states.[9]

3. *Governmental efforts to increase the population.* A few governments have deliberately sought to bring about a population increase with a view to enhancing their power. A number of complementary policies are available for this purpose. Governments can forbid abortion and the manufacture and sale of contraceptives. They can adopt or improve public health programs. They can adopt any or all of a wide variety of economic measures designed to encourage marriage and the birth of children; among them are discriminatory tax policies, monetary grants to parents upon the birth of a child, wage differentials based on the number of children whom the worker supports, loans to newlyweds which can be paid off through child-bearing, and so on. They can designate as "mother heroines" women who bear many children, and adopt other propaganda devices to encourage an increase in the size of families. They can forbid emigration, urge the return of those who have emigrated in the past, and encourage new immigration. Italy under Mussolini and Germany under Hitler provide outstanding examples of such policies.

Especially where death rates have been high, public health measures may have a sharp impact on population trends. In countries which are attractive to immigrants, appropriate immigration policies may likewise produce a significant population increase. It is much more questionable, however, whether policies deliberately aimed at increasing the birth rate have actually been successful. Nowhere have they been pursued rigorously enough or long enough to permit valid conclusions; such minor increases as were recorded in Hitler's Germany may well have reflected influences other than those which the government deliberately brought to bear.[10]

[9] Notestein, *op. cit.*, pp. 117-138.
[10] Thompson, *op. cit.*, Chapter XXII.

Productive Capacity: Resources and Plant

Power requires production. A country which lacks resources and plant for the production of great quantities of goods is doomed to weakness; a country with extensive resources and a well-developed plant for utilizing them possesses a major element of power. It is likely to be all the stronger if its productive capacity is high not only in absolute but also in per capita terms. At a given time, the human and material resources of a country may or may not be employed to any considerable extent for the maintenance of military power, but the resources for this must be available if the state is to possess a commanding position on the world stage. As Sherman Kent puts it, the amount of fat, slack, and flexibility present in an economy is important to the mobilization of military power. By fat he means the possession of various kinds of resources in such abundance that a substantial proportion of them can be diverted to military purposes without intolerable sacrifice. By slack he means latent, unused productive power: "such things as the 40-hour week, twelve to sixteen years of education for youth, small proportion of women in the labor force, unemployment of both labor and capital, only partial utilization of equipment, etc." By flexibility he means "the capacity of the economy to beat plowshares and pruning hooks into swords, and that in jig time." [11]

Productive capacity is important not only as it contributes to the actual or potential military power of the country possessing it; it is also important, as we shall see in Chapter 13, because it provides a basis for exerting influence on other states. Especially during and since World War II, for example, the United States has used its productive capacity as a major weapon, selling or giving goods to favored states and withholding goods from others. The discriminatory treatment of other states in economic matters has proved to be a major weapon in the power struggle.

The correlation between productive capacity and power is not necessarily direct, any more than is the correlation between population and power. To possess power states must not only produce, but they must also utilize what they produce for power purposes. During World War II both Japan and the Soviet Union developed power which, by western standards, was greatly disproportionate to their production of material things, largely because they used so great a portion of their output for military purposes. Similarly the production of goods gives a state an opportunity to manipulate international economic relationships for power purposes, but taking effective advantage of the opportunity depends on human purpose and ingenuity. Productive capacity sets limits

[11] Sherman Kent, *Strategic Intelligence for American World Policy* (Princeton, Princeton University Press, 1949), p. 51.

to the level of power that can be achieved but does not govern with any precision the level that will be achieved.

Transportation and Communications

Railway and highway networks, navigable rivers and canals, air transport, and the various kinds of electronic communication devices are all elements of a country's power. Transportation and communication facilities are essential to production, to the movement of goods and men, to the coordination of domestic activities, and to the preservation of unity. The greatest of states would become helpless almost immediately if all mechanical means of transportation and communication could somehow be suddenly destroyed. In fact, it is scarcely conceivable that large countries such as the United States and the Soviet Union could even remain united for long if the integrating forces based on transportation and communication systems should disappear. Questions of logistics (procuring needed materials, and delivering them to the points where they are needed) are among the major problems of war; their solution depends in part on the facilities that are available for transportation and communication.

Scientific and Inventive Potentialities

Just as the present power of a state depends to quite an extent on inventions and scientific discoveries of the past, so does its power-potential depend on the inventions and scientific discoveries of the present and future. Suppose, for example, that in 1930 the states which later became allies in World War II had somehow been compelled to put a stop to all new inventions and discoveries within their borders, and Germany had continued to press scientific investigations to the limit. Presumably, the Allied powers would then have fought World War II (if they had dared to fight it at all) without radar and without many other electronic devices. The aircraft and other weapons and vehicles of 1930 would not have been substantially improved, and new ones would not have been developed. Atomic weapons would not have become available to them. Antibiotics would not have been discovered, and other developments relating to public health would not have occurred. In Germany the situation would have been different. German aircraft would have developed so as to give Hitler mastery of the skies over Europe and Britain. German weapons and vehicles would almost certainly have become superior to those at the disposal of Britain and the United States. Had the war lasted, Germany might first have developed atomic weapons. Although certainty in such matters is not possible, the odds are that Germany would have won the war, laying Britain, the Soviet Union, and the whole continent at her feet. If so, the inference is that a decade of Allied research meant the difference between victory and defeat.

Now suppose that in 1946 the West had imposed a moratorium on further inventions and scientific discoveries and the Soviet Union had taken an opposite course. What would the effect have been on power relationships today? At the least, the West would have no thermonuclear weapons, no weapons depending on fission other than the atomic bomb itself, and nothing but very primitive guided missiles and jet aircraft. Again, it is quite conceivable that less than a decade, during which scientific research occurred on one side but not on the other, might have tipped the scales of military power.

Assuming that not all inventions and scientific discoveries have yet been made, it seems likely that the same considerations may operate for the indefinite future. Although it is not to be expected that any state would put a complete stop to scientific progress, as suggested in the examples above, governments may well differ in the extent and effectiveness of their attention to the problem. It is a sobering thought that Hitler would probably have won World War II and that the continent of Europe might now be under his heel had some twist of fate put atomic weapons in his hands at Christmas time, let us say, in 1941. It is sobering to think of Sir Winston Churchill's remark crediting the safety of Europe in the postwar years to the American monopoly of atomic weapons. Such thoughts illustrate the possibility that both the distribution of power among states and the course of subsequent history may be drastically affected if one side or the other neglects science or manages somehow to bring off a great scientific or inventive coup.

The Political System

Effectiveness of governmental organization and administration within a state is another element of its power. How stable is the government? Does it exercise effective control over its entire territory and command the loyalty of those under its jurisdiction? To what extent, if at all, are its operations impeded by factional or party strife? To what extent is it free, in terms of the constitution and in terms of public opinion, to do those things which concern for the power position of the state may demand? Do the various agencies of government cooperate well with each other? Does the government command knowledge of the resources and capacities of the country sufficient to permit it to exploit and allocate resources wisely? Is it organized so as to be able to reach decisions with reasonable speed? Is the decision-making process one which gives reasonable assurance that decisions will be wise? Does the administrative structure facilitate efficient operations? Are the civil servants trustworthy and competent?

Questions such as these often lead to different answers in relation to different countries. Some, such as Britain, emerge from scrutiny in a favorable light, but weaknesses are revealed in many. For decades, China was weak because, among other reasons, the central government lacked effective control over major portions of the country. Political power in France in recent decades has been divided among a number of political parties. This has not only led to frequent cabinet crises but has rendered it difficult for the French government to pursue positive and resolute policies. Political power in the Soviet Union is concentrated in the hands of one party, which is the major unifying force in the state. "If anything were ever to occur to disrupt the unity and efficacy of the Party as a political instrument, Soviet Russia might be changed overnight from one of the strongest to one of the weakest and most pitiable of national societies." [12] Relatively new governments, such as those of India, Pakistan, and Indonesia, are commonly handicapped by the inexperience of many of their political leaders and civil servants.

Whether dictatorship or democracy is best for a country from a power point of view is a question on which opinions differ. The usual argument in favor of dictatorships is that they can act with speed and with whatever consistency or flexibility the situation seems to demand. The usual argument in favor of democracies in connection with power politics is that public criticisms and widespread participation in the decision-making process make it more probable that decisions will be sound. Both arguments are questionable. Sometimes democracies act with greater speed than a dictator, and sometimes a dictator may act more wisely than a democracy. The evidence is not sufficient to permit the establishment of a general rule. In World Wars I and II the democratic regimes seem generally to have fared better than those which were autocratic or dictatorial, excepting the Soviet Union. However, prolonged war or prolonged international tension tends to undermine democracy and to accentuate movements for regimentation and dictatorial controls.[13]

The Economic System

Effective economic organization is likewise important. To what extent do the economic system and surrounding practices stimulate and facilitate economic development? Would changed practices substantially increase production? How effective are the stimulants to inventiveness and ingenuity, and to the making of investments which involve risk? How does the per capita rate of production compare with that prevailing in similar industries in other countries? Is the economic system reasonably stable, or is it subject to debilitating crises? To what extent do relationships between various groups involved in production, for example, management and labor, involve actual and potential cooperation or strife?

[12] George F. Kennan, "The Sources of Soviet Conduct," reprinted in his *American Diplomacy, 1900-1950* (Chicago, The University of Chicago Press, 1951), p. 125.
[13] Quincy Wright, *A Study of War* (Chicago, The University of Chicago Press, 1942) Vol. II, pp. 833-848.

Is the system flexible enough to permit rapid and effective conversion to war purposes? To what extent will peacetime economic practices also serve power purposes, and to what extent must new practices be inaugurated and tested when and if the maximum mobilization of power becomes the object?

Again, questions such as these lead to different answers in relation to different countries, and thus are suggestive of actual or potential power differentials. Some countries are economically stultified, whereas others are surging forward in terms of capital investment and economic development. Production, both on an absolute and on a per capita basis, varies tremendously between countries. Some countries are plagued by industrial strife far more than others, though even where open strife does not appear there may be considerable underlying discontent, which is potentially significant to power. Most major countries have by now become experienced in some degree of economic planning, which has proved to be vital if military power is to be sharply increased, but differentials still exist in the acceptability of planning and the skill with which it is handled.

It is, of course, a major question whether socialist or relatively free economic systems will in the long run provide a better base for state power. Marxists contend that "capitalist" countries inevitably experience periodic depressions and that they are doomed to weakness and ultimate destruction. Exponents of free enterprise make analogous dire predictions concerning socialism. The issue may well prove to be a fateful one. Should the American economy seriously falter in the next several decades while the Soviet economy booms, or vice versa, the effect might be decisive to the outcome of the East-West struggle.

Strategic Position

Strategic position is in part an aspect of the elements of power already discussed. We have seen that geography has definite implications for the military-strategic position of a country and that resources and supplies may govern a country's strategic position from an economic point of view; it may be able to exert influence or pressure on other states simply by regulating its international trade.

There are numerous other factors which also affect the strategic position of a country, whether for purposes of persuasion or coercion. The variety of counters that can be employed in international bargaining, and the variety of leverages that can be used for coercive purposes, is almost endless. Illustrations from interpersonal relations may shed light on the point. A dentist is in a good strategic position in relation to a person with a toothache. A skilled workman is in a good strategic position when two employers are in urgent need of his services. A person with a legal right to a piece of property is in a good strategic position in relation to another person who is desperately eager to obtain the property and who restricts himself to legal methods. A college student requesting tuition money from his father is in a good strategic position if the father has the money and is committed to the desirability of a college education. A blackmailer may hold a good strategic position, derived from knowledge or documents which he possesses. A kidnapper is in a good strategic position as long as the kidnapped person is at his mercy.

Similar situations occur in international politics. One state may derive strategic advantage from the commitment of another to legal or moral principles or by playing on the desires, interests, fears, or aversions of another; it may derive advantage from the rivalries of others. Panama, though physically far weaker than the United States, can bargain effectively with the United States concerning air bases outside the Canal Zone because its legal position is impregnable and because the United States is committed to law observance. Western Germany, though unarmed, can negotiate effectively with the West because it possesses manpower and other bargaining counters which the West regards as valuable. After the Korean armistice, Syngman Rhee could bargain with the United States on the basis of the threat that unless he received concessions he would precipitate a renewal of the war. The Soviet Union at the time of the collapse of Germany in World War II could bargain concerning the fate of Eastern Europe and certain Far Eastern matters more effectively than otherwise because of the American desire to secure Soviet help and to reduce the loss of American lives in connection with the defeat of Japan. Communist China could intervene in the Korean War and give aid to the rebels in Viet Nam because of fears in the West that drastic action against China might bring on World War III. Iran could nationalize the Anglo-Iranian Oil Co. and defy a militarily more powerful Britain both because British military intervention might have been countered by the Soviet Union and because it would have cost Britain good will in many parts of the world. Britain, in turn, could take advantage of its control of oil tankers and shipping lanes to exclude Iranian oil from the world markets and so induce Iran to come to terms. The United States, militarily preponderant in the British Isles during part of World War II, might conceivably have made Britain an American colony; the probability that few, if any, Americans thought of doing this or would have wanted to do it was an asset in Britain's strategic position.

The list of such situations could be expanded indefinitely. Often the ability of a state to make its will prevail, that is, to exercise power, may have little to do with its command over violence. Countries which are physically small and weak sometimes occupy a strategic position of some sort which permits them virtually to dictate terms to great powers, or they can negotiate without regard to military power relationships, knowing that the character of the issue or of surrounding circumstances is such that military power will not be resorted to. Switzerland, for example, knows with practical certainty that the United States will not use military power in an effort to bring about a reduction of Swiss trade barriers. This means that great powers sometimes find themselves in situations where vast armed strength does them little good. However, governments must be cautious in relying on a strategic position which is not based on physical strength. Pushed too far, the physically strong may flout the law or moral principle, or may sacrifice some hopes and forget some fears, in order to get what they want.

Ideas

Napoleon is said to have taken the view that the pen is mightier than the sword. Machiavelli's observation was somewhat different: that all armed prophets have conquered, and unarmed prophets have failed. Some endorse the epigram that you can't stop ideas with bullets, whereas others observe that, since ideas are commonly spread by means of bullets, they might also be stopped in the same way. Certainly the fate of communist ideas would have been somewhat changed had Kerensky commanded enough bullets to prevent the Bolsheviks from seizing power in Russia in 1917, or had other countries intervened against the Bolsheviks in a more determined fashion in 1918-1919, or had Hitler won World War II. It was bullets which stopped the extension of communism to South Korea after the North Korean attack in 1950.

Whether the pen is more or less mighty than the sword, it clearly has might. Ideas and ideologies are elements in the power of a state.[14] In the first place, the ideas that a government champions do a good deal to determine the extent of popular sympathy and support for it at home and abroad. In the second place, ideas influence the development and use of command over power and violence.

To be strong, a government must stand for ideas which command support at least at home, and it will be stronger if they also command support abroad. We have already noted the role of nationalism in providing unity, and therefore strength, for the nation-state. Where a nation is not yet united, the appeal to nationalism may strengthen it in a struggle to redeem an Irredenta, and by the same token the appeal is likely to weaken the state which includes the Irredenta. Colonial peoples derive strength from the appeal of nationalism, and by the same token imperial countries are weakened. We have noted that the ideologies of liberalism, fascism, and communism have international appeal. Hitler took advantage of this fact by organizing fifth columns abroad, seeking to use them as adjuncts of German power. Soviet leaders have done the same thing, creating a world-wide network of communist parties which

[14] Bertrand Russell, *Power, a New Social Analysis* (New York, Norton, 1938), pp. 145-156.

are loyal to Moscow largely because of belief and faith in the ideas which Moscow champions. Liberal governments have not generally sought to organize adherents abroad in a formal fashion, but they engage in propaganda designed to win them foreign sympathy and support.

Ideas may also weaken a state. Nazism certainly aroused more antagonism and hostility abroad than sympathy and support. It is perhaps too early to say what the result will be for Soviet communism in the long run, but certainly the advantage from a power point of view is not all on Moscow's side. Neither does liberalism always evoke a positive response.

The means which a state has at its disposal for advertising and propagating its ideology should be counted, as well as the ideology itself, among the elements in its power position. Thus the facilities employed in Voice of America broadcasts are elements of American power; similar facilities, as well as foreign communist parties, are elements of Soviet power.

Closely intertwined with ideas as a source of power is consent. Where consent is given, the state may make its will prevail without coercion. Efforts to coerce are themselves more likely to succeed if at least some of the interested parties consent that they are legally or morally justified. Opposition will at least be allayed, and positive support may be forthcoming.[15]

As suggested above, ideas not only help to determine the extent of popular sympathy and support for a government, but they also influence the development and use of command over power and violence. As an extreme illustration, suppose that the people and government of a state adopt a completely liberal and humanitarian outlook; they believe in the brotherhood of man and seek to promote the welfare of men on the basis of the "golden rule." Violence and bloodshed are regarded as evil. Now suppose the opposite: that the people and government of the same state reject liberal and humanitarian virtues. Whether for the greater glory of Allah or for the vindication of the rights of a master race or for the liberation of the peoples of the world from capitalism and imperialism, they are determined to impose their rule wherever possible and are unscrupulous on the question of methods. They regard violence as inevitable and aversion to violence as a sign of weakness. They are contemptuous of systems of law or morality which stand in their way. They are willing to shed unlimited quantities of blood to achieve their goal.

Which of these two sets of ideas would probably contribute most to the power of the state? The answer is not certain. Brutal and bloody aggressiveness might arouse so much antagonism as to be self-defeating, as Hitler learned. Yet, barring this possibility, it seems likely that the

[15] Louis J. Halle, *Civilization and Foreign Policy* (New York, Harper, 1955), pp. 53-82.

state will have more power if it is inspired by militant and aggressive rather than by pacific and humanitarian ideas.

Intelligence

We are not using the word *intelligence* here to refer to the mental ability of political leaders, though this clearly would have something to do with the power position of the state. Rather, in this connection the word *intelligence* refers to knowledge and to the activities designed to produce knowledge. The knowledge referred to is not all knowledge, of course, but rather whatever knowledge will contribute to the wisdom of governmental decisions concerning foreign affairs. As Sherman Kent puts it in relation to American intelligence operations, the aim is to produce "the kind of knowledge our state must possess regarding other states in order to assure itself that its cause will not suffer nor its undertakings fail because its statesmen and soldiers plan and act in ignorance." [16]

Such knowledge is power. This is most obvious in time of war, when advance knowledge of the time, place, and strength of an enemy attack may contribute more to victory in the battle than will an armored division. Similarly, knowledge of specific weaknesses of the enemy may contribute more to defeating him than will many bomber wings. It is not so obvious, but it is nevertheless true, that knowledge may also be power in times of peace. Suppose that the object is to strengthen or weaken a country economically or militarily. The activities which ensue must not be aimless. Intelligence must provide knowledge of the particular things which it is feasible to do and which will most effectively promote the objective; in the absence of such knowledge, the objective is not likely to be achieved. Suppose that the object is to induce another state to accept a treaty of alliance. Again knowledge may be power. In fact, the very decision to seek the alliance is presumably based on intelligence reports to the effect (*a*) that the power position of the state is weaker than it should be in view of the intentions and capabilities of a potential enemy, and (*b*) that the particular alliance sought would significantly improve the situation. Once negotiations get under way, the negotiator who knows nothing of the fears and hopes and capabilities of the country with which he is dealing is in a difficult position indeed. He cannot tell what he can reasonably demand and what he may be obliged to concede. He cannot tell what timing to employ, what bargaining counters are available and useful, what promises or threats may be effective. Failure in such a situation is to be expected. Conversely, a negotiator who is fully cognizant of all relevant data is much more likely to succeed.

Put more broadly, a government without an effective and reliable

[16] Kent, *op. cit.*, p. 3.

intelligence service may go without warning of potential dangers, and thus may fail either to forestall them or to prepare itself against them, or it may become the victim of false fears, and might even plunge itself and others into unnecessary war. Governments which are blind and deaf, which fail to see and hear, live dangerously, if they survive at all. Knowledge may not provide omnipotence, but it enhances the prospect that objectives will be wisely selected and effectively promoted.

Armed Establishments and Military Leadership

One of the more obvious facts about power is that it is expressed, among other ways, in armed establishments and given its ultimate test in war. States commonly maintain armed establishments even in time of peace, and expand them substantially in time of war.

The problem of calculating the actual and potential power of an armed establishment without actually testing it on the battlefield is a complex one, for so many elements are involved—including almost all those which we are discussing under other headings. However, certain restricted aspects of the problem might be noted. The actual number of men under arms, the availability of trained and untrained reserves, the quality and quantity of weapons and other equipment on hand and potentially available, the training and morale of personnel, the teamwork of the various branches of the armed forces, and the quality of military leadership are all of vital importance. So is the vulnerability of the state to specific forms of military action, such as blockade and atomic bombardment. Such general statements can easily be made, but they by no means solve the problem of appraising military power. For example, what is the effect on total military power of different ratios of civilian to military manpower? What proportion of men under arms and what proportion left in civilian pursuits will provide maximum power? What is the effect on power of different methods of handling the problem of reserves? Is it better from a power point of view to give, say, three years of training to half the military manpower available, or eighteen months of training on a universal basis? So far as weapons are concerned, which ones are likely to be most emphasized in the next war and how will they be used? Which ones are actually available and in what quantity? How quickly and how much can production of weapons be expanded? To what extent should resources be tapped to stockpile weapons, and to what extent should they be employed in a program of research and development for the purpose of producing better weapons? What allocation of resources between the various branches of the armed forces is most likely to meet the needs of future war? What degree of cooperation and what degree of friction among the army, navy, and air force can be expected? Are the staff officers planning imaginatively and realistically for future war, or simply planning in terms of the last war? What kinds of planning and what kinds of strategies are most likely to pay off when and if war comes?

Military men, intelligence agents, and others are constantly seeking answers to such questions. They must be answered as a part of the effort to determine what the actual and potential power position of a state is. That they are difficult to answer, and that reliable answers can scarcely be counted upon, seems plain.

Lest the task of appraising armed establishments be made to appear even more complex and difficult than it is, note might be made of the fact that certain kinds of significant knowledge are ordinarily obtainable. For example, each country knows with some degree of accuracy how many divisions others have under arms and what the fire power of a division is; each one knows, at least roughly, what the size and composition of the air and naval forces of the others are. Each knows within limits what weapons the others have available or in prospect, and what military strategies and tactics appear to find favor. The knowledge shared by both the United States and the Soviet Union that each possesses both thermonuclear weapons and aircraft capable of delivering them to all the major civilian and military centers of the other constitutes considerable knowledge of reciprocal military capabilities.

The Wisdom of Leadership

We have mentioned leadership as an element of power in connection with the military establishment. It is even more important in the political sphere, for it is in this sphere that the most fateful policy decisions are made, including decisions on high military strategy. Political leaders determine in what proportions to allocate resources between military and civilian programs, that is, how great the military-power-in-being should be. They allocate appropriations among the branches of the armed services. They determine when to seek alliances, with which states to seek them, and on what terms. They decide when and what to concede in relations with other states, and whether and when to stand firm. They declare war and make peace. What they do or fail to do may have a fundamental and lasting impact on the power of the state and, for that matter, on the whole course of history.

Illustrations of the point abound. Of course, many changes in the power positions of states have resulted from forces of history completely beyond the control of the political leaders of any one country or time, but usually there are alternatives to the decisions which statesmen make. Suppose, for example, that the United States had joined the League of Nations and participated actively in efforts to promote security and peace in Europe and the world thereafter. Suppose that Britain's leaders had supported Poincaré of France in a vigorous enforcement of the Treaty of Versailles. Suppose that neighboring countries had taken mil-

itary action against Hitler's Germany at the time Hitler announced
German rearmament or at the time of the remilitarization of the Rhineland. Suppose that toward the close of World War II American intelligence estimates concerning the need for Soviet support against Japan
had been more accurate, and that American leaders had then taken a
firmer stand against Soviet policies in Eastern and Southeastern Europe.
Suppose that President Truman had not ordered American intervention
in the Korean war or had sided with those who opposed the development of thermonuclear weapons. Defining political leadership as inclusive of both executive and legislative personnel, it is reasonable to assume
that most or all of the above-mentioned alternatives to choices actually
made were within the realm of the possible, and had such alternative
policies been pursued, the distribution of power among states would
today undoubtedly be much different than it is. Hitler's decisions led
to a series of events after 1933 which first transformed Germany from
a weak into a very powerful state and then transformed her once more
from a dominant European power to a defeated, divided, and virtually
helpless power. Serious internecine strife among the leaders of the Kremlin might conceivably lead to a similar transformation in the power
position of the Soviet Union.

Thus calculations of power must include evaluations of the actual and
potential quality of a country's leadership. A country is bound to be
stronger and to have a greater power potential if it is led by men of
strength and wisdom who are united in service to what is regarded as
the national cause than if it is led by those who are weak or rash or
stupid or divided against themselves in pursuit of personal or partisan
advantage. The capacity of a political system to bring able leaders to
the top and then actually permit them to lead is one of the tests of its
effectiveness from a power point of view.

SHORT CUTS IN THE CALCULATION OF POWER

The above analysis of the elements of power is stated in very broad
terms; a thorough effort to estimate the power of a given state would
require the categories listed to be broken down in considerable detail.
The task would be huge, so huge that there is a temptation to avoid it
in favor of short cuts. In truth, there are so many uncertainties even in
thorough calculations that some short cuts may produce results that have
an equal degree of reliability. Perhaps the best short cut is to consider
the record of a state in wars which have actually been fought. Recent
war is especially useful in this connection; barring special circumstances,
the odds are that the factors which made for great strength or great
weakness in a recent war will persist and will thus make for similar
strength or weakness again. That this short cut is not always reliable,

however, has been proved again and again; an example is the changed fortunes of France and Russia in the two world wars.

Steel production and productive capacity are also often considered as yardsticks of power, or at least as yardsticks of power-potential. The device has some merit, too. Steel is a vital sinew of strength. Quantitatively, it is probably the most important element in the weapons and equipment with which armies are provided. Moreover, the amount produced, measured in both absolute and per capita terms, is likely to reflect a great many of the attributes of the state: its resources of many kinds, its technological level and the skills of its population, its manufacturing capacity. Again, however, this index of power is not always reliable, for the proportion of steel that is or can be devoted to power purposes may vary considerably from country to country.

The United States Department of State has made computations on the production and consumption of energy in political units throughout the world. The results are even more indicative of the various qualities of a state than are statistics on steel production. The computations cover both animate sources of energy (human and animal labor power) and inanimate sources (coal, oil, water power, etc.). For statistical purposes, all sources are transformed into kilowatt-hours of electricity equivalent; it is assumed, for example, that a ton of coal or a cubic meter of natural gas is equivalent to a certain amount of electricity. On this basis it is possible to state in an understandable way how much energy is produced and used, and what visible reserves of energy are available for the future. It is also possible to show what proportion of the energy used comes from animate sources, and what proportion comes from inanimate sources. Such statistics tell a great deal about the level of technology within a country, about the amount of physical power that a state can muster, and about power-potential. The published results of these computations, based on the situation as of 1937, are now obsolete, but a few of them can be cited for illustrative purposes. The United States in 1937 consumed about 35 per cent of all the energy consumed on earth for productive purposes; the United Kingdom consumed about 10 per cent; the Soviet Union 9 per cent; Germany 9 per cent; France 5 per cent; Japan 4 per cent. Thus, some 72 per cent of all energy consumed for productive purposes was consumed by six great powers, and almost half this total was consumed by the United States alone. Middle and South America consumed 3 per cent of the world's total, Africa 2 per cent. The approximate figures on per capita use of energy in kilowatt-hours of electricity equivalent were as follows: the United States, 7000; the United Kingdom, 5500; Germany, 3500; France, 3000; the U.S.S.R., 1500; Japan, 1000. Over 97 per cent of all the energy used in the United States for productive purposes came from inanimate sources; the corresponding figures for the United Kingdom, Germany, and France were all over 95 per cent, and the figures for Japan and the U.S.S.R. were 91 per cent and 88 per cent, respectively. Only 1 per cent of the energy used for productive purposes in Afghanistan came from inanimate sources.[17]

Consumption of energy for productive purposes changed markedly in the period from 1937 to 1946. Generally, countries remote from theaters of war used considerably more, and those in war areas used less. The Soviet Union, now including the Baltic states, was a partial exception to this generalization, for its consumption of energy increased by 31 per cent despite the fighting on its soil. The increase for the United States was 35 per cent. France showed a decline of 19 per cent, and Britain of 5 per cent.[18]

Statistics on visible reserves of fuel and power as of 1937 reveal a different situation than do statistics on actual use of energy in that year. The United States possessed 29 per cent of the world total, the Soviet Union 23 per cent, Canada 7 per cent, China 4 per cent, Germany 3.6 per cent, the Union of South Africa 2.4 per cent, French Equatorial Africa 2.1 per cent, and the United Kingdom 2.0 per cent.[19]

Such figures are suggestive of actual or potential power relationships, just as figures on steel production are, but they must be treated with some caution. Countries which consume vast quantities of energy may use a large part of it to provide for the comforts and luxuries of life, whereas countries which consume relatively less may devote it largely to military purposes. Thus actual power relationships would depart considerably from the relationships the statistics suggest. Similarly, countries with relatively small visible reserves of energy may use those reserves up at a rapid rate, producing more power than might be expected. Despite these qualifications, however, consideration of the distribution and allocation of energy resources provides a useful short cut in power calculations.

THE RELATIVITY OF POWER

Whether short cuts are resorted to or not, the calculation of power is even more complex than has so far been suggested. The reason for this is that the amount of a state's power in an absolute sense is not the significant thing. A person able to run 100 yards in 10 seconds may or may not win the race, depending on the conditions under which the race is held and the speed of the competing runners. Similarly a state possessing x units of power may or may not have enough.

For power calculations to be significant they must be relative. It is not so much the absolute power of a state as its power position in relation

[17] Department of State, *Energy Resources of the World* (Washington, Government Printing Office, 1949), pp. 102-103.
[18] *Ibid.*, p. 27.
[19] *Ibid.*, pp. 120-121.

to other states which counts. Thus power calculations must encompass all those states whose power may or will be brought to bear when a test of power comes.

Further, to be really significant, the calculation must be made in relation to a specific form of power and a specific situation in which that form of power is to be brought to bear. For example, the power of the United States to induce the General Assembly to adopt Resolution X is likely to differ from its power to induce the adoption of Resolution Y. The power to induce the adoption of any resolution is likely to differ from the power to induce France to lower a specific trade barrier or to ratify a particular treaty. American economic power over Panama differs in extent from American economic power over the Soviet Union. American power to influence opinion abroad differs among various countries and on various issues.

Military power must also be considered in relative terms. American military power is not the same at all geographical points. We might be overwhelmingly strong in relation to all conceivable opposition if the test of strength occurred in New Jersey or California. If the test of strength occurred in Western Europe, we would not be so strong, and if it occurred in Iran or Thailand we would be still weaker. Moreover, our relative power position would depend not only on our armed forces and on our ability to transport military units to the scene of struggle, but also on the attitudes and strength of other countries. Presumably, the more allies we had the stronger would our relative power position be, and the more enemies we confronted the weaker would it be. If, for example, the problem is to determine the probable relative power position of the United States if war should break out with the Soviet Union next year, it would not be enough simply to calculate American power, or even to calculate both American and Soviet power and compare the two. In addition, specific assumptions would have to be made concerning the probable relationship of other states to the struggle, and calculations of their power would have to be made. The relative power position of the United States would thus largely reflect the relative power of the two alliance systems. Uncertainties in the calculation of such relative power positions would clearly be numerous.

SUGGESTED READINGS

HALLE, Louis J., *Civilization and Foreign Policy* (New York, Harper, 1955).

HILSMAN, Roger, *Strategic Intelligence and National Decisions* (Glencoe, Free Press, 1956).

JONES, Stephen B., "The Power Inventory and National Strategy," *World Politics*, Vol. 6 (July, 1954), pp. 421-452.

KENT, Sherman, *Strategic Intelligence for American World Policy* (Princeton, Princeton University Press, 1949).

KNORR, Klaus, *The War Potential of Nations* (Princeton, Princeton University Press, 1956).

MACKINDER, Sir Halford J., *Democratic Ideals and Reality* (New York, Holt, 1942).

MOODIE, A. E. *Geography Behind Politics* (London, Hutchinson's University Library, 1947).

SPROUT, Harold and Margaret, *Foundations of National Power* (New York, Van Nostrand, 1951).

SPYKMAN, Nicholas J., "Geography and Foreign Policy," *American Political Science Review*, Vol. 32 (February and April, 1938), pp. 28-50, 213-236.

SPYKMAN, Nicholas J., *The Geography of the Peace* (New York, Harcourt, Brace, 1944).

STRAUSZ-HUPÉ, Robert, *Geopolitics* (New York, Putnam, 1942).

CHAPTER 11

The Distribution and Balancing of Power

WE HAVE SAID that politics is a struggle for power but rarely an all-out struggle for maximum power. Governments seek power, but they also must be concerned with the promotion of other values. Only a part of the resources at their disposal are marshaled for the development and preservation of power; other resources are devoted to other purposes. What should the allocation of resources be? How much power is enough? What kind of a relative power position do statesmen regard as satisfactory? And how do they go about securing or preserving a satisfactory, relative power position? These are the questions to which this chapter is addressed.

Official definitions of a satisfactory power position are rarely clear-cut. Statesmen rarely say with any precision how much power they will regard as enough. Generally, however, answers to the question fall into two categories, depending on the objectives which are being pursued. Statesmen following defensive policies, desiring mainly to preserve and protect existing rights and interests, commonly regard what is called a balance of power as satisfactory. Those following aggressive policies, desiring to extend the rights and privileges of the state, commonly seek a preponderance of power. In other words, states aiming to preserve the status quo ordinarily want enough power to check those who might challenge it, whereas states aiming to upset the status quo seek a decisive power advantage for themselves. The difference is not as great as these words suggest, as we shall see. In this context, power is thought of as capacity to wage war.

THE PURPOSES OF BALANCING POWER

The main purpose of a state seeking to establish or maintain a balance of power is to protect its vital rights and interests. Vital rights and in-

199

terests are those for which the state is willing to wage war if necessary. Thus the desire for a balance of power becomes a desire for a distribution of power that will permit a state to avoid defeat, if not to win victory, in war.

Stated in more general terms, the object of the balancing of power is to establish or maintain such a distribution of power among states as will prevent any one of them from imposing its will upon another by the threat or use of violence.

The idea is an old one.[1] When Carthage was at war with Rome, Syracuse sent aid to Carthage "lest by its fall the remaining [Roman] power should be able, without let or hindrance, to execute every purpose and undertaking." The principle was that no state which might ultimately attack Syracuse should be allowed to amass sufficient power to do so with assurance of success. Fenelon stated a similar principle, writing in the seventeenth century to instruct a grandson of Louis XIV. His assumption was that in international politics the strongest state will in the long run tend to prevail over the others and overthrow them unless they unite to establish a balance. And he declared that "to hinder one's neighbor from becoming too strong is not to do harm; it is to guarantee one's self and one's neighbors from subjection. . . . The excessive aggrandizement of any one [nation] may mean the ruin and subjection of all the [others]." Vattel, an early writer on international law, defined the balance of power as "an arrangement of affairs so that no state shall be in a position to have absolute mastery and dominate over the others." In a famous memorandum written for the British Foreign Office in 1907, Sir Eyre Crowe explained the idea of the balance of power as follows: [2]

History shows that the danger threatening the independence of this or that nation has generally arisen, at least in part, out of the momentary predominance of a neighbouring state. . . . The only check on the abuse of political predominance . . . has always consisted in the opposition of an equally formidable rival, or of a combination of several countries forming leagues of defense. The equilibrium established by such a grouping of forces is technically known as the balance of power, and it has become almost a historical truism to identify England's secular policy with the maintenance of this balance by throwing her weight now in this scale and now in that, but ever on the side opposed to the political dictatorship of the strongest single state or group at a given time.

Peace is sometimes said to be the purpose of the balancing of power. Perhaps it is correct to classify it as a secondary purpose, or, even better, as an incidental result which the balancing process sometimes brings

[1] See Sidney B. Fay, "Balance of Power," *Encyclopedia of the Social Sciences*, Vol. II, pp. 395-399.
[2] Great Britain, Foreign Office, *British Documents on the Origins of the War, 1898-1914* (London, H. M. Stationery Office, 1926-1938), Vol. III, p. 403.

about. Peace, however, is not the prime purpose. In fact, as will be seen, states sometimes deliberately resort to war for the purpose of establishing or preserving a balance.

ASSUMPTIONS UNDERLYING THE PRINCIPLE OF THE BALANCE OF POWER

Five major assumptions underlie the principle of the balance of power.[3] Some of them are obviously valid, and others are questionable.

The first is that states are determined to protect their vital rights and interests by the means at their disposal, including war. It is up to each state to decide for itself which of its rights and interests are vital.[4] They commonly include such values as independence, territorial integrity, security, preservation of the domestic political and economic system or the domestic way of life, and the protection of certain legal rights, like the right to the freedom of the seas. If states were not determined to protect some such rights and interests, they would logically have to be indifferent to power relationships and willing to accede to whatever demands were made upon them by other states. Complete self-abnegation is extremely rare, if it ever occurs at all. The nearest approach to it comes when one state voluntarily accepts absorption by another, as with the Republic of Texas. In general, the first of the assumptions must be regarded as sound.

The second underlying assumption of the balance-of-power principle is that vital interests of the state are or may be threatened. Otherwise, there would be no need for a state which wants to preserve the status quo to concern itself with power relationships. The validity of the assumption is obvious. All history shows that threats to the vital interests of states sometimes arise. They may be ever-present.

The third underlying assumption is that a balance of power will either deter the threatening state from launching an attack or permit the victim to avoid defeat if an attack should occur. In other words, it is assumed that states are not likely to attack unless they command a preponderance of power, or, if they do attack, that they cannot win. The latter part of the proposition—that preponderance is necessary to victory—is obvious. The first part—that the existence of balance will deter attack—is probably true, but still questionable. The implication is that acts of state are rationally controlled, which may not always be true. Another implication is even more dubious: that the existence of a balance of power or the

[3] Cf. Quincy Wright, *A Study of War* (Chicago, The University of Chicago Press, 1942), Vol. II, pp. 743-759; Ernest B. Haas, "The Balance of Power as a Guide to Policy Making," *Journal of Politics*, Vol. 15 (August, 1953), pp. 370-398.

[4] Martin Wight, *Power Politics*, "Looking Forward" Pamphlets, No. 8 (London, Royal Institute of International Affairs, 1946), pp. 36-39.

possession of a preponderance of power is something which can be determined with considerable assurance in advance of war. In fact, calculations of power cannot be very precise. An aggressive state may think that it possesses a preponderance of power, only to be proved wrong; or an aggressive state, facing uncertain power relationships, may simply take a gamble on war, hoping that the distribution of power will turn out to be in its favor.

The fourth underlying assumption is that relative power positions can be measured with a significant degree of accuracy, and that these power calculations can be projected into the future. If such measurement and projection could not be made, a conscious effort to balance power would be out of the question.

The analysis of the elements of power contained in the preceding chapter has already demonstrated that the calculation of power is a complex problem. Some of the elements are quite intangible and therefore difficult to assess. How does one measure the power a government derives at home and abroad from the ideas which it champions? How does one measure the effect on power of the quality of military and political leadership, and how can this factor be projected into the future? How can one know whether treaties of alliance will be honored, or new ones made? Questions like these indicate that estimates of power can be no more than approximations. The probable margin of error is rather wide.

Nevertheless, if governments are determined to preserve their vital interests and if these interests are in any danger of attack, power calculations must perforce be made. There is no real choice. Without a calculation or a guess, governments would have no basis for deciding what proportion of their resources to allocate to an armed establishment and military preparations. They therefore, in fact, engage in calculations and in guessing, even though they know that the results will not be entirely accurate. The more thorough the calculations are, the narrower becomes the area in which pure guesswork prevails.

This fourth assumption, though questionable, is probably sound. The relative power position of a state is of such vital importance that any power calculations which reduce the area of guesswork will be significant. It is obviously better to have foreign policy decisions made by those who know that the Soviet Union and Luxembourg are different in size, for size has implications for power. Similarly, it is better to have decisions made by those who know as much as can be known about the other elements which affect the power position of states.

The fifth underlying assumption of the idea of balancing power is that statesmen can and will make foreign policy decisions intelligently on the basis of power considerations. If this were not possible, the deliberate balancing of power could not occur.

AN EXAMINATION OF THE FIFTH ASSUMPTION

The Problem of Identifying Vital Interests

A number of factors militate against the deliberate and intelligent balancing of power. In the first place, if the vital interests of the state are to be protected through the balancing of power, those vital interests must be known and clearly defined; there must be some measure of agreement on the part of decision-makers in identifying them. Such agreement always exists to some extent, but it is rarely complete. All American decision-makers agree, for example, that the preservation of the independence and territorial integrity of the United States is a vital interest. Is it also a vital interest, that is, one for which the United States should fight, if necessary, that all countries should treat American citizens within their borders according to the requirements of an international standard of justice? Is it a vital interest that American traders should have access to certain foreign markets? Is it a vital interest that democracy should be preserved, as a good in itself, in Italy? Is it a vital interest that protection should somehow be extended to Jewish or other minority groups whom a foreign dictator is exterminating? Such questions are not unanswerable, but the answers are not always obvious. Different groups within the United States, and different persons and groups among the decision-makers in Washington, are likely to come up with different answers. A government which defines the concept of vital interests one way this year may conclude next year that the definition was wrong. During the early part of World War I, for example, the United States regarded the preservation of certain neutrality rights as a vital matter, only to abandon those rights voluntarily just before World War II. Given such problems in identifying the interests to be protected, it is difficult to make intelligent decisions on the amount of power that may be needed.

The Problem of Identifying and Assessing Threats

In the second place, a government pursuing a balance-of-power policy must not only know what its vital interests are but must also be able to determine whether and when a threat to them exists or is likely to develop. In other words, it must be able to determine what the capabilities and intentions of other states are and are likely to be. Are other states able to attack or encroach upon interests regarded as vital? What is the prospect that they actually will do so unless somehow prevented?

We have already noted that it is difficult to assess the power of states with accuracy, and this in itself militates against the intelligent application of balance-of-power principles. It is often even more difficult to assess their intentions. Further, the two problems become vastly more difficult when anticipation of the future is required, as it often is in balance-of-power operations.

For example, in the chapter "War and the Expectation of War," we saw that before World War I Russia and France agreed that the acquisition of territory by Austria-Hungary might affect the balance of power in Europe, so that when Austria-Hungary later attacked Serbia, Russia mobilized, partly on the assumption that the conquest of Serbia would strengthen Austria-Hungary and make it more threatening to Russia. This kind of assumption is commonly made. Britain has repeatedly acted on the assumption that conquest of the Low Countries by a major European power would threaten her. She entered World War II on the assumption that Hitler's Germany would become an intolerable threat if Poland were conquered. In the United States, Secretary of State Robert Lansing desired American participation in World War I on the ground that a victorious Germany would be a threat to vital American interests, and before Pearl Harbor President Franklin D. Roosevelt assumed that an Axis victory would endanger this country. American policy since World War II has been based on the assumption that any extension of communism would be a threat to the United States, because it would enhance Soviet and communist power.

Such assumptions and anticipations may or may not be correct. Had Austria-Hungary been permitted to conquer Serbia in 1914, would she in fact have been strengthened? Might she not have had so much trouble governing unruly Serbs that the conquest would have weakened her? Might she not have become less rather than more dangerous to Russia? Suppose that the United States had not entered World War I. Would the outcome have been such as to endanger the United States? To the extent that America's entry was based on balance-of-power considerations, were these considerations sound? Suppose that we had not entered World War II. How likely is it that, in this event, the Soviet Union and Germany might have exhausted and destroyed each other, leaving the United States in a better power position than she obtained by fighting? Suppose that since World War II the United States had done nothing to halt the spread of communism. How much would it have spread? How much would this have endangered the United States? Is it not possible that the more communism is extended the more difficulties the Kremlin will have in keeping the movement integrated and strong? Might not divisive forces within the communist movement weaken rather than strengthen it as it comes to dominate more and more countries? Is Tito necessarily the sole successful Titoist?

It takes a very good crystal ball to answer such questions, yet the balance-of-power principle requires on occasion that they be answered. On this basis, can a balance of power be intelligently pursued?

Not only does the intelligent pursuit of a balance of power require an ability to predict the future capacity of other states to threaten vital interests, but it also requires an ability to divine their intentions. This is not always easy. For example, after Hitler came to power in 1933 he took a series of steps which greatly strengthened Germany. He announced German rearmament in 1935. In 1936 he remilitarized the Rhineland. In 1938 in the name of the principles of nationalism and self-determination he took Austria, and a few months later the Sudetenland. He had made statements claiming for the Nordic race the right to rule the world, yet at the same time he had repeatedly professed a love of peace and had assured the world after each territorial acquisition that this was his last demand. Further, according to principles endorsed throughout the Western world, there was some justice in Hitler's demands down to the spring of 1939. As the British Prime Minister, Neville Chamberlain, put it,[5] "there was something to be said, whether on account of racial affinity or of just claims too long resisted . . . for the necessity of a change in the existing situation." The question was, could Hitler be appeased by conceding to his just demands, or would concessions simply lead to the making of new demands without end? Did Hitler really threaten Britain and other states? Down to the spring of 1939 Chamberlain was not entirely convinced that he did, and he therefore followed an appeasement policy and did not rigorously pursue a balance of power. Then, concluding that Hitler's intentions were definitely menacing to Britain, he switched to an emphasis on power.

A similar problem confronts the countries outside the Moscow-Peking orbit today. What are the intentions of the Soviet and Chinese Communists? Granting their control over great military power, how do they intend to use it? What relative stress should other countries give to mustering power on the one hand and seeking a settlement which would permit coexistence on the other? To what extent, if at all, are the two lines of action incompatible? If the Soviet Union and the United States go to war with each other, what roles can such countries as China, Britain, France, Germany, Italy, and India be expected to play? The intelligent pursuit of a balance of power requires that such questions be answered.

The Problem of Contradictory Principles: Balance vs. Law, Morality, and Justice

Once statesmen pursuing a balance of power have defined the vital interests which they want to defend and have determined what threats exist or are in prospect, they have met two of the prerequisites of the intelligent application of the balance-of-power principle, but there are still others. The third one is that the balance of power be pursued regard-

[5] Neville Chamberlain, *In Search of Peace* (New York, Putnam, 1939), p. 274.

less of considerations of law, morality, or justice. Otherwise a balance may be destroyed, or prove unobtainable. The question is whether statesmen and peoples are prepared to do what an intelligent application of balance-of-power principles sometimes requires.

Suppose, for example, that in a free election France should go communist, presumably meaning that it would withdraw from the North Atlantic Treaty Organization and enter the Soviet alliance system. The probability is that the example set by the French people and government would be followed in other European countries, such as Italy, which are now aligned with the United States. What would the United States do, if anything? Intervention to set aside the verdict of the polls would be difficult to justify in the light of America's endorsement of both law and democracy, yet intervention would probably be required by the principle of the balance of power. It might be said that the United States, on the basis of balance-of-power and other considerations, should seek to influence opinion in France long before the election occurs so as to prevent the development of the dilemma; still, such dilemmas sometimes arise regardless of preventive action.

Suppose that it were feasible to come to an understanding with the Soviet Union concerning the establishment of mutually satisfactory power relationships. Suppose, however, that a division of the world into spheres of interest is a necessary aspect of the understanding; this would imply that the United States would not interfere in any way with action taken by the Soviet Union to preserve or extend communist domination within its sphere. This aspect of the agreement would be widely regarded in the United States and elsewhere as immoral. If it seemed desirable on the basis of balance-of-power considerations, would it nevertheless be accepted?

Suppose that Yugoslavia or Greece or Turkey should deliberately attack Bulgaria. Let us assume that the aggression is clearly illegal and that it is generally regarded in the United States as immoral or unjust. Military events quickly make it plain that the aggressor, left unaided, will be defeated. The almost certain consequence of defeat will be the reduction of the aggressor to the status of a satellite of the Soviet Union. The power of the Soviet Union will thus presumably be enhanced, and this threatens to upset a preexisting balance of power. What would such countries as the United States do? Under balance-of-power considerations, they would have to act. They might attempt to secure a termination of the war short of a communist victory, or, failing that, they might have to enter the war on the side of the aggressor. The question is, would they do so? Would devotion to the principle of balancing power lead to an abandonment of the principles of law and morality which the aggressor has violated?

Franco's Spain provides an actual case in point, and consideration of the issue has produced different answers in different Western countries. Various attributes of Franco's regime make it morally distasteful to many people and governments. At the same time, Spain controls some resources and possesses a strategic location which are of value to the West in the East-West struggle. Should Spain be brought within the Western alliance structure? The French and British have said no, largely on moral grounds. The United States has said yes.

Reference might also be made to events in 1956 revolving around Egypt and the Suez Canal, although, in view of the incompleteness of the data at the time of writing, only tentative statements can be made. The events were precipitated by an Israeli attack on Egypt, which put Britain and France, and subsequently the United States, on the horns of a dilemma. On the one hand, Egypt had been following policies which Britain and France regarded as menacing to their vital interests; from a power point of view they could only wish for Egypt's defeat and for the downfall of the government in Egypt which was hostile to them. On the other hand, Israel's attack raised serious legal and moral questions; the answers were not clear-cut, but a good case could be made for the view that Israel had violated relevant legal obligations. If Britain and France were to pursue their power interests various courses were open to them, including as an extreme the launching of an attack on Egypt on their own part. If they were to guide themselves by legal and moral considerations their course of action would have depended on their answers to the legal and moral questions posed, but surely they would not have supported the Israeli attack. The decision Britain and France made was to guide themselves by power considerations, regardless of law and morality; they attacked Egypt. The consequent American dilemma was not clear-cut. Concern for law and morality suggested that the United States must at least dissociate itself from Britain and France. From a power point of view such action would weaken bonds with these two states, but the loss might be counterbalanced in some degree by gains in relationships with the Arab and other states of the free world. The decision of the United States was to guide itself largely by its conception of the requirements of law and morality. It therefore denounced the attacking states. At the same time it obviously hoped for the best in the realm of power and demonstrated its concern for power by opposing any form of Soviet aid for Egypt.

The Problem of Domestic Political Conditions and Attitudes

A fourth prerequisite to an intelligent application of balance-of-power principles is that domestic political conditions and attitudes should be suitable. Sometimes they are not. In fact, sometimes they militate against, and even preclude, effective balance-of-power operations. This occurs particularly in democracies, where political leaders are apt to regard

victory at the polls as the primary objective. If public opinion or influential party leaders oppose the kind of action required for a balancing
of power, those primarily responsible for safeguarding the rights and
interests of the state find themselves in a difficult position. If they take
or advocate the action required, they may lose the next election. If they
temporize, accepting risks for the state, they may reduce electoral risks
for themselves. The same dilemma arises when public opinion or influential party leaders demand action which is incompatible with balance-
of-power considerations.

For example, in the first years of the Hitler regime the government in
London realized that dangers to Britain were increasing, but feared that
public opinion would not support rearmament. It therefore delayed
action. Lord Baldwin, the Conservative leader and Prime Minister, later
declared that at the time the issue arose "there was probably a stronger
pacifist feeling running through this country than at any time since the
War," and that if the party had championed rearmament the loss of the
elections in 1935 would have been certain. Not until after the elections
(and, it should be added, not until after the German menace became
plainer to all) did the British government push a rearmament program.[6]

Except for the period since World War II, American public opinion
has generally prevented the United States government from engaging in
a balancing of power—and even now it must be done in the name of
collective security, which seems to be a more acceptable term. According
to Colonel E. M. House, Woodrow Wilson said privately in 1915 that he
"had never been sure that we ought not to take part in [World War I],
and if it seemed evident that Germany and her militaristic ideas were
to win, the obligation upon us was greater than ever."[7] Yet he fought
the electoral campaign of 1916 with the slogan, "He kept us out of war."
After the outbreak of World War II, President Roosevelt gave clear and
sharp warnings of the dangers of an Axis victory for the United States,
but in the interests of electoral victory in 1940 felt obliged to pledge
that American boys would not be called upon to fight in foreign wars.[8]
The tradition of isolation and neutrality was so strong in the United
States that many were blind to the possibility that events abroad might
produce serious threats to vital American interests. Had Wilson and
Roosevelt urged in an election year that balance-of-power considerations
required participation in war, the electoral victory which each in fact
won would clearly have been put in jeopardy.

Not only must domestic political conditions and attitudes permit inter-

[6] E. H. Carr, *Britain, a Study of Foreign Policy* (New York, Longmans Green,
1939), pp 159-160.
[7] Charles Seymour, *The Intimate Papers of Colonel House* (Boston, Houghton
Mifflin, 1926), Vol. II, p. 84.
[8] Franklin D. Roosevelt, *The Public Papers and Addresses of Franklin D. Roosevelt,*
1940 volume (New York, Macmillan, 1941), p. 517.

vention in war, but they must also permit conducting the war and terminating it in the interest of the balance of power. This may involve peace without victory, a slogan which Wilson championed before America's intervention in World War I only to abandon it later. It may require that a Kaiser or a Hirohito or a Stalin be allowed to remain in office on the basis of a negotiated peace.

George Kennan, in his appraisal of American diplomacy, poses the question whether a democracy can either wage war or make peace on the basis of the cold calculations which the balancing of power requires.[9]

I sometimes wonder whether in this respect a democracy is not uncomfortably similar to one of those prehistoric monsters with a body as long as this room and a brain the size of a pin: he lies there in his comfortable primeval mud and pays little attention to his environment; he is slow to wrath—in fact, you practically have to whack his tail off to make him aware that his interests are being disturbed; but, once he grasps this, he lays about him with such blind determination that he not only destroys his adversary but largely wrecks his native habitat. You wonder whether it would not have been wiser for him to have taken a little more interest in what was going on at an earlier date and to have seen whether he could not have prevented some of these situations from arising instead of proceeding from an undiscriminating indifference to a holy wrath equally undiscriminating.

Difficulties in applying the balance-of-power principle may well be accentuated where peoples and governments are committed to any of a number of fixed points of view. A tradition of isolation, a prejudice against colonialism, a belief that in war there is no substitute for victory, an insistence that aggression is always wrong, a conviction that the requirements of law and morality are always to be observed, and a deep yearning for peace are among the many attitudes likely at one time or another to impede an effective balancing of power.

The Problem of Choice of Method

Finally, it is one thing to conclude that balance-of-power considerations require action of some sort, and quite another thing to decide precisely what the action should be. Statesmen may be intelligent about the choice of objective but mistaken in their choice of method for reaching it. For example, in appraising American policy in relation to World War I, George Kennan does not criticize response to the principle of the balance of power but rather the timing and precise character of the response. He argues that we should have recognized before 1914 that troubles were brewing in Europe which threatened American interests, and that we should therefore have seen to it [10] "that this country provided itself right then and there with something in the way of an armed

[9] George F. Kennan, *American Diplomacy, 1900-1950* (Chicago, The University of Chicago Press, 1951, copyright 1951 by the University of Chicago), p. 66.
[10] *Ibid.*, pp. 71-72.

establishment, so that our word would carry some weight and be listened to in the councils of the powers."

When the war broke out, you could have ignored the nonsensical timidities of technical neutrality and used our influence to achieve the earliest possible termination of a war that nobody could really win. Admittedly, if there were any possibility of this, it was in the first months of the war, and we would have had to be armed. If this had not succeeded, then you would have had to carry on through the war, exercising what moderating influence you could, avoiding friction with the belligerents on minor matters, holding your power in reserve for the things that counted. And if you finally had to intervene to save the British from final defeat (which I am quite prepared to accept as a valid ground for intervention), then you could have gone in frankly for the avowed purpose both of doing this and of ending the war as rapidly as possible; you could have refrained from moralistic slogans, refrained from picturing your effort as a crusade, kept open your lines of negotiation to the enemy, declined to break up his empires and overthrow his political system, avoided commitments to the extremist war aims of your allies, retained your freedom of action, exploited your bargaining power flexibly with a view to bringing its full weight to bear at the crucial moments in order to achieve the termination of hostilities with a minimum prejudice to the future stability of the Continent.

How often have states and statesmen, attempting to pursue the principle of balancing power, made mistakes in the way in which they went about it? Many of the failures in the balancing process have no doubt resulted less from the principle involved than from poor judgment on the part of those applying it.

The stress so far has been on factors which militate against the validity of the fifth assumption underlying the balance-of-power principle, that statesmen can and will make foreign policy decisions intelligently on the basis of power considerations. Such factors exist in good number. For good or ill, states which desire to establish or preserve a balance of power are also guided by other desires, some of which may be incompatible with the balancing of power. Nevertheless, the record shows that states can and do follow the principle. They may not always do it with coldly calculated precision and with uniform success, but they do it. This will become abundantly clear through an analysis of the methods of balancing power—methods which every major power and many others have at one time or another employed.

METHODS EMPLOYED IN THE BALANCING OF POWER

The Adjustment of Power by Domestic Measures

A number of methods are employed in the balancing of power. The adjustment of national power by domestic measures is prominent among them. A state which feels threatened by the growing power of another may simply bring about a growth of its own power in order to maintain a balance. It may build up its armaments; it may initiate or expand an economic program designed to enhance its fighting capacity; it may develop a domestic propaganda campaign designed to stimulate love of country and hatred of the potential enemy; it may, in fact, go through the whole inventory of the elements of power, seeking to increase its strength in every way that is reasonably possible. When and if the other state ceases to be so powerful or so threatening, these measures may be relaxed and national power allowed to decline.

For example, the United States, after engaging in demobilization at the end of World War II to a much greater extent than the Soviet Union, became convinced that the Soviet Union was a potential enemy state. It therefore began a program of rearmament, which it greatly intensified both after it became clear that the Soviet Union had developed atomic weapons and after the North Korean aggression in 1950 gave increased evidence of communist hostility. Fat, slack, and flexibility in the American economy made it possible through purely domestic measures to do a good deal to redress the balance between East and West. This method of pursuing a balance of power, however, is not always adequate or feasible. Where there is a vast discrepancy in the power-potential of two states, it is futile for the weaker of the two to seek to establish balance by its own unaided action. Domestic American measures might, but domestic Iranian measures could not, bring about a balancing of Soviet power.

Winning and Strengthening Friends and Allies

If domestic measures are inadequate, and perhaps in any event, they may be supplemented by measures taken abroad. The range of action which can be taken abroad is at least as great as the range of action which can be taken at home. Treaties of alliance may be concluded, providing for various degrees of cooperation in military and related affairs. Treaties of neutrality and non-aggression may be concluded, designed to give assurance that the power of neither party will be directed against the other. A state may extend military or economic aid, or both, to another in order to strengthen it, on the assumption that an increase in the power of the recipient will contribute to a balancing of power. Propaganda campaigns may be launched to win support for the national cause abroad and to deprive the potential enemy of support. In fact, once again, the state seeking a balance of power can go through the whole inventory of the elements of power, seeking to strengthen actual or potential allies in every way that is reasonably possible.

Treaties of alliance should be noted especially as devices employed in the balancing process. Selected illustrations follow. In 1892 France and Russia completed their alliance by signing a military convention. In the preamble they affirmed their common desire to preserve the peace and declared that they had "no other aim than to prepare for the necessities of defensive war." Article 1 then provided:

If France is attacked by Germany, or by Italy supported by Germany, Russia shall employ all her available forces to fight Germany.

If Russia is attacked by Germany, or by Austria supported by Germany, France shall employ all her available forces to fight Germany.

In 1899 France and Russia added to this an understanding that they would seek to maintain "the European balance of power." Still later there was a tacit agreement that a territorial acquisition on the part of Austria would affect the general balance of power in Europe.[11] When Austria then attacked Serbia, Russia mobilized, and France stood by her. Moreover, the Tsar sent a telegram to the King of England appealing for British aid in the name of the balance of power. The object of the Austrian ultimatum to Serbia, he said,[12]

was to crush Serbia and make her a vassal of Austria. Effect of this would have been to upset balance of power in Balkans, which is of such a vital interest to my Empire as well as to those Powers who desire maintenance of balance of power in Europe. . . . I trust your country will not fail to support France and Russia in fighting to maintain balance of power in Europe.

Before World War II the British Prime Minister issued an oral guarantee to Poland, pledging to support Poland "in the event of any action which clearly threatened Polish independence, and which the Polish Government accordingly considered it vital to resist with their national forces." This guarantee was later transformed into a formal alliance, the two parties pledging themselves to give one another all the support in their power in the event that either became "engaged in hostilities with a European Power in consequence of aggression by the latter against that Contracting Party."[13] In 1939, also, Germany and Italy made an alliance with thinly veiled aggressive intentions. The treaty included the following article: [14]

If, contrary to the wishes and hopes of the contracting parties, it should happen that either of them is involved in military entanglements with another Power or Powers, the other contracting party will immediately rally to its side as ally and support it with all its military resources on land, at sea and in the air.

The most notable treaty since World War II aiming at a balance of power is the North Atlantic Treaty. In the chapter "Ideological Moti-

[11] Bernadotte E. Schmitt, *The Coming of the War* (New York, Scribner, 1930), Vol. I, pp. 10, 18-21.

[12] Great Britain, Foreign Office, *op. cit.*, Vol. XI, p. 276.

[13] *Documents on International Affairs 1939-1946* (New York, Oxford University Press, 1951), Vol. I, pp. 126, 469.

[14] *Ibid.*, p. 169.

vations and Objectives," we have already noted the expressed aims of the treaty. In promoting these objectives, the parties pledge themselves "separately and jointly, by means of continuous and effective self-help and mutual aid, [to] maintain and develop their individual and collective capacity to resist armed attack." They further agree "that an armed attack against one or more of them in Europe or North America shall be considered an attack against them all." Consequently, each party agrees to "assist the Party or Parties so attacked by taking forthwith, individually and in concert with the other Parties, such action as it deems necessary, including the use of armed force, to restore and maintain the security of the North Atlantic area." Similar provisions are included in the Rio Pact of 1947 among the American republics. The treaty of 1951 between the United States, Australia, and New Zealand involves a more limited obligation. In it "each Party recognizes that an armed attack in the Pacific area on any of the Parties would be dangerous to its own peace and safety and declares that it would act to meet the common danger in accordance with its constitutional processes." [15]

Most treaties of alliance are deliberately couched in somewhat vague language because the governments concluding them are motivated by conflicting desires. They want to give strong warning to the potential enemy, but at the same time want to assume only a weak obligation. They want to receive assurances that their allies will spring to their aid, yet many of them wish at the same time to retain the right to decide by their own constitutional processes whether and when the circumstance calling for action (i.e., the *casus foederis*) has arisen. They want assurances of maximum help from an ally while retaining freedom to decide how much help they themselves will give. Finally, they have to reconcile aggressive intent, if it exists, with the necessity of appearing to aim only at the defense of peace, security, and other socially accepted values.

Curbing the Power of the Potential Enemy

In pursuit of a balance of power, positive measures to build up power at home or through alliances are likely to be supplemented by negative measures designed to curb the power of the potential enemy. Thus, the United States, while granting extensive aid to its allies, has attempted to cut off the flow of strategic materials to the countries behind the Iron Curtain. It has spread propaganda in those countries designed to keep popular support for their governments at a minimum. It welcomed Yugoslavia into the Western fold after Tito split with Stalin in 1948.

[15] The treaties here mentioned are Nos. 1964, 1838, and 2493 in U. S. Department of State, *Treaties and Other International Acts Series* (Washington, Government Printing Office, 1946–). Cf. Appendix of this book, pp. 476–478, and Francis O. Wilcox and Thorsten V. Kalijarvi, eds., *Recent American Foreign Policy, Basic Documents 1941-1951* (New York, Appleton-Century-Crofts, 1952).

It offered economic aid to Poland in 1956 when it appeared that Poland was gaining a greater degree of freedom from Moscow's control. Perhaps it might have done more than it in fact has done to prevent the Soviet Union from gaining new allies or to encourage Titoism.

Negotiating Agreements with the Potential Enemy

Additional kinds of measures may also be taken in pursuit of a balance of power. They may involve negotiations with the potential enemy.

1. *The level of armaments.* Particularly since World War I states have negotiated persistently over the level of armaments to be maintained—the central factor in a balance of power. Among the many objectives of such negotiations two are relevant here. In the first place, disarmament may be proposed as a propaganda maneuver designed to demonstrate one's own desire for peace and friendship among nations and to reveal to all the world the intransigence and bellicosity of the potential enemy. It thus may be designed to affect the balance of power by influencing public opinion in various countries. In the second place, it may be proposed in the hope, which is usually forlorn, that agreement on a mutually satisfactory distribution of military power can be reached. We shall see in a subsequent chapter how difficult and unlikely it is that agreement can be achieved.

2. *Applying the principle of compensation.* Negotiations concerning the balance of power have on occasion involved what is called the principle of compensation. The best illustration dates from the partition of Poland in the last part of the eighteenth century. Prussia, Russia, and Austria-Hungary, which surrounded the weak state of Poland, each knew that the other two would not permit it to conquer Poland, for that would upset the balance of power among them; yet Poland was a tempting morsel for all of them. In the end they agreed upon successive partitions, each one taking a portion of Poland deemed equivalent in terms of power to the portions taken by the others; each was "compensated" for the enhancement of the power of the others by gaining a similar increment of power for itself. The power of all three was presumably increased, but the ratio of power among them presumably remained the same.

3. *Buffer states, spheres of influence, and neutralization.* Whether or not as a result of negotiations, buffer zones or buffer states sometimes play a role in the balancing of power.[16] Buffers are areas which are weak but which possess considerable strategic importance to two or more stronger powers. Each of the stronger powers may seek to bring the buffer within its sphere, but regards it as important, if not vital, that no other strong power be permitted to do so. If one of them manages to bring the buffer within its sphere, the usual result is annexation, or the

16 Wight, *op. cit.*, pp. 52-55.

establishment of a protectorate, or the conclusion of an alliance. Otherwise, the stronger powers will seek to maintain the independence and neutrality of the buffer. Formal neutralization may occur.

Korea, for example, has served as a buffer between Japan, China, and Russia. After defeating both China and Russia around the turn of the present century, Japan annexed Korea, only to be ousted after World War II. Then Korea, divided at the thirty-eighth parallel, became a buffer between the United States and the Soviet Union, later joined by Communist China. When North Korea attacked and threatened to take all of Korea into the Moscow-Peking sphere, the United States intervened on behalf of South Korea. The tentative result is the continued division of the country, with the southern part allied to the United States and the northern part allied to the Soviet Union and Communist China.

Iran has historically been a buffer between Britain and Russia, and more recently has become a buffer between East and West. To minimize their rivalries in connection with the formation of the Triple Entente, Britain and Russia in 1907 agreed to a division of Iran into three zones. The northern and southern zones were to be Russian and British spheres of influence, respectively, each country pledging itself not to seek political or commercial concessions in the sphere of the other. In the central zone, neither country was to seek concessions except in agreement with the other.[17] After Russian power had collapsed because of World War I and the Bolshevik Revolution, Britain concluded a treaty with Iran which made it a virtual protectorate. (A protectorate has all the rights and powers of an independent state, except those taken away by international agreement. Among other things, the agreement usually restricts the freedom of the protectorate in the conduct of its foreign relations.) Iran subsequently repudiated this agreement, regaining full independence, and for the last several decades the Soviet Union and Britain—the latter now joined by the United States—have jealously sought to preserve the independence of Iran, at least against encroachments from the other side.[18] Each side wants to deny to the other the strategic advantages which would come from control over Iranian territory.

Belgium has historically been a buffer between France and Germany. When it first achieved independence, it was neutralized. A neutralized state is "one whose integrity has been permanently guaranteed by international treaty, conditionally on its maintaining a perpetual neutrality save in its own defense."[19] In other words, the states accepting the

[17] Sidney B. Fay, *The Origins of the World War* (New York, Macmillan, 1932), Vol. I, p. 220.
[18] George Lenczowski, *Russia and the West in Iran, 1918-1948* (Ithaca, Cornell University Press, 1949), pp. 42-47.
[19] J. L. Brierly, *The Law of Nations* (Oxford, Clarendon, 1949), p. 121; cf. Fred Greene, "Neutralization and the Balance of Power," *American Political Science Review*, Vol. 47 (December, 1953), pp. 1041-1057.

neutralization agreement pledge not to attack the neutralized state, and it in turn pledges not to attack, or to join in an attack, on them; theoretically, then, each of the guarantors is assured that none of the others will gain a power advantage through relationships with the neutralized state. Germany violated Belgium's neutrality in 1914, and after German power had been laid low in World War I France concluded a military alliance with Belgium.

History provides numerous other illustrations of the use of buffer states or buffer zones in the balancing of power. Since World War II, however, with the tightening of alignments between East and West, such areas have tended to disappear.

War, and the Terms of Peace

War is the most extreme method of pursuing a balance of power. We have already seen that Britain has historically sought to prevent any strong and potentially hostile power from gaining control over the Low Countries or from gaining mastery over Europe as a whole; she repeatedly has waged balance-of-power wars to execute one or another of these purposes. Russia went to the aid of Serbia in 1914 partly for balance-of-power reasons. Secretary of State Lansing desired American participation in World War I as a means of preventing Germany from gaining domination on the continent, on the assumption that Germany would thus be strengthened and that she would eventually become hostile to the United States. President Roosevelt and others favored aiding the Allies in the early part of World War II largely on the basis of the same considerations as moved Secretary Lansing, and as the war progressed the United States took such strong measures to affect its outcome that Japan attacked at Pearl Harbor in retaliation, and Germany then also declared war. Balance-of-power considerations were among those which influenced American intervention in Korea after the North Korean attack in 1950, the fear being that communist success in Korea would encourage attacks elsewhere until eventually the United States might find itself in a very disadvantageous power position. Some have favored "preventive war" against the Soviet Union on the basis of balance-of-power considerations: that if we do not strike now, Soviet power may become so great as to preclude effective defense of vital American rights and interests later on.

Just as war may be fought, so may peace be made with the balance of power in mind. The Peace of Utrecht (1713) contained arrangements made with the expressly stated purpose *ad conservandum in Europa equilibrium.* The same consideration was a major element in the settlement made at the Congress of Vienna a century later, and is reflected also, implicitly or explicitly, in other treaties as well.

The Holder of the Balance

The happiest position for a state in the balancing process is that of the holder of the balance—or that of the "laughing third party" as it is sometimes called.[20] For example, suppose that in a system including only three states, A and B are approximately equal in power and are so bitterly hostile to each other that an alliance between them is out of the question. State C can then become the laughing third party. If it lines up with A, the two could crush B, or if it lines up with B, the two could crush A. Both A and B are therefore likely to woo C diplomatically, and C can commit itself or remain noncommittal as its interests seem to dictate. Neither A nor B is likely to be able to make a major move without making sure in advance that C would not be alienated thereby. State C can thus largely dictate relationships among the three where she chooses to bring her power to bear.

In practice, it is rare for a state to enjoy a position as favorable as the one we have assigned to C in the above illustration, but sometimes states achieve somewhat analogous positions. Britain has traditionally played the role of a holder of the balance in relation to the continent of Europe, "throwing her weight now in this scale and now in that." It is thus that she came to be known as perfidious Albion. Since World War II, no state or group of states can really be described as a holder of the balance. The ideological conflict makes it extremely difficult for a state to switch sides in the East-West struggle, though Tito has proved that it can be done. Whether any state could switch into the Soviet camp without establishing a communist dictatorship remains to be seen, but seems doubtful. The modern equivalent of the laughing third party is probably the fearful and reluctant ally, who does not threaten to switch sides but who does blow hot or cold on the plans of the dominant partner in the alliance.

THE SEARCH FOR A PREPONDERANCE OF POWER

We have been discussing the purposes, the underlying assumptions, and the methods of balancing power. As we have said, however, not all states seek balance. Those desiring to upset the status quo seek a preponderance of power. If they can get it, they want a decisive power advantage for themselves.

Mutatis mutandis, many of the same considerations apply to the search for preponderance as to the search for balance. The purpose is not to defend, but to gain. The assumption is that a decisive power advantage

[20] Carl J. Friedrich, *Foreign Policy in the Making* (New York, Norton, 1938), p. 126.

will permit gain, whether through intimidating or defeating other states. The methods are essentially the same as those employed in the balancing of power. The state seeking preponderance will take extensive domestic measures to build up and maintain its armed power. It may seek allies and help to strengthen them. It will do all that can reasonably be done to keep or render the potential victim weak. It may engage in economic manipulations for this purpose. It may propose disarmament—in those weapons in which the potential victim is strong. It will try to frustrate efforts of the potential victim to secure or keep allies. It is likely to employ propaganda designed to show that it stands for justice and progress, whereas the prospective victim blocks progress and defends injustice. It may picture itself as the bulwark of peace, whereas the prospective victim obstructs a settlement which would bring peace.

Some of the devices of Hitler's Germany in the 1930's and of the Soviet Union since World War II are in point here. Both involve vast domestic economic, psychological, and military preparations, designed to bring national power to a high level. Both involve efforts to obtain allies. Hitler sought quite deliberately to isolate his potential victims. When he took Austria, he assured Czechoslovakia that he had no designs on her. When he took the Sudetenland, he gave assurances that he had no designs on the rest of Czechoslovakia, and when he took the rest he gave assurances that he had no designs on Poland. Generally, he attempted to persuade Britain and France that his aims were limited, involving no threat to them. Before attacking Poland he concluded a treaty of neutrality and non-aggression with the Soviet Union, supplemented by a secret agreement which reflected the principle of compensation by dividing eastern Europe into spheres of interest. In other words, Hitler sought to convince other states that his aggressions involved no danger to them which justified an application of balance-of-power principles.[21]

Perhaps the most striking feature of Soviet diplomacy, aside from the use of communist parties abroad, is the effort to prevent the United States from building a strong alliance system. The Kremlin resorted to thinly veiled threats in an effort to dissuade some states from accepting the North Atlantic Treaty. It has protested certain measures for implementing the treaty, such as the establishment in Denmark of bases available to the American Air Force. It has prevented the reunification of Germany on a democratic basis, at least partly out of fear that a reunited and democratic Germany would align itself with the United States. It made numerous protests and proposals designed to deter France, especially, from ratifying the treaties providing for the creation of a European Defense Community. It has tried to drive a wedge between the United States and its European allies by picturing the United States as an ag-

[21] Crane Brinton, "The Pattern of Aggression," reprinted in Harold and Margaret Sprout, Foundations of National Power (New York, Van Nostrand, 1951), pp. 30-38.

gressive, warmongering, imperialist power interested in Europe mainly because of the profits and the cannon fodder available there. The Soviet Union has repeatedly protested its own love of peace, assuring other states, in effect, that no danger threatens them from Moscow and that they therefore have no need to apply balance-of-power principles in relation to Moscow. The result is that many people wonder just how dangerous the Soviet Union is—and with some semblance of reason— just as they did with regard to Hitler.

AN APPRAISAL OF THE BALANCE-OF-POWER PRINCIPLE

In analyzing the purposes and the underlying assumptions of the balance-of-power principle, we have already engaged in some appraisal of it, but some additional remarks are called for.

What Does Balance Mean?

We have been using the term *balance* without defining it, as if everybody knew what it meant. In fact, it is not far from the truth to say that nobody knows what it means. In everyday usage the term has two distinct meanings which are relevant here. Sometimes it denotes an equilibrium, as when a scale is brought into balance by adjusting the weights. Sometimes it refers to a remainder—an amount left over when one sum is deducted from another, as when one speaks of his bank balance, and it is still a balance whether the amount involved is one cent or a million dollars.

In the introduction to this chapter, we posed the question, how much power is enough, and answered it by saying that states seeking a balance of power want enough to check states which seek to upset the status quo. Later, the statement was made that the desire for a balance of power becomes a desire for a distribution of power which will permit a state to avoid defeat, if not to win victory, in war. Such vague answers are the best which can be given, but still they are not very satisfactory.

The tendency is for those who seek a balance of power to seek something more than equilibrium. After all, equilibrium would presumably give the potential aggressor an even chance of winning. More important, everyone knows that power calculations are not very accurate. Thus, statesmen are inclined to allow for possible error by building up more power than seems to be necessary to match that of the potential adversary. Further, though something less than a matching of power may deter attack, and equilibrium is even better, a clear preponderance gives the greatest assurance of both peace and safety. Woodrow Wilson may have been thinking along these lines when he described the "great game" of the balance of power as "forever discredited"; in the League of

Nations he sought legal and institutional arrangements assuring that there would be a preponderance of power on the side of law and order. (The relationship between the balance-of-power principle and the League system of "collective security" will be discussed in a later chapter.) The French statesman, Edouard Herriot, was similarly influenced when he said that the League (meaning France?) was determined "to put an end to the old policy of equilibrium and balance which in the past has, in effect, engendered more wars than it has averted." [22] He wanted a preponderance of power in the hands of the satisfied. Similarly, Winston Churchill in 1946, facing the Soviet threat, was quite blunt in rejecting balance in the sense of equilibrium. "The old doctrine of a balance of power is unsound," he said. "We cannot afford, if we can help it, to work on narrow margins, offering temptations to a trial of strength." [23]

The upshot, then, is that the satisfied powers are inclined to seek the same thing as the dissatisfied: a preponderance of power, whether or not they call it a balance. Their contentment may make their concern for power less urgent and zealous, and they are likely to be more reluctant to resort to war. Further, they may be more restrained than the dissatisfied in the pursuit of preponderance because of the knowledge that excessive power in their hands is likely to make them appear menacing to others and thus to call countervailing power into existence. Nevertheless, they want such a distribution of power as will give reasonable safety to their vital interests, and this calls for some degree of preponderance if it can be obtained without undue sacrifice.

The similarity in the attitudes of the satisfied and the dissatisfied toward power has led some writers to use the term *balance* as if it referred simply to the distribution of power, whatever it may be. Some give it an even broader meaning. Thus Grant and Temperley declare that in the early nineteenth century: [24]

The nations of Europe faced one another as armed and distrustful rivals, recognising no rule of conduct except their own advantage, and entering into transitory alliances on the promptings of fear or gain. These unstable relationships among the states of Europe have received the name of the Balance of Power. This has been idealised by some as a safeguard for European peace and the protection of the world against despotism; it has been denounced by others as the cause of the wars of Europe. It was, in truth, neither the one nor the other. It is simply a convenient name for the way in which states act towards one another when there is no influence to persuade them to concord,

[22] Arnold Wolfers, *Britain and France Between Two Wars* (New York, Harcourt, Brace, 1940), p. 173.

[23] Winston Churchill, *The Sinews of Peace, Post-War Speeches* (Boston, Houghton Mifflin, 1949), p. 103.

[24] A. J. Grant and Harold Temperley, *Europe in the Nineteenth and Twentieth Centuries* (New York, Longmans Green, 1952), p. 2.

nor force to coerce them, nor any court whose authority they are all prepared to recognise. . . . The most obvious feature of the state system of Europe under the influence of this idea is the recurring alliance of the weaker powers against any state that seemed to exercise or claim a supremacy in Europe.

Unnecessary War, and the Unnecessary Extension of War

The major criticism of the balance of power as a policy of the satisfied states is not that it really calls for preponderance; in fact, this is less a criticism than an element in the definition of the concept. The major criticism is that the principle probably leads to unnecessary war, and to the unnecessary extension of war. Recall that the application of the principle requires that the capabilities of other states be estimated and their intentions divined. Recall that it also requires prediction of the probable effect on power relationships of hypothetical future events. Such estimates and divinations and predictions may be wrong. States may fear power which isn't there. They may seek to counteract intentions which do not exist. They may enter an existing war, which otherwise might have been localized, because of fear for the future which may not be justified.

When threats are putative rather than direct and immediate, statesmen are in fact in a dilemma in relation to the balance of power. If they attempt to counteract a putative threat, they may actually increase present danger, perhaps becoming involved in a war which could have been avoided. Yet if they take no action they may find themselves helpless when and if the putative threat materializes. Which way out of the dilemma do they, and should they, take?

From hindsight, we know that the Russian Tsar in 1914 took the wrong way out; at least, his personal fate and the fate of Russia could hardly have been worse had he refused to go to Serbia's defense. He transformed a hypothetical future danger into an immediate catastrophe. Did France likewise take the wrong way out? Once Austria-Hungary and Germany were lined up against Serbia and Russia, what should France have done? By going to war, she incurred great risk and suffered tremendous losses, but what would her fate have been had she abstained from a war which the Central Powers won? No one can know; France may or may not have chosen the lesser evil.

What of the choices made after the rise of Hitler to power in Germany in 1933? From hindsight it seems clear that Britain and France (and the United States) made mistakes in failing to anticipate the future danger; they could have acted against Hitler with very little risk at the time he announced the rearmament of Germany in 1935 or at the time he reoccupied the Rhineland and set about remilitarizing it in 1936. Here it was a lack of sufficient concern for power relationships which led to "the unnecessary war," as Churchill once suggested that World War II be called. Suppose that Britain and France had also refused to act against Hitler when the invasion of Poland occurred. They would at least have delayed their own participation in war. In the long run would they then have been worse off or better off?

And what of the choices being made since World War II? The United States, for example, has been increasing present dangers for itself by the course which it has been pursuing. At least, it seems very likely that the danger that the Soviet Union might start dropping atomic bombs on New York, Pittsburgh, and Chicago would be less if the United States had reverted to isolationism. But what of the long-run prospect? If the United States reverted to isolationism, what are the odds that it might some time be confronted with such overwhelming Soviet and communist power as to render impossible the preservation of vital American interests?

Assuming that the balance-of-power principle sometimes leads to unnecessary war, or to the unnecessary extension of existing war, it would be rash to conclude that statesmen should ignore the principle. If they ignore it, they may also bring on unnecessary war, or find that another state or coalition of states has mustered such overwhelming power that resistance to its demands is hopeless. At bottom, the question is not whether statesmen should be concerned with the distribution of power and with the achievement of a satisfactory relative power position; as long as states exist and are determined to preserve vital interests which may be attacked, prudence dictates that this should be done. The question is how wise the choices of the decision-makers will be. When they are wise, unnecessary wars are unlikely to occur, and vital rights and interests are likely to be preserved.

Balance and Bipolarity

Our world in recent years is said to have become bipolar. This is not strictly true, even though the number of great powers has substantially declined and even though power is concentrated more than ever before in the hands of only two states, the United States and the Soviet Union. A number of new states have been created, especially in southern Asia, and China under the Communists comes closer to deserving the title of a great power than it ever did before. But assuming that the tendency is toward bipolarity, what may the effects be on the balancing process? On the one hand, bipolarity may facilitate the balancing process, for under it both the source and the extent of potential threats are likely to be clearer than when power is distributed more nearly evenly among many states. On the other hand, bipolarity may make for instability and war. Quincy Wright explains this as follows: [25]

[25] Quincy Wright, *The Study of International Relations* (New York, Appleton-Century-Crofts, 1955), p. 143.

The greater the number of states and the more nearly equal their power, the more stable is the equilibrium. In a system composed of a large number of equal states, no one can defy all successfully. Consequently, if all are ready to curb aggression, no aggression can be successful. As the number of states diminishes, the relative power of each against the whole becomes greater, and the hope of successful aggression by the more powerful increases. When bipolarity is reached each of the centers of power fears attack by the other. No [new] allies are possible, because all are now associated with one or the other center of power and consequently the center of power against which time appears to be running is likely to start a war. Eventual war is likely to be considered inevitable and consequently, even though the chances of success are not good, it would be better to run the risk now than later. Such conditions have in the past often led to a termination of a system of power politics by the establishment of a universal state through conquest.

Balance and the Arts of Civilization

Wright comes to the same general conclusion—that the balancing process is likely to break down in a war for world conquest—on the basis of the assumption that there is a tendency "toward economic and cultural interdependence, constitutionalism, democracy, and attention to the arts of civilization rather than of war."

. . . The result is that many states become less self-sufficient, less centralized, and less able to shift alliances, to threaten war and to engage in the maneuvers necessary for maintenance of a stable equilibrium. Democratic and constitutional statesmen cannot easily follow Machiavelli's advice to pay first attention to the arts of war. Their constituencies demand more attention to the arts of peace. In such a situation, opportunities are presented to the autocratic states that remain. The development of civilized characteristics by most of the states provides an opportunity to the barbarians, who have acquired the arts of war developed by the civilization, but not the antipathy to war which is, likely to be an ultimate fruit of civilization. As a consequence, the system of power politics becomes less stable.

The effect of these tendencies has been to deteriorate the stability of balance of power systems. There are fewer states, all are more worried, all are more vulnerable, and many are thinking of security in terms of a universal law or a universal culture. The consequence has usually been a universal conquest, after efforts to establish an effective regime of law by general consent have failed.[26]

Balance and Nuclear Weapons

What is the relationship between the development of nuclear weapons and the prospect of a stable balance of power? The question is a crucial one, but the answer is not known. It seems possible that the existence of nuclear weapons might counteract the tendencies which Wright describes above.

This possibility rests on the hypothesis that nuclear weapons tend to

[26] *Ibid.*, pp. 144-145.

equalize the power of the states possessing them. This hypothesis in turn is based on several assumptions: that the possessors of nuclear weapons may use them against the major cities of the enemy, that such use would substantially terminate industrial activities in the cities attacked, and that the destruction of major cities would itself be of such overwhelming importance that all lesser exercise of military power would be relatively insignificant. In short, the assumption is that, when each side has the power to destroy the cities and industrial centers of the other, there is a substantial equality of power regardless of the lesser damage which either side might be able to inflict.[27] The tendency of nuclear weapons to equalize power among the possessors is presumably all the greater if each possessor is able, through the diffusion of radioactive materials, to wipe out a substantial portion of the population of other states or to exterminate a substantial portion of the human race. These assumptions do not involve a prediction that nuclear weapons will be used for the suggested purposes; they simply involve a recognition of possibilities.

Given such possibilities, it is doubtful whether any state can rationally hope to gain by launching a war in which both sides make unrestricted use of nuclear weapons; such a war might well involve simply an exchange of catastrophically destructive blows. Moreover, threats against a state which lacks nuclear weapons may also be of dubious utility, for they would presumably lead such a state to secure an atomically armed ally.

If these assumptions and propositions are true, nuclear weapons make war less likely. The existence of such weapons tends to create or reinforce a balance of power. By the same token, it tends to reinforce the status quo, giving protection to existing rights and interests against the threat or use of violence.

These statements are cautiously phrased, and should be cautiously interpreted. There is no prediction that nuclear weapons preclude further war. Wars have been fought in Korea and in Indochina despite the existence of nuclear weapons. Other such limited wars may well occur. Moreover, wars have resulted in the past from mistakes and from irrational behavior, and the existence of nuclear weapons gives no assurance that men will become both wise and rational in what they do. The principal point made here is that the prospect of terrible destruction in nuclear war is likely to make rational statesmen less inclined to regard war as a useful instrument of policy.

If nuclear weapons make war less likely, this does not mean that they are leading to an abatement of the power struggle among states; the reasons for the struggle persist. Rather, it means that states pursuing contradictory objectives are likely to emphasize methods other than violence for obtaining what they want. They are likely to prefer cold war

[27] Bernard Brodie, ed., *The Absolute Weapon* (New York, Harcourt, Brace, 1946), esp. pp. 74-76.

to hot war, stressing economic manipulations, organized subversion, and propaganda. These methods of states will be examined below.

Balance and the Inevitability of Change

A final consideration relating to the balancing of power should be mentioned. A policy of balancing power is a means by which states seek to preserve existing rights and interests. In a dynamic world society, however, it is out of the question that all existing vital rights and interests can be preserved indefinitely. Change could be avoided only if the world were static. The manipulation of power can be no more successful among countries than within countries in freezing the status quo. The question is not whether but how change will be brought about. The balancing process must therefore be supplemented somehow so as to permit adjustment or change, or it will break down. Possibilities along these lines will also be examined below.

SUGGESTED READINGS

CARR, E. H., *Britain, a Study of Foreign Policy* (New York, Longmans Green, 1939).

GRANT, A. J., and TEMPERLEY, Harold, *Europe in the Nineteenth and Twentieth Centuries* (New York, Longmans Green, 1952).

GREENE, Fred, "Neutralization and the Balance of Power," *American Political Science Review*, Vol. 47 (December, 1953), pp. 1041-1057.

GULICK, Edward Vose, *Europe's Classical Balance of Power* (Ithaca, Cornell University Press, 1955).

HAAS, Ernst B., "The Balance of Power as a Guide to Policy Making," *Journal of Politics*, Vol. 15 (August, 1953), pp. 370-398.

KENNAN, George F., *American Diplomacy, 1900-1950* (Chicago, The University of Chicago Press, 1951).

LANGER, William L., *European Alliances and Alignments, 1871-1890* (New York, Knopf, 1931).

WOLFERS, Arnold, *Britain and France Between Two Wars* (New York, Harcourt, Brace, 1940).

WRIGHT, Quincy, *The Study of International Relations* (New York, Appleton-Century-Crofts, 1955).

WRIGHT, Quincy, *A Study of War* (Chicago, The University of Chicago Press, 1942).

CHAPTER 12

Armaments and Disarmament

INTELLIGENT consideration of the question of armaments and disarmament in international relations must be based on the premise that armed establishments serve useful functions and important purposes. States do not ordinarily engage lightly either in arming or in disarming. Irrationality and perversity play a part in this area of human activity as they do in many others, but they are not the controlling factors. It is a mistake to think that states arm themselves out of capriciousness or to think that disarmament would occur if decision-makers could only be made to see the light of right reason.

THE FUNCTIONS AND PURPOSES
OF ARMED FORCES

The possible functions and purposes of armed forces have already been mentioned, implicitly or explicitly, at various points, but a brief summary is in place here. In the domestic field, governments regularly seek to command such armed forces as will give them reasonable security against rebellion. They may, if they choose, manipulate expenditures on armed forces as a means of regulating the national economy—expanding armies to avoid or relieve unemployment and reducing the amount spent on armed forces as a means of combating inflation. They can confer officers' commissions as a means of assuring prestige and income to influential persons who otherwise might be fractious and even rebellious. There have been rulers and other leading personages to whom an army was a source of pride and pleasure, to be drilled and commanded and paraded for the psychological satisfaction involved; even in modern democratic societies there are individuals and perhaps sizable portions of the population which enjoy and take pride in military ceremony and panoply. It is plain that some of these domestic functions of military establishments are important, but means do not exist for measuring their importance with any precision; it naturally varies at different times and in different countries.

The functions and purposes of armed establishments in the international field are generally more important. The over-all purpose is to protect and promote what are regarded as the rights and interests of the state. To accomplish this purpose, the possession and display of armed strength may be enough, but the record shows that states have also frequently found it necessary or desirable to resort to violence, whether in military action short of war or in war itself.

The possession, display, and employment of armed strength are so important in international affairs that they deserve to be dwelt upon. They do much to govern the extent to which a state can work its will. Consider, for example, the position of the belligerents at the end of a war. If the test of war has proved one side to be militarily inferior, and if it has therefore capitulated, it is at the mercy of the victors. They may seize and annex territory, occupy remaining territory, insist on changes in the personnel of the government or in the form of the political and social system, take an indemnity or reparations, disarm the defeated, and impose other measures as they see fit. Among the victors themselves, influence over the terms of the peace is apt to be proportionate to the military power at their command. Cuba and the United States, for example, both declared war against Germany in the two world wars, but the equality of their legal status by no means led to equality of influence over the terms of the peace. The influence of the Soviet Union in Eastern and Southeastern Europe after World War II, and the influence of the United States in Japan, derived not from righteousness or virtue but from the fact of military dominance. The role of military power in determining relative influence over peace settlements is illustrated also by Winston Churchill's remark at the Yalta Conference, toward the end of World War II, that the conference was "a very exclusive club, the entrance fee being at least five million soldiers or the equivalent." [1]

The conclusion of a peace settlement by no means terminates the significance of armed power. Its influence is still likely to be great. After World War II the peace settlement affecting Eastern and Southeastern Europe involved the reestablishment of Czechoslovakia as an independent, democratic state, yet a few years later Czechoslovakia fell under the control of a Communist dictatorship; among the factors operating to produce this result, the relative armed strength of the Soviet Union and the United States in the region of Czechoslovakia was certainly important. At about the same time as Czechoslovakia fell, there was some danger that the Italian people might vote a Communist government into office. The United States used various means in seeking to avert this

---

[1] James F. Byrnes, *Speaking Frankly* (New York, Harper, 1947), p. 25.

development. Among other things, American bombers engaged in practice flights over Italy, and American war vessels paid courtesy calls at Italian ports, granting shore leave to Marine contingents aboard. The clear object was to encourage the friends of the West and to discourage those tempted to vote Communist.

As tension with the Soviet Union mounted after World War II, the United States resorted increasingly to developing and displaying its military strength. It continued manufacturing atomic bombs and developing other atomic weapons. Periodically, it has tested such weapons; although these tests are staged in part for scientific purposes, they are also designed to reassure friends and to warn potential enemies. They may be timed and publicized with a view to influencing particular diplomatic negotiations. Along with the tests of atomic weapons, the Strategic Air Command has been sending its bombers on non-stop flights half way around the globe, partly to train the crew and test efficiency but also to demonstrate the ability of the United States to deliver atomic bombs to Moscow and beyond. Similarly, both the Army and Navy have engaged in war exercises and war games, which commonly involve political purposes. The geographical location of the game and the strategic problem posed are both likely to be selected with a view to impressing and intimidating a given prospective enemy.

The importance of armaments in times of peace is brought out especially by Salvador de Madariaga.[2]

The fact is that armaments are more useful in time of peace than in time of war. The normal wielders of armaments are not the soldiers, but the diplomats. The gun that does not shoot is more eloquent than the gun that has to shoot and above all than the gun which has shot. There is a Spanish light comedy in which a man is made to agree with a particular course of action by the liberal exhibition of a revolver before his frightened eyes, and as the victim is asked by a third party whether he has at last been convinced: "Yes. He brought me round by means of a 5-bullet argument." Yet no shot had been fired. The diplomacy of the great powers is carried out not exclusively, not always openly, not even always consciously, but always nevertheless on such a principle. The foreign secretary of this or that nation may be the most conciliatory man on earth; yet the minimum which will be granted to him by his adversaries will be considerably higher for the fact of his armaments. At their lowest, therefore, armed forces are one of the most formidable tacit elements in international policy; at their highest . . . the determining factor.

States not only gain their ends simply by possessing armed power; sometimes they actually use it. The steps taken may be short of war. On many occasions strong naval powers have established a so-called pacific blockade as a means of coercing weaker countries; by such a blockade, vessels of the blockaded state are prevented from entering or leaving

[2] Salvador de Madariaga, *Disarmament* (New York, Coward-McCann, 1929), pp. 57-58.

home ports. The hope is that the disruption of commerce will bring the weaker state to terms. Especially in the decades from 1910 to 1930, the United States repeatedly engaged in military intervention in several of the Caribbean republics, virtually assuming the prerogatives of government in some instances. Time and again, too, states which believe that their legal rights have been violated have used their military forces to inflict reprisals.

Whether to avert a war by balancing power or to create power relationships in which aggressive war can be launched with the best prospect of success, states also arrange, as we have seen, to combine their physical strength by making alliances, pledging cooperative military operations in certain contingencies.

The ultimate function of armed establishments is, of course, the waging of war. War is the ultimate means by which states defend their rights and interests. It is also the ultimate means by which states prosecute what they consider to be justice, that is, by which they seek to gain new rights against the opposition of others. It is analogous to revolution in the domestic field, and is likely to be regarded as necessary and useful in international politics at least as long as revolutions are thought to be necessary and useful in domestic politics. War may also be thought of as a substitute for legislative, executive, and judicial agencies; it is a means of enforcing law, and a means of determining whose desires shall prevail concerning the content and interpretation of law.

There are likely to be differences of opinion concerning the importance of some of the domestic uses of armed power. It may not seem vital to gratify the ego of certain persons by giving them troops to command, or vital to arouse patriotic spirit through military panoply. There is less room for disagreement, however, on the importance of armed strength for purposes of international relations. States which do not have good arms or good friends, or both, are apt to live in considerable jeopardy, if they survive at all. It is no wonder that such a large proportion of the money spent by national governments goes to military establishments. Neither is it any wonder that international negotiations concerning disarmament have produced little result, even though they have occupied much of the time of statesmen and diplomats of the twentieth century.

REGULATING AND LIMITING ARMAMENTS

Disarmament is a popular word. At the same time, it is a misleading one. In a literal sense, governments never disarm and cannot be expected to. They always need some armed power at their disposal, if for no other reason than to guard the frontier against bandit forays. When people discuss disarmament, they are therefore really discussing the regulation and limitation of armaments, not the complete abolition of armed power.

Armaments may be regulated and limited on the basis of either unilateral action or international agreement.

Unilateral Action Affecting Armed Power at Home and Abroad

Unilateral action occurs on the basis of the fact that general international law leaves each government free to choose its weapons and to arm
itself with them as heavily or as lightly as it pleases. A government may
confine itself to spears, or may concentrate on thermonuclear bombs. It
may maintain a bare minimum of armed power, or it may devote so
much of its resources to military purposes that a substantial portion of
its population starves. Within countries, governments may specify the
kind and quantity of weapons that private persons may legally possess.
Among countries no agency has developed which exercises comparable
functions. Such international regulations as exist concerning armaments
depend on treaties agreed to by the affected states.

Not only can states take unilateral action determining the extent of
their own military preparations, but they can also take unilateral actions
which affect the military strength of others. Specifically, under general
international law each state is free in time of peace to export and import
armaments and other war materials as it sees fit. It may buy peashooters
and battleships from anyone who will sell them, and it may sell or give
such weapons to anyone who will take them. It may also refuse to buy
or sell, and it is free to do so on a discriminatory basis. A government
which wishes to strengthen the economy or productive power of an ally
may place orders with it or its citizens for matériel, and may withhold
such orders from uncooperative or unfriendly states. Likewise, a government may regulate the exportation of its own products so as to make
them available to favored states and unavailable to others. Again, such
international regulations as exist concerning these matters depend on
treaties agreed to by the affected states.

Such rights and powers have been exercised increasingly in recent
years, as we shall see in the next chapter. The United States, for example,
refuses to sell strategic materials to the Soviet Union and its allies, and
it has brought strong pressure to bear on recipients of American aid to
follow the same policy. The communist states enforce analogous trade
restrictions. The result is that trade in strategic materials between East
and West has substantially ceased. Presumably both sides are somewhat
weaker militarily than they would be if such trade restrictions did not
exist, yet the effect is necessarily marginal. If most of the world were to
join in prohibiting the sale of strategic materials to a small country, that
country would presumably be condemned to weakness. However, when
the prohibition operates against a group of states commanding great

resources of their own, they are still likely to be able to develop great power.

Unilateral action is unlikely to lead to general disarmament. For various reasons, some states voluntarily refrain from arming themselves heavily, but many others fail to show similar restraint. Governments usually seem more inclined to sacrifice welfare for power than to forego power for the sake of welfare. And the greater the danger which they think they confront, or the greater their dissatisfaction with the status quo, the more heavily they are likely to arm. Moreover, unilateral efforts to limit the power of other states by imposing restrictions on international trade can scarcely have a drastic effect on the general level of armaments.

International Agreements on Armaments

International agreements are commonly regarded as a more promising basis for disarmament than unilateral action. Such agreements may be concluded in several types of circumstances: (1) those existing at the end of a war in which one side has achieved victory and can largely dictate the terms of peace; (2) those existing in the absence of an expectation of war; and (3) those existing in the presence of an expectation of war.

1. *Imposing disarmament on the defeated.* It is common for victors in war to disarm the defeated. Both the incentive and the power to do so are there. Victors normally wish to reduce to a minimum any prospect that the defeated might rebuild their power and seek revenge, and they therefore include in the treaty of peace provisions which impose more or less strict limits on the possession of armed power. After World War I, for example, the Allies reduced Germany's army to 100,000 men and restricted the German navy to a total of 36 ships. The air force was completely abolished, and Germany was prohibited from possessing certain specified weapons—tanks, for example. The whole Rhineland region, a rich industrial region lying along Germany's border with France and Belgium, was demilitarized, meaning that Germany could neither build fortifications nor station troops there. In effect, this made the Rhineland a hostage to Germany's good behavior, open to military occupation at the will of France and Belgium. After World War II, the Allies divided Germany and subjected it to military occupation, eliminating German armed power completely. Japanese armed power was likewise destroyed, and the armed establishments of other defeated countries were severely limited.

After neither of the world wars has the disarmament of the defeated countries proved to be enduring. After World War I the Allies failed to adopt effective means of detecting and preventing evasions and violations of the treaty on the part of Germany. Moreover, as time went on they gradually lost their determination to enforce the disarmament which they had imposed. Persistent evasions and violations finally led in 1935 to an open announcement by Hitler that Germany would no longer regard itself as bound by the disarmament provisions of the Treaty of Versailles, and in the following year he similarly repudiated the provisions calling for the demilitarization of the Rhineland. By 1936, therefore, Germany had thrown off the limitations on its armed power with impunity.

The disarmament of the defeated in World War II has likewise been short-lived. With the coming of the East-West struggle, victors on both sides have sought allies wherever they could find them, even among the former enemy states, and they have naturally not wished to enforce the disarmament of an ally. The problem has been not how to enforce disarmament but how and under what conditions to bring about rearmament.

In short, powerful forces work to undermine imposed arrangements for unequal disarmament. Victors tend to lose their determination to enforce such arrangements; they tend also to become divided against each other, and then some or all of them may reverse themselves and actively seek the rearmament of former enemies who are willing to co-operate. Moreover, the defeated states which have been disarmed are likely to chafe under the restrictions imposed upon them and to seek release, whether with the connivance or against the opposition of other states.

If the disarmament of the defeated is unlikely to endure, it is still less likely to lead to general disarmament, even when the victors regard themselves as peace-loving states which have now eliminated the power of the warlike. The victors normally either retain fear of the defeated or develop fear of each other, or both. Despite professions of a love of peace, some of them may also develop aggressive aspirations, which require that they be armed and that others retain arms in self-defense.

2. *Agreements between states not expecting war with each other.* The second of the types of circumstances in which disarmament may be sought is characterized by an absence of an expectation of war. Unfortunately for the prospects of disarmament, the absence of this expectation is never a general condition. Two states, or even a grouping of a number of states, may enjoy such harmonious relationships that they have no expectation of war with each other. They may therefore leave boundaries which they have in common substantially unguarded and may estimate their military needs without regard to the possibility of war among themselves. Canada and the United States provide the usual example of this kind of situation; under the Rush-Bagot agreement of 1817 the Great Lakes remain demilitarized, and by tacit accord the prin-

ciple of demilitarization has been extended to the remainder of the common boundary as well. A similar situation, though not based on formal agreement, exists in the relationships of a number of other states, for example, Norway and Sweden. But neither Canada and the United States nor any other combination of states live in the complete absence of an expectation of war. Though Canada and the United States may have no fear of each other, they both have had to recognize the possibility of war with outside powers—with Germany or Japan or the Soviet Union. The disarmament to which their mutual trust has led has therefore been strictly limited. Assured of peace with each other, they can simply devote their resources more fully to military preparedness against an outside power.

3. *Negotiations between potential enemies.* The last of the three types of circumstances in which disarmament may be sought is characterized by the existence of an expectation of war among the parties trying to negotiate the disarmament agreement. They may seek a general, across-the-board reduction or limitation of armaments. They may seek an agreement affecting only one branch of the armed forces, as at several of the interwar conferences aimed at limiting the naval power of the participants. They may seek agreements regarding the use of specified territories for military purposes, as when Britain, France, Japan, and the United States agreed in 1922 to maintain the status quo so far as the fortification of certain Pacific islands was concerned; or they may seek limitations on specific weapons or kinds of weapons, which is usually referred to as "qualitative" disarmament: for example, there have been efforts to limit the possession of "aggressive" weapons or weapons of mass destruction, such as the atomic bomb. Though hundreds of able men have devoted thousands of hours to thought, discussion, and negotiation about the problems involved in concluding agreements along these lines, the results have so far been very meager. States acting on the assumption that they may become involved in war with each other find it very difficult to agree on any plan for regulating and limiting their armed power. In the sections below we shall see why this is so.

WHY STATES PROPOSE DISARMAMENT

States which propose general agreements for disarmament do so for various reasons. Some, but not all, of them are good reasons, compatible with the end sought.

To Save Money

The desire to save money or, more properly, to permit the diversion of resources to purposes which are socially more desirable is a common reason for disarmament proposals. Anyone familiar with governmental budgets will realize that a very large proportion of national expenditures is devoted to defense. The figures given vary, depending on what is included in the defense category. For the United States, President Eisenhower has said that "64 per cent of the expenditures in the fiscal year 1957 will be for deterring possible aggression." [3] He included not only the costs of the American armed establishment but also all other costs connected with the defense program, for example, aid to foreign countries. If only the costs of the national armed establishment are counted, the major powers devote from about 20 per cent to about 35 per cent of their budgets to defense.[4] The Economic Commission for Europe once transformed expenditures into the equivalent in terms of man-years of industrial labor, with the results indicated in the table below.

Defense Expenditures Expressed in Terms of Industrial Years *

(Rough Estimates)

Country	Defense Expenditures, thousands of man-years		Defense Expenditures, man-years per 1,000 inhabitants	
	1949	1951	1949	1951
France	1,600	2,200	38	51
Netherlands	250	475	25	46
Poland	275	450	11	18
United Kingdom	2,300	4,200	46	82
U.S.S.R.	8,400	10,200	42	49
United States	4,700	11,400	31	74

* *Source:* U.N. Department of Economic Affairs, *Economic Survey of Europe in 1950*, prepared by the Economic Commission for Europe (Geneva, 1951), pp. 136-138.

The figures indicate that in 1951 the defense expenditures of the United States, for instance, were great enough to pay average industrial wages to 11,400,000 men for a year; they also show that, for every 1000 men, women, and children in the country, the labor of 74 average industrial workers was devoted to the defense effort.

The burden of defense expenditures is also sometimes measured by determining what proportion of the Gross National Product they will buy. Illustrative statistics appear in the table on p. 235.

However computed and compared, the burden of maintaining armed strength is clearly a heavy one for most states. Expenditures for armaments are, for the most part, unproductive. The millions of men recruited for the armed forces of various countries do not produce things which make life better either for themselves or for the remainder of the popu-

[3] *State Department Bulletin*, Vol. 34 (January 30, 1956), p. 147.
[4] U.N. Department of Economic Affairs, *Economic Survey of Europe in 1950*, prepared by the Economic Commission for Europe (Geneva, 1951), pp. 136-137.

lation. On the contrary, they consume the production of others. Resources devoted to the building of battleships and aircraft carriers cannot be devoted to the construction of schools and hospitals. Men who are manning guns cannot at the same time make refrigerators and air-conditioning units. Talents devoted to the science and art of war cannot, except as an incidental byproduct, improve the social and cultural well-being of a people. While millions and millions of people throughout the world are poorly clothed, poorly fed, poorly housed, poorly educated, and poorly safeguarded from disease, millions and millions of others devote themselves to developing means of destroying life and property. The tragic anachronism is so obvious that demands for disarmament naturally follow. Except perhaps where armament programs serve as regulators of the domestic economy, this motive for disarmament is genuine.

Defense Expenditures as a Percentage of Gross National Product *

	1938	1952-1953	1955
Denmark	0.9	3.9	4
France	7.3	10.7	7
Italy	6.0	6.1	3
Netherlands	2.3	7.7	6
United Kingdom	6.5	10.8	8
United States	1.2	17.8	11

* Data for 1938 and 1952-1953 are taken from: U.S. Senate, Committee on Foreign Relations, *The Mutual Security Act of 1952*, Report ... No. 1490, 82d Congress, 2d Session (Washington, 1952), p. 22. For countries other than the United States, data for 1955 are taken from: U.N. Department of Economic and Social Affairs, *Economic Survey of Europe in 1955*, prepared by the Economic Commission for Europe (Geneva, 1956), p. 7. The figure for the United States in 1955 is computed from federal statistics on Gross National Product and defense expenditures.

To Reduce Tensions and the Danger of War

The desire to reduce international tensions is another reason for proposals for disarmament. This desire is no doubt often as genuine as the desire to reduce costs, but it rests on one or more assumptions which do not always hold true and which, even when true, are often not as significant as they are held to be. One set of related assumptions is that armaments themselves induce or exacerbate tensions, that the possession of power creates a temptation to wield it, and, most particularly, that the development of an armaments race increases the probability of war. Another assumption relates specifically to atomic and other weapons of mass destruction: it is that agreement concerning the possession and use of such weapons, presumably involving their outlawry, might reduce tensions based on fear of a holocaust, whether wrought in a surprise attack or after the outbreak of war has given due warning. Those accepting such assumptions as these hope that a reduction and limitation of armaments by international agreement would diminish both the probability and the destructiveness of war.

1. Do armaments cause tension and war? There is, of course, something to be said for these assumptions. When a government arms, it gives tangible evidence of thoughts of war; this very fact may increase the fears of another government, forcing it also to think in terms of war and leading it to arm itself more heavily. A vicious circle (or spiral) may thus be created, in which the military preparations of one state accentuate the fears of another, leading it to engage in military preparations, which in turn accentuate the fears of the first. As we have seen, a balance of power may be maintained in which neither state will feel that it dares to resort to war. But those who are militarily minded will have been brought to the fore. A military machine and perhaps a military class or caste may have been created which may feel the need of war; Schumpeter's theory of imperialism should be recalled in this connection. If time seems to be running against one side in the armaments race, even those among its leaders who are peacefully inclined may conclude that the risks of postponing a showdown are too great. Thus, though an armaments program may contribute to a balancing of power, it may also exacerbate tensions and accentuate forces making for war.

Yet, though there is some basis for the assumption that disarmament might relieve tensions and reduce the dangers of war, there are considerations of a more fundamental sort which must be taken into account. We have already seen that states arm themselves for various reasons, and that not all these reasons can be denounced as capricious. A state may arm itself in a desire to bring about changes in the status quo, in which case it will hardly be attracted to disarmament by the thought that disarmament might relieve international tensions. Another state may arm itself to preserve existing rights and interests, in which case it will understandably insist on a reduction or elimination of dangers as a prerequisite to disarmament. In other words, armaments are a symptom more than a cause. The tensions and the dangers of war which go with armaments are to be attributed to the forces that produce armaments programs more than to the armaments themselves. The argument that disarmament would make war less likely is (if a slight exaggeration is permitted) somewhat akin to the argument that the elimination of doctors and hospitals would make sickness less likely. It involves some confusion between cause and effect; it involves the transformation of correlations into causal relations.

Quincy Wright even suggests that the quantitative reduction of armaments, in itself, "would probably tend to increase the frequency of war." He reasons that war is more likely to lead into a mutually destructive stalemate when states are heavily armed than when they are lightly armed, in other words, that a quantitative reduction of armaments increases the prospect that one side or the other can win a relatively inexpensive victory.[5]

2. *Would outlawry of nuclear weapons make war less likely?* The hope that agreements outlawing or otherwise regulating the possession and use of weapons of mass destruction would significantly reduce international tensions and so make war less likely is probably also misplaced. In the first place, it is doubtful whether such agreements would significantly reduce dangers of a devastating surprise attack, unless they were accompanied by rascal-proof means of detecting violations quickly. This has been a principal contention of the United States in the negotiations on an international agreement for the elimination or regulation of nuclear weapons.

Even if it were possible to achieve by treaty the complete elimination of all existing bombs and all plants and stockpiles of fissionable materials, the fears and suspicions of nations would still not be removed. While it is true that the absence of bombs would seem to remove any opportunity to embark on adventures in atomic warfare, it would at the same time create the ideal opportunity for a nation bent on aggression to achieve a complete monopoly of atomic power. In a world made bombless by treaty, the first to violate the treaty would gain an enormous advantage. Under such conditions the opportunities for world dominance would be breath-taking! Hence we come to the paradox that the further the nations go by international agreement in the direction of eliminating bombs and installations, the stronger becomes the temptation to evade the agreement.[6]

In the absence of a really effective system of inspection and detection, one or more states might well succumb to such temptation. Governments which themselves wished to observe the agreement in good faith would inevitably fear that other governments might not do so, and the consequent uncertainties, suspicions, and fears might have a more corrosive effect on international relations than would the certain knowledge that various states possessed the awesome weapons. A number of governments might feel obliged to violate the agreement secretly simply because of a belief (verified by espionage or not) that one or more other governments were doing so. Whatever the reason for secret violations, the danger of devastating surprise attack would remain. Nor is it likely that the situation would be substantially different if the international agreement provided that weapons of mass destruction could be possessed only by an international agency. Individual states might still violate the agreement. Moreover, the stocks of weapons possessed by the international agency would naturally have to be located somewhere on earth,

[5] Quincy Wright, *A Study of War* (Chicago, The University of Chicago Press, 1942), Vol. II, p. 802.
[6] Frederick Sherwood Dunn, in Bernard Brodie, ed., *The Absolute Weapon: Atomic Power and World Order* (New York, Harcourt, Brace, 1946), p. 15.

and then they would be subject to seizure by one or more national governments.

3. *Would outlawry make the use of nuclear weapons less likely?* It is still less likely that outlawing or otherwise regulating the possession and use of weapons of mass destruction would restrain states once they became involved in war. Suppose, for example, that an international agreement existed which prohibited the possession and use of atomic or thermonuclear bombs. Suppose, further, that up to the outbreak of war every belligerent had observed the agreement. There would then be several possibilities.

In the first place, the agreement might conceivably be respected even in wartime, but this is unlikely.

In the second place, one or more belligerents might willfully violate the agreement. Each one might think that it could produce nuclear weapons faster than the enemy, so that it would for a time enjoy a monopoly position. Even if the monopoly were due to last for only a few days, it might well determine the outcome of the war. Through an ultimatum or through an actual, devastating attack, the belligerent which enjoyed the monopoly might force the capitulation of the enemy. It is obvious that such a possibility would sorely tempt the belligerents, and it seems probable that one or more of them would succumb to the temptation. In this case, a peacetime agreement outlawing the possession and use of atomic or thermonuclear bombs might simply lead to a race to manufacture them once war got under way, and whoever won the race might well win the war.

The third possibility is that one or more belligerents might violate the agreement regretfully rather than willfully. The situation might be similar to the one cited above, prevailing in peacetime. Various belligerents might believe or fear, rightly or not, that others would violate the agreement in search of a decisive power advantage. If only to avoid being placed in a position of hopeless inferiority, they would thus probably feel compelled to violate the agreement themselves. Thus, here too, the peacetime agreement outlawing weapons of mass destruction would lead to a wartime race to manufacture them.

In short, the desire to reduce international tensions through disarmament agreements, though often genuine, is based to quite an extent on a failure to engage in cogent and realistic thinking. In all probability the means chosen (disarmament) would not contribute significantly to the achievement of the end desired; it might even accentuate suspicions and tensions rather than relax them. If that is true, it is clear why this reason for proposing disarmament has not proved to be very compelling.

To Achieve a Power Advantage

The desire of states to improve their relative power position, or to avert a decline in relative power, is another factor which prompts disarmament proposals. In the discussion of the balancing of power, we have already seen that statesmen seek a satisfactory, relative power position for their states. One possible way of achieving or preserving it is through international agreements on the reduction and limitation of armaments. It is obviously less costly from several points of view to weaken a potential enemy at a conference, if it can be done there, than to attempt it on the battlefield. But a conference at which each participant is seeking greater relative strength for himself, and greater relative weakness for others, is not a conference which has good prospects of success. Where one state's gain is another state's loss, and where nothing can be done except by unanimous consent, impasse is the most likely result.

This, in fact, has been the usual outcome of disarmament conferences and proposals. The first of the great modern disarmament conferences, held at The Hague in 1899, was called by the Russian Tsar. Among the considerations influencing him and his government was the fact that Germany was equipping its army with rapid-firing artillery and that the state of Russian finances made it very difficult for Russia to keep pace. Moreover, the Russian Foreign Minister felt that the distribution of power at the time was favorable and that "an agreement not to increase forces would leave Russia her great preponderance." [7] Naturally, however, the Tsar found the Germans (and others) uncooperative about limiting their armed power for the advantage of Russia. The results, in terms of agreement on armaments, were negligible. The conference did, however, succeed in concluding a series of conventions (treaties) codifying the laws and customs of war.

The situation was reversed at the time of the Conference on the Reduction and Limitation of Naval Armaments, held in Washington in 1921-1922.[8] The initiator this time was the United States, which had no fear of being outdistanced by others; in fact, it had a naval building program under way which other states could scarcely have matched. They were therefore receptive to American proposals. Moreover, the possibility of war among the participants in the Washington Conference was rather far in the background, and this facilitated agreement. Notwithstanding the favorable circumstances, however, agreement was reached

[7] William L. Langer, *The Diplomacy of Imperialism. 1890-1902* (New York, Knopf, 1935), Vol. II, p. 583.

[8] See Harold and Margaret Sprout, *Toward a New Order of Sea Power* (Princeton, Princeton University Press, 1940).

only on the number of capital ships (battleships and heavy carriers) that the parties might have.

Subsequent conferences, called to extend the arrangement so as to make it cover all kinds of naval vessels, proved futile for various reasons, and Japan terminated the Washington agreement as soon as it was legally free to do so. The record largely justifies the conclusion that "a naval disarmament conference becomes . . . a paper war in which each delegation tries to preserve its own fleet and to sink as much of the other fleets as possible." [9]

The desire of states to improve their relative power position, or to avert a decline in relative power, operated also in connection with the efforts of the League of Nations to bring about general disarmament. It became evident, as the same observer put it, that "states are always perfectly willing to disarm provided their potential enemies disarm more." [10] When many states tacitly insist on such a proviso, it is obviously improbable that agreement can be reached. In fact, the League's efforts resulted in complete failure.

Negotiations since World War II concerning nuclear weapons have been influenced by the same desire. Particularly during the period when the United States enjoyed a monopoly of atomic weapons, the Kremlin's proposals to outlaw their possession and use were obviously calculated to improve the relative power position of the Soviet Union. Even since the termination of the American monopoly, outlawry would still presumably work to the advantage of the states in the Moscow-Peking sphere. Given their totalitarian controls, they could probably violate the agreement with less risk of detection. Moreover, if the agreement were observed, an important counterweight to their tremendous manpower would be removed. On the other side, the proposals championed by the United States and by the non-communist members of the United Nations Atomic Energy Commission would probably have worked to the advantage of the West from a power point of view, for several reasons. In the first place, neither the specific agreement proposed nor any other could have deprived the United States of the advantage which it held for a time in terms of scientific knowledge and technical, manufacturing know-how; had the Soviet Union accepted the American proposals when they were first made, it probably could not have caught up with the United States as fast as it seems to have done by retaining full freedom of action. In the second place, the Western proposals would probably have worked out to the power advantage of the West through decisions concerning the location of atomic plants and laboratories, if not also through decisions concerning the location of nuclear weapons placed in the hands of a

[9] Nicholas J. Spykman, *America's Strategy in World Politics* (New York, Harcourt, Brace, 1942), p. 168.
[10] *Ibid.*

United Nations agency. It is a fair guess, at least, that the West would have sought criteria for locating and manning nuclear installations so as to give itself an advantage if seizures of such installations ever occurred. In the third place, a power advantage would probably have accrued to the West from the very extensive piercing (if not the elimination) of the Iron Curtain, for which the American proposals called. If it is true that the proposals of each side would have worked to the disadvantage of the other from a power point of view, it is understandable why agreement has not been reached.

To Achieve a Propaganda Advantage

Another common reason for proposals of disarmament relates to public opinion. As we have seen, public attitudes at home and abroad are an element in the power position of a state. The common assumption is that the public favors disarmament. It is therefore assumed that people at home and abroad will be inclined to give sympathy and support to a government which champions disarmament, and be inclined to withhold sympathy and support from a government which can be made to appear to obstruct disarmament. Disarmament proposals may therefore be made with no expectation whatever that they will be accepted, but only for the purpose of winning friends and influencing people. For example, after the Soviet Union proposed total disarmament in 1927, a world congress of the Communist International explained that there had been no expectation that the proposal would be accepted. Rather, the objectives had been to enlist sympathy for the Soviet Union as the champion of peace, to expose the "imperialists" as enemies of peace, to eradicate alleged pacifist illusions, and to provide a basis for propaganda in support of "the only way toward disarmament and the abolition of war, viz., arming the proletarian dictatorship." [11] The aim at disarmament conferences may thus be more to secure good publicity for one's own side and bad publicity for the potential enemy than to secure agreement. When this is the situation, it is not surprising that agreement is not reached.

In sum, proposals for disarmament by international agreement are based on one or more desires: (1) to save money, or to permit the use of resources for more constructive purposes; (2) to reduce tensions and so to diminish the danger of war; (3) to improve the relative power position of the state, or to avert a decline in power; and (4) to gain a propaganda advantage. Of these desires, only the first is well reasoned and fully compatible with the successful achievement of the declared objective. Vast resources are in fact allocated for essentially unproductive military purposes that could be used to promote ends which are socially more

[11] *International Press Correspondence,* Vol. 8 (November 28, 1928), pp. 1596-1597.

desirable. The remaining reasons for discussions of disarmament are unlikely actually to promote agreement. Tensions and war dangers are largely created by factors other than armaments; they would persist even if agreement were reached on the reduction and limitation of armaments, and might be accentuated. The desire to gain a power advantage by means of a disarmament agreement can be effectuated only if the other side is willing or if its calculations of the effect of the agreement on power relationships differ. The search for a propaganda advantage can obviously contribute little or nothing to the actual achievement of agreement.

OBSTACLES TO AGREEMENT ON DISARMAMENT

Voluntary agreement on disarmament is difficult to achieve only in part because the underlying desires are not all well-reasoned and fully compatible with the objective. There are additional obstacles.

Armaments Are Needed

A fundamental one relates to a consideration advanced at the beginning of this chapter: that armaments have useful functions and that they serve a number of important purposes. States depend upon them, and are not likely to give them up or accept serious restrictions on them until alternative means of serving the same functions and purposes have been established. During the interwar period, there was a prolonged and important argument over the order in which arbitration, security, and disarmament should be sought. (The term *arbitration* in this context referred to the various means by which the peaceful settlement of international disputes is assured.) As matters turned out, the half-measures adopted to promote arbitration and security proved to be an inadequate basis for disarmament. Most of the states involved believed that they had to remain armed to safeguard their own rights and interests. They believed that they needed armed power both as an inducement to other states to accept the peaceful settlement of disputes and as something to fall back on in the event that efforts to achieve satisfactory peaceful settlement failed. Further, as events proved, a few of the states wanted to retain and build up their armaments for purposes of aggression.

In other words, one of the major obstacles to disarmament is the absence of reliable substitutes for armed power for the achievement of a number of the objectives which states seek. Within countries, people disarm only after a police force has been established to assure them protection, and only after executive, legislative, and judicial methods have been adopted by which rights and interests can be safeguarded and promoted. Analogous substitutes for armed power will probably have to be found internationally before states can be induced to disarm.

The Problem of Agreement on Ratios of Strength

Another fundamental obstacle to disarmament by voluntary consent derives from the fact that agreement on disarmament presupposes agreement on ratios of strength among armed establishments. What basis is there for determining the ratios which ought to prevail? By what criteria is it to be decided that one state "needs" or ought to be allowed to have fifteen units of armed power, another state twelve units, and another state two?

Attempts to answer the question fall into two general categories. The first category includes answers plainly designed to serve the power interests of a particular state or group of states. Salvador de Madariaga tells of negotiations which once occurred over the limitation of naval armaments. Various states, including Great Britain, had built up their naval power during World War I. Others, including Spain, had been unable to do so. Britain wanted Spain to accept the status quo so far as relative naval strength was concerned, but Spain was reluctant.

One day the Spanish Admiral accosted the British Admiral at the end of the sitting and declared himself ready to accept the status quo. His British colleague was very much elated. Then the Spaniard added: "But we must discuss one point, the year to be chosen to define the status quo." "Why," said the Englishman, "1921." "Oh, no," said the Spaniard: "I suggest 1588." [12]

A state which finds existing power ratios satisfactory to it and its allies will naturally want to preserve them. It is likely to be favorably disposed toward a standstill arrangement or toward the reduction of armed strength on a percentage basis. It will thus preserve a favorable position. By the same token, states which regard the existing power ratio as unsatisfactory are likely to reject it as a basis for agreement. If they favor disarmament at all, it will be on the basis of a more advantageous ratio which prevailed in earlier years, or on the basis of a new ratio considered desirable for the future. The same kinds of considerations operate when qualitative disarmament is considered; states are likely to favor disarmament in those weapons in which potential enemy states have an advantage.

The second category of answers includes those seriously designed to bring about the reduction and limitation of armaments on an equitable basis. They reflect the subjective judgments of individuals—based on a wide variety of possible considerations—on the question of appropriate and acceptable power ratios. If the judgments are wise, and particularly if, in addition, war seems remote, the proposals might be accepted. However, this combination of circumstances is very rare. What judgments about ratios of power can be wise when most or all of the

[12] de Madariaga, *op. cit.*, p. 106.

states involved want to gain or maintain a power advantage at the expense of the others?[13]

The Problem of Implementing Agreement on Ratios

Even if there were agreement on the ratios of power which ought to prevail among states seeking disarmament, there would still be great obstacles to agreement. The above reference to units of power was euphemistic. There is no such thing. Weights and distances can be measured; speed can be clocked; the energy available in coal and oil can be transformed arithmetically into kilowatt-hours of electricity equivalent, but there is no standard unit for computing power. If all states had precisely the same weapons and trained equally capable men in precisely the same way, it would be more nearly possible to say what quantities of this and that would produce the agreed ratios of power. But this is not the situation. Some states have thermonuclear bombs and others do not. Some have atomic artillery and others do not. Some stress tanks that are heavy and slow, and others stress tanks that are light and fast. Some naval powers are strong in submarines; others are strong in battleships. Some give relatively brief periods of training to vast numbers of men; others give more intensive training to fewer men. How many submarines equal one battleship in terms of power? How many mortars equal one thermonuclear bomb? How many poorly trained soldiers equal one professional? No precise and reliable answer to such questions is possible. There is no known way of reducing the power of battleships, submarines, atomic artillery, and rifles to comparable terms. Moreover, as we have seen, armed establishments are not the only elements of national power, and, once armaments are reduced, other elements of power become proportionately more important. How much allowance should be made for the fact that the frontiers of one state are naturally less defensible than the frontiers of another? What weight should be given in the scales of power to such items as commercial aircraft and merchant ships, which can be converted for military purposes when need arises? How much allowance should be made for the prospect that, if a disarmament agreement were violated, one state would be able to rearm more rapidly than another? As Salvador de Madariaga says, the destruction of the eggs of armaments would still leave some states in a favored position in terms of the possession of hens. Given good feeling and an absence of expectation of war, problems of this kind would be easily resolved, and it would not matter much how they were resolved. But an expectation of war necessitates jealous regard for every aspect of the power position of the state; even if we assume that there has been an agreement on what the ratio of power should be, this attitude is likely

[13] Wright, *op. cit.*, Vol. II, p. 803.

to lead states into an impasse when it comes to determining precisely how many men each may have under arms in each branch of the armed forces and precisely how many of which weapons each may have.

The Problem of Distrust

Even if all these obstacles were somehow overcome, there would still be another which might block agreement. Frequently governments do not trust each other. This is particularly true in relationships between communist and non-communist states; it may be true even among allies, as the current French attitude toward the regulation of the armed power of Western Germany indicates. In questions as important as the level of armaments, the parties to an agreement want and need assurances that the agreement will be observed. How can such assurances be obtained?

This problem has been especially acute in relation to the question of the international control of atomic energy. As we have already suggested, the temptation to violate an agreement on nuclear weapons would be especially strong. The negotiating states have therefore simply assumed that they could not rely on each other's good faith. In fact, the non-communist countries, led by the United States, insisted on very sweeping arrangements designed to prevent and detect evasions. The plan provided that an international control agency would own all source material of atomic energy from the moment it was removed from the ground, that the agency would own and manage dangerous facilities capable of producing or utilizing nuclear fuel, that it would license (and thus be in a position to control) most other activities relating to the production of nuclear fuel, and that it could engage in unlimited inspections within participating countries, including ground and aerial surveys. Only by such devices, it was felt, could adequate assurances be secured against the secret production and stockpiling of nuclear weapons. From the Soviet point of view, the proposed arrangements constituted an infringement of sovereignty. For this and for other reasons the Soviet Union refused to endorse the plan, and no agreement for the international control of atomic energy has been reached.

Where distrust runs so deep that no reliance is placed on the good faith of other states, this kind of result is very likely. The search for sure guarantees against violation leads almost necessarily to plans of inspection and control which involve extensive foreign interference and participation in the domestic affairs of states. In the best of situations, the interference and participation is likely to be very unwelcome, and it is likely to be completely unacceptable when hatred and distrust of some of the foreigners who would be engaged in inspection and control activities is intense. In other words, another vicious circle is involved. Severe tension and distrust make extensive international interference in domestic affairs necessary if disarmament is to be achieved, but the same tension and distrust make such interference unacceptable. Even if the Soviet Union had accepted the United Nations plan for the international control of atomic energy, it is questionable whether two-thirds of the United States Senate would have permitted American ratification of the treaty, in view of the prospect that it would bring many Russian Communists into the United States.

DISARMAMENT AND POLITICAL SETTLEMENT

The problem of disarmament may be tackled either directly or indirectly. We have already explored the difficulties in the way of the direct approach. When states regard armaments as useful and necessary, whether to give latent support to peaceful diplomacy or to provide strength in war, they are naturally reluctant to disarm, and determined that any disarmament which occurs shall not have an adverse effect on their power position. To expect states to disarm before the need for armaments is removed or reduced is like expecting an American frontiersman to abandon his musket in the face of a threat from the Indians and in the absence of police protection.

For the frontiersman, disarmament was brought about largely by indirect means. Threats from Indians and from other sources were reduced or eliminated. Police forces were organized. Legislative, executive, and judicial agencies were established through which rights and interests could be protected or promoted. The frontiersman became a citizen in an organized community, and then he no longer needed to rely on private weapons.

Something similar is probably necessary if disarmament by international agreement is ever to occur on an extensive scale. As Salvador de Madariaga put it,[14] "The problem of disarmament is not the problem of disarmament. It really is the problem of the organization of the World-Community." Quincy Wright comes to a similar conclusion: [15]

Successful disarmament treaties have always been accompanied by political arrangements which were believed by the parties to augment their political security or to settle their outstanding political problems. The two have gone hand in hand, and, considering the conditions of successful negotiation, it is unlikely that agreement will ever be reached on the technical problems of disarmament unless the parties have lessened tensions by political settlements or by general acceptance of international procedures creating confidence that such settlements can be effected peacefully.

Likewise, the Commission for Conventional Armaments, established by the Security Council of the United Nations, concluded in 1948 that [16]

[14] de Madariaga, op. cit., p. 56.
[15] Wright, op. cit. (copyright 1942 by the University of Chicago), Vol. II, pp. 800-801.
[16] Andrew Martin, Collective Security (Paris, UNESCO, 1952), p. 83.

A system of regulation and reduction of armaments and armed forces can only be put into effect in an atmosphere of international confidence and security. Measures for the regulation and reduction of armaments which would follow the establishment of the necessary degree of confidence might in turn be expected to increase confidence and so justify further measures of regulation and reduction.

The possibility of organizing the world community or of establishing the political prerequisites of disarmament is a topic which will be explored in later chapters.

SUGGESTED READINGS

BERNARD, Stephan, "Some Political and Technical Implications of Disarmament," *World Politics*, Vol. 8 (October, 1955), pp. 71-90.

CAVERS, David F., "The Challenge of Planning Arms Controls," *Foreign Affairs*, Vol. 34 (October, 1955), pp. 50-66.

CLARK, Grenville, *A Plan for Peace* (New York, Harper, 1950).

DE MADARIAGA, Salvador, *Disarmament* (New York, Coward-McCann, 1929).

"Disarmament: Proposals and Negotiations, 1946-1955," *World Today*, Vol. 11 (August, 1955), pp. 334-348.

FRYE, William R., *Disarmament; Atoms into Plowshares?* Headline Series, No. 113 (New York, Foreign Policy Association, 1955).

SPINGARN, Jerome H., *Is Disarmament Possible?* Public Affairs Pamphlet, No. 235 (New York, Public Affairs Committee, 1956).

SPROUT, Harold and Margaret, *Toward a New Order of Sea Power* (Princeton, Princeton University Press, 1940).

TATE, Merze, *The Disarmament Illusion, the Movement for a Limitation of Armaments to 1907* (New York, Macmillan, 1942).

TATE, Merze, *The United States and Armaments* (Cambridge, Harvard University Press, 1948).

WHEELER-BENNETT, John W., *The Pipe-Dream of Peace: The Story of the Collapse of Disarmament* (New York, Morrow, 1935).

CHAPTER 13

The Pursuit of Objectives by Economic Means

THE FOCUS in the last several chapters has been on power. We have studied the elements of power, the balancing of power, and the problem of armaments and disarmament in relation to the power position of states. Now it is time to recall that not all the objectives of states are power objectives. Governments are concerned with ideologies. They seek the preservation of a given way of life at home; sometimes they also seek to preserve or extend a political or economic system abroad. Moreover, governments are concerned with the well-being or prosperity of people; their concern may be restricted to the well-being of only a portion of the population of the home state, or it may extend to the whole population, or it may extend to people abroad as well.

Whatever the objective, proper action in the economic field is likely to promote its achievement. Certainly the economic policies of a government will have a marked impact on the amount of power that it can muster; similarly, the economic policies of one government may have considerable effect on the power that other governments can command. Ideologies and economics are also intertwined; economic deprivations help make people susceptible to the appeals of extremist political movements, whereas economic satisfaction reinforces the going system. Obviously, a government's policies in the economic field are likely to have much to do with the level of domestic well-being achieved; they may also affect well-being abroad.

In this book on international politics we are not concerned with the whole field of economics or even with all the economic policies of governments. Most aspects of the subject are best left to the economists and to students of domestic politics. We are, however, concerned with economic policies which enter directly into the field of international relations—with those economic means by which governments seek to promote foreign policy objectives or by which they seek to promote other objectives in

cooperation or conflict with foreign states. This means that we are concerned with national policies and international agreements relating to:
(1) foreign exchange, that is, the purchase or sale of the money of one
state in exchange for the money of another; (2) the international exchange
of goods and services; and (3) foreign investments.

These subjects are vast. Again it is best to leave a substantial portion of
the relevant material to the economists, especially the discussion of the
rather complex theories which are associated with foreign economic policies. We can, however, draw on some conclusions of the economists, and
we can see what states in fact do, and what they hope to accomplish, in
promoting or regulating international commercial transactions.

Note might be made at the outset of the fact that general international
law (i.e., law applicable to all states, as distinct from treaty law, which
is applicable only to the parties to the treaty) leaves each government
substantially free to regulate international commercial transactions as it
sees fit. It may monopolize the field itself, establishing state trading
agencies and prohibiting its nationals from engaging in international trade
on a private basis. If it permits private trade, it may fix the conditions on
the basis of which it occurs. It may prohibit either the import or export
of some or all goods, or adopt less severe regulations—for example, regulations permitting goods to be imported only if a tariff duty is paid. A
government, within the limits of its jurisdiction, may prohibit or regulate
the purchase or sale of its currency. With some qualifications to be noted
later, each government is free to prohibit or regulate the commercial
activities of foreigners in its territory. Measures taken to regulate international trade may discriminate among foreign states; thus a higher tariff
rate may be imposed on wood products from the Soviet Union than on
the same products from Canada, and the export of oil may be made legal
or illegal, depending on whether the destination of the oil is China or
Britain. It goes without saying that economic aid of various kinds may
be extended to one state though denied to another. The freedom of states
to regulate international commercial activities, and to do so on a discriminatory basis, means that economics can easily be made a weapon in deal-
ings with foreign states.

FOREIGN EXCHANGE

Some Bases for Governmental Action

The obvious fact should be stressed that international economic activities involve relationships among different economies. Each sovereign state
maintains its own monetary system, pursues its own fiscal and tax policies,
and develops its own price and income structure. Nevertheless, the very
fact that goods, services, and capital are exchanged means that the various
national economies are not entirely independent of each other. The expan-

sion and contraction of foreign commerce are factors which affect both the level of well-being and the level of power that states attain.

Though barter deals among countries occur, international transactions generally involve the use of money. The importer pays for what he gets either in the currency of his own country or in the currency of the exporter, depending on the terms of the bargain. For one party or the other, a foreign currency is thus involved. If the importer is to pay in foreign currency, he will presumably have to buy it first. If the exporter is paid in a foreign currency, he may want to sell it and repatriate the proceeds. The buying and selling of foreign currency are foreign exchange transactions. The price of one currency in terms of another is its foreign exchange rate.

Governments may interfere or participate in foreign exchange transactions just as they may interfere or participate in foreign trade. A government may, for example, permit its currency to be bought and sold freely, in which case its currency is said to be freely convertible, or it may impose limitations and restrictions. It may take action to fix or regulate the foreign exchange rate of its currency.

Now obviously the convertibility of a currency and its foreign exchange rate have much to do with the foreign trade of the country involved. A Frenchman who cannot convert his francs into dollars faces an obstacle if he wants to make a purchase in the United States. He may or may not be able to find an American exporter who is willing to receive inconvertible francs. If conversion is possible, the foreign exchange rate becomes all-important. Is the rate a stable one? Stability is generally regarded as the best basis for trade, though speculators may be attracted to the gambling possibilities of a situation in which rates are fluctuating. Is the rate high or low? The more dollars a British subject can buy with his pounds sterling, the more he will be encouraged to make purchases in the United States; conversely, the fewer pounds Americans can buy with dollars, the less will they want to import from Britain. These statements assume some elasticity of demand.

Closely associated with the problem of exchange rates is the problem of the balance of payments, that is, the relationship between payments and receipts in connection with the international exchange of goods, services, and capital. The so-called balance may or may not be in equilibrium. When all of a country's exports pay for all of its imports, with gold holdings and other reserves neither increased nor reduced, equilibrium exists; otherwise there is disequilibrium. Over any short term, some disequilibrium is virtually inevitable. Over a long period, however, substantial equilibrium must be maintained, for nations must pay their way.[1]

[1] See Harry G. Brainard, *International Economics and Public Policy* (New York, Holt, 1954), esp. pp. 227-255; Lawrence W. Towle, *International Trade and Commercial Policy* (New York, Harper, 1948), pp. 155-214.

What kinds of actions do governments take concerning the convertibility and the exchange rates of their currencies? What objectives do they seek to serve in so doing? We shall not attempt to explore and explain many of the forces at work in influencing governmental policies, for an understanding of them requires considerable knowledge of economics. Neither shall we describe all the possible lines of governmental action. A few will be sufficient.

Governmental Policies: The Gold Standard and Its Abandonment

Up to 1914 and during some of the interwar years most governments based their money on the gold standard, meaning that they stood ready to buy or sell gold at a fixed price and to permit the gold to be imported and exported freely. With almost all countries fixing the value of their currencies in terms of gold, a common denominator existed; foreign exchange rates became obvious and stable. There was some fluctuation in the rates, depending on supply and demand, but any considerable deviation from the standard rate simply led to a shipment of gold. The theory was that such adjustments as were needed to keep the balance of payments in substantial equilibrium should occur in the domestic economies of the various states. They were to allow domestic price and income levels to rise and fall, and this in turn would encourage or discourage exports and imports. If deflation and unemployment occurred, it was unfortunate.

With the gold standard, and indeed under any system in which there is an effort to maintain a fixed exchange rate, governments may devalue their currency, meaning that they may cut its price. The United States devalued its currency during the depression simply by raising the price at which it bought and sold gold. Each dollar thereafter was worth less in terms of gold, as well as in terms of other currencies. Although the action was mainly induced by concern for the domestic price level, there was also hope that devaluation would encourage exports by permitting foreigners to get more dollars with the same amount of their own currency or of gold. From the point of view of the foreigner, the effect of devaluation was a cut in the price of all American goods and services. One hope was that he would thus be induced to buy more in the American market, providing employment for American workers; as some put it, the idea was to export unemployment. The difficulty was that many other countries also devalued their currencies, and competitive devaluations turned out to be a losing game.

Regardless of the possibility of manipulating the price of gold, the international gold standard broke down, and for many reasons. The principal one was that, as World War I and the depression disrupted trade patterns, governments became unwilling to allow the violent fluctuations in the domestic economy which adherence to the gold standard entailed.

Generally, they determined to stress domestic stability and full employment, seeking equilibrium in the international balance of payments, or "controlled disequilibrium," through actions affecting foreign exchange.[2]

Various policies in this area are possible. Governments may adopt a paper currency standard, under which foreign exchange rates find their own level through the operation of the law of supply and demand, and under which considerable fluctuation in exchange rates may occur. Alternatively, governments may adopt regulatory devices or controls of one kind or another. They may seek to "peg" foreign exchange rates, which means that they seek to modify the fluctuations to which a paper currency standard might lead by entering the foreign exchange market themselves, buying and selling (within limits) to compensate for shifts in supply and demand. They may adopt exchange control.

Governmental Policies: Exchange Control

Under a thorough system of exchange control, the government monopolizes the buying and selling of foreign currency. Those needing foreign currency may get it only from the government, and those who acquire foreign currency must sell it to the government. This puts the government in a position to control and direct all legal international commercial transactions, including foreign travel on the part of its citizens. It may provide foreign exchange for purchases in one country, but refuse to provide it for purchases in another. It may provide foreign exchange for the importation of one type of goods, but refuse to provide it for the importation of another type. If foreigners acquire currency of the country, "blocked accounts" may develop, that is, currency holdings which cannot be converted. Differential foreign exchange rates may be adopted, meaning that the government may make foreign exchange available at a bargain rate for certain purposes, and charge a stiff price in other connections.

Exchange control may apply only to certain foreign currencies, whereas free convertibility into others is allowed. For many years, for example, a "sterling bloc" has existed, that is, a group of countries which allow the free conversion of their currency into the British pound sterling at a fixed rate, while exercising control over conversion into American dollars and certain other currencies. The European Payments Union (EPU), though not providing for free convertibility, significantly facilitates the handling of foreign exchange problems among its members. British membership in the EPU means that a kind of marriage between it and the sterling bloc has occurred, increasing the number of countries among which international trade can occur with relative freedom from exchange control.

Through exchange control, if it is rigorous enough, a government can

[2] Lloyd A. Metzler, "The Theory of International Trade," in Howard S. Ellis, ed., *A Survey of Contemporary Economics* (Philadelphia, Blakiston, 1948), pp. 211-240.

achieve equilibrium in the international balance of payments, or it may maintain "controlled disequilibrium." It will forego the advantages of buying in the cheapest market and selling in the dearest, and will thus sacrifice one of the bases of domestic prosperity, but at the same time it can prevent developments in the field of international commerce which might have an adverse effect on the domestic economy. There may be political compensations, too. The very fact of stability in the domestic economy has domestic political advantages; governments which permit deflation and unemployment on a substantial scale jeopardize the support on which their continuance in office may depend. Moreover, exchange controls permit governments to direct international trade so as to serve diplomatic ends. They can refuse to make foreign exchange available for purchases in unfriendly states, and can encourage trade with other states. They can use control over foreign exchange as a bargaining counter in negotiations with other governments, whatever the main issue in the negotiations may be. Germany under Hitler manipulated exchange controls and blocked accounts in such a way as to obtain a strangle hold on the economies of some of the states of southeastern Europe. If such ends could not also be promoted by other means, such as boycotts, embargoes, quotas, and the licensing of imports and exports, which we shall soon discuss, it is probable that exchange control would become even more widespread than it is.[3]

International Agreement: The International Monetary Fund

Toward the end of World War II the International Monetary Fund was created, now inclusive of most of the states of the free world. The arrangement was that participants, though not on the gold standard, would price their currencies in terms of gold. Thus exchange rates could be tentatively fixed. Those participants in a position to do so would then allow free convertibility; the United States and a very few other states have complied. Others, in specified circumstances, might "manage" their currency, usually by a combination of partial exchange control and the use of a stabilization fund, that is, a fund with which the member government can enter the foreign exchange market with a view to compensating for shifts in supply and demand. The International Monetary Fund itself is a stabilization fund, to which the members make contributions and from which they can obtain assistance in counteracting short-term pressures against the exchange rate of their currency. If a fundamental disequilibrium appears which these measures do not counteract, a member may devalue its currency; a devaluation by not more than 10 per cent may occur through unilateral action, but a more severe devaluation requires the consent of the Fund. Voting rights in the Fund are weighted

[3] Brainard, *op. cit.*, pp. 48-72, 418-448; Yuan-li Wu, *Economic Warfare* (New York, Prentice-Hall, 1952), pp. 109-145.

on the basis of various criteria, the United States alone casting 30 per cent of the votes. A common interest in the stability of exchange rates has thus been recognized, and qualified assurances have been exchanged against the competitive devaluation of currencies.[4]

THE INTERNATIONAL EXCHANGE OF
GOODS AND SERVICES

Governments pursue various kinds of policies in connection with the international exchange of goods and services, depending on the economic system of the state, the objectives pursued, and estimates of the probable effect of given lines of action.

Free Trade

Where free enterprise prevails, governments may allow free trade. A country is said to follow a policy of free trade when its government interposes no special obstacles to the international exchange of goods and services. There may be low tariffs on imports for the purpose of raising revenue, but there will be none designed to give domestic enterprise protection against foreign competition, nor will other protective measures be adopted. There will be no bounties or subsidies to encourage exports. Private traders will be allowed to buy and sell abroad as they please, importing or exporting freely for their own profit or pleasure.[5] Of course, even with free trade governments adopt policies which affect foreign exchange rates, and, as we have seen, this means that governments fix an important condition on which trade proceeds.

Though the ideal of the classical economists, free trade has never been generally accepted by governments. Great Britain came closest to doing so during most of the nineteenth and the early part of the twentieth century, and others approached the policy more or less closely.[6] Now none do so. The general rule now is that governments regulate, and participate in, international commercial activities. The reasons for this will appear as we see what kinds of policies they in fact pursue.

The National Regulation of Imports

1. Tariffs and the reasons for adopting them. Outside the communist world, governments generally adopt protective tariffs on imports. They do so for various purposes. The desire of governing groups to promote

---

[4] Towle, *op. cit.*, pp. 717-727; Raymond F. Mikesell, "The International Monetary Fund 1944-49: A Review," *International Conciliation*, No. 455 (November, 1949), pp. 828-874.

[5] Towle, *op. cit.*, pp. 84-127.

[6] A descriptive history of the commercial policies of many states may be found in Asher Isaacs, *International Trade: Tariff and Commercial Policy* (Chicago, Irwin, 1948).

their own domestic political advantage is important among them. After all, these groups face pressures for the adoption of tariffs. For all the glorification of competition which capitalism involves, few free enterprisers really want it. If they can eliminate or reduce competition by inducing the government to adopt a high tariff, they are usually glad to do so, and they are ready to give or withhold support to a political party or faction, depending on its willingness to go along. The adoption of a protective tariff generally means that consumers will have to pay higher prices than otherwise for the protected items, but this loss is spread among many who are often hardly aware of the fact that they are being burdened with it. The gain goes to a few, to whom the matter may be really vital. Support from those who want a tariff may in turn be vital to an officeholder, a party, or a government.

Protective tariffs may also be adopted for other reasons. It would be quite difficult to establish some productive activities in a country, even if it were well suited for them, unless protection were afforded against established foreign competition; this is the "infant industry" argument for tariffs, which, though often misused, is theoretically defensible. In the interest of domestic economic stability, tariffs may be adopted to give protection against "dumping," that is, against the sporadic importation of products sold by a foreign merchant at prices lower than those he charges to buyers in his own country. Tariffs are sometimes designed to improve the terms of trade for the country imposing them, that is, through them in some circumstances it may be possible to pay for more imports with fewer exports. The possibility of gaining this advantage through tariffs is reduced, however, when many countries attempt it at the same time.[7] Governments sometimes adopt tariffs simply as a measure of retaliation, perhaps with a view to negotiating reciprocal reductions with other governments. Entirely aside from the question of favoring the producers of certain items at the expense of consumers, governments may adopt tariffs as a means of affecting the distribution of income among various economic groups in the population; for example, the portion of the national income going to labor or to agriculture may be increased or reduced, depending on the tariff policy pursued.[8] Power considerations may also lead to the adoption of tariffs. The governments of sovereign states must think in terms of the possibility of war, defensive if not offensive. They must therefore manage economic affairs so as to be prepared for war, which sometimes means that they must develop and maintain domestic sources of supply even though it is uneconomic to do so. Frequently the tariff is chosen as a means by which this can be done.

Whatever the original objective in adopting tariffs, governments are

[7] Towle, *op. cit.*, pp. 271-371; Metzler, *op. cit.*, pp. 241-244.
[8] Metzler, *op. cit.*, pp. 244-249.

necessarily cautious about reducing or eliminating them once they have been established. If a protected industry were suddenly deprived of its protection, considerable unemployment and loss of invested capital might well occur; these are developments which governments are understandably loath to bring about.

2. *Other devices.* Governments frequently supplement tariffs with other devices for restricting or regulating imports. A tariff does not fix the quantity of an item which may be imported; those willing to pay the price may import as much as they please. Other devices, such as quotas, licensing systems, and exchange controls, involve quantitative restrictions. When a government fixes import quotas, it specifies the amount of a commodity that can be imported within a given period of time; the quota may be global, or it may be fixed on a country-by-country basis. Under licensing systems, importers bring specified goods into a country only on the basis of licenses which the government may grant or withhold as it sees fit. Exchange controls have already been described.

These supplementary devices for regulating imports may be applied for exactly the same purposes as tariffs. They have generally been adopted, however, in response to special situations. The United States has employed quotas mainly in connection with its program of giving price support to certain agricultural products; it is willing to give the American farmer the benefit of artificially high prices at the expense of the taxpayers and consumers, but does not want to extend the benefit to foreign producers.[9] Most countries have placed quantitative restrictions on imports because of balance-of-payments difficulties. They have not been able to export enough to pay for all the desired imports, and so they have simply curtailed imports rather than accept the economic consequences of imbalance. At the same time, they have exercised their controls so as to avoid frittering away scarce foreign exchange and so as to require that it be devoted only to the purchase of imports regarded as necessary. Especially after World War II, many governments used quotas, licenses, and foreign exchange controls to make sure that only those things would be imported which would contribute most to national rehabilitation and recovery.

As suggested earlier, all these devices for regulating imports may be applied on a discriminatory basis. A government can select the countries from which it is willing to have imports come; it can exclude certain foreign countries from its markets, completely or partially, and it can adopt measures to facilitate the importation of goods from others. Thus it can affect the level of well-being and power that it is possible for other countries to achieve.

---

[9] See D. Gale Johnson, "Agricultural Price Policy and International Trade," *Essays in International Finance* (Princeton, Princeton University, Department of Economics and Social Institutions, International Finance Section), No. 19, June, 1954.

3. *Indirect restrictions.* So far, we have been speaking mainly of direct restrictions on the importation of goods. There are also indirect restrictions. The very process of clearing goods through customs sometimes impedes international trade more than the customs duty itself, for it often involves uncertainty about the tariff rate which will be applied and delay in making the decision. Propaganda may be issued to induce popular boycotts of goods made in certain countries. The law may require that imports bear a label indicating their country of origin, and sometimes this requirement has proved to be very onerous. The United States government insists on the "Buy American" principle, meaning that federal agencies (and many state and local agencies as well) commonly procure what they need from domestic producers, even if the same item can be purchased abroad at a substantial saving. Quarantine and sanitary requirements, ostensibly designed to protect domestic plant and animal life from disease, may be administered so as to make them primarily instruments for protecting domestic producers against foreign competition. Thus American beef producers have been protected from Argentine competition by a ruling which excludes fresh beef from any part of Argentina because of the presence of hoof-and-mouth disease in one part.

International Agreements on Import Policies

International trade is regulated not only by national but also by international action. General international law contains a number of rules and principles regulating the treatment of persons engaged in travel, trade, and commerce outside the boundaries of the state of which they are nationals. In addition, most states have found it desirable to conclude treaties with each other on the subject.

1. *General treaties of commerce and navigation.* Such treaties have traditionally dealt with any or all of a wide variety of problems: the rights of the ships of one party in the ports of the other; the rights of nationals of one party engaged in travel, trade, or commerce in the territory of the other; protection by one government of the patent, copyright, and similar rights assured by the other government to its nationals; fishing rights; consular activities; tariffs.

Two principles are especially common in commercial treaties. One calls for "national treatment" and the other for "most-favored-nation treatment."

A pledge of national treatment is a pledge by one party to treat the nationals of the other party as well as it treats its own nationals; the pledge is usually reciprocal. In all matters to which it relates, equal rights and privileges are to be afforded. Thus the nationals of one state may be assured of the right to engage in commercial activities in the territory of the other, free from any discrimination because they are aliens. Reservations or exceptions may, however, be made; the United

States, for example, regularly refuses to extend national treatment to foreigners so far as participation in the coastwise carrying trade is concerned. Similarly, exceptions to the principle may be made for the benefit of foreigners, as when they are exempted from military service.

The most-favored-nation clause in a treaty obliges one party to treat nationals of the other party as well as it treats the nationals of any third state; as in the case of national treatment, the pledge is usually reciprocal. The general object is equal and non-discriminatory treatment. The principle may be adopted in relation to any or all aspects of international commercial relationships; it is most commonly related to tariff rates. Suppose, for example, that France and the United States are bound in tariff matters to extend most-favored-nation treatment to each other. France then makes a special tariff concession to Belgium, which makes Belgium most favored. France will then be obliged to extend the same concession to the United States. There are, however, two forms, or two interpretations, of the most-favored-nation clause. Sometimes the obligation is unconditional, and sometimes it is conditional. When unconditional, it requires that each party automatically extend to the other any tariff concession which it extends to a third state. When conditional, it requires the extension of the concession only for the same or equivalent compensation, if any, which the third state has granted. Thus the conditional form may or may not produce equal and non-discriminatory treatment.

2. *Special trade agreements.* In addition to general treaties on trade, navigation, and commerce, states also conclude special treaties of various kinds dealing with international economic relations. Bilateral agreements providing for the reciprocal reduction of specific tariff rates have long been common. The promotion of such agreements became a regular feature of American foreign policy in 1934, with the adoption of the Reciprocal Trade Agreements program. Under this program the President may conclude agreements with other states reducing American tariffs by as much as 50 per cent in return for satisfactory reciprocal tariff concessions; after most of the possible reductions had been made on the basis of the 1934 tariff rates, Congress permitted further reductions of as much as 50 per cent of the 1945 rates. The agreements include the most-favored-nation clause in its unconditional form.

3. *The GATT.* By 1954 thirty-four states, conducting about 80 per cent of the world's international trade, had become parties to the General Agreement on Tariffs and Trade (GATT), originally concluded in 1947. The principal purpose of the GATT is to increase international trade by reducing trade barriers. The treaty was originally concluded after elaborate bargaining on a multilateral basis to secure reductions in tariff rates; several tariff-bargaining conferences have been held subsequently.

In addition to reducing their tariffs, the states involved have agreed, in principle, to eliminate all quantitative restrictions on imports, but have hedged their agreement with many reservations and exceptions. They have also recognized the need to simplify and expedite the process of clearing goods through customs barriers.[10]

4. *Preferential tariff arrangements and customs unions.* We have already mentioned the fact that tariffs and other trade restrictions may be applied on a discriminatory basis unless this is forbidden by special treaty agreement. The result at times has been the adoption of preferential tariff systems. In 1932 Britain and its Dominions concluded the Ottawa Agreements under which they granted each other special tariff concessions not extended to other states. The United States has preferential tariff arrangements with both Cuba and the Philippines.[11]

Customs unions carry the idea of preferential tariff arrangements to the limit. They involve the elimination of all tariffs on trade among countries joining in the union and the establishment of common tariffs for all of them on imports from other states. There has been more talk than action concerning such unions. At the end of World War II, Belgium, the Netherlands, and Luxembourg agreed in principle to join in a customs union, but they hedged the agreement about with many reservations and exceptions; progress in implementing the principle has been slow, though the Benelux customs union is formally in existence. Likewise after World War II, France and Italy explored the possibility of joining in a customs union, but abandoned the idea in favor of a piecemeal approach to the reduction of trade barriers.[12]

5. *The European Coal and Steel Community.* Perhaps the most ambitious scheme of the sort, involving a partial customs union, has taken shape in the European Coal and Steel Community, including France, Italy, Germany, and the Benelux countries; the object is the creation of a common market among the six countries for coal and steel. All tariffs and other trade restrictions on these commodities are abolished, and arrangements are made to prevent nationalist discriminations of any sort. An elaborate supranational structure of agencies supervises the implementation of the agreement. The objectives of the coal and steel community are not only economic but also political. It is designed to bring about a more efficient use of resources and thus contribute to the welfare

[10] Raymond Vernon, "America's Foreign Trade Policy and the GATT," *Essays in International Finance,* No. 21, October, 1954; Wytze Gorter, "GATT After Six Years: An Appraisal," *International Organization,* Vol. 8 (February, 1954), pp. 1-18.

[11] Isaacs, *op. cit.,* pp. 360-361, 549-550.

[12] F. Gunther Eych, "Benelux in the Balance," *Political Science Quarterly,* Vol. 69 (March, 1954), pp. 65-91; Klaus Knorr, "Problems of a Western European Union," *Review of Politics,* Vol. 11 (April, 1949), pp. 131-152; Jacob Viner, *The Customs Union Issue* (New York, Carnegie Endowment for International Peace, 1950).

of the populations involved; it is also designed to reduce the possibility of war among the parties by bringing about a thorough integration of vital portions of their national economies.[18]

The National Regulation of Exports

In addition to measures taken affecting the importation of goods, governments may act either to expand or to curtail exports.

The expansion of exports may be brought about in various ways and for various purposes. Governments sometimes provide bounties to encourage exports, perhaps for the purpose of stimulating prosperity at home. They sometimes subsidize service activities, such as merchant shipping, perhaps so that the ships will be available under the national flag in the event of war. They sometimes extend loans to make the export of goods possible. The United States, for example, operates the Export-Import Bank, which extends loans primarily to foreign governments but also to both domestic and foreign corporations engaged in foreign trade. The principal purpose is to facilitate the export of American goods. Obviously, too, measures which a state takes to encourage imports, such as a reduction in its tariffs, are likely to increase exports, for the foreigners who have sold the goods imported will acquire money with which to buy goods which they want in return.

Loans by one wartime ally to another have long been common. During World War II, the United States engaged in extensive "lend-lease" operations, supplying vital goods and services to most of the states of the world to enhance their military strength and their determination to resist the Axis powers. The period since World War II has witnessed a whole series of programs in which the United States has played the leading role and in connection with which the exportation of goods and services has occurred on a vast scale. There were American loans to individual governments. There was the United Nations Relief and Rehabilitation Administration (UNRRA). There was the program of aid to Greece and Turkey under the Truman Doctrine. There was the extensive European Recovery Program (the Marshall Plan). The latter was supplemented and eventually supplanted by other programs of economic and military aid. All these postwar programs have involved very extensive grants of funds and of goods and services by the United States.[14] We shall describe them more fully in Chapter 17, "Substitutes for War."

The major purposes of American aid programs have been military and political. During World War II the obvious purpose was to contribute to the defeat of the Axis powers. Since the war, and especially after the

[13] John Goormaghtigh, "European Coal and Steel Community," *International Conciliation*, No. 503 (May, 1955), pp. 343-408.
[14] William Adams Brown and Redvers Opie, *American Foreign Assistance* (Washington, Brookings, 1953).

enunciation of the Truman Doctrine, the dominant purpose has been to keep the free world free; more specifically, it has been to improve economic conditions abroad so as to render people less susceptible to the appeals of communism and to enhance the political and military strength of non-communist states so as to render them less susceptible to Soviet blandishments and pressures. Foreign economic operations have become a major method of political warfare.

Other purposes have also been pursued. There has been a belief that the long-run prosperity of the United States would be promoted by economic recovery and development in other countries with which trade might later be conducted on a mutually profitable basis. Humanitarian motivations have played a part, especially in connection with the UNRRA program. To a very slight extent, programs of economic and military aid may have been supported in the belief that they might ward off unemployment and economic recession. Sometimes the programs have provided occasions for disposing of surplus products. The various purposes and the extent to which they have been achieved will be discussed in Chapter 17.

Conversely, governments may also impose restrictions or prohibitions on exports. The object may simply be to keep goods at home which are regarded as vital to military preparedness. It may be to deny the goods to other states, so as to avoid assisting them in the development of their welfare or their power. In recent years, especially under the Battle Act, the United States has imposed an embargo on the shipment of a long list of strategic goods to the Soviet Union and to communist states friendly to it, and has insisted that foreign countries receiving American aid impose similar embargoes. A government may make it illegal for its nationals to sell goods to other states, even though the goods never enter its territory. It may prohibit ships flying its flag from carrying forbidden goods to another state, and can bar foreign ships from its ports when engaged in obnoxious trading operations. It can freeze the assets which foreign governments and their nationals have deposited in its territory, thus preventing further purchases. Needless to say, lesser measures may also be taken, such as prohibiting the sale to a country of a greater quantity of a given item than is thought necessary to it for serving normal or proper purposes.[15]

State Trading

So far the discussion of trade arrangements has assumed that the system was one in which government stands apart from private enterprise, imposing regulations and restrictions on private operators. How-

[15] Wu, *op. cit.*, esp. pp. 16-85. For a study of American policies of economic warfare during World War II, see David L. Gordon and Royden Dangerfield, *The Hidden Weapon* (New York, Harper, 1947).

ever, considerable state trading also occurs. The international trade of communist states is conducted exclusively by agencies under governmental control, and in many other countries governments are merchants. In connection with the European Recovery Program, for example, the United States government played the role of merchant on a considerable scale; among other things, it engaged in "offshore procurement," purchasing goods in Latin America, say, for delivery to European recipients of American aid. The United States Atomic Energy Commission purchases uranium from foreign sources. Merchant shipping is frequently government-owned and -operated.

If anything, state trading enhances opportunities to make economics a weapon. The possibility is implicit in every bargain which is made or avoided. Unfriendly states can be boycotted, and friendly states can be patronized. The terms of the bargains which are made can be generous or hard. Goods can be bought abroad simply to prevent them from falling into the hands of another state which also wants them; they can be sold or otherwise disposed of in such a way as to disrupt the economy of another state or to help it out of difficulties. The possible political advantages are obvious. At the same time, there are dangers, for a system which gives political significance to all commercial transactions may well increase international friction.

FOREIGN INVESTMENTS

So far in this chapter we have been asking how governments can pursue whatever objectives they have by actions directly affecting foreign exchange and international trade in goods and services. The international exchange of capital also occurs, and offers further means by which the achievement of public objectives can be promoted. Foreign investments may be made by private persons, by governments themselves, or by international agencies established by governments.

Policies of Capital Exporters

1. *Encouraging investments abroad.* Governments have various means at their disposal for encouraging, regulating, or restricting foreign investments by private persons. Both the means and the objectives which governments hope to promote in this way have been exhaustively analyzed and illustrated by Eugene Staley, in his *War and the Private Investor*.[16] Governments themselves may participate along with private

[16] Treatment of the subject here is based largely on Staley's work. See especially his Chapters 4 and 10: "How Investments Serve Diplomacy," and "How Governments Influence Their Investors." See also Jacob Viner, "International Finance and Balance of Power Diplomacy, 1880-1914," *Southwestern Political and Social Science Quarterly*, Vol. 9 (March, 1929), pp. 407-451; *idem*, "Political Aspects of International Finance," *Journal of Business*, Vol. 1 (April, 1928), pp. 141-173.

investors in financing foreign projects in order to encourage private investments or to serve other interests of state. For example, the Japanese government for several decades owned a controlling interest in the Oriental Development Co., engaged in extensive overseas commercial operations. The British government in 1913 acquired stock in the Anglo-Iranian Oil Co., and held it until the property was nationalized by Iran. Private capital participates to some extent in the loans extended by the American Export-Import Bank.[17] Governments also sometimes subsidize private companies engaged in investment and other activities abroad. Sometimes they guarantee a foreign investment or earnings on the investment, or the convertibility of earnings (i.e., the opportunity to repatriate earnings by exchanging a foreign currency for money of the home state). They may either encourage or discourage foreign investing and foreign economic operations of all kinds by the tax policies which they pursue, and by the arrangements which they make with other governments (or fail to make) concerning double taxation. They may offer informal inducements to private lending, government officials taking advantage of personal, social, and business connections, appealing to patriotism, or tacitly holding out the possibility of public distinction and prestige to investors who serve their country well. Promises of firm diplomatic and consular support may be made. Governments of investing countries normally insist vigorously that other governments adhere to the legal principle that private property is not to be nationalized without just compensation.

2. *Discouraging investments abroad.* Governments may also exert negative influences over foreign investments. The objection of a government is in itself usually enough to induce bankers and others to refuse to make a loan to foreign governments. The law may preclude the listing of foreign securities on the stock exchange unless prior authorization is received from the appropriate governmental agency. In 1934 Congress enacted the Johnson Act, making it a criminal offense to lend money to a foreign government in default on its financial obligations to the United States government. The various American "neutrality" acts of the 1930's prohibited the lending of money to belligerents under certain stipulated conditions.

3. *Objectives served by governmental measures.* Governments may pursue many objectives through their influence or control over the direction and size of foreign investments. Foreign investments, whether private or public, may contribute to the prosperity of the creditor country in various ways, for example, by making available raw material or other resources which otherwise would have gone untapped. They usually enhance the creditor country's prestige and power. Investments in

[17] Brainard, *op. cit.,* p. 266.

backward and weak areas, especially, may facilitate the extension of the civilization and culture of the more advanced country. Foreign investments have frequently been instruments for penetrating and acquiring political influence in foreign areas. They have provided excuses for intervention and have sometimes been the prelude to conquest. Both Russia and Japan, for example, have at different times acquired great influence and control in Manchuria through the contractual rights which went along with the construction and operation of railways in the region. In the early decades of this century, the United States frequently intervened in various Caribbean republics to protect the rights of investors there. The knowledge of foreign areas gained by citizens who are active in commercial operations abroad is sometimes of considerable value from an intelligence point of view. The threat that loans would be denied or that existing short-term loans would be withdrawn has, on occasion, served as a bargaining weapon. At times, one government has been able to bring about the downfall of another by preventing the extension of loans to it, and frequently embargoes on loans, like embargoes on trade, have presumably impeded the economic or military strengthening of unfriendly states. Investments directed toward friendly and allied states may, of course, enhance both their welfare and their power. For example, Congress once enjoined the Export-Import Bank to make loans designed "to assist in the development of the resources, the stabilization of the economies, and the orderly marketing of the products of the countries of the Western Hemisphere." [18] The bank makes both general purpose and special project loans, and is influenced in its decisions by both commercial and diplomatic considerations.

4. *The International Bank for Reconstruction and Development.* At the close of World War II a number of Allied nations joined in establishing the International Bank for Reconstruction and Development (the IBRD, or World Bank), of which most states of the free world are members. The members contribute capital to the bank and have voting power on its Board of Governors roughly in proportion to their contributions. The bank may extend loans to member governments or, if the member government involved guarantees the loan, to private corporations. Loans must be for specific projects which will contribute to economic growth and development in the borrowing country; in practice, the bank has acted primarily to develop transportation facilities and to increase the output of electric power. In comparison with the vast sums expended by the United States in various foreign aid programs, the investments of the bank have been relatively small. It is nevertheless a useful agency for the promotion of economic progress. The interna-

[18] *Ibid.*, p. 263.

tional character of the bank limits the extent to which any one member can discriminate among potential borrowers to serve national political purposes.[19]

Policies of Capital Importers

So far we have spoken of international investments mainly in terms of the policies and purposes of the investor. Borrowers, of course, are also involved, and they may do various things to attract or repel investors. They can attract foreign investments by the stability of their political and economic system, by their reputation for reliability in the payment of debts, and, of course, by the opportunities for profit which they provide. They can adopt tax policies which make investment in their territory attractive. Tariffs which they adopt sometimes induce foreign enterprises to make what are called direct investments, that is, the foreign enterprise establishes a branch factory inside the tariff wall. Governments desiring to attract investors may give guarantees that earnings from investments can be converted from their own currency into the currency of the investor and then repatriated. By treaty or contract they can give assurances against nationalization. If none of these conditions or policies prevails, foreign investors are likely to stay away.

Many advanced countries have taken measures against the alienation of control over certain enterprises, and these steps restrict foreign investment. They may regulate or prohibit ownership by aliens of certain kinds of resources, such as land and coal mines. Governments, or private corporations themselves, sometimes require that leading officers of corporations shall not be foreigners. Similarly, less advanced or politically weak countries sometimes seek to protect themselves against economic penetration in various ways. They may use the same devices as the advanced countries. When they need capital or foreign skills, they may give preference to nationals of states deemed least likely to take advantage of the situation for imperialistic purposes. They have also sought acceptance of certain legal principles; they have, in fact, succeeded in establishing the principle that force shall not be used to collect public contract debts, but have not fared so well in efforts to establish the principle, often expressed in a "Calvo clause" in contracts, that the foreign investor shall have no right of diplomatic protection from his home government. Of course, the nationalization or socialization of enterprises or of resources precludes foreign investment in them unless the socializing government itself decides to borrow foreign capital.[20]

---

[19] *Ibid.*, pp. 269-278; Klaus Knorr, "The Bretton Woods Institutions in Transition," *International Organization*, Vol. 2 (February, 1948), pp. 19-38.

[20] For a discussion of protective measures taken by capital-importing countries, see Staley, *op. cit.*, pp. 406-414.

ECONOMIC NATIONALISM AND
ECONOMIC INTERNATIONALISM

Foreign economic policies can be classified in several ways. Most frequently they are labeled by the terms *economic nationalism* and *economic internationalism*. Neither term has a fixed and precise meaning.

The term *economic nationalism* is sometimes used to denote policies aimed to produce *Autarkie* or economic self-sufficiency, the object being to reduce or eliminate dependence upon foreign markets and foreign sources of supply. This in turn may be desired to promote the financial gain of influential groups which wish to be shielded against foreign competition, or to insulate the domestic economy from foreign economic instability, or to prepare the country for war, when its foreign commercial ties would be severed in any event.

The term is also sometimes given a broader meaning, to denote "the point of view that it ought to be the object of statesmanship in economic matters to increase the power rather than the economic well-being of a given society." So defined, economic nationalism complements political nationalism, so far as both seek to consolidate and enhance the power of the state.

Whatever the definition, the methods adopted are selected from those which have already been discussed in this chapter. Tariffs, quotas, exchange controls, and the licensing of foreign trade may be chosen. State subsidies may be granted to encourage domestic enterprises, such as the production of synthetic oil. Such foreign trade as continues and such foreign investments as are made may be so directed as to favor potential allies and to avoid strengthening potential enemies. Pronatalist and other population policies may be pursued to increase the manpower available for war.

Economic internationalism is an even vaguer concept. Generally it connotes an emphasis on economic well-being rather than on power, and a belief that well-being can best be promoted by an extensive and a reasonably free international exchange of goods, services, and capital. The economic internationalist accepts the idea that each country should specialize in the production of those things which it is economically best fitted to produce, and should then exchange its products for those which can be produced most advantageously abroad. Barriers to trade and commerce are to be kept at a minimum, and such barriers as exist are to be non-discriminatory. Immigration and emigration should be free. Mass production is to occur for a world market. Through an international division of labor and reasonably free trade, it is hoped, the world's resources can be exploited and allocated in such a way as to provide the maximum well-being for all. The economic internationalist tends toward the extreme of seeking an integrated world economy, rather than a series of national economies more or less poorly integrated with each other.

The actual policies of states usually fall somewhere between the two extremes. Economic nationalism has generally proved to be more attractive than economic internationalism, especially in relationships among states which regard themselves as potential enemies. Among friends and allies, economic nationalism is likely to be considerably modified. Though the countries of the West since World War II have not exactly pursued a policy of economic internationalism as defined above, they have implemented many cooperative and sometimes very generous policies designed to promote both their well-being and their power.

SUGGESTED READINGS

BRAINARD, Harry G., *International Economics and Public Policy* (New York, Holt, 1954).

BROWN, William Adams, and OPIE, Redvers, *American Foreign Assistance* (Washington, Brookings, 1953).

CHALMERS, Henry, *World Trade Policies* (Berkeley, University of California Press, 1953).

GOORMAGHTIGH, John, "European Coal and Steel Community," *International Conciliation,* No. 503 (May, 1955).

GORDON, David L., and DANGERFIELD, Royden, *The Hidden Weapon* (New York, Harper, 1947).

HIGHLEY, Albert E., *The First Sanctions Experiment* (Geneva, Geneva Research Centre, 1938).

International Sanctions, Royal Institute of International Affairs (London, Oxford, 1938).

MASON, Henry L., *The European Coal and Steel Community* (The Hague, Nijhoff, 1955).

METZLER, Lloyd A., "The Theory of International Trade," in ELLIS, Howard S., ed., *A Survey of Contemporary Economics* (Philadelphia, Blakiston, 1948).

VINER, Jacob, *Studies in the Theory of International Trade* (New York, Harper, 1937).

VINER, Jacob, *The Customs Union Issue,* Studies in the Administration of International Law and Organization, No. 10 (New York, Carnegie Endowment for International Peace, 1950).

CHAPTER 14

Diplomacy and Settling International Disputes

DIPLOMACY IS "the management of international relations by means of negotiation; the method by which these relations are adjusted and managed by ambassadors and envoys; the business or art of the diplomat." [1] Whatever the objectives a state pursues, diplomacy is sure to be employed as a method of promoting their achievement. The sending and receiving of diplomats is the common practice.

It is through diplomacy that states arrange alliances called for by balance-of-power considerations or seek to isolate a potential victim of attack. Through diplomacy they negotiate concerning the level and type of armaments to be maintained. Through diplomacy they seek to coordinate economic policies designed to enhance their welfare or power, or designed to restrict the welfare or power of other states. Through diplomacy they contribute to the development of international law and appeal to the law when it is useful to them. Through diplomacy they establish international organizations, like the United Nations, in which they conduct more diplomacy. There is hardly an aspect of international affairs on which diplomacy does not touch.

Diplomacy may, of course, be reinforced and supplemented in various ways. In fact, in classifications of the methods of international politics, diplomacy as such scarcely figures as a major, separate category. The cynical are inclined to classify methods under the headings of force, fraud, and favor. The more lighthearted refer to the method of the carrot, figuratively dangled in front of the donkey's nose, and the method of the stick, applied at the other end; they may vary the figure of speech and speak of the "big stick" and the "sugar stick." The more serious speak of persuasion and coercion—perhaps adding corruption, though corruption

---

[1] Harold Nicolson, *Diplomacy* (New York, Harcourt, Brace, 1939), p. 15.

might be subsumed under the other two. Harold Lasswell classifies political methods into four categories: those which employ symbols, violence, goods, and practices, respectively.[2] A symbol may be a thing, like the national flag, or a word, like *freedom*. When states use propaganda to get what they want, they are manipulating symbols. The method of violence is self-explanatory, in the extreme taking the form of war. The use of goods as a method of achieving objectives has been discussed in the preceding chapter, taking the form, perhaps, of trade regulations designed to strengthen or weaken other states. Lasswell's fourth method includes such practices as those which are observed by legislative and executive branches of government in formulating and implementing policies.

Diplomacy may apply, or be supplemented and reinforced by, all these methods. Between some states at some times, diplomacy may be completely supplanted by other methods, as when states formally declare war.

Whether or not diplomacy is classified as a major political method, it is obviously a prominent element in international relations. As such, it deserves separate attention. Moreover, the methods available to governments for seeking the settlement of international disputes also need to be examined if the processes of international politics are to be understood.

RECOGNITION AND THE ESTABLISHMENT
OF DIPLOMATIC RELATIONSHIPS

Recognition of What? When?

The question of extending recognition arises both in relation to foreign states and in relation to foreign governments. The recognition of a state remains effective regardless of changes in the character and composition of its government. Governments are recognized as they come to power. Whether there is an obligation to recognize either a state or a government (and whether the other party has a corresponding right to demand recognition) is a vexing question on which students of international law differ. In practice, most governments deny any obligation. The practice is for each government to decide for itself whether and when to extend recognition, and to base the decision on whatever grounds seem expedient.[3]

[2] Harold D. Lasswell, *Politics, Who Gets What, When, How* (New York, Whittlesey House, 1936).

[3] Hersh Lauterpacht, ed., *International Law*, 7th ed. (New York, Longmans Green, 1948-1952); Ti-chiang Chen, *The International Law of Recognition* (New York, Praeger, 1951).

The Exchange of Diplomatic Missions

Given mutual recognition, governments normally enter into diplomatic relationships; each one sends a diplomatic mission to the other. However, if either government decides that it would like to sever diplomatic relationships, it is free to dismiss the mission which it has received and to recall the one which it has sent.

General and Special Reasons for Recognition

When a new state comes into existence with the consent of the government from whose territory it has been carved, other governments normally accord recognition. Over the last several decades a number of new states have come into existence, in the crescent extending from Syria and Lebanon to the Philippines. Once the "mother country" acquiesced, recognition of the new states by others generally followed without question. Similarly, when a new government comes into power by orderly processes, or when it in fact exercises uncontested jurisdiction in the state, other governments normally extend recognition. There is never any question, for example, whether the United States will recognize a new government in Britain or in Canada.

The reason for this is that governments generally find it to their advantage to recognize and to establish diplomatic relationships with other states and governments. The security and welfare of each state depends in part on establishing and maintaining satisfactory relationships with other states with which there is contact. Through diplomatic relationships one government may be able to influence the policies of another. It may build up good will for itself and perhaps obtain positive support for the policies which it chooses to pursue. It may allay hostility and reduce or eliminate obstacles to the achievement of its objectives. Advantageous commercial and cultural exchange may be promoted. The interests of citizens who travel and do business abroad can be more surely protected. Valuable information can perhaps be secured which might otherwise be unobtainable. Other advantages may accrue as well. The calculation of advantage turns out in favor of extending recognition and establishing diplomatic relationships so regularly that these actions ordinarily occur as a matter of course.

Sometimes governments have very special reasons for extending recognition. They may combine recognition with other measures to encourage or support a change which they desire, and when they do this they may meet opposition from governments which are against the change. France recognized the United States in 1778 as a means of weakening Britain, and accompanied recognition with an alliance which meant participation in war. Theodore Roosevelt, frustrated by Colombia's stand regarding the construction of a trans-isthmian canal, encouraged revolution in Panama; once revolution occurred he promptly extended recognition and took other measures to assure the survival of the new state. During World War I the Allies recognized a government of the new state of Czechoslovakia before it had actual control over any territory at all. Early in the Spanish Civil War, both Italy and Germany extended recognition to Franco's rebel faction as one of a number of measures to assure its victory. During World War II the Soviet Union coupled recognition with other measures to make sure that the government of its choice would survive in Poland after the war. In such circumstances as these, recognition takes on special significance, but it is hardly recognition itself which determines whether or not the desired change will occur; the measures which accompany or follow recognition are more important.

Some Reasons for Withholding Recognition

Sometimes when governments oppose or dislike a change, they withhold recognition. The United States has been especially prone to do this in connection with revolutionary governments. At one time or another it has refused to recognize a number of Latin American regimes because they came to power by unconstitutional means. Similarly, it has been very reluctant to recognize communist governments, usually on the ground of their unwillingness to abide by international obligations but partly also because of a dislike for communism and an assumption that recognition would enhance the strength or prestige of the government recognized. There is a feeling, with regard to newly established communist regimes, that the withholding of American recognition may encourage domestic opposition to them and perhaps bring about their overthrow, whereas recognition would stamp them as stable. So far as the Communist government of China is concerned, the withholding of recognition is also a part of a program designed to prevent that government from displacing the Nationalist government as the representative of China in the United Nations.

The refusal of the United States to extend recognition to certain Latin American governments in times past has caused them difficulties, particularly when they wanted to borrow money from American bankers, and has even contributed on occasion to their downfall. But with communist governments non-recognition has proved so far to be rather ineffective as a weapon. Apparently it has not weakened any of them seriously, nor has it induced any of them to make significant changes in policy. On the contrary, it may have intensified their hostility toward the outside world, and certainly it has deprived the United States itself of the usual advantages of diplomatic relationships. After more or less protracted delays, the United States has, in effect, admitted the failure of the policy of non-recognition and has extended recognition; China remains the outstanding exception.

The Severance of Diplomatic Relationships

Sometimes the question is not whether to recognize a government and establish relations with it but whether to sever or curtail relationships. Disputes between states sometimes become so bitter that one or the other of them severs diplomatic relations as a mark of its hostility or as a means of exerting pressure. Thus the United States severed diplomatic relations with Bulgaria in 1950 in retaliation for restrictions placed on American diplomats in Sofia, and Iran severed relations with Great Britain in 1951 in the course of the Anglo-Iranian oil dispute. Frequently, though not always, the severance of relationships is a prelude to war. Displeasure with the Franco regime in Spain after World War II led the General Assembly of the United Nations to recommend that members of the United Nations should withdraw their ambassadors from Madrid, leaving diplomatic missions in the hands of officers of lower rank. The hope was that the action might lead to the downfall or reform of Franco's government, but his position in Spain seems to have been strengthened rather than weakened.

Consular Relationships

International relations are not entirely intergovernmental. Citizens engage in travel and trade abroad and are frequently in need of some kind of assistance. To serve them, governments normally seek to station consuls in the principal foreign centers. Assent of the foreign government involved is necessary and is ordinarily granted, especially where diplomatic relationships exist. Again, however, assent may be withheld, or the number of consuls permitted to operate may be limited, as a means of exerting pressure on the sending government.

SOME GROUND RULES OF DIPLOMATIC RELATIONSHIPS

Questions of rank, precedence, and protocol once plagued international relations. Sometimes they seriously delayed the conduct of diplomatic business. Persistently they led to friction, and on occasion even brought on the threat of war. In a more or less conscious effort to reduce such difficulties, states have gradually developed certain rules and principles governing diplomatic intercourse. In other words, they have developed international laws defining common interests and putting certain relationships on an orderly and predictable basis. Law thus serves, however effectively, as a method of pursuing certain objectives and, once developed, as a limiting condition of subsequent actions.

As a result of an agreement originally made at the Congress of Vienna in 1815, subsequently modified, diplomatic agents are divided into four categories and ranked as follows: ambassadors, ministers, ministers resident, and chargés d'affaires. Within each rank, precedence is based upon the date of the official notification of the arrival of the diplomat in the receiving country.[4] A diplomatic post headed by an ambassador is called an embassy, and a post headed by a person of lower rank is called a legation. States exchanging diplomats agree on the rank to be accorded them. The original expectation was that the great powers would exchange ambassadors among themselves, and the lesser powers would send and receive diplomats of lesser rank. Largely because of sensitivity to signs of prestige, however, states of all degrees of power are inclined more and more to exchange ambassadors. Approximately four-fifths of the diplomatic agents sent and received by the United States have this rank.[5]

The individual diplomat must be *persona grata* in the eyes of the receiving government, that is, he must be personally acceptable. The practice of *agréation* has thus developed: the sending state asks for assurance in advance that the diplomat whom it proposes to send will be received. Once received, a diplomat who becomes *persona non grata* may be dismissed, or his recall may be requested. It might be mentioned in this connection that diplomats are not to interfere in any way in the domestic affairs of the country to which they are accredited, and it is up to the receiving government to determine what kinds of actions constitute interference.

The general principle is accepted that states receiving diplomatic missions will permit them to exercise their duties free from local interference and will assure them safety and respect. The implications of this principle are numerous. For example, diplomats are to be free to communicate with their home governments; diplomatic personnel cannot be sued or prosecuted, nor can diplomatic premises be invaded by the police; protection must be accorded to diplomatic personnel and property in proportion both to the needs of the situation and the means at the disposal of the receiving state. Questions persistently arise over the meaning of such rules in particular circumstances; still, the existence of the rules clearly serves to facilitate diplomatic intercourse.

Consuls likewise have some immunity from local jurisdiction, but on a much less extensive scale.

THE FUNCTIONS OF DIPLOMATS AND CONSULS

Governments assign a number of different functions to their diplomats. Most prominently, the diplomat is expected to conduct negotiations with the government to which he is accredited. He may deliver formal notes

[4] Sir Ernest Satow, *A Guide to Diplomatic Practice* (London, Longmans Green, 1922), Vol. I, pp. 237-248. See also Lassa F. L. Oppenheim, *International Law,* 7th ed., Hersh Lauterpacht, ed. (New York, Longmans Green, 1948-1952), Vol. I, pp. 687-757.

[5] Graham H. Stuart, *American Diplomatic and Consular Practice,* 2nd ed. (New York, Appleton-Century-Crofts, 1952), p. 127.

prepared in the foreign office to which he is responsible. He may negotiate verbally, under whatever instructions he has received. He receives communications similarly from the foreign government and dispatches them home, perhaps along with information and advice which will presumably be helpful to those at home who are directly concerned with the matter. The end-point in intergovernmental negotiations naturally varies. Perhaps it is simply the discovery of areas of agreement or disagreement; perhaps it is the settlement of a dispute, or agreement on a method to be followed in seeking settlement; perhaps it is to induce the other state to act, or to refrain from acting, in a particular way; perhaps it is the signature of a treaty; perhaps it is to create circumstances in which war can be waged with the greatest prospect of success. The objective of the diplomat in negotiating should be the objectives of his government. He conducts negotiations in such a way as to maximize the prospect that the desires of his own government will be achieved, whatever they may be.

The diplomat is likewise an intelligence agent in a foreign country charged with the duty of observing and reporting on everything which may be of interest to his home government. He or members of his mission normally report on a multitude of subjects: on all kinds of political developments in the country to which he is assigned, on relationships between it and other foreign states, on all aspects of its military posture and potentialities, on the facts and trends of agricultural and industrial production, on the attitudes and activities of leading public figures and on personal relationships among them, on public attitudes, and so on.

Another major function of the diplomat is to provide information concerning his country to the people of the country in which he is stationed. So far as possible the diplomat usually seeks to develop public understanding and sympathy for the policies of his government and appreciation of various aspects of life in the country which he represents. He may stress its power, its cultural achievements, its economic or scientific progress, or its future potentialities. He sponsors and attends social gatherings, gives speeches, holds press conferences, issues printed materials, participates in or provides radio and television programs, and spreads propaganda favorable to his country in every possible way. In conjunction with the American diplomatic service, libraries of information are maintained in many foreign centers, containing materials on all aspects of American life. All these informational and propaganda activities are conducted, of course, only with the consent of the government of the receiving state, which can restrict or curtail them at will.

Finally, the diplomat shares with the consul certain duties concerning nationals of his own state. He assists them in relations with the government to which he is accredited and provides information which may be helpful to them in commercial or other pursuits.

It is sometimes said that the diplomat, in contrast to the general, is a man of peace, that his first and most important duty is to maintain friendly relations with the government to which he is accredited. Such idealization of the diplomat is inaccurate and misleading. The diplomat is an agent of his government, promoting its objectives and following methods which he is instructed to follow. Of course, the information which he supplies, and perhaps the recommendations which he offers, may influence the selection of ends and means by those to whom he reports, and the discretion left to him in the performance of his duties may give him an opportunity to deflect the course of events somewhat in the direction of peace or war, as he chooses. However, he is not primarily a policy-making official. Rather, he is an instrument, used by those who appoint him to promote whatever ends they have. His primary duty is not to promote friendly relations and peace but to serve his government faithfully. If the government's policies make for peace, the diplomat can be a man of peace; otherwise that is hardly possible, and he may be guilty of contumacy if he attempts it. In some circumstances, it may be his assigned task to set the stage for war. This is certainly what Hitler and Mussolini called upon some of their diplomats to do.

Consuls ordinarily have little to do with intergovernmental relations. Their primary functions relate to commerce, industry, and navigation. They are stationed abroad to collect information on commercial matters, to promote the commerce of the sending state, to perform various duties relating to ships flying the flag of the sending state, and to give assistance of various kinds to the nationals of the sending state. Generally, they are an expression of the interest of the sending state in the economic well-being of its people.

AMICABLE METHODS OF HANDLING INTERNATIONAL PROBLEMS

States have developed a number of different ways of handling international problems, diplomacy and the diplomat being involved in some of them, but not in all. The methods may be classified as amicable and non-amicable. The amicable methods are either political, involving negotiations, or judicial, involving arbitration or adjudication. The principal distinction between them is that negotiations imply no obligation to reach or accept a settlement, whereas resort to judicial procedures implies an obligation to accept an award or decision as binding.

Political Methods

1. *Direct negotiations.* The political method of handling problems is normally the first one attempted and often the only one needed. The negotiations required may be conducted by exchanging notes, by conver-

sations between a diplomat and a spokesman for the government to which he is accredited, or by conference. Conferences, to be discussed more fully below, are now resorted to more and more, especially in connection with issues involving a number of states. The course and the techniques of negotiation vary widely in different circumstances, and few generalizations can be made. Proposals and perhaps counterproposals will be made. Each side will presumably buttress and support its position as best it can, combining varying mixtures of persuasion and coercion. Concession and compromise may occur. Since the Munich Conference in 1938 the term *appeasement* has come into prominence in this connection. Originally a neutral word designating efforts to relieve tensions and reduce the danger of war by a policy of concession and compromise, *appeasement* thereafter became a bad word. As a bad word, its meaning is not very precise. The Munich connotation is that appeasement occurs when a concession is made (perhaps at the expense of a third state) in fear of force and in violation of avowed principle, on the assumption that the demanding state has only a limited objective and will be pacified by the concession when in fact the demanding state has extensive or unlimited objectives and will react to the concession by presenting new demands. So defined, appeasement is obviously something to be avoided. The problem which the negotiator faces is to determine when a concession will constitute appeasement in the neutral sense and when it will constitute appeasement in the bad sense. In any event, the end-point in negotiations concerning international problems is usually agreement, however it is arrived at and however satisfied or dissatisfied the parties to the agreement may be.

2. *The use of third parties: good offices, mediation, and conciliation.* A third party sometimes supplements or facilitates negotiations. The third party may be a government not directly involved, or several governments acting jointly, or an international agency such as the Security Council of the United Nations, or individual persons appointed somehow, for example, by the Security Council. The third party may provide good offices or mediation, or it may engage in an investigation of the facts or in conciliation. Distinctions between these roles are not always agreed upon or observed. The term *good offices* usually denotes various kinds of actions by a third party designed to bring about negotiations or a resumption of them. If two disputing states have severed diplomatic relations, for example, a third party may offer its good offices, meaning that, as a minimum, it will transmit messages back and forth. The term *mediation* usually applies to active participation in the negotiations by the third party, who proposes terms of settlement. A "commission of inquiry" may seek to ascertain the facts relevant to the issue and report on them, on the assumption that impartial findings of fact may facilitate negotiation and agreement. If the commission not only reports on rele-

vant facts but also proposes terms of settlement, it is usually said to engage in conciliation.[6]

It should be emphasized that, when third parties are employed in any of the capacities described above, their function is strictly limited. They arrive at findings or make suggestions which the disputants are free to reject. Commissions of inquiry, mediators, and conciliators are not empowered to make awards or decisions which will be binding on the disputants. Their function is to facilitate agreement, not to impose terms of settlement.

Judicial Methods

Amicable methods of handling international problems include not only the political methods described above but also judicial methods: arbitration and adjudication. The end-point in judicial procedures is a determination and application of existing law.

1. Arbitration. The term *arbitration* is used rather loosely. Sometimes it denotes all methods of peaceful settlement, as in the debate in the interwar period over the order in which "arbitration, security, and disarmament" should be sought. When it denotes a judicial procedure, however, the meaning is much narrower. An appropriate definition appears in the first Hague Convention of 1907. "International arbitration," it says, "has for its object the settlement of disputes between states by judges of their own choice on the basis of respect for law. Recourse to arbitration implies an engagement to submit in good faith to the award."

States referring a dispute to an arbitral tribunal normally draw up a *compromis,* which is a written agreement specifying the various arrangements and conditions under which arbitration will occur. It is usually agreed that each party to the case will name two arbitrators, no more than one of whom is to be its national, and that the four arbitrators so named shall select a fifth. Each party is expected to argue its case before the tribunal, and the tribunal arrives at its ultimate award by a majority vote. Once the dispute is disposed of, the tribunal dissolves. The first Hague Convention provided for the establishment of a Permanent Court of Arbitration, but the name is misleading. The so-called Permanent Court is simply a list of persons deemed qualified to serve as arbitrators and presumably available for appointment to arbitral tribunals.

2. Adjudication. Arbitration is an age-old method of settling international disputes. Adjudication, the second of the judicial methods, developed on a significant scale only after World War I. Then a Permanent Court of International Justice was established, succeeded after World War II by the International Court of Justice. The latter is one of the principal organs of the United Nations, and membership in the United

---

[6] Oppenheim, *op. cit.,* Vol. II, pp. 3-20.

Nations automatically involves adherence to the Statute of the Court. Non-members of the United Nations may also adhere. Headquarters of the Court are at The Hague, Netherlands.

The International Court of Justice consists of fifteen judges elected for nine-year terms by the concurrent action of the Security Council and the General Assembly. They are not representatives of the states from which they come. No two are to be nationals of the same state, and elections occur on the basis of the principle that "the representation of the main forms of civilization and of the principal legal systems of the world should be assured." The Court may make binding decisions settling legal disputes between states, and may give advisory opinions to various agencies of the United Nations or to independent organizations associated with the United Nations. Decisions and opinions are arrived at by majority vote.

The Distinction Between Political and Justiciable Disputes

What kinds of disputes are suitable for judicial settlement (i.e., justiciable), and what kinds are essentially political in character? In other words, when is a dispute to be handled by a court and when is it to be handled by other means?

This question has caused great perplexity. There is scarcely a topic which has not at some time somewhere been brought before courts. Whether the issue concerns the location of a boundary line, jurisdictional rights, obligations to other states, or whatever, the chances are that the subject involved is one which at some time or other has been submitted to adjudication. This suggests that all disputes are justiciable.

In truth, if the only factor considered is the character of the subject matter, all disputes are justiciable. But the nature of the subject is not the only consideration. An even more important consideration is the attitude of the parties in the dispute. The nature of a dispute, whether justiciable or political, depends on their attitudes. If they are willing, at least tentatively, to accept the judgment of a court, the dispute becomes justiciable. If not, it is political. To put it another way, if the parties in dispute are willing to formulate the issue in legal terms, so as to involve conflicting claims of right, their dispute is justiciable. But if at least one of them insists on particular terms of settlement regardless of existing law, the dispute is political.[7]

Suppose, for example, that states A and B are in dispute over a given piece of territory. Assume first that A has a clear legal title to the territory; B admits this but wants the territory anyway. The issue therefore

[7] See P. E. Corbett, *Law and Society in the Relations of States* (New York, Harcourt, Brace, 1951), pp. 77-79; J. L. Brierly, *The Outlook for International Law* (Oxford, Clarendon, 1944), pp. 122-123.

does not involve conflicting claims of legal right. In this situation it would be absurd to seek judicial settlement, for the tribunal or court could only confirm the already admitted fact that A's claim is valid and that B's claim has no basis in law. Such a dispute must be handled by political rather than by judicial means. Perhaps B can negotiate the purchase of the territory from A, or perhaps B will go to war.

Assume in the second place that A and B both base their claims to the territory on assertions of legal right. Each one professes to think that the law is on its side. Then the dispute is theoretically justiciable. There can be resort to arbitration or adjudication, and an authoritative interpretation of the law will be handed down.

Suppose, however, that B, though advancing a legal claim, is not really confident that it could win a favorable decision, and it does not want to risk an adverse judgment. What then? This introduces another very significant question: Who determines not only which disputes are suitable for judicial settlement but also which ones will actually be submitted for judicial settlement? Under what circumstances, if any, is a state under an obligation to accept judicial settlement? Under what circumstances, if any, is one state free to arraign another in court?

Consent as a Prerequisite to the Use of Judicial Methods

1. Ad hoc consent. Answers to the preceding questions and to similar questions derive from the practice of states, and in many areas of operation states have been very jealous of their freedom of action. The general principle which they have maintained in this particular connection is that each state is free to decide for itself whether or not to permit the submission of a dispute to judicial settlement. In other words, the general principle is that there is no obligation to refer any dispute of any kind to arbitration or adjudication. In general, then, one state has no right to arraign another in court.

When arbitration or adjudication occurs, therefore, it occurs with the consent of the parties to the dispute. Unless they agree to arbitrate, no arbitral tribunal will be formed. Unless they agree to adjudicate, the International Court of Justice will refuse to hear the case; one party cannot bring a case to the Court without the consent of the other.

2. Advance consent in various treaties. However, states may and do make agreements in which they consent in advance to the judicial settlement of specified kinds of disputes. Treaties often include a provision obliging the parties to submit disputes over their meaning to arbitration or to the International Court of Justice. A considerable proportion of the cases over which the Court has exercised compulsory jurisdiction have been brought to it on the basis of such treaty obligations. For arbitration, advance consent may also be expressed in what are called general arbitration treaties, specifying that all or certain kinds of future disputes shall be submitted to arbitral tribunals.[8] The obligation usually applies, of course, only to justiciable disputes, and normally there are reservations potentially excluding some of them. In concluding general arbitration treaties, states usually promise to submit all future legal disputes to arbitration excepting those affecting their vital interests, their independence, their honor, or the interests of third states. The exceptions are far-reaching. States insisting on them become "Indian givers," promising to arbitrate but taking back the promise by attaching reservations. There is no objective way of determining which disputes fall into one or more of the reserved categories. Each state can decide for itself, so that if a state wants to prevent arbitration it can simply declare that its vital interests or honor are involved. Advance consent given on such conditions means no more than a promise to arbitrate when and if arbitration appears desirable.

3. *Advance consent in the optional clause.* Advance consent can also be given to adjudication at the hands of the International Court of Justice. As already mentioned, treaties often provide that disputes over the meaning of their terms shall be referred to the Court, thus giving it compulsory jurisdiction and permitting one state to arraign another in court even though it objects at the time. Further, Article 36 of the Statute includes a so-called optional clause, as follows: [9]

The states parties to the present Statute may at any time declare that they recognize as compulsory *ipso facto* and without special agreement, in relation to any other state accepting the same obligation, the jurisdiction of the Court in all legal disputes concerning:

    a. the interpretation of any treaty;
    b. any question of international law;
    c. the existence of any fact which, if established, would constitute a breach of an international obligation;
    d. the nature or extent of the reparation to be made for the breach of an international obligation.

In the event of a dispute as to whether the Court has jurisdiction, the matter shall be settled by the decision of the Court.

Over half the parties to the Statute have granted the Court compulsory jurisdiction by making the unilateral declarations invited by this article. The United States, Britain, and France are among them. The Soviet Union is not.

4. *The significance of the optional clause.* Such declarations have some significance. Legal disputes do arise which fall within one or more

[8] Helen May Cory, *Compulsory Arbitration of International Disputes* (New York, Columbia University Press, 1932).
[9] International Court of Justice, *Yearbook 1952-1953* (Leyden, Sijthoff, 1953), pp. 39-40, 170-182. The full text of the Statute appears on pp. 450-462 of this book.

of the four enumerated categories, and states which have accepted the compulsory jurisdiction of the Court have on occasion been required to observe the obligation despite their objections.

At the same time, the significance of the declarations is limited. By no means do they involve an obligation to submit all disputes to adjudication, but only legal disputes. Although the Court itself is empowered to decide whether a dispute comes within one of the four enumerated categories, it can do so only on the basis of the claims and counterclaims which have been put forward by the parties. If each of them has stated its case in such a way as to bring the dispute within the enumerated categories, the Court can assume jurisdiction. However, if one party is demanding what it thinks ought to be or what it thinks it ought to have, the issue is not a legal one and the Court is precluded from assuming jurisdiction.

Further, in making declarations under Article 36, most states have added reservations. Great Britain, for example, included among its reservations one restricting compulsory jurisdiction to disputes arising in the future. The United States excluded from the Court's compulsory jurisdiction "disputes with regard to matters which are essentially within the domestic jurisdiction of the United States as determined by the United States." Such reservations obviously restrict the significance of the acceptance of obligations under Article 36.[10]

The Problem of Judicial Bias

When states refer a dispute to judicial settlement they may agree to permit a judgment *ex aequo et bono,* that is, based on equity and justice. This rarely occurs. The general rule, which holds in the absence of special agreement to the contrary, is that arbitral tribunals and the Court will render their decisions on the basis of existing law. Political expediency, political, social, and economic preferences, and even the judge's sense of fairness are theoretically not supposed to influence his decision. He is supposed to be an unprejudiced, dispassionate, impartial interpreter of the law, which may or may not make him an instrument of justice. There is no doubt that judges commonly try conscientiously to live up to the standards fixed for them. In truth, however, the cards are stacked against them in this respect, and the standards are extraordinarily difficult to maintain. The very existence of a legal dispute suggests that the law on the point in question is vague or uncertain. Perhaps several meanings can be read into it equally well. In this situation it is likely that the

[10] Edvard Hambro, "Some Observations on the Compulsory Jurisdiction of the International Court of Justice," *The British Yearbook of International Law,* Vol. 25 (1948), pp. 133-157; Ruth C. Lawson, "The Problem of the Compulsory Jurisdiction of the World Court," *American Journal of International Law,* Vol. 46 (April, 1952), pp. 219-238.

decision of the judge, consciously or unconsciously, will be influenced by his background and preferences.[11] In rejecting judicial settlement as much as they have, communist governments have no doubt been influenced in part by fear of this bias.

Single-package Agreements for Peaceful Settlement

Since World War I there has been a strong movement for single-package agreements providing for the peaceful settlement of all disputes, and a number of treaties of this type have been concluded. The usual requirement is that the parties will seek settlement through negotiations first of all. Negotiations failing, they will refer justiciable disputes to arbitration or adjudication, and non-justiciable or political disputes to conciliation. Great Britain, France, Holland, Belgium, and Luxembourg bound themselves to such an arrangement in 1948 in the Treaty of Brussels. The General Act for the Pacific Settlement of International Disputes, signed in 1928 and binding on more than twenty states, contains a similar requirement, along with a curious and controversial provision concerning disputes which conciliation fails to settle. Such disputes are to be submitted to an arbitral tribunal which will settle them on the basis of law if an applicable rule of law exists; otherwise the tribunal will decide *ex aequo et bono*. The question is, who decides, and on what basis, whether a rule of law is applicable.[12] The single-package arrangements for peaceful settlement contained in the League of Nations Covenant and the United Nations Charter will be discussed below.

NON-AMICABLE METHODS OF SETTLEMENT

We have already noted that negotiations among states may involve both persuasion and coercion. The two, in fact, are often difficult to distinguish, for the power to coerce ordinarily enhances the ability to persuade. States may achieve what they want ostensibly on the basis of persuasion when in fact their latent power to coerce is the principal persuasive factor. Moreover, it is not uncommon for negotiations to be accompanied and supplemented by active efforts to coerce, including ultimately the threat of war. Those who bargain are likely to use more than verbal blandishments if they are in a position to do so. States often resort to economic pressures of all degrees of severity to induce compliance with their wishes. In some circumstances appeal to opinion, perhaps involving subversive efforts, may put another government in a position in which it is virtually obliged to accept a settlement. Military leverages and threats may be employed.

[11] Frederick Sherwood Dunn, *The Protection of Nationals* (Baltimore, Johns Hopkins Press, 1932), esp. pp. 95, 98-112, 200.
[12] Oppenheim, *op. cit.*, Vol. II, pp. 92-96.

Since coercion is not uncommon in negotiations, there is no sharp dividing line between amicable and non-amicable means of settling international disputes. The one category merges into the other. Coercion, however, is the characteristic, dominant, and perhaps the exclusive feature of non-amicable methods.

There are four types of non-amicable means: retorsion, reprisal, intervention, and war.

An act of retorsion is a legal but deliberately unfriendly act with a retaliatory or coercive purpose. For example, the severance of diplomatic relations or an embargo on the exportation of strategic materials to a particular state may constitute acts of retorsion.

An act of reprisal is an illegal and deliberately unfriendly act with a retaliatory or coercive purpose, deemed justified by prior violation of law by the other party; war is not intended but may follow if the victim of the reprisal chooses to fight. For example, Hitler felt that German rights were violated when bombs dropped by Loyalist airplanes during the Spanish Civil War fell on a German war vessel in port in the Balearic Islands. In retaliation, he ordered his navy to shell the Loyalist port city of Almería. The shelling of the city was an act of reprisal. After Japan invaded Manchuria in 1931, the Lytton Commission, appointed by the League of Nations, came to the conclusion that the action should be classified as a measure of reprisal.

Intervention denotes dictatorial interference by one state in the internal or external affairs of another. States resort to intervention for various purposes, among them the settlement of disputes and, more generally, the imposition of their will upon other states. Intervention may involve, for example, the occupation of some of the territory of another state, as when President Wilson ordered the occupation of Veracruz upon the refusal of the Mexican government to make amends for a violation of American rights. It may involve establishment of a blockade, as when Great Britain and France blockaded the coast of Holland in 1833 to force it to acknowledge the independence of Belgium. It may involve the dictatorial interference of a third state in the dispute of two other states, designed to force a settlement on them, as when Hitler's government required Rumania to give up Transylvania to Hungary. The forms and purposes of intervention are numerous. Sometimes it is legal and sometimes illegal. Both the League of Nations and the United Nations, as well as other international agencies, have engaged in collective intervention to terminate hostilities or defeat aggression. This aspect of the subject will be treated below.

War itself is the ultimate means of settling international disputes. More generally, it is the ultimate means by which states seek to impose their will on each other. When all other means have failed them, or even before other means have been exhausted, states may resort to war to get what they want. The fact that war serves a function and that it is not a purposeless activity is an obvious and an important fact—a fact which those who wish to reduce its role in world affairs must not forget. If war served no function, it might simply be outlawed; people could get along without a useless activity. But reducing the role of an activity which has a useful purpose—in fact, many useful purposes—is a more complex and difficult matter.

DIPLOMACY BY CONFERENCE

The Increasing Use of the Conference Method

So far in the discussion of diplomacy we have confined ourselves to its traditional form, the exchange of diplomatic agents on a bilateral basis. Periodically in history, however, and especially after wars, diplomacy has been conducted in conferences, and diplomacy by conference has taken on ever-increasing importance since the time of World War I.[13] During that war the Allies established many joint groups which functioned more or less continuously to determine and implement common policies on different aspects of the war effort. After the war came the establishment of the League of Nations, and under it there were annual and special conferences of all the members (meeting as the Assembly of the League) and more frequent conferences of a selected group (meeting as its Council). In addition, there were meetings of a number of international agencies associated with the League, as well as many conferences, such as several of the disarmament conferences, outside the framework of the League.

During World War II there was a great elaboration of the conference method of handling international problems among the Allies. The heads of the governments of the Big Three met on several occasions. Foreign ministers likewise conferred directly and personally. Britain and the United States maintained a Combined Chiefs of Staff to plan and guide the execution of military strategy. A number of other joint international agencies were also in operation. Though there was no general peace conference after the war, the conference technique has been applied to draft treaties and to handle other problems emanating from the war.

At the close of the war came the establishment of the United Nations. Its Security Council, consisting of eleven members, is so organized as to function continuously. Its General Assembly, in which all members are represented, meets several months each year. The Economic and Social Council (ECOSOC) is a principal organ of the United Nations, and associated with the United Nations are many specialized agencies the activ-

---

[13] Frederick Sherwood Dunn, *The Practice and Procedure of International Conferences* (Baltimore, Johns Hopkins Press, 1929); Nicolson, *op. cit.*, pp. 155-178.

ities of which involve numerous conferences. Description and discussion of the nature and functions of the various bodies will be found in subsequent chapters.

The Necessity of the Conference Method

Diplomacy by conference is necessary. It has become necessary because of the great increase in diplomatic business. Technological changes and various human proclivities have brought an astounding multiplication of international contacts and have produced problems simultaneously affecting many states. States are becoming more and more interdependent. The fortune and fate of one are becoming more and more interlocked with the fortune and fate not simply of one or two neighbors but of many states. So many urgent problems are common to so many states that it would be almost impossible to handle them by bilateral negotiations through ordinary diplomatic channels.

The Advantages of the Conference Method

Diplomacy by conference is not only necessary but also predominantly good, whatever the criteria of judgment selected. The main advantage lies in the possibility of relatively speedy agreement and action, or the speedy discovery of areas of agreement and disagreement. Moreover, a conference includes a built-in provision for mediation and other forms of third-party action. In a conference of any size, the probability is that some participants will not be committed to a particular position on every issue, and they can quietly employ good offices, mediation, or even intervention to bring about settlement of disputes which arise. Conferences by their very nature facilitate personal contacts among statesmen from different countries; the effects of this may, of course, be varied, probably including the development of personal antipathies as well as personal friendships. On the assumption that knowledge and understanding are desirable, however, personal contacts are probably also desirable, whatever their effects.

The usual rule of diplomacy is that each state decides for itself whether or not to take a particular action and whether or not to permit a modification of its legal rights. Of course, its decision, though technically a free one, may be made under various internal and external pressures. The conference method often adds to the pressures, for good or ill. Some of them come from within the conference itself, where there is pressure to go along with—or at least not to obstruct—the majority. Though a state is free to say no while all the others say yes, it is likely to hesitate before using such freedom; isolation is not ordinarily agreeable. Other pressures come from outside the conference. Public attention in the home countries of the diplomats is likely to focus somewhat more on a conference than on bilateral negotiations, and it is commonly assumed, whether rightly or not, that the public is more concerned with the appearance of agreement than with the terms of agreement. Moreover, governments which are concerned with the issues being discussed at the conference, but which are not represented, will also watch the results. This intensifies pressures for agreement. The various pressures may really produce agreement which might not otherwise have been obtained, or they may induce the statesmen involved to resort to what is called a diplomatic formula —a statement which registers agreement, but which is so vague that no one knows precisely what the agreement is. Each party hopes to have its own meaning read into the agreement later on. This may or may not solve the problem.

Finally in connection with diplomacy by conference there is a strong tendency to modify the unanimity rule formally.[14] The Charter of the United Nations provides that the Security Council may make its decisions on the basis of seven votes out of the eleven. On procedural questions any seven votes will suffice, and on non-procedural questions the seven must include the votes of the permanent members (China, France, Great Britain, the U.S.S.R., and the United States). Either way, the vote of the seven is binding on all eleven and, for that matter, on all United Nations members. The General Assembly decides some questions by an absolute majority and others by a two-thirds majority; in neither case is there any requirement that the great powers be included in the majority. Theoretically, all the great powers might be in the defeated minority. Similarly, aside from the Security Council and the General Assembly, other international agencies and conferences operate on something other than a unanimity rule.

As we shall see when we discuss the United Nations in later chapters, these qualifications to the general rule that states must consent to measures affecting them are not as important as they appear at first sight. Yet they are not without their significance. The development of diplomacy by conference is having a corrosive effect on the general rule. The tendency is toward the development of voting rules for conferences that are analogous to the voting rules in parliaments, and the development of such rules is bound to have a profound effect on the meaning of sovereignty and on the nature of international politics. They reflect the growth of a conception of an international public interest, to which national interest must in some degree give way.

---

[14] Cromwell A. Riches, *The Unanimity Rule and the League of Nations* (Baltimore, Johns Hopkins Press, 1933); *idem, Majority Rule in International Organization* (Baltimore, Johns Hopkins Press, 1940); Wellington Koo, Jr., *Voting Procedures in International Political Organizations* (New York, Columbia University Press, 1947).

THE CHOICE OF METHODS

In this chapter we have made a brief survey of practices concerning recognition, of ground rules on the basis of which diplomatic relationships are maintained, of the methods of settling international disputes, and of conferences as a method of diplomacy. We divided the methods of settling disputes into those regarded as amicable and those regarded as non-amicable. The amicable means are political, featuring negotiations in which third parties may or may not take part, or judicial. The non-amicable means include measures of retorsion and reprisal, intervention, and war. Diplomacy by conference, though discussed separately, belongs in the category of political methods.

What considerations influence states in their choice of methods? The question will arise repeatedly in subsequent chapters, and we shall attempt only a partial answer here.

The nature of the objective pursued may have considerable influence on the choice of method. At the end of Chapter 9, we described the various categories into which states are sometimes classified—the welfare states and the power states, the "haves" and the "have-nots," the satiated and the unsatiated, the status quo states and the revisionists, the status quo states and the imperialist states. The point was made there that states in the first category in each classification system are inclined toward peaceful methods, and states in the second category are inclined toward aggressive methods, including war.

As a general rule, a status quo state will naturally want to rely on peaceful methods rather than on war. In negotiations, the status quo state is theoretically free to preserve the status quo. It can refuse concessions and reject compromises; as long as the other side restricts itself to peaceful methods, the status quo power is normally in a position to preserve what it wants to preserve. If it feels that it might be at a disadvantage in bilateral negotiations, it can call for third-party participation or seek a general conference, especially if the third-party or the members of the conference seem likely to side with it. Or the status quo power is likely to be happy to have disputes settled by judicial means, for the law to be interpreted and applied is itself a part of the status quo.

The revisionist or imperialist power is likely to have the opposite attitudes. If it is strong, it may favor negotiations, and then mix considerable coercion with its efforts to induce concessions. It is likely to prefer bilateral negotiations to those involving third powers, for an isolated state will be more likely to succumb to pressures. It is likely to prefer political rather than judicial methods of settlement, for settlement on the basis of law is not likely to be as favorable as settlement according to power. If the other party stubbornly refuses to make the desired concessions, the strong imperialist power can give more and more signs of a willingness to abandon persuasion and resort to coercion, perhaps to war.

Although helpful and largely true, these generalizations are also hazardous. A status quo power may resort to preventive war if time seems to be on the side of a rising, imperialist power. Moreover, a state which is generally an upholder of the status quo may want to upset a particular aspect of it, and then it will choose the methods of imperialism in a portion of its relationships. Furthermore, the usefulness of these generalizations depends upon the reliability of the classifying process; it is not always possible to tell whether a state is satiated or unsatiated, and even if this could be determined for any one month or year, sudden changes might be brought about by either external or internal developments.

SUGGESTED READINGS

BRIERLY, J. L., *The Outlook for International Law* (Oxford, Clarendon, 1944).

CORBETT, P. E., *Law and Society in the Relations of States* (New York, Harcourt, Brace, 1951).

CORY, Helen May, *Compulsory Arbitration of International Disputes* (New York, Columbia University Press, 1932).

DUNN, Frederick Sherwood, *The Protection of Nationals* (Baltimore, Johns Hopkins Press, 1932).

LISSITZYN, Oliver J., *The International Court of Justice,* United Nations Studies, No. 6 (New York, Carnegie Endowment for International Peace, 1951).

McCAMY, James L., *The Administration of American Foreign Affairs* (New York, Knopf, 1950).

NICOLSON, Harold, *Diplomacy* (New York, Harcourt, Brace, 1939).

NICOLSON, Harold, *The Evolution of Diplomatic Method* (New York, Macmillan, 1955).

OPPENHEIM, Lassa F. L., *International Law,* 7th ed., Hersh Lauterpacht, ed., 2 vols. (New York, Longmans Green, 1948-1952).

ROSENNE, S., "International Court and the United Nations: Reflections on the Period 1946-1954," *International Organization,* Vol. 9 (May, 1955), pp. 244-256.

CHAPTER 15

International Law, Morality, and Peaceful Change

IN VARIOUS CHAPTERS we have already made some references to both law and morality. The immediately preceding chapter contained a brief summary of certain legal principles, especially those relating to the exchange of diplomatic agents. In Chapter 2 there was a discussion of the nature of law within countries and an appraisal of its role in preserving domestic peace. Many aspects of international politics involve legal and moral questions.

In this chapter the general object is to appraise law and morality as limitations on the behavior of states and as instruments which they use in pursuing their interests. To what extent and in what ways do they contribute to peace, and why do they not assure peace? What relationships exist between law, morality, peaceful change, and power? To answer such questions we shall consider what international law is, what kinds of rules it contains, how they are brought into existence and enforced, and what purposes they serve. We shall also briefly examine the role of morality in international affairs. The discussion of these topics will provide a suitable background for an analysis of the important problem of peaceful change.

WHAT IS INTERNATIONAL LAW?

Some doubt that anything exists which deserves to be called international law. The question is hardly worth arguing, for the answer depends upon the definition with which one starts. Some definitions of law—for example, those requiring the existence of a determinate superior enforcing authority—lead to the conclusion that there is nothing which can properly be called international law. Other definitions lead to the opposite conclusion. Since all Foreign Offices talk and act as if international law exists, it seems best to adopt a definition which permits it to exist. The following is as good as any: [1]

The term international law may fairly be employed to designate the principles and rules of conduct declaratory thereof which states feel themselves bound to observe and, therefore, do commonly observe in their relations with each other.

International law is said to be general when it applies to all states; it is said to be particular when it binds only some of them. Thus customary rules concerning the immunities of diplomatic agents constitute a part of general international law. A bilateral treaty constitutes particular international law, binding only the parties. From another point of view, international law is divided into three branches: the law of peace, the law of war, and the law of neutrality. Students of international law call the whole field of domestic law (national, state, and local) municipal law.

THE INTERNATIONAL LEGISLATIVE PROCESS

States bring international law into existence mainly through custom and treaties, though judicial agencies and scholarly research do a good deal to clarify and even to expand the law thus established.

The Development of Customary Law

The process of establishing customary law is somewhat analogous to the one by which English common law was created. If a number of states are repeatedly faced with a particular issue and if they accept the same rule for solving the problem over a considerable period, they establish what is known as a usage. When they begin to follow this rule out of a sense of obligation, the usage is transformed into custom and therefore into law. Or a state may assert a claim of right with regard to an issue and may be willing reciprocally to acknowledge that other states possess the same right. When enough states have acknowledged that the right exists, it becomes a part of international law. It is as difficult to say when states create customary law as it is to say when people who walk across a lawn create a path. No one knows how many states must accept a particular principle for how long a time before a customary rule of law can be said to have been created. At best, however, the process is a slow and uncertain one; a number of decades are likely to be required. Further, there are often so many variations in the circumstances surrounding the precedents or the claims of right that customary law is frequently vague or ambiguous.

It has been noted that [2] "such [customary] law as has emerged has

---

[1] Charles Cheney Hyde, *International Law Chiefly as Interpreted and Applied by the United States* (Boston, Little, Brown, 1945), Vol. I, p. 1.

[2] Edwin D. Dickinson, "International Law: An Inventory," *California Law Review*, Vol. 33 (December, 1945), p. 539.

rested both theoretically and practically upon a well-nigh universal consent or acquiescence. This is to say, of course, that the law has made substantial progress where there was no substantial controversy. . . ."

Legislating by Making and Terminating Treaties

Law may be brought into existence more deliberately and more rapidly through treaties and other international agreements.[3] Treaty-making normally includes several steps. First, a treaty is initialed or signed by representatives of the states which expect to become parties to it; this usually follows negotiations among them all, but with treaties of peace may result from the dictation of the winning side. Ratification is the second step, accomplished by each state through its own constitutional processes. Finally, instruments attesting to ratification are exchanged or are deposited with a designated party. If the treaty is between only two states, it normally comes into effect when they exchange ratifications. When many states are involved, the terms of the treaty normally specify how many of them must exchange or deposit instruments of ratification in order to bring it into effect among the ratifying powers. Once a treaty has come into effect, states which were not among the original signatories may be permitted to adhere to it.

As suggested above, a treaty creates law only for those states which become party to it. France and Belgium may make a treaty creating law for themselves, but they cannot thereby add to or take away from the legal rights of the Netherlands. Even if a majority of states adhere to a treaty, they are still creating particular rather than general international law. However, treaties may be designed to be declaratory of existing general law. Further, treaties are said to create general international law when they are ratified by nearly all states. The Kellogg-Briand Pact outlawing war, for example, was ratified by so many states that its principles no doubt constitute a part of general international law. Sometimes treaties ratified by a large number of states are described as constituting "international legislation," but the practice is misleading; actually all treaties, unless they are simply declaratory of existing law, are legislative so far as the parties are concerned.

The principle *pacta sunt servanda* (agreements are to be observed) is a basic one in international law. A state cannot free itself at will from the obligations of a treaty. Nevertheless, treaties can be terminated, and their termination is an aspect of the legislative process. They may be terminated in accordance with their own terms; for example, the treaty may provide for its expiration after a specified period of years or on notice from one party that it desires termination. They may be terminated by the general consent of the parties; the technical requirement

---

[3] The term *treaty* is commonly interchangeable with a number of other terms, such as *pact* and *convention*.

that *all* parties consent is frequently ignored. Violation of the treaty by one party gives the other party a right to denounce it; assuming that respect for treaties is desirable, the difficulty here is that each state decides for itself whether another has violated its obligations, and the judgment rendered may not be unprejudiced. Nazi Germany, for example, presumed to free itself from a number of treaties on the basis of the dubious assertion that another party had previously violated them. Other conditions in which termination is legitimate theoretically exist but rarely occur in practice. A treaty may not be terminated simply because it was initially accepted under duress; otherwise, most treaties of peace would not be binding.

"Legislative" Functions of Judicial Agencies and Scholars

Theoretically, judicial agencies (the International Court of Justice, arbitral tribunals, and national courts) do not participate in the legislative process. Their task is to determine what the law is, not to create new law. Yet, the very fact that a case has come before a judicial agency usually means that the law is not clear on the point in question, and when a judicial agency clarifies the law or reads meaning into a legal principle, it engages in something closely akin to a law-making function. Theoretically, the research work of scholars does not make law either, but the convenience of their findings and the thoroughness of their work often give them considerable influence on moot points.

The Problem of Codification

Implicit in the above is the fact that the evidences of law are widely scattered. There is no comprehensive official code to which one can turn to find a statement of what the law is. The Hague Conferences of 1899 and 1907 led to the conclusion of a number of conventions which codified certain portions of international law, notably portions concerned with war and neutrality; many of the rules have, however, become obsolete because of technological and other changes. The League of Nations took it upon itself to promote the codification of international law, and called a conference in 1930 for the purpose of drawing up codes in the three areas deemed most ripe for codification: (1) nationality; (2) territorial waters; and (3) the responsibility of states for damage done in their territory to the person or property of foreigners. The results were meager. A few special conventions on certain questions pertaining to nationality were agreed upon (subsequently ratified by only ten states), but there was much disagreement on the other topics and no comprehensive code was accepted on any of the three.[4] The Charter of the United Nations

[4] Lassa F. L. Oppenheim, *International Law*, 7th ed., Hersh Lauterpacht, ed. (New York, Longmans Green, 1948-1952), Vol. I, pp. 57-59; P. E. Corbett, *Law and Society in the Relations of States* (New York, Harcourt, Brace, 1951), pp. 48-49.

instructs the General Assembly to "initiate studies and make recommendations for the purpose of . . . encouraging the progressive development of international law and its codification." Progress is likely to be slow.

THE SCOPE AND CONTENT OF INTERNATIONAL LAW

Although it would be impossible in a few pages to state the rules of international law which have developed as a result of the legislative process described above, some knowledge of the scope and content of the law is essential to an understanding of international politics.[5] At a number of different points, in fact, we have already been obliged to refer to the legal rules and principles which states accept.

The Law of Peace

1. Sources, sanctions, persons. Textbooks which survey international law commonly include a discussion of the sources and evidences of law, which we have referred to above under the heading of the legislative process. They discuss sanctions, which we shall take up shortly. They define the persons, mainly states, subject to international law, and discuss the rules and principles relating to the birth of states and the recognition of states and governments.

2. The extent of the national domain. International law includes rules and principles concerning property and control. States are said to have dominion over territory. The boundaries of a state's domain are fixed under customary law or by treaty. In a surprising number of cases, however, especially in less civilized areas, legal rights to territory are in dispute, and in many other cases one state asserts a political claim to territory in the possession of another. There is agreement that the domain of maritime states includes a maritime belt, but disagreement on the width of the belt. Rules governing the use of straits, international waterways like the Suez Canal,[6] and international rivers are commonly fixed by treaties. The air space above a state is under its exclusive control; among other things, this means that aircraft from one state may fly over the territory of another only with its consent and under such regulations as it chooses to impose. The high seas, outside the domain of any state, are said to be free. Various legal methods exist, of course, by which states may acquire additional territory; the law includes rules concerning the transfer of rights and obligations when one state takes over all or part of the territory of another.

---

[5] The article by Dickinson, cited in footnote 2 above, contains a good brief survey of international law. See also J. L. Brierly, *The Law of Nations* (Oxford, Clarendon, 1949).

[6] Cf. Hugh J. Schonfield, *The Suez Canal in World Affairs* (New York, Philosophical Library, 1953).

3. *Jurisdiction and its limits.* Within the national domain states enjoy very extensive freedom and, with minor qualifications, exercise exclusive jurisdiction. Under general international law they have retained the right to deal with domestic affairs as they see fit, even in many areas where their actions have profound implications for foreign states and peoples. They remain free to adopt the political and economic system of their choice; whether a government is fascist or communist or liberal, or whether the economy is socialized or free, makes no difference in general international law. With minor qualifications governments may adopt whatever domestic policies they choose to adopt, and may make actions within their borders legal or illegal as they wish; each state has exclusive police power within its own territory. As we saw in Chapter 12, governments may permit the private manufacture of armaments on an unlimited scale and may themselves manufacture whatever armaments they can. They may allow or engage in the exportation and importation of armaments. They may maintain armed establishments of any composition and size, and may locate all or part of their armed establishment on the vulnerable border of another state. Pistols and thermonuclear weapons are on the same plane, so far as general international law is concerned. As we saw in Chapter 13, governments are free to regulate the movement of goods, capital, and persons across national frontiers, even though the regulations inflict injury abroad.

There are, of course, limitations on the jurisdictional rights of a state even within its own domain. A large body of law exists regulating the treatment of agents of one state who enter the domain of another. Foreign diplomats and consuls, for example, are largely immune from the jurisdiction of the state in which they operate. War vessels paying a friendly visit in a foreign port remain under the jurisdiction of the flag state. Merchant ships in a foreign port come under the jurisdiction of the foreign state for some purposes and remain under the jurisdiction of the flag state for other purposes. Jurisdiction over the maritime belt is qualified by the requirement that foreign vessels be granted a right of "innocent passage." On the high seas, each state asserts jurisdiction over ships flying its flag, but such jurisdiction is not exclusive; it is shared to an uncertain extent with other maritime states, which assert jurisdiction even over foreign vessels where they consider it necessary for their safety or the enforcement of their laws.

The jurisdiction of a state extends over its nationals abroad, and even for some purposes over non-nationals abroad, though enforcement of this jurisdiction is often impossible. Through treaties, states generally accept an obligation to extradite those found under their jurisdiction who have fled from justice in another state, though a right to grant asylum to political refugees is recognized.

4. Other topics. International law also deals with the problem of determining the nationality of persons and with the problems which may arise when the same person is a national of two or more states. States commonly extend diplomatic protection to their nationals abroad, and this practice has given rise to an extensive body of law concerning the responsibility of states for injury to aliens or for damage to their property. We shall refer to this subject again.

Another important area of international law is concerned with inter-governmental communication, particularly with rules and regulations governing the status and treatment of diplomats. As we have already indicated, international law also fixes rules and procedures for the conclusion and termination of agreements among states and for the settlement of disputes which arise among them.

The Law of War

The above topics are covered in the law of peace. States have also allowed a "law of war" to develop, regulating the conduct of hostilities and the treatment of enemy nationals and their property. They have, however, reserved the right to act in conformity with military necessity, regardless of the law; moreover, they have had difficulty in keeping the law adjusted to changing technological conditions. As scientific developments bring new weapons into existence and permit the adoption of more effective military strategies, those rules concerning the conduct of hostilities which are rendered obsolete receive scant attention.

The Law of Neutrality

Along with the law of war, states have developed a "law of neutrality," defining the rights and obligations of neutrals and belligerents in relationships with each other. A state is neutral when it does not participate in a war which is in progress and when it treats the belligerents impartially. The law of neutrality represents a compromise between the desire of neutrals to keep wartime interference with normal practices and pursuits at a minimum and the desire of belligerents to prevent the enemy from bolstering its strength by receiving supplies or other forms of aid from foreign sources. It gives no assurance that the neutral will refrain from entering the war or that the belligerent will refrain from attacking. Neutrals have in fact frequently abandoned their neutrality and have become belligerents; belligerents have frequently decided that they could gain more by attacking a neutral than by respecting its rights. But the law of neutrality facilitates the preservation of peace between neutrals and belligerents when both desire peace. It minimizes the possibility that the war will be extended simply because of the absence of rules on the basis of which special wartime conflicts of interest can be resolved.

The Law Concerning Resort to War

Aside from concluding treaties vaguely pledging friendship and eternal peace, the various states did not permit the development of any serious legal restriction on their freedom to go to war until after World War I. When they chose to be at peace with each other, the law of peace prevailed; when they chose to go to war, the laws of war and neutrality came into operation. The law was indifferent to the choice which was made. Thus a monstrous situation existed in which states were "legally bound to respect each other's independence and other rights, and yet free to attack each other at will." [7] States were entitled to rights, provided that other states did not take them away by war. Moreover, since the law recognized the freedom of states to go to war, it could scarcely be clear in prohibiting coercive measures short of war. On many occasions, states resorted to intervention (dictatorial interference) in the affairs of other states, thus infringing on their independence or other rights, and the problem of classifying acts of intervention as legal or illegal was a vexing one.

The Covenant of the League of Nations severely restricted the freedom of the members of the League to resort to war, though leaving "gaps" through which war might legally be waged. Nearly all the states of the world ratified the Kellogg-Briand Pact of 1928. In it the parties "condemn recourse to war for the solution of international controversies, and renounce it as an instrument of national policy." Further, they pledge never to seek the settlement of any dispute except by pacific means. Similarly, the United Nations Charter binds the members to "settle their international disputes by peaceful means" and to "refrain in their international relations from the threat or use of force against the territorial integrity or political independence of any state."

It is obvious that these treaties have not prevented states from resorting to war. We shall discuss some of the reasons for the failure later on. Suffice it to point out here that a right of self-defense is always assumed. The Charter explicitly provides that nothing in it "shall impair the inherent right of individual or collective self-defense if an armed attack occurs. . . ." In practice, states regularly claim to be fighting in self-defense, however flimsy the claim may be. Moreover, war may arise out of essentially domestic struggles, as when two governments claim jurisdiction in the same state and when each of them secures the aid of outside states in attempting to vindicate its claim. Further, when a belief exists that justice or vital interests can be promoted or protected effectively only by the threat or use of force, the strain on obligations to eschew force is very great.

[7] J. L. Brierly, *The Outlook for International Law* (Oxford, Clarendon, 1944), p. 21.

RESPECT FOR LAW AND THE ENFORCEMENT OF LAW

Voluntary Observance

By and large, international law is freely observed. The methods by which it is established suggest that this would be so. Customary law develops out of the practice of states, reflecting rules which they have proved themselves willing to observe. As Brierly puts it,[8] "... states have only allowed [customary] law to control their relations in matters which, though they are not unimportant in themselves, are of secondary importance, and therefore present them with no very strong temptation to defy it." Most treaties are also concluded on a thoroughly voluntary basis, establishing rules of action which the parties expect to be of benefit to them. States thus commonly observe law because they find it advantageous to do so.

Nevertheless, disputes arise. They do not arise so much because of deliberate defiance of the law, for this is relatively rare, as because of vagueness or ambiguity in the law, or because, on many questions, alternative legal principles are applicable. Where vagueness or ambiguity or alternative choices exist, it is rather natural, even when two states are equally willing to observe the law, that each will take the legal stand which is most advantageous to it.[9] Moreover, each state may be so convinced of the rightness of its own stand that it will regard the different stand of the other party as contrary to law.

Sanctions and Self-help

Respect for international law does not depend entirely on the willingness of states to abide by it. Action designed to induce respect can occur, that is, sanctions can be applied. A wide variety of sanctioning measures are available. A state which seeks to induce another to observe the law may protest an impending or actual violation. If it chooses, it may threaten and take retaliatory action of various kinds. Among the possibilities are the severance of diplomatic relations, a boycott of the products of the offending state, an embargo on the shipment of some or all goods to that state, a prohibition of loans to it, or a freezing of its assets. Sanctioning measures may also take the form of military action. The United States has on many occasions intervened militarily in certain Latin American countries, occupying some or all of their territory, to prevent or terminate what it regarded as a violation of international law; some other great powers have done the same thing. Blockades have been used. If the offending state chooses to fight back against the military

[8] *Ibid.*, p. 17.
[9] Frederick Sherwood Dunn, *The Protection of Nationals* (Baltimore, Johns Hopkins Press, 1932), pp. 25-26; Brierly, *The Law of Nations*, pp. 72-77.

force brought to bear upon it, the ensuing hostilities may or may not be regarded as war. When the initial violation of law takes the form of a military invasion, war is the likely result, and, from the point of view of the invaded state, the war will be designed as a sanction of law. Sanctioning measures short of war can be classified as measures of retorsion or reprisal, defined in the preceding chapter.

Assuming the desirability of law and order in international affairs, it is obviously objectionable to have the offended state stand over the offending state as policeman, prosecutor, judge, jury, and executioner. It is as if, within countries, each individual were allowed to decide for himself whether his rights were threatened or violated, and, if so, to take such preventive or punitive action as he saw fit. The principle that every man defines and defends his own rights is a principle that prevails only in societies without effective government, which is precisely the characteristic of the society of nations.

Of course, disputing states have always been free, on the basis of mutual consent, to refer disputes over their respective rights to arbitration, and they have often availed themselves of this procedure. Since the establishment of the Permanent Court of International Justice after World War I and the International Court of Justice after World War II, the voluntary submission of disputes to adjudication has also been easily possible. As indicated in the preceding chapter, many states have accepted the optional clause of the Court's Statute, binding themselves in advance to submit legal disputes to the Court. Thus, if states are willing to do so, they can avoid sitting in judgment on their own cause and can, instead, secure the presumably impartial judgment of a third party. Even so, however, the enforcement of a judgment is left to the benefited state. Neither an arbitral tribunal nor the International Court of Justice has the right or power to apply sanctions. The absence of such a right is not as serious as it might be, however, for when states accept third-party judgment they also normally accept the results; enforcement action is rarely needed.

Sanctions Under the United Nations

The proposition that each state is its own policeman, prosecutor, judge, jury, and executioner has been modified by various treaties, such as the League of Nations Covenant, the Kellogg-Briand Pact, and the United Nations Charter, restricting the freedom of states to resort to war. Under the United Nations Charter members are free to enforce respect for their rights only so long as they confine themselves to peaceful means, except in a case of self-defense against armed attack. When there is a "threat to the peace, breach of the peace, or act of aggression" the United Nations itself becomes concerned. The Security Council may identify the guilty state. The guilty state may be the one which is trying to enforce respect for its rights, if the means used are impermissible, or the one which is threatening or infringing upon the rights of another. Once the guilty state has been identified, the Security Council may call upon members of the United Nations to apply sanctions against it. Article 41 of the Charter specifies that these measures "may include complete or partial interruption of economic relations and of rail, sea, air, postal, telegraphic, radio, and other means of communication, and the severance of diplomatic relations." If these measures are not adequate, the Security Council under Article 42 "may take such action by air, sea, or land forces as may be necessary to maintain or restore international peace and security. Such action may include demonstrations, blockade, and other operations by air, sea, or land forces of Members of the United Nations." Similarly, the General Assembly may recommend sanctions, though it has no right or power to order them.

In short, under the United Nations Charter each state still defines and defends its own rights. But where the issue is serious, peaceful settlement must be sought, and in the event of threats to the peace, breaches of the peace, and acts of aggression the sanctioning measures taken by a member may be reinforced through action of the Organization. This subject —the role of the United Nations and the principle of "collective security" —will be discussed more fully in a later chapter.

Strains on Treaty Obligations

The problem of maintaining respect for treaty obligations is often a special one. Strains on treaty obligations are often very great, especially as concerns treaties which affect the power position of a state or other interests which it regards as vital. Dictated treaties of peace offer an extreme illustration; imposed through violence, they are likely to be defied when the victor loses either the strength or the determination to enforce their terms. E. H. Carr speaks more generally on the subject: [10]

The element of power is inherent in every political treaty. The contents of such a treaty reflect in some degree the relative strength of the contracting parties. Stronger states will insist on the sanctity of the treaties concluded by them with weaker states. Weaker states will renounce treaties concluded by them with stronger states so soon as the power position alters and the weaker state feels itself strong enough to reject or modify the obligation.

Even after treaties have been quite voluntarily accepted, states sometimes conclude that they will gain more by violating than by observing them. This is especially true of treaties of alliance; a state which finds that time has seriously reduced the benefits of an alliance or increased its risks is not likely to abide by its obligation.

[10] E. H. Carr, *The Twenty Years' Crisis 1919-1939* (London, Macmillan, New York, St. Martin's, 1949), p. 190.

Since the possible effect of an alliance is to draw a third party into a war which is not of his doing, the strain on the treaty is very great unless *both* allies feel at the time that they are equally threatened. It seems too much to expect that a nation which has no interest in the outcome of a war will risk its very life merely to fulfill a promise contained in a treaty of alliance.[11]

As we have seen, one of the fears associated with proposals to outlaw the possession of nuclear bombs is that the temptation to violate the agreement would be too great to be resisted.

In a world made bombless by treaty, the first to violate the treaty would gain an enormous advantage. Under such conditions the opportunities for world dominance would be breathtaking! Hence we come to the paradox that the further the nations go by international agreement in the direction of eliminating bombs and installations, the stronger becomes the temptation to evade the agreement.[12]

Machiavelli's advice was that "a prudent ruler ought not to keep faith when by so doing it would be against his interest and when the reasons which made him bind himself no longer exist." The injunction seems to deny that prudent rulers should ever be moved simply by a desire to maintain good faith. In practice states commonly regard it as one of their interests that the principle *pacta sunt servanda* should be maintained. They know that, if they violate treaties, others will do the same. And a world in which no state's word could be counted on would be an undesirable world for all. This is not to say that treaties are always honored. Violations do occur, but they are the exception rather than the rule.

THE FUNCTIONS OF LAW

International law is useful to states. If it were not useful, they would not have created it, nor would they be adding to it and clarifying it as time goes on. In what ways is it useful? Is it equally useful to all? What role does law play in world affairs?

Law Within Countries as the Instrument of the Strong

In Chapter 2 we gave a partial answer to these questions in relation to the political struggle within countries. Some of what was said there needs now to be recalled.

The general theme there developed was that law is largely an instrument of the strong, reflecting the desires of the strong. The theme was similar to one advanced by Rousseau, that [13] "the spirit of the laws of all countries is always to favor the strong against the weak and him that has against him that has not." The notion that there can be a "rule of

---

[11] Frederick Sherwood Dunn, "The Common Problem," in Bernard Brodie, ed., *The Absolute Weapon* (New York, Harcourt, Brace, 1946), p. 9.

[12] *Ibid.*, p. 15.

[13] Carr, *op. cit.*, p. 176.

law, and not of men" was rejected. The contention was that even under the rule of law, law remains an instrument of men; more specifically, it is used by those men who command power. Although their power may derive from different sources, such as control over wealth, control over skills, or adherence to ideas which command support, it is ultimately expressed in force and violence. As Brierly puts it,[14] "There is no such phenomenon in human society as 'the rule of law' in the literal sense of that term; force rules always. . . ."

Strength and Law in Unstable Countries

This view of politics and of the role of law is most easily illustrated by reference to countries which are politically unstable. In some countries of Latin America and in some in the Middle East control over government (and therefore over law-making and law-enforcing authority) is commonly obtained by those who command a preponderance of violence; the correlation between political power and military power is direct and plain. When a person or group which has seized control of the government loses command over a preponderance of violence, a revolution or *coup d'état* is likely; through it, those who have somehow gained control over a preponderance of violence achieve political power, which means that they achieve law-making and law-enforcing authority. They can enact or amend law as they please. It will reflect their desires. The truth of this is not changed if they choose to buttress their political power by shaping the law so as to placate those who might otherwise rebel against them.

Every civil war provides an illustration of the proposition that the law is a reflection of the desires of the strong. When the Bolsheviks achieved victory in Russia, they obviously changed the law to make it reflect their will. The outcome of the Civil War in Spain in the late 1930's gave law-making authority to Franco. Civil war in China determined that the Communists would rule. Often, also, governments retain law-making and law-enforcing authority not because their actions reflect the desires of most of the people whom they rule but because revolutionary elements are unable to muster sufficient military power to make rebellion feasible.

Strength and Law in Democratic Countries

What of countries like the United States and Britain, where scarcely a thought is given to the possibility of civil war? Does the law here likewise reflect the desires of the strong? The answer must be that it does, but the strong must be identified in several ways.

1. The strong defined as those sharing the constitutional consensus. The outstanding characteristic of stable, democratic societies is that a moral and constitutional consensus exists, accepted and supported by

[14] *The Outlook for International Law*, pp. 73-74.

practically the entire population. This means that the population shares
fundamental desires and values, including the desire that governmental
affairs shall be conducted in accordance with agreed constitutional procedures and within agreed constitutional limitations. On the level of
fundamental principles and procedures, then, the strong include all those
who share the consensus. Their strength is so great and so nearly uncontested that it is forgotten. When all agree—when violence is not needed
—the fact that it is available fades from men's minds.

2. *The strong defined as the winners in elections.* On the level of
action under the constitution, the strong are identified and defined somewhat differently. At least in democratic countries, strength is measured
in terms of votes. The more votes a party wins the stronger it is said to be
and the more nearly complete does its control over law-making become.
With sufficient electoral support, it can bring about drastic legislative
and even constitutional changes. When no one person or no one mono-
lithic party wins complete control over government, the law must reflect
a compromise or adjustment of the desires of competing groups. This
appears most clearly in a parliamentary democracy where a coalition
controls the government and where legislation necessarily reflects bargaining among parties in the coalition. Collectively they are the strong,
but their strength is qualified both by the existence of an opposition and
by some degree of disunity among themselves. Compromise on the law
becomes essential, and it comes to reflect common elements in the desires
of various groups.

Whether strength is defined in terms of command over violence or in
terms of command over votes, it should not be assumed that the desires
of the strong necessarily go against the desires of the weak. In some
areas, the desires of the two coincide, and then the law will serve what
is generally regarded as the common good. Moreover, when the strong
face an opposition and when they are more or less divided among themselves, compromises and adjustments prevent the law from reflecting the
narrow desires of any one group.

3. *The strong defined as the victors in civil war.* Though command
over violence may fade into the background in a democratic society
operating under a constitutional consensus, the importance of violence
should not be ignored. In a large society, no consensus is ever complete.
At a minimum, there will be criminal elements which reject it, and it is
taken for granted that they are to be suppressed. Probably, too, there will
be political elements which reject some or all aspects of the constitutional
consensus. Sometimes this leads to a gradual change in the consensus
through a process of agreement, but when the challenge to the consensus
is revolutionary (as the communist challenge is, for example), the chal-
lengers are considered subversive. As such, they may or may not be
tolerated. When they are suppressed, the act reflects strength, even

though expressed by legal means. If they are not suppressed and if, instead, they gain great strength themselves, force and violence are likely to come to the fore again as the ultimate means of determining whose will is to prevail. As many revolutions attest, the counting of votes or the use of other peaceful devices for determining who is entitled to exercise law-making and law-enforcing authority provides only a tentative decision. The tentative decision may prevail, but if it is challenged the ultimate decision will be made on the battlefield.

Strength and the Law in International Politics

If the above statements are true of the relationship between strength and law within countries, are they also true in the international realm? The answer must be in the affirmative.

1. The strong and customary law. It is inconceivable that a rule of customary law could develop against the opposition of powerful states. The rules of law which are created through usage, or through the assertion of a claim of right on the basis of reciprocity, must be rules which are at least acceptable to the powerful. If they reject the usage, they prevent it from crystallizing into law, and if they deny the asserted right it is doubtful that it can be established. Customary law may reflect the desires and interests of all states; it may be in the common good, but the crucial fact is that it is acceptable to the strong.

The powerful cannot create customary law quite as readily as they can prevent its creation, but when they are not divided against each other the possibility exists. They have substantially had their way, for example, on the question of an international standard of justice concerning the treatment of aliens. Weak and ill-governed countries have generally taken the view that aliens are on the same basis as citizens so far as the protection of the laws is concerned, entitled only to local remedies for any injury allegedly done to them; in other words, they have held that aliens can expect only such justice as the local law provides, and that other states have no right to insist on any other standard. Powerful states (the United States among them) have refused to accept this principle, asserting that there is a minimum international standard of justice which all states are to be expected to meet. They have extended diplomatic protection to their nationals abroad, interceding verbally and sometimes resorting to military intervention to make sure that justice was done. Faced with such attitudes and actions, the weak have perforce succumbed to the pressures of the strong. They have had to accept the dictation of the strong and, in a sense, have been fortunate when the strong chose law rather than overt force and violence as the instrument of their will.

There is no reason at all to believe that, in the absence of the institution [of diplomatic protection], the stronger states would have been content to stand by and do nothing while their citizens in Latin American countries were receiving treatment which appeared unjust or improper. . . . In other parts of the world, territorial conquest was then taking place on much slighter provocation than was being offered in some Latin American countries. . . . The legal institution of diplomatic protection, in other words, served as a substitute for territorial conquest in bringing the Latin American states within the orbit of international trade and intercourse. . . .[15]

Powerful states have thus contributed significantly to the development of law concerning diplomatic protection and international claims; in particular circumstances they have forced acceptance of legal principles which took the place of outright violence in the achievement of their desires.

2. *The strong and treaty law.* Similarly, power relationships have much to do with treaty law. Frequently, of course, treaties reflect the common desires of the parties and are thus equally acceptable to the strong and the weak. Where differing desires exist, however, the strong have an obvious advantage, whether they exert strength by means of the "big stick" or the "sugar stick"; in the geographical region where the Soviet Union can most easily bring its power to bear, it has both imposed treaties on the weak and prevented them from concluding treaties which were objectionable. Other great powers have acted similarly. Negotiations for peace provide an extreme illustration of the role of power in determining treaty law. It is a commonplace that states which share in fixing the terms of peace have influence in rough proportion to the power which they are thought to command. If one state has emerged the victor, it can dictate terms. Allied states which have won victory must bargain among themselves, weapons in hand, over the terms to impose on the defeated. If it is a peace without victory, belligerents from both sides will presumably share in fixing the terms of settlement, and the terms agreed upon are likely to reflect their expectations in the event of resumption of war.

3. *Some qualifications.* The proposition that the law reflects the desires of the strong must be qualified in relation to international law just as in relation to municipal law. On some points the strong and weak agree. Further, it is not to be assumed that strong states are always united against weak states in determining the content of the law. Strong states may be divided against each other, and may adjust their conflicts by accepting legal principles which weak states can invoke in their own favor. Moreover, strong states struggling with each other may seek the support of weaker states, and may therefore champion principles which the weaker states likewise favor. The strong are not, in fact, always guided by narrow and ruthless self-interest. They commonly prefer that their self-interest be "enlightened"; the term is a vague one, but it pre-

[15] Dunn, *The Protection of Nationals,* pp. 57-58.

sumably involves a belief that self-interest is best served through some regard for the desires and interests of others in the society. Moreover, the strong join others in claiming to act in accordance with the requirements of morality and justice; though definitions of the moral and the just often differ, they also often include common elements. The result is that international law does not bestow its favors quite as unequally as the general proposition suggests. Treaties, and above all treaties of peace, often discriminate harshly against the weak, but many rules of law serve the weak as well as the strong. More or less unwittingly, the power struggle often produces rules which reflect common interests.

The Uses of Law

In which ways is law useful? The answer can be the same whether with reference to international or to municipal law. Law helps to establish and preserve order and regularity in public affairs. It permits prediction of the consequences of certain acts and warns subjects of the law not to commit those acts which would be followed by consequences they wish to avoid. It "is a means of enabling the day-to-day business of states to be conducted in normal times along orderly and predictable lines, and that is no small service." [16] Where the law is clear, it reduces the possibility that conflicting legal claims will be advanced, and it thus reduces the occasion for friction. To the extent that it promotes order and regularity in public affairs, it provides a framework within which commercial, cultural, and personal interchange can occur and interdependence can develop; such interchange and interdependence may, of course, lead to friction, but it also may create or reinforce common bonds, contributing to the development of a society. Finally, it should be noted that throughout history those who have made and enforced law have sought to make it hallowed. They have sought to inculcate the idea that obedience to law is a virtue. To the extent that they have succeeded, a final function can be assigned to the law: that it carries an air of sanctity and therefore lends sanctity even to the achievements of force and violence.[17]

THE ROLE OF MORALITY

What role do principles of morality play, either as a limitation on the actions of states or as an instrument for promoting national advantage?

Although those acting in the name of states may sometimes do things which they themselves regard as immoral, it is reasonable to assume that this is uncommon. Certainly statesmen regularly claim that they act in accordance with high moral principles. As a general rule, it can be

[16] Brierly, *The Outlook for International Law,* p. 17.
[17] Cf. George W. Keeton and Georg Schwarzenberger, *Making International Law Work* (London, Stevens, 1946), pp. 31-48.

assumed that the moral principles endorsed by decision-makers influence the decisions they make. People commonly act in accordance with their conception of the good and the right.

The Tendency Toward Egocentric Definitions of the Good and Right

But within what frame of reference are the good and the right defined? And what definitions are arrived at? If all those who influence decisions affecting international relations were inspired and guided by a desire to promote the good and the right equally for all mankind, and if their conceptions of the good and the right coincided, the world would be far different than it is. In fact, the tendency is very strong to focus on the nation or state, rather than on all mankind, in defining the good and the right; it is the national society which counts primarily, rather than a putative world society. There is a very marked reluctance to take the view that the nation or state is a unit in a world society whose good transcends the good of its individual parts.[18] The result is that those who act in the name of the state tend to regard the state as an end in itself. Supreme moral value becomes attached to such objectives as the establishment, the preservation, and perhaps the aggrandizement of the nation-state, to the way of life and the ideology for which the state stands, and to the welfare or prosperity of some or all the people within the state.

The Morality of Satiated States

Given the national frame of reference within which the requirements of morality are defined, it is not surprising that there should be a correlation between the desires of a government and the moral principles it accepts. States which are satiated, or states which in the main wish to preserve the status quo, generally place a high moral value on peace. Thus the French Foreign Minister, Aristide Briand, speaking in the days when France was favored by the Treaty of Versailles, declared that "peace comes before all; peace comes even before justice." [19] Thus also Prime Minister Neville Chamberlain of Britain, faced with Hitler's challenge to the status quo, declared that [20]

His Majesty's Government have constantly advocated the adjustment, by way of free negotiation between the parties concerned, of any difficulties that may arise between them. . . . In their opinion there should be no question incapable of solution by peaceful means, and they would see no justification for the substitution of force or threats of force for the method of negotiation.

[18] Carr, *op. cit.*, pp. 166-169; see also Hans J. Morgenthau, *In Defense of the National Interest* (New York, Knopf, 1951), and George F. Kennan, *Realities of American Foreign Policy* (Princeton, Princeton University Press, 1954), pp. 47, 50.
[19] Carr, *op. cit.*, p. 73.
[20] Neville Chamberlain, *In Search of Peace* (New York, Putnam, 1939), p. 279.

There is no need to doubt the sincerity of either Briand or Chamberlain; at the same time it can scarcely be pure coincidence that the moral values which they espoused tended to reinforce the favored positions which their countries held.

The Morality of Unsatiated States

Hitler was not impressed by the morality of the status quo powers.

. . . Either the wealth of the world is divided by force, in which case this division will be recorrected from time to time by force.

Or else the division is based on grounds of equity and therefore also of common sense. . . .

But to assume that God has permitted some nations first to acquire a world by force and then to defend this robbery with moralizing theories is perhaps comforting and above all comfortable for the "haves," but for the "have-nots" it is just as unimportant as it is uninteresting and lays no obligation upon them. . . . At bottom it is only a question of power, in which common sense and justice receive no consideration.[21]

Rejecting the moral conceptions of the satisfied states, Hitler advanced moral conceptions of his own. He said that the "folkish" view

. . . by no means believes in an equality of the races, but with their differences it also recognizes their superior and inferior values, and by this recognition it feels the obligation in accordance with the Eternal Will that dominates this universe to promote the victory of the better and stronger, and to demand the submission of the worse and the weaker. . . . It cannot grant the right of existence to an ethical idea, if this idea represents a danger for the racial life of the bearers of higher ethics. . . .

Hitler also declared that "peoples which bastardize themselves, or permit themselves to be bastardized, sin against the will of eternal Providence, and their ruin by the hand of a stronger nation is consequently not an injustice that is done to them, but only the restoration of right." [22]

Similarly the communists, dissatisfied with a status quo in which capitalism survives, adopt a moral outlook which permits resort to revolution and war to accomplish their purposes. Thus Lenin long ago declared that [23] "if war is waged by the proletariat after it has conquered the bourgeoisie in its own country and is waged with the object of strengthening and extending socialism, such a war is legitimate and 'holy.'" Along the same line, Lenin and Stalin both included among "just wars" those wars which are waged "to liberate people from capitalist slavery or . . . to liberate colonies and dependent countries from the yoke of imperialism."

[21] Adolf Hitler, *Speech Delivered in the Reichstag January 30th, 1939* (Berlin, Müller, n.d.), pp. 27-29.

[22] Adolf Hitler, *Mein Kampf* (New York, Reynal & Hitchcock, 1939), pp. 452, 579-580.

[23] See above, p. 80.

Egocentric Morality as a Limit on Behavior

The existence of divergent conceptions of morality does not necessarily mean that morality is without effect in limiting the behavior of states. As suggested above, the adoption of moral principles implies the voluntary acceptance of certain limitations on conduct. Hitler's moral principles permitted him to seek the extermination of the Jews, but not the extermination of Danes and Norwegians. Moral principles now prevailing in the United States render an attack upon Canada unthinkable and preclude any attempt to establish imperial control over Latin America. Many Englishmen favored granting dominion status to India and Pakistan because they regarded the action as morally right and even imperative. Moral principles endorsed by the Soviet Union did not prevent it from seizing eastern Poland in 1939, but they caused considerable discomfort in those who had to concoct a justification of the action.

Egocentric and International Morality

Neither does the existence of divergent conceptions of morality necessarily mean that morality is exclusively national. International morality exists just as international law exists, consisting of moral principles which a number of states endorse. In fact, customary international law is to quite an extent a reflection of principles of morality which states jointly accept; it is sanctioned international morality. Similarly, the United Nations Charter reflects international morality in many of its provisions—for example, in calling for respect for human rights and fundamental freedoms without distinction as to race, sex, language, or religion. The moral desirability of peace is formally affirmed almost universally, though with provisos and conditions attached.

Those rules of morality which have not crystallized into law are even more vague and ambiguous than those which have. Moreover, as in connection with law, there are often several moral principles which are applicable in a concrete situation, permitting choice of the one to be stressed. The result is that national governments are left with considerable discretion in interpreting the requirements of international morality. In the exercise of this discretion, the decision-makers within a country may find it expedient to give heed to moral conceptions held abroad, for it is not always safe to commit acts which foreign governments and peoples regard as morally outrageous; still, the interpretation of the requirements of international morality is likely to be influenced primarily by the moral outlook prevailing at home.

The vague nature of what Carr calls the "code" of international morality is indicated by the following statements: [24]

[24] Carr, *op. cit.*, p. 154.

One of the most important and clearly recognized items in this code is the obligation not to inflict *unnecessary* death or suffering on other human beings, i.e., death or suffering not necessary for the attainment of some higher purpose which is held, rightly or wrongly, to justify a derogation from the general obligation.

When is the infliction of death or suffering "necessary"? What "higher purpose" may justify it? These questions are answered, in the first instance at least, by national governments. They are guided by some widely accepted standards, a number of which have crystallized into law, but considerable freedom of choice remains. It is needless to say that the "higher purpose" which is taken to justify the infliction of death or suffering is likely to be a national purpose.

The Universal Validity of Egocentric Principles

These observations on the role of morality in international politics involve no judgment on whether there are absolute and universally applicable moral standards which spring from either divine or natural sources. For present purposes there is no need to make such a judgment. Regardless of the existence or non-existence of absolute moral standards, the fact is that the same moral standards are not everywhere accepted. Even among individuals and groups within national societies there are marked differences of moral outlook, and the differences are all the greater where different societies and cultures are involved.

Nevertheless, the tendency of governments, like the tendency of individuals, is to claim universal validity for the moral principles which they accept. They picture themselves as promoting the good not only for their own peoples but for other peoples as well, perhaps for all mankind, and they seek to heap moral opprobrium on governments which pursue adverse policies. Thus conceptions of morality become not only guides to action but also instruments of struggle, each government seeking to strengthen its position by claiming moral credit for itself and seeking to weaken the position of unfriendly states by casting moral discredit upon them.

Morality as a Basis for Harmony and for Strife

Where moral standards are similar, as they are among the countries of the English-speaking world, for example, they do much to facilitate harmony and cooperation; they reinforce law by providing an international constitutional consensus. Such a consensus virtually prevents certain kinds of disputes from arising and provides a basis on which the issues that do arise can be resolved. Where moral standards clash, as they did between the fascist states and others, and as they do between the communist and non-communist worlds, the area of consensus is bound to be very narrow, if it exists at all, and the possibilities of friction and conflict are correspondingly enhanced. The danger is particularly great when a moral outlook calls for national aggrandizement or for the liberation of foreign peoples from the evil system under which they are thought to live.

Morality and Power

Differing conceptions of morality have been in competition with each other throughout history. Many factors affect the outcome of the competition, including the ability of the moral idea to commend itself and secure acceptance. Certainly, however, the power factor operates here, just as it does in law. Moral ideas provide one of the elements of power, and power in turn does much to determine which moral conceptions will prevail.

THE PROBLEM OF PEACEFUL CHANGE

Changing Power Relationships Require Changing Law

In dynamic societies power relationships change. Neither the weak nor the strong forever maintain the same relative power position. Within countries the strength of political parties waxes and wanes; some parties go out of existence, and others are created. Over the years, too, the strength of those who support the constitutional consensus and the strength of the subversives change. Among countries change is also the rule. The history of world affairs is, among other things, a history of the rise and fall of states. Some weak states have grown strong, and, sooner or later, all strong states have grown weak. The process of change continues.

If law is largely a reflection of the desires of the strong, and if strength shifts from party to party or from state to state, it is to be expected that the law would change. This does not mean that every rule of law must be replaced by another, for many of them endure indefinitely. The desires of those who are rising in power often coincide in many ways with the desires of those whose power is declining, and the same rule of law may thus serve successive wielders of power equally well. But the newly strong do not always agree with those whom they are displacing, and where their desires differ, they will insist that the law be changed. As President Eisenhower once said,[25] "We must not think of peace as a static condition in world affairs.... Change is the law of life, and unless there is peaceful change, there is bound to be violent change."

Peaceful Change and Its Limits Within Countries

One of the outstanding characteristics of societies operating under a constitutional consensus is that provision is made for peaceful change.

[25] *State Department Bulletin*, Vol. 33 (September 5, 1955), p. 376.

Within a country the consensus may be that a king has a divine right to rule and that others are to obey; then the king may change the law; perhaps he will act in accordance with his own arbitrary will or perhaps in response to pressures brought to bear upon him. The consensus may be that a communist or fascist dictatorship should prevail; then the party or the individual dictator may shape the law. The consensus may call for democracy; then the law may be changed by those who win elections. Nowhere within countries does the rule prevail that the law may be changed only by the slow process of developing custom or by the unanimous consent of the affected parties.

At the same time it should be noted that the possibility of peaceful change within countries is ordinarily not unlimited. Fear of various forms of resistance, including rebellion, limits even the dictator in what he can do. Within democratic countries, the constitution or the constitutional consensus imposes limits. In most federal systems, for example, the central government is not free to alter the boundary lines of the constituent units without their consent.[26] If New Jersey should adamantly demand that part of Pennsylvania be handed over to it, there is apparently no way in which this transfer can be peacefully accomplished unless Pennsylvania agrees, or unless the Constitution is amended. In effect, the problem of peaceful change is handled within countries in part by a tacit or explicit agreement that certain kinds of change will not be demanded. If they are demanded nevertheless, the demand constitutes a challenge to the constitutional system, and if such a challenge is pressed it may lead to civil war.

In short, peace within countries depends not only on the existence of machinery for peaceful change but also on the absence of adamant demands for certain kinds of change.

Change Among Countries: Peaceful and Violent

Among countries, the machinery for peaceful change is more primitive. The law can be changed through the slow accumulation of precedents, shaping customary law. It can be changed through the voluntary conclusion of treaties. Disputes may be handled in the ways described in the preceding chapter. Direct negotiations may occur. Countries may try mediation, conciliation, or commissions of inquiry. International conferences or the agencies of an international organization may be used. Yet these devices can lead to a settlement only with the consent of the parties. Sometimes consent to change can be obtained, but on vital matters the consent of the party adversely affected is likely to be withheld. States are particularly reluctant to accept a change which deprives them of territory or which reduces their power or prestige. If they refuse to give their consent, what happens then?

[26] Brierly, *The Outlook for International Law*, pp. 134 ff.

Confronted by the opposition of others, a state demanding change may give up the attempt, resigning itself to a continuation of the legal status quo. But if it regards the change as urgent and vital, and if it commands sufficient power, it may resort to coercion, including military intervention and war itself. "The use or threatened use of force is . . . a normal and recognized method of bringing about important political change. . . . Normally, the threat of war, tacit or overt, seems a necessary condition of important political changes in the international sphere." [27] Heinrich von Treitschke came to a similar conclusion: [28]

When a state realizes that existing treaties no longer express the actual relations between the Powers, then, if it cannot bring the other contracting state to acquiescence by friendly negotiations, there is nothing for it but the international lawsuit—War.

Peaceful Change Under the League

The framers of the League of Nations Covenant recognized that some provision should be made for peaceful change in addition to such devices as negotiation, mediation, and conciliation. They therefore specified in Article 19 that that the Assembly of the League might "advise the reconsideration . . . of treaties which have become inapplicable and the consideration of international conditions whose continuance might endanger the peace of the world." Note that the Assembly was empowered only to advise; it could not enact or amend law, nor could it enforce acceptance of its advice. Interpreters of the Covenant disagree on the voting rules under which advice might have been rendered, but the details of the dispute are scarcely worth examining now.[29]

Article 19 and the League devices for peaceful change broke down not so much because of voting rules and inadequacies in the machinery as because of the attitudes of states. There was no constitutional consensus fixing the limits within which change might occur, as there commonly is within countries. There was no agreement to bow to the recommendations of the Assembly in certain matters; in fact the states were jealous of their sovereignty and fearful of anything resembling an international legislature. Neither was there renunciation of demands for change which were sure to be resisted. In fact, the demands for change that led to war (particularly Italy's demands on Ethiopia and Albania, and Germany's demands on Poland) were demands that no conceivable system of peaceful change could have been expected to satisfy.

I cannot see any real connection between the rigidity and consequent impracticability of Article 19 and the wars which have been waged against

[27] Carr, *op. cit.,* pp. 215-216.
[28] Quoted by Brierly, *op. cit.,* p. 19.
[29] Frederick Sherwood Dunn, *Peaceful Change* (New York, Council on Foreign Relations, 1937), pp. 106-111.

Members of the League in the course of the last years. No matter how generously the framers of the Covenant might have provided for the pacific revision of international treaties, they could not have made legally possible such events as the rape of Manchuria, Abyssinia [Ethiopia], Czechoslovakia, Albania, and Poland.[30]

In the absence of recognized limits within which the system of peaceful change might operate and beyond which it could not be expected to operate, Article 19 was a dead letter from the first.

Peaceful Change Under the United Nations

The United Nations Charter in various articles similarly empowers the General Assembly to make recommendations for peaceful change. The recommendations may be made on the basis of a two-thirds vote, making action possible despite the opposition of a few adversely affected parties. Recommendations made by such a majority, particularly when supported by the major powers, necessarily carry considerable moral authority, but still they are only recommendations. As with the League Assembly, the United Nations General Assembly cannot enact or amend law, nor can it enforce acceptance of its recommendations. However, if the Security Council finds that the rejection of a recommendation of the General Assembly constitutes a threat to the peace, breach of the peace, or act of aggression, it can order enforcement action. The theoretical possibility thus exists that the General Assembly and the Security Council, acting in cooperation, might assume the role of a legislature and an executive, providing for change in the law and for such enforcement action as might be necessary to assure acceptance of the change, that is, the possibility exists that peaceful change among countries might be made more nearly what it is within countries: policeful change.[31]

We shall discuss this possibility more fully in a subsequent chapter. Suffice it to refer here to the principal case in which the possibility has been tested. In 1947 the General Assembly was confronted with the problem of Palestine. The area had been a British mandate, but Britain had announced its determination to give up its role as the mandatory power. Change of some kind was thus made unavoidable, and the Arabs and Jews who inhabited the area could not agree on a new governmental arrangement. After considerable deliberation the Assembly recommended that separate Arab and Jewish states be created in the area, but the Arabs rejected the recommendation and resisted Jewish efforts to implement it. War between the two groups resulted. When the matter came before the Security Council, various members took the view that the Charter did not authorize them to enforce recommendations of the

[30] William E. Rappard, *The Quest for Peace* (Cambridge, Harvard University Press, 1940), p. 176.
[31] See Chapter 2 above, pp. 15-18.

General Assembly. Moreover, the Security Council failed to rule that the fighting in Palestine involved a threat to the peace, breach of the peace, or an act of aggression. Enforcement of the General Assembly's recommendation was thus left to the party which wanted the recommendation carried out, the Jews themselves.

Peaceful change occurs among nations, of course. Common interests frequently lead to its acceptance. The moral authority of an agency such as the General Assembly might induce a state to accept change even at some sacrifice, if the sacrifice is not too great. A state which finds itself in a position of hopeless military weakness may accept great sacrifice—as Czechoslovakia did when Britain and France joined Germany and Italy at the Munich Conference in 1938 in advising Czechoslovakia to cede part of its territory to Germany. But there is nothing in the record of the League of Nations, of the United Nations, or of diplomacy generally to give the basis for hope of peaceful change in situations where a state having the power to resist is asked to give up something which it regards as vital. On matters regarded as important, change is likely to remain a function of the power relations between states which demand it and states which oppose it.

If the problem of peaceful change among nations is ever solved, the solution will probably have to include both the elements which are ordinarily present within countries. Machinery for change is not enough. There must also be agreement on the limits within which peaceful change will be allowed to occur. If demands for change going beyond these limits are not renounced, the issue will presumably become one of naked power, as with revolutionary challenges to the constitutional consensus within countries.

THE OUTLAWRY OF WAR

We have noted that the League of Nations Covenant, the Kellogg-Briand Pact, and the United Nations Charter all contain restrictions on the freedom of states to go to war. War nevertheless occurs. One of the major reasons for this is now clear. If the law goes drastically against the desires of the strong on matters which the strong regard as vital, and if effective means for changing the law peacefully do not exist, the issue is likely to be submitted to the arbitrament of the sword.

Merely to outlaw war, as the Kellogg-Briand Pact presumed to do, cannot possibly solve the problem. War and the threat of war have in fact proved useful to states. They have been useful, among other ways, as methods of forcing change in the law. Until alternative methods for bringing about change have been developed, and until conditions permit those methods to be effective, it cannot be expected that war and the threat of war will in practice be abandoned.

This is all the more true because war, whether legal or illegal, is not always considered morally wrong. Most systems of morality justify defensive war, and men are ingenious in finding reasons for classifying the wars they fight as defensive. Some systems of morality glorify war and call for aggression, and even those which condemn aggressive war as evil often permit it to be considered a lesser evil. The good which men hope to accomplish through war is taken to justify the evil which war itself involves.

. . . The attempt to make a moral distinction between wars of "aggression" and wars of "defense" is misguided. If a change is necessary and desirable, the use or threatened use of force to maintain the status quo may be morally more culpable than the use or threatened use of force to alter it. . . . The moral criterion must be not the "aggressive" or "defensive" character of the war, but the nature of the change which is being sought and resisted. "Without rebellion, mankind would stagnate and injustice would be irremediable." Few serious thinkers maintain that it is always and unconditionally wrong to start a revolution; and it is equally difficult to believe that it is always and unconditionally wrong to start a war.[32]

A mature legal system must be expected to include a prohibition of revolution against itself. In the international realm this means that a mature system of international law must be expected to include a prohibition of war. Yet the prohibition is not likely to be respected if effective alternatives to war are not provided for the accomplishment of change.

International law is a means which states employ in the power struggle, and a limitation on their behavior. It is a means by which they arrange to conduct a host of relationships in an orderly and peaceful fashion. It is a means by which they define common interests and through which they adjust conflicting claims and expectations. It is a means which the strong employ to register and define their will—a means by which they give status to the achievements of power. At the same time, in defining rights and imposing obligations, law limits the claims which states can rightfully assert and the actions in which they can rightfully indulge.

Law can be effective in limiting the behavior of states either as long as its rules reflect the common desires of affected states or as long as they reflect the desires of states which have both the strength and the determination to enforce them. Otherwise legal limitations on state behavior are not likely to be effective, and change of some kind will almost certainly occur. With existing attitudes and organizational arrangements, especially with divergent and essentially national conceptions of morality, there is no assurance that change can be peacefully accomplished.

[32] Carr, *op. cit.*, p. 208. The quotation within the quotation is from Bertrand Russell.

If it cannot be, those states which desire change and which have sufficient power are likely to seek it by threatening or using coercive measures, perhaps including war.

SUGGESTED READINGS

BRIERLY, J. L., *The Outlook for International Law* (Oxford, Clarendon, 1944).
BRIERLY, J. L., *The Law of Nations* (Oxford, Clarendon, 1949).
CARR, E. H., *The Twenty Years' Crisis 1919-1939* (London, Macmillan, New York, St. Martin's, 1949).
CORBETT, P. E., *Law and Society in the Relations of States* (New York, Harcourt, Brace, 1951).
CORBETT, P. E., *The Study of International Law* (Garden City, Doubleday, 1955).
CORBETT, P. E., *Morals, Law & Power in International Relations* (Los Angeles, the John Randolph Haynes and Dora Haynes Foundation, 1956).
CRUTTWELL, C. R. M. F., *A History of Peaceful Change in the Modern World* (New York, Oxford, 1937).
DICKINSON, Edwin D., *What Is Wrong with International Law?* (Berkeley, Gillick, 1947).
DUNN, Frederick Sherwood, *The Protection of Nationals* (Baltimore, Johns Hopkins Press, 1932).
DUNN, Frederick Sherwood, *Peaceful Change* (New York, Council on Foreign Relations, 1937).
FERRERO, Guglielmo, *The Principles of Power: The Great Political Crises of History* (New York, Putnam, 1942).
International Sanctions, Royal Institute of International Affairs (London, Oxford, 1938).
KEETON, George W., and SCHWARZENBERGER, Georg, *Making International Law Work* (London, Stevens, 1946).
KENNAN, George F., *Realities of American Foreign Policy* (Princeton, Princeton University Press, 1954).
LAUTERPACHT, Hersh, *The Function of Law in the International Community* (Oxford, Clarendon, 1933).
MORGENTHAU, Hans J., *In Defense of the National Interest* (New York, Knopf, 1951).
NIEBUHR, Reinhold, *Moral Man and Immoral Society, a Study in Ethics and Politics* (New York, Scribner, 1932).
NIEBUHR, Reinhold, *Christianity and Power Politics* (New York, Scribner, 1940).
OPPENHEIM, Lassa F. L., *International Law,* 7th ed., Hersh Lauterpacht, ed., 2 vols. (New York, Longmans Green, 1948-1952).
RAPPARD, William E., *The Quest for Peace* (Cambridge, Harvard University Press, 1940).
WELDON, T. D., *States and Morals* (New York, McGraw-Hill, 1947).
WOLFERS, Arnold, "Statesmanship and Moral Choice," *World Politics,* Vol. 1, (January, 1949), pp. 175-195.
WRIGHT, Quincy, *Contemporary International Law: A Balance Sheet* (Garden City, Doubleday, 1955).

CHAPTER 16

The Utility of War

REPEATED REFERENCES have been made throughout this book to the fact that states find war useful. War is the ultimate means by which they seek to make their will prevail—the ultimate expression of power. It is used by those seeking change in the status quo, and by others in defense. It is used by those seeking domination, and by others seeking to establish or preserve a distribution of power which gives them a reasonable chance of preserving independence and other values.

War has occurred persistently throughout history, so persistently that some are inclined to question whether war rather than peace should not be regarded as normal. It has survived new inventions, new scientific discoveries, and new technologies, which have repeatedly brought new and more devastating weapons to the fore. It has survived progress in education, culture, and political organization. War and the threat of war remain a regular preoccupation of the major states of the world, and of many lesser states as well.

War has been so important an instrument of states that the fact deserves to be dwelt upon; we shall do so briefly in this chapter. Then we shall ask what the costs of war have been and whether trends in the costs permit any conclusion as to the probable utility of war in the future. Finally, we shall attempt an appraisal of the probable effects of the development of weapons of mass destruction, especially nuclear weapons, on the usefulness of war.

THE POLITICAL IMPORTANCE OF WAR

War and the Birth, Growth, and Extinction of States

The general rule is that states are born in war and that war plays a major role in determining where their boundary lines shall be. In addition, war is a common cause of the extinction of states.

These generalizations are applicable to both ancient and modern times and to all geographical regions of the world.

The United States itself provides a good illustration. The North American continent was wrested from the Indians by violence. Wars among the colonizing countries largely determined what territory in North America each would hold. The thirteen colonies established their independence from Britain by a revolutionary war, which became an international war when France joined. The first great extension of the territory of the United States was accomplished through purchase, the Louisiana Purchase, but France's fear that she would lose the territory in war was a powerful factor in inducing her to sell. Russia was influenced by somewhat similar considerations when she agreed to sell Alaska. Threats of war were a factor in the settlement of the Oregon boundary controversy. The annexation of Texas led to outright war, as a result of which the entire Southwest was added to the Union. Puerto Rico and the Philippines were acquired by war with Spain. Hawaii was acquired peacefully, but only after American settlers overthrew the native government by force and asked for annexation. World War II led to the establishment of an American trusteeship over the Caroline, Marshall, and Marianas Islands in the Pacific and to American control over Okinawa. In addition, the fact should be recalled that the United States has fought two wars, the War of 1812 and World War I, which produced no change in its boundaries, and it fought a Civil War which determined whether the Union would be preserved.

War has likewise played a powerful role in the history of Russia and the Soviet Union. Muscovy began in the twelfth century as a relatively small principality. By the end of the fifteenth century it had thrown off the yoke of the Mongol hordes and had expanded, largely through violence, to the Arctic, the Ural Mountains, the Caspian Sea, and Lake Ladoga. In subsequent centuries Russia fought many wars, especially with various states of Europe and with the Ottoman Empire, and her boundaries fluctuated back and forth (but in the main were pushed outward) as a result of defeat and victory. World War I brought the collapse of the tsarist regime, made possible the Bolshevik seizure of power, and led to a contraction of the boundaries of the state. World War II not only decided whether the Soviet regime could survive but brought renewed expansion, accomplished both by the formal annexation of territory and by the establishment of communist satellite regimes in Eastern and Southeastern Europe. What began as Muscovy is now a Soviet empire which includes or dominates the tremendous area stretching from the Elbe River in the heart of Europe to the Kurile Islands lying north of Japan.

Similarly, war has played a powerful role in the history of the German people. Frederick the Great succeeded to the throne of the small kingdom of Prussia in 1740, and forthwith precipitated the War of the Austrian Succession, in the course of which he seized Silesia. The Seven Years' War, involving practically all of Europe as well as North America, soon followed. Later in Frederick's reign he engaged in a brief war with Austria-Hungary. Prussia was, of course, heavily involved in the wars of the French Revolution and Napoleon, in the course of which the French conqueror consolidated many of the small states into which the German people had been divided. Bismarck brought the remaining German states into one Reich through a series of wars—with Denmark, with Austria-Hungary, and with France. World War I brought a reversal of German fortunes, including the loss of considerable territory to surrounding states. Hitler took Austria and Czechoslovakia more by the threat than by the use of violence, and in World War II established a short-lived empire stretching from the Pyrenees to the gates of Stalingrad. His defeat led not only to the collapse of his regime and to the loss of great territories but to the end of Germany as a united state.

War and the Fate of Ideologies, Cultures, and Civilizations

In broader terms, war has also played a powerful role in the struggles among ideologies, cultures, and civilizations. It figured prominently in the process through which Christianity was extended over Europe and over the western hemisphere. Islam spread to a large extent through war, and was prevented from engulfing Europe mainly because of the greater military power which the Christian states of Europe proved able to command. The civilizations of the Aztecs and Incas collapsed and disappeared as a result of European barbarism and violence. Western ideas and western technology have accompanied western imperialism in penetrating Africa and Asia. The strongest of the extant ideologies, nationalism, has achieved its triumphs largely in war. Fascism and Nazism were appealing as long as they were powerful, but have been discredited by defeat. Communism has spread through war, and both the communist and the non-communist worlds view the problem of their survival largely in military terms.

War, then, has been the instrument by which most of the great facts of political national history have been established and maintained. . . . The map of the world today has been largely determined upon the battlefield. The maintenance of civilization itself has been, and still continues to be, underwritten by the insurance of army and navy ready to strike at any time where danger threatens. Thus, even in peace, the war system has to a large degree determined not only international relationships but the character and history of the nations themselves.[1]

[1] James T. Shotwell, *War as an Instrument of National Policy* (New York, Harcourt, Brace, 1929), p. 15.

Similarly, war has played a powerful role in domestic politics.

There is hardly a national state in this world community, including our own, whose ultimate origins did not lie in acts of violence. The source of every governmental claim to legitimacy will be found to rest in some situation created originally by the arbitrary exertion of armed might. There is hardly a constitution that does not trace its origin to some act which was formally one of insurrection or of usurpation.[2]

The picture should not be overdrawn. After all, historical developments of great significance occur without war. The spread of Buddhism provides an example in one field, and the Industrial Revolution in another. Some states have achieved independence in peace—the Philippines, for example. Still, war has been a tremendously powerful force in history —a weapon which peoples and states have persistently used.

THE INCIDENCE AND COSTS OF WAR

The Difficulty of Determining Costs

No study is available of the incidence and costs of war throughout the world, even for very recent times. In truth, it is extremely difficult for students of the subject to arrive at reliable findings. Many costs, such as the moral and cultural costs and the costs resulting from wartime dislocations of production and trade, can scarcely be measured in quantitative terms. Estimates of property damage can be no more reliable than the judgment of the many individuals who make the estimates. Governmental expenditures relating to a specific war generally begin long before war breaks out and continue long after it is over, and the selection of the expenditures which should be included in a computation of costs is bound to be somewhat arbitrary. Usually in the case of civilians and often in the case of soldiers it is difficult to determine how many have died as a direct result of a war; if indirect losses are to be included, such as those resulting from wartime epidemics, arbitrary decisions and estimates again become involved. Further, although the absolute costs of war are of interest, relative costs have greater historical significance. For example, it is more significant to know what proportion of the population of a state dies from war than to know precisely how many die, and it is more significant to know what proportion of the national income is expended on war than to know precisely how much is spent. This means that additional data must be taken into account, and often the additional data are either unavailable or unreliable. For example, reliable statistics on population, even in western Europe, do not go very far back in history, and statistics permitting conclusions on the proportion of the national income devoted to war are not available in some countries even in relation to World War II.

[2] George F. Kennan, *Realities of American Foreign Policy* (Princeton, Princeton University Press, 1954), p. 37.

Findings of Quincy Wright

The best available summary treatment of the incidence and costs of war is to be found in *A Study of War,* by Quincy Wright. Published in 1942, it does not take World War II into account. Wright gives attention "to (1) spacial and (2) temporal variations in the intensity of war and to general trends with respect to (3) the quantity and (4) quality of war during the modern period." [3] His study is largely confined to the European states.

1. Spacial and temporal variations in incidence. Wright finds that "the great powers have been the most frequent fighters." From 1480 to 1940 he counts about 2600 important battles involving European states. "Of these 2600 battles France participated in 47%; Austria-Hungary in 34%; Germany (Prussia) in 25%; Great Britain and Russia each in about 22%; Turkey in 15%; Spain in 12%; the Netherlands in 8%; Sweden in 4%; and Denmark in 2%." The special warlike character of the great powers is also demonstrated by an analysis of participation in military campaigns from 1900 to 1930.

This analysis indicates that the seven great powers had averaged 46 campaigns each during these thirty years and that each campaign averaged fourteen months. Eight secondary powers of Europe and Asia had averaged 19 campaigns each of an average duration of eight months. The remaining states, nine noncolonial small powers of northern Europe, averaged only one campaign each of five months' average duration. Several of these—Denmark, Sweden, Norway, Switzerland, Estonia—had not fought any campaign at all in this period.

As to temporal variations, Wright finds that several centuries ago practically all battles occurred during daytime and during the months from April to November, whereas in both world wars men fought day and night the year around. From 1450 to 1930 he counts 278 wars in which the principal European powers engaged, and finds that their average length was 4.4 years. "Perhaps four or five years of the strain of war is as much as people can stand without resting. Signs of break in internal morale are almost certain to appear in one or both of the belligerents after that period."

2. Various quantitative trends. Wright did what he could to discover quantitative trends relating to the size of armies, the proportion of war years to peace years, the intensity and extensity of war, and the costs of war.

"The size of armies has tended to increase during the modern period both absolutely and in proportion to population." In the seventeenth

[3] Quincy Wright, *A Study of War* (Chicago, The University of Chicago Press, 1942, copyright 1942 by the University of Chicago), Vol. I, p. 220. The quotations and data which follow come from the same volume, pp. 220-248.

century the European states kept about three persons per thousand under arms, which is approximately the same ratio as prevailed under the Roman Empire. Before World War I the proportion had risen to about five per thousand, and in 1937 it was about nine per thousand. Individual countries, of course, exceeded the general average; in 1937 "France, with less than half the population of the Roman Empire, maintained almost twice as big an army, some nineteen to one thousand of her European population."

It is clear that during the modern period there has been a trend toward an increase in the absolute and relative size of armies whether one considers the peace army, the number mobilized for war, the number of combatants engaged in battle, or the number of the military and civil populations devoting themselves to war work.

The major European states have been formally at war during a smaller and smaller proportion of the time in the past several centuries. They were at war about 65 per cent of the time in the sixteenth and seventeenth century; about 38 per cent of the time in the eighteenth; about 28 per cent in the nineteenth; and about 18 per cent from 1900 to 1940. But this tendency to be at peace a greater proportion of the time has been more than counteracted, for the tendency has been to fight harder during war. Battles themselves have lasted longer, and the number of battles per war year has increased. "As a result the total number of battles fought in a century has tended to increase." War has tended to increase not only in intensity but also in extensity, that is, more states tend to become involved. Wright counts 126 wars from 1475 to 1940.

Of these 126 wars, the 42 which began in the late fifteenth and in the sixteenth centuries averaged 2.4 participants each; the 19 which began in the eighteenth century averaged 4.8 participants each; the 32 which began in the nineteenth century averaged 3.1 participants each; and the 11 which began in the twentieth century averaged 5.6 participants each.

Only in the twentieth century have wars occurred which deserved to be called world wars. Although most battles continue to be fought in Europe, an increasingly large proportion occur in other areas.

The net result of various trends is that the human costs of war have increased, both absolutely and relative to population. True, a smaller and smaller proportion of those who participate in battle die as a direct result of battle, and military deaths from disease have been strikingly reduced. Moreover, down to World War II civilian deaths resulting directly from battle tended to decline. Yet, as we have already seen, the proportion of the population mobilized and the number of battles fought have tended to increase. "As a result, the proportion of the population dying as a direct consequence of battle has tended to increase."

Taking all factors into consideration the proportion of deaths attributable to military service and to hostilities has probably increased among European countries from about 2% in the seventeenth to about 3% in the twentieth century.

Wright suggests the probability "that the total of deaths indirectly due to war have been three times as great as direct war deaths in twentieth-century Europe. . . . Probably at least 10% of the deaths in modern civilization can be attributed directly or indirectly to war." Moreover, war has become "progressively more detrimental to the quality of population."

For the reasons cited above, reliable comprehensive statistics on the direct and indirect economic costs of war are not available. Certainly these costs have increased tremendously in an absolute sense, and in all probability they have increased disproportionately to increases in the production of wealth. Both world wars consumed vast quantities of labor, skills, and material resources. In battle areas both caused enormous damage to property of all kinds. Whole nations were impoverished. In many countries economic dislocations occurred from which recovery proved to be very difficult and which might have led to even greater political changes than actually came about, had it not been for the fact that the American economy survived both wars as a source of succor and strength.

3. *Qualitative costs.* Trends in the general social and cultural costs of war are, as Wright says, "even less susceptible to objective measurement." His "highly subjective" conclusion is that:

Wars of large magnitude have been followed by anti-intellectual movements in art, literature, and philosophy; by waves of crime, sexual license, suicide, venereal disease, delinquent youth; by class, racial, and religious intolerance, persecution, refugees, social and political revolution; by abandonment of orderly processes for settling disputes and changing law; and by a decline in respect for international law and treaties.

Wright grants that the standards of some people and groups have been stimulated in the opposite direction, but feels that serious deterioration has been the general rule.

PROSPECTIVE COSTS OF NUCLEAR WARFARE

The Destructiveness of Nuclear Weapons

The development of atomic and thermonuclear weapons makes it very doubtful whether past costs and trends in those costs provide much of a guide for the future. The differences between the new weapons and those hitherto used are so great as to involve destructive power of an entirely new order of magnitude. The differences are so great as to become differences not merely in degree but in kind. Moreover, within the realm of nuclear weapons the period since the end of World War II has witnessed very striking advances. The plain fact is that a fundamental scientific and technological revolution has occurred. Unrestricted use of the new weapons would completely transform the character of war and involve the destruction of life, property, and cultural values on an unprecedented and unimaginable scale.

The bombs dropped on Hiroshima and Nagasaki at the end of World War II made the giant blockbusters hurled at Hitler's Germany seem like firecrackers by comparison. Since then, apparently, atomic bombs have been improved to the point where they release some 25 times the explosive power of their prototypes. Hard on the heels of this revolution has come a second one, which is also of gargantuan importance: the development of thermonuclear weapons. Apparently thermonuclear bombs exist, or can certainly be produced, 2500 times as powerful as the atomic bombs used against Japan. As if this were not enough to stagger the statesmen and generals in the calculations they must make, it is also possible to manufacture and explode thermonuclear weapons so as to spread radioactive particles through the atmosphere; these radioactive particles will then be carried by the wind, only to drop down to earth with potentially lethal effects over wide areas.[4] Moreover, the production of atomic energy for peacetime uses involves, as a byproduct, the creation of a radioactive ash, a "death dust," which, if released in the atmosphere in proper quantities, would have the same lethal effects as the fall-out associated with thermonuclear explosions. Every state operating nuclear power stations will be able to accumulate such death dust; it is expected that by 1985 it will exist in abundance. "Any industrialized nation with the necessary technicians—no matter how small, no matter if it lacks armed forces—will be able to inflict deadly damage on another nation."[5]

The nuclear revolution has apparently also gone in another direction since Hiroshima, that is, toward the development of weapons with less explosive power than the bombs dropped on Japan. The nuclear arsenal thus evidently includes quite a variety of weapons with a considerable range of destructive power. Troops using the least powerful nuclear weapons, it is said, might fight their way through a city like Des Moines without completely destroying it, whereas just one thermonuclear bomb might destroy all life, for example, in Great Britain.[6]

[4] Ralph E. Lapp, "Civil Defense Faces New Peril," *Bulletin of the Atomic Scientists,* Vol. 10 (November, 1954), pp. 349-351.

[5] Hans Thirring, "The Noiseless Weapon," *Harper's,* Vol. 211 (October, 1955), p. 44.

[6] A. T. Hadley, "Low-Yield Atomic Weapons: A New Military Dimension," *Reporter,* Vol. 14 (April 19, 1956), pp. 23-25. The diameter of the circle of "severe" blast of various nuclear weapons is said to range from a few hundred feet to between 15 and 20 miles. See Roger Hilsman, "Strategic Doctrines for Nuclear War," in William W. Kaufmann, ed., *Military Policy and National Security* (Princeton, Princeton University Press, 1956), p. 67.

President Eisenhower in 1953 made a statement which was striking at the time: [7]

Today, the United States' stockpile of atomic weapons, which, of course, increases daily, exceeds by many times the explosive equivalent of the total of all bombs and all shells that came from every plane and every gun in every theatre of war in all the years of World War II.

Two years later a group of scientists could make an even more chilling statement, in reference to the prospect that thermonuclear bombs (H-bombs) would throw radioactive particles into the atmosphere.

No one knows how widely such lethal radioactive particles might be diffused, but the best authorities are unanimous in saying that a war with H-bombs might quite possibly put an end to the human race. It is feared that if many H-bombs are used there will be universal death—sudden only for a minority but for the majority a slow torture of disease and disintegration.[8]

It is said that the number of thermonuclear explosions necessary to produce this result is a "large" one and that this "large" number is "not likely to be reached unless the war is fought in an entirely irrational way." [9] Still, the possibility that all human life could be destroyed suggests the revolutionary character of the weapons which some governments command.

The Possibilities of Defense

Once bombing planes have taken off with a load of nuclear weapons, or once nuclear missiles have been launched against their target, what are the possibilities of defense? Apparently they are not good. During World War II the defenders generally thought they were doing well if they allowed no more than 90 per cent of the attacking bombing planes to get back to home territory. Even if defense measures could be improved to the point where 90 per cent were destroyed, the remainder of the bombers dropping thermonuclear bombs on urban centers could wreak catastrophic destruction. Adequate defense against nuclear attack requires the shooting down of practically all bombing planes before they can release their bombs. Apparently, developments have already made it conceivable that this might be accomplished in the event of a "small-scale attack," but the solution to the problem of a "large coordinated attack" does not appear to be in sight.[10] Moreover, even if successful means of defense against bombers could be devised, there are alternative means of attack with which it would be extremely difficult to cope. Coastal cities could be bombarded from hostile submarines which rise to

[7] State Department Bulletin, Vol. 29 (December 21, 1953), p. 848.
[8] New York Times, July 10, 1955, p. 25, col. 4.
[9] Paul H. Nitze, "Atoms, Strategy and Policy," Foreign Affairs, Vol. 34 (January, 1956), p. 190.
[10] Ibid., p. 194.

the surface many miles from shore. Various types of long-range missiles, fitted with nuclear warheads and traveling at great heights and at speeds many times the speed of sound, are likely weapons of the future. How effectively such methods of attack can be countered remains to be seen. Passive defense measures can of course be taken, such as the dispersion of industry and the development of civil defense programs, to increase a country's capacity to absorb attack without being knocked out of a war immediately. Especially with new productive facilities, there is reason for governments to insist that they be located away from existing industrial centers.[11] At best, however, feasible measures of passive defense can scarcely be of more than marginal importance.

The Potentially Suicidal Character of Unrestricted Nuclear War

The theoretical possibilities of destruction in nuclear war, of course, offer no sure basis of predicting what would happen if a test should actually come. Much would depend upon the strategies adopted and on the speed with which one side could substantially destroy the capacity of the other to deliver nuclear weapons over significant targets. If each side should drop thermonuclear weapons on the major urban and industrial centers of the other, the destruction would be catastrophic. Sir Winston Churchill was apparently assuming that this type of strategy would be employed when he declared that [12]

Major war of the future will differ from anything we have known in the past in this one significant respect, that each side at the outset will suffer what it dreads the most—the loss of everything that it has ever known.

Air Marshal Slessor seems to accept the same assumption in saying: [13]

We are living through a complete revolution in human affairs and at last are reaching the point—which admittedly men have thought before that they were reaching—when war would be general suicide and the end of civilization as we know it.

Bernard Brodie does not necessarily accept the assumption that nuclear weapons will be directed at urban centers, but indicates that, if this does happen, the war would be both catastrophic and short.[14]

The minimum destruction one can reasonably expect from any unrestricted strategic attack will inevitably be too high to permit further meaningful mobilization of resources, perhaps too high even to permit the effective use of surviv-

[11] Klaus Knorr, "Passive Air Defense for the United States," in Kaufmann, *op. cit.*, pp. 75-101.
[12] *New York Times*, March 2, 1955, p. 8, col. 6.
[13] Sir John Slessor, *Strategy for the West* (New York, Morrow, 1954), p. 14.
[14] Bernard Brodie, "Strategy Hits a Dead End," *Harper's*, Vol. 211 (October, 1955), p. 35.

ing military units. . . . If strategic bombing occurs on the grand scale, other kinds of military operations will prove either unfeasible or superfluous and most likely both.

The problem of the survivors of an all-out nuclear attack will be to continue to live. "They are unlikely to be much concerned with the further pursuit of political-military objectives." The implication is that values which had seemed so precious, including those on behalf of which the war was undertaken, are likely to become relatively insignificant to those surviving, after nuclear weapons have transformed the conditions under which life proceeds.

The Possibility of Limited Nuclear Warfare

What are the chances that nuclear weapons could be used in major war, but not in an all-out, unlimited manner? Liddell Hart holds out some prospect of this. He takes the view that [15]

. . . where both sides possess atomic power, "*total* warfare" makes nonsense. Total warfare implies that the aim, the effort, and the degree of violence are unlimited. . . . An unlimited war waged with atomic power would make worse than nonsense; it would be suicidal. . . . It is likely that any future warfare will be less unrestrained and more subject to mutually agreed rules. Within such limits it may develop new forms.

Liddell Hart credits aggressors with a desire "to achieve their gains with the least possible damage, both to themselves and to their acquisitions," and he cites Hitler's efforts to avert the general bombardment of cities.[16] In such situations it is for the defenders to decide whether to accept the limitations tacitly or explicitly suggested.

If the Soviet Union should make a nuclear attack on the United States, or vice versa, it is an open question whether any significant limitations would be observed. Some hold out hope that they might be. The argument is that in the initial exchange of blows each side would aim to destroy the capacity of the other to engage in strategic bombing.[17] This means that they would aim to destroy not urban centers but air bases, nuclear weapons, and the means of delivering the weapons. If either side gained a substantial advantage in this destructive process, it is argued, the war would become increasingly one-sided as the advantage was exploited. Anticipating this, the initial loser would

. . . face a truly agonizing decision. It may still have the capability of destroying a few of the enemy's cities. But the damage it could inflict would be indecisive and out of all proportion to the annihilation which its own cities could expect to receive in return.[18]

[15] B. H. Liddell Hart, *The Revolution in Warfare* (New Haven, Yale University Press, 1947), p. 99.
[16] *Ibid.*, pp. 89, 100.
[17] Nitze, *loc. cit.*, pp. 192-193.
[18] *Ibid.*, p. 193.

What would it then do? The thought is that it might capitulate. The damage would no doubt be enormous already, for even an attack designed to destroy the ability of the enemy to retaliate might well involve the destruction of some cities. An early capitulation, whatever its other consequences, would at least put a halt to destruction before extreme limits were reached.

It is not out of the question that prudence might lead to such meager limitations. It is also possible that the side which foresees the destruction of its capacity to wreak nuclear vengeance would attack the urban centers of the other while there was yet time. It would have to expect retaliation in kind. The result might be so catastrophic to both sides that neither would find it possible, in the end, to impose its will upon the other.[19]

If war were to break out in a way not involving the direct exchange of blows between the Soviet Union, on the one hand, and the United States or any North Atlantic Treaty country, on the other, the possibility of limiting it would be somewhat greater. The Korean war provides a precedent. The United States might have used nuclear weapons in that war, but refrained. Similarly the Soviet Union refrained from supplying nuclear weapons to North Korean and Chinese Communist forces. Both sides followed policies which reflected a desire to keep hostilities confined to a limited area. Britain and France followed a similar policy in their military action against Egypt in 1956. It is in these respects, that is, in the weapons employed and the area engulfed, that limitations seem most likely to be possible.

Policy Requirements for Limiting Nuclear Warfare

Suppose that the United States in peacetime should wish to follow policies designed to maximize the prospect of limiting any future Korea-like wars. What could it do? Kaufmann has spelled out some of the major requirements.[20] "Certainly a first requirement during peacetime," he says, "is that forces be available to cope with an attack, and that they be able to move into the battle area with great rapidity and strength." The point is that the aggressor must not be allowed to gain a dominant military position at the outset, from which he can be dislodged only by extensive and intensive fighting. The second requirement is closely related. It is "that the forces of countries vulnerable to Communist aggression should be supported and strengthened wherever possible, even when the countries in question refuse to ally themselves with the United States." Not only would this help prevent the aggressor from gaining a dominant military position at the outset, but it would increase the prospect that the war could be confined to "local forces clashing over local issues." The

---

[19] Roger Hilsman, *loc. cit.*, pp. 56-57.
[20] William W. Kaufmann, "Limited Warfare," in Kaufmann, *op. cit.*, pp. 102-136.

third more general requirement is "that American policy exhibit a high degree of reasonableness." Among other things, the United States might let it be known in peacetime that wars in which it becomes engaged will not necessarily be fought through to an unconditional surrender and punishment of the enemy, to say nothing of an imposed transformation of the political and economic system in the defeated state.

Similarly, if the United States actually becomes involved in war, the strategy pursued might be calculated to keep the war limited, provided, of course, that the enemy is willing to pursue a comparable strategy. Decisions concerning the weapons to be employed, the area to be engulfed, the specific targets to be attacked, and the war aims to be pursued could all be made with a view to maximizing the prospect that peace could be restored, presumably through negotiations, without catastrophe for either side.

Massive Retaliation?

In 1954 Secretary of State John Foster Dulles seemed to repudiate a policy aimed at limiting war. He referred to the various areas in which communist aggression might occur and to the high costs of a policy of meeting aggression at points on the periphery of the Sino-Soviet orbit. Although granting that "local defense" would always be important, he said that it "must be reinforced by the further deterrent of massive retaliatory power." And he said that the United States had made a "basic decision": "To depend primarily upon a great capacity to retaliate, instantly, by means and at places of our choosing." [21] The implication was that another act of aggression similar to the one in Korea might lead the United States to initiate nuclear warfare against the Soviet Union or Communist China. Dulles left the question unanswered whether urban centers might be the targets, and whether weapons throwing radioactive particles into the atmosphere might be employed.

The pronouncement has been subjected to searching criticism.[22] It is generally agreed that a massive nuclear attack by the Soviet Union would have to be answered in kind. But to choose massive retaliation where war might otherwise be limited is to take massive risk, and it is doubtful whether massive risk can be justified except in the most compelling circumstances.

Graduated Deterrence

Associated with the idea of limited war is the principle of "graduated deterrence." The term is a vague one, calling generally for measures of

---

[21] *State Department Bulletin*, Vol. 30 (January 25, 1954), pp. 107-110.
[22] William W. Kaufmann, "The Requirements of Deterrence," in Kaufmann, *op. cit.*, pp. 12-38; cf. Lester B. Pearson, *Democracy in World Politics* (Princeton, Princeton University Press, 1955), pp. 9-39.

deterrence or defense proportionate to the extent of the danger, or for the minimum necessary violence.[23] Presumably this means that aggression would be countered, wherever possible without the use of nuclear weapons and without unnecessarily extending the area of hostilities. Where nuclear weapons are considered essential, preference would be given to those with the minimum necessary destructive power, and targets would be selected on the basis of a compromise between the desire for the maximum reduction of the enemy's military strength and the minimum destruction of life and property. The deliberate bombardment of urban centers outside the battle zone and the use of thermonuclear weapons or of any weapon which spreads dangerous quantities of radioactive particles through the atmosphere would be regarded as measures of last resort.

The Communist Record in Waging Limited War

Not only in Korea but also in other circumstances Communist leaders have exhibited a willingness to limit war. The Soviet Union fought major engagements with Japan toward the end of the 1930's, but on a localized basis and without even a severance of diplomatic relations.[24] It gave assistance to the Spanish Loyalists without committing its prestige to their victory. Soviet satellite countries supported Communist rebels in Greece after World War II, but so limited their actions that the rebels could be crushed without overt international war. Both in Korea and in Indochina the Communist leaders of China restricted themselves to something less than all-out war. In truth, they did not formally commit themselves at all, alleging that the Chinese forces which fought abroad consisted of "volunteers." Moreover, one of Moscow's threats in connection with the Middle Eastern crisis of 1956 was that Soviet "volunteers" might go to the support of Egypt. These precedents give no assurance for the future, but they suggest the possibility that the Communists may be willing to confine themselves to tests of strength falling short of the extreme limits of thermonuclear war.

DOES WAR REMAIN A USEFUL INSTRUMENT?

What are the implications of the existence of nuclear weapons for the usefulness of war? After all, states engage in war because of an expectation that through it they can gain or keep more than they will lose. Is such an expectation still tenable?

[23] Rear Admiral Sir Anthony W. Buzzard, "Massive Retaliation and Graduated Deterrence," *World Politics*, Vol. 8 (January, 1956), pp. 228-237.
[24] Clark W. Tinch, "Quasi-War between Japan and the U.S.S.R., 1937-1939," *World Politics*, Vol. 3 (January, 1951), pp. 174-199.

Where Both Sides Lack Nuclear Weapons

Obviously, it is still a tenable expectation among states which do not possess nuclear weapons. Although the costs of "conventional" warfare have increased, they have not become prohibitive. North and South Korea went to war in 1950, and Israel and Egypt fought in 1956; in these contests each side knew that the other lacked nuclear weapons, and at the outset each presumably thought it possible to gain or keep more than would be lost. India and Pakistan are without nuclear weapons, and presumably judge questions of war and peace between themselves without much thought to the possibility of atomic destruction. The same is true of many states. In other words, war remains approximately as useful and as possible as ever for a considerable proportion of the states of the world. How long this will be true remains to be seen. In the not-too-distant future it may be that most or all governments will have nuclear weapons in their arsenals.

Where Only One Side Possesses Them

If war remains useful in situations where nuclear weapons are lacking on both sides, does it also remain useful where one side possesses them and the other side does not? Addressing himself to this question, Liddell Hart says flatly that [25] "if one side possesses atomic power and the other does not, embattled resistance makes nonsense. That spells the disappearance of warfare in such cases." Similarly, Sir Winston Churchill has said that a small quantity of plutonium "would suffice to produce weapons which would give indisputable world domination to any great power which was the only one to have it." [26] He obviously assumed that states without nuclear weapons would not dare resist a state which possessed them.

The assumptions underlying these statements, however, are unrealistic. Though the possession of nuclear weapons is obviously important, it is not necessarily decisive. A willingness to use them (or a reputed willingness) is more important. Egypt in 1956 resisted first the demands and later the attack of Britain and France despite its lack of nuclear weapons. Further, no state has a nuclear monopoly; several already possess the dread weapons, and many more will come to possess them. It is unlikely that the world will be divided so that all possessors are united on one side. Rather, the possessors are likely to continue to be divided against themselves, and if one of them threatens a state which lacks nuclear weapons it must consider the possibility that the threatened state may obtain the support of another possessor. Thus American possession of nuclear weap-

[25] Liddell Hart, *op. cit.*, p. 98.
[26] *New York Times*, March 2, 1955, p. 8, col. 1.

ons does not necessarily give preponderance over Communist China, for in the event of war Peking might obtain Moscow's support, and the Soviet Union does not necessarily have clear preponderance over Japan, for in the event of war Japan might gain American support. Surely the potential threat of Soviet nuclear power was among the factors inducing Britain, France, and Israel to abandon their military effort and accept a cease-fire in Egypt in 1956. The state which lacked nuclear weapons (Egypt) could thus sustain itself.

This means that no flat generalization can safely be made about the usefulness of war where one side possesses nuclear weapons and the other side does not. The answer depends on whether and how nuclear weapons would be employed and whether the state lacking such weapons would receive support from a state possessing them.

Where Both Sides Possess Them

Now suppose that both sides in a dispute possess nuclear weapons and the capacity to deliver them. Has war then become prohibitively costly? Again the answer depends upon whether and how nuclear weapons would be used.

In a war involving the United States on one side and the Soviet Union on the other, it seems likely that nuclear weapons would be used. The parties to the North Atlantic Treaty, fearing the advantage which the Soviet Union has in manpower, have instructed their Supreme Headquarters to plan the defense of Europe on this assumption. Air Marshal Slessor declares that [27] "in the unlikely event of another great war, [nuclear weapons] would unquestionably be used." Sir Winston Churchill as Prime Minister warned that [28] "it would be folly to suppose that they would not be used. Our precautionary dispositions must therefore be based on the assumption that, if war should come, these weapons would be used."

We have already discussed whether the use of nuclear weapons would be unlimited, though with inconclusive results. Those who assume that nuclear warfare would be unlimited are inclined to doubt whether it will occur at all. Thus in 1953, Sir Winston Churchill said that he sometimes had [29]

... the odd thought that the annihilating character of these agencies [nuclear weapons] may bring an utterly unforeseeable security to mankind. ... It may be that when the advance of destructive weapons enables everyone to kill everybody else no one will want to kill anyone at all.

[27] Slessor, op. cit., p. 18.
[28] New York Times, March 2, 1955, p. 8, col. 5.
[29] Quoted by Slessor, op. cit., p. 1.

In 1955, taking the development of thermonuclear weapons into account, Churchill reverted to the same thought.[30]

> After a certain point has been passed, it may be said, the worse things get the better. . . . Then it may be that we shall, by a process of sublime irony, have reached a stage in this story where safety will be the sturdy child of terror, and survival the twin brother of annihilation.

Similarly, Air Marshal Slessor holds that [31] "the continued existence of atomic weapons gives us an almost certain chance of preventing another world war. . . ."

Such hopes rest not only on the assumption that nuclear warfare will be unlimited but also on others: (1) that the potential victim of attack will have the capacity to inflict devastating retaliation on the aggressor; (2) that the potential aggressor will be aware of this and will therefore be deterred; and (3) that the potential belligerents will exercise sufficient control over all relevant developments to avoid being caught up in war except through deliberate choice. If the first additional assumption did not hold true, there is a possible alternative: that the potential victim which lacks the capacity to deter a nuclear attack will yield without a struggle.

Sooner or later hopes based on such assumptions are likely to prove false. Conceptions of honor may prevent states from yielding without a struggle, even though the odds are hopeless. Accidents may happen, and states may lose control over the course of events. Bluffs may be made and called. Nuclear and other capabilities may be miscalculated. A psychopathic individual may achieve the power of decision in an important government. In other words, even if unrestricted nuclear warfare is suicidal, it is still possible that it will occur.

Further, as suggested above, it is among the possibilities that nuclear warfare might somehow be limited. Powerful pressures will work in this direction. On the one hand, occasions will certainly arise in the future, as in the past, when war is regarded as a necessary means of promoting the objectives of the state. On the other hand, unlimited warfare is likely to be regarded as suicidal. The obvious solution to the dilemma is to accept limitations on the methods of waging war. As Bernard Brodie puts it,[32] "In a world still unprepared to relinquish the use of military power, we must learn to effect that use through methods that are something other than self-destroying."

We have confined this discussion to the impact of the development of nuclear weapons. Note should also be made, however, of the possibility that chemical or bacteriological weapons might be equally disastrous.

[30] *New York Times*, March 2, 1955, p. 8, col. 4.
[31] Slessor, *op. cit.*, p. 18.
[32] Bernard Brodie, *loc. cit.*, p. 37.

NUCLEAR WEAPONS AND THE LEVEL OF ARMAMENTS

Official and unofficial study and discussion of the problem of armaments and disarmament have taken on increased intensity since the development of nuclear weapons. Some of the proposals made, and the difficulties involved in securing adoption of them, have been discussed in Chapter 12. Now a new consideration can be added. As suggested above, it is probable that a state would launch nuclear warfare only if it expected that its initial blow would substantially curtail the ability of the victim to retaliate. States that want to avoid war must therefore place great emphasis on developing and preserving their retaliatory power. No doubt both the United States and the Soviet Union are attempting to do this by all feasible means. They could presumably do it more surely if they were to agree on a plan under which each could be assured against surprise; in other words, each side is more likely to be able to preserve a capacity to retaliate if it gets advance warning of an attack.

These considerations have led to the proposal that the United States, the Soviet Union, and perhaps other states should join in establishing an "early warning system" under which each government would be kept continuously informed of the military strength and posture of the others. Each might engage at will in aerial reconnaissance and on-the-ground investigation in the territory of the others, and have observers stationed at points from which attack might be launched. The agents of one government in the territory of the others would have complete freedom of communication, and so presumably could give early warning of impending danger. The theory is that, if surprise could thus be ruled out, the initial attack is less likely to be paralyzing and therefore is not likely to occur. Peace would be preserved.

As with most plans relating to armament and disarmament, however, the advantages seem to be unequal. They are less for the state that might launch a surprise attack than for a state that is unlikely to do so; they are less for the state that has the better espionage service or is otherwise most likely to obtain early warning without benefit of an international agreement designed to make it possible. These considerations are no doubt among those which have induced the Soviet Union to reject the plan.

There is speculation that there may be less need to maintain vast armed establishments when states can hold each other at bay through the threat of nuclear destruction, and that therefore the possibilities of some degree of disarmament in conventional weapons may be increased. Unilateral American policies lend some credence to this view, for there has been a tendency to stress air-atomic power and to devote a lower proportion of the total defense outlay to ground forces. Similarly the

Soviet Union has announced significant reductions in the size of the Red Army.

It should be noted that reliance on nuclear weapons as a basis for disarmament, that is, reliance on a "balance of terror," inherently limits the possibilities. If this is the source of safety, it is obvious that disarmament cannot be carried too far. Each side must retain the power to inflict devastating retaliation if it should be attacked—at least until other bulwarks of peace have developed. It is this consideration which led Air Marshal Slessor to say that [33] "the greatest disservice that anyone could possibly do to the cause of peace would be to abolish nuclear armaments on either side."

It is even more important to note that there are great dangers in placing primary reliance on nuclear weapons. By so doing, states might make war less likely, but at the same time they would make it more likely that the wars which are fought would be catastrophic. If the aim of limiting warfare is to be vigorously pursued, it is imperative that states keep themselves in a position to choose weapons and strategies appropriate to the occasion. So-called brush-fire wars might be fought exclusively with conventional weapons or with the strictly tactical use of only the less powerful nuclear weapons. The burden of developing and maintaining nuclear weapons and delivery systems may have to be a supplement to, rather than a substitute for, the burden of maintaining conventional armed establishments.

The prospect that nuclear warfare would be catastrophic may also have implications outside the field of military policy. Methods of struggle other than war have always existed. If nuclear weapons reduce the usefulness of war, one obvious implication is that greater reliance may be placed on other methods: on propaganda and subversion, on fifth columns, and on economic measures. Possibilities along these lines will be explored in the following chapter.

SUGGESTED READINGS

BRODIE, Bernard, ed., *The Absolute Weapon; Atomic Power and World Order* (New York, Harcourt, Brace, 1946).

BRODIE, Bernard, "Strategy Hits a Dead End," *Harper's*, Vol. 211 (October, 1955), pp. 33-37.

BUZZARD, Rear Admiral Sir Anthony W., "Massive Retaliation and Graduated Deterrence," *World Politics*, Vol. 8 (January, 1956), pp. 228-237.

EARLE, Edward M., ed., *Makers of Modern Strategy* (Princeton, Princeton University Press, 1944).

FALLS, Cyril, *A Hundred Years of War* (New York, Macmillan, 1954).

KAUFMANN, William W., ed., *Military Policy and National Security* (Princeton, Princeton University Press, 1956).

[33] Slessor, *op. cit.*, p. 14.

LIDDELL HART, B. H., *The Revolution in Warfare* (New Haven, Yale University Press, 1947).

MIKSCHE, Lieut.-Col. F. O., *Atomic Weapons and Armies* (New York, Praeger, 1955).

NEF, John U., *War and Human Progress* (Cambridge, Harvard University Press, 1950).

NITZE, Paul H., "Atoms, Strategy and Policy," *Foreign Affairs*, Vol. 34 (January, 1956), pp. 187-198.

PEARSON, Lester B., *Democracy in World Politics* (Princeton, Princeton University Press, 1955).

PULESTON, Captain W. D., *The Influence of Force in Foreign Relations* (New York, Van Nostrand, 1955).

SLESSOR, Sir John, *Strategy for the West* (New York, Morrow, 1954).

SOROKIN, Pitirim A., *Social and Cultural Dynamics*. Vol. III, *Fluctuation of Social Relationships, War and Revolution* (New York, American Book, 1937).

TINCH, Clark W., "Quasi-War between Japan and the U.S.S.R., 1937-1939," *World Politics*, Vol. 3 (January, 1951), pp. 174-199.

WRIGHT, Quincy, *A Study of War* (Chicago, The University of Chicago Press, 1942).

CHAPTER 17

Substitutes for War

IF THE TITLE of this chapter were taken literally, the subject would be very broad—virtually as broad as politics itself. We have seen that politics is a struggle to determine whose will is to prevail in connection with group concerns; its essence is conflict, and the ultimate form of conflict is war. All methods of struggle short of war can therefore be regarded as substitutes for war.

We shall not actually interpret the subject so broadly. Instead, we shall confine ourselves to two possible substitutes: (1) the dissemination of education, information, and propaganda, including particularly the possibility of aggression by subversion; and (2) the use of economic blandishments and penalties.

Theoretically action in one or both of these areas might permit a state to shape the course of events so as to render a war unnecessary. The action might be designed to forestall developments which would lead to war if they occurred, or it might be designed to bring about developments for which war would otherwise be required. Suppose, for example, that the United States is determined to fight, if need be, to prevent the Soviet Union and its communist cohorts from achieving political control of the continent of Europe. If this development can be forestalled by propaganda and economic action, these weapons would have served as substitutes for war. Or suppose that the Soviet Union wants to annex Finland; for this kind of step, military conquest is the usual preliminary. If annexation can be accomplished by means of verbal and economic weapons, they would have served as a substitute for war.

It should be noted that in this chapter we shall not discuss the possibility of changing fundamental attitudes over the world or of bringing about some sort of universal moral transformation to reduce or eliminate conflict. Neither shall we discuss the problem of developing an international organization or a world government through which conflicts might be resolved without war. These subjects will be treated in later chapters. In this chapter we shall assume that sovereign states will continue to exist and continue to struggle with each other without drastic change in the existing political framework; further, we shall consider efforts to change human attitudes in relation to the continuing international struggle rather than in relation to the problem of establishing universal harmony.

THE DISSEMINATION OF EDUCATION, INFORMATION, AND PROPAGANDA

Methods of Dissemination

There are a number of methods or channels through which states disseminate education, information, and propaganda with a view to influencing foreign people. Some seek to reach foreigners within the proselyting country, and others involve efforts to influence foreigners in their home countries.

The presence of foreigners within a country obviously provides an opportunity to influence their attitudes. Consequently, some governments encourage foreigners to come. Soviet practices provide illustrations. Soon after the October Revolution in 1917, the Bolsheviks spread communist propaganda among prisoners of war over whom they had inherited control, and succeeded in indoctrinating some who later became leaders in the communist movement in their home countries. Subsequently various schools in the Soviet Union became centers for training foreign students. Though knowledge of Soviet practices in this respect is scant, apparently a considerable portion of the prominent Communists throughout the world have attended these schools. As of 1945, for example, 57 per cent of the members of the Central Committee of the Chinese Communist Party were persons who had received some of their education in the Soviet Union.[1]

The United States engages in similar activities. Rather than collect the indemnity due it after the Boxer uprising in China, it chose to make the funds available to Chinese students who wished to attend American universities. After World War II, the United States launched a relatively extensive program by which foreign students and teachers receive financial assistance to come to American educational centers. Moreover, leaders in public life from many parts of the world are also encouraged to visit the country, frequently receiving financial grants which make the visits possible.[2] The obvious hope is that experience in the United States will

[1] Frederick C. Barghoorn, "The Ideological Weapon in Soviet Strategy," in C. Grove Haines, ed., The Threat of Soviet Imperialism (Baltimore, Johns Hopkins Press, 1954), pp. 91-92.

[2] Department of State, International Educational Exchange Service, Partners in International Understanding, Department of State Publication 5853, International Information and Cultural Series 40 (Washington, 1955).

create or reinforce attitudes favorable to the country and to the principles
for which it stands, and that those who gain such experience will on their
return home influence others to adopt similar attitudes. The more such
attitudes can be made to prevail in given foreign countries, the less likely
is it that they will succumb to communism and the more likely that they
will follow foreign policies friendly to the United States.

It is difficult to measure the actual effects of efforts to influence foreigners who come into the proselyting country. Possibly the Communist
leaders who have been schooled in the Soviet Union would have been
Communist leaders in any event. And who can tell what the political
effects will be if a student from France or India or Formosa spends a year
or two in the United States? In all probability, however, the programs
have been significant, and they may well take on increasing significance.
Certainly there would be considerable alarm in the United States if a large
proportion of the students from the free world who seek an education
abroad should begin to choose Soviet rather than American universities.

Aside from encouraging foreigners to come into the country, a proselyting state can take actions designed to affect the attitudes of people abroad.
The United States, in conjunction with its efforts to bring foreigners into
the country, also sponsors programs under which Americans receive grants
to go abroad as students or teachers, or on special trips as good-will
ambassadors. Both governmental and private agencies have assisted in
financing schools abroad where foreign students can secure learning,
which presumably will be of political advantage to the United States.
The dissemination of information and propaganda favorable to the home
country is one of the normal functions of diplomatic missions. They often
distribute journals and bulletins. They provide speakers for public occasions, or provide radio and TV programs. The United States government
maintains libraries of information at many centers abroad, containing
sizable collections of books, journals, and documents. The Soviet Union
has sent ballet dancers and other artists abroad; in fact, numerous governments have engaged in comparable activities. Governments may help
arrange for the exhibition of various types of national products at commercial fairs held abroad, in part for commercial reasons but also in part
because of the political implications which such exhibits often have. The
United Nations and the agencies connected with it provide forums for the
dissemination of propaganda. The investigations undertaken, the resolutions presented, and the speeches made are frequently designed more to
influence opinion in various parts of the world than to influence United
Nations action; efforts along these lines are reported to the world both
in official United Nations documents and through news services.

Private news services such as the Associated Press and Reuters have
long been active in the field of international information and propaganda.
Even though they distribute "straight" news, it is commonly assumed that

they play a significant role in shaping foreign opinion in a way favorable to the home country. Many governments have subsidized news services or established official services. Soviet agencies have apparently gone further and have actually given financial and other assistance to approved newspapers and publishing houses in other countries. In many countries both private and public agencies have engaged increasingly in broadcasting radio programs designed for foreign audiences. The Soviet Union has long maintained an extensive program of foreign language broadcasts, and more recently the United States has entered the field with the Voice of America.

Special propaganda campaigns are sometimes conducted by extraordinary methods. Some governments have, on occasion, engaged in outright bribery to influence the foreign press and even the officials of foreign states. Americans of Italian extraction apparently exerted appreciable influence over the outcome of the Italian national elections in 1948 by writing letters to friends and relatives in Italy urging them to vote against the Communist Party. Other Americans have subsequently maintained a program under which information and propaganda are carried behind the Iron Curtain by free-floating balloons.

The periodic Olympic games have acquired rather vague but no doubt real political significance, for their outcome affects the prestige of the nations involved.

Objectives in Influencing Foreign Opinion

The objectives in disseminating education, information, and propaganda differ, just as do the channels and methods of dissemination. A state engaged in the activity may aim: (1) to promote and consolidate friendly relations with another state, without reference to any specific policy problem; (2) to influence another state to follow, or not to follow, a specific course of action, without challenge to the existence or integrity of the other state and without challenge to its fundamental values and basic institutions; or (3) to bring about some kind of fundamental change which the government in the target state opposes—perhaps the overthrow of that government or the overthrow of the whole economic and political system within which it operates.

A large proportion of the international activity in this realm falls into the first category. By disseminating education, information, and propaganda to citizens of other countries, governments often seek simply to promote good will, to win respect for domestic institutions and practices, or to nurture cultural affinities. Even such apparently mild activities, however, may be part of a program substituting for war. For example, the United States and the Soviet Union are engaged in competitive propaganda campaigns in many in-between countries. Each seeks in a positive sense to win good will, and each uses good-will propaganda, among other things, to counteract what are regarded as the hostile or subversive activities of the other. If through its activities the Soviet Union can set the stage in any country for the triumph of communism there, or if the United States can detach a communist country from the Soviet camp, a victory will have been achieved comparable to one which might have been achieved in war.

Activity in the second category, designed to influence another state to follow, or not to follow, a specific course of action, is also common, and may help either to avert war or to accomplish objectives for which war might otherwise have been required. Propaganda spread by the United States in Britain during the American Civil War probably influenced the British to withhold diplomatic recognition from the Confederate government, and so helped avert war between Britain and the United States. American efforts to influence the Italian elections in 1948 apparently helped bring about the defeat of the Communists and so helped to avert what otherwise would have become a very tense international situation. Nazi Germany used propaganda extensively, sometimes including threats of war in it, to reinforce diplomatic demands—for example, to obtain the acquiescence of Britain and France to the transfer of the Sudetenland from Czechoslovakia to Germany. Generally speaking, informational and propaganda programs can serve as supplements to diplomacy in making known the wishes and demands of governments. Such programs thus provide others with a basis for calculating the risks of war connected with the pursuit of certain policies, and this in turn may lead to the adoption of policies which keep such risks at a minimum.

Sometimes international action in the realm of education, information, and propaganda falls into the third category, that is, it is subversive, involving a challenge to the existence of a government, to the integrity of a state, or to its fundamental values or basic institutions. Action of this type usually constitutes ideological warfare. The weapons are words and other symbols rather than guns or bombs, but aggression by subversion may involve struggle no less fateful to the state than aggression by military means.

Ideological Warfare and Fifth Columns: Subversion as a Substitute for War

Ideological warfare, or aggression by subversion, is age-old. In modern times it achieved considerable prominence in Europe after the French Revolution. Since then, nationalist movements have frequently brought ideological struggles between governments seeking to bring about the unity and independence of a nation and governments seeking to prevent such a development. Cavour, Prime Minister of Sardinia-Piedmont and chief architect of the unification of Italy a century ago, employed nationalist propaganda against governments standing in the way of unity, inciting domestic insurrection against them. In the decades preceding World War I, the government and private parties in Serbia spread nationalist propaganda in the Austro-Hungarian Empire, trying to induce Slavic people there to transfer their loyalty from the Emperor in Vienna to the idea of a united Serbian (or South Slavic) nation. In the 1930's Hitler and the German Nazis tried to make Nazis out of German-speaking people in other countries—especially in Austria and Czechoslovakia; they used nationalist and other appeals in subversive attacks which threatened the very existence of these countries.

The principal ideological struggle currently in progress is that between the communist and non-communist worlds. The communist program calls for the "liberation" of the masses in all countries from what the communists regard as capitalist oppression and exploitation, and the liberation of colonial peoples from the "yoke of imperialism." Some influential leaders in the non-communist world, especially in the United States, feel a comparable urge to liberate those under communist control from what they regard as a system of tyranny based on deception and hate. Moreover, on each side the missionary spirit is reinforced by other considerations, notably by the belief of each side that it will gain many advantages for itself (e.g., greater security) if those who champion a hostile ideology on the other side are overthrown.

Subversive efforts may have various objectives. They may be designed simply to bring pressure to bear on another government in order to influence its policies. They may be designed to weaken the target state so that it can be defeated more easily in war. Or they may be employed as a substitute for war. If we ask under what conditions, if any, subversive action can serve as a substitute for war, the answer will also shed light on the usefulness of subversion as an instrument for the achievement of lesser objectives.

1. *The need for support from within the target state.* In the first place, if subversion is to substitute for war (or, really, if it is to serve any purpose), the "attacking" state must champion an ideology and a program of action which evoke support within the territory of the victim. In "real" war, a state may win exclusively through the use of its own personnel against the united opposition of the enemy, but in subversion the aggressor must rally people to its cause within the victim state. It is essential in subversion that the people in the target country become disunited, some of them adhering to the enemy.

This requirement poses a question implicitly. What renders people in one country susceptible to subversive appeals emanating from another? An answer can be given in the form of an illustration, drawn from a study of *The Appeals of Communism*, by Gabriel Almond.[3] He classifies the

---

[3] Gabriel A. Almond, *The Appeals of Communism* (Princeton, Princeton University Press, 1954), esp. pp. 235-242.

needs and interests which render individuals susceptible to communist appeals into four major groups: (1) neurotic needs, (2) self-related interests, (3) group-related interests, and (4) ideological interests. The neurotic may, for example, feel rejected by the society in which he lives and may reject it in turn; he may express his rejection in various ways, adherence to an external enemy being among them. Self-related interests include career interests, companionship, and intellectual satisfaction. Group-related interests are illustrated by the example of the trade union official who joins the Communist Party in the belief that he will then be able to promote the objectives of his union more effectively, or by the Negro leader who believes that he can serve his race best by helping to overthrow the system under which it suffers discrimination. Ideological interests which render an individual susceptible to subversive propaganda are exemplified in the person who believes in liberty and equality, but who also believes that these values are not and cannot be adequately realized under the existing social order.

Obviously, the extent of susceptibility to subversive propaganda (i.e., the extent to which the needs and interests of the above types are left unsatisfied) will be different for different persons, different groups or classes, different countries, and different times. Many influencing factors operate. Probably the two most common ones relate to scales of living and to the satisfaction of nationalist aspirations. Susceptibility is likely to be accentuated when people are persistently denied a scale of living that meets their expectations. It is also likely to be accentuated when nationalist aspirations are thwarted—when nations do not enjoy political unity and independence. Communist subversion plays particularly on these vulnerable features of the position of non-communist states. It also plays on the popular desire for peace, based on the allegation that peace is unobtainable as long as capitalism survives.

2. *The need for organization and coordination.* If aggression by subversion is to substitute for war, it is necessary, in the second place, that the adherents of the "attacking" state in the target country be organized; it is also necessary that they be willing to coordinate their actions with those of the "attacker" or, better, to subordinate themselves to its control. Given these conditions, they are said to constitute a *fifth column,* a term stemming from the remark of a rebel leader in the Spanish Civil War that he controlled four armed columns for an attack on Madrid, plus a fifth column inside the city which would assist him from within. If people abroad are to allow themselves to be used as a fifth column, they must not only believe in the ideology and program of the attacker, but must also obtain, or hope to obtain, assistance from him. Afghanistan would have difficulty winning the support of a fifth column in France, regardless of the merits of the ideology and program it championed, because few Frenchmen would expect Afghanistan to be able to give

them aid. The Soviet Union faces much less difficulty. The Soviet Union would probably have some fifth columns abroad even if it did nothing to encourage their development, for people who believe in the need for a communist revolution in their country would naturally seek to identify themselves with Soviet power and would conduct themselves so as to maximize the prospect of attracting Soviet support.

3. *The need to deter or withstand retaliation.* The third main requirement if aggression by subversion is to substitute for war is that the aggressor must be in a position to deter or withstand retaliatory action by its intended victim, whether the retaliatory action take the form of an ideological counteroffensive, economic pressure, or war. In truth, aggression by subversion is most likely to succeed when the "attacking" state also is able to get what it wants by other methods.

This point is easily illustrated. For some years before 1914 the government of Serbia allowed its territory to serve as a base for subversive propaganda against Austria-Hungary; being militarily more powerful, Austria-Hungary was unwilling to confine the struggle to the ideological level, and finally responded with a declaration of war. Conversely, in the 1930's Hitler's Germany was powerful in every way, whereas Austria was weak; this permitted Hitler to resort to subversion without fear of retaliation and finally led to a bloodless conquest in which, in truth, German military power played a role at least as important as the role of the fifth column which Hitler had nurtured in Austria. Similarly, after World War II, the Soviet Union was in a virtually unassailable position in relation to the countries of Eastern and Southeastern Europe; it could therefore sponsor fifth-column activities in those countries with impunity. Egypt, Syria, and Saudi Arabia, inciting nationalism throughout North Africa and the Middle East and therefore accentuating antagonisms against Britain and France especially, are in a more vulnerable position, though the events of 1956 proved that both the United Nations and Soviet power give them some degree of safety from retaliatory military action.

4. *The requirement that domestic defenses be ineffective.* Governments threatened by subversion may defend themselves not only by retaliation against the external source of danger but also by purely domestic measures. Thus there is a fourth requirement for successful subversion: that domestic defense measures either not be adopted or not be effective.

Domestic defense measures may be either positive or negative, that is, they may be designed to inculcate loyalty or to prevent subversion. All governments adopt positive defense measures of some sort, however successfully or unsuccessfully. In most countries the major positive defense against subversion is the domestic educational system, together with the various means of mass communication. Through these agencies governments and supporting private agencies exert tremendous influence over political attitudes. Schools commonly inculcate respect for the culture of the country and the political and economic principles on which its social life is based. Similarly, newspapers, periodicals, and radio and TV broadcasts, whether controlled by private persons or public agencies, commonly inculcate and reinforce national loyalties. Even where academic freedom is complete, and where there is complete freedom of speech and press, a strong bias in favor of the prevailing national ideology is the normal thing; usually, though obviously not always, attitudes of loyalty are so thoroughly implanted that subversive appeals emanating from abroad or from a fifth column within the country evoke little response.

Governments which fear that positive domestic measures to inculcate loyalty may not be sufficient are free to adopt negative measures to curtail the flow of subversive ideas from abroad. Different kinds of negative measures can be taken. Contacts with foreigners can be reduced to a minimum by preventing them from coming into the country and by preventing citizens from going abroad. The importation and circulation of printed materials can be regulated. The cultural and informational activities of foreign diplomatic missions can be curtailed. Foreign radio broadcasts can be jammed, or it can be made a criminal offense to listen to such broadcasts. If a foreign government is officially engaged in subversive activities abroad, there is basis for diplomatic protest on the ground that the requirements of international law are being violated. Governments are rarely completely successful in cutting off the flow of ideas and information from abroad, but they can reduce it very drastically.

Moreover, governments are free to suppress fifth-column activities within their own territory, and strong governments determined to do so have generally succeeded. The dictatorial governments of Europe in the interwar period, for example, outlawed communist parties and introduced police agents into the underground communist organizations so successfully that Soviet fifth-column activities became insignificant. Virtually the same results have been achieved in the United States since World War II without the formal outlawry of the Party. Yet, though governments are theoretically free to suppress fifth columns, sometimes they do not act. Perhaps they fail to see the danger. Perhaps they are beset by so many domestic problems and so much domestic opposition that they are simply unable to act effectively. Fear of retaliation may lead a weak country to refrain from suppressing a fifth column sponsored by a powerful neighbor. Difficulties involved in distinguishing a loyal political party from a fifth column may induce a policy of toleration; thus Communists are sometimes regarded as constituting a political party entitled to democratic freedoms, and sometimes they are regarded as members of an international conspiratorial movement aiming at the violent overthrow of non-communist governments. In short, though each government seems theoretically to have the advantage on its own soil in connection with the problem of fifth columns—as well as in all aspects of struggle in the field of education, information, and propaganda— circumstances sometimes arise which throw the advantage the other way.

The upshot is that a state tempted to resort to war may or may not find that subversion is a feasible substitute. Subversion may be a feasible substitute: (1) if the aggressor champions an ideology and a program of action which command significant support in the target country, (2) if those supporting the aggressor within the target country are effectively organized and willing to subordinate their actions to the influence or control of the aggressor, (3) if the aggressor can deter or withstand any retaliatory action which attempts at subversion may provoke, or, still better, if the aggressor and its fifth column possess a clear preponderance of military power over the government of the target country, and (4) if the victim is for some reason unable to exploit its natural defensive advantage effectively in thwarting or suppressing subversive activity. This combination of circumstances is relatively rare. Most wars which have been fought arose in circumstances which precluded the use of subversion as a substitute. Even if opportunities to employ subversion increase in the future, and even if "real" war is therefore reduced, it seems unlikely that a complete substitution can be made.

This should not be interpreted to mean, however, that the international dissemination of education, information, and propaganda (whether or not it is subversive) is lacking in significance. If it influences the policies which states pursue and the balance of power among them, its importance is obvious. Also, conquest through subversion, even though rare, is as fateful to the countries involved as conquest through war.

ECONOMIC BLANDISHMENTS AND PENALTIES

Types of Measures Available

In Chapter 13 we have already mentioned the kinds of policies that a state engaged in economic warfare may pursue. They all relate, of course, to the international flow of goods, services, and capital, and more particularly to controlling that flow so as to confer benefits on favored states and inflict deprivations on others. A government may give economic aid to some states and deny it to others. It may make or permit loans to some, and deny them to others. By means of various devices, it can regulate exports from its own territory, and establish controls over its ports, its shipping, and its transportation and communication facilities, so as to help some states and hurt others. It can regulate imports so as to channel purchases to favored states, and so enhance their prosperity, and, having created a situation in which the other states are dependent on access to its markets, it can close off its markets. Such measures as these may be taken by a state acting alone, or they may be taken by a number of states acting in concert; the concerting of policies may itself be either quite voluntary or the result of economic pressures which one or more governments bring to bear on others. For influence to be exerted it is not always necessary that such actions actually be carried out; the mere prospect of benefits or the threat of deprivations may suffice. Aside from measures of the above types, a government which controls a fifth column abroad may be able to use it in economic warfare; this possibility is most obvious where the fifth column controls trade unions, which can be called out on strike.

The Granting or Withholding of Loans

The kinds of measures that can be taken (whether to win or hold friends, or to strengthen allies, or to avoid strengthening unfriendly states) can easily be illustrated.

It has long been common for governments to grant or withhold loans, and to regulate private foreign lending, on the basis of political considerations. In wartime, of course, governments lend money to allies and refuse to lend to enemies. The same thing can and does occur in times of peace. Before World War I, France contributed to the strength of its Russian ally by permitting and encouraging Frenchmen to buy Russian bonds. After World War I, France led the way in insisting, in connection with an international rehabilitation loan for Austria, that Austria reaffirm an obligation not to alienate her independence and that she undertake not to enter into economic agreements with other countries which might compromise that independence; the object was to prevent Germany from strengthening itself by uniting with Austria.

The United States has made extensive use of its ability to lend capital. On several occasions before Pearl Harbor it extended loans to the government of China both to encourage it in the prosecution of war and to warn Japan. In 1946, both for political and for economic reasons, it extended a loan of $3¾ billion to Britain and, in effect, refused to extend a similar loan to the Soviet Union. The European Recovery Program, to be described more fully below, was conducted in part on the basis of loans. Political considerations, among others, have been important in guiding the foreign lending operations of the Export-Import Bank. In 1955 competition between the Soviet Union and the Western countries for the favor of Egypt led several of the latter to consider—for a time favorably —making capital available to Egypt for the giant Aswan Dam project.

Gifts (Economic Aid)

1. The Lend-Lease Program. Foreign aid programs have been a major feature of American economic warfare. The first great program was adopted early in 1941 as a means of countering the challenge of the Axis powers. Hoping to stay out of the "real" war which was under way but nevertheless believing that its own security was threatened by Axis aggression, the United States decided to participate in the struggle through economic action. Among other steps, Congress enacted the Lend-Lease Bill under which the President provided services and gave vast quantities of goods of military value to countries the defense of which he considered vital to the defense of the United States. The theory was that, if the United States could assure their survival, or still better their victory, by providing them with the sinews of war, American military participation might be avoided. The Japanese attack at Pearl Harbor dashed such hopes, but the Lend-Lease program continued as an adjunct to military measures and played an important part in the war.[4]

2. Aid to Greece and Turkey. Since World War II the United States has engaged in a series of foreign aid programs, mainly as an instrument of struggle in the cold war. Faced with the challenge of the Soviet Union and its fifth columns abroad, the United States responded not only with defense preparations of a military type but also with economic aid to threatened countries. In 1947 the government in Greece was struggling both against economic difficulties greatly accentuated by wartime devastation and against an overt Communist rebellion; Turkey was menaced directly by the Soviet Union. In this situation President Truman called upon the United States "to help free peoples to maintain their free institutions and their national integrity against aggressive movements that seek to impose upon them totalitarian regimes." He declared,[5]

> The seeds of totalitarian regimes are nurtured by misery and want. They spread and grow in the evil soil of poverty and strife. They reach their full growth when the hope of a people for a better life has died.

He therefore took the view that "our help should be primarily through economic and financial aid which is essential to economic stability and orderly political processes." Congress responded then and for several years thereafter by appropriating money which was used to promote economic rehabilitation in Greece and to enhance the military strength of both Greece and Turkey.

---

[4] For descriptions of various American aid programs, see William Adams Brown and Redvers Opie, *American Foreign Assistance* (Washington, Brookings, 1953).

[5] Francis O. Wilcox and Thorsten V. Kalijarvi, eds., *Recent American Foreign Policy, Basic Documents 1941-1951* (New York, Appleton-Century-Crofts, 1952), pp. 814-819.

3. *The European Recovery Program.* Similar considerations led later in the same year to the adoption of an interim aid program for countries in Western Europe and in 1948 to the adoption of the European Recovery Program. Especially in France and Italy there seemed to be danger that communism might triumph. If either or both of these countries succumbed, it seemed quite possible that all the rest of the European continent might do so as well. If all Europe went communist, aligning itself with the Soviet Union, the potential power of the Soviet camp would have been so great as to place the United States in acute jeopardy. Acting in large part on the basis of the same belief that Truman expressed in connection with his request for aid to Greece and Turkey—that "the seeds of totalitarian regimes are nurtured by misery and want"—the United States set about attempting to reduce misery and want in Europe. During the four-year period of the ERP it provided over $12 billion of assistance to the 16 recipient countries, about three-fourths of this in the form of outright grants and the rest in loans. The goods and services provided came mainly from the United States, leading Paul G. Hoffman to say that "in one very real sense, today's contest between freedom and despotism is a contest between the American assembly line and the Communist Party line." [6]

In addition, some offshore procurement occurred (e.g., the United States bought goods in Latin America for delivery to Europe), thus spreading the economic stimulation which the program afforded. The object was to provide those goods and services which would contribute most effectively to economic recovery. Receiving countries were required to put into a special fund—a "counterpart fund"—the money received from the sale of products given to them, and money from the counterpart fund was itself in turn spent for projects—such as the development of hydroelectric power—which would contribute to economic recovery.

Appraisal of the results of the ERP is difficult. So many factors were at work affecting the rate of economic recovery and the strength of communist parties that it is impossible to say precisely which effects were caused by the American program. The fact is, however, that by the end of 1951 industrial production in the recipient countries had risen by almost two-thirds above the level of 1947, and agricultural output had made a 25 per cent gain. [7] Communist parties did not grow in strength during the period of the ERP; in fact, though they remained strong especially in France and Italy, the general record was one of decline.

4. *Subsequent American aid programs.* Official termination of the

---

[6] Paul G. Hoffman, *Peace Can Be Won* (Garden City, Doubleday, 1951), p. 87.

[7] Harry G. Brainard, *International Economics and Public Policy* (New York, Holt, 1954), pp. 613-620. For a more comprehensive account and appraisal of the ERP, see Harry Bayard Price, *The Marshall Plan and Its Meaning* (Ithaca, Cornell University Press, 1955).

European Recovery Program did not by any means bring American foreign aid programs to an end. In fact, even before its termination, two other programs had already been launched, and have been continued since then. Under one of them, originally called the Mutual Defense Assistance Program, the aid given has been designed explicitly to enhance the military power of allies and potential allies of the United States; in fact, under the North Atlantic Treaty the program has been made a reciprocal one, for the treaty obliges all the parties to engage not only in self-help but also in "mutual aid" to maintain and develop their individual and collective capacity to resist armed attack. The program has involved a large-scale pooling of resources for defense and a concerting of defense policies in the use of those resources. The American contribution has been heavy.

The second program was enunciated by President Truman as Point Four in his State of the Union message in 1949. He called for "a bold new program for making the benefits of our scientific advances and industrial progress available for the improvement and growth of underdeveloped areas." Truman left the political objectives of such a program unexpressed, specifying only that it be implemented to help "free" and "peace-loving" peoples, but it was quickly classified, like the ERP, as designed to reduce susceptibility to the appeals of communism. In comparison with the ERP and the military aid programs, the Point Four program has been conducted on a relatively small scale. In the mid-1950's, however, after the Soviet Union had entered the picture as a serious contender for the favor of the peoples of the Middle East and South Asia, the program seemed likely to be given somewhat greater emphasis; it appeared possible that Moscow and Washington would engage in a competitive struggle for support in this region, each side using propaganda and economic measures as its major weapons.

5. *The question of discrimination and conditions.* Adopted mainly to serve American political purposes (i.e., to bring about developments which would affect the distribution of power favorably or to forestall developments which would affect it unfavorably), American aid programs are conducted on a discriminatory and conditional basis. They are discriminatory in that aid goes only to friends and allies and, more broadly, to states which do not seem to be irrevocably unfriendly or hostile. The greatest amount of aid has gone to those countries which are committed to the United States and which are most important militarily and strategically; lesser amounts have gone to others, and none to the Soviet Union or to states aligned definitely with it. Yugoslavia received aid only after its break with the Soviet Union in 1948, and talk of aid to Poland occurred only after hope developed in 1956 that it might be detached from the Soviet camp. The discriminatory policy no doubt has had some effect in winning or keeping friends. Thus, voters in the 1948 elections in

Italy were no doubt influenced by the American announcement that, if the Communists won, American aid would be withdrawn.

The most notable condition of American aid concerns the shipment of strategic materials to the Soviet orbit. To be eligible for economic and military aid, receiving countries must adopt embargo and other control measures similar to those enforced by the United States. Other conditions are sometimes attached on an *ad hoc* basis to influence the action of receiving countries with regard to specific international issues. Thus ERP funds for the East Indies were once blocked in an effort to influence Dutch policy, and aid to Israel under the Mutual Security Program was once suspended in an effort to induce Israel to obey an order of the United Nations Truce Supervisor. Some conditions under which American aid is extended relate to domestic policies—mainly fiscal and commercial policies—in the receiving countries, and there is basis, at least, for exerting informal pressures on behalf of political reform.[8] Nevertheless considerable circumspection is required in efforts to influence domestic policies. Recipient states, like others, are jealous of their independence and sensitive about intervention in their affairs. If objectionable conditions were attached to aid, or if objectionable pressures were exerted they themselves might withdraw from the program; they would thus lose its benefits, but the United States would then have failed to promote its own paramount objective. The extent to which measures of economic warfare can serve to promote the achievement of secondary objectives is thus limited.

Expansion or Curtailment of Trade

Direct control over the flow of trade is also often used as a weapon in economic warfare. It was largely through such control that the founders of the League of Nations hoped to provide "collective security," a concept which will be discussed below. Article 16 of the Covenant of the League obliged all members to cut off all trade and financial relations with any member which resorted to war in violation of the Covenant. The hope was that no state would dare resort to war in the face of such a threat or that, isolated economically, it would be unable to win. The fate of this provision of the Covenant will be discussed later. Members interpreted the article so as to minimize their obligations under it. In several circumstances where they might have applied it, they failed to do so. And in the one situation where implementation was attempted, after the Italian invasion of Ethiopia in 1935, only half-measures were adopted, and they proved insufficient to defeat the aggression. The crucial element in the explanation is that economic warfare involves costs and risks. A state which cuts off trade and financial relations with an-

[8] Raymond F. Mikesell, *United States Economic Policy and International Relations* (New York, McGraw-Hill, 1952), pp. 264-268.

other loses something itself. Moreover, it risks retaliation, perhaps in the form of a military attack. The members of the League were unwilling to accept the costs and face the risks which a broader interpretation and a more sweeping application of Article 16 would have involved. Whether bolder policies in the economic field would have deterred or defeated such aggressions as the one launched by Italy, without involving League members in military conflict, will never be known. Experience in the United Nations may provide an answer in future cases, for the United Nations Charter permits action along the same lines as that called for by Article 16 of the Covenant.

Quite aside from a general application of economic sanctions, individual states or groups of states may expand or curtail trade with others as an aspect of economic warfare. In 1940 the United States enacted an Export Control Act under which the President was empowered to license the exportation of strategic materials, and the President then exercised that power to restrict exports to the Axis powers and to channel them to countries which he wished to strengthen.[9] In 1941 he froze Japanese assets in the United States, which precluded further Japanese purchases of any kind. Since World War II, the United States has resumed the practice of regulating the exportation of strategic goods, prohibiting or restricting shipments to unfriendly states and facilitating shipments to friends; further, as we have seen, it has insisted that countries receiving economic and military aid adopt similar policies. Offshore procurement under the European Recovery Program was a way of expanding the foreign trade, and therefore contributing to the economic well-being, of the countries in which the purchases were made.

Nazi Germany secured considerable influence over various governments in southeastern Europe, which in the 1930's faced serious economic problems; plagued by unemployment and overproduction, these governments desperately needed a foreign market and became politically dependent upon Germany in some degree when it provided the market. One of the fears connected with Japan's position since the Communists came to power in China is that a large-scale resumption of Sino-Japanese trade would render Japan vulnerable to Chinese pressures. In Soviet foreign policy economic weapons have so far played a relatively minor role, but economic progress in the Soviet Union makes it ever more possible that by expanding or curtailing its purchases and sales in a given country it may be able to secure considerable influence. In 1955, for example, it attempted to cultivate Burmese friendship by promising to buy rice which Burma could not sell advantageously elsewhere.

A final and rather unusual illustration of possibilities in connection with the expansion or curtailment of trade can be found in events following

[9] *Ibid.*, pp. 102-105.

the nationalization of the Anglo-Iranian Oil Co. in 1951. Actually, Iran's own policies, especially the expulsion of British administrative and technical personnel, doomed the nationalized company to relatively unprofitable operations for some time to come. Even had this not occurred, however, the British government, the Anglo-Iranian Oil Co., and other oil concerns were in a position to accomplish the same result. To make operations profitable, Iran had to sell most of its oil and oil products abroad. How could they be shipped? The oil tankers were under the control of the Anglo-Iranian and other foreign oil concerns, which had no desire to assist Iran. Moreover, the British government took the view that the act of nationalization was illegal, and that the oil products remained the property of the Anglo-Iranian Oil Co.; thus these products were liable to seizure if brought into British ports or into the ports of other countries willing to take the British view. The result was that Iran could not market such oil as it was able to produce, and the Iranian government was deprived of what had been a very important source of revenue.[10]

Fifth Columns

The Soviet Union has been able to use fifth columns as a means of bringing economic pressure to bear against other governments for political purposes. The outstanding example came in connection with Soviet efforts to defeat the European Recovery Program, above all in France. Strikes were the means employed. Communists loyal to Moscow led a large proportion of the French trade unions, and in the fall of 1947 they took advantage of their positions to call strikes wherever they could. For some weeks they came close to paralyzing the whole French economy, but the French government stood firm, and the workers were unable or unwilling to stay out on strike indefinitely. Though imposing losses on France greater than the value of many months of American aid, the strike movement did not compel a withdrawal from the ERP, nor did it bring the Communists to power in Paris. Later efforts of the French Communists to induce longshoremen to refuse to unload ships carrying military aid to France had even less success. Nevertheless, though the Soviet Union never achieved complete success in its use of strikes as a weapon of diplomacy, the effort and the possibility are noteworthy.

Facilitating and Limiting Conditions

To engage in economic warfare, a state must obviously control something of value to one or more other states. The control may be over resources which another state wants, or it may be over markets in which the other state can sell its goods and services. The ideal for the state

[10] George Lenczowski, "Iran's Deepening Crisis," *Current History*, Vol. 24 (April, 1953), pp. 230-236; Harlan Cleveland, "Oil, Blood, and Politics: Our Next Move in Iran," *Reporter*, Vol. 9 (November 10, 1953), pp. 11-19.

engaged in economic warfare is to have exclusive control over resources and markets vitally important to another state. The ideal, of course, is rarely if ever achieved in practice.

The other principal condition permitting and limiting warfare by economic action is a willingness and an ability to suffer the costs and accept the risks involved. Costs and risks are sometimes minimal, as when money is loaned or when goods and services are bought or sold on a normal commercial basis. Gifts, however, are obviously costly, at least on a short-term basis; few governments are both able and willing to impose substantial sacrifices on people under their jurisdiction in order to make gifts possible. The imposition of economic penalties is also often costly to the state which imposes them, since it forgoes the advantages of normal trade. Moreover, there is risk of untold additional cost should the target country retaliate.

Military retaliation, that is, resort to war, is the most serious of the possibilities. The likelihood that it will occur varies with (1) the extent to which the economic penalties threaten interests of the target country, (2) the importance which it attaches to those interests, and (3) the relative power position of the two sides. The greater the threat, the more important the interest threatened, and the greater the relative power of the target country, the more likely is it that military retaliation will occur. If it occurs, the economic penalties have obviously not served as a substitute for war.

The Italo-Ethiopian case provides an illustration of the problem. As already indicated, the economic penalties (constituting sanctions) which the League members imposed on Italy were relatively mild. There was discussion, however, of more severe measures, especially the imposition of an oil embargo. Dependent on foreign sources of oil, Mussolini might have been defeated by such an embargo, and, if defeated, it is possible that he and his government might have been overthrown. In other words, an oil embargo would have been a serious threat to vital interests. Alive to the danger, Mussolini let it be known that if an oil sanction were imposed he would attack the British Mediterranean fleet, forcing Britain and presumably other League members into war.[11] In the end, they proved unwilling to accept this risk. In the eyes of the British Prime Minister, Stanley Baldwin, the experience confirmed an observation which he had made earlier, "that there is no such thing as an [economic] sanction which will work and which does not mean war." It supplied evidence to support Carr's view that [12] "economic power is impotent if the military weapon is not held in readiness to support it."

[11] Arnold J. Toynbee, *Survey of International Affairs,* 1935, Vol. II, *Abyssinia and Italy* (London, Oxford, 1936), p. 292.
[12] E. H. Carr, *The Twenty Years' Crisis 1919-1939* (London, Macmillan, New York, St. Martin's, 1949), p. 119.

It might be pointed out that there was no possibility for Mussolini to get what he wanted from Ethiopia either through the dissemination of education, information, and propaganda or through economic blandishments and penalties. The same would be true in relation to many of history's wars. Many of the purposes for which states have fought, and many of the situations in which they have fought, have precluded the effective use of substitutes. It may be that the development of nuclear and other weapons of mass destruction will lead statesmen to ask themselves more seriously than in the past whether the purposes they are pursuing justify a war. Even if they conclude that war is justifiable, they may seek more persistently than ever before to accomplish their purposes without it; at times they may be able to do it by resorting to one or both of the methods discussed in this chapter. There is no prospect, however, that these substitute methods will work in promoting all the purposes for which war might be fought in all the situations in which it might occur.

SUGGESTED READINGS

ALMOND, Gabriel A., *The Appeals of Communism* (Princeton, Princeton University Press, 1954).

BINGHAM, Jonathan B., *Shirt-Sleeve Diplomacy: Point 4 in Action* (New York, Day, 1954).

BOWLES, Chester, *The New Dimensions of Peace* (New York, Harper, 1955).

BRAINARD, Harry G., *International Economics and Public Policy* (New York, Holt, 1954).

BROWN, William Adams, and OPIE, Redvers, *American Foreign Assistance* (Washington, Brookings, 1953).

BARGHOORN, Frederick C., "The Ideological Weapon in Soviet Strategy," in HAINES, C. Grove, ed., *The Threat of Soviet Imperialism* (Baltimore, Johns Hopkins Press, 1954).

CARR, E. H., *The Twenty Years' Crisis 1919-1939* (London, Macmillan, New York, St. Martin's, 1949).

GORDON, David L., and DANGERFIELD, Royden, *The Hidden Weapon* (New York, Harper, 1947).

MIKESELL, Raymond F., *United States Economic Policy and International Relations* (New York, McGraw-Hill, 1952).

PRICE, Harry Bayard, *The Marshall Plan and Its Meaning* (Ithaca, Cornell University Press, 1955).

STEPHENS, Oren, *Facts to a Candid World* (Stanford, Stanford University Press, 1955).

THORP, Willard, *Trade, Aid, or What?* (Baltimore, Johns Hopkins Press, 1954).

CHAPTER 18

International Organization for Peace and Security

AT VARIOUS POINTS we have already referred to the League of Nations and the United Nations, and to some of the hopes and possibilities of achieving peace and security through them. The League of Nations was, and the United Nations is, based on the hope that somehow through international organization states may be able to accomplish the peaceful settlement of their disputes and peaceful change in their rights; even if this should be impossible, the hope has been that through international organization resort to war can be deterred or aggression defeated.

Enough has been said in preceding chapters to suggest that it is questionable whether such hopes can be realized, but the importance of the two organizations entitles them to more coherent analysis than they have so far been given, and the urgency of the problem of war dictates investigation of every possible solution.

There will be no effort here to deal with all aspects of the two organizations. Some—especially efforts through international organization to promote human welfare in ways having little immediate bearing on the problems of war and peace—will be discussed in the following chapter. Here the focus will be on provisions in the League Covenant and the United Nations Charter for (a) peaceful settlement and peaceful change, and (b) collective security.

These terms are plagued with ambiguity. It is not always clear when settlement or change is "peaceful," for the threat of violence frequently lies in the background, and sometimes "peaceful" action is possible only because of some prior use of violence—as when the United States secured the right to construct the Panama Canal. The terms *settlement* and *change* are sometimes used interchangeably. The definition of "peaceful change" offered in Chapter 2 (p. 18) could serve equally as a definition

356

of "peaceful settlement." Yet, though settlement may involve change, it does not always require it. Settlement may involve simply a clarification of existing rights, whereas change necessarily involves the acquisition of a new right by one state and, perhaps, its loss by another. Settlement may, and often does, occur through judicial processes; change is normally sought through legislative or executive action. Settlement is reached by more or less voluntary agreement between the disputing states (perhaps aided by third parties); change connotes action likely to be opposed in some manner by the state(s) adversely affected.[1]

The term *collective security* has too many possible meanings to permit an elaboration of them. Broadly speaking, it denotes a system in which a number of states join in collective efforts to promote each other's individual security against aggression. More specific meanings will appear as we analyze the Covenant and Charter.

THE LEAGUE OF NATIONS: STRUCTURE AND POWERS

The League of Nations was established "in order to promote international cooperation and to achieve international peace and security." Sixty-two members joined the League, though the total membership was never that high at any one time. The United States was the only major power which did not join. The principal organs of the League were the Council, the Assembly, and the Secretariat. The great powers that were members of the League had permanent seats on the Council, and other members were elected from time to time by the Assembly; through the years the total number of states represented on the Council at any one time varied from eight to fifteen. All members were entitled to representation in the Assembly. In each body, members had one vote and, with certain exceptions, the unanimity rule prevailed. The Assembly normally met once a year, and the Council at three- or four-month intervals. The Secretariat was the League's civil service, consisting of up to 800 permanent employees drawn from all over the world.

The Covenant contained several articles dealing with peaceful settlement. In the event of "any dispute likely to lead to a rupture," the members obliged themselves to submit the matter either to arbitration or judicial settlement or to inquiry by the Council. They bound themselves "to carry out in full good faith" any award or decision made by an arbitral tribunal or a court. If a dispute went to the Council, it was to make a report. If the report was agreed to by all members other than one or more of the parties to the dispute, the members agreed not to go to war against

---

[1] Frederick Sherwood Dunn, *Peaceful Change* (New York, Council on Foreign Relations, 1937), pp. 2-3; C. R. M. F. Cruttwell, *A History of Peaceful Change in the Modern World* (New York, Oxford, 1937).

any party which complied with the recommendations of the report. If the report was not endorsed by all Council members other than the parties, war might legally occur, except that all members were bound "in no case to resort to war until three months after the arbitral award, and judicial decision, or the report by the Council." Thus there were provisions both for peaceful settlement and for a "cooling off" period after the conclusion of efforts to reach a peaceful settlement.

We have already noted in Chapter 15 that the Covenant included a provision for peaceful change, permitting the Assembly to "advise the reconsideration . . . of treaties which have become inapplicable and the consideration of international conditions whose continuance might endanger the peace of the world."

Article 11 of the Covenant related potentially both to peaceful settlement and peaceful change, on the one hand, and to collective security on the other. It specified that:

> Any war or threat of war . . . is hereby declared a matter of concern to the whole League, and the League shall take any action that may be deemed wise and effectual to safeguard the peace of nations.

Given this right to take "any action . . . deemed wise and effectual," the League theoretically faced very few limits in what it could do either to ward off a threat of war or to repress aggression.

Articles 10 and 16, providing for sanctions, are generally regarded as the heart of the League's collective security system. In Article 10 the members undertook "to respect and preserve as against external aggression the territorial integrity and the existing political independence" of all other members. Article 16 specified that a "resort to war" by a member would be deemed an act of war against all members. All members then undertook "immediately" to cut off "all" commercial relationships between the guilty state and the rest of the world. Moreover, the Council was to recommend "what effective military, naval, or air force" the members were to contribute to the armed forces to be used to protect the Covenant of the League.

A HYPOTHETICAL "MAXIMALIST" INTERPRETATION OF THE PROVISIONS FOR COLLECTIVE SECURITY

Although the Covenant was generally said to provide for a system of collective security, no one could quite tell from the words precisely what collective security meant. Like the words in the American Constitution, those in the Covenant were subject to interpretation. Suppose that they had been given a "maximalist" interpretation, that is, an interpretation making for the strongest and most effective system of collective security permitted by the Covenant. What would have been the characteristics of such a system?

The Characteristics of Maximalist Collective Security

Consider some of the terms of the Covenant quoted above. Article 11 specified that a threat of war came within the cognizance of the League. Theoretically, the members might have interpreted this article to permit the issuance of something analogous to injunctions, perhaps requiring a state to put a halt to a program of action which increased the danger of war. Article 10 required members to "respect" each other's territorial integrity and political independence; even more, it required them to "preserve" each other against external aggression. The word *preserve* could have been interpreted to require all members to resort to any necessary extremity, including all-out war, to save a victim of aggression. The inviolability of all frontiers throughout the world might have become as precious to each member as the inviolability of its own frontiers. Article 16 embodied the principle that war against one was an act of war against all. It might have been interpreted to require all members, if war occurred, to place themselves in a state of war with the aggressor and to act at once to isolate the aggressor economically; moreover, as under Article 10, they might have regarded themselves as bound to bring their full military power to bear in order to defeat the aggression. Under a maximalist interpretation of Articles 10 and 16, a state contemplating aggression would have faced the sure prospect of struggle not simply with one victim but with all League members, which would have thrown in all their resources and fought to exhaustion if need be.[2]

Maximalist Collective Security and the Balance of Power

How would a maximalist system of collective security have differed from the traditional balance-of-power system? Several distinctions are clearly discernible.

Most obviously, a state pursuing a balance-of-power policy seeks at most to organize selected states into an alliance arrangement against one or more other states. A division of states into more or less hostile camps is assumed. Though balance may not mean equilibrium, as we have seen, the usual expectation is that a distribution of power will exist which leaves each side short of overwhelming preponderance. But a maximalist collective security system can aim to include all states, as the League in fact did. If all or almost all states join, the clear possibility exists that they will be able to confront any aggressor with an overwhelming preponderance of power.

Closely related to the above distinction is another: that in a balance-of-power system there is an obligation to act only against one or more enemies, which have been more or less specifically identified in advance,

2 Cf. Howard C. Johnson and Gerhart Niemeyer, "Collective Security: The Validity of an Ideal," *International Organization*, Vol. 8 (February, 1954), pp. 19-35.

whereas in a maximalist collective security system there is an obligation to act against any state which commits aggression. Put in other words, states joined in a balance-of-power arrangement agree to defend certain selected frontiers, whereas states joined in a maximalist collective security system agree to defend all frontiers of all members throughout the world. In the one case the obligation is more limited, and advance planning can occur for the coordination of defense measures; in the other the obligation is virtually unlimited, and, since the potential aggressor is unknown, advance planning of common defense measures is practically impossible.

Further, a balance-of-power system permits neutrality and the localization of war; a maximalist collective security system precludes neutrality on the part of members and requires that all take action against the aggressor.

An important difference in underlying assumptions is inherent in the above. The state seeking a balance of power through alliance arrangements assumes that it has vital interests in common with selected states, but not with all states; in fact, it may seek safety at the expense of the territorial integrity or political independence of some states. There is no assumption that an integrated society exists in which each member is obliged to help protect the rights of all. Such an assumption is, however, fundamental to a maximalist system of collective security.

Obstacles to the Acceptance of a Maximalist Interpretation

Many hoped that the Covenant would be interpreted in a maximalist fashion. They wanted states to abandon narrow conceptions of self-interest as a guide to policy and to regard themselves as units in a world society having an interest in preserving law and order everywhere. They wanted states to accept the view that there was a common vital interest in repressing an illegal resort to war, just as, within countries, there is said to be a common vital interest in repressing crime. If one state illegally attacked another, they saw no more basis for neutrality than when one individual murders or robs another. They wanted to eliminate the balance-of-power system. The hope was that, if a potential aggressor knew in advance that resort to war would lead all other units in the world society to spring to arms, aggression would not occur, or, if it did occur, it would be defeated.

1. The absence of a sense of membership in a united world society. There were, however, serious obstacles to an interpretation of the Covenant conforming to the maximalist conception of collective security. The basic one was that states really did not regard themselves as members of one society having a common vital interest in protecting and preserving each other's rights. Did it really matter much to Japan if Paraguay and Bolivia destroyed each other in war? Was it vital to Chile that Bulgaria should not attack Rumania, or that the attack should be defeated? Within countries, analogous questions are answered in the affirmative; all citizens are said to have a vital interest in supporting the system of law enforcement. But the sovereign states which interpreted the League Covenant were not willing to give affirmative answers, nor are the sovereign states of today willing to do so. They were willing to "preserve" selected states and to defend selected frontiers, but the principle of "one for all and all for one" did not commend itself.

2. *The costs and risks of collective security.* Another obstacle to a maximalist interpretation of the League Covenant's provisions for collective security was that the problem of enforcing peace is far greater among countries than among individuals within countries. Governments can enforce law against individuals with little fear. Except in very unusual circumstances, the worst that may happen is that a robber will shoot a policeman. The individual lawbreaker is so nearly helpless in the face of the might which government commands that he must perforce adopt hit-and-run tactics, depending on surprise and concealment; he cannot resist the government in an open, frontal fashion. Moreover, the government, through the tax structure and otherwise, can see to it not only that citizens share the costs and burdens of law enforcement but that they do it on what is considered an equitable basis; the costs and burdens do not become unduly heavy for anyone.

Internationally, however, the situation is quite different. Disparities of power are much greater. Theoretically, it might be easy for a world society to defeat aggression by a small power like Denmark, but what if one of the great powers turns aggressor? Repression of the aggression of the Central Powers after 1914 and of the Axis powers after 1939 might have been called a police action in each case, but the police actions would have been world wars nevertheless. If a substantial proportion of the total military might of the world is concentrated in any one state, and if that state turns aggressor, the repression of aggression becomes an extremely costly and hazardous undertaking to which other states are understandably loath to commit themselves in advance. It is one thing for a government to enforce law against a relatively helpless individual, and another thing for a League of Nations to try to enforce the law against a state which may be almost as strong as the rest of the world combined. The expectation that a world society united against any aggressor member would always command an overwhelming preponderance of power is not necessarily valid.

3. *Probable inequities in sharing costs and risks.* Further, there can be no real assurance that the costs and burdens would be shared equitably and without undue hardship to individual units. The criteria for determining equity themselves are vague, and even a maximalist interpretation of the League Covenant would not have provided a reliable method either of fixing the criteria or of applying them. Moreover, even if the

requirements of equity were determined, there is no real assurance that states, being sovereign, would actually contribute to enforcement measures in conformity with them. In any event, a weak state adjacent to a great power aggressor would be especially exposed to retaliation if it joined in enforcement measures.

4. *Recognition of the need for change.* Another problem in a maximalist interpretation of the concept of collective security is the reconciliation of security with change. Within countries, governments do not try to enforce unchanging law. Rather, they combine executive power for the enforcement of law with legislative power to change the law, and, as we saw in Chapter 2, timely adjustments in the law may well contribute as much to the preservation of domestic peace as does provision for enforcement action. Those who drafted the Covenant, however, quite deliberately refrained from making effective provision for peaceful change. (See the discussion in Chapter 15.) They were too concerned for their own sovereignty and for their own territorial and other rights to be willing to give legislative power to an international agency. But though they were unwilling to provide for change, they knew that it was inevitable and often desirable. How, then, could they agree to a maximalist conception of collective security which seemed to require a freezing of the status quo?

5. *Defense and ancillary ambitions.* Still another difficulty with a maximalist system of collective security stems from the fact that states which go to war to defend themselves or others against aggression often either have or develop ancillary ambitions. Given a loose and flexible system, states can take such actual or potential ambitions into account in deciding whether or not joint action against aggression should occur, but a maximalist system would not permit choice.

This consideration can easily be illustrated by reference to the contemporary scene. Suppose, for example, that Pakistan should attack India, and suppose that the Soviet Union were quite willing to send the Red Army through Afghanistan and Iran into Pakistan in the name of collective security. Judging by communist principles and by the record of the Soviet Union after World War II, it seems likely that Moscow would not confine itself to an effort to defeat an aggressor but would attempt to satisfy an ancillary ambition: the establishment of communist control over areas that the Red Army enters. The same kind of possibility would exist for the Soviet Union if France should attack Germany, or if Western Germany should attack the Communist regime in Eastern Germany. Had the United Nations authorized the Soviet Union to go to the defense of Egypt in 1956, the imposition of communist or pro-Soviet control over one or more of the Middle Eastern states would have been a likely consequence. Similarly, if Bulgaria should attack Yugoslavia, the United States might be willing, in the name of collective security, to take action against the aggressor, but there is a question whether resistance to aggression would be kept separate from the ancillary ambition of liberating a Soviet satellite.

Under a maximalist system of collective security, the United States would presumably be obliged to accept and endorse Soviet action against aggression by Pakistan, and the Soviet Union would presumably be obliged to accept and endorse American action against aggression by Bulgaria. For this reason the United States and the Soviet Union, each fearing the ancillary ambitions of the other, can scarcely favor maximalist collective security. Maximalist collective security, being ideologically blind, is hardly acceptable to states engaged in ideological struggle.

Another aspect of the same point was illustrated in the Korean war. Suppose for the moment that the official objective of various powers, including the United States, was to "preserve" South Korea. South Korea wanted to be preserved, of course, but at the same time it wanted to expand—to absorb the territory of the aggressor. How could military action designed to defeat aggression be distinguished from military action designed to extinguish the aggressor government and absorb its territory? In fact, the two objectives were not disentangled until after the intervention of the Chinese Communists rendered the unification of Korea impossible.[3]

Similar problems seem likely to attend every effort to implement maximalist conceptions of collective security. Action taken primarily to resist aggression is also likely to serve other purposes. "It is one of the fallacies of the theory of collective security that war can be waged for the specific and disinterested purpose of 'resisting aggression.'"[4] Where those supporting the principle of collective security are agreed not only on the main objective but also on all other objectives, the problem is a minor one, but this is rare. As a general rule, there is disagreement over ancillary ambitions and objectives. This constitutes a serious obstacle to the acceptance of the relatively inflexible concept of maximalist collective security. In fact, it constitutes a problem whenever principles of collective security are applied.

All these difficulties connected with the maximalist system of collective security suggest that, even if one were established, it could not be relied upon. States would still have to depend for their security on their own power and on alliances; in other words, balance-of-power arrangements would have to exist side by side with collective security arrangements. This would involve still further difficulties, for the requirements of a balance-of-power policy are not always compatible with the requirements

[3] Leland M. Goodrich, "Korea: Collective Measures Against Aggression," *International Conciliation*, No. 494, October, 1953.

[4] E. H. Carr, *The Twenty Years' Crisis 1919-1939* (London, Macmillan, New York, St. Martin's, 1949), p. 113.

of collective security. And there would be danger that the pursuit of incompatible principles would prevent either one from being followed successfully.

ACTUAL INTERPRETATIONS AND APPLICATIONS OF PROVISIONS FOR COLLECTIVE SECURITY

Not all these considerations were advanced in the debates which occurred during the early days of the League over the interpretations to be given to the Covenant. Some of them were, and the result was that the system of collective security which emerged was much weaker than it might theoretically have been.[5] Even before the League's debates, the United States had already given the idea of a strong collective security system a blow by refusing to join in one at all; the American decision was the result of complex forces, but among them was the belief, held especially by some Senators, that Article 10 might involve the country in unnecessary risks and sacrifices. On the one hand, they felt that the United States was reasonably secure, with little to gain from a guarantee that others would "preserve" its territorial integrity and political independence. On the other hand, they saw that if this country joined in extending such a guarantee to others the potential costs in American life and treasure might be enormous.

The refusal of the United States to share the potential burdens of League membership meant that, if these burdens were assumed at all, they would be all the greater for those who undertook them. Moreover, there was the possibility that, if the League members ever attempted to isolate an aggressor economically, as Article 16 seemed to require, the United States might object to the interruption of its trade. Canada considered itself to be in a particularly difficult position, for it did not want to be involved in an effort to enforce collective security against the opposition of the United States.

The Attack on Article 10

The first meetings of the Assembly, therefore, witnessed successful efforts to give certain articles of the Covenant a minimalist interpretation. In truth, Canada proposed flatly that Article 10 be deleted from the Covenant. Failing to secure acceptance of this proposal, Canada sought an interpretation of Article 10 which would free it from an obligation to send troops abroad in the event of aggression. Prolonged negotiations and debates led to the development of a formula in which it was declared to be the right of each member to decide for itself in what degree it was

[5] The discussion which follows is based largely on William E. Rappard, *The Quest for Peace Since the World War* (Cambridge, Harvard University Press, 1940), esp. pp. 208-334.

bound to assure the execution of the obligation of Article 10 by the employment of its military forces; the formula made it clear that the Council had no more than an advisory role in connection with the implementation of Article 10, and enjoined the Council in making its recommendations "to take account ... of the geographical situation and of the special conditions of each State."

Superficially, the formula left the obligation of Article 10 intact—all the more so since it technically failed of adoption in the Assembly because of a single negative vote cast by Persia. Nevertheless, the spirit of the debate and of the formula itself demonstrated that many members had little enthusiasm for Article 10. This made it questionable whether, if a test came, the League members would in fact "preserve" a state which had been attacked.

The Interpretation of Article 16

A similar fate befell Article 16. It was to be implemented if any member resorted to war in violation of the Covenant. Who was to decide which acts constituted "war" and whether a resort to war had actually occurred? Some commentators initially took it for granted that the Council would decide these questions, and that its decisions would be binding upon all members. But some members demurred, with the result that the Assembly adopted an interpretation similar to the one already mentioned in connection with Article 10: each member was to satisfy itself that a resort to war had actually occurred, and only then would it be bound to act under Article 16. The interpretation emphasized something which the retention of the principle of state sovereignty made inevitable in any event: that there would be no real assurance of united action.

Moreover, the provision of Article 16 that a resort to war against any member would constitute an act of war against all members was interpreted so as to prevent the latter from being plunged automatically into a state of war; they became entitled to declare themselves at war with the aggressor if they chose to do so, but the spirit of the League was said to call for the avoidance of war and the restoration of peace by economic pressure.

Further, the requirement of an *immediate* severance of *all* commercial and financial relations between the aggressor and other states was interpreted to mean something other than the words clearly seemed to say. Under the interpretation, action was to be considered "immediate" if it occurred on the date recommended by the Council. "All" commercial relationships were not necessarily to be severed, but only certain kinds of relationships; if the initial economic sanctions did not bring the aggressor to book, measures of increasing stringency could be taken, but the cutting off of the food supplies of the civil population of the defaulting state was to be regarded as an extremely drastic measure which would only be applied if other measures were clearly inadequate. Moreover, some states (presumably those especially vulnerable to retaliation) might be excused in whole or in part from applying economic sanctions.

The Resulting Uncertainty

Thus the United States and a number of League members refused to accept the view that aggression anywhere would necessarily threaten their own interests so seriously that they should bind themselves in advance to take drastic action against the aggressor. They refused to create a world society which could require its members to take effective joint action against law violators. The League members preferred a rather loose and flexible arrangement by which they would be free to act against aggression in the name of law and noble principle but by which their concrete obligations would be minimal. This meant that the world might or might not array itself against an aggressor. Members could comfort themselves that their membership need not turn out to be burdensome and dangerous. Aggressors could hope that they would not meet the overwhelming power of a united League if they resorted to war. At the same time, states fearing for their security were forewarned that they could not rely upon the League but would have to assure themselves so far as possible through their own measures of defense and through alliances. Arrangements to establish and maintain a balance of power remained necessary, yet even the weak interpretation of the Covenant left members under some obligations which were incompatible with a free application of balance-of-power principles.

The Record of Collective Security Under the League

Actual developments in the period of the League conformed generally to expectations based on these early interpretations of the Covenant. No one can say what wars might have occurred in the absence of the League, but there is no reason to think that it prevented any, save perhaps one, where two small states (Greece and Bulgaria) resorted to hostilities and and where there seemed to be a possibility that France and Britain might support League action vigorously. In this case the request of the President of the Council for a cease-fire was honored. On the other hand, Italy bombarded the Greek island of Corfu, and Poland seized the city of Vilna, each with impunity so far as the League was concerned. When Japan attacked in Manchuria in 1931, the agreement in the League was to regard the action as a measure of reprisal rather than as a resort to war. Article 16 was therefore not applied at all, and there was no serious effort through the League to "preserve" China's territorial integrity in accordance with Article 10. China was remote from the leading League powers, and they did not regard its fate as of vital concern to them.

When Italy attacked Ethiopia in 1935, most of the members of the

League acknowledged that a resort to war in violation of the Covenant had occurred. However, they did not take the view that this had plunged them into war with Italy, nor did they make a very serious effort to preserve Ethiopia's territorial integrity and independence. They were more concerned about the possibility of German aggression in Europe than with the fact of Italian aggression in Africa. They hoped to retain Italy's help in a balance-of-power arrangement against Germany, and therefore hesitated to act vigorously in implementing principles of collective security on behalf of Ethiopia. At the worst, Italy would not become more dangerous to them simply because of the conquest of a remote and backward African state; it might even become less dangerous, for the African territory would, in a sense, be a hostage at Britain's mercy, subject to seizure if Italy behaved badly in the future. The result was the adoption of some mild economic sanctions against Italy, discussed in the preceding chapter. The sanctions irritated Italy and drove it out of the balance-of-power alignment against Germany, but they did not save Ethiopia. The League members fell between two stools when faced with the dilemma of choosing between the principle of balancing power and the principle of collective security as a guide to their conduct.

This episode, plus the fact that military intervention by Mussolini and Hitler in the so-called Civil War in Spain was not declared to be a violation of the Covenant, sounded the death knell of the League of Nations. A number of members expressed the view publicly that, though the Covenant still permitted them to attempt to enforce peace and repress aggression if they chose, the provisions calling for the application of sanctions had acquired a non-obligatory character. When Hitler seized Austria and Czechoslovakia in 1938 and 1939, no member of the League chose to invoke the Covenant. Neither was there League action against Hitler for the attack upon Poland which started World War II. States which had failed to apply the Covenant faithfully when others were attacked were stopped from appealing to it when they themselves became victims of aggression. Those who were permitting the organization to die pumped enough life back into it to bring about the expulsion of the Soviet Union from membership after its attack upon Finland in the fall of 1939, but that was all. Formally, the League lingered on through World War II, playing no role in the great political events of the period, only to be dissolved after the establishment of the United Nations.

THE UNITED NATIONS:
PURPOSES, STRUCTURE, AND POWERS

The failure of the members to make the League of Nations an effective instrument of collective security, even in a minimalist sense, did not lead them to abandon the idea that an international organization was needed and that it might be made useful. They therefore established another in 1945, even before World War II was over.

Purposes

The purposes of the United Nations are similar to the purposes of the League. The first purpose listed in the Charter, and the one with which we are primarily concerned in this chapter, is: [6]

To maintain international peace and security, and to that end: to take effective collective measures for the prevention and removal of threats to the peace, and for the suppression of acts of aggression or other breaches of the peace, and to bring about by peaceful means, and in conformity with the principles of justice and international law, adjustment or settlement of international disputes or situations which might lead to a breach of the peace.

"The Organization is based on the principle of the sovereign equality of all its Members." Members bind themselves to "settle their international disputes by peaceful means in such a manner that international peace and security, and justice, are not endangered." They pledge themselves to "refrain in their international relations from the threat or use of force against the territorial integrity or political independence of any state. . . ."

Eighty political entities have subscribed to the above purposes and pledges by joining the United Nations. Switzerland and several divided states (Germany, Korea, and Vietnam) are the principal non-members.

The Principal Organs

Like the League of Nations, the United Nations has a General Assembly, a Security Council, and a Secretariat; in addition, several other agencies are formally declared to be "principal organs": the Economic and Social Council, the Trusteeship Council, and the International Court of Justice. All members of the United Nations are entitled to representation in the General Assembly. The Charter specifies that the Security Council shall consist of eleven members. Five are named in the Charter as permanent members (China, France, the U.S.S.R., the United Kingdom, and the United States), and the other six are elected for two-year terms by the General Assembly.

Powers of the Security Council

The Charter requires that the Security Council be "so organized as to be able to function continuously," and assigns it "primary responsibility for the maintenance of international peace and security." It has extensive rights to act both in the field of the pacific settlement of international disputes and in the field of enforcement action. Where a dispute exists

---

[6] The full text of the Charter will be found in the Appendix.

which might endanger international peace, the Security Council may call upon the parties to seek pacific settlement, may "recommend appropriate procedures or methods of adjustment," or may recommend terms of settlement. The Security Council is also empowered to "determine the existence of any threat to the peace, breach of the peace, or act of aggression." If it finds any such threat, breach, or act, it has wide discretionary powers. It may call upon the parties concerned to comply with provisional measures designed to prevent an aggravation of the situation, or it may apply sanctions. The sanctions "may include complete or partial interruption of economic relations and of rail, sea, air, postal, telegraphic, radio, and other means of communication, and the severance of diplomatic relations." If such measures are considered inadequate, the Security Council "may take such action by air, sea, or land forces as may be necessary to maintain or restore international peace and security." Sanctioning measures are to be applied by all United Nations members, or by some of them, as the Security Council determines. The Charter assumed that the Security Council would make special agreements with individual United Nations members by which those members would provide "armed forces, assistance, and facilities" necessary for enforcement action, but no such agreements have actually been concluded.

Voting Rules in the Security Council

The voting rules of the Security Council are of crucial importance. The Charter gives each member one vote. It sets up two categories into which questions are to be classified: "procedural" and "other"; the "other" questions are commonly referred to as "non-procedural" or "substantive." The arrangement is that decisions on procedural matters require an affirmative vote of any seven members. Decisions on substantive matters also require seven votes out of the eleven, but the seven must include the concurring votes of the permanent members; in other words, the five permanent members plus any two of the non-permanent members may make substantive decisions. The word *veto* does not appear in the Charter, but its use arises from the voting rules. Where a resolution is defeated by the negative vote of a single permanent member, it is said to have been vetoed. The question whether an issue before the Security Council is procedural or substantive is itself considered substantive. Thus a "double veto" is possible—the first negative vote of the permanent member preventing the matter from being classified as procedural, and the second preventing the adoption of the resolution. A custom has developed permitting a permanent member to abstain from voting without blocking action, and action is also not blocked if the delegate of a permanent member deliberately absents himself. When the Security Council is attempting to bring about the pacific settlement of a dispute, parties to the dispute are to abstain from voting. When it is considering enforcement action, however, all members of the Security Council may vote; thus a permanent member is free to veto enforcement action against itself or against any other state.

The General Assembly: Powers and Voting Rules

The General Assembly of the United Nations meets annually and in special sessions. It may "discuss any questions or any matters within the scope of the present Charter or relating to the powers and functions of any organs" of the United Nations. More particularly, it may "recommend measures for the peaceful adjustment of any situation, regardless of origin, which it deems likely to impair the general welfare or friendly relations among nations." There is a proviso of minor significance in the Charter which, though not curtailing the freedom of the General Assembly to discuss disputes or situations being considered by the Security Council, prohibits it from making recommendations thereon, except by special request of the Security Council.

In the General Assembly, as in the Security Council, each member has one vote. Again the Charter sets up two categories into which questions are to be classified: "important questions" and "other questions." Decisions on "important questions" can be made only by a two-thirds majority of the members present and voting, whereas decisions on "other questions" can be made by a bare majority. The Charter itself lists some questions which are to be considered important, and specifies that additional questions may be placed in this category by a bare majority; in other words, a bare majority may require that a question be so classified that a two-thirds majority is necessary for a decision.

The Right of Self-defense

It might be noted that the framers of the Charter, fearing that the members of the United Nations might not use it effectively to provide security for each other, included the following statement in Article 51: "Nothing in the present Charter shall impair the inherent right of individual and collective self-defense if an armed attack occurs against a Member...." [7]

PEACEFUL CHANGE AND PERMISSIVE ACTION FOR COLLECTIVE SECURITY

In this and in previous chapters we have already presented considerations which bear directly on the question of the meaning of the Charter and the potential significance of the United Nations. Some of these con-

[7] For a discussion of the meaning of the various articles of the United Nations Charter, see Leland M. Goodrich and Edvard Hambro, *Charter of the United Nations, Commentary and Documents* (Boston, World Peace Foundation, 1949).

siderations can now be brought into clearer focus, and others can be added.

The Use of Force and Peaceful Change

Recall that the members of the United Nations pledge themselves to "refrain in their international relations from the threat or use of force against the territorial integrity or political independence of any state." The pledge is similar to one in the League Covenant and in the Kellogg-Briand Pact. If the pledge were honored, members would be confined in their struggles with each other to such methods as those discussed in the preceding chapter, namely, to the use of propaganda, fifth columns, and economic measures. A substantial degree of collective security would automatically exist. To what extent does it exist as an actuality or as a probability?

One glance at the armed establishments and alliance systems which many of the members maintain is sufficient to indicate that they have little confidence that the pledge will be honored. Everywhere states seek to equip themselves to withstand the threat or use of force, if not actually to threaten or use force themselves. Those demanding change and those determined to protect their rights obviously do not really expect to achieve their objectives through the United Nations.

The United Nations, of course, has served, and presumably will continue to serve, as an agency which promotes the peaceful settlement of international disputes. It provides a meeting place for diplomats. It facilitates communication. It increases the possibilities that third parties will act, by suggestions and moral pressures, to bring disputing states to agreement either on terms of settlement or on procedures to be followed in arriving at such terms. On several occasions, United Nations action has served to ameliorate difficult situations, sometimes seeming to avert hostilities which apparently threatened, or inducing the suspension of hostilities once begun. So far, however, the members have not interpreted the Charter in such a way as to permit the imposition of terms of settlement on unwilling parties. Their voluntary agreement is required, and there is no guarantee that it will be forthcoming.

Neither is there any assurance that peaceful change can be accomplished through the United Nations; in fact, it is highly doubtful whether it can be. Experience in the Palestine situation, described in Chapter 15, is not encouraging. The General Assembly recommended change, but the Security Council refused to act on the suggestion that resistance to implementation of the plan should be regarded as a threat to the peace, calling for enforcement action; the General Assembly itself also refrained from recommending measures of compulsion, though such restraint may not have been required by the Charter. The recommendation of the General Assembly served not to bring about peaceful change but to give some shadow of justification to the use of violence by the party desiring the change. In practically all cases where recommendations for change are made, it is to be expected that adversely affected parties will resist, making peaceful change impossible.

Not only are recommendations unlikely to be accepted by adversely affected parties, but in connection with many demands for change they are unlikely to be made at all. A high proportion of the demands which have actually led to war in history have been demands which an international organization of sovereign states could scarcely have been expected to endorse.

The Security Council and Enforcement Action

Since dissatisfaction with various aspects of the status quo persists, and since the possibilities of peaceful settlement and peaceful change are limited, it is not to be expected that states will observe their pledge to refrain from the threat or use of force. Danger of war and war itself are sure to occur in the future, as in the past. Provisions of the Charter concerning collective security, which have already been cited, are therefore of some importance.

These provisions differ somewhat from analogous provisions of the League Covenant. The Covenant was so worded that it appeared to require members to act against an aggressor without waiting for a decision by any League organ, whereas the Charter makes it clear that an obligation to act arises only as a result of a decision by the Security Council. If the Security Council decides that action is called for, it has great leeway in determining precisely what action should occur. The Charter does not oblige members to "preserve" each other, nor does it oblige them to take any specific measures once the existence of a threat to the peace, breach of the peace, or act of aggression has been determined. The choice of measures is left to the discretion of the Security Council.

The Security Council acts, of course, only on the basis of a vote. Under the voting rules, as we have seen, any one permanent member or any five of the non-permanent members can block action. As a practical matter, then, the Charter permits action but by no means assures it. Perhaps it would be more realistic, in view of the strains and tensions in the world, especially in East-West relations, to say that effective action against an aggressor through the Security Council, though possible, is most unlikely. Obviously, each permanent member would veto enforcement action against itself. In all probability, too, each would veto enforcement action against a friend or ally. More generally, it is probable that the United States and the Soviet Union would each block any action by the Security Council which would call for the use of the armed forces of the other outside the homeland. It is difficult to think of any situation in which the communist and non-communist states would have a common interest in carrying out enforcement action through the United Nations.

True, enforcement action through the United Nations occurred after North Korea attacked South Korea in 1950. But this was possible only because the Soviet delegate at the time was boycotting the meetings of the Security Council. Had he been present, he presumably would have vetoed any action against North Korea. Moreover, the action of the United States and of other United Nations members which supported enforcement action does not necessarily reflect a commitment to resist aggression simply out of belief that the principle of collective security deserved support.

Instead of being a case of nations fighting "any aggressor anywhere" and for no other purpose than to punish aggression and to deter potential aggressors, intervention in Korea was an act of collective military defense against the recognized number-one enemy of the United States and of all the countries which associated themselves with its action.[8]

Had South Korea been the aggressor, it seems unlikely that the non-communist states in the United Nations would have endorsed enforcement action for the benefit of the Communist regime in North Korea.

The General Assembly and Enforcement Action

Anticipating that the Security Council would rarely, if ever, be able to provide for enforcement action, the United States joined with several other states in 1950 in proposing the "Uniting for Peace" resolution to the General Assembly, and it was adopted. This resolution was, in the main, an announcement that, if the Security Council should be unable to act against an aggressor because of the veto, the General Assembly itself would consider the matter with a view to recommending collective measures. The General Assembly could make such recommendations by a two-thirds vote, permitting action despite the opposition of a great power or even against a great power which had committed aggression. The possibility that the United Nations might be used as an agency for authorizing enforcement action was thus markedly increased.

It probably makes little difference that the General Assembly can only recommend enforcement action whereas the Security Council can order it. Though imposing a legal obligation, a Security Council order would, as a practical matter, leave states free to respond or not, as they saw fit. This being so, a recommendation might well be as effective (or as ineffective) as a binding decision. As a matter of fact, the Security Council itself, when it acted in the Korean case, confined itself to the making of recommendations.

[8] Arnold Wolfers, "Collective Security and the War in Korea," *Yale Review,* Vol. 43 (June, 1954), p. 492. Cf. Alexander L. George, "American Policy-Making and the North Korean Aggression," *World Politics,* Vol. 7 (January, 1955), pp. 209-232.

The Permissive Nature of the United Nations Security System

The main conclusion to be derived from this discussion is perhaps already clear. It is that the United Nations system of collective security, like the League system that finally evolved, is essentially permissive.[9] If seven members of the Security Council, including the five permanent members, want to take action in the face of a threat to the peace, breach of the peace, or act of aggression, they may do so. Similarly, if two-thirds of the members of the General Assembly want to recommend action, they may do so. Application of the Charter's provisions for collective security depends more on considerations of expediency than on adherence to principle. It depends on the way in which members of the United Nations define their interests in particular circumstances.

The fact that the United Nations system of collective security is permissive means, among other things, that the members have little assurance of United Nations support should they become victims of aggression. They must rely on their own resources and on such alliances as they find it desirable and possible to make. In no sense has the United Nations system of collective security replaced the balance-of-power system. Article 51 of the Charter, confirming "the inherent right of individual and collective self-defense," has turned out to be one of its most important provisions, assuring members, as it does, that such arrangements as those contained in the North Atlantic Treaty are permissible.

The United Nations Security System and the Balance of Power

What, then, is the relationship between the traditional concept of the balance of power and the concept of collective security as reflected in the United Nations? The answer is that the arrangements for collective security stand both as potential supplements and as potential obstacles to the pursuit of a balance of power, depending on whether the balance-of-power action is defensive or aggressive. States determined to resist aggression, for whatever reasons, may come to the United Nations for endorsement of their actions; by the same token, states which pursue balance by aggressive action may find themselves confronted by a victim whose resistance is endorsed and perhaps supported by the United Nations. To some extent, of course, this corresponds to the hopes of the exponents of the principle of collective security, but it falls short of the maximalist interpretation of the principle in that the prospect and the character of action by the United Nations are so uncertain.

If action occurs, it may have significance. The side credited with acting

[9] Ernst B. Haas, "Types of Collective Security: An Examination of Operational Concepts," *American Political Science Review,* Vol. 49 (March, 1955), pp. 47-54.

in self-defense derives a propaganda advantage, for self-defense and assistance to a state engaged in self-defense are generally regarded as virtuous. The side branded as aggressive suffers a corresponding disadvantage, for aggression is generally regarded as evil. United Nations action may have more tangible significance, too, for the Charter specifies that

All members shall give the United Nations every assistance in any action it takes in accordance with the present Charter, and shall refrain from giving assistance to any state against which the United Nations is taking preventive or enforcement action.

Presumably this obligation exists only if the action is endorsed by the Security Council and not if it occurs in harmony with a recommendation of the General Assembly, but a vote for a recommendation in the General Assembly involves at least a moral commitment.

At the same time, endorsement by the United Nations gives its members a claim to a share of influence over the political and military policies of the states that assume the primary burdens of the enforcement effort. They may urge policies designed to restrict or localize the police action. They may assume the mediator's role, trying to discover terms on the basis of which hostilities can be brought to a close.

The relationship between the concept of the balance of power and the United Nations concept of collective security is illustrated by the Korean dispute. Balance-of-power and other considerations induced the United States to go to the defense of South Korea. In effect, the Security Council was asked to endorse American action and permit it to occur in the name of the United Nations. For propaganda purposes, endorsement rendered the United States less vulnerable than it might otherwise have been to charges that it was acting out of imperialistic motivations. Practically, though the action of the Security Council did not deter the Soviet Union from giving assistance to North Korea, it did give the United States leverage in soliciting support from other United Nations members. Along with this, of course, went the fact that since the United States was acting in the name of the United Nations it was subject to pressure from United Nations members in connection with questions concerning the conduct and termination of the war. Some members, especially India, though nominally supporting the United Nations action, came to be called neutrals, and sought the adoption of policies that would bring about a restoration of peace once minimal United Nations objectives were achieved.

Action in connection with the Middle Eastern crisis of 1956 also illustrates the relationship between the balance-of-power concept and the United Nations concept of collective security. Israel, Britain, and France, presumably influenced by balance-of-power considerations, made what

they regarded as preventive attacks on Egypt. More than two-thirds of
the members of the United Nations, for whatever reasons, opposed their
action. The General Assembly called for a cease-fire and a withdrawal of
troops. Within and outside the framework of the United Nations, both
the Soviet Union and the United States brought pressure to bear against
the attacking states. Israel accomplished its minimum objectives (that is,
it defeated Egyptian forces and occupied the Sinai Peninsula) before
deterrent action could be effective, but Britain and France succumbed
to the protests and threats, accepting a cease-fire without achieving their
objectives. Temporarily, at least, a victory had been scored for the principle of collective security.

The prospects of the United Nations are highly uncertain. The organization has fundamental flaws and perhaps fatal weaknesses both in the
field of peaceful settlement and peaceful change and in the field of
collective security. Lacking real legislative and judicial authority, it can
scarcely be counted upon to settle disputes peacefully; least of all is it to
be expected to keep law adjusted to the desires of the strong. Executive
action to apply the principle of collective security can occur only if the
necessary votes are obtained and can be effective only if the individual
members choose to make it effective. Many considerations, above all
those related to the East-West struggle, make the prospects uncertain.
Neither East nor West is likely to support action through the United
Nations that would seriously weaken it in relation to the other. Either
side can block such action in the Security Council, but in the General
Assembly the states of the free world have a voting advantage. They have
a better chance than the states of the Soviet orbit to prevent action
detrimental to their relative power position. But if the application of the
principle of collective security is regularly adjusted to the power interests
of the West, it is questionable how long the principle will last and how
long the communist states will choose to remain members of the organization.

World War III, if it should come, would obviously have a profound
effect on the United Nations. Let it be assumed that the states of the
Soviet orbit would be ranged against states of the free world. If the act
of aggression should come from the free world, the United Nations would
probably be disrupted; many considerations would prevent the endorsement of the communist cause, and the principles of the Charter would
prevent endorsement of aggression. If the act of aggression should come
from a state of the Soviet orbit, the General Assembly might endorse the
cause of the free world. Presumably this would lead to the withdrawal
or expulsion of the communist states from the United Nations, making it
in effect a military coalition of the remaining members. The fortunes of
war would then determine the fate of the organization.

SUGGESTED READINGS

CLAUDE, Inis L., *Swords into Plowshares* (New York, Random House, 1956).

GEORGE, Alexander L., "American Policy-Making and the North Korean Aggression," *World Politics*, Vol. 7 (January, 1955), pp. 209-232.

GOODRICH, Leland M., "Korea: Collective Measures Against Aggression," *International Conciliation*, No. 494, October, 1953.

GOODRICH, Leland M., and HAMBRO, Edvard, *Charter of the United Nations, Commentary and Documents* (Boston, World Peace Foundation, 1949).

GOODRICH, Leland M., and SIMONS, Anne P., *The United Nations and the Maintenance of International Peace and Security* (Washington, Brookings, 1955).

HAAS, Ernst B., "Types of Collective Security: An Examination of Operational Concepts," *American Political Science Review*, Vol. 49 (March, 1955), pp. 40-62.

HAVILAND, H. Field, *The Political Role of the General Assembly*, United Nations Studies No. 7 (New York, Carnegie Endowment for International Peace, 1951).

JIMÉNEZ DE ARÉCHAGA, Eduardo, *Voting and the Handling of Disputes in the Security Council*, United Nations Studies No. 5 (New York, Carnegie Endowment for International Peace, 1950).

JOHNSON, Howard C., and NIEMEYER, Gerhart, "Collective Security: The Validity of an Ideal," *International Organization*, Vol. 8 (February, 1954), pp. 19-35.

KOO, Wellington, Jr., *Voting Procedures in International Organizations* (New York, Columbia University Press, 1947).

LEVI, Werner, *Fundamentals of World Organization* (Minneapolis, University of Minnesota Press, 1950).

LIE, Trygve, *In the Cause of Peace* (New York, Macmillan, 1954).

McINTYRE, Elizabeth, "Weighted Voting in International Organizations," *International Organization*, Vol. 8 (November, 1954), pp. 484-497.

MANGONE, Gerard J., *The Idea and Practice of World Government* (New York, Columbia University Press, 1951).

MANGONE, Gerard J., *A Short History of International Organization* (New York, McGraw-Hill, 1954).

MARTIN, Andrew, *Collective Security* (Paris, UNESCO, 1952).

NIEMEYER, Gerhart, "A Query About Assumptions on International Organization," *World Politics*, Vol. 7 (January, 1955), pp. 337-347.

RAPPARD, William E., *The Quest for Peace* (Cambridge, Harvard University Press, 1940).

RICHES, Cromwell A., *Majority Rule in International Organization* (Baltimore, Johns Hopkins Press, 1940).

SCHIFFER, Walter, *The Legal Community of Mankind* (New York, Columbia University Press, 1954).

TOYNBEE, Arnold J., *Survey of International Affairs, 1935*, Vol. II, *Abyssinia and Italy* (London, Oxford, 1936).

WOLFERS, Arnold, "Collective Security and the War in Korea," *Yale Review*, Vol. 43 (Summer, 1954), pp. 481-496.

WRIGHT, Quincy, *Problems of Stability and Progress in International Relations* (Berkeley, University of California Press, 1954).

CHAPTER 19

International Organization for Welfare

WE HAVE REPEATEDLY NOTED that states commonly pursue a number of objectives. Some of them, such as security, relate primarily to the state itself. Others, such as prosperity, relate primarily to individuals. There is often an interrelationship between the pursuit of objectives on behalf of the state and their pursuit on behalf of individuals, for the efforts may be mutually reinforcing.

Interrelated concern for the state and for the individual has led governments to cooperate for what can be labeled broadly as the promotion of welfare. Sometimes the immediate concern of each cooperating government is with the welfare of its own citizens. Sometimes some of the governments involved are concerned with people abroad, usually on the basis of mixed motives. One of the motives "is undoubtedly a human sympathy which makes the spectacle of pain in others a pain to the spectator." [1] There was a time when pain abroad could be ignored because it was unknown, but the communication network of the modern world calls much of it to the attention of people in a position to extend help. Another motive operating in the more advanced countries is more directly related to the ideological struggle. The United States, for example, is willing to join in international welfare activities for the benefit of people abroad partly so as to make it less likely that they will go communist. The long-run economic interests of advanced countries may also be at stake.

. . . Our highly industrialized countries are approaching ever more critical shortages of raw materials. To ensure supplies, we must win and preserve the friend-

---

[1] P. E. Corbett, *The Individual and World Society* (Princeton, Center for Research on World Political Institutions, 1953), p. 15.

ship of countries now underdeveloped, we must provide initial capital and technical assistance, and we must help in setting up the training necessary for sustained production. Success in this endeavor demands improved sanitation, better and more abundant food, stable and tolerable legal orders. The chain of reasoning, with its statistical backing, reveals our concrete and inescapable interest in the whole economic, social, and political development of the world's "backward areas." [2]

Moreover, international welfare activities are also often called for in the name of peace. Thus the Charter assigns welfare functions to the United Nations "with a view to the creation of conditions of stability and well-being which are necessary for peaceful and friendly relations among nations." Similarly, the constitution of the United Nations Educational, Scientific, and Cultural Organization (UNESCO) provides for what we are broadly calling welfare activities, declaring that they are to be undertaken to promote peace and security. "Since wars begin in the minds of men, it is in the minds of men that the defenses of peace must be constructed."

Those viewing the promotion of welfare as a path to peace may do so for either or both of two reasons. They may contend that better educated, more prosperous, and more healthy people are more likely to be contented and therefore peaceful, even though the world continues to be divided into sovereign states. Or they may contend that as people learn the value of international cooperation for the advancement of welfare they will come to think of themselves more as members of a world society and less as members of distinct national societies. The hope is that "functional integration" will occur, that is, that people all over the world will become united by cooperating in international organizations to perform functions which contribute directly to better living, and, further, that integration at this level may lead to the development of a sense of social unity throughout the world (perhaps even to political integration), thus rendering war less likely.

Numerous motivations and objectives thus combine to produce international cooperation for the promotion of welfare, and the criteria for judging success are therefore complex.

Perhaps it should be noted at the outset of the discussion of international organizations engaged in the promotion of welfare that none of them is empowered to exercise jurisdiction over individuals or to oblige member states to do anything against their will. They are agencies through which voluntary cooperation occurs rather than agencies having an independent existence and a capacity to impose decisions. They can accomplish no more than their members are willing to have them accomplish—and often not as much.

[2] *Ibid.*

THE GENERAL ASSEMBLY AND THE
ECONOMIC AND SOCIAL COUNCIL

The United Nations has been assigned extensive welfare functions. It is charged with promoting:

a. higher standards of living, full employment, and conditions of economic and social progress and development;

b. solutions of international economic, social, health, and related problems; and international cultural and educational cooperation; and

c. universal respect for, and observance of, human rights and fundamental freedoms for all without distinction as to race, sex, language, or religion.

These objectives are to be pursued primarily by the General Assembly and the Economic and Social Council (ECOSOC). Some of them are also the responsibility of "specialized agencies" (i.e., international organizations established outside the framework of the United Nations rather than by the United Nations). These agencies have been brought into relationship with the United Nations through agreements with ECOSOC. Several of them are much older than the United Nations itself.

ECOSOC consists of eighteen members of the United Nations elected for three-year terms by the General Assembly. Reelection being permitted, the major powers are regularly represented. Meetings are held semiannually, and decisions are made by a simple majority of those present and voting.

The division of responsibility among the General Assembly, ECOSOC, and the various specialized agencies is not clear-cut. The General Assembly, if it chose, could do virtually everything that ECOSOC can do, and either agency may act in some of the same fields with which the specialized agencies are concerned. The General Assembly and ECOSOC actually concern themselves more or less with the entire range of international welfare activities, but where a specialized agency assumes primary responsibility the United Nations bodies confine themselves largely to discussing reports received, making recommendations, and, perhaps, providing financial assistance for special types of projects. Since membership in the various agencies overlaps, conflict among them is kept at a minimum, and, in fact, considerable cooperation occurs.

As the Charter requires, the General Assembly and ECOSOC give attention to a number of types of economic problems. They are provided, by the United Nations Secretariat and otherwise, with a variety of statistical and analytical reports on economic affairs throughout the world and in particular countries or regions. Their discussions concern such problems as the expansion of international trade, full employment, economic stability, the development of underdeveloped countries, increasing productivity, conservation, the utilization of water resources, equitable relationships between the prices of primary commodities and capital goods, developing and freeing international transport and communications, and so on. Often there is no more than an exchange of information and points of view. Sometimes recommendations are adopted, directed perhaps to all United Nations members or perhaps to some other international agency. Sometimes operational programs are launched.

Perhaps the best example of an operational program is the program of technical assistance which the United Nations has undertaken jointly with a number of the specialized agencies. Appropriations for the program are made out of the regular United Nations budget, and an "expanded program" is in progress based on special contributions. In 1954 under the expanded program "the United Nations and the specialized agencies jointly sent out 1,584 experts of 63 different nationalities to 71 countries and territories. A total of 1,524 scholarships and fellowships were awarded to nationals of more than 86 countries and territories for study in 70 countries." [3] We shall refer to this program later when the specialized agencies are discussed.

For several regions ECOSOC has established special economic commissions on which appropriate governments are represented: the Economic Commission for Europe (ECE), the Economic Commission for Asia and the Far East (ECAFE), and the Economic Commission for Latin America (ECLA). These commissions (or their staffs and committees) make studies and reports on special problems, and provide forums for the exchange of views; international agreements facilitating economic development often emerge.

In the social field, probably the most publicized activity of ECOSOC concerns human rights and fundamental freedoms. It established a Commission on Human Rights in 1946 which set for itself the objective of formulating an "International Bill of Human Rights," to consist of three parts: a declaration, a covenant, and measures of implementation. A "Universal Declaration of Human Rights" was formulated, and secured the endorsement of the General Assembly in 1948. It includes provisions commonly found in the bills of rights of Western countries. In addition, there is said to be a right to: "(1) democratic government, with participation secured by free, periodic, and 'genuine' elections, universal suffrage, and equal access to public office; (2) social security; (3) work, coupled with free choice of employment, equal pay for equal work, the right to form and join trade unions, rest, leisure, holidays with pay, and a standard of living adequate to sustain the health and well-being of

[3] *Yearbook of the United Nations, 1954* (New York, Columbia University Press, 1947–), p. 137. Information concerning the work of ECOSOC may also be obtained from the reports which it submits annually to the General Assembly.

worker and family; (4) education, participation in the cultural life of the community, and protection of literary, artistic, or scientific authorship." [4]

The Declaration is a statement of the rights which, in the view of the General Assembly, ought to be afforded to human beings all over the world, but it is not a treaty and does not impose a legal obligation. Nevertheless, as Corbett points out, "the whole text presupposes a universal sense of community, common ideas of justice, and some means of bringing to bear a world-wide collective influence upon recalcitrant states." [5]

Efforts to complete the International Bill of Rights have so far failed. The Commission on Human Rights has formulated Covenants which, if ratified, would transform the moral principles of the Declaration into law. The Covenants have been transmitted through ECOSOC to the General Assembly, but the General Assembly has not given them its endorsement.

The General Assembly and ECOSOC have also concerned themselves with many other social and political problems: the "right" of peoples and nations to self-determination, the prevention of discrimination and the protection of minorities, forced labor, slavery, freedom of information, the status of women, the plight of refugees, and various social welfare questions. In 1951 the General Assembly established the Office of the United Nations High Commissioner for Refugees, which has sought to improve the lot of refugees in various countries. A United Nations Children's Fund (UNICEF) engages in mass health and feeding programs, promotes maternal and child welfare, and grants emergency aid. Several agencies associated with ECOSOC concern themselves with the production and international shipment of narcotic drugs, seeking to reduce their diversion into illicit channels and to combat drug addiction.

THE SPECIALIZED AGENCIES

As suggested above, many of the activities in which the General Assembly and ECOSOC might theoretically engage are actually regarded as the primary responsibility of various specialized agencies, existing independently but associated with the United Nations. The organizational structure of the agencies is similar. A conference is the supreme body in all of them; the conferences of the different organizations meet at various intervals (once a year, once every other year, or once in five years), and in them each member has one vote. Decisions are sometimes taken by a simple majority, sometimes by a two-thirds majority. The conference elects a smaller body which directs the affairs of the organization until

[4] Summary by Corbett, op. cit., p. 39.
[5] Ibid., p. 41. The text of the Declaration appears on pp. 471–475 of the present book.

the next conference occurs. Each organization also has a secretariat or staff. The regular expenses of the organizations are borne by the members roughly in accordance with presumed ability to pay—the proportions ranging from a fraction of 1 per cent up to 30 per cent. Some of the organizations receive subventions from the United Nations to implement technical assistance programs. Brief sketches of some of the specialized agencies follow.[6] Organizations which have been dealt with elsewhere (e.g., the International Monetary Fund) are here ignored.

International Transportation and Communication: UPU, ITU, ICAO

Problems which can easily be imagined developed long ago in connection with the international exchange of mail. To assist in their solution a number of states joined in 1875 in establishing what is now called the Universal Postal Union (UPU), with over 90 members. "The purpose of the Union," according to its constitution, "is to assure the organization and improvement of the various postal services and to promote, in that sphere, the development of international cooperation." The members regard themselves as constituting a single postal territory. Each accepts mail for delivery abroad. Each assures a right of transit across its domain. Agreements have been reached concerning a multitude of details, for example, the permissible size of envelopes. "Regular" international mail is handled on the basis of substantially uniform rules throughout the world, and many countries are party to arrangements under which special services are provided, for example, sending money abroad through international money orders. The UPU itself does not carry mail, but the members have been highly successful through it in their efforts to arrange for smooth and efficient cooperation in postal matters.

The UPU is based upon a main Convention which is at once a constitution and a code of rules for handling regular mail; agreements supplementary to the main Convention provide for special services. Although adherence to the supplementary agreements is optional, all members must perforce accept the main Convention. In this connection a form of international majority rule has in effect developed, for the Congress (i.e., the conference of members) may amend the main Convention by a two-thirds vote. Theoretically, states which are outvoted may withdraw from the organization, but in practice they regularly bow to the will of the majority rather than lose the benefits of membership. The work of the organization is generally regarded as technical and administrative rather than political; at least, it has so little to do with national prestige and power that members are commonly represented at the Congresses not

---

[6] Summary sketches of the work of the various specialized agencies may be found in the annual editions of the *Yearbook of the United Nations*. Fuller statements may be found in the annual reports issued by each agency.

by personnel from the diplomatic service but rather by postal officials. There is no doubt that the welfare of individuals throughout the world is served. No one has ever been able to determine to what extent these international postal services contribute to the development of a sense of membership in a world society, but it seems plausible that some contribution occurs.

Similarly, problems developed with the coming of the telegraph, the telephone, radio, and TV. On the basis of what kind of arrangements would telegraph and telephone systems in one country handle messages originating in another? What technical specifications should be recommended, for example, concerning the type and quality of equipment used? What radio frequencies should be reserved for different kinds of purposes? What could be done to minimize interference between broadcasting stations? Ninety or more political entities throughout the world now attempt to handle problems of these types through the International Telecommunication Union (ITU), which stems from an organization founded in the nineteenth century. They have succeeded pretty well in cooperating in the fields of the telegraph and telephone, for the problems have been mainly technical and administrative in character. Success in connection with radio broadcasting, however, has been more limited. So far, the scientists have not devised means by which each country can do all the broadcasting it wishes to do without interfering with foreign stations, especially in the high-frequency bands, and there is no scientific or technical way of deciding what allocation of frequencies would be equitable; for that matter, even if the rules of equity could be determined, some states might not wish to accept them, for international broadcasting is related to questions of prestige and power. The ITU engages in a continuous attack on problems of the type referred to above; many have been solved, but new problems are always arising and some old ones have proved to be intractable.

The development of aviation also produced problems in the international field. On the basis of what conditions might civil aircraft from one country fly over or land in the territory of another? Should the aircraft of one country be allowed to transport passengers and goods between two other countries? What flight rules should be fixed? What navigational aids should interested countries cooperate in establishing and maintaining? Should they cooperate in collecting and exchanging weather information, and, if so, how? What standards of airworthiness should aircraft meet, and what standards of fitness should pilots and crew members meet? With special regard to financing the purchase and operation of aircraft, what rules should the various countries observe concerning property rights? What rules should be fixed in connection with the problems arising from the loss of life and property because of accidents?

To promote agreement on these and other problems, over sixty political entities have joined the International Civil Aviation Organization (ICAO), which formally came into existence in 1947. In addition to promoting agreement among states on common problems, it responds to the requests of members for technical assistance in organizing and operating their aeronautical services and in training personnel.

The International Labor Organization

At the end of World War I, the victors founded not only the League of Nations and a world court but also an International Labor Organization (ILO). It survived World War II and exists today with approximately 70 members. The reason given for the establishment of the ILO was that peace cannot be attained without "social justice," and that to achieve social justice labor conditions must be regulated by international agreement.

The constitution of the ILO lists areas of action for the organization and the general principles to be pursued. The following summary of this portion of the constitution is by P. E. Corbett.[7]

The first and guiding principle is that "labor should not be regarded merely as a commodity or article of commerce." Then follow the right of association; wages "adequate to maintain a reasonable standard of life" as this is understood in the worker's time and country; "an eight hours day or a forty-eight hours week as the standard to be aimed at where it has not already been attained"; a twenty-four hours weekly rest; abolition of child labor and limitation of the labor of young persons to permit continuation of education and ensure proper physical development; equal pay for men and women for work of equal value; equitable economic treatment of all legally resident workers; in every State a system of inspection, with women taking part, to ensure enforcement of laws protecting the employed.

In addition, the constitution lists some "urgently required" improvements.

These specify "the regulation of the labor supply"; "the prevention of unemployment"; "the protection of the worker against sickness, disease, and injury arising out of his employment"; the protection of women; "provision for old age and injury"; "protection of the interests of workers when employed in countries other than their own," and "the organization of vocational and technical education."

Experience demonstrated that the problem of establishing social justice for workers along the above lines was a wide-ranging one, affecting many aspects of the social structure. The ILO therefore became concerned with the question of the kind of society that would have to exist to make its objectives in the realm of labor realizable. In a General Conference in 1946 the members defined such a society as one in which "all human beings, irrespective of race, creed, or sex, have the right to pursue both

[7] Corbett, op. cit., p. 18.

their material well-being and their spiritual development in conditions of freedom and dignity, of economic security and equal opportunity. . . ." They declared that the attainment of these conditions was the "central aim" of all national and international policies and measures. "The welfare of the individual in society was thus affirmed as the primary purpose of all social organization on any plane." [8]

The ILO is distinctive in the composition of its leading organs. To the General Conference the government of each member state appoints four delegates, two being governmental representatives and the other two being representatives of workers and employers, respectively. The smaller Governing Body also includes representatives of governments, workers, and employers.

As suggested by the summary of the constitutional provisions given above, members carry on activities through the ILO falling under three main headings: (1) the development of labor and social standards, and the adoption of measures to promote their acceptance; (2) assistance to members in improving living standards; and (3) the compilation, analysis, and dissemination of information on social questions.

In the realm of labor and social standards, the Secretariat of the ILO or a special committee engages first of all in studies pertaining to specific, selected labor problems. Studies have occurred, for example, on the problem of increasing labor productivity, the vocational rehabilitation of the disabled, the regularization of production and employment at a high level in the metal trades, and improving social security legislation. One of the most notable studies of recent years was made by an *Ad Hoc* Committee on Forced Labor, established jointly in 1951 by the ILO and ECOSOC, which studied practices with regard to forced labor, especially in colonial areas and in communist states.[9] Such studies commonly lead either to a recommendation on the subject by the General Conference or to the formulation of a convention. If two-thirds of the delegates composing a General Conference endorse a convention, it must be referred to the official or agency authorized in each country to consider it for ratification. If a state chooses to ratify, it is, of course, expected to abide by the standards fixed, and is subject to pressures (theoretically including positive sanctions) if it fails to do so.

An example of such a convention and of action under it may be in order. The ILO has endorsed a "Freedom of Association and Protection of the Right to Organize Convention, 1948," and a "Right to Organize and Collective Bargaining Convention, 1949." A considerable number of

[8] *Ibid.,* p. 19.
[9] International Labour Office, *Report of the Ad Hoc Committee on Forced Labour,* No. 36, in the *Studies and Reports* (New Series) of the International Labour Office (Geneva, 1953).

states have ratified. To keep check on the implementation of these conventions the Governing Body of the ILO has established a Committee on Freedom of Association. If, for example, the International Confederation of Free Trade Unions believes that the convention is being violated in any state, it may lodge a complaint with the Committee. The Committee then investigates the question and takes such action as it deems appropriate. If it concludes that the complaint is well founded, the most likely action is the submission of recommendations or observations to the accused government. Reliance is thus placed mainly on persuasion rather than on coercive enforcement measures. Where the action of lesser agencies is not considered adequate, the Governing Body may "recommend to the Conference such action as it may deem wise and expedient to secure compliance" with conventions which have been ratified.

Since its establishment the General Conference has endorsed over 100 conventions on various subjects, of which no less than 86 have been ratified by enough states to bring them into force. The total number of ratifications is approximately 1500.[10]

The activity of the ILO in the second category listed above, assistance to members in improving living standards, has also been extensive. Such assistance is given on the request of members. ILO experts have surveyed the handicrafts and small-scale industries in Afghanistan and have assessed their prospects. They have advised the government of Thailand on the development of consumer cooperatives. A number of governments, including those of Guatemala and Peru, have received assistance in developing social security programs. Libya secured the services of an ILO expert in revising, codifying, and applying its entire body of labor legislation. Technical assistance has gone to the governments of Burma, Pakistan, Thailand, and Turkey in the field of occupational safety. Venezuela secured the services of a vocational training expert to prepare training programs in the country's iron and steel industries. In fact, a considerable number of countries have received technical assistance in the general field of manpower organization, including vocational training. Many types of assistance have thus been provided to members all over the world.

Activity of the third type, the compilation, analysis, and dissemination of information, requires little comment. Studies undertaken as a preliminary to the formulation of recommendations and conventions commonly have value in themselves. The ILO publishes a *Yearbook of Labour Statistics,* as well as many special reports.

There is no doubt that purely national activities in the field of labor are of more vital significance than the activities conducted internationally

[10] International Labour Organisation, *Ninth Report of the International Labour Organisation to the United Nations* (Geneva, 1955), pp. 61-62.

through the ILO. Yet it cannot be doubted either that through international cooperation the welfare of labor in many countries has been improved.

The Food and Agriculture Organization

The Food and Agriculture Organization (FAO), now with more than 70 members, was established at the close of World War II. The preamble of the Constitution of the FAO declares that the members are "determined to promote the common welfare by furthering separate and collective action for the purposes of"

raising levels of nutrition and standards of living of the peoples under their respective jurisdictions,

securing improvements in the efficiency of the production and distribution of all food and agricultural products,

bettering the condition of rural populations,
and thus contributing toward an expanding world economy.

To promote these purposes, FAO is active over much of the world in the fields of agriculture, fisheries, forestry, nutrition, and education and information; it also collects and disseminates statistics relevant to its purposes and undertakes studies concerning the distribution and marketing of agricultural products.

A large proportion of its work, performed in cooperation with ECOSOC, takes the form of technical assistance, provided to members on their request. For example, Iraq has received FAO assistance in connection with the problem of soil erosion. India has received assistance in training mechanics in the maintenance of agricultural machinery and irrigation equipment. A number of European countries have secured FAO help in connection with the introduction and development of hybrid seed corn. The entire Middle East, as well as some countries in other regions, have benefited from the locust-control activities of FAO. Egypt and other countries have secured the services of FAO experts regarding problems connected with the production of rice. Widespread cooperation has occurred through FAO in combating various animal and plant diseases. Agricultural extension specialists have been assigned to a number of the fundamental education centers sponsored by UNESCO. Turkey has received assistance in improving the organization and administration of its fishing industry, and Ceylon, India, and Liberia have sought FAO help in improving fishing gear and methods. Missions have been sent to Brazil, Chile, Paraguay, Libya, and Ethiopia to advise on forestry policy. In cooperation with the World Health Organization, FAO has attacked the problem of Kwashiorkor in Africa, a children's disease resulting from malnutrition. These are simply examples of the types of technical assistance that FAO provides. In conjunction with such assistance and in addition to it, FAO conducts extensive educational and information activities, and sponsors conferences of experts on numerous problems in its field.[11]

The World Health Organization

The World Health Organization (WHO), with over eighty members, formally came into existence in 1948. As with FAO, a large part of its work takes the form of technical assistance to members. Many countries have received assistance in combating such diseases as malaria, syphilis, yaws, and tuberculosis. WHO has also concerned itself with the field of mental health, with maternal and child health, with training programs for nurses, midwives, and doctors, and with health education programs. In 1954 a total of 334 WHO projects were under way in more than 76 different countries, frequently producing remarkable results on the basis of relatively small expenditures.

The United Nations Educational, Scientific, and Cultural Organization

The United Nations Educational, Scientific, and Cultural Organization (UNESCO), now including more than 70 members, came into existence at the end of World War II, and is active in the fields indicated by its name. Most member states have established National Commissions which seek to promote the purposes of UNESCO within their territory.

As with the other specialized agencies, the work of UNESCO can only be illustrated briefly here. In the field of education, UNESCO seeks to promote free and compulsory primary education in countries that do not already provide it. ("There are over two hundred million children in the world for whom no school facilities exist.") It does this, among other ways, by sending educational missions to countries requesting them, mainly to give assistance in teacher-training programs. Similarly, UNESCO sponsors a "fundamental education" program, promoting the training of teachers who will assist uneducated adults to gain the minimum knowledge necessary for improving their living conditions. International understanding and knowledge of the United Nations are promoted in various ways.

Other activities relate to the natural and social sciences. UNESCO helps to finance private international organizations in both areas—for example, the International Council of Scientific Unions. It facilitates the international exchange of information concerning scholarly research (for example, by assisting in the publication of *International Political Science Abstracts*) and in other ways promotes liaison among scientists of different countries. It publishes studies of research and teaching in various

[11] See Gove Hambidge, *The Story of FAO* (New York, Van Nostrand, 1955).

science fields throughout the world. In the social sciences it has sponsored a study of social tensions, especially tensions affecting international understanding. In both the natural and the social sciences it seeks to stimulate improvements in teaching.

Many cultural activities of UNESCO are conducted through non-governmental organizations which it helps finance, such as the International Council for Philosophy and Humanistic Studies and the International Music Council. In addition, it seeks to promote the "preservation and utilization of the cultural heritage of mankind," to improve international arrangements for the protection of copyrights, to make the notable literature of various countries available in translation, to assist in the international exchange of publications, and to perform other services contributing to inter-cultural understanding and progress. In all areas, it seeks to promote freedom of communication among the peoples of the world. Its Constitution is reprinted on pp. 463-470 of this book.

THE VALUE OF INTERNATIONAL WELFARE ACTIVITIES

Welfare for the Sake of Welfare

At the beginning of this chapter mention was made of the fact that international cooperation for the promotion of welfare occurs for a number of reasons. There is no doubt that the achievement of some of the objectives is being promoted. Certainly it is a convenience and an economic asset to have postal systems integrated and to have arrangements under which international transportation and communication are facilitated. Certainly a humanitarian interest is served when labor standards are improved, when agricultural and industrial production is increased in underdeveloped areas, and when health is promoted. It is generally assumed that the extension of education, science, and culture is good in itself. Very probably the long-run economic advantage both of the advanced and of the less developed countries is served by measures which enhance the possibilities of future trade among them. The United Nations and the specialized agencies are promoting all these objectives. Some of the services performed are indispensable if a mode of living involving international exchange and interdependence is to be maintained.

International Welfare Activities and National Political Objectives

The extent to which cooperative international welfare activities promote the achievement of objectives that are more definitely political is less certain. These objectives may be classified as "national" and "world-social."

The United States, for example, pursues certain national political objectives in supporting international welfare activities. It wants to reduce the appeals of communism and to win or keep friends. But it can, and does, seek to promote the same objectives through a national aid program—the Point Four program. What considerations guide it in giving emphasis to one line of action or the other? Through which line of action is the greatest political advantage likely to be derived? On the one hand, a national program permits the allocation of aid among foreign countries in accordance with their political and strategic importance to the United States, and it permits the United States to gain the benefit of whatever good will is created. On the other hand, it would scarcely be compatible with support for the United Nations as an organization for the promotion of peace and security if support were denied to its activities in the economic and social realm. Moreover, the fact is that some countries are reluctant to receive aid directly from the United States for fear that it will lead to interference in their affairs or for fear that it will unduly identify them with the United States in the East-West struggle. If aid is to reach them, with the presumed result of reducing the appeals of communism, use of an international agency as an intermediary is indicated.

These considerations do not lead to a clear-cut answer to the questions asked. There are political advantages and disadvantages in both national and world-social technical assistance programs, which perhaps suggests that both are to be supported for the advantages which they respectively offer.

International Welfare Activities and the Development of a World Society

The world-social objectives which some expect international welfare activities to promote relate to the idea of functional integration and to the hope that enhanced well-being throughout the world will contribute to peace.

It is obvious, in the first place, that the development of a sense of membership in a unified world society is bound to be slow. There has been and there will be no sudden transformation of attitudes because it is possible to mail a letter to Yemen or to telephone a friend in Vienna. Nationalism, communism, and other divisive forces constitute powerful obstructions to world unity, and, if they are overcome at all by the methods discussed in this chapter, it can only be by a very gradual process of erosion.

In the second place, cooperative international welfare activities are least extensive and effective where, from a world-social point of view, they are most needed. Though the greatest need is to bridge the gap between East and West, such progress as has occurred has been largely "in the direction of a welfare society of the 'free world,' particularly as it has been greatly stimulated by the desire to build up resistance to Moscow-directed communism." [12] True, the Soviet Union is a member of the United Nations, ECOSOC, UPU, and ITU. In recent years it has become a member of the ILO and UNESCO. Yet, the suspicion and distrust between East and West are so sharp and probably so well founded that little basis seems to exist for optimism concerning the peaceful emergence of a sense of membership in a united world society.

In the third place, the problem of war is much more than a problem of educating people and making them healthy and prosperous. Educated, healthy, and prosperous people have often been engaged in war. To bring the peoples of the world up to the social, economic, and cultural standards that have long prevailed in Europe might simply equip them to fight more effectively and destructively, unless somehow the process is accompanied by the development of common attitudes and value patterns which involve stress on tolerance, unity, cooperation, and peace.

Considerations such as the above do not encourage optimism about the possibility that cooperative international welfare activities might create a peaceful world. However, it should be remembered that no other line of action seems promising enough to encourage optimism either. Certainly the direct attacks which have been made on the problem of assuring peace and security—whether in the name of the balance of power or in the name of collective security—have produced very meager results; where they have produced results, they have contributed more to the relative advantage of a few states than to the development of a unified world society. The problem of producing such a society is overwhelmingly difficult. This situation prevailing, even very slight contributions toward its solution are precious. Thus there is reason to emphasize cooperative international welfare activities, for they can be justified in the name of welfare alone, and they may, after all, have supplementary value.

In a period when the mechanisms hopefully devised for universal security are stalled by resurgent conflict, increased emphasis may with profit be placed upon social and humanitarian work. The welfare of the individual in society should be recognized as an end in itself and the purpose of all organization, national or international. But the direct effort to promote it may also prove the speediest road to general and enduring peace.[13]

SUGGESTED READINGS

BECKEL, Graham, *Workshops for the World: The Specialized Agencies of the United Nations* (New York, Abelard-Schuman, 1954).

CORBETT, P. E., *The Individual and World Society* (Princeton, Center for Research on World Political Institutions, 1953).

[12] Corbett, *op. cit.*, p. 16.
[13] *Ibid.*, p. 59.

Dunn, Frederick Sherwood, *War and the Minds of Men* (New York, Harper, 1950).

Freeman, Harrop A., and Paullin, Theodore, *Road to Peace: A Study in Functional International Organization* (Ithaca, Pacifist Research Bureau, 1947).

Hambidge, Gove, *The Story of FAO* (New York, Van Nostrand, 1955).

Mitrany, David, *A Working Peace System* (London, Royal Institute of International Affairs, 1944).

Yearbook of the United Nations (New York, Columbia University Press, 1947–).

CHAPTER 20

The Treatment of
Dependent Peoples

IN VARIOUS CHAPTERS, especially in Chapters 6 and 7, we have already discussed why states pursue imperialistic policies. The question to be discussed now concerns not so much the motivations leading to imperialism as the policies pursued in relation to the fruits of imperialism. Once an imperialistic goal has been achieved (i.e., once extranational territorial expansion has occurred or some degree of dominance has been achieved over an alien people), what happens? What types of policies and principles are associated with empire? What trends exist in the realm of imperial relationships? What problems?

Imperialism bears different kinds of fruits, and we shall not be concerned with all of them. It may give an "advanced" state control over foreign people who are also "advanced," as with Hitler's temporary conquest of Europe. It may involve the establishment of a territorially united multinational state, the inhabitants of which are all regarded as belonging to the main body politic, however oppressed some of them may be; the old Austro-Hungarian Empire provides an example. Or it may lead to colonial and quasi-colonial types of relationships. It is with the latter that we shall be concerned.

The general rule is that the treatment of colonies is a matter falling within the domestic jurisdiction of states, but increasingly questions pertaining to colonial and quasi-colonial relationships have entered the international realm. The acquisition and loss of colonies and the establishment and termination of quasi-colonial relationships have, of course, frequently been accompanied by international rivalries. Even before the establishment of the League of Nations, treaties had been concluded dealing with the treatment of colonial peoples. Under the League a mandate system was established, specifically bringing the treatment of a restricted group of dependent territories into the field of international politics. The United

Nations Charter goes even further, laying down principles in accordance with which all non-self-governing territories are to be treated and establishing a trusteeship system, more or less as a substitute for the League's mandate system. The East-West struggle is so all-pervasive that it necessarily includes struggle over the fate of colonial areas. Thus at least some aspects of the general subject of colonialism are definitely part of the subject matter of international politics.

TRADITIONAL TYPES OF COLONIAL AND QUASI-COLONIAL RELATIONSHIPS

Types of colonial and quasi-colonial relationships which have been established vary considerably. They range from those in which the "advanced" state is given, or claims, relatively minor special privileges to those in which it exercises complete control.

Spheres of Interest

In a legal sense, perhaps the mildest form of quasi-colonial relationship comes from the assertion by an "advanced" state that all or part of the territory of another state falls within its sphere of influence or interest. Ordinarily, the assertion that such a sphere exists involves no formal transfer of rights. The sovereignty of the state whose territory is said to be within the sphere of interest of another state remains unimpaired. Thus, as we have noted in Chapter 11, Britain and Russia once agreed to divide Persia (Iran) into zones, each party agreeing not to seek political or commercial concessions in the zone assigned to the other. So far as Britain and Russia were concerned, each had its sphere of interest carved out, but each could act within its sphere only with the consent of the Persian government, which was not a party to the agreement.

Extraterritoriality

In relations with certain states of Africa and Asia, "advanced" countries have sometimes concluded treaties, called capitulations, endorsing the principle of extraterritoriality, that is, they provided that citizens of the advanced country would be outside the jurisdiction of the other even when on its territory. If an American citizen in China was accused of a criminal offense, for example, he was to be tried not in a Chinese court but in an American consular court. Such "unequal" treaties, placing one party in a position of inferiority, have now been terminated.

Leased Territory

States sometimes lease territory to each other, thus transferring certain jurisdictional rights over it. For example, a number of western countries leased territory in China before World War I. Such arrangements do not necessarily imply anything like colonialism, for "advanced" countries sometimes lease territory to each other, but when China was concerned they were taken again to reflect a status of its inferiority. Similarly, arrangements by which one state collects the customs of another or controls the customs rates, or secures other special privileges touching on the sovereignty of the other, may be marks of a quasi-colonial status.

Protectorates

The establishment of a protectorate, which usually occurs by treaty agreement, is a more extreme form of imperialist encroachment. The protected country remains a state, and usually retains considerable autonomy in the management of its domestic affairs. The protecting power regularly manages the foreign affairs of the protectorate and provides for its defense, and it may gain other prerogatives as well. For a number of decades Tunisia, for example, was a protectorate of France; Morocco was divided into Spanish and French protectorates. Aden is a British protectorate.

These types of relationships are generally considered quasi-colonial. The weaker state, though placed in a status which implies inferiority or subordination, nevertheless remains a state. Colonial relationships are different in that the colony is a part of the domain of the imperial power, lacking sovereignty of its own. Thus the thirteen American colonies were a part of the domain of the British Crown, and thus also the Virgin Islands are now a part of the domain of the United States.

Colonies

There is generally no difficulty about identifying a colony. Its territory is usually not regarded as an integral part of the home territory of the imperial power, and its inhabitants are usually considered to be outside the main body politic. Usually colonial people are ethnically and culturally distinct from those of the imperial country and are relatively backward. In fact, one of the common features of colonialism is that it involves a control relationship between societies which are alien to each other and which are at different levels of development in terms of technology, culture, and social organization.

These identifying marks do not always provide a satisfactory guide. Algeria, for example, possesses most of the characteristics of a colony, with the major exception that the French government considers it an integral part of France. Similarly, "all territories and peoples under Portugese rule in Europe, Africa, and elsewhere are equally part of Portugal one and indivisible." [1] From Portugal's point of view, it has no colonies.

[1] Thomas R. Adam, *Modern Colonialism: Institutions and Policies* (Garden City, Doubleday, 1955), p. 20.

Some of the peoples that form an integral part of the Soviet Union are so backward and so much under the tutelage of more advanced elements in the population that they hold a colonial status in all but name. Whether a French territory like Algeria, a Portugese territory like Goa, or a Soviet territory like the Uzbek Republic should be classified as colonial are questions to which different people give different answers.

COLONIAL IMPERIALISM AND NATIVE WELFARE

Colonial imperialism has come to be a term of opprobrium in the eyes of many, connoting the forceful imposition of alien rule on weak and backward peoples who are then oppressed politically and exploited economically. There is, of course, some historic basis for such attitudes, but the record of the imperial countries in treating colonial peoples is by no means all black.

Laissez Faire at Home and in the Colonies

It should be recalled that within the imperial countries themselves governments have not always adhered to the standards which have come to be associated with the modern, democratic welfare state. Political tyranny and oppression, and economic exploitation, are not to be identified exclusively with colonies. Laissez faire was long the dominant principle guiding relationships between government and economic life; the principle was pursued within a legal framework which gave economic advantage to the few, and often when the principle was abandoned it occurred as a result of the political pressures of the few and served to accentuate their advantage. In a sense, governments have simply been umpires in a prize ring within which individuals struggled for their own profit, the stronger and more influential fighters at times getting help from the umpire in their struggle. The result was the development of an economic hierarchy, with a few at the top enjoying great wealth and many at the bottom finding life rather miserable and barren.

Scales of living for natives have generally been low in colonial areas, even lower than for those at the bottom of the economic hierarchy in imperial countries. This is partly due to the fact that the native peoples have lacked the knowledge, the skills, the attitudes, and the capacity for planned and organized effort which are required for economic progress.[2] Imperial countries have also been in part responsible, for they have been slow to undertake remedial measures. That this is true should not be surprising, for governments have also been slow to adopt measures designed to promote mass welfare within their metropolitan territories.

[2] Eric A. Walker, *Colonies* (Cambridge, Cambridge University Press, 1944), pp. 18-22.

If people at home were left to look out for themselves, pursuing their own profit and living in varying degrees of deprivation and degradation when they failed to achieve it, it was not unnatural that little solicitude would be shown for people in colonies. If private advantage was pursued at home even at the expense of others, it is no wonder that in colonies this occurred as well. Moreover, if governments sometimes enacted laws which benefited special interests at the expense of the mass of the people at home, it is hardly surprising that they engaged in similar actions at the expense of colonial peoples. The tendency to regard alien, colored, and backward people as inferior beings made exploitative and even in-human practices all the more acceptable.

Long ago higher principles were advanced in accordance with which, it was contended, native peoples should be treated. Edmund Burke pro-tested against the treatment meted out to portions of India by the East India Co., and urged that the British exercise a "sacred trust" in govern-ing colonial peoples. The very notion of the White Man's Burden and of a *mission civilisatrice* reflected a sense of obligation to promote native welfare. Accepting the General Act of the Berlin Conference (1885), which dealt with colonialism in Africa, most of the European powers and the United States bound themselves "to protect the natives in their moral and material well-being ... [and] to further the education and civilization of the natives." [3]

Actual implementation of such principles was slow in coming, but con-siderable progress has occurred. The very process of economic exploita-tion involved some benefit for colonial peoples. Western traders, to make profits for themselves, had to contribute to the development of the col-onies in which they operated. Communication and transportation facil-ities had to be developed. Public health measures had to be taken, even if primarily for the benefit of Europeans. Agriculture has been improved, industrialization has begun, and native workers have had to be equipped with such skills as their jobs required, if not with some minimum amount of education.

The Promotion of Welfare at Home and in the Colonies

As governments have come to assume responsibility for the education, health, and welfare of their citizens at home, so have they tended, though haltingly and with a considerable time lag, to assume similar responsi-bilities in their colonies. Liberal and socialist elements which have pressed for the abandonment of laissez faire and for the development of the welfare state have also generally pressed for improved treatment for

[3] Parker T. Moon, *Imperialism and World Politics* (New York, Macmillan, 1927), p. 84.

dependent peoples. Improved communications, making the plight of such peoples more widely known, have stimulated demands for reform. Members of the League of Nations, through the Covenant and through the Mandates Commission (to be discussed below), supported principles and practices with reference to mandated territories some of which were generally applicable and to a degree were actually applied to other colonies.[4] In the period between the two world wars and especially during and after World War II, the more advanced colonial peoples pressed for improvements in their status, sometimes demanding complete independence. Members of the United Nations, through the Charter, the Trusteeship Council, and the General Assembly, are supporting principles and practices, as we shall shortly see, that call for reform not only in trust territories but also in all non-self-governing territories. In the General Assembly and elsewhere small countries which are fearful of imperialist powers, and former colonial countries which are now independent, can and do act as champions of what they assume to be the welfare of dependent peoples. Finally, as a force working for improvement and reform in the field of colonial welfare, are the cold war and the threat of communism. With the Soviet Union, Communist China, and the international communist movement championing the "liberation" of colonies from the "yoke of imperialism," competition for the favor of colonial peoples has developed, which implies enhanced attention to their needs and desires.

Despite the progress which has occurred and is occurring, it should not be thought that the colonies are treading a primrose path toward the achievement of the good society. Where white settlers have entered colonies inhabited by colored people, racial prejudices have sometimes developed; especially in certain African territories, the race problem is explosive. Further, in some areas the whites have achieved privileged economic positions, and fear the results of improvements in the status of the natives. Progress is necessarily slow even where it is seriously desired by all parties. Illiteracy, ignorance, ill-health, poverty, and technological backwardness take time to overcome. The human and material resources of many colonial areas are scarcely sufficient, whether in quality or quantity, to provide a basis for rapid progress without substantial outside aid, and, though giving some aid for colonial improvements, the advanced countries have so far not evidenced a willingness to make serious sacrifices for the purpose. There is thus no expectation of a quick solution to the problem of colonial welfare—any more, for that matter, than there is an expectation of a quick solution to the problem of welfare in many independent countries.

[4] H. Duncan Hall, *Mandates, Dependencies and Trusteeship* (Washington, Carnegie Endowment for International Peace, 1948), p. 65.

ARRANGEMENTS FOR GOVERNING COLONIES

Arrangements for governing colonies vary, depending on many factors, among them the level of social advancement of the inhabitants, the degree of social unity achieved, and the expectations or hopes of the imperial country concerning long-term relationships. Backward or primitive peoples have generally been placed under governors who, though subject to control by the appointing government, have wielded powers approaching the dictatorial. Similarly, when the inhabitants of a colony are so sharply divided among themselves that tolerant cooperation in political affairs is difficult to achieve, the tendency has been for the imperial country to exercise more or less autocratic control, however beneficent or harsh. This situation is not uncommon, for many colonies are plural societies, that is, the population is divided, perhaps along tribal, ethnic, linguistic, or religious lines, perhaps by color, or perhaps by the levels of cultural development achieved. Backwardness and sharp social cleavages in colonies have led all imperial countries toward autocratic rule, even though something other than autocracy may be the professed goal.[5]

Where colonial peoples are more advanced and where they constitute a unified society, governmental arrangements have depended more on the expectations or hopes of the imperial country for long-term relationships. Britain and France provide examples of two extremes. Increasingly since the revolt of the American colonies, Britain has envisaged an arrangement under which colonies become self-governing or achieve dominion status, but remain associated under the Crown in the Commonwealth and Empire. Colonies settled largely by Englishmen possessed some measure of self-government nearly from the first, and most of them have emerged from colonial status and have become Dominions, equal in status to Britain itself within the Commonwealth. In colonies with largely non-British inhabitants, the development of self-government has been slower, but advances have been made and are being made. Burma, Ceylon, India, and Pakistan, which were all colonies, are no longer in this status; Burma is independent, and the other three are Dominions. Other colonies, at different rates of speed, are traveling the same road.

In contrast to Britain, France has hoped to assimilate its colonies, that is, to transfer its culture to colonial peoples with a view to their integration into a greater France. Where assimilation seemed to be only a distant possibility, France has pursued a policy of "association" as a step toward the ultimate goal, the object of association being the transfer of French culture to a native elite, which would presumably give support and aid in governing the area in question and which would serve as a carrier of

[5] Adam, *op. cit.*, pp. 29-30; Walker, *op. cit.*, pp. 71-77.

French culture to the rest of the population. However, in some areas these hopes have been difficult to realize; France abandoned them in 1956 with regard to her territories in sub-Sahara Africa by giving them an enlarged measure of autonomy.

The French Union, established after World War II, reflects mixed desires.[6] The French Republic is its principal component, including not only Metropolitan France but also certain Overseas Departments and Overseas Territories. All portions of the Republic are represented, though on a discriminatory basis, in the French parliament. From the French governmental point of view, the Overseas Departments and some of the Overseas Territories are now assimilated in France and are not colonies. As already indicated, Algeria holds this position, though very restively. In addition to the French Republic, the French Union includes the Cameroons, held under trusteeship as an Associated Territory, and Togoland, which became a self-governing republic in 1956. Formerly the French Union included certain Associated States (French Morocco, Tunisia, Cambodia, Laos, and Vietnam), but they are now independent.

The English-speaking countries that possess colonies, including the United States, generally follow the British pattern in governing them. The Soviet Union aims, as France did, at the assimilation of peoples who, if they were overseas, would certainly be regarded as colonial. Belgium seeks to promote economic development in her colonies, but does very little by means of education or otherwise to stimulate progress toward self-government.

THE LEAGUE OF NATIONS MANDATE SYSTEM

Background Considerations

During World War I the Allies seized Germany's colonies. Though one of Wilson's fourteen points called for "a free, open-minded, and absolutely impartial adjustment of all colonial claims," it was simply assumed that Germany should not be permitted to regain what she had lost. Likewise during World War I, the Ottoman Empire collapsed, and at the end of the war the Allies were in possession of its Near Eastern territories. The peace conference thus faced the question what to do with these spoils of war.

Traditionally after wars the victors have simply annexed some or all colonies of the defeated, and there were demands at the peace conference that this policy should be followed, but in many quarters colonialism was already in disrepute. In some aspects it contradicted Christian, liberal, and democratic principles; moreover, at least in relation to the more

[6] O. R. Taylor, *The Fourth Republic of France* (London, Royal Institute of International Affairs, 1951), pp. 65-71; *France Overseas* (New York, French Embassy, Press and Information Division, 1956).

advanced colonial peoples, it contradicted the nationalist principle that each nation should be united in an independent state. Further, Woodrow Wilson had justified the war in the name of high moral principle rather than for territorial or other tangible gain, and, in any event, the United States was uninterested in acquiring additional colonies for itself and anticolonialist generally. When a suggestion was made that territories taken from the Ottoman Empire, rather than being annexed, should be placed under the temporary tutelage of individual victors by being mandated to them, Wilson insisted that the same general principle should also be applied to the former German colonies, and his view prevailed.

Provisions of the League Covenant

The League Covenant therefore included the provision that the colonies and territories, which had been taken from Germany and the Ottoman Empire and which were "inhabited by peoples not yet able to stand by themselves under the strenuous conditions of the modern world," should be placed under the tutelage of advanced nations, these nations to act as "Mandatories on behalf of the League." The League and its mandatories accepted the principle that "the well-being and development of such peoples form a sacred trust of civilization." To make it possible for the League to check on the implementation of this principle, the Covenant obliged each mandatory to submit an annual report on its mandated territories; it also provided for the establishment of a Permanent Mandates Commission to receive and examine the reports and to advise the League Council on matters pertaining to them.

The Mandates Commission

As it turned out, the Mandates Commission operated, however wisely and efficiently, within rather strict limits. Its rule was to consider the past, that is, the period covered by the reports submitted to it, though it might express hope that subsequent reports would show improvement. If it considered a report incomplete, it might ask for additional information. It could give publicity to the information received. However, it could not visit and inspect the mandated territories, nor could it receive petitions from their inhabitants unless they were forwarded by the mandatory power. Theoretically, the general endorsement by League members of the principle of the sacred trust and the arrangements made for checking on the implementation of the principle in the mandated territories constituted very significant developments. Whether they led the mandatory powers in practice to treat native peoples better than they would have done in any event is difficult to say.[7]

---

[7] For descriptions and appraisals of the mandate system, see Quincy Wright, *Mandates Under the League of Nations* (Chicago, University of Chicago Press, 1930); and Hall, *op. cit., passim.*

Types of Mandates

Mandated territories fell into three categories, A, B, and C, depending largely on their level of cultural development. Into the A Category went former territories of the Ottoman Empire which, according to the Covenant, had reached "a stage of development where their existence as independent nations can be provisionally recognized subject to the rendering of administrative advice and assistance by a Mandatory until such time as they are able to stand alone." They were thus to have considerable autonomy and were encouraged to look forward to the attainment of complete independence. At the other extreme were the C mandates, including one of the former German colonies in Africa and all the former German insular possessions in the Pacific, which were to be "administered under the laws of the Mandatory as integral portions of its territory." This came as close as could be to outright annexation within the limits of the mandate system. The B mandates, obviously, were given an in-between status, the characteristics and potentialities of which were left undefined; in regulating their trade and commerce, however, the mandatory power was obliged to secure equal opportunities for all League members.

The implied pledge of independence for the A mandates was observed. Iraq and Transjordan, both mandated to Britain, became independent in 1932 and 1946, respectively. The status of Palestine was not so smoothly changed, as we have observed in earlier chapters. Britain gave up its mandate in 1948 in the absence of full agreement by the interested parties in the fate of the territory, and only through war did Israel set itself up in part of Palestine as an independent state. Syria and Lebanon, mandated to France, achieved independence in the course of World War II. It is perhaps only fair to say that changed power relationships, as well as the good faith of the mandatory powers, played a considerable role in these developments. In any event, of the mandated territories only those in the B and C categories were in a position to be transferred into the United Nations trusteeship system when it replaced the mandate system.

THE UNITED NATIONS AND COLONIALISM

By the end of World War II, the forces working against colonialism were much stronger than ever before. The United States, though behaving somewhat inconsistently, remained anticolonialist. The Soviet Union took a similar view for reasons of its own, and wherever socialists had influence they generally exerted it in support of the idea that self-government and welfare in the colonies ought to be promoted. A number of small countries, fearful and resentful of various manifestations of imperialism, threw such influence as they had into the anti-imperialist scales. Moreover, some imperial countries emerged from World War II relatively weaker than before, and some colonial peoples were both more restive and relatively stronger. Finally, widespread acceptance of the principle that government, rather than following a policy of laissez faire, should actively promote welfare at home led rather naturally to demands that the same principle should be applied in behalf of colonial peoples.

Provisions of the Charter

The result was that the United Nations Charter went much further than the League Covenant in the provisions relating to the treatment of dependent peoples. Aside from the provisions concerning mandates, the Covenant had confined itself to the requirement that League members give "just treatment" to natives. The Charter expresses concern for all non-self-governing territories. It specifies that

Members of the United Nations which have or assume responsibilities for the administration of territories whose peoples have not yet attained a full measure of self-government recognize the principle that the interests of the inhabitants of these territories are paramount, and accept as a sacred trust the obligation to promote to the utmost . . . the well-being of the inhabitants of these territories.

To this end, members also agree, among other things, (1) to insure the political, economic, social, and educational advancement of such peoples, (2) to develop self-government, to take due account of the political aspirations of the peoples, and to assist them in the progressive development of their free political institutions, and (3) to transmit information regularly to the Secretary-General relating to economic, social, and educational conditions in the non-self-governing territories.

In two articles of the Charter the members affirm their "respect for the principle of equal rights and self-determination of peoples." Both the meaning of the principle and the question whether and under what circumstances it is applicable to colonial peoples are left in doubt.

In addition to the Charter's provisions concerning all non-self-governing territories, there are also provisions concerning the trusteeship system. The objectives of the system are: (1) to promote international peace and security; (2) to promote the political, economic, social, and educational advancement of the inhabitants of the trust territories, and their progressive development towards self-government or independence; (3) to encourage respect for human rights and fundamental freedoms; and (4) to insure equal treatment in social, economic, and commercial matters for all United Nations members.

To check on the extent to which these objectives are being promoted in the trust territories and, in effect, to replace the League's Permanent Mandates Commission, the United Nations has established a Trusteeship Council. On it are represented: (1) states administering trust territories; (2) any other permanent members of the Security Council; and (3) enough additional states, elected by the General Assembly for three-year terms, to secure an equal division in the Trusteeship Council between administering and non-administering members. Decisions are by simple majority of those present and voting.

Territories Under Trusteeship

Territories are placed under trusteeship by agreement between the parties directly concerned, on the one hand, and the General Assembly, on the other, except for "strategic" territories or areas. (Actually, there is only one strategic trust territory, the Pacific Islands, formerly mandated to Japan and now held by the United States. When a territory is designated "strategic," all functions which the General Assembly would otherwise exercise are assigned to the Security Council.) With one exception, all former mandated territories which have not gained independence have been made trusteeships, the exception being the former German colony of South-West Africa, which the Union of South Africa holds under mandate and wishes to annex. The Charter also permits the inclusion of territories detached from enemy states in World War II, as well as any other colonial territories, but only one such territory (Italian Somaliland) has in fact been included.

Supervision of the Trust Power

The Trusteeship Council has somewhat fuller access to information concerning trust territories than the Permanent Mandates Commission had. It not only receives annual reports which respond to its own questionnaire, but it also provides for periodic visits to the trust territories and receives petitions concerning them. On the basis of its examination of the affairs of a trust territory, it may offer criticisms and suggestions to the administering power, perhaps including them in its report to the General Assembly. Members of the General Assembly, in turn, are free to make such comments as they please, and the General Assembly as a body may enact resolutions concerning relationships between the administering powers and their trust territories. (Again it might be noted that the Security Council displaces the General Assembly for strategic territories.)

Non-self-governing Territories Other than Trusteeships

The fact that all non-self-governing territories have come within the purview of the United Nations is probably more significant than the fact that a few of them are trusteeships. To be sure, the relevant provisions of the Charter are rather vague. Who decides, and on the basis of what criteria, which territories are non-self-governing? Does the requirement that imperial countries transmit information concerning economic, social, and educational conditions in such territories include a requirement that political information be transmitted? When information is received by the Secretary-General, what may he and the United Nations do? In agreeing to provide information, in promising to treat non-self-governing territories on the basis of the principle that the interests of the inhabitants are "paramount," and in promising to develop self-government in such territories, have the imperial countries made themselves accountable to the United Nations for their actions? These and other questions have been the basis for some conflict. Generally, the imperial countries want to decide for themselves which of their territories have become self-governing; they want to exclude political information from their reports; they resist the contention that they have rendered themselves internationally accountable; and they are inclined to resent United Nations action. The imperial countries do not, however always present a united front, for there are disagreements among them. The United States is in an especially ambivalent position; it possesses colonies itself and is allied to other imperial powers whose support it values, yet it is anticolonialist. Moreover, the imperial countries are outnumbered in the General Assembly by the others, many of which are definitely anticolonialist. Most states lying in the arc extending from the eastern end of the Mediterranean through South Asia to the Philippines have recently been colonies themselves, and they are resentful of colonialism. They gain support not only from communist states but also from many small countries which, though long free, have been inclined to regard themselves as menaced by imperialism. The tendency of these states is to try, in effect, to extend the trusteeship system to all colonies and to hold the imperial countries accountable for their stewardship. Their chief preoccupation, both for territories held formally in trust and for all other colonies, is with the obligation to promote self-government or independence or, more generally, with the "right" of self-determination.[8] The principle that imperial countries hold colonies in a kind of national trust under their domestic jurisdiction is attacked in the name of the principle that they hold colonies under international trust and are internationally accountable for what they do or fail to do.

It should not be inferred from this that the imperial countries are necessarily malevolent and selfish exploiters and enslavers who are resisting the noble efforts of more unselfish and enlightened states in behalf of colonial peoples. As already suggested, as governments have become more active in promoting health, education, and welfare at home they have also become more active in the same fields in their colonies.[9] In recent years, their efforts have been supplemented, with their full support and concurrence, by technical assistance programs, including those con-

[8] See Benjamin Rivlin, "Self-Determination and Dependent Areas," *International Conciliation,* No. 501 (January, 1955).

[9] See, for example, Annette Baker Fox, *Freedom and Welfare in the Caribbean* (New York, Harcourt, Brace, 1949).

ducted through the United Nations and the specialized agencies. In some areas, of course, there have been, and are, acute differences between imperial states and their colonies, especially in connection with demands for independence. Since World War II, the Netherlands has been compelled to give up its control of Indonesia, and France has been compelled to grant independence to the states of Indochina and to Tunisia and French Morocco. The racialism of the Union of South Africa makes for an explosive situation not only within the Union but, potentially, in mandated South-West Africa. Nevertheless, these are exceptional situations. Generally speaking, imperial countries are following policies in their colonies which deserve to be called enlightened. It is striking that over 650 million people who were non-self-governing in 1945 had by 1956 become 18 independent and sovereign nations.

The Aim of Self-government or Independence

There can be quite honest differences of opinion on the question of the speed with which self-government or independence should be established, however these terms are defined. If all colonies were suddenly given their freedom, who would be made free? Frequently it would be a native elite which is as yet relatively inexperienced and incompetent in managing public affairs. Government placed in their hands would necessarily be inefficient, and perhaps it would be oppressive and corrupt as well. As a matter of fact, some colonies that have achieved independence, and some states that have long been independent, have regimes which may glory in the possession of sovereignty, but which are so reactionary, corrupt, oppressive, inefficient, or unstable that the people are worse off, and have less freedom, than people in many colonies. It is one of the ironies of the United Nations situation that governments guilty of practices which would not be tolerated in a well-run colony can use the United Nations as a forum for criticizing colonial powers. The argument is sometimes advanced that self-government is preferable to good government, and there are things to be said for this point of view, but it is well to ask what elements of the population will be included in the self and what the prospect is that self-government can become good government.

Moreover, it is questionable whether it would make sense, especially in Africa, to regard all existing colonies as suitable units for independent statehood. The boundaries of colonies were not drawn with this in mind. They sometimes divide ethnically similar people and unite the ethnically dissimilar. They sometimes flout requirements of economic viability. If independence were suddenly granted to existing units, years of trouble might follow as Africa got itself sorted out and divided up on more desirable lines. Of course, it is also a question whether such problems can or will be solved while European powers still have control.

The problem of colonialism brings up not only questions pertaining to the advancement and welfare of the colonial peoples but also questions pertaining to power relationships and, more particularly, the East-West struggle. As long as the free world and the communist world are engaged in mortal struggle—and, for that matter, as long as states think of war as a distinct possibility—power considerations will at least compete with, if they do not take priority over, all others in relation to the colonial issue. If a colony were to be made free only to fall under communist control, the development would obviously be disadvantageous to the free world, and it is not surprising, especially in the light of events since World War II in Korea and Indochina, that colonial powers are concerned with the possibility. Further, some colonies have great strategic importance, whether simply because of their location or because, in addition, military bases have been established on their territory. If such colonies were to assert neutrality on becoming independent, or switch to the other side, the consequences might be grave. Memories of the attitude of the Irish Republic during World War II, endangering Britain and the whole free world by its neutrality, are still fresh, and they militate against grants of freedom to other areas if comparable results were likely to ensue. Power considerations in part explain communist opposition to colonialism, for a termination of colonialism would no doubt weaken the free world. At the same time, they also in part explain the determination of some states to retain control of their colonies. If the defense of freedom against communism is vital, and if independence for certain colonies would impair that defense, the attitude of imperial countries becomes understandable.

Just as with the League mandate system, it is difficut to say how much effect the actions of the Trusteeship Council and General Assembly have had on the treatment accorded to non-self-governing and trust territories. Neither agency can do more than ask questions, express opinions, and make recommendations. There can be appeals to pride and conscience. Efforts can be made to mobilize public opinion against an imperial power which is deemed remiss. The non-communist, anticolonialist states can refuse to be cooperative in the United Nations and elsewhere unless they secure concessions. Such pressures may have some effect. However, the fate of the colonial areas is likely to be influenced even more by the fact that governments have come to accept increasing responsibility for individual welfare and by the fact that the East-West struggle makes the support of colonial peoples important. "Nowadays, the good will rather than the subjection of the inhabitants of underdeveloped areas has become the prize which the West seeks to secure against its Soviet rival. Modern colonial policy, then, is limited to a choice between bankruptcy and partnership."[10]

[10] Adam, *op. cit.*, p. 77.

SUGGESTED READINGS

ADAM, Thomas R., *Modern Colonialism: Institutions and Policies* (Garden City, Doubleday, 1955).

APTER, David E., *The Gold Coast in Transition* (Princeton, Princeton University Press, 1955).

CHOWDHURI, R. N., *International Mandates and Trusteeship Systems* (The Hague, Nijhoff, 1955).

FOX, Annette B., *Freedom and Welfare in the Caribbean* (New York, Harcourt, Brace, 1949).

FOX, Annette B., "The United Nations and Colonial Development," *International Organization*, Vol. 4 (May, 1950), pp. 199-218.

HAAS, Ernst B., "The Attempt to Terminate Colonialism: Acceptance of the United Nations Trusteeship System," *International Organization*, Vol. 7 (February, 1953), pp. 1-21.

HALL, H. Duncan, *Mandates, Dependencies and Trusteeship* (Washington, Carnegie Endowment for International Peace, 1948).

MOON, Parker T., *Imperialism and World Politics* (New York, Macmillan, 1927).

RIVLIN, Benjamin, "Self-Determination and Dependent Areas," *International Conciliation*, No. 501, January, 1955.

WALKER, Eric A., *Colonies* (Cambridge, Cambridge University Press, 1944).

WRIGHT, Quincy, *Mandates Under the League of Nations* (Chicago, The University of Chicago Press, 1930).

Part IV

PROSPECTS FOR PEACE

CHAPTER 21

The Prospects of Peace:
A Balance Sheet

THE ANALYSIS "Domestic Politics, Peace, and Civil War," in Chapter 2, indicated that government and attitudes are crucial in determining whether peace will prevail within countries or whether civil war will occur.

Governments, it was said, contribute to domestic peace in several ways. In the first place, they seek to establish and maintain power relationships within countries which are conducive to peace; specifically, they seek to establish and maintain police and military power that is overwhelming in relation to the physical power that could be mustered by any rebellious group. In the second place, they provide peaceful procedures—executive, legislative, and judicial—by which change can be brought about and by which what is regarded as justice can be achieved. In the third place, they provide a system of law which tends to reinforce peace by providing a reasonably clear definition of rights and duties and by providing a basis for the development of a network of social relationships.

Certain types of attitudes were likewise found to contribute to peace within countries, the general proposition being that peace is more secure the more widely a set of fundamental attitudes is shared. In the first place, belief in the desirability of law and order, belief in peace, is important. There must be a desire for peace that is stronger than a desire for change which could be brought about only by violence. In the second place, a constitutional consensus is important, reflecting generally accepted fundamental rules and principles in accordance with which social and political life should proceed. In the third place, it is helpful if there is a feeling of membership in a society whose good transcends the good of individuals and groups within it—a belief that in some circumstances it is proper to require individuals and groups within the society to undertake risks and make sacrifices for the good of the whole. Finally, loyalty to the state, a loyalty superseding other loyalties in the event of conflict, contributes to domestic peace.

It is difficult to say whether government or attitudes are more important as bases of peace. Theoretically, either one might suffice at least for a time. Governments might be able to maintain peace within countries even though supporting attitudes were weak or held only by a small portion of the population. Similarly, a common set of shared attitudes might provide a basis of peace among members of large groups, even in the absence of government. Peace, however, is most secure when government and attitudes reinforce each other.

Likewise it is difficult to say which comes first in the development of a peaceful society. There is an interaction, governments seeking to foster the general acceptance of certain common attitudes, and the existence of common attitudes helping to make it possible for governments to exist.

The argument in both Chapters 1 and 2 was that within countries the strong rule. Politics is not a process which is always carried on in a spirit of harmony and cooperation; conflict is an inevitable element in it. Various methods are used in the political struggle within countries, and various tests serve to measure strength and allocate the right to rule. The ultimate test is violence—civil war. Those who win in civil war secure control of government and therefore the right to say what the law shall be. The generalization was made that law within countries commonly reflects the desires of the strong.

Presumably the conditions of peace among countries are similar to the conditions of peace among individuals and groups within countries. In Parts II and III we have, in effect, been asking to what extent those conditions exist in the international field. Now the purpose is to engage in a summary and stock-taking, and to inquire into the prospects of bringing about organizational and attitudinal changes in the world which might render peace more secure than it in fact is.

THE PROBLEM OF GOVERNMENT FOR THE WORLD

A book on international politics was scarcely required to demonstrate the fact that the world is controlled by many governments, not by one. Rather than being concentrated overwhelmingly in central hands, power is dispersed over the world among sovereign states, all of which are potential rebels, potential aggressors. Throughout history international politics, like domestic politics, has involved a power struggle, but the international power struggle has not been mitigated, regulated, and rendered peaceful in anything like the same degree as the power struggle within most states. Naked violence has been much more prominent.

The substitutes which have been developed for world government are pallid and weak. During most of modern history there has been nothing remotely resembling an international executive; there has been no central agency for administering and enforcing the law. States and alliances of states have relied upon their own power to enforce portions of the law that are of interest to them. The system has been one of self-help. The victors of World War I attempted to modify the system by creating the League of Nations, and after it broke down the victors of World War II established the United Nations. In a sense the Security Council of the United Nations is a kind of international executive for the protection of United Nations members against threats to the peace, breaches of the peace, and acts of aggression, but we have seen how restricted and attenuated its powers in practice are. When seven or more members of the Security Council, including the permanent members, agree that they want to take enforcement action, they may do so. There is no assurance that they will want to, or that members will supply sufficient power to make the action effective. The United Nations is less an international executive than an agency from which states wishing to engage in self-help may perhaps obtain a blessing and a basis for appealing for the help of others.

During most of modern history the international legislative process has operated without a legislature. Law could be developed and changed only with the explicit or tacit consent of the states to which it applied, given voluntarily or under all sorts of coercive pressures, including war. The United Nations has modified the methods of making and changing law even less than it has the methods of enforcing it. It incorporates the old devices of mediation and conciliation, and the General Assembly may make such recommendations as it pleases. Peaceful change in the law may follow, but only if the affected states consent, and the consent of the adversely affected is rarely given.

During the same period, also, the international judicial process has operated without a judiciary. States involved in legal disputes might somehow reach agreement by negotiation, or by resort to *ad hoc* arbitral tribunals. Since World War I an international court has existed (now named the International Court of Justice); as we have seen, advance consent gives it some compulsory jurisdiction, and the extent of its compulsory jurisdiction is increasing, but in the main the Court can decide a dispute only if the parties at the time consent.

Since World War I states have agreed in various documents, most notably in the United Nations Charter, to restrict themselves to peaceful methods of pursuing their needs and wants. But the agreements have been unreliable, and it was predictable that they would be. Peace is not maintained within countries simply through an exchange of promises not to go to war, and there is no hope of maintaining it throughout the world by this means.

In the world as a whole, as within countries, the strong are to be expected to demand that the law reflect their desires. The development of conditions and procedures by which they can achieve this peacefully has been a slow process within countries, and it is probably a never-ending one. Some countries have been far from successful, as the occurrence and the threats of civil war attest. Internationally the process has barely begun. Though there has been some erosion of the unanimity rule, there is nothing comparable to the elections staged in democratic countries as measurements of strength and therefore as methods of allocating law-making and law-enforcing authority. For that matter, there is no agreement on a set of constitutional powers and limitations within which the strong could exercise such authority even if they could be peacefully identified. The established test of strength and therefore of the "right" to shape law is military power and war.

THE PROBLEM OF ATTITUDES

Just as the world is poorly organized for peace, so are prevailing attitudes poorly shaped. Over the world there has not existed in the past, and there does not exist today, a desire for peace which is stronger than a desire for change. Periodically, one state or another has wanted change with sufficient urgency to feel justified in resorting to violence to get it, and it is to be expected that adamant demands for change will continue to be made, now by this state and now by that. Such demands are more likely to be deterred by a belief that the risks and costs of pressing them are too great (i.e., by a belief that power relationships are unfavorable) than by dedication to peace. The threat of nuclear warfare may be especially effective as a deterrent. Yet, even within countries, where governments exist which attempt to preserve a monopoly of violence, it has often proved impossible to maintain such a deterrent, and the difficulties of doing it are much greater in a world of sovereign states. It takes only one aggressive government to plunge others—perhaps all the rest of the world—into war.

A constitutional consensus exists among some states, just as a strong desire for peace exists within some. Among those states which share a constitutional consensus, peace has a good chance of prevailing. The United States and Canada share such a consensus, as do Norway and Sweden; there are other such combinations of states as well. It is difficult to say just what elements must be included in a constitutional consensus to provide a basis for peace. Presumably there must be substantial agreement among the states involved in defining their respective rights and interests; some interests must be shared, and those which are not shared (particularly if they are regarded as vital) must at least be compatible. Given agreement in defining rights and interests, there must be mutual respect for them. Agreement on interests would presumably include agreement concerning objectives to be pursued and the methods to be adopted in pursuing them. There must be tolerance of some degree of diversity, and there must be no thought of settling such disputes as arise by anything other than peaceful means.

Although such elements of consensus exist among restricted groups of states, there is no one consensus for the world as a whole, as the record of international tension and war demonstrates. Attitudes frequently differ on questions pertaining to legal rights and obligations, and on the importance of paying attention to law. They differ on the location of boundary lines, on the question of freedom for colonies, on the question of reuniting divided states, on the question of permitting nations to be united in independent states, and on a myriad of other questions. Conflicting aspirations are pursued, and, even where objectives are agreed to, there may be differences over the choice of method in striving to achieve them. Prestige and power, so widely sought, are values which can be obtained only at the relative expense of others. Communists want a world of communists, and liberals want a world of liberals. So many conflicts of important and vital interests exist that threats of war are regularly present in one area or another, and somewhere in the world war is usually being fought. The expectation of war leads to additional tensions and conflicts, as states try to maintain or improve their relative power positions. The absence of a world constitutional consensus means that the world lacks an important basis of peace.

Within countries, we have seen, people are expected to regard themselves as members of a society whose good transcends the good of individual parts. They are expected to make sacrifices, voluntarily or on demand, for the good of the society, including the risk of life itself. For the world as a whole, such expectations are weak, if they exist at all. Individuals may have a vague feeling that they belong to something called the human race, and they may feel some affinity to mankind. Both privately and through governments they sometimes respond to charitable impulses to help those in distress and to uplift the benighted. Statesmen, as we have seen, frequently justify policies they pursue in the name of universal values, and they speak of duties to mankind. Still, when help is given to those beyond the borders of the state, it is given to people who are regarded as foreign, rather than to people who are regarded as comembers of one society; when help is received across political boundaries, it is received from foreigners. The sense of disunity, reflecting differences in culture, in value patterns, and in social and political organization, seems to be much stronger than any sense of unity. It is even doubtful whether a world society can be said to exist.

There is even less sign of anything that could be called world loyalty than there is of a sense of membership in a world society. Literally none of the forces and conditions which give rise to loyalty to states and lesser groups operate significantly to produce world loyalty. The closest approximation occurs in connection with the United Nations, to which some small degree of loyalty may have developed because of the hope that it would serve effectively as a means of preserving peace. Such loyalty as the United Nations has aroused may or may not be maintained, depending on attitudes toward its utility.

Thus the principal generalization which can be made is that the attitudinal basis for peace over the world as a whole is very weak.

Persistence of this situation is not necessarily inevitable. Theoretically it is possible to develop in all men attitudes that would provide a basis for peace. This is so because attitudes are not congenital but socially and culturally determined. They develop through the learning process. They result from communications of some kind reaching individuals after their birth. This is true of loyalty as well as of other attitudes. If the right things were communicated—if the learning process were properly controlled—all mankind could be led to adopt attitudes conducive to peace. Hope of this is implicit in the constitution of UNESCO which, as we have seen, assumes that wars begin in the minds of men and that it is in those minds that the defenses of peace must be constructed.

However, results which are theoretically possible are often difficult to achieve in practice, and this is true above all with the problem of changing attitudes. Who would decide which attitudes to sponsor? Could the Soviet Union and the United States agree in selecting them? Would other states agree? It seems virtually out of the question. Nationalists would have to cease being nationalists, and communists would have to cease being communists (or at least the adherents of these and other ideologies would have to accept severe modifications of them) if agreement on the attitudes essential to peace were to be reached. Governments would have to risk and perhaps accept subversion. Notions of the sources of prestige and glory, or of the importance of these values, would have to be changed. The obstacles to agreement are formidable. Again, even if agreement could be reached on the nature of the attitudes to be sponsored, who would sponsor them, and how? What chance is there that all people throughout the world whose attitudes are important to peace could be reached and induced to accept attitudes somehow agreed upon? Even if totalitarian controls governed an indoctrination process, it is doubtful whether success could be achieved, and such controls would be unacceptable to significant portions of mankind in any event. The development of appropriate attitudes in free and thinking minds, which would probably be essential to a stable peace, would require a very long time, tremendous effort, and unwonted cooperation among many governments and vast numbers of people.

SECURITY-COMMUNITY

The concept of the security-community has been suggested in connection with the problem of war and peace.

A security-community is considered to be a group which has become integrated, where integration is defined as the attainment of a sense of community, accompanied by formal or informal institutions or practices, sufficiently strong and widespread to assure peaceful change among members of a group with "reasonable" certainty over a "long" period of time.[1]

Security-communities are described as amalgamated and pluralistic. The United States is an amalgamated security-community, having come into existence as a single entity under one government through the merger of formerly independent entities. The United States and Canada together comprise a pluralistic security-community, pluralistic because they are under separate governments.

The fact that security-communities have somehow come into existence in the past suggests that the process is one which might be repeated and extended. States which are not now security-communities might be integrated so as to constitute one, or existing security-communities might be expanded through the addition of other states. The thought is that the development of security-communities would at least solve the problem of war among the members, and that if one security-community could come to encompass most or all of the world the problem of war would be solved for mankind.

The process and the possibility have already been discussed, though the term *security-community* has not appeared. The problems involved have been shown to be tremendous. A further point might be added. It is that the problem of developing a series of security-communities is no doubt much less difficult than the problem of expanding one such community over most or all of the world. This is demonstrated by the very fact that some security-communities, each including a few states, have come into existence, whereas obviously none has spread over the world. Various factors which we have already discussed, to be described collectively as common interests, have repeatedly brought a few states into stable and peaceful relationships with each other. Many alliances are among states which constitute a security-community. Yet, just as alliances tend to produce counteralliances, so is it likely that security-communities would tend to produce rivals. Even if the whole world were organized in a series of security-communities, the likelihood is that at least one of them would define its interests in such a way as to create

---

[1] Richard W. Van Wagenen, *Research in the International Organization Field, Some Notes on a Possible Focus* (Princeton, Center for Research on World Political Institutions, 1952), pp. 10-11.

friction and a danger of war with others. Consensus among such diverse alignments of states as those in the North Atlantic Treaty Organization and those in the communist world seems remote.

WORLD FEDERALISM

Plans for joining sovereign states in some kind of international organization which would to some degree substitute for world government have been proposed throughout the centuries. The League of Nations was, and the United Nations is, such an organization. A number of proposals have been made to go beyond them in the establishment of international or world government. Such plans usually contemplate a federal structure. Some are "partialist," in that they call for including only a part of the states of the world in the structure; others are "universalist." Some are "minimalist," in that they would assign few powers to the federal government; others are "maximalist." The plan of the United World Federalists has been given most prominence in the United States. It is universalist and minimalist. The powers to be given to the world federation, at least at the outset, are substantially limited to the achievement and enforcement of disarmament. It is proposed that the federation come into existence through amendments to the United Nations Charter, that is, through the consent of two-thirds of the United Nations members, including all five permanent members of the Security Council.

For the foreseeable future, such plans have no chance of adoption. Reasons for this conclusion have been presented, implicitly or explicitly, throughout this book. Several of the most important deserve emphasis.

In the first place, the minimum essential attitudinal basis for world federation does not exist and seems unlikely to be created for a long time to come.

In the second place, no acceptable and feasible solution has been found to the problem of allocating votes (or, more generally, shares of control over decisions) within a world federal structure. The authority of a world federation would have to be exercised in conformity with the desires of the strong, just as within countries. One of the assumptions on which democracy rests, that men are equally strong and therefore entitled to equal voting power, is not acceptable on a world scale. People in the more advanced and powerful countries, extending through the geographic region from the Soviet Union to the United States, would not accept a distribution of votes in a world federal structure in proportion to population; they would not believe that India should have more than double the voting strength of the United States, or Indonesia double the voting strength of Britain or France. To give each state in the federal structure one vote would be even more absurd, since states vary so greatly in strength. If either of these "solutions" could somehow be adopted, it would almost inevitably break down, for those with a majority of the votes would not control a preponderance of power. An apportionment of votes according to the distribution of military strength has much to commend it, but it involves many difficulties; among them is the probability that the principle would not be acceptable to weaker peoples and the fact that it provides no basis for reapportionment in the period following the hoped-for disarmament of the units in the federal structure.

In the third place, it is very difficult to internationalize power or to transfer it to a world federal structure. Many elements of power (plants for producing nuclear fuel, for example) are geographically fixed, and the units and weapons of any armed establishment must be geographically located. States within a world federal structure would necessarily retain some power, actual and potential, power of their own and power ostensibly under the command of the federal government but subject to seizure. Closely related is the fact that potential rebels against the world federation would not be geographically interspersed with supporters of the federation. Within countries, potential rebels are usually interspersed with other elements of the population and lack a geographical base for preparing their rebellion. Within a world federation, each unit would not only command some power inevitably but would also have a definite geographic base as a staging area for revolutionary operations.

The final obstacle to world federation which we shall name is

... the unwillingness of governments and peoples to abandon their means of self-defense until they are certain that a world federation can protect them, and the certainty that a world federation cannot protect them until the most powerful have abandoned these means.[2]

The same dilemma has been described in other words.

The status of the international community calls to mind the two trains which met at a crossing where neither would proceed until the other had passed. No state can give up its power of self-defense, or the right to decide when it shall be used, until almost every other state has done the same.[3]

CRISIS

Clearly the peoples and governments of the world today face a crisis. Comfort may be derived from the fact that they have pretty regularly faced crises throughout history, yet somehow have survived, but today's crisis seems to be of a different order of magnitude from any which have been faced before.

In varying degrees sovereign states perform useful functions. They

[2] Quincy Wright, *Problems of Stability and Progress in International Relations* (Berkeley, University of California Press, 1954), p. 235.

[3] Van Wagenen, *op. cit.*, p. 17.

provide a stable order for large groups of people over the world, and within the framework of the stable order they provide for peaceful change. They afford protection for life and property. They permit and stimulate educational, scientific, and cultural pursuits, and the development of systems of production and distribution. If by some evil incantation the sovereign state and its agent, government, could somehow be destroyed and if no substitute were provided (i.e., if complete anarchy could be brought into existence), unimaginable damage would be done.

In rough measure the division of the world into sovereign states reflects actual diversities among men. Men differ in the languages they speak, the religions they profess, the aspirations which they pursue, the skills which they have acquired, the social customs which they follow, the ideologies to which they adhere, the loyalties which they develop, and in a multitude of other ways. They have differing and often conflicting values. On many fundamental questions they hold attitudes which sharply clash. Even within many states differences and conflicts are so great and fundamental that stability and order are difficult to maintain; civil wars occur. Among many states, though not between all of them, the differences and conflicts are still greater. The system of sovereign states is to a considerable degree adapted to the diversities among men, permitting different societies to be governed more or less in accordance with the characteristics which are peculiar to them.

At the same time, whereas sovereign states perform useful and important functions within their own territory, it is obvious that for the world as a whole the system of sovereign states fails to provide adequately for stability, order, and individual welfare. In a multitude of ways the things done by men in one state affect men in other states. Many aspirations can be pursued only through cooperation or conflict with people abroad. And the system of sovereign states does not provide (in fact, it seems to preclude the development of) effective world agencies, comparable to government within countries, for facilitating cooperation and regulating conflicts.

The statement was just made that comfort might be taken from the fact that men have survived crises in the past. The statement should be qualified by recognizing that some states, and even some civilizations, have not survived. A number have perished, and prominent among the reasons has been the inadequacy of interstate arrangements for stability, order, and peaceful change. "The failure to solve the problem of war has been the death of most civilizations that have died since civilizations first came into existence." [4]

The great powers of today, and the civilizations which they help main-

---

[4] Arnold J. Toynbee, as quoted by Kenneth W. Thompson, "Mr. Toynbee and World Politics: War and National Security," *World Politics*, Vol. 8 (April, 1956), p. 383.

tain, face greater danger of cataclysmic destruction than have any of the states or civilizations which have perished in the past. For the first time in history, the possibility exists that war may bring death to people by the hundreds of millions, if not to all mankind. Although science and technology have produced a revolutionary increase in the dangers men face, the methods which men have been willing to adopt to ward off the dangers have improved relatively little for decades and centuries. Better methods are known, but prevailing attitudes make them unacceptable and would probably doom them to failure even if an attempt could somehow be made to use them.

Though a crisis exists for which no acceptable solution is in sight, the prospects are not necessarily hopeless. There have been prolonged periods of substantial peace in the past (witness the century from 1815 to 1914), which suggests that they are possible in the future even if no major change in the political structure of the world occurs. When war comes, as it undoubtedly sometime will, it is not to be assumed that it will necessarily involve the unrestricted use of nuclear weapons or other weapons of mass destruction. The longer utter catastrophe can be postponed, the greater is the possibility that attitudes can be shaped over the world in such a way as to make the postponement indefinite. Moreover, though the prospect now seems remote, changing attitudes plus creative imagination may yet lead to the development of some kind of a world political system which will provide for both stability and change.

More somber possibilities also exist. Surely very drastic changes will occur if major powers engage in unrestricted nuclear warfare. If one side should succeed in laying waste the other while remaining relatively unscathed itself, it might conceivably unite the world politically through the threat of its power; men who are unwilling to agree to something akin to world government might find themselves included in a world empire dominated by the victor. If the belligerents succeed in laying each other waste without destroying all human life, leadership in what is left of the world may well be transferred to peoples now on the periphery of the power struggle, to peoples who are now too weak or backward or uncivilized to take part in suicidal war.

SUGGESTED READINGS

BRINTON, Crane, *From Many One: The Process of Political Integration. The Problem of World Government* (Cambridge, Harvard University Press, 1948).

CARR, E. H., *Nationalism and After* (London, Macmillan, 1945).

CORBETT, Percy E., *Post-War Worlds* (Los Angeles, Institute of Pacific Relations, 1942).

DEUTSCH, Karl W., *Political Community at the International Level, Problems of Definition and Measurement* (New York, Doubleday, 1954).

DUNN, Frederick Sherwood, *War and the Minds of Men* (New York, Harper, 1950).

GROSS, Feliks, *Foreign Policy Analysis* (New York, Philosophical Library, 1954).

GUETZKOW, Harold, *Multiple Loyalties: Theoretical Approach to a Problem in International Organization* (Princeton, Center for Research on World Political Institutions, 1955).

HEMLEBEN, Sylvester J., *Plans for World Peace Through Six Centuries* (Chicago, The University of Chicago Press, 1943).

MARRIOTT, J. A. R., *Commonwealth or Anarchy? A Survey of Projects of Peace from the Sixteenth to the Twentieth Century* (New York, Columbia University Press, 1939).

NORTHROP, F. S. C., *The Taming of the Nations* (New York, Macmillan, 1952).

SCHUMAN, F. L. *The Commonwealth of Man* (New York, Knopf, 1952).

STREIT, Clarence K., *Freedom Against Itself* (New York, Harper, 1954).

THOMPSON, Kenneth W., "Mr. Toynbee and World Politics: War and National Security," *World Politics*, Vol. 8 (April, 1956), pp. 374-391.

VAN WAGENEN, Richard W., *Research in the International Organization Field, Some Notes on a Possible Focus* (Princeton: Center for Research on World Political Institutions, 1952).

WRIGHT, Quincy, *Problems of Stability and Progress in International Relations* (Berkeley, University of California Press, 1954).

WYNNER, Edith, and LLOYD, Georgia, *Searchlight on Peace Plans* (New York, Dutton, 1944).

Appendix

INTERNATIONAL DOCUMENTS

Charter of the United Nations

WE THE PEOPLES
OF THE UNITED NATIONS
DETERMINED

> to save succeeding generations from the scourge of war, which twice in our lifetime has brought untold sorrow to mankind, and

> to reaffirm faith in fundamental human rights, in the dignity and worth of the human person, in the equal rights of men and women and of nations large and small, and

> to establish conditions under which justice and respect for the obligations arising from treaties and other sources of international law can be maintained, and

> to promote social progress and better standards of life in larger freedom,

AND FOR THESE ENDS

> to practice tolerance and live together in peace with one another as good neighbors, and

> to unite our strength to maintain international peace and security, and

> to ensure, by the acceptance of principles and the institution of methods, that armed force shall not be used, save in the common interest, and

> to employ international machinery for the promotion of the economic and social advancement of all peoples,

HAVE RESOLVED TO
COMBINE OUR EFFORTS TO
ACCOMPLISH THESE AIMS.

> Accordingly, our respective Governments, through representatives assembled in the city of San Francisco, who have exhibited their full powers found to be in good and due form, have agreed to the present Charter of the United Nations and do hereby establish an international organization to be known as the United Nations.

CHAPTER I

PURPOSES AND PRINCIPLES

Article 1

The Purposes of the United Nations are:

1. To maintain international peace and security, and to that end: to take effective collective measures for the prevention and removal of threats to the peace, and for the suppression of acts of aggression or other breaches of the peace, and to bring about by peaceful means, and in conformity with the principles of justice and international law, adjustment or settlement of international disputes or situations which might lead to a breach of the peace;

2. To develop friendly relations among nations based on respect for the principle of equal rights and self-determination of peoples, and to take other appropriate measures to strengthen universal peace;

3. To achieve international cooperation in solving international problems of an economic, social, cultural, or humanitarian character, and in promoting and encouraging respect for human rights and for fundamental freedoms for all without distinction as to race, sex, language, or religion; and

4. To be a center for harmonizing the actions of nations in the attainment of these common ends.

Article 2

The Organization and its Members, in pursuit of the Purposes stated in Article 1, shall act in accordance with the following Principles.

1. The Organization is based on the principle of the sovereign equality of all its Members.

2. All Members, in order to ensure to all of them the rights and benefits resulting from membership, shall fulfil in good faith the obligations assumed by them in accordance with the present Charter.

3. All Members shall settle their international disputes by peaceful means in such a manner that international peace and security, and justice, are not endangered.

4. All Members shall refrain in their international relations from the threat or use of force against the territorial integrity or political independence of any state, or in any other manner inconsistent with the Purposes of the United Nations.

5. All Members shall give the United Nations every assistance in any action it takes in accordance with the present Charter, and shall refrain from giving assistance to any state against which the United Nations is taking preventive or enforcement action.

6. The Organization shall ensure that states which are not Members of the United Nations act in accordance with these Principles so far as may be necessary for the maintenance of international peace and security.

7. Nothing contained in the present Charter shall authorize the United Nations to intervene in matters which are essentially within the domestic jurisdiction of any state or shall require the Members to submit such matters to

settlement under the present Charter; but this principle shall not prejudice the application of enforcement measures under Chapter VII.

Chapter II

MEMBERSHIP

Article 3

The original Members of the United Nations shall be the states which, having participated in the United Nations Conference on International Organization at San Francisco, or having previously signed the Declaration by United Nations of January 1, 1942, sign the present Charter and ratify it in accordance with Article 110.

Article 4

1. Membership in the United Nations is open to all other peace-loving states which accept the obligations contained in the present Charter and, in the judgment of the Organization, are able and willing to carry out these obligations.

2. The admission of any such state to membership in the United Nations will be effected by a decision of the General Assembly upon the recommendation of the Security Council.

Article 5

A Member of the United Nations against which preventive or enforcement action has been taken by the Security Council may be suspended from the exercise of the rights and privileges of membership by the General Assembly upon the recommendation of the Security Council. The exercise of these rights and privileges may be restored by the Security Council.

Article 6

A Member of the United Nations which has persistently violated the Principles contained in the present Charter may be expelled from the Organization by the General Assembly upon the recommendation of the Security Council.

Chapter III

ORGANS

Article 7

1. There are established as the principal organs of the United Nations; a General Assembly, a Security Council, an Economic and Social Council, a Trusteeship Council, an International Court of Justice, and a Secretariat.

2. Such subsidiary organs as may be found necessary may be established in accordance with the present Charter.

Article 8

The United Nations shall place no restrictions on the eligibility of men and women to participate in any capacity and under conditions of equality in its principal and subsidiary organs.

Chapter IV

THE GENERAL ASSEMBLY

Composition

Article 9

1. The General Assembly shall consist of all the Members of the United Nations.

2. Each Member shall have not more than five representatives in the General Assembly.

Functions and Powers

Article 10

The General Assembly may discuss any questions or any matters within the scope of the present Charter or relating to the powers and functions of any organs provided for in the present Charter, and, except as provided in Article 12, may make recommendations to the Members of the United Nations or to the Security Council or to both on any such questions or matters.

Article 11

1. The General Assembly may consider the general principles of cooperation in the maintenance of international peace and security, including the principles governing disarmament and the regulation of armaments, and may make recommendations with regard to such principles to the Members or to the Security Council or to both.

2. The General Assembly may discuss any questions relating to the maintenance of international peace and security brought before it by any Member of the United Nations, or by the Security Council, or by a state which is not a Member of the United Nations in accordance with Article 35, paragraph 2, and, except as provided in Article 12, may make recommendations with regard to any such question to the state or states concerned or to the Security Council or to both. Any such question on which action is necessary shall be referred to the Security Council by the General Assembly either before or after discussion.

3. The General Assembly may call the attention of the Security Council to situations which are likely to endanger international peace and security.

4. The powers of the General Assembly set forth in this Article shall not limit the general scope of Article 10.

Article 12

1. While the Security Council is exercising in respect of any dispute or situation the functions assigned to it in the present Charter, the General Assembly shall not make any recommendations with regard to that dispute or situation unless the Security Council so requests.

2. The Secretary-General, with the consent of the Security Council, shall notify the General Assembly at each session of any matters relative to the maintenance of international peace and security which are being dealt with by the Security Council and shall similarly notify the General Assembly, or the Members of the United Nations if the General Assembly is not in session, immediately the Security Council ceases to deal with such matters.

Article 13

1. The General Assembly shall initiate studies and make recommendations for the purpose of:

a. promoting international cooperation in the political field and encouraging the progressive development of international law and its codification;

b. promoting international cooperation in the economic, social, cultural, educational, and health fields, and assisting in the realization of human rights and fundamental freedoms for all without distinction as to race, sex, language, or religion.

2. The further responsibilities, functions and powers of the General Assembly with respect to matters mentioned in paragraph 1(b) above are set forth in Chapters IX and X.

Article 14

Subject to the provisions of Article 12, the General Assembly may recommend measures for the peaceful adjustment of any situation, regardless of origin, which it deems likely to impair the general welfare or friendly relations among nations, including situations resulting from a violation of the provisions of the present Charter setting forth the Purposes and Principles of the United Nations.

Article 15

1. The General Assembly shall receive and consider annual and special reports from the Security Council; these reports shall include an account of the measures that the Security Council has decided upon or taken to maintain international peace and security.

2. The General Assembly shall receive and consider reports from the other organs of the United Nations.

Article 16

The General Assembly shall perform such functions with respect to the international trusteeship system as are assigned to it under Chapters XII and XIII, including the approval of the trusteeship agreements for areas not designated as strategic.

Article 17

1. The General Assembly shall consider and approve the budget of the Organization.

2. The expenses of the Organization shall be borne by the Members as apportioned by the General Assembly.

3. The General Assembly shall consider and approve any financial and budgetary arrangements with specialized agencies referred to in Article 57 and shall examine the administrative budgets of such specialized agencies with a view to making recommendations to the agencies concerned.

Voting

Article 18

1. Each member of the General Assembly shall have one vote.

2. Decisions of the General Assembly on important questions shall be made by a two-thirds majority of the members present and voting. These questions

shall include: recommendations with respect to the maintenance of international peace and security, the election of the non-permanent members of the Security Council, the election of the members of the Economic and Social Council, the election of members of the Trusteeship Council in accordance with paragraph 1(c) of Article 86, the admission of new Members to the United Nations, the suspension of the rights and privileges of membership, the expulsion of Members, questions relating to the operation of the trusteeship system, and budgetary questions.

3. Decisions on other questions, including the determination of additional categories of questions to be decided by a two-thirds majority, shall be made by a majority of the members present and voting.

Article 19

A Member of the United Nations which is in arrears in the payment of its financial contributions to the Organization shall have no vote in the General Assembly if the amount of its arrears equals or exceeds the amount of the contributions due from it for the preceding two full years. The General Assembly may, nevertheless, permit such a Member to vote if it is satisfied that the failure to pay is due to conditions beyond the control of the Member.

Procedure

Article 20

The General Assembly shall meet in regular annual sessions and in such special sessions as occasion may require. Special sessions shall be convoked by the Secretary-General at the request of the Security Council or of a majority of the Members of the United Nations.

Article 21

The General Assembly shall adopt its own rules of procedure. It shall elect its President for each session.

Article 22

The General Assembly may establish such subsidiary organs as it deems necessary for the performance of its functions.

CHAPTER V

THE SECURITY COUNCIL

Composition

Article 23

1. The Security Council shall consist of eleven Members of the United Nations. The Republic of China, France, the Union of Soviet Socialist Republics, the United Kingdom of Great Britain and Northern Ireland, and the United States of America shall be permanent members of the Security Council. The General Assembly shall elect six other Members of the United Nations to be non-permanent members of the Security Council, due regard being specially paid, in the first instance to the contribution of Members of the United Nations to the maintenance of international peace and security and to the other purposes of the Organization, and also to equitable geographical distribution.

2. The non-permanent members of the Security Council shall be elected for a term of two years. In the first election of the non-permanent members,

however, three shall be chosen for a term of one year. A retiring member shall not be eligible for immediate re-election.

3. Each member of the Security Council shall have one representative.

Functions and Powers
Article 24

1. In order to ensure prompt and effective action by the United Nations, its Members confer on the Security Council primary responsibility for the maintenance of international peace and security, and agree that in carrying out its duties under this responsibility the Security Council acts on their behalf.

2. In discharging these duties the Security Council shall act in accordance with the Purposes and Principles of the United Nations. The specific powers granted to the Security Council for the discharge of these duties are laid down in Chapters VI, VII, VIII, and XII.

3. The Security Council shall submit annual and, when necessary, special reports to the General Assembly for its consideration.

Article 25

The Members of the United Nations agree to accept and carry out the decisions of the Security Council in accordance with the present Charter.

Article 26

In order to promote the establishment and maintenance of international peace and security with the least diversion for armaments of the world's human and economic resources, the Security Council shall be responsible for formulating, with the assistance of the Military Staff Committee referred to in Article 47, plans to be submitted to the Members of the United Nations for the establishment of a system for the regulation of armaments.

Voting
Article 27

1. Each member of the Security Council shall have one vote.

2. Decisions of the Security Council on procedural matters shall be made by an affirmative vote of seven members.

3. Decisions of the Security Council on all other matters shall be made by an affirmative vote of seven members including the concurring votes of the permanent members; provided that, in decisions under Chapter VI, and under paragraph 3 of Article 52, a party to a dispute shall abstain from voting.

Procedure
Article 28

1. The Security Council shall be so organized as to be able to function continuously. Each member of the Security Council shall for this purpose be represented at all times at the seat of the Organization.

2. The Security Council shall hold periodic meetings at which each of its members may, if it so desires, be represented by a member of the government or by some other specially designated representative.

3. The Security Council may hold meetings at such places other than the seat of the Organization as in its judgment will best facilitate its work.

Article 29

The Security Council may establish such subsidiary organs as it deems necessary for the performance of its functions.

Article 30

The Security Council shall adopt its own rules of procedure, including the method of selecting its President.

Article 31

Any Member of the United Nations which is not a member of the Security Council may participate, without vote, in the discussion of any question brought before the Security Council whenever the latter considers that the interests of that Member are specially affected.

Article 32

Any Member of the United Nations which is not a member of the Security Council or any state which is not a Member of the United Nations, if it is a party to a dispute under consideration by the Security Council, shall be invited to participate, without vote, in the discussion relating to the dispute. The Security Council shall lay down such conditions as it deems just for the participation of a state which is not a Member of the United Nations.

CHAPTER VI

PACIFIC SETTLEMENT OF DISPUTES

Article 33

1. The parties to any dispute, the continuance of which is likely to endanger the maintenance of international peace and security, shall, first of all, seek a solution by negotiation, enquiry, mediation, conciliation, arbitration, judicial settlement, resort to regional agencies or arrangements, or other peaceful means of their own choice.

2. The Security Council shall, when it deems necessary, call upon the parties to settle their dispute by such means.

Article 34

The Security Council may investigate any dispute, or any situation which might lead to international friction or give rise to a dispute, in order to determine whether the continuance of the dispute or situation is likely to endanger the maintenance of international peace and security.

Article 35

1. Any Member of the United Nations may bring any dispute, or any situation of the nature referred to in Article 34, to the attention of the Security Council or of the General Assembly.

2. A state which is not a Member of the United Nations may bring to the attention of the Security Council or of the General Assembly any dispute to which it is a party if it accepts in advance, for the purposes of the dispute, the obligations of pacific settlement provided in the present Charter.

3. The proceedings of the General Assembly in respect of matters brought to its attention under this Article will be subject to the provisions of Articles 11 and 12.

Article 36

1. The Security Council may, at any stage of a dispute of the nature referred to in Article 33 or of a situation of like nature, recommend appropriate procedures or methods of adjustment.

2. The Security Council should take into consideration any procedures for the settlement of the dispute which have already been adopted by the parties.

3. In making recommendations under this Article the Security Council should also take into consideration that legal disputes should as a general rule be referred by the parties to the International Court of Justice in accordance with the provisions of the Statute of the Court.

Article 37

1. Should the parties to a dispute of the nature referred to in Article 33 fail to settle it by the means indicated in that Article, they shall refer it to the Security Council.

2. If the Security Council deems that the continuance of the dispute is in fact likely to endanger the maintenance of international peace and security, it shall decide whether to take action under Article 36 or to recommend such terms of settlement as it may consider appropriate.

Article 38

Without prejudice to the provisions of Articles 33 to 37, the Security Council may, if all the parties to any dispute so request, make recommendations to the parties with a view to a pacific settlement of the dispute.

Chapter VII

ACTION WITH RESPECT TO THREATS TO THE PEACE, BREACHES OF THE PEACE, AND ACTS OF AGGRESSION

Article 39

The Security Council shall determine the existence of any threat to the peace, breach of the peace, or act of aggression and shall make recommendations, or decide what measures shall be taken in accordance with Articles 41 and 42, to maintain or restore international peace and security.

Article 40

In order to prevent an aggravation of the situation, the Security Council may, before making the recommendations or deciding upon the measures provided for in Article 39, call upon the parties concerned to comply with such provisional measures as it deems necessary or desirable. Such provisional measures shall be without prejudice to the rights, claims, or position of the parties concerned. The Security Council shall duly take account of failure to comply with such provisional measures.

Article 41

The Security Council may decide what measures not involving the use of armed force are to be employed to give effect to its decisions, and it may call upon the Members of the United Nations to apply such measures. These may include complete or partial interruption of economic relations and of rail, sea, air, postal, telegraphic, radio, and other means of communication, and the severance of diplomatic relations.

Article 42

Should the Security Council consider that measures provided for in Article 41 would be inadequate or have proved to be inadequate, it may take such action by air, sea, or land forces as may be necessary to maintain or restore international peace and security. Such action may include demonstrations, blockade, and other operations by air, sea, or land forces of Members of the United Nations.

Article 43

1. All Members of the United Nations, in order to contribute to the maintenance of international peace and security, undertake to make available to the Security Council, on its call and in accordance with a special agreement or agreements, armed forces, assistance, and facilities, including rights of passage, necessary for the purpose of maintaining international peace and security.

2. Such agreement or agreements shall govern the numbers and types of forces, their degree of readiness and general location, and the nature of the facilities and assistance to be provided.

3. The agreement or agreements shall be negotiated as soon as possible on the initiative of the Security Council. They shall be concluded between the Security Council and Members or between the Security Council and groups of Members and shall be subject to ratification by the signatory states in accordance with their respective constitutional processes.

Article 44

When the Security Council has decided to use force it shall, before calling upon a Member not represented on it to provide armed forces in fulfillment of the obligations assumed under Article 43, invite that Member, if the Member so desires, to participate in the decisions of the Security Council concerning the employment of contingents of that Member's armed forces.

Article 45

In order to enable the United Nations to take urgent military measures, Members shall hold immediately available national air-force contingents for combined international enforcement action. The strength and degree of readiness of these contingents and plans for their combined action shall be determined, within the limits laid down in the special agreement or agreements referred to in Article 43, by the Security Council with the assistance of the Military Staff Committee.

Article 46

Plans for the application of armed force shall be made by the Security Council with the assistance of the Military Staff Committee.

Article 47

1. There shall be established a Military Staff Committee to advise and assist the Security Council on all questions relating to the Security Council's military requirements for the maintenance of international peace and security, the

employment and command of forces placed at its disposal, the regulation of armaments, and possible disarmament.

2. The Military Staff Committee shall consist of the Chiefs of Staff of the permanent members of the Security Council or their representatives. Any Member of the United Nations not permanently represented on the Committee shall be invited by the Committee to be associated with it when the efficient discharge of the Committee's responsibilities requires the participation of that Member in its work.

3. The Military Staff Committee shall be responsible under the Security Council for the strategic direction of any armed forces placed at the disposal of the Security Council. Questions relating to the command of such forces shall be worked out subsequently.

4. The Military Staff Committee, with the authorization of the Security Council and after consultation with appropriate regional agencies, may establish regional subcommittees.

Article 48

1. The action required to carry out the decisions of the Security Council for the maintenance of international peace and security shall be taken by all the Members of the United Nations or by some of them, as the Security Council may determine.

2. Such decisions shall be carried out by the Members of the United Nations directly and through their action in the appropriate international agencies of which they are members.

Article 49

The Members of the United Nations shall join in affording mutual assistance in carrying out the measures decided upon by the Security Council.

Article 50

If preventive or enforcement measures against any state are taken by the Security Council, any other state, whether a Member of the United Nations or not, which finds itself confronted with special economic problems arising from the carrying out of those measures shall have the right to consult the Security Council with regard to a solution of those problems.

Article 51

Nothing in the present Charter shall impair the inherent right of individual or collective self-defense if an armed attack occurs against a Member of the United Nations, until the Security Council has taken measures necessary to maintain international peace and security. Measures taken by Members in the exercise of this right of self-defense shall be immediately reported to the Security Council and shall not in any way affect the authority and responsibility of the Security Council under the present Charter to take at any time such action as it deems necessary in order to maintain or restore international peace and security.

CHAPTER VIII

REGIONAL ARRANGEMENTS

Article 52

1. Nothing in the present Charter precludes the existence of regional arrangements or agencies for dealing with such matters relating to the maintenance of international peace and security as are appropriate for regional action, provided that such arrangements or agencies and their activities are consistent with the Purposes and Principles of the United Nations.

2. The Members of the United Nations entering into such arrangements or constituting such agencies shall make every effort to achieve pacific settlement of local disputes through such regional arrangements or by such regional agencies before referring them to the Security Council.

3. The Security Council shall encourage the development of pacific settlement of local disputes through such regional arrangements or by such regional agencies either on the initiative of the states concerned or by reference from the Security Council.

4. This Article in no way impairs the application of Articles 34 and 35.

Article 53

1. The Security Council shall, where appropriate, utilize such regional arrangements or agencies for enforcement action under its authority. But no enforcement action shall be taken under regional arrangements or by regional agencies without the authorization of the Security Council, with the exception of measures against any enemy state, as defined in paragraph 2 of this Article, provided for pursuant to Article 107 or in regional arrangements directed against renewal of aggressive policy on the part of any such state, until such time as the Organization may, on request of the Governments concerned, be charged with the responsibility for preventing further aggression by such a state.

2. The term enemy state as used in paragraph 1 of this Article applies to any state which during the Second World War has been an enemy of any signatory of the present Charter.

Article 54

The Security Council shall at all times be kept fully informed of activities undertaken or in contemplation under regional arrangements or by regional agencies for the maintenance of international peace and security.

CHAPTER IX

INTERNATIONAL ECONOMIC AND SOCIAL COOPERATION

Article 55

With a view to the creation of conditions of stability and well-being which are necessary for peaceful and friendly relations among nations based on respect for the principle of equal rights and self-determination of peoples, the United Nations shall promote:

a. higher standards of living, full employment, and conditions of economic and social progress and development;

b. solutions of international economic, social, health, and related problems; and international cultural and educational cooperation; and

c. universal respect for, and observance of, human rights and fundamental freedoms for all without distinction as to race, sex, language, or religion.

Article 56

All Members pledge themselves to take joint and separate action in cooperation with the Organization for the achievement of the purposes set forth in Article 55.

Article 57

1. The various specialized agencies, established by intergovernmental agreement and having wide international responsibilities, as defined in their basic instruments, in economic, social, cultural, educational, health, and related fields, shall be brought into relationship with the United Nations in accordance with the provisions of Article 63.

2. Such agencies thus brought into relationship with the United Nations are hereinafter referred to as specialized agencies.

Article 58

The Organization shall make recommendations for the coordination of the policies and activities of the specialized agencies.

Article 59

The Organization shall, where appropriate, initiate negotiations among the states concerned for the creation of any new specialized agencies required for the accomplishment of the purposes set forth in Article 55.

Article 60

Responsibility for the discharge of the functions of the Organization set forth in this Chapter shall be vested in the General Assembly and, under the authority of the General Assembly, in the Economic and Social Council, which shall have for this purpose the powers set forth in Chapter X.

CHAPTER X

THE ECONOMIC AND SOCIAL COUNCIL

Composition

Article 61

1. The Economic and Social Council shall consist of eighteen Members of the United Nations elected by the General Assembly.

2. Subject to the provisions of paragraph 3, six members of the Economic and Social Council shall be elected each year for a term of three years. A retiring member shall be eligible for immediate re-election.

3. At the first election, eighteen members of the Economic and Social Council shall be chosen. The term of office of six members so chosen shall expire at

the end of one year, and of six other members at the end of two years, in accordance with arrangements made by the General Assembly.

4. Each member of the Economic and Social Council shall have one representative.

Functions and Powers

Article 62

1. The Economic and Social Council may make or initiate studies and reports with respect to international economic, social, cultural, educational, health, and related matters and may make recommendations with respect to any such matters to the General Assembly, to the Members of the United Nations, and to the specialized agencies concerned.

2. It may make recommendations for the purpose of promoting respect for, and observance of, human rights and fundamental freedoms for all.

3. It may prepare draft conventions for submission to the General Assembly, with respect to matters falling within its competence.

4. It may call, in accordance with the rules prescribed by the United Nations, international conferences on matters falling within its competence.

Article 63

1. The Economic and Social Council may enter into agreements with any of the agencies referred to in Article 57, defining the terms on which the agency concerned shall be brought into relationship with the United Nations. Such agreements shall be subject to approval by the General Assembly.

2. It may coordinate the activities of the specialized agencies through consultation with and recommendations to such agencies and through recommendations to the General Assembly and to the Members of the United Nations.

Article 64

1. The Economic and Social Council may take appropriate steps to obtain regular reports from the specialized agencies. It may make arrangements with the Members of the United Nations and with the specialized agencies to obtain reports on the steps taken to give effect to its own recommendations and to recommendations on matters falling within its competence made by the General Assembly.

2. It may communicate its observations on these reports to the General Assembly.

Article 65

The Economic and Social Council may furnish information to the Security Council and shall assist the Security Council upon its request.

Article 66

1. The Economic and Social Council shall perform such functions as fall within its competence in connection with the carrying out of the recommendations of the General Assembly.

2. It may, with the approval of the General Assembly, perform services at the request of Members of the United Nations and at the request of specialized agencies.

3. It shall perform such other functions as are specified elsewhere in the present Charter or as may be assigned to it by the General Assembly.

Voting

Article 67

1. Each member of the Economic and Social Council shall have one vote.

2. Decisions of the Economic and Social Council shall be made by a majority of the members present and voting.

Procedure

Article 68

The Economic and Social Council shall set up commissions in economic and social fields and for the promotion of human rights, and such other commissions as may be required for the performance of its functions.

Article 69

The Economic and Social Council shall invite any Member of the United Nations to participate, without vote, in its deliberations on any matter of particular concern to that Member.

Article 70

The Economic and Social Council may make arrangements for representatives of the specialized agencies to participate, without vote, in its deliberations and in those of the commissions established by it, and for its representatives to participate in the deliberations of the specialized agencies.

Article 71

The Economic and Social Council may make suitable arrangements for consultation with non-governmental organizations which are concerned with matters within its competence. Such arrangements may be made with international organizations and, where appropriate, with national organizations after consultation with the Member of the United Nations concerned.

Article 72

1. The Economic and Social Council shall adopt its own rules of procedure, including the method of selecting its President.

2. The Economic and Social Council shall meet as required in accordance with its rules, which shall include provision for the convening of meetings on the request of a majority of its members.

CHAPTER XI

DECLARATION REGARDING NON-SELF-GOVERNING TERRITORIES

Article 73

Members of the United Nations which have or assume responsibilities for the administration of territories whose peoples have not yet attained a full measure of self-government recognize the principle that the interests of the inhabitants of these territories are paramount, and accept as a sacred trust the obligation to promote to the utmost, within the system of international peace and security established by the present Charter, the well-being of the inhabitants of these territories, and, to this end:

a. to ensure, with due respect for the culture of the peoples concerned, their political, economic, social, and educational advancement, their just treatment, and their protection against abuses;

b. to develop self-government, to take due account of the political aspirations of the peoples, and to assist them in the progressive development of their free political institutions, according to the particular circumstances of each territory and its peoples and their varying stages of advancement;

c. to further international peace and security;

d. to promote constructive measures of development, to encourage research, and to cooperate with one another and, when and where appropriate, with specialized international bodies with a view to the practical achievement of the social, economic, and scientific purposes set forth in this Article; and

e. to transmit regularly to the Secretary-General for information purposes, subject to such limitation as security and constitutional considerations may require, statistical and other information of a technical nature relating to economic, social, and educational conditions in the territories for which they are respectively responsible other than those territories to which Chapters XII and XIII apply.

Article 74

Members of the United Nations also agree that their policy in respect of the territories to which this Chapter applies, no less than in respect of their metropolitan areas, must be based on the general principle of good-neighborliness, due account being taken of the interests and well-being of the rest of the world, in social, economic, and commercial matters.

Chapter XII

INTERNATIONAL TRUSTEESHIP SYSTEM

Article 75

The United Nations shall establish under its authority an international trusteeship system for the administration and supervision of such territories as may be placed thereunder by subsequent individual agreements. These territories are hereinafter referred to as trust territories.

Article 76

The basic objectives of the trusteeship system, in accordance with the Purposes of the United Nations laid down in Article 1 of the present Charter, shall be:

a. to further international peace and security;

b. to promote the political, economic, social, and educational advancement of the inhabitants of the trust territories, and their progressive development towards self-government or independence as may be appropriate to the particular circumstances of each territory and its peoples and the freely expressed wishes of the peoples concerned, and as may be provided by the terms of each trusteeship agreement;

c. to encourage respect for human rights and for fundamental freedoms for all without distinction as to race, sex, language, or religion, and to encourage recognition of the interdependence of the peoples of the world; and

d. to ensure equal treatment in social, economic, and commercial matters for all Members of the United Nations and their nationals, and also equal treatment for the latter in the administration of justice, without prejudice to the attainment of the foregoing objectives and subject to the provisions of Article 80.

Article 77

1. The trusteeship system shall apply to such territories in the following categories as may be placed thereunder by means of trusteeship agreements:

a. territories now held under mandate;

b. territories which may be detached from enemy states as a result of the Second World War; and

c. territories voluntarily placed under the system by states responsible for their administration.

2. It will be a matter for subsequent agreement as to which territories in the foregoing categories will be brought under the trusteeship system and upon what terms.

Article 78

The trusteeship system shall not apply to territories which have become Members of the United Nations, relationship among which shall be based on respect for the principle of sovereign equality.

Article 79

The terms of trusteeship for each territory to be placed under the trusteeship system, including any alteration or amendment, shall be agreed upon by the states directly concerned, including the mandatory power in the case of territories held under mandate by a Member of the United Nations, and shall be approved as provided for in Articles 83 and 85.

Article 80

1. Except as may be agreed upon in individual trusteeship agreements, made under Articles 77, 79, and 81, placing each territory under the trusteeship system, and until such agreements have been concluded, nothing in this Chapter shall be construed in or of itself to alter in any manner the rights whatsoever of any states or any peoples or the terms of existing international instruments to which Members of the United Nations may respectively be parties.

2. Paragraph 1 of this Article shall not be interpreted as giving grounds for delay or postponement of the negotiation and conclusion of agreements for placing mandated and other territories under the trusteeship system as provided for in Article 77.

Article 81

The trusteeship agreement shall in each case include the terms under which the trust territory will be administered and designate the authority which will exercise the administration of the trust territory. Such authority, hereinafter called the administering authority, may be one or more states or the Organization itself.

Article 82

There may be designated, in any trusteeship agreement, a strategic area or areas which may include part or all of the trust territory to which the agreement applies, without prejudice to any special agreement or agreements made under Article 43.

Article 83

1. All functions of the United Nations relating to strategic areas, including the approval of the terms of the trusteeship agreements and of their alteration or amendment, shall be exercised by the Security Council.

2. The basic objectives set forth in Article 76 shall be applicable to the people of each strategic area.

3. The Security Council shall, subject to the provisions of the trusteeship agreements and without prejudice to security considerations, avail itself of the assistance of the Trusteeship Council to perform those functions of the United Nations under the trusteeship system relating to political, economic, social, and educational matters in the strategic areas.

Article 84

It shall be the duty of the administering authority to ensure that the trust territory shall play its part in the maintenance of international peace and security. To this end the administering authority may make use of volunteer forces, facilities, and assistance from the trust territory in carrying out the obligations towards the Security Council undertaken in this regard by the administering authority, as well as for local defense and the maintenance of law and order within the trust territory.

Article 85

1. The functions of the United Nations with regard to trusteeship agreements for all areas not designated as strategic, including the approval of the terms of the trusteeship agreements and of their alteration or amendment, shall be exercised by the General Assembly.

2. The Trusteeship Council, operating under the authority of the General Assembly, shall assist the General Assembly in carrying out these functions.

Chapter XIII

THE TRUSTEESHIP COUNCIL

Composition

Article 86

1. The Trusteeship Council shall consist of the following Members of the United Nations:

    a. those Members administering trust territories;

    b. such of those Members mentioned by name in Article 23 as are not administering trust territories; and

    c. as many other Members elected for three-year terms by the General Assembly as may be necessary to ensure that the total number of members of the Trusteeship Council is equally divided between those Members of the United Nations which administer trust territories and those which do not.

2. Each member of the Trusteeship Council shall designate one specially qualified person to represent it therein.

Functions and Powers

Article 87

The General Assembly and, under its authority, the Trusteeship Council, in carrying out their functions, may:

a. consider reports submitted by the administering authority;

b. accept petitions and examine them in consultation with the administering authority;

c. provide for periodic visits to the respective trust territories at times agreed upon with the administering authority; and

d. take these and other actions in conformity with the terms of the trusteeship agreements.

Article 88

The Trusteeship Council shall formulate a questionnaire on the political, economic, social, and educational advancement of the inhabitants of each trust territory, and the administering authority for each trust territory within the competence of the General Assembly shall make an annual report to the General Assembly upon the basis of such questionnaire.

Voting

Article 89

1. Each member of the Trusteeship Council shall have one vote.

2. Decisions of the Trusteeship Council shall be made by a majority of the members present and voting.

Procedure

Article 90

1. The Trusteeship Council shall adopt its own rules of procedure, including the method of selecting its President.

2. The Trusteeship Council shall meet as required in accordance with its rules, which shall include provision for the convening of meetings on the request of a majority of its members.

Article 91

The Trusteeship Council shall, when appropriate, avail itself of the assistance of the Economic and Social Council and of the specialized agencies in regard to matters with which they are respectively concerned.

CHAPTER XIV

THE INTERNATIONAL COURT OF JUSTICE

Article 92

The International Court of Justice shall be the principal judicial organ of the United Nations. It shall function in accordance with the annexed Statute, which is based upon the Statute of the Permanent Court of International Justice and forms an integral part of the present Charter.

Article 93

1. All Members of the United Nations are *ipso facto* parties to the Statute of the International Court of Justice.

2. A state which is not a Member of the United Nations may become a party to the Statute of the International Court of Justice on condition to be determined in each case by the General Assembly upon the recommendation of the Security Council.

Article 94

1. Each Member of the United Nations undertakes to comply with the decision of the International Court of Justice in any case to which it is a party.

2. If any party to a case fails to perform the obligations incumbent upon it under a judgment rendered by the Court, the other party may have recourse to the Security Council, which may, if it deems necessary, make recommendations or decide upon measures to be taken to give effect to the judgment.

Article 95

Nothing in the present Charter shall prevent Members of the United Nations from entrusting the solution of their differences to other tribunals by virtue of agreements already in existence or which may be concluded in the future.

Article 96

1. The General Assembly or the Security Council may request the International Court of Justice to give an advisory opinion on any legal question.

2. Other organs of the United Nations and specialized agencies, which may at any time be so authorized by the General Assembly, may also request advisory opinions of the Court on legal questions arising within the scope of their activities.

CHAPTER XV

THE SECRETARIAT

Article 97

The Secretariat shall comprise a Secretary-General and such staff as the Organization may require. The Secretary-General shall be appointed by the General Assembly upon the recommendation of the Security Council. He shall be the chief administrative officer of the Organization.

Article 98

The Secretary-General shall act in that capacity in all meetings of the General Assembly, of the Security Council, of the Economic and Social Council, and of the Trusteeship Council, and shall perform such other functions as are entrusted to him by these organs. The Secretary-General shall make an annual report to the General Assembly on the work of the Organization.

Article 99

The Secretary-General may bring to the attention of the Security Council any matter which in his opinion may threaten the maintenance of international peace and security.

Article 100

1. In the performance of their duties the Secretary-General and the staff shall not seek or receive instructions from any government or from any other authority external to the Organization. They shall refrain from any action which might reflect on their position as international officials responsible only to the Organization.

2. Each Member of the United Nations undertakes to respect the exclusively international character of the responsibilities of the Secretary-General and the staff and not to seek to influence them in the discharge of their responsibilities.

Article 101

1. The staff shall be appointed by the Secretary-General under regulations established by the General Assembly.

2. Appropriate staffs shall be permanently assigned to the Economic and Social Council, the Trusteeship Council, and, as required, to other organs of the United Nations. These staffs shall form a part of the Secretariat.

3. The paramount consideration in the employment of the staff and in the determination of the conditions of service shall be the necessity of securing the highest standards of efficiency, competence, and integrity. Due regard shall be paid to the importance of recruiting the staff on as wide a geographical basis as possible.

CHAPTER XVI

MISCELLANEOUS PROVISIONS

Article 102

1. Every treaty and every international agreement entered into by any Member of the United Nations after the present Charter comes into force shall as soon as possible be registered with the Secretariat and published by it.

2. No party to any such treaty or international agreement which has not been registered in accordance with the provisions of paragraph 1 of this Article may invoke that treaty or agreement before any organ of the United Nations.

Article 103

In the event of a conflict between the obligations of the Members of the United Nations under the present Charter and their obligations under any other international agreement, their obligations under the present Charter shall prevail.

Article 104

The Organization shall enjoy in the territory of each of its Members such legal capacity as may be necessary for the exercise of its functions and the fulfillment of its purposes.

Article 105

1. The Organization shall enjoy in the territory of each of its Members such privileges and immunities as are necessary for the fulfillment of its purposes.

2. Representatives of the Members of the United Nations and officials of the Organization shall similarly enjoy such privileges and immunities as are neces-

sary for the independent exercise of their functions in connection with the Organization.

3. The General Assembly may make recommendations with a view to determining the details of the application of paragraphs 1 and 2 of this Article or may propose conventions to the Members of the United Nations for this purpose.

CHAPTER XVII

TRANSITIONAL SECURITY ARRANGEMENTS

Article 106

Pending the coming into force of such special agreements referred to in Article 43 as in the opinion of the Security Council enable it to begin the exercise of its responsibilities under Article 42, the parties to the Four-Nation Declaration, signed at Moscow, October 30, 1943, and France, shall, in accordance with the provisions of paragraph 5 of that Declaration, consult with one another and as occasion requires with other Members of the United Nations with a view to such joint action on behalf of the Organization as may be necessary for the purpose of maintaining international peace and security.

Article 107

Nothing in the present Charter shall invalidate or preclude action, in relation to any state which during the Second World War has been an enemy of any signatory to the present Charter, taken or authorized as a result of that war by the Governments having responsibility for such action.

CHAPTER XVIII

AMENDMENTS

Article 108

Amendments to the present Charter shall come into force for all Members of the United Nations when they have been adopted by a vote of two-thirds of the members of the General Assembly and ratified in accordance with their respective constitutional processes by two-thirds of the Members of the United Nations, including all the permanent members of the Security Council.

Article 109

1. A General Conference of the Members of the United Nations for the purpose of reviewing the present Charter may be held at a date and place to be fixed by a two-thirds vote of the members of the General Assembly and by a vote of any seven members of the Security Council. Each Member of the United Nations shall have one vote in the conference.

2. Any alteration of the present Charter recommended by a two-thirds vote of the conference shall take effect when ratified in accordance with their respective constitutional processes by two-thirds of the Members of the United Nations including all the permanent members of the Security Council.

3. If such a conference has not been held before the tenth annual session of the General Assembly following the coming into force of the present Charter, the proposal to call such a conference shall be placed on the agenda of that

session of the General Assembly, and the conference shall be held if so decided by a majority vote of the members of the General Assembly and by a vote of any seven members of the Security Council.

CHAPTER XIX

RATIFICATION AND SIGNATURE

Article 110

1. The present Charter shall be ratified by the signatory states in accordance with their respective constitutional processes.

2. The ratifications shall be deposited with the Government of the United States of America, which shall notify all the signatory states of each deposit as well as the Secretary-General of the Organization when he has been appointed.

3. The present Charter shall come into force upon the deposit of ratifications by the Republic of China, France, the Union of Soviet Socialist Republics, the United Kingdom of Great Britain and Northern Ireland, and the United States of America, and by a majority of the other signatory states. A protocol of the ratifications deposited shall thereupon be drawn by the Government of the United States of America which shall communicate copies thereof to all the signatory states.

4. The states signatory to the present Charter which ratify it after it has come into force will become original Members of the United Nations on the date of the deposit of their respective ratifications.

Article 111

The present Charter, of which the Chinese, French, Russian, English, and Spanish texts are equally authentic, shall remain deposited in the archives of the Government of the United States of America. Duly certified copies thereof shall be transmitted by that Government to the Governments of the other signatory states.

IN FAITH WHEREOF the representatives of the Governments of the United Nations have signed the present Charter.

DONE at the city of San Francisco the twenty-sixth day of June, one thousand nine hundred and forty-five.

Statute of the International Court of Justice

Article 1

The International Court of Justice established by the Charter of the United Nations as the principal judicial organ of the United Nations shall be constituted and shall function in accordance with the provisions of the present Statute.

CHAPTER I

ORGANIZATION OF THE COURT

Article 2

The Court shall be composed of a body of independent judges, elected regardless of their nationality from among persons of high moral character, who possess the qualifications required in their respective countries for appointment to the highest judicial offices, or are juris-consults of recognized competence in international law.

Article 3

1. The Court shall consist of fifteen members, no two of whom may be nationals of the same state.

2. A person who for the purposes of membership in the Court could be regarded as a national of more than one state shall be deemed to be a national of the one in which he ordinarily exercises civil and political rights.

Article 4

1. The members of the Court shall be elected by the General Assembly and by the Security Council from a list of persons nominated by the national groups in the Permanent Court of Arbitration, in accordance with the following provisions.

2. In the case of Members of the United Nations not represented in the Permanent Court of Arbitration, candidates shall be nominated by national groups appointed for this purpose by their governments under the same condi-

tions as those prescribed for members of the Permanent Court of Arbitration by Article 44 of the Convention of The Hague of 1907 for the pacific settlement of international disputes.

3. The conditions under which a state which is a party to the present Statute but is not a Member of the United Nations may participate in electing the members of the Court shall, in the absence of a special agreement, be laid down by the General Assembly upon recommendation of the Security Council.

Article 5

1. At least three months before the date of the election, the Secretary-General of the United Nations shall address a written request to the members of the Permanent Court of Arbitration belonging to the states which are parties to the present Statute, and to the members of the national groups appointed under Article 4, paragraph 2, inviting them to undertake, within a given time, by national groups, the nomination of persons in a position to accept the duties of a member of the Court.

2. No group may nominate more than four persons, not more than two of whom shall be of their own nationality. In no case may the number of candidates nominated by a group be more than double the number of seats to be filled.

Article 6

Before making these nominations, each national group is recommended to consult its highest court of justice, its legal faculties and schools of law, and its national academies and national sections of international academies devoted to the study of law.

Article 7

1. The Secretary-General shall prepare a list in alphabetical order of all the persons thus nominated. Save as provided in Article 12, paragraph 2, these shall be the only persons eligible.

2. The Secretary-General shall submit this list to the General Assembly and to the Security Council.

Article 8

The General Assembly and the Security Council shall proceed independently of one another to elect the members of the Court.

Article 9

At every election, the electors shall bear in mind not only that the persons to be elected should individually possess the qualifications required, but also that in the body as a whole the representation of the main forms of civilization and of the principal legal systems of the world should be assured.

Article 10

1. Those candidates who obtain an absolute majority of votes in the General Assembly and in the Security Council shall be considered as elected.

2. Any vote of the Security Council, whether for the election of judges or for the appointment of members of the conference envisaged in Article 12,

shall be taken without any distinction between permanent and non-permanent members of the Security Council.

3. In the event of more than one national of the same state obtaining an absolute majority of the votes both of the General Assembly and of the Security Council, the eldest of these only shall be considered as elected.

Article 11

If, after the first meeting held for the purpose of the election, one or more seats remain to be filled, a second and, if necessary, a third meeting shall take place.

Article 12

1. If, after the third meeting, one or more seats still remain unfilled, a joint conference consisting of six members, three appointed by the General Assembly and three by the Security Council, may be formed at any time at the request of either the General Assembly or the Security Council, for the purpose of choosing by the vote of an absolute majority one name for each seat still vacant, to submit to the General Assembly and the Security Council for their respective acceptance.

2. If the joint conference is unanimously agreed upon any person who fulfils the required conditions, he may be included in its list, even though he was not included in the list of nominations referred to in Article 7.

3. If the joint conference is satisfied that it will not be successful in procuring an election, those members of the Court who have already been elected shall, within a period to be fixed by the Security Council, proceed to fill the vacant seats by selection from among those candidates who have obtained votes either in the General Assembly or in the Security Council.

4. In the event of an equality of votes among the judges, the eldest judge shall have a casting vote.

Article 13

1. The members of the Court shall be elected for nine years and may be re-elected, provided, however, that of the judges elected at the first election, the terms of five judges shall expire at the end of three years and the terms of five more judges shall expire at the end of six years.

2. The judges whose terms are to expire at the end of the above-mentioned initial periods of three and six years shall be chosen by lot to be drawn by the Secretary-General immediately after the first election has been completed.

3. The members of the Court shall continue to discharge their duties until their places have been filled. Though replaced, they shall finish any cases which they may have begun.

4. In the case of the resignation of a member of the Court, the resignation shall be addressed to the President of the Court for transmission to the Secretary-General. This last notification makes the place vacant.

Article 14

Vacancies shall be filled by the same method as that laid down for the first election, subject to the following provision: the Secretary-General shall, within one month of the occurrence of the vacancy, proceed to issue the invitations provided for in Article 5, and the date of the election shall be fixed by the Security Council.

Article 15

A member of the Court elected to replace a member whose term of office has not expired shall hold office for the remainder of his predecessor's term.

Article 16

1. No member of the Court may exercise any political or administrative function, or engage in any other occupation of a professional nature.

2. Any doubt on this point shall be settled by the decision of the Court.

Article 17

1. No member of the Court may act as agent, counsel, or advocate in any case.

2. No member may participate in the decision of any case in which he has previously taken part as agent, counsel, or advocate for one of the parties, or as a member of a national or international court, or of a commission of enquiry, or in any other capacity.

3. Any doubt on this point shall be settled by the decision of the Court.

Article 18

1. No member of the Court can be dismissed unless, in the unanimous opinion of the other members, he has ceased to fulfil the required conditions.

2. Formal notification thereof shall be made to the Secretary-General by the Registrar.

3. This notification makes the place vacant.

Article 19

The members of the Court, when engaged on the business of the Court, shall enjoy diplomatic privileges and immunities.

Article 20

Every member of the Court shall, before taking up his duties, make a solemn declaration in open court that he will exercise his powers impartially and conscientiously.

Article 21

1. The Court shall elect its President and Vice-President for three years; they may be re-elected.

2. The Court shall appoint its Registrar and may provide for the appointment of such other officers as may be necessary.

Article 22

1. The seat of the Court shall be established at The Hague. This, however, shall not prevent the Court from sitting and exercising its functions elsewhere whenever the Court considers it desirable.

2. The President and the Registrar shall reside at the seat of the Court.

Article 23

1. The Court shall remain permanently in session, except during the judicial vacations, the dates and duration of which shall be fixed by the Court.

2. Members of the Court are entitled to periodic leave, the dates and duration of which shall be fixed by the Court, having in mind the distance between The Hague and the home of each judge.

3. Members of the Court shall be bound, unless they are on leave or prevented from attending by illness or other serious reasons duly explained to the President, to hold themselves permanently at the disposal of the Court.

Article 24

1. If, for some special reason, a member of the Court considers that he should not take part in the decision of a particular case, he shall so inform the President.

2. If the President considers that for some special reason one of the members of the Court should not sit in a particular case he shall give him notice accordingly.

3. If in any such case the member of the Court and the President disagree, the matter shall be settled by the decision of the Court.

Article 25

1. The full Court shall sit except when it is expressly provided otherwise in the present Statute.

2. Subject to the condition that the number of judges available to constitute the Court is not thereby reduced below eleven, the Rules of the Court may provide for allowing one or more judges, according to circumstances and in rotation, to be dispensed from sitting.

3. A quorum of nine judges shall suffice to constitute the Court.

Article 26

1. The Court may from time to time form one or more chambers, composed of three or more judges as the Court may determine, for dealing with particular categories of cases; for example, labor cases and cases relating to transit and communications.

2. The Court may at any time form a chamber for dealing with a particular case. The number of judges to constitute such a chamber shall be determined by the Court with the approval of the parties.

3. Cases shall be heard and determined by the chambers provided for in this Article if the parties so request.

Article 27

A judgment given by any of the chambers provided for in Articles 26 and 29 shall be considered as rendered by the Court.

Article 28

The chambers provided for in Articles 26 and 29 may, with the consent of the parties, sit and exercise their functions elsewhere than at The Hague.

Article 29

With a view to the speedy despatch of business, the Court shall form annually a chamber composed of five judges which, at the request of the parties, may hear and determine cases by summary procedure. In addition, two judges shall be selected for the purpose of replacing judges who find it impossible to sit.

Article 30

1. The Court shall frame rules for carrying out its functions. In particular, it shall lay down rules of procedure.

2. The Rules of the Court may provide for assessors to sit with the Court or with any of its chambers, without the right to vote.

Article 31

1. Judges of the nationality of each of the parties shall retain their right to sit in the case before the Court.

2. If the Court includes upon the Bench a judge of the nationality of one of the parties, any other party may choose a person to sit as judge. Such person shall be chosen preferably from among those persons who have been nominated as candidates as provided in Articles 4 and 5.

3. If the Court includes upon the Bench no judge of the nationality of the parties, each of these parties may proceed to choose a judge as provided in paragraph 2 of this Article.

4. The provisions of this Article shall apply to the case of Articles 26 and 29. In such cases, the President shall request one or, if necessary, two of the members of the Court forming the chamber to give place to the members of the Court of the nationality of the parties concerned, and, failing such, or if they are unable to be present, to the judges specially chosen by the parties.

5. Should there be several parties in the same interest, they shall, for the purpose of the preceding provisions, be reckoned as one party only. Any doubt upon this point shall be settled by the decision of the Court.

6. Judges chosen as laid down in paragraphs 2, 3, and 4 of this Article shall fulfil the conditions required by Articles 2, 17 (paragraph 2), 20, and 24 of the present Statute. They shall take part in the decision on terms of complete equality with their colleagues.

Article 32

1. Each member of the Court shall receive an annual salary.

2. The President shall receive a special annual allowance.

3. The Vice-President shall receive a special allowance for every day on which he acts as President.

4. The judges chosen under Article 31, other than members of the Court, shall receive compensation for each day on which they exercise their functions.

5. These salaries, allowances, and compensation shall be fixed by the General Assembly. They may not be decreased during the term of office.

6. The salary of the Registrar shall be fixed by the General Assembly on the proposal of the Court.

7. Regulations made by the General Assembly shall fix the conditions under which retirement pensions may be given to members of the Court and to the Registrar, and the conditions under which members of the Court and the Registrar shall have their traveling expenses refunded.

8. The above salaries, allowances, and compensation shall be free of all taxation.

Article 33

The expenses of the Court shall be borne by the United Nations in such a manner as shall be decided by the General Assembly.

Chapter II

COMPETENCE OF THE COURT

Article 34

1. Only states may be parties in cases before the Court.

2. The Court, subject to and in conformity with its Rules, may request of public international organizations information relevant to cases before it, and shall receive such information presented by such organizations on their own initiative.

3. Whenever the construction of the constituent instrument of a public international organization or of an international convention adopted thereunder is in question in a case before the Court, the Registrar shall so notify the public international organization concerned and shall communicate to it copies of all the written proceedings.

Article 35

1. The Court shall be open to the states parties to the present Statute.

2. The conditions under which the Court shall be open to other states shall, subject to the special provisions contained in treaties in force, be laid down by the Security Council, but in no case shall such conditions place the parties in a position of inequality before the Court.

3. When a state which is not a Member of the United Nations is a party to a case, the Court shall fix the amount which that party is to contribute towards the expenses of the Court. This provision shall not apply if such state is bearing a share of the expenses of the Court.

Article 36

1. The jurisdiction of the Court comprises all cases which the parties refer to it and all matters specially provided for in the Charter of the United Nations or in treaties and conventions in force.

2. The states parties to the present Statute may at any time declare that they recognize as compulsory *ipso facto* and without special agreement, in relation to any other state accepting the same obligation, the jurisdiction of the Court in all legal disputes concerning:

   a. the interpretation of a treaty;

   b. any question of international law;

   c. the existence of any fact which, if established, would constitute a breach of an international obligation;

   d. the nature or extent of the reparation to be made for the breach of an international obligation.

3. The declarations referred to above may be made unconditionally or on condition of reciprocity on the part of several or certain states, or for a certain time.

4. Such declarations shall be deposited with the Secretary-General of the United Nations, who shall transmit copies thereof to the parties to the Statute and to the Registrar of the Court.

5. Declarations made under Article 36 of the Statute of the Permanent Court of International Justice and which are still in force shall be deemed, as between the parties to the present Statute, to be acceptances of the compulsory jurisdiction of the International Court of Justice for the period which they still have to run and in accordance with their terms.

6. In the event of a dispute as to whether the Court has jurisdiction, the matter shall be settled by the decision of the Court.

Article 37

Whenever a treaty or convention in force provides for reference of a matter to a tribunal to have been instituted by the League of Nations, or to the Permanent Court of International Justice, the matter shall, as between the parties to the present Statute, be referred to the International Court of Justice.

Article 38

1. The Court, whose function is to decide in accordance with international law such disputes as are submitted to it, shall apply:

   a. international conventions, whether general or particular, establishing rules expressly recognized by the contesting states;

   b. international custom, as evidence of a general practice accepted as law;

   c. the general principles of law recognized by civilized nations;

   d. subject to the provisions of Article 59, judicial decisions and the teachings of the most highly qualified publicists of the various nations, as subsidiary means for the determination of rules of law.

2. This provision shall not prejudice the power of the Court to decide a case *ex aequo et bono,* if the parties agree thereto.

CHAPTER III

PROCEDURE

Article 39

1. The official languages of the Court shall be French and English. If the parties agree that the case shall be conducted in French, the judgment shall

be delivered in French. If the parties agree that the case shall be conducted in English, the judgment shall be delivered in English.

2. In the absence of an agreement as to which language shall be employed, each party may, in the pleadings, use the language which it prefers; the decision of the Court shall be given in French and English. In this case the Court shall at the same time determine which of the two texts shall be considered as authoritative.

3. The Court shall, at the request of any party, authorize a language other than French or English to be used by that party.

Article 40

1. Cases are brought before the Court, as the case may be, either by the notification of the special agreement or by a written application addressed to the Registrar. In either case the subject of the dispute and the parties shall be indicated.

2. The Registrar shall forthwith communicate the application to all concerned.

3. He shall also notify the Members of the United Nations through the Secretary-General, and also any other states entitled to appear before the Court.

Article 41

1. The Court shall have the power to indicate, if it considers that circumstances so require, any provisional measures which ought to be taken to preserve the respective rights of either party.

2. Pending the final decision, notice of the measures suggested shall forthwith be given to the parties and to the Security Council.

Article 42

1. The parties shall be represented by agents.

2. They may have the assistance of counsel or advocates before the Court.

3. The agents, counsel, and advocates of parties before the Court shall enjoy the privileges and immunities necessary to the independent exercise of their duties.

Article 43

1. The procedure shall consist of two parts: written and oral.

2. The written proceedings shall consist of the communication to the Court and to the parties of memorials, counter-memorials and, if necessary, replies; also all papers and documents in support.

3. These communications shall be made through the Registrar, in the order and within the time fixed by the Court.

4. A certified copy of every document produced by one party shall be communicated to the other party.

5. The oral proceedings shall consist of the hearing by the Court of witnesses, experts, agents, counsel, and advocates.

Article 44

1. For the service of all notices upon persons other than the agents, counsel, and advocates, the Court shall apply direct to the government of the state upon whose territory the notice has to be served.

2. The same provision shall apply whenever steps are to be taken to procure evidence on the spot.

Article 45

The hearing shall be under the control of the President or, if he is unable to preside, of the Vice-President; if neither is able to preside, the senior judge present shall preside.

Article 46

The hearing in Court shall be public, unless the Court shall decide otherwise, or unless the parties demand that the public be not admitted.

Article 47

1. Minutes shall be made at each hearing and signed by the Registrar and the President.

2. These minutes alone shall be authentic.

Article 48

The Court shall make orders for the conduct of the case, shall decide the form and time in which each party must conclude its arguments, and make all arrangements connected with the taking of evidence.

Article 49

The Court may, even before the hearing begins, call upon the agents to produce any document or to supply any explanations. Formal note shall be taken of any refusal.

Article 50

The Court may, at any time, entrust any individual, body, bureau, commission, or other organization that it may select, with the task of carrying out an enquiry or giving an expert opinion.

Article 51

During the hearing any relevant questions are to be put to the witnesses and experts under the conditions laid down by the Court in the rules of procedure referred to in Article 30.

Article 52

After the Court has received the proofs and evidence within the time specified for the purpose, it may refuse to accept any further oral or written evidence that one party may desire to present unless the other side consents.

Article 53

1. Whenever one of the parties does not appear before the Court, or fails to defend its case, the other party may call upon the Court to decide in favor of its claim.

2. The Court must, before doing so, satisfy itself, not only that it has jurisdiction in accordance with Articles 36 and 37, but also that the claim is well founded in fact and law.

Article 54

1. When, subject to the control of the Court, the agents, counsel, and advocates have completed their presentation of the case, the President shall declare the hearing closed.

2. The Court shall withdraw to consider the judgment.

3. The deliberations of the Court shall take place in private and remain secret.

Article 55

1. All questions shall be decided by a majority of the judges present.

2. In the event of an equality of vote, the President or the judge who acts in his place shall have a casting vote.

Article 56

1. The judgment shall state the reasons on which it is based.

2. It shall contain the names of the judges who have taken part in the decision.

Article 57

If the judgment does not represent in whole or in part the unanimous opinion of the judges, any judge shall be entitled to deliver a separate opinion.

Article 58

The judgment shall be signed by the President and by the Registrar. It shall be read in open court, due notice having been given to the agents.

Article 59

The decision of the Court has no binding force except between the parties and in respect of that particular case.

Article 60

The judgment is final and without appeal. In the event of dispute as to the meaning or scope of the judgment, the Court shall construe it upon the request of any party.

Article 61

1. An application for revision of a judgment may be made only when it is based upon the discovery of some fact of such a nature as to be a decisive factor, which fact was, when the judgment was given, unknown to the Court and also to the party claiming revision, always provided that such ignorance was not due to negligence.

2. The proceedings for revision shall be opened by a judgment of the Court expressly recording the existence of the new fact, recognizing that it has such a character as to lay the case open to revision, and declaring the application admissible on this ground.

3. The Court may require previous compliance with the terms of the judgment before it admits proceedings in revision.

4. The application for revision must be made at latest within six months of the discovery of the new fact.

5. No application for revision may be made after the lapse of ten years from the date of the judgment.

Article 62

1. Should a state consider that it has an interest of a legal nature which may be affected by the decision in the case, it may submit a request to the Court to be permitted to intervene.

2. It shall be for the Court to decide upon this request.

Article 63

1. Whenever the construction of a convention to which states other than those concerned in the case are parties is in question, the Registrar shall notify all such states forthwith.

2. Every state so notified has the right to intervene in the proceedings; but if it uses this right, the construction given by the judgment will be equally binding upon it.

Article 64

Unless otherwise decided by the Court, each party shall bear its own costs.

Chapter IV

ADVISORY OPINIONS

Article 65

1. The Court may give an advisory opinion on any legal question at the request of whatever body may be authorized by or in accordance with the Charter of the United Nations to make such a request.

2. Questions upon which the advisory opinion of the Court is asked shall be laid before the Court by means of a written request containing an exact statement of the question upon which an opinion is required, and accompanied by all documents likely to throw light upon the question.

Article 66

1. The Registrar shall forthwith give notice of the request for an advisory opinion to all states entitled to appear before the Court.

2. The Registrar shall also, by means of a special and direct communication, notify any state entitled to appear before the Court or international organization considered by the Court, or, should it not be sitting, by the President, as likely to be able to furnish information on the question, that the Court will be prepared to receive, within a time limit to be fixed by the President, written statements, or to hear, at a public sitting to be held for the purpose, oral statements relating to the question.

3. Should any such state entitled to appear before the Court have failed to receive the special communication referred to in paragraph 2 of this Article, such state may express a desire to submit a written statement or to be heard; and the Court will decide.

4. States and organizations having presented written or oral statements or both shall be permitted to comment on the statements made by other states or organizations in the form, to the extent, and within the time limits which the Court, or, should it not be sitting, the President, shall decide in each particular case. Accordingly, the Registrar shall in due time communicate any such written statements to states and organizations having submitted similar statements.

Article 67

The Court shall deliver its advisory opinions in open court, notice having been given to the Secretary-General and to the representatives of Members of the United Nations, of other states and of international organizations immediately concerned.

Article 68

In the exercise of its advisory functions the Court shall further be guided by the provisions of the present Statute which apply in contentious cases to the extent to which it recognizes them to be applicable.

Chapter V

AMENDMENT

Article 69

Amendments to the present Statute shall be effected by the same procedure as is provided by the Charter of the United Nations for amendments to that Charter, subject however to any provisions which the General Assembly upon recommendation of the Security Council may adopt concerning the participation of states which are parties to the present Statute but are not Members of the United Nations.

Article 70

The Court shall have power to propose such amendments to the present Statute as it may deem necessary, through written communications to the Secretary-General, for consideration in conformity with the provisions of Article 69.

Constitution of the United Nations Educational, Scientific and Cultural Organisation

THE GOVERNMENTS of the States parties to this Constitution on behalf of their peoples declare

that since wars begin in the minds of men, it is in the minds of men that the defences of peace must be constructed;

that ignorance of each other's ways and lives has been a common cause, throughout the history of mankind, of that suspicion and mistrust between the peoples of the world through which their differences have all too often broken into war;

that the great and terrible war which has now ended was a war made possible by the denial of the democratic principles of the dignity, equality and mutual respect of men, and by the propagation, in their place, through ignorance and prejudice, of the doctrine of the inequality of men and races;

that the wide diffusion of culture, and the education of humanity for justice and liberty and peace are indispensable to the dignity of man and constitute a sacred duty which all the nations must fulfil in a spirit of mutual assistance and concern;

that a peace based exclusively upon the political and economic arrangements of governments would not be a peace which could secure the unanimous, lasting and sincere support of the peoples of the world, and that the peace must therefore be founded, if it is not to fail, upon the intellectual and moral solidarity of mankind.

For these reasons, the States parties to this Constitution, believing in full and equal opportunities for education for all, in the unrestricted pursuit of objective truth, and in the free exchange of ideas and knowledge, are agreed and determined to develop and to increase the means of communication between their peoples and to employ these means for the purposes of mutual understanding and a truer and more perfect knowledge of each other's lives;

In consequence whereof they do hereby create the United Nations Educational, Scientific and Cultural Organisation for the purpose of advancing, through the educational and scientific and cultural relations of the peoples of the world, the objectives of international peace and of the common welfare of mankind for which the United Nations Organisation was established and which its Charter proclaims.

ARTICLE I

PURPOSES AND FUNCTIONS

1. The purpose of the Organisation is to contribute to peace and security by promoting collaboration among the nations through education, science and culture in order to further universal respect for justice, for the rule of law and for the human rights and fundamental freedoms which are affirmed for the peoples of the world, without distinction of race, sex, language or religion, by the Charter of the United Nations.

2. To realise this purpose the Organisation will:

a. collaborate in the work of advancing the mutual knowledge and understanding of peoples, through all means of mass communication and to that end recommend such international agreements as may be necessary to promote the free flow of ideas by word and image;

b. give fresh impulse to popular education and to the spread of culture;

by collaborating with Members, at their request, in the development of educational activities;

by instituting collaboration among the nations to advance the ideal of equality of educational opportunity without regard to race, sex or any distinctions, economic or social;

by suggesting educational methods best suited to prepare the children of the world for the responsibilities of freedom:

c. maintain, increase and diffuse knowledge;

by assuring the conservation and protection of the world's inheritance of books, works of art and monuments of history and science, and recommending to the nations concerned the necessary international conventions;

by encouraging cooperation among the nations in all branches of intellectual activity, including the international exchange of persons active in the fields of education, science and culture and the exchange of publications, objects of artistic and scientific interest and other materials of information;

by initiating methods of international cooperation calculated to give the people of all countries access to the printed and published materials produced by any of them.

3. With a view to preserving the independence, integrity and fruitful diversity of the cultures and educational systems of the States Members of this Organisation, the Organisation is prohibited from intervening in matters which are essentially within their domestic jurisdiction.

ARTICLE II

MEMBERSHIP

1. Membership of the United Nations Organisation shall carry with it the right to membership of the United Nations Educational, Scientific and Cultural Organisation.

2. Subject to the conditions of the agreement between this Organisation and the United Nations Organisation, approved pursuant to Article X of this Constitution, States not members of the United Nations Organisation may be admitted to membership of the Organisation, upon recommendation of the Executive Board, by a two-thirds majority vote of the General Conference.

3. Members of the Organisation which are suspended from the exercise of the rights and privileges of membership of the United Nations Organisation shall, upon the request of the latter, be suspended from the rights and privileges of this Organisation.

4. Members of the Organisation which are expelled from the United Nations Organisation shall automatically cease to be members of this Organisation.

ARTICLE III

ORGANS

The Organisation shall include a General Conference, an Executive Board and a Secretariat.

ARTICLE IV

THE GENERAL CONFERENCE

A. *Composition*

1. The General Conference shall consist of the representatives of the States Members of the Organisation. The Government of each Member State shall appoint not more than five delegates, who shall be selected after consultation with the National Commission, if established, or with educational, scientific and cultural bodies.

B. *Functions*

2. The General Conference shall determine the policies and the main lines of work of the Organisation. It shall take decisions on programmes drawn up by the Executive Board.

3. The General Conference shall, when it deems it desirable, summon international conferences on education, the sciences and humanities and the dissemination of knowledge.

4. The General Conference shall, in adopting proposals for submission to the Member States, distinguish between recommendations and international conventions submitted for their approval. In the former case a majority vote shall suffice; in the latter case a two-thirds majority shall be required. Each of the Member States shall submit recommendations or conventions to its competent authorities within a period of one year from the close of the session of the General Conference at which they were adopted.

5. The General Conference shall advise the United Nations Organisation on the educational, scientific and cultural aspects of matters of concern to the latter, in accordance with the terms and procedure agreed upon between the appropriate authorities of the two Organisations.

6. The General Conference shall receive and consider the reports submitted periodically by Member States as provided by Article VIII.

7. The General Conference shall elect the members of the Executive Board, and, on the recommendation of the Board, shall appoint the Director-General.

C. Voting

8. Each Member State shall have one vote in the General Conference. Decisions shall be made by a simple majority except in cases in which a two-thirds majority is required by the provisions of this Constitution. A majority shall be a majority of the Members present and voting.

D. Procedure

9. The General Conference shall meet annually in ordinary session; it may meet in extraordinary session on the call of the Executive Board. At each session the location of its next session shall be designated by the General Conference and shall vary from year to year.

10. The General Conference shall, at each session, elect a President and other officers and adopt rules of procedure.

11. The General Conference shall set up special and technical committees and such other subordinate bodies as may be necessary for its purposes.

12. The General Conference shall cause arrangements to be made for public access to meetings, subject to such regulations as it shall prescribe.

E. Observers

13. The General Conference, on the recommendation of the Executive Board and by a two-thirds majority may, subject to its rules of procedure, invite as observers at specified sessions of the Conference or of its commissions representatives of international organisations, such as those referred to in Article XI, paragraph 4.

ARTICLE V

EXECUTIVE BOARD

A. Composition

1. The Executive Board shall consist of eighteen members elected by the General Conference from among the delegates appointed by the Member States, together with the President of the Conference who shall sit *ex officio* in an advisory capacity.

2. In electing the members of the Executive Board the General Conference shall endeavour to include persons competent in the arts, the humanities, the sciences, education and the diffusion of ideas, and qualified by their experience and capacity to fulfil the administrative and executive duties of the Board. It shall also have regard to the diversity of cultures and a balanced geographical distribution. Not more than one national of any Member State shall serve on the Board at any one time, the President of the Conference excepted.

3. The elected members of the Executive Board shall serve for a term of three years, and shall be immediately eligible for a second term, but shall not serve consecutively for more than two terms. At the first election eighteen members shall be elected of whom one-third shall retire at the end of the first year and one-third at the end of the second year, the order of retirement

being determined immediately after the election by the drawing of lots. Thereafter six members shall be elected each year.

4. In the event of the death or resignation of one of its members, the Executive Board shall appoint, from among the delegates of the Member State concerned, a substitute, who shall serve until the next session of the General Conference which shall elect a member for the remainder of the term.

B. *Functions*

5. The Executive Board, acting under the authority of the General Conference, shall be responsible for the execution of the programme adopted by the Conference and shall prepare its agenda and programme of work.

6. The Executive Board shall recommend to the General Conference the admission of new Members to the Organisation.

7. Subject to decisions of the General Conference, the Executive Board shall adopt its own rules of procedure. It shall elect its officers from among its members.

8. The Executive Board shall meet in regular session at least twice a year and may meet in special session if convoked by the Chairman on his own initiative or upon the request of six members of the Board.

9. The Chairman of the Executive Board shall present to the General Conference, with or without comment, the annual report of the Director-General on the activities of the Organisation, which shall have been previously submitted to the Board.

10. The Executive Board shall make all necessary arrangements to consult the representatives of international organisations or qualified persons concerned with questions within its competence.

11. The members of the Executive Board shall exercise the powers delegated to them by the General Conference on behalf of the Conference as a whole and not as representatives of their respective Governments.

Article VI

SECRETARIAT

1. The Secretariat shall consist of a Director-General and such staff as may be required.

2. The Director-General shall be nominated by the Executive Board and appointed by the General Conference for a period of six years, under such conditions as the Conference may approve, and shall be eligible for re-appointment. He shall be the chief administrative officer of the Organisation.

3. The Director-General, or a deputy designated by him, shall participate, without the right to vote, in all meetings of the General Conference, of the Executive Board, and of the committees of the Organisation. He shall formulate proposals for appropriate action by the Conference and the Board.

4. The Director-General shall appoint the staff of the Secretariat in accordance with staff regulations to be approved by the General Conference. Subject to the paramount consideration of securing the highest standards of integrity, efficiency and technical competence appointment to the staff shall be on as wide a geographical basis as possible.

5. The responsibilities of the Director-General and of the staff shall be exclusively international in character. In the discharge of their duties they shall not seek or receive instructions from any government or from any authority external to the Organisation. They shall refrain from any action which might prejudice their position as international officials. Each State Member of the Organisation undertakes to respect the international character of the responsibilities of the Director-General and the staff, and not to seek to influence them in the discharge of their duties.

6. Nothing in this Article shall preclude the Organisation from entering into special arrangements within the United Nations Organisation for common services and staff and for the interchange of personnel.

ARTICLE VII

NATIONAL COOPERATING BODIES

1. Each Member State shall make such arrangements as suit its particular conditions for the purpose of associating its principal bodies interested in educational, scientific and cultural matters with the work of the Organisation, preferably by the formation of a National Commission broadly representative of the Government and such bodies.

2. National Commissions or national cooperating bodies, where they exist, shall act in an advisory capacity to their respective delegations to the General Conference and to their Governments in matters relating to the Organisation and shall function as agencies of liaison in all matters of interest to it.

3. The Organisation may, on the request of a Member State, delegate, either temporarily or permanently, a member of its Secretariat to serve on the National Commission of that State, in order to assist in the development of its work.

ARTICLE VIII

REPORTS BY MEMBER STATES

Each Member State shall report periodically to the Organisation, in a manner to be determined by the General Conference, on its laws, regulations, and statistics relating to educational, scientific and cultural life and institutions, and on the action taken upon the recommendations and conventions referred to in Article IV, paragraph 4.

ARTICLE IX

BUDGET

1. The budget shall be administered by the Organisation.

2. The General Conference shall approve and give final effect to the budget and to the apportionment of financial responsibility among the States Members of the Organisation subject to such arrangement with the United Nations as may be provided in the agreement to be entered into pursuant to Article X.

3. The Director-General, with the approval of the Executive Board, may receive gifts, bequests, and subventions directly from governments, public and private institutions. associations and private persons.

Article X

RELATIONS WITH THE UNITED NATIONS ORGANISATION

This Organisation shall be brought into relation with the United Nations Organisation, as soon as practicable, as one of the specialised agencies referred to in Article 57 of the Charter of the United Nations. This relationship shall be effected through an agreement with the United Nations Organisation under Article 63 of the Charter, which agreement shall be subject to the approval of the General Conference of this Organisation. The agreement shall provide for effective cooperation between the two Organisations in the pursuit of their common purposes, and at the same time shall recognise the autonomy of this Organisation, within the fields of its competence as defined in this Constitution. Such agreement may, among other matters, provide for the approval and financing of the budget of the Organisation by the General Assembly of the United Nations.

Article XI

RELATIONS WITH OTHER SPECIALISED ORGANISATIONS AND AGENCIES

1. This Organisation may cooperate with other specialised inter-governmental organisations and agencies whose interests and activities are related to its purposes. To this end the Director-General, acting under the general authority of the Executive Board, may establish effective working relationships with such organisations and agencies and establish such joint committees as may be necessary to assure effective cooperation. Any formal arrangements entered into with such organisations or agencies shall be subject to the approval of the Executive Board.

2. Whenever the General Conference of this Organisation and the competent authorities of any other specialised inter-governmental organisations or agencies, whose purposes and functions lie within the competence of this Organisation, deem it desirable to effect a transfer of their resources and activities to this Organisation, the Director-General, subject to the approval of the Conference, may enter into mutually acceptable arrangements for its purpose.

3. This Organisation may make appropriate arrangements with other inter-governmental organisations for reciprocal representation at meetings.

4. The United Nations Educational, Scientific and Cultural Organisation may make suitable arrangements for consultation and cooperation with non-governmental international organisations concerned with matters within its competence, and may invite them to undertake specific tasks. Such cooperation may also include appropriate participation by representatives of such organisations on advisory committees set up by the General Conference.

Article XII

LEGAL STATUS OF THE ORGANISATION

The provisions of Articles 104 and 105 of the Charter of the United Nations Organisation concerning the legal status of that Organisation, its privileges and immunities shall apply in the same way to this Organisation.

ARTICLE XIII

AMENDMENTS

1. Proposals for amendments to this Constitution shall become effective upon receiving the approval of the General Conference by a two-thirds majority; provided, however, that those amendments which involve fundamental alterations in the aims of the Organisation or new obligations for the Member States shall require subsequent acceptance on the part of two-thirds of the Member States before they come into force. The draft texts of proposed amendments shall be communicated by the Director-General to the Member States at least six months in advance of their consideration by the General Conference.

2. The General Conference shall have power to adopt by a two-thirds majority rules of procedure for carrying out the provisions of this Article.

ARTICLE XIV

INTERPRETATION

1. The English and French texts of this Constitution shall be regarded as equally authoritative.

2. Any question or dispute concerning the interpretation of this Constitution shall be referred for determination to the International Court of Justice or to an arbitral tribunal, as the General Conference may determine under its rules of procedure.

ARTICLE XV

ENTRY INTO FORCE

1. This Constitution shall be subject to acceptance. The instruments of acceptance shall be deposited with the Government of the United Kingdom.

2. This Constitution shall remain open for signature in the archives of the Government of the United Kingdom. Signature may take place either before or after the deposit of the instrument of acceptance. No acceptance shall be valid unless preceded or followed by signature.

3. This Constitution shall come into force when it has been accepted by twenty of its signatories. Subsequent acceptances shall take effect immediately.

4. The Government of the United Kingdom will inform all members of the United Nations of the receipt of all instruments of acceptance and of the date on which the Constitution comes into force in accordance with the preceding paragraph.

IN FAITH WHEREOF, the undersigned, duly authorised to that effect, have signed this Constitution in the English and French languages, both texts being equally authentic.

DONE in London the sixteenth day of November 1945 in a single copy, in the English and French languages, of which certified copies will be communicated by the Government of the United Kingdom to the Governments of all the Members of the United Nations.

Universal Declaration of Human Rights

PREAMBLE

WHEREAS recognition of the inherent dignity and of the equal and inalienable rights of all members of the human family is the foundation of freedom, justice and peace in the world,

WHEREAS disregard and contempt for human rights have resulted in barbarous acts which have outraged the conscience of mankind, and the advent of a world in which human beings shall enjoy freedom of speech and belief and freedom from fear and want has been proclaimed as the highest aspiration of the common people,

WHEREAS it is essential, if man is not to be compelled to have recourse, as a last resort, to rebellion against tyranny and oppression, that human rights should be protected by the rule of law,

WHEREAS it is essential to promote the development of friendly relations between nations,

WHEREAS the peoples of the United Nations have in the Charter reaffirmed their faith in fundamental human rights, in the dignity and worth of the human person and in the equal rights of men and women and have determined to promote social progress and better standards of life in larger freedom,

WHEREAS Member States have pledged themselves to achieve, in cooperation with the United Nations, the promotion of universal respect for and observance of human rights and fundamental freedoms,

WHEREAS a common understanding of these rights and freedoms is of the greatest importance for the full realization of this pledge,

NOW, THEREFORE,

THE GENERAL ASSEMBLY

proclaims

This Universal Declaration of Human Rights as a common standard of achievement for all peoples and all nations, to the end that every individual and every organ of society, keeping this Declaration constantly in mind, shall strive by teaching and education to promote respect for these rights and freedoms and by progressive measures, national and international, to secure their universal and effective recognition and observance, both among the peoples of Member States themselves and among the peoples of territories under their jurisdiction.

Article 1

All human beings are born free and equal in dignity and rights. They are endowed with reason and conscience and should act towards one another in a spirit of brotherhood.

Article 2

Everyone is entitled to all the rights and freedoms set forth in this Declaration, without distinction of any kind, such as race, colour, sex, language, religion, political or other opinion, national or social origin, property, birth or other status.

Furthermore, no distinction shall be made on the basis of the political, jurisdictional or international status of the country or territory to which a person belongs, whether it be independent, trust, non-self-governing or under any other limitation of sovereignty.

Article 3

Everyone has the right to life, liberty and security of person.

Article 4

No one shall be held in slavery or servitude; slavery and the slave trade shall be prohibited in all their forms.

Article 5

No one shall be subjected to torture or to cruel, inhuman or degrading treatment or punishment.

Article 6

Everyone has the right to recognition everywhere as a person before the law.

Article 7

All are equal before the law and are entitled without any discrimination to equal protection of the law. All are entitled to equal protection against any discrimination in violation of this Declaration and against any incitement to such discrimination.

Article 8

Everyone has the right to an effective remedy by the competent national tribunals for acts violating the fundamental rights granted him by the constitution or by law.

Article 9

No one shall be subjected to arbitrary arrest, detention or exile.

Article 10

Everyone is entitled in full equality to a fair and public hearing by an independent and impartial tribunal, in the determination of his rights and obligations and of any criminal charge against him.

Article 11

1. Everyone charged with a penal offence has the right to be presumed innocent until proved guilty according to law in a public trial at which he has had all the guarantees necessary for his defence.

2. No one shall be held guilty of any penal offence on account of any act or omission which did not constitute a penal offence, under national or international law, at the time when it was committed. Nor shall a heavier penalty be imposed than the one that was applicable at the time the penal offence was committed.

Article 12

No one shall be subjected to arbitrary interference with his privacy, family, home or correspondence, nor to attacks upon his honour and reputation. Everyone has the right to the protection of the law against such interference or attacks.

Article 13

1. Everyone has the right to freedom of movement and residence within the borders of each state.

2. Everyone has the right to leave any country, including his own, and to return to his country.

Article 14

1. Everyone has the right to seek and to enjoy in other countries asylum from persecution.

2. This right may not be invoked in the case of prosecutions genuinely arising from non-political crimes or from acts contrary to the purposes and principles of the United Nations.

Article 15

1. Everyone has the right to a nationality.

2. No one shall be arbitrarily deprived of his nationality nor denied the right to change his nationality.

Article 16

1. Men and women of full age, without any limitation due to race, nationality or religion, have the right to marry and to found a family. They are entitled to equal rights as to marriage, during marriage and at its dissolution.

2. Marriage shall be entered into only with the free and full consent of the intending spouses.

3. The family is the natural and fundamental group unit of society and is entitled to protection by society and the State.

Article 17

1. Everyone has the right to own property alone as well as in association with others.

2. No one shall be arbitrarily deprived of his property.

Article 18

Everyone has the right to freedom of thought, conscience and religion; this right includes freedom to change his religion or belief, and freedom, either alone or in community with others and in public or private, to manifest his religion or belief in teaching, practice, worship and observance.

Article 19

Everyone has the right to freedom of opinion and expression; this right includes freedom to hold opinions without interference and to seek, receive and impart information and ideas through any media and regardless of frontiers.

Article 20

1. Everyone has the right to freedom of peaceful assembly and association.

2. No one may be compelled to belong to an association.

Article 21

1. Everyone has the right to take part in the government of his country, directly or through freely chosen representatives.

2. Everyone has the right of equal access to public service in his country.

3. The will of the people shall be the basis of the authority of government; this will shall be expressed in periodic and genuine elections which shall be by universal and equal suffrage and shall be held by secret vote or by equivalent free voting procedures.

Article 22

Everyone, as a member of society, has the right to social security and is entitled to realization, through national effort and international cooperation and in accordance with the organization and resources of each State, of the economic, social and cultural rights indispensable for his dignity and the free development of his personality.

Article 23

1. Everyone has the right to work, to free choice of employment, to just and favourable conditions of work and to protection against unemployment.

2. Everyone, without any discrimination, has the right to equal pay for equal work.

3. Everyone who works has the right to just and favourable remuneration ensuring for himself and his family an existence worthy of human dignity, and supplemented, if necessary, by other means of social protection.

4. Everyone has the right to form and to join trade unions for the protection of his interests.

Article 24

Everyone has the right to rest and leisure, including reasonable limitation of working hours and periodic holidays with pay.

Article 25

1. Everyone has the right to a standard of living adequate for the health and well-being of himself and of his family, including food, clothing, housing and medical care and necessary social services, and the right to security in the event of unemployment, sickness, disability, widowhood, old age or other lack of livelihood in circumstances beyond his control.

2. Motherhood and childhood are entitled to special care and assistance. All children, whether born in or out of wedlock, shall enjoy the same social protection.

Article 26

1. Everyone has the right to education. Education shall be free, at least in the elementary and fundamental stages. Elementary education shall be compulsory. Technical and professional education shall be made generally available and higher education shall be equally accessible to all on the basis of merit.

2. Education shall be directed to the full development of the human personality and to the strengthening of respect for human rights and fundamental freedoms. It shall promote understanding, tolerance and friendship among all nations, racial or religious groups, and shall further the activities of the United Nations for the maintenance of peace.

3. Parents have a prior right to choose the kind of education that shall be given to their children.

Article 27

1. Everyone has the right freely to participate in the cultural life of the community, to enjoy the arts and to share in scientific advancement and its benefits.

2. Everyone has the right to the protection of the moral and material interests resulting from any scientific, literary or artistic production of which he is the author.

Article 28

Everyone is entitled to a social and international order in which the rights and freedoms set forth in this Declaration can be fully realized.

Article 29

1. Everyone has duties to the community in which alone the free and full development of his personality is possible.

2. In the exercise of his rights and freedoms, everyone shall be subject only to such limitations as are determined by law solely for the purpose of securing due recognition and respect for the rights and freedoms of others and of meeting the just requirements of morality, public order and the general welfare in a democratic society.

3. These rights and freedoms may in no case be exercised contrary to the purposes and principles of the United Nations.

Article 30

Nothing in this Declaration may be interpreted as implying for any State, group or person any right to engage in any activity or to perform any act aimed at the destruction of any of the rights and freedoms set forth herein.

North Atlantic Treaty

THE PARTIES to this Treaty reaffirm their faith in the purposes and principles of the Charter of the United Nations and their desire to live in peace with all peoples and all governments.

They are determined to safeguard the freedom, common heritage and civilization of their peoples, founded on the principles of democracy, individual liberty and the rule of law.

They seek to promote stability and well-being in the North Atlantic area.

They are resolved to unite their efforts for collective defense and for the preservation of peace and security.

They therefore agree to this North Atlantic Treaty:

Article 1

The Parties undertake, as set forth in the Charter of the United Nations, to settle any international disputes in which they may be involved by peaceful means in such a manner that international peace and security, and justice, are not endangered, and to refrain in their international relations from the threat or use of force in any manner inconsistent with the purposes of the United Nations.

Article 2

The Parties will contribute toward the further development of peaceful and friendly international relations by strengthening their free institutions, by bringing about a better understanding of the principles upon which these institutions are founded, and by promoting conditions of stability and well-being. They will seek to eliminate conflict in their international economic policies and will encourage economic collaboration between any or all of them.

Article 3

In order more effectively to achieve the objectives of this Treaty, the Parties, separately and jointly, by means of continuous and effective self-help and mutual aid, will maintain and develop their individual and collective capacity to resist armed attack.

Article 4

The Parties will consult together whenever, in the opinion of any of them, the territorial integrity, political independence or security of any of the Parties is threatened.

Article 5

The Parties agree that an armed attack against one or more of them in Europe or North America shall be considered an attack against them all; and consequently they agree that, if such an armed attack occurs, each of them, in exercise of the right of individual or collective self-defense recognized by Article 51 of the Charter of the United Nations, will assist the Party or Parties so attacked by taking forthwith, individually and in concert with the other Parties, such action as it deems necessary, including the use of armed force, to restore and maintain the security of the North Atlantic area.

Any such armed attack and all measures taken as a result thereof shall immediately be reported to the Security Council. Such measures shall be terminated when the Security Council has taken the measures necessary to restore and maintain international peace and security.

Article 6

For the purpose of Article 5 an armed attack on one or more of the Parties is deemed to include an armed attack on the territory of any of the Parties in Europe or North America, on the Algerian departments of France, on the occupation forces of any Party in Europe, on the islands under the jurisdiction of any Party in the North Atlantic area north of the Tropic of Cancer or on the vessels or aircraft in this area of any of the Parties.

Article 7

This Treaty does not affect, and shall not be interpreted as affecting, in any way the rights and obligations under the Charter of the Parties which are members of the United Nations, or the primary responsibility of the Security Council for the maintenance of international peace and security.

Article 8

Each Party declares that none of the international engagements now in force between it and any other of the Parties or any third state is in conflict with the provisions of this Treaty, and undertakes not to enter into any international engagement in conflict with this Treaty.

Article 9

The Parties hereby establish a council, on which each of them shall be represented, to consider matters concerning the implementation of this Treaty. The council shall be so organized as to be able to meet promptly at any time. The council shall set up such subsidiary bodies as may be necessary; in particular it shall establish immediately a defense committee which shall recommend measures for the implementation of Articles 3 and 5.

Article 10

The Parties may, by unanimous agreement, invite any other European state in a position to further the principles of this Treaty and to contribute to the security of the North Atlantic area to accede to this Treaty. Any state so invited may become a party to the Treaty by depositing its instrument of accession with the Government of the United States of America. The Government of the United States of America will inform each of the Parties of the deposit of each such instrument of accession.

Article 11

This Treaty shall be ratified and its provisions carried out by the Parties in accordance with their respective constitutional processes. The instruments of ratification shall be deposited as soon as possible with the Government of the United States of America, which will notify all the other signatories of each deposit. The Treaty shall enter into force between the states which have ratified it as soon as the ratifications of the majority of the signatories, including the ratifications of Belgium, Canada, France, Luxembourg, the Netherlands, the United Kingdom and the United States, have been deposited and shall come into effect with respect to other states on the date of the deposit of their ratifications.

Article 12

After the Treaty has been in force for ten years, or at at any time thereafter, the Parties shall, if any of them so requests, consult together for the purpose of reviewing the Treaty, having regard for the factors then affecting peace and security in the North Atlantic area, including the development of universal as well as regional arrangements under the Charter of the United Nations for the maintenance of international peace and security.

Article 13

After the Treaty has been in force for twenty years, any Party may cease to be a party one year after its notice of denunciation has been given to the Government of the United States of America, which will inform the Governments of the other Parties of the deposit of each notice of denunciation.

Article 14

This Treaty, of which the English and French texts are equally authentic, shall be deposited in the archives of the Government of the United States of America. Duly certified copies thereof will be transmitted by that Government to the Governments of the other signatories.

IN WITNESS WHEREOF, the undersigned plenipotentiaries have signed this Treaty.

DONE at Washington, the fourth day of April, 1949.

INDEX

Acheson, Dean, 66-70
Adam, Thomas R., 408
Adjudication, 277-278
Adler, Alfred, 137
Aggrandizement, objective of states, 156-159; *see also* Aggression, Imperialism, Nationalism
Aggression, psychological explanations, 135 ff.
Alliances, and the balancing of power, 211-213
Animism, definition and implications, 143-144
Appeasement, defined, 276
    of Hitler by Chamberlain, 205
    outgrowth of the desire for peace, 160
Arbitration, 277
Armaments, armament races, 118
    and the balancing of power, 211, 214
    cause of war, 235-237
    costs, 234-235
    and power, 192
    purposes and importance, 226-229
Attitudes, defined, 134
    and domestic peace, 20 ff., 413-414
    and world peace, 416-418

Balance of power, appraisal, 219-225
    assumptions underlying principle, 201-210
    and collective security, 359-360, 367, 374-376
    and the expectation of war, 116 ff.
    meaning, 219-220
    methods of achieving, 210-217
    vs. preponderance, 217-218
    purposes, 199-201
    U. S. attitudes toward, 208-209, 216
Banse, E., 127
Beveridge, Sen. Albert J., 53, 94
Brierly, J. L., 297
Buffers, and the balancing of power, 214-215

Capitalism, communist view, 76-78
    and imperialism, 76-78, 129-130

Carr, E. H., 299, 309, 315, 363
Churchill, Sir Winston, 68
Cobban, Alfred, 64
Coexistence, meanings, 81
Collective security, defined, 357
    under the League of Nations, 364-367
    "maximalist," 358-364
    under the United Nations, 370-376
    See also Security
Colonies, arrangements for governing, 400-401
    meaning of the concept, 396-397
    native welfare, 397-399
    treatment of, 394 ff.
    and the United Nations, 403-408
Commerce and navigation, treaties of, 257-258
Communism, basic principles, 75 ff.
    compared to liberalism, 86-87
Conciliation, 276
Consensus, *see* Attitudes
Corbett, P. E., 378-379, 381-382, 385, 391-392
Crowe, Sir Eyre, 200

Davie, Maurice R., 144
Democracy, communist definition, 78-79
    and liberalism, 62-64
Diplomacy, by conference, 284-286
    defined, 268
    functions of diplomats and consuls, 273-275
    law concerning, 272-273
    methods of settling disputes, 275-277
Disarmament, defined, 229
    conditioning circumstances, 230-233
    conferences on, 239-240
    and nuclear weapons, 334-335
    obstacles to agreement on, 242-246
    and political settlement, 246-247
    why proposed, 233-242
Dulles, John Foster, 68, 329-330
Dunn, Frederick Sherwood, 18, 148, 237, 300, 303-304
Durbin, E. F. M., and John Bowlby, 141, 144-145

479

Economic and Social Council, composition and functions, 380-382
Eisenhower, Dwight D., 70, 164
Equality of states, definition and significance, 32-33, 155-156
European Coal and Steel Community, 259-260
European Recovery Program, 260, 349
Extraterritoriality, 395

Fascism, implications, 74-75
    principles, 73-74
Food and Agriculture Organization, 388-389
Frederick the Great, 125, 188
Freedom, objective of liberal statesmen, 67-70; see also Human Rights
Freud, Sigmund, 136
Fromm, Erich, on political motivations, 138-139
Frustration-aggression theory, 140 ff.

GATT, 258-259
General Assembly, enforcement action, 373
    powers and voting rules, 370
    promotion of welfare, 380-382
    See also United Nations
Glory, political behavior and the desire for, 125, 137-138, 166-167, 418
Good offices, 276
Government, and domestic peace, 15 ff., 413
    for the world, 414-416

Hawtrey, R. G., 111
Hitler, Adolf, diplomatic strategy, 205, 218
    moral principles, 307
    motivations, 138
    quoted, 74-75, 158
Hobbes, Thomas, on the desire for power, 166
Hobson, J. A., on imperialism, 103-104
Horney, Karen, on political motivations, 137-138
Human Rights, Commission on, 381
    text of Declaration, 471-475
    Universal Declaration of, 381-382

Ideology, basis for cooperation and conflict, 60-61
    defined, 135
    objective of protecting or promoting, 162-163

and power, 189-191
    See also Communism, Fascism, Liberalism, Nationalism
Imperialism, American, 93-95
    defined, 52, 170
    and the desire for wealth, 89 ff.
    economic theories, 102 ff.
    Hobson's explanation, 103-104
    Keynes's explanation, 104-105
    Lenin's explanation, 76-77, 105-108
    and nationalism, 52-54
    and population pressure, 92-93
    relative influence of economic and political causes, 95-96
    Schumpeter's explanation, 127-130
    and the treatment of dependent peoples, 394-408
Intelligence, an element of power, 191-192
Interests, communist claim to knowledge of, 75 ff.
    definition, 7-8
    determination, 135
    vital, 199-200, 203
International Bank for Reconstruction and Development, 264-265
International Civil Aviation Organization, 385
International Court of Justice, composition and functions, 277-278
    optional clause, 280-281
    text of Statute, 450-462
International Labor Organization, 385-388
International Monetary Fund, 253-254
International Telecommunication Union, 384
Internationalism, economic, 266-267
    proletarian, 83
Irredentas, see Nationalism, general

Jingoism, definition and influence, 123
Justice, common objective of states, 163-164
    problem of definition, 163-164

Kellogg-Briand Pact, 296, 371
Kennan, George F., 186, 209, 210, 320
Kent, Sherman, 191
Keynes, John M., 104-105
Kipling, Rudyard, 53

Lansing, Robert, 41, 121, 216
Lasswell, Harold D., on political methods, 269
    on the "political type," 145-149
    on values, 9, 146

Law, international, and armaments, 230
    codification, 292-293
    defined, 290
    and diplomatic relationships, 272-273
    instrument of the strong, 303-305
    and international commerce, 249
    legislative methods, 290-293
    observance and enforcement, 297-300
    and resort to war, 296
    scope and content, 293-295
    See also Peaceful change
Law, municipal, importance of procedures for change, 17-18
    instrument of the strong, 16-18, 300-303
    reinforcement of peace, 19
League of Nations, collective security, 358-367
    the mandate system, 401-403
    and peaceful change, 312-313
    structure and powers, 357-358
Lend-Lease program, 348
Lenin, V. I., 75, 78, 79-80, 307
    theory of imperialism, 105-108
Liberalism, basic principles, 62-64
    compared to communism, 86-87
    declared objectives of liberal statesmen, 66-72
Loyalty, basis for domestic peace, 22, 58
    definitions, 55-57
    inculcation, 57-58
    national and international, 58, 417-418
    requirement of nationalism, 54-57

Machiavelli, 189, 300
Mackinder, Sir Halford, on geography and power, 180
"Mad Caesars," 150-151, 167
Madariaga, Salvador de, 228
Mandate system, 401-403
Marxism, as a science, 75-76; see also Communism
Mediation, 276
Mercantilism, 97-98
Militarism, definition and implications of, 123-127
Morality, and the balancing of power, 205-207
    communist attitude toward, 77
    influence on foreign policy, 71-72, 306-310
Mussolini, Benito, 73, 74, 127

Napoleon, 158
Nation, the problem of definition, 43-45; see also Nationalism

National minorities, see Nationalism, general
Nationalism, economic, 266
    fascist, 73-75
    general, communist attitudes toward, 82-83
    development of, 42
    and imperialism, 52-54, 97
    importance and definition, 41
    and Irredentas, 46-47
    and national minorities, 46-49
    source of conflict, 44 ff.
Nationalism, liberal, declared objectives of liberal statesmen, 66-72
    nature and implications of, 62-66
Nazism, see Fascism
Neutrality, defined, 295
Neutralization, definition and relationship to balancing of power, 215-216
North Atlantic Treaty, mutual aid, 350
    terms and objectives of, 68, 69, 212-213
    text, 476-478
Nuclear weapons, destructiveness, 323-324, 423
    outlawry, 237-238
    relationship to balancing of power, 223-224

Objectives of states, basis of classifying states, 168-171
    summary discussion, 153-168
    See also Aggrandizement, Imperialism, Liberalism, Morality, Nationalism, Security, Self-preservation

Parry, J. H., 91
Peace, assumed as a value, 13
    and attitudes, 20-23
    and the balance of power, 200-201
    and coexistence, 81
    common objective of states, 159-161
    definitions, 159, 160
    and government, 15-20
    objective of liberal statesmen, 66
    prospects, 413-423
    and welfare, 379
    See also Collective security, War
Peaceful change, and collective security, 362
    defined, 18, 356
    need and provisions for, 16-18, 310-314, 358, 371-372
Peaceful settlement, defined, 356
    judicial methods, 277-282
    and the League of Nations, 357-358
    political and justiciable disputes, 278-279

Peaceful settlement (*cont.*)
  political methods, 275-277
  single-package agreements, 282
  and the United Nations, 371
Point Four program, and economic warfare, 350
  objectives, 67-68
  and the United Nations, 391
Politics, a focus of study, 12-13
  international and domestic, compared, 14 ff.
  nature and definition, 4 ff.
  a pursuit of interests, 7-8
  a struggle for power, 6-12
  a struggle for the realization of values, 8-9
Population, policies, 182
  pressure, and imperialism, 92-93
Power, defined, 6, 164-165, 199
  elements of, 175 ff.
  end and means, 11-12, 165-166
  and fascism, 74
  how much desired, 166-168
  "power politics," 6, 166
  its relativity, 196-197
  short cuts in calculation of, 194-196
  sources of craving for, 147-149
  vs. welfare, 168
  See also Armaments, Balance of power, Politics, Rule of the strong
Propaganda, substitute for war, 338 ff.
Prosperity, common objective of states, 161-162
  and international commerce, 248 ff.
  See also Imperialism, Well-being
Protection, of domestic economy, 97-99
  of nationals abroad, 89-90, 94-95
Protectorate, 396

Recognition, 269-271
Roosevelt, Franklin D., 121
Rule of the strong, within countries, 15-18, 23-25, 300-303, 414
  in international affairs, 303-305, 415-416
Russell, Bertrand, 166-167

Sanctions, defined, 297
  economic, 351-352, 354
  under the League of Nations, 358
  and self-help, 297-298
  under the United Nations, 372-373
Schumpeter, Joseph A., on imperialism, 127-130
Security, common objective of states, 154-156
  and competing interests, 36-38
  defined, 35

objective of liberal statesmen, 66-67
  policy problems relating to, 35-36
  See also Collective security
Security-community, 419-420
Security Council, enforcement action, 372-373
  powers and voting rules, 368-370
  See also United Nations
Self-determination, defined, 41-42
  difficulties in application of principle, 42 ff.
  plebiscites as instruments of, 49-51
  and the United Nations, 404-408
  Wilson and Lansing on, 41-42
Self-preservation, characteristics of the "self," 29-34
  objective of states, 29, 36
  and security, 154-156
Settlement, non-amicable methods, 282-284
  See also Peaceful settlement
Sovereignty, defined, 30-32
  preservation as an objective of states, 30-32, 154-156
  reflection of diversity and basis of war, 38-39
Sphere of influence, and balancing of power, 214-215
  quasi-colonial relationship, 395
Staley, Eugene, 96
Stalin, J. V., 75
  sick personality, 150
States, characteristics, 29-34
  common objectives, 153-171
  implications of division of world into, 38-39, 421-423
  as instruments, 40-41
  objective of self-preservation, 29
  relationship to nation, 41 ff.

Technical assistance, objectives, 67-68
  and Point Four, 350
  through the United Nations, 381
Trade, international, foreign exchange problems and practices, 249-254
  policies on foreign investments, 262-265
  regulation of exports, 260-261
  state trading, 261-262
  tariffs and other controls, 254-259
Truman, Harry S., 69, 70
  aid to Greece and Turkey, 348
Trusteeship system, 404-408

UNESCO, organization and functions, 389-390
  text of Constitution, 463-470

United Nations, colonialism, 403-408
  diplomacy by conference, 284-286
  peaceful change, 313-314, 371-372
  promotion of welfare, 378 ff.
  prospects, 376
  purposes, structure, and powers, 367 ff.
  text of Charter, 427-449
Universal Postal Union, 383-384
UNRRA, 260-261

Values, defined, 8-9
  listed and discussed by Lasswell, 145-
    149
  relationship to attitudes and interests,
    134-135
Van Wagenen, Richard W., 18, 419
Viner, Jacob, 95, 98, 101, 102

War, as a cause of war, 111 ff.
  economic causes, 88 ff., 161-162
  economic substitutes for, 346-355
  good in itself, 126-127
  ideological, 341-346
  incidence and costs, 320 ff.
  influence of expectation of, 116 ff.
  instrument of policy, 229
  instrument of revolution, 79-81
  and jingoism, 123
  method of settling disputes, 283-284
  and militarism, 124-127

  nuclear, 323-335
  outlawry, 296, 314-315, 371
  political importance, 54, 317-320
  problem of, within countries, 15 ff.
  propaganda as a substitute for, 337-341
  psychological factors, 131 ff.
  ratio of civil to international, 14
  source of glory, 125
  unifying activity, 125-126
Welfare, in colonies, 397-399
  international organization for, 378-393
  See also Well-being
Well-being, common objective of states,
    161-162
  objective of liberal statesmen, 70
  See also Welfare
Wight, Martin, 159, 166
Wilson, Woodrow, 41
Wolfers, Arnold, 35
  on the goals of states, 171
World federalism, 420-421
World Health Organization, 389
World War I, and balance of power, 221
  and expectation of war, 120-121
World War II, and balance of power,
    221-222
  and expectation of war, 121
  holy war, 164
Wright, Quincy, 5, 109, 122, 222-223,
    246
  on incidence and costs of war, 321-323

United Nations, relationships, 402-409
   diplomacy by conference, 294-296
   peaceful change, 312-314, 371-372
   permanent alteration, 373 ff.
   proposal, 370
   purpose, structure, and policies, 367 ff.
   Uniting for Peace Charter, 312-314
   Universal Postal Union, 352-354
UNESCO, 355-361

Value, defined, 8 ff.
   ideal and the real, by J. Laserson, 137-
   139
   relationship to attitude and interests,
   124-133
Van Wagenen, Richard W., 36, 113
Viner, Jacob, 96, 98, 101, 105

War, as a means of war, 111 ff.
   automatic cause of, 95 ff. 101-106
   economic ambitions for, 96-98
   good or not, 124-127
   philosophical goals, 1 ff.
   inclination and ends, 95 ff.
   influence of expectation of, 116 ff.
   instrument of policy, 356
   instrument of revolution, 75-85
   and fragment, 141
   medium of settling disputes, 280-281
   and influence, 124-127

nuclear, 202-233
   military, 280, 314-317, 371
   political importance, 314-317, 320
   problem of, within capitalism, 15 ff.
   megalomania as a substitute for, 327-341
   predilection of force, 141 ff.
   ratio of end to... rationalized, 14
   sources of glory, 125
   nihilism in Italy, 133-139
Wilson, in relation, 387-391
   International organization for, 378-391
   See also Will to...
Well-being, common objective of state,
   161-181
   objective of liberal democracy, 70
   See also Welfare
Wirt, Walter, 1931 106
Wilson, Woodrow, 41
Welfare, herald, 55
   on the goals of states, 176
   World Revolution, 409-411
   World Health Organization, 400
   World War I, as balance of power, 321
   and aggression of war, 120-121
   World War II, and balance of power,
   321 ff.
   and expectation of war, 121
   Italy, war, 141
Wright, Quincy, 3, 161, 172, 226-227,
   246
   on the human and social war, 221-222